ISBN 978-1-330-38673-6
PIBN 10047828

This book is a reproduction of an important historical work. Forgotten Books uses
state-of-the-art technology to digitally reconstruct the work, preserving the original format
whilst repairing imperfections present in the aged copy. In rare cases, an imperfection in
the original, such as a blemish or missing page, may be replicated in our edition. We do,
however, repair the vast majority of imperfections successfully; any imperfections that
remain are intentionally left to preserve the state of such historical works.

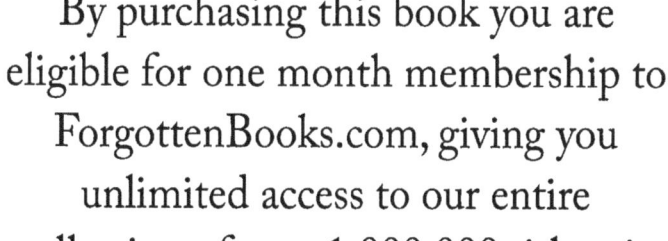

English
Français
Deutsche
Italiano
Español
Português

www.forgottenbooks.com

Mythology Photography **Fiction**
Fishing Christianity **Art** Cooking
Essays Buddhism Freemasonry
Medicine **Biology** Music **Ancient
Egypt** Evolution Carpentry Physics
Dance Geology **Mathematics** Fitness
Shakespeare **Folklore** Yoga Marketing
Confidence Immortality Biographies
Poetry **Psychology** Witchcraft
Electronics Chemistry History **Law**
Accounting **Philosophy** Anthropology
Alchemy Drama Quantum Mechanics
Atheism Sexual Health **Ancient History**
Entrepreneurship Languages Sport
Paleontology Needlework Islam
Metaphysics Investment Archaeology
Parenting Statistics Criminology
Motivational

A HISTORY

OF

CLASSICAL LITERATURE.

A HISTORY

OF

LASSICAL LITERATURE.

BY

R. W. BROWNE, M.A.,

PREBENDARY OF ST. PAUL'S,
AND PROFESSOR OF CLASSICAL LITERATURE IN KING'S COLLEGE, LONDON.

Σπουδαῖον οὐδὲν in sermone, φιλόλογα multa.

Cic. *Ep.* ad Att.

GREEK LITERATURE.

PHILADELPHIA:
NCHARD AND LEA.
1852.

PHILADELPHIA:
T. K. AND P. G. COLLINS, PRINTERS.

PREFACE.

In entering upon a general survey of Classical Literature, that of Greece first engages the attention, not only as constituting the oldest literature of Europe, but as the source from which Rome derived all her mental culture. The literature of Rome was distinguished not by originality of talent, but by cultivation of taste. Rome owed to Greece all her genius for poetry, her knowledge of philosophy, her skill in historical composition. To Greece, then, the scholar first turns, in order to seek for the germs of that intellectual excellence, which, when expanded and matured, has influenced and formed the taste of the most civilized nations in Europe.

In forming a correct estimate of Greek Literature, the nation in which it took its rise must be viewed in two different, and, as it at first sight appears, somewhat contradictory aspects; first, in its oneness as a nation, next in its subdivision into different races, distinct enough to give rise to almost opposite intellectual phenomena, but not enough to destroy nationality. Unity and combination against the non-Greek, or, as the Greeks called it, the Barbarian element of the human race, and jealousy between the opposing sections of the Hellenic portion, constitute the key to Greek Political History, and it is the leading principle also in Greek Intellectual and Literary History. In everything relating to Greece this tendency to union, accompanied with an insurmountable principle of disunion and division of race, is discernible. The natural boundaries of river and mountain presented at one and the same time obstacles to physical and moral amalgamation, and yet, notwithstanding this separation, there was a sympathy between Greek and Greek which never existed between **Greek and Barbarian.**

In literature, as in their political and social relations, the author, to whatever race he might belong, found common sympathies, to which he could appeal, and which he was sure to awaken. Hence each poet, although local in blood, in prejudices, in principles, was boasted of by Greece universal as the common property of the Hellenic name. No one could fail to observe the difference between Ionian, Æolian, Dorian, Bœotian, and Sicilian; and yet to see in all, the common features which distinguish the Greek nation from the other nations of the world. It is in the earliest phase of Greek literature that nationality is most manifest. Homer was an Ionian, and displays all the intellectual characteristics of the Ionian race, yet he unites in himself the peculiarities of the other races likewise. He is the representative of the Greek national mind. The versatility which could paint all the varied elements which go to make up Greek character, must have been the attribute of a nature possessing in itself somewhat of each of them. In the Homeric poems the terse, rude, and satiric wit of the Dorian occasionally appears amid the graceful polish of the Ionian. Achilles, the chieftain of the Thessalian mountaineers, Ulysses, the monarch of the enduring and wily islanders, are portraits evidently the work of one who could understand and sympathize with the feelings of both of them.

But whilst it is necessary to bear in mind the unity and nationality of Greek literature, it is also important to remark the different intellectual peculiarities which characterize the great races into which Greece was divided. The refined and energetic mind of the Ionian developed itself in the epic, elegiac and iambic poetry; and their poetical genius reached its zenith in the activity and life-like representations of the Attic tragedy and comedy. In prose, the same mind was the first to exercise its acuteness and ingenuity in philosophical speculations, and to satisfy its inquisitive thirst after knowledge in the wide field of historical inquiry; for with them history, as the name implies (ἱστορία), was at first not mere compilation (συγγραφή), but original investigation. The same structure of the ear which led to the modulation of Ionic poetry, gave birth to the melodious dialect in which Herodotus and Hecatæus narrated their stories; and when a modern dialect succeeded, and literature was transplanted to the soil of Attica, we recognize the same, or even greater, sweetness in Attic purity and simplicity. The philosophical spirit there combined with the habit of historical research, and Ionian Athens gave birth to Thucydides, the father of philosophical history, as Asiatic Ionia did to Herodotus, the father of the history of induction and inquiry.

Again, the same talent developed itself in the critical faculty which was so strong in Aristotle, which could analyze the principles of beauty and of taste, and thus reduce to rule and system, and bring within the province of art and science the laws which in these matters regulate the operations of the human mind. And lastly, the imagination, combined with the logical power, produced oratory, which shed a lustre upon the decline and fall of Greek liberty.

Such was the career of Ionian and Attic intellect, far superior in every point of view but one to that of the Dorian and Æolian races; for their characteristics, as might be expected from their origin, were the same. But there was one excellence peculiar to themselves. The palm in lyric poetry was due to the Æolians of Lesbos. They could boast of the passionate emotions of Alcæus, in which love, though full of tenderness, breathes an almost chivalrous respect for the beloved object, and is elevated far above a mere sensual passion. Theirs were the burning strains of Sappho, whose simplicity, whatever may have been her faults, could not disguise her most secret thoughts and feelings.

Again, the Dorian originated and cultivated the religious and fervid enthusiasm of the dithyrambic chorus, and then modifying and adapting it to the drama, handed down those beautiful odes which adorn the texture of Attic tragedy. They consecrated the lyric muse to the service of religion, and to the celebration of the victors in the national games of Greece. The prolific talent of Simonides exhibited itself in his numerous epinician odes, and still more in his plaintive and pathetic threni. And the lofty Pindar far outstripped his contemporary, Simonides, if not in feeling, at least in grandeur. Such were the claims of the Dorian race to literary reputation; but these were all. Their very chorus was not finished and brought to perfection by themselves, but by the genius of the Attic dramatists. They had no history, no oratory, no philosophy.

The literature of Greece has been stamped, by universal testimony, as beyond comparison with that of subsequent periods. We admire and imitate the Greeks, but we cannot equal them. We take their works as models, not arbitrarily, but after putting them to the test of those principles of taste which form part of our nature; and when put to this test they never fail.

But Greek literature is not only admirable, as presenting a picture of the human intellect in its highest state of perfection, but also for its moral value. It is a monument to all ages of unselfish industry, of enthusiastic devotion to a great purpose. Each author seems impressed with the idea that he has a duty to perform, a message to deliver. The lower motives which too often give an impulse to the literature of modern times, did not influence them. The poet, the philosopher, the historian, were urged on by an irresistible devotion to their work, or at least felt no motive more selfish than a desire to be loved and admired by their contemporaries, or to enjoy an undying reputation in after ages. Private means were, in many cases, only considered valuable as affording to the possessor an opportunity for indulging his tastes, and undertaking a literary career. They were ungrudgingly expended in procuring a liberal education and the advantages of foreign travel, for their own sakes, and not with any hope of a pecuniary return. Few writers think so little of self as the ancients; their minds and thoughts are absorbed in that of which they write, their sentiments are freely revealed in their works; but it is very difficult to derive from them any information respecting themselves. Although, therefore, it is impossible not to admire the unselfishness from which this results, it is a cause of regret that, for the same reason, the sources from which their private histories are derived are often of doubtful credit.

Only a few words are necessary respecting the author's object in giving to the public this work, and the mode in which he has carried it into effect. He feels that apologies are due for venturing on a field in which so many, superior to himself in abilities and learning, have already successfully labored; but he wished to collect within a moderate compass such facts and observations as might be interesting to the general reader, but which are now scattered over a wide surface, and cannot be brought together without pains and trouble.

To the researches of his predecessors in the history of ancient literature, and to the labors of modern philologers, especially Mr. Donaldson, he acknowledges the deepest obligation. As the present work is the result of reading and study during a period in which, from the position which he has occupied, it has been his duty to collect information from all possible sources, he cannot always say to whose investigations particular statements are due, nor can he always separate his own original observations from those which he has derived from other authorities.

Owing to the limits within which he has wished to confine himself, he has often stated the conclusions to which he has come, without entering into the grounds and reasons on which they are based. He hopes, therefore, that this apology will be accepted, for some parts of the work being in a dogmatic form, instead of that controversial one which, to the minds of some readers, appears more satisfactory.

From the same desire to economize space, he has almost always contented himself with giving references to illustrative passages, instead of quoting the passages themselves; whilst, at the same time, he has inserted translations, in order that the sense and spirit of the author may be conveyed to those who are unacquainted with the language of the original.

If the reader recognizes in this work statements which are already familiar to him, and observations which appear trite, they will be found, it is hoped, such as could not be omitted in a work which professes to be a history. If, on the contrary, he observes what he considers important omissions, let him remember that it was the author's duty to exercise his judgment, to the best of his power, in making a selection from a vast mass of materials. It will readily be believed that one of the principal difficulties which the author has encountered in his task, has been the making this selection, and determining what might be omitted, without violating the fidelity of history.

In most instances the author believes that his statements are justified by competent authority ; wherever he has given his own views and opinions, he offers them with diffidence, as to their correctness, although he has adopted them as the result of deliberate conviction.

CONTENTS.

BOOK I.

FIRST ERA OF GREEK LITERATURE.

CHAPTER I.

CHAPTER II.

CHAPTER III.

CHAPTER IV.

CHAPTER V.

CHAPTER VI.

CHAPTER VII.

CHAPTER XII.

CHAPTER XIII.

CHAPTER XIV.

CHAPTER XV.

BOOK II.

SECOND OR FLOURISHING ERA OF GREEK LITERATURE.

CHAPTER I.

CHAPTER II.

CHAPTER III.

CHAPTER IV.

CHAPTER V.

CHAPTER VI.

2

CHAPTER XI.

CHAPTER XII.

CHAPTER XIII.

CHAPTER XVII.

CHAPTER XVIII.

CHAPTER XIX.

CHAPTER XXVI.

A HISTORY

OF

CLASSICAL LITERATURE.

PART I.

·GREEK LITERATURE.

___

BOOK I.

FIRST ERA OF GREEK LITERATURE.

___

CHAPTER I.

LIMITS OF THIS WORK.—ITS TWOFOLD DIVISION.—ORIGIN AND AFFINITIES OF THE GREEK LANGUAGE.—INDO-EUROPEAN AND SEMITIC RACES.—THEIR LANGUAGES COMPARED.—THE GREEK DIALECTS.—CONNECTION OF THE IONIANS WITH THE PELASGIANS.—ORIGIN OF THE GREEK ALPHABET.

THE Classical literature of a nation includes, strictly speaking, only the works of its best authors. Its era is that during which the national intellect is in its greatest vigor and health ; when the language, which is the exponent of that intellect, exhibits the most perfect refinement and purity ; when Poetry, Philosophy, and History are in the most flourishing condition.

This definition excludes the period of its rise and progress towards perfection, as well as that of its decline and fall ; but it is obvious that a history, even of its flourishing period, although it naturally terminates when that period comes to a close, must trace its growth and development from the earliest times.

3

An inquiry, therefore, into the Classical literature of Greece divides itself into two heads :—

I. The era which extends from the infancy of literature, unwritten as well as written, to the time of the Pisistratidæ. It includes the time when the Ionian Greeks were struggling against the overwhelming power of Cyrus, and terminates with their subjugation towards the end of the sixth century before Christ.

II. The era at which the national literature had attained its highest state of perfection. During this era the Tragic Drama rapidly arrived at maturity, and suddenly became extinct; Comedy flourished; History assumed its most perfect form, and Athens came to be considered the home of Philosophy. This period commences with Simonides, and ends with Aristotle. It includes the Persian and Peloponnesian wars, the subsequent years during which Grecian liberty was in a tottering state, and had a hard struggle for existence, until at length the supremacy of Macedon completed its destruction.

At this point, then, will end that portion of this work which is devoted to the history of Greek Classical literature.

But the history of a nation's literature implies some account of its language, and the important philological investigations which have distinguished the present age, furnish the materials for tracing the origin of the Greek language, and its affinities with other languages of the civilized world.

Language is the material of literature, in the same way that the marble gives visible existence to the ideas and feelings of the sculptor. As the artist converts the shapeless block into a lifelike statue, so the poet, the philosopher, and the historian breathe life into the dead letter of mere words.

Again, the beauty of sculpture depends in no small degree on the fitness of the material for expressing and giving reality to the ideas of the artist. And in the same way, on the genius of a language, the character of a national literature will frequently depend.

The first step towards exhibiting the origin of the Greek language, is to trace the earliest migrations of the human race. From Armenia there proceeded two great families. One, the Aramaic, or Semitic, gradually occupied the plains of Mesopotamia, and thence overspread Syria, Arabia, and North Africa, including Egypt; the other, the Iranian, or Indo-European, moved westward to Asia Minor, thence to India, and skirting in its migrations the northern shores of the Euxine and Caspian, penetrated into the colder and less fertile regions of Europe. These two races were equally gifted both corporeally and intellectually; to them are owing the literature and civilization of the world.

To the Indo-European race we are indebted for the vocabulary and grammatical structure of the languages of civilized Europe. To the Semitic we owe the alphabet and the means of committing ideas to writing.

But whilst the Semitic race possessed, far earlier than the Indo-European, a phonetic alphabet of such power and perfection as to satisfy the requirements of both races, and to be capable of expressing and representing every sound, its comparative superiority, in point of language, ends here. The varied structure of the Indo-European languages, the power of combination in their elements, the perfection of their grammatical principles, endowed them with greater capacity for forming a widely diffused and extended literature. The written literature of the Semitic race is of greater antiquity than that of the other, as is evident from a critical study of the sacred volume, an antiquity likewise established by the whole course of modern discovery; but the varied power of inflexion, the luxuriant copiousness of grammatical forms in the Indo-European tongues, gave them a superior facility of accommodating themselves to the various modes of thought and feeling in different nations.

In the Semitic languages, the roots are few in number, and composed of only two or three letters, and the formation of words by means of prefixes and affixes is simple, and in most cases similar; hence, although there is weight and dignity, there is an absence of that variety of sound which, in the Classical languages, falls so agreeably upon the ear, even although we are ignorant of the true pronunciation. Hebrew poetry, for example, is probably metrical, but we cannot discover those nice shades of rhythm and scansion, which in Greek and Latin are capable of being reduced to such exact rules. The only poetical peculiarities discoverable, are antitheses in sense and equally balanced periods, or sentences.

The slightest acquaintance with the Classical languages of antiquity is sufficient to show the advantage of varied grammatical inflexion, both as to sense and sound. The mind recognizes with satisfaction the philosophical exactness with which they were able to express the most refined distinctions of human thought, the means which were at their disposal by composition and derivation, for forming a complete nomenclature in any science—a power which modern languages are obliged to borrow from them.

Doubtless, the Greeks were distinguished by a vast amount of mental energy and subtlety of discrimination, but it is clear, that, whilst these natural gifts assisted in the rapid development of their language, the accommodating structure of the Indo-European languages was a powerful instrument to mould and educate their mental powers.

Muller[1] says on this subject, "That in the ancient languages the words with their inflexions, clothed, as it were, with muscles and sinews, come forward like living bodies full of expression and character; while in the modern tongues, the words seem shrunk up into mere skeletons."

The ear, even of the uninitiated, is struck with the harmonious variety perceptible in the Greek language, and its fitness at once for the loftiest strains of heroic and dithyrambic poetry, the sweet pathos of the lyric muse, the rhythmical character of oratorical prose composition, and the simple homeliness and elegant perspicuity of narrative and conversation. But whilst this is the charm resulting from variety of inflexion, the ear is also effectually addressed by the systematic rule which regulates these inflexions. Every different idea and relation has its different sound, but at the same time, as a general rule, every similar and kindred idea has a similar or kindred oral development. The ear, attuned as that of the Greek was to catch at every minutest difference in sound, and to discriminate with the nicest accuracy, was at once conscious of the sound, and the mind as readily recognized the mutual relation of ideas, the adaptation

[1] History of Greek Literature, p. 5.

of the parts, the dependence upon each other of the words in the sentence. The Greek language, then, was especially adapted to an age when literature and a literary taste were disseminated far more by oral transmission than by writing.

Even when the art of writing was discovered, and writing materials became sufficiently abundant, convenient means for a rapid and easy multiplication of copies were not at hand until the invention of printing; hence recitation, and oratory, and the drama, and lectures, and the public and private conversations of philosophers, were, for the most part, the vehicles of literature. It was most important, therefore, to the formation of a national literature, that the language should be one which addressed itself to the ear rather than to the eye.

There was, besides the variety of inflexion, and the symmetry of principle which regulated inflexion, another important advantage which the Greek possessed over modern languages. The grammar was the natural offshoot and product of the human mind; it was the grammar of attraction rather than of government; it presented itself as the natural normal form in which ideas strive for utterance rather than as artificial trammels to restrain and correct inaccuracies of expression. To write accurate grammar was natural to them.

The reverse would, as it were, have done violence to their nature. The very inaccuracies of the poets, and of so rapid a thinker as Thucydides, can be accounted for on the common laws which regulate human thought; even the familiar and conversational dialogues of Plato, and the jottings down of Aristotle's note-books, are free from grammatical inaccuracies which we frequently meet with even in the polished essays of modern times.

With the ancients, the order of thought was that in which the thoughts were expressed. The plastic nature of their languages allowed the thoughts to flow in words precisely as nature dictates. The arrangement of the words in a Latin or Greek sentence is determined by the relative importance of the ideas, and therefore the classical is in fact the natural order, whilst the grammatical order is that which is determined by artificial rule.

The same facility which assisted the ear in the appreciation of

the sense, and led the hearer gradually onward together 'with the
speaker, so that he grasped the ideas precisely as they originated
in the speaker's mind, constituted one of the charms of Greek
poetry.   The laws of metre and of rhythm might fairly be more
strict where the grammatical structure of a sentence did not
fetter or circumscribe the order in which the words might be arranged ; and at the same time regular metrical analysis was perfectly compatible with the infinite variety which classical metre
is capable of assuming.   Hence a determinate quantity could be
affixed by rule, or by authority, to every syllable which the
tutored ear of modern scholars, even amid all the disadvantages
under which we labor, is able to appreciate, but which must have
spoken to the musical ear of the Greek in accents of which we
can form no adequate idea.

There can be little doubt, that, although the dialects of early
Greece were very numerous, a variety of which Homer[1] was aware,
the Greek language was originally the result of one regular plan.
The manner in which Hellas originally became settled is of itself
sufficient to account for the rise of many various forms out of one
common matrix.   The same causes which interfered with the
mixture of races would produce difference of dialects and present
a barrier to their fusion.   The physical features of a country exercise an important influence in perpetuating or causing distinctions of dialect, on the one hand, and in preventing one language
from being split into many cognate varieties, on the other.

The vast open plains inhabited by the Semitic nations softened
down the differences of languages and encouraged a similarity
and uniformity in their structure, whilst the rivers and mountains
which intersected Greece produced and maintained the characteristic forms of her several dialects, and hindered their amalgamation into one common Hellenic tongue.   The following is the
account which some philologists have given of its origin.   The
Pelasgi, who were the oldest inhabitants of Greece, and who,
according to the authority of Herodotus,[2] spoke a barbarian, i. e.,
a foreign language, were allied to the Iranian tribes in the north
of India; and consequently that element in the Greek language
which exhibits an affinity for the Sanscrit is the Pelasgic, and

---

[1] Iliad, ii. 804; iv. 437.   [2] Herod. i. 57.

hence the numerous resemblances in words and inflexions which
are found to exist between the two languages. It is to this oldest
element that the Latin is allied, which is now universally allowed
to be the older language of the two, and to resemble the Greek
in the earliest phase of its existence.

The Hellenes subsequently migrated into Greece, and the Hellenic element being added to the other, caused the older Pelasgian
language to be looked upon as barbarous, when the Hellenes, who
were an Ionian race, became the possessors of Attica. This element of the Greek language is said to have had an affinity to the
Persian.

A distinguished modern scholar[1] brings forward the examples
of Democedes[2] and Themistocles[3] as proofs of some similarity existing between Greek and Persian; and thus accounts for the
facility with which these persons are represented as having learnt
the latter language.

According to this theory, then, the common or older element
in the Greek and Latin languages would be the Pelasgian, and
would have a close affinity with the Sanscrit; whereas the new element which distinguishes the Greek from the Latin would be the
Hellenic, and be closely related to the Persian.

When tradition, following the universal practice of legendary history, named races after imaginary patriarchs, and made
Dorus, Æolus, and Ion the offspring of Hellen, it was symbolizing
the fact that the subdivisions of the Hellenic race were the Dorians, Æolians, and Ionians. The Dorians, as their name implies,
which has an affinity to other words signifying mountains—such as
Tor and Taurus—were the mountaineers. The Æolians—whose
habits and modes of thought, and therefore their literature, as
seen in the compositions of the lyric poets of Lesbos, exhibit some
mixture of Dorian feeling—sprang probably from an union of
Dorian races with the Pelasgians of Thessaly. For that reason
they were termed Αἰόλεις, or a mixed race. The Ionians are so
called, because they inhabited the coast (ἠιών). It was to their
local habitation, and consequently their commercial and maritime
pursuits, and their intercourse with foreigners that they owed
those peculiar characteristics, which distinguished them by so

[1] Donaldson's New Cratyl.   [2] Herod. iii. 130.   [3] Thuc. i.

broad a line of demarcation from the Dorians and Æolians. Hence sprang their activity of mind, their enterprising disposition, their love of foreign travel, their restless desire of change, their liberal spirit, and attachment to free institutions, the versatility of their intellectual powers, which is reflected in the wide extent and varied nature of their literature.

Of the ancient Pelasgian race little certain is known, although their traces are visible throughout Europe and Asia, marking, wherever they are found, the progress of civilization.

Herodotus asserts that they were barbarians;[1] that they were the occupiers of the whole of Hellas; that the inhabitants of Attica were once called Pelasgians;[2] that the Athenians afterwards shared that country with them, and learnt from them some of their customs; that their gods had no names;[3] that judging from the Pelasgian settlements, which existed in his own day, their language was barbarous;[4] that they were expelled from Attica, and settled in Lemnos;[5] and that, together with change of race, the language of Attica changed also;[6] that a wall attributed to Pelasgians existed at Athens,[7] a fact which is also alluded to by Thucydides, who speaks of a district of the city called the Pelasgian.[8] Such is the imperfect account transmitted to us by the father of history. The mighty works which have marked their migration—the fortifications which they built (for their vastness called Cyclopean), relics of which even still remain—the undoubted fact that they were the founders of those nations amongst whom literature and the arts have most flourished, forbid the belief that they or their language were barbarian.

Doubtless the Pelasgians were a civilized and peaceful race, whilst the Hellenes were a warlike and conquering people; both sprang from one common origin; and their languages were sufficiently similar, so that, when the races lived together as a conquering and subject people, they were capable of amalgamation, and in the process of reconstruction formed the Greek language in the earliest state in which it was applied to the purposes of literature.

Possibly the assertion of Herodotus is, after all, the true one,

[1] Herod. i. 57. [2] Ibid. viii. 44. [3] Ibid. ii. 51.
[4] Ibid. vi. 137. [5] Ibid. v. 64. [6] Ibid. i. 57.
[7] Ibid. i. 57. [8] Thuc. lib. i.

that the Athenians were not a Hellenic but a Pelasgian race.[1] The Dorians, we know, were Hellenians; and the opposition between the Dorian and Ionian mind and character leads us to expect that in the Ionian race are to be found the descendants of that marvellous people which Italy, as well as Greece, acknowledges for its founders.

Such appears to have been the origin of the Greek nation and its great subdivisions, and such the sources from which its language was derived. But whilst the Greek language belongs to the Indo-European family, the alphabet is of Semitic origin. Tradition represents Cadmus, a Phœnician, as having introduced an alphabet, of sixteen letters, into Greece,[2] and there are good reasons for believing that the ancient Greeks were accustomed to call the Semitic nations Phœnicians. The truth, which the mythical history symbolizes, was probably the following.

The Phœnician, or Syro-Chaldean, cities of Tyre and Sidon were, in very early times, important commercial communities. It is probable that through them, principally, the trade between the East and West was carried on. The antiquity of our own sacred writings proves that the existence of a Semitic written literature was at least coeval with their commerce; and thus it was not long before the Greek merchants derived from the descendants of Shem, the signs which they used, and which they adapted to the representation of the sounds of their own native tongue.

The Semitic alphabet was doubtless at first pictorial, and afterwards, in process of time, became phonetic. Even after it had undergone this improvement, the ancient names of the things which the letters depicted still remained; and although the form became gradually altered, some rude resemblance to the original picture form can be still detected. For example א, the first letter in the present Hebrew alphabet, was called Aleph, or *ox;* and in the character, and still more in the older Phœnician form ∢, the rude picture of an ox's head may be traced. So ב, Beth, signified a *house;* ג, Gimel, a *camel;* and so forth. The letter ע, Ain, the *eye,* corresponds to the European vowel O ; and the oldest form in which it was written was ⊙, or ◯, as representing

<hr/>

[1] Herod. viii. 44. [2] Ibid. v. 28.

a rude resemblance to the human eye. Other instances of the pictorial character may be traced in some of the letters of the Hebrew and cognate alphabets.

Tradition informs us that the Phœnician or Semitic alphabet, introduced into Greece by Cadmus, consisted of sixteen letters, and the grammarians asserted that these sixteen were α, β, γ, δ, ε, ι, κ, λ, μ, ν, ο, π, ς, σ, τ, υ;[1] but the same philologer, whose authority has been already referred to, has unanswerably proved that this is impossible, and that the original letters must have been those which appear in the extant Hebrew alphabet, under the following names and symbols :—

Hebrew.			Greek.
א	H	first breathing,	A.
ב	B	⎫	B.
ג	G	⎬ middle sounds (mediæ),	Γ.
ד	D	⎭	Δ.
ה	H	second breathing,	E.
ו	Bh	⎫	F, digamma.
ח	Gh	⎬ aspirated sound,	H.
ט	Dh	⎭	Θ.
ל	L	⎫	Λ.
מ	M	⎬ liquids,	M.
נ	N	⎭	N.
ס	S.	the sibilant,	Σ.
ע	O	third breathing,	O.
פ	P		Π.
ק	Q	⎬ smooth sounds (tenues),	Φ.
ת	T	⎭	T.

The following specimens of Greek, Phœnician, and Samaritan characters, will show the transition from the Semitic and Greek[2] forms :—

Hebrew.	Samaritan.	Phœnician.	Greek.
א		✦	A.
ב	9		B.
ג	ㄱ		Γ.
ד		۹	Δ.

---

[1] Donaldson's New Cratyl. i. 5.
[2] See Penny Cyclopædia, art. Alphabet.

Hebrew.	Samaritan.	Phœnician.	Greek.
ה	א		E.
ו		7	F, digamma.
ז			
ח	אy		H.
ט			Θ.
י			
כ		ע	K.
ל		∠	Λ.
מ		¥	M.
נ		)	N.
ס			Ξ. (?)
ע		O	O.
פ			Π.
צ	ﬡﬡ		Z.
ק	Y		Φ.
ר			P.
ש	ﬠﬡ		Σ.
ת	ﬡ		T.

From a mere inspection of these alphabets thus compared together, it is plain that the resemblance between the letters of the Semitic alphabets and the corresponding Greek characters is very great, due allowance being of course made for the fact that the Semitic nations wrote from right to left, and the Greek characters with which we are familiar were used at the time when the Greeks wrote as we do—from left to right. Hence the letters B, Γ, E, &c., are turned exactly the contrary way to their original Semitic types.

In the earliest times, as may be proved from old inscriptions, the Greeks wrote precisely in the same direction as the Semitic nations, and afterwards they wrote alternately from right to left, and from left to right. This transition state of writing was designated by the characteristic term βουστροφηδον, i. e., the way in which oxen plough.

With respect to their sixteen original characters, and the other omitted letters of the present Greek alphabet, the following observations may be made.

1. E ה. Although this was first the common aspirate h, it afterwards became the vowel e. The Greeks had originally, like the

Latins, only one *e*—the introduction of the long *e*, as well as the long ω, being due to later times. The earliest instances[1] of the Ω which are extant, are on some coins of Gelon, tyrant of Syracuse ; and therefore it must have been in use some time previous to the date of his death, B.C. 478 : and the H is also found in some very ancient coins of Rhegium. With respect, however, to the comparative antiquity of these two letters, there is every reason for supposing that the Ω was of later introduction than the H. Wordsworth[2] observed an inscription in the Grotto of the Nymphs, on Mount Hymettus, on the way from Athens to Sunium, in which H is used, but Ω does not occur. Neither of these letters, however, is found in Attic inscriptions earlier than C.C. 403. The ω is evidently a double letter, artificially composed of two o's.

2. Ϝ. This letter, from its being apparently made up of two 's, was fancifully termed the digamma. Its power is *w*, or *v*. It retained its place in the numerical alphabet as the symbol of the figure 6, and is then generally written ς', and commonly called the stigma, from its resemblance to the character which represents στ. Although it has gone out of use in the written or spoken language, its presence may still be detected in those Latin words which have an affinity for Greek words, in which it originally occurred, *e. g.* οἶνος, *vinum ;* οἶκος, *vicus.* In the same way the Koppa, which, like the ρ, is a combination of κ and υ, and the Sanpi ϡ, a combination of σ and π, after they ceased to be letters, remained as the representatives of numbers.

3. H η. When this character ceased to be used as an aspirate, it was divided into two parts, ⊢ and ⊣, of which the first designated the aspirate; the other was prefixed to unaspirated vowels in the cursive and more familiar form of (') and ('); the character was then used to represent the long *e*, and its place amongst the aspirates was supplied by X.

4. K Ϙ. When the Koppa was disused, this became its substitute.

5. The Hebrew ז corresponds to the old Greek letter San, which enters into the composition of Sanpi ϡ, a numeral, but not, so far as we have any evidence, an alphabetic character.

---

[1] Payne Knight.   [2] "Athens and Attica."

6. The only point which appears doubtful and difficult of adjustment in this theory is, whether the ◘ corresponds to Σ, and ʊ to ᗶ, or the reverse. The place which ◘ occupies seems to indicate that its Greek correlative is ᗶ, since it stands in a similar position in the Greek alphabet; and, moreover, the form of the Samaritan ᴟ is precisely similar to the Greek Σ. On the other hand, the whole theory of Donaldson, who adopts the contrary view, is so complete, and supported by such powerful arguments, as to render it almost impossible to propose any deviation.

With regard to the sibilant letter generally, it may be observed that it may be classed with the aspirates, instead of being, as grammarians have termed it, a letter of its own power (*suæ potestatis*). Experiment will prove that a very strong expiration has a tendency to produce a hissing sound. It is probably for this reason that, in Latin, the *s* is the representative of the aspirate in some words which have an affinity with aspirated words in Greek, *e. g.* in ὗς, *sus*, and ὕλη, *sylva*.

It is a remarkable fact, which must not be passed over whilst speaking of the Greek alphabet, that, until the downfall of the Thirty Tyrants—although the new alphabet of twenty-four letters had been long in use—the laws of Solon were still written in the sixteen old Attic letters. This defect Archinus proposed to remedy, when it was determined that this code should be transcribed and set up to public view, on the partial restoration of the old constitution.

CHAPTER II.

POETRY PRECEDES PROSE LITERATURE.—FIRST DEVELOPMENTS OF GREEK POETRY
RELIGIOUS.—WORSHIP OF NATURE.—GREEK CLIMATE.—WORSHIP OF THE SUN-GOD.—
ANCIENT TRADITIONS.—LINUS.—HYLAS —LITYERSES.—ADONIS.—BARDS.—TESTIMONY
OF HOMER.—ORPHEUS. — EUMOLPUS. — THAMYRIS. — MUSÆUS. — CHRYSOTHEMIS.—
PHILAMMON.—OLEN.

THE earliest species of literature is poetry. It is the natural
outpouring of the heart, the language in which imagination and
passion seek for utterance, whilst prose implies more reflection
and logical exactness, and therefore an advanced state of intellectual power.

This may at first appear a startling and paradoxical assertion.
Men converse in prose, and therefore it might be thought that
the first works which they intended to outlive them would have
taken the most natural form, and not have been bound by the
fetters of verse. But the histories of all nations prove the contrary, and the following brief considerations will account for the
phenomenon. The hearers, whether engaged in a private and
social, or a public and religious ceremony, whether at the banquet or the altar, would demand a species of composition adapted
for a musical accompaniment. Nor would metrical arrangement
constitute a practical difficulty to the composer. The aid which
metre is to the memory, which then had not the artificial help of
writing, far surpassed the inconvenience arising from the trammels of verse. It must be remembered, also, that the great
variety of position which the words in ancient languages are permitted to assume, greatly diminished the difficulty of versification.
This advantage is denied by the more rigid rules which regulate
the syntactical order of modern languages.

The first developments of Greek poetry were immediately
connected with religion; and that worship, the enthusiastic devotion of which was embodied in poetry, was the worship of Nature.

The Greek inhabited a land well suited to foster and nurture the fancy and imagination. His was a country of varied and picturesque beauty; a land of the mountain and the flood. Its shores were indented by numerous beautiful bays and inlets, and almost in every part washed by the sea, which naturally suggests to the mind images sometimes of the calmest beauty, sometimes of the grandest sublimity. The climate was as beautiful as the country. The ancient poets constantly speak of its transparency. A modern scholar and traveller[1] thus writes of the sky and atmosphere of Greece.

"It is impossible to describe the varied tints which dye the marbles of Hymettus, which bathe the islands of the Ægean, and fringe the crests of the mountains. So magnificent are these effects of light, that even Homer has not attempted to paint a sunrise or a sunset. He has substituted metaphor for details, which his pencil could not trace. He has spoken to us of the rosy fingers of Aurora, to distract our attention and make us forget that he has never described Aurora herself."

"Nor does the light of the sun in Greece alone defy description; the night has its own peculiar brilliance. The stars shine like fire. The rays of the moon are not of silver, as in the cold North. The attributes of Phœbe are similar to those of her brother; the poets with truth encircle her brows with a crown of gold."

This bright and cheerful climate was supposed by the ancients to exert an influence over the mental powers, and Cicero attributes the clearness of Attic wit to that of the Attic atmosphere.

The Greek mythology, therefore, connected the legends which tradition handed down, with the local scenery of their fatherland; it peopled every river, and fountain, and hill, with deities and nymphs, and other supernatural beings. Every scene upon which the eye of the Greek rested, was, in his imagination, haunted by mysterious essences; and thus, even the perishable and transitory things of this world were stamped, as it were, with immortality. Hence the first poems—the existence of which is made known to us by tradition—were solemn hymns, addressed as acts of worship and adoration to these deified phenomena of nature.

[1] Ampère.

In its infancy, poetry realized the definition of Strabo[1]—'Η ποιητικὴ πᾶσα ὑμνητική, all poetry should consist of hymns of praise. These effusions, though unwritten, were nevertheless, to that early age, its literature. They were rhythmical poetical compositions, delighting the ear and charming the intellect, long before the Greek nation became acquainted either with the letters of the alphabet or the art of writing.

The deity who represented the Sun-god—the giver of life and heat, the cause of plenty and fertility—was the earliest object of poetical worship. When the shortest days of winter were just passing away, hymns of joy and welcome were sung in his honor, in token that the days were lengthening, and the brighter seasons of spring and summer approaching. Again, a little later, the same god, under the name of Apollo, was celebrated in the hymn Ie Pæan (ἰὴ Παιῆον),[2] and the approach of the vernal equinox, when nature began to look gay and smiling, was hailed with spring pæans (εἰαρινοὶ παιᾶνες).[3]

Such were the hymns, the burden of which was distinguished by ἰή, the cry of joy; but there were others distinguished by the burden αἰ Λίνε (alas! Linus)[4] the subject of which was sad and melancholy. As the songs of joy were sung in honor of reviving nature, so these laments symbolized the withering and perishing of nature's life and vigor.[5] Tradition represents Linus as a beautiful boy, whom matrons and maidens bewailed. Legends told that he was brought up in infancy with the lambs, and torn to pieces by dogs. The lamentation for his untimely fate was sung to an accompaniment on the harp, in a low and solemn chant.

Ηάντες μὲν θρηνοῦσιν ἐν εἰλαπίναις τε χοροῖς τε,
'Αρχόμενοι δὲ Λίνον καὶ λήγοντες καλέουσι.—HES. *Fragm.*

    Where dance and feast are sparkling gay,
    His is the melancholy lay ;
    Ere they begin and when they close
    They call on Linus' name, they tell of Linus' woes.
                                                    ANSTICE.

---

[1] Strabo, x. p. 468.   [2] Hymn to Apollo, 21.
[3] See Müller's History of Greek Literature.
[4] See Æsch. Agam. 120.
[5] See Müller's Dorians, xi. 12.

The Egyptians marked the period of the greatest heat by the sign Thoth, or the watch-dog, as giving warning of the rising of the Nile, and hence those days were called the days of Thoth, or the dog-days; and the constellation, afterwards called Sirius by the Greeks, which rose heliacally at that period, was called the dog-star. At this period of the year, when the raging heat of summer parches up the exhausted powers of nature, and the spring in which the lambs sport over the green meadows is no more, the shepherds sang the lament of Linus, and hence the legend derived its origin. In Asia Minor there were many dirges embodying similar stories. The lament for Hylas, borne away by the nymphs of the Mysian fountains; the θρῆνος of the Mariandyni for the beautiful Bormus, whose fate was the same as that of Hylas; the song of Lityerses, in Phrygia; and, lastly, that of Adonis, which was sung throughout the coasts of the Mediterranean. At the Egyptian Pelusium, also, a dirge was sung in honor of Maneros, an Egyptian prince, cut off in early youth, which Herodotus[1] considers as identical with that of Linus. But the bard and the song were present not only at all seasons of public rejoicing or mourning, but on those occasions in private life which are closely connected with religion, and which call up ideas of a religious nature. At marriages the song of joy was as customary as at the more solemn rites and ceremonies relating to the gods. In the following passage Homer describes a nuptial procession accompanied by a hymeneal song :—

> Two splendid cities also there he formed,
> Such as men build. In one were to be seen
> Rites matrimonial solemnized with pomp
> Of sumptuous banquets ; from their chambers fôrth
> Leading the brides they ushered them along
> With torches through the streets, and sweet was heard
> The voice around of hymeneal song.
> Here striplings danced in circles to the sound
> Of pipe and harp.
>
> *Il.* xviii. 490 (COWPER).

And at funerals hired singers led the dirge or coronach for the dead, and others followed them with an accompaniment of

[1] Herod. ii. 79.

4

wailing.   At the funeral of Achilles the Muses are the leaders (ἔξαϛχοι)[1] and the Nereids accompany their strains.

Choral dances too, and the music of the harp accompanied these songs, but the dance was poetical or imitative; it did not merely consist of graceful gestures or rhythmical movements, but the action described by the song was dramatically represented by the dancer; it resembled, indeed, in some degree the ballet-dancing of modern times.   The cheerful festive scene depicted on the shield of Achilles, in the "Iliad," and the entertainment at the court of Menelaus, in the "Odyssey," well illustrate the nature of this triple union of music, pantomime, and poetry.

> They with well-tutored step now nimbly ran
> The circle, swift, as when, before his wheel
> Seated, the potter twirls it with both hands
> For trial of its speed, now crossing quick
> They passed at once into each other's place.
> On either side spectators numerous stood
> Delighted ; and two tumblers rolled themselves
> Between the dancers, singing as they rolled.
> <div align="right"><i>Il.</i> xviii. 599 (Cowper).</div>

> A sacred bard sang sweetly to his harp,
> While in the midst two dancers smote the ground
> With measured steps, responsive to his song.
> <div align="right"><i>Od.</i> iv. 18 (Cowper).</div>

If, then, the earliest poetry was either consecrated to the service of the gods, or designed to sympathize with the joys and sorrows of domestic life, it is clear what the engrossing subjects of these strains would be.   They must have been the praises of the gods, the melancholy legends interwoven with the popular mythology, the exploits of warriors and heroes, the joys of love and wine.

The deities with whose worship these plaintive strains and joyful songs were especially connected, were Apollo, Demeter, Dionysus, and Cybele.

Little as we know of the early minstrels or bards, it is certain that, as the composers of hymns and the only depositaries of family legends, they occupied a high place in the respect and veneration of the people.   The bard was gifted not only with

---

[1] Od. xxiv. 59.

poetic inspiration, but with the knowledge of futurity, and therefore he was the prophet and the seer, and both officers were signified by one common name. As their leader in common worship
and the keeper of their traditions, he was also, as it were, the
priest, the historian, the instructor of the laity. Not only did
he minister to their amusement, but his position was also one of
considerable influence and authority. Frequently he was the
political adviser of the prince, who confided to him the most
delicate duties. Agamemnon, for example, when he took the
command of the Trojan expedition, confided to a minstrel bard
his young and then virtuous wife, Clytemnestra.

The earliest of these bards and composers of hymns, whose
names have come down to us, are Orpheus, Eumolpus, Thamyris,
Musæus, Chrysothemis, Philammon, Olen, and some others.[1]
Philammon is said to have been a Delphian, Chrysothemis a
Cretan, Olen a Lycian, and the compositions of all are reported
to have referred to the worship of Apollo. Herodotus[2] tells us
that the hymns of Olen were sung in honor of Apollo, at Delos.
The other bards were, in Greek tradition, commonly called
Thracians. The probability is, that they were not natives
of Thrace Proper, but of Pieria, the district situated between
Macedonia, Thessaly, and Mount Olympus. These Pierians had
also southern settlements near Mount Helicon, in Bœotia; and
we learn from Herodotus,[3] that Xerxes, in his Thracian expedition, found fortresses belonging to them in Thrace itself. It was
to these districts, inhabited by these Pierian bards, that the
localities and names attributed to the Muses owe their origin.
Parnassus, Helicon, Pimpla, Libethra, Hippocrene, thus became
consecrated as the favorite haunts of the goddesses of song.

The poets, or rather minstrels, whose names have been mentioned, belong so entirely to the age of fable, that the legends
in which their history is incorporated, must be sought for in the
Greek mythology. Orpheus, the power of whose lyre over all
animate and inanimate nature, is celebrated throughout the writings of the ancient poets, was probably the author of religious
poetry. The worship which he celebrated was that of Dionysus,[4]

---

[1] Matthiæ, Hist. of Liter. part i. sect. 2.   [2] Herod. iv. 35.
[3] Ibid. vii. 112.   [4] Ibid. ii. 81.

not the jovial wine-god, but one dwelling in the darkness of the
lower world.   The ceremonies of it were of a mysterious nature,
like those of Eleusis, and those who took part in them were
admitted by solemn rites of initiation.   Hence, probably, arose
the legend of his descent to Hades in search of his beloved Eurydice.   The marked contrast between the solemn and pure worship
of this Dionysus Zagreus, and the wild orgies of the wine-god,
may have exposed him to the fierce enmity of a rival priesthood,
and given rise to the legend of his death at the hands of the
Thracian bacchanals.   The Orphic worship was of a pure and
self-denying character, its legends spoke of the soul's immortality,
its chief priests at Athens were the noble family of the Lyconidæ,
who professed to be the keepers of its traditions.   The literature
which bears the name of this fabulous poet was believed by some
to be the genuine productions of the Pre-Homeric age, but has
now been proved to consist partly of forgeries, partly of genuine
fragments belonging to a later period.

Eumolpus doubtless owes his existence to family vanity.   He
is the mythical patriarch of the Eumolpidæ, a noble Athenian
family, who were the high priests of the Eleusinian mysteries.
These, as their name implies (beautiful singers), claimed to be
descended from a line of holy bards, at the head of which they
placed this mythical poet.   Thamyris was said to have been the
son of Philammon, who, in his turn, boasted of Apollo as his
father.   Musæus was the reputed son of Orpheus, who, by birth
a Thracian, migrated to Athens.   His name typifies the first rise
of poetry, the earliest devotion paid to the Muses in the Grecian
capital.   Chrysothemis, if he existed at all, was probably one of
the founders of the Apollinarian worship, as the legend makes
him the son of a Cretan priest of that deity.

Olen is represented by the legend, not as a Greek, but a Lycian, or, as some say, a Hyperborean.   In either case, then, he
typifies the foreign origin of the worship of Apollo, and in the
former, that Lycian, or Lycean, worship alluded to in the most
common of all the epithets attributed to him by the poets.   Ancient art, in this case, as in many others, illustrates literature.[1]
Mure states, from his own observation, that the Lycian sculptures

---

[1] Hist. of Greek Literature, viii. 56.

of which England now possesses such valuable specimens, are precisely similar to those found at Mycenæ in the present day. Hence confirmation is given to the Homeric legend of an intercourse between Lycia and Argolis in mythical times, and to the popular tradition that the sculpture at Mycenæ, which bears obvious reference to the rites of Apollo, were the works of Lyeian artists.

CHAPTER III.

NO ACTUAL LITERATURE BEFORE HOMER.—HIS BIRTH-PLACE.—DIFFERENT TRADITIONS
RECONCILED.—ARGUMENT IN FAVOR OF SMYRNA.—DIFFICULT TO DETERMINE WHE-
THER HE WAS AN IONIAN OR AN ÆOLIAN.—LIFE BY HERODOTUS AND SUIDAS.—IMPORT-
ANCE OF THIS LEGENDARY BIOGRAPHY.—THE CHORIZONTES, OR SEPARATORS.—THEIR
DOCTRINES REVIEWED.—PAYNE KNIGHT.—NITZSCH.

ALTHOUGH, in the earliest ages, the religious aspirations of
man sought and found utterance in song, we cannot affirm the
actual existence of Greek poetic literature until the time of
Homer. The bards, his predecessors, may have done much for
the formation of a polished and harmonious language, they may
have handed down, from age to age, a store of heroic legends to
interest, wise sayings to instruct, and beautiful imagery to delight
their hearers; but it is to the author of the Homeric poems that
we are indebted for the first blending together all those parts in
one harmonious whole. These poems present the first instance
of a perfect systematic plot, a unity of design, steadily keeping
one end in view, and persevering until it is attained, a plot carried out by characters, whose consistency is maintained to the
conclusion of the poem. Such is that wonderful and almost
superhuman work the epic poem, of which there are but few in
the whole circle of the world's literature, and of which the
authors stood out in bold relief as the exceptions to the rest of
their kind. Homer, Virgil, Dante, Tasso, Milton, the. author of
the " Cid," are poets whose existence can scarcely be expected,
except at intervals of centuries.

Seven cities contended for the honor of being the birth-place
of Homer.

Smyrna, Chios, Colophon, Salamis, Rhodos, Argos, Athenæ,
   Orbis de patriâ certat, Homere, tuâ.

K. O. Muller[1] supposes that there is by no means such discrepancy in these traditions as at first sight appears. Athens claimed the honor as pretending to be the mother city of Smyrna.[2] In Chios lived a society called Homeridæ. They were probably, judging from the sense in which the word is used in Plato, admirers and imitators of Homer, but the patronymic form of the word caused them to be considered as his descendants, and hence tradition represented Homer as

The blind old man of Scio's rocky isle.

Again, Ephesus was connected with Smyrna, as having sent thither the first band of colonists; and these, when driven out by an invading party of Æolians, sought and obtained refuge at Colophon. Thus Smyrna, after all, appears to be the stem from which branch forth the majority of the seven claims.

The prevailing opinion among the ancients was that he was a Smyrnean; his epithet, Melesigenes, being derived from the river Meles, in the neighborhood of Smyrna. Upon the whole, notwithstanding it has been argued that he was a European, and by Briant that he was a native of Ithaca, all his local descriptions, his feelings and prejudices, displayed in his works, are in favor of the supposition that he was an Asiatic, and probably an Ionian.[3] His accurate and graphic descriptions of the Asiatic coast of the Ægean, and the scenery of the adjacent islands, are those of one long and familiarly acquainted with them. His statement that the west wind blows the waves in shore, is the language of one accustomed to the coast of the Levant.

" The swans of Cayster—the Asian meadows—and other scenes in Ionia, are described with the faithfulness and feeling of one who connected them with his earliest recollections."[4]

He shows the greatest reverence for the Ionian theology.[5] Poseidon is recognized by him as the deity of the Ionian league. Ajax is represented as an Attic (and therefore an Ionic) hero, instead of being described, according to the Dorian usage, as of the same family with Achilles.

[1] Literature of Greece, chap. v.
[2] Bekker's Anecdota, vol. ii. p. 768.
[3] See Plato, De Legg. iii. p. 680.
[4] Müller, c. v.   [5] Ibid. c. v.

The Homerides, his principal admirers, inhabited Chios, which was situated off the Ionian coast; and the Cyclic poets, who, in their feeble imitations, prolonged his strain, were likewise Ionians. With the exception of one passage (Il. δ´, 40) he has avoided any allusion to the Dorian conquest of the Peloponnesus,[1] for the Dorians were the enemies of the Ionian race; and, lastly, the only Heraclid chieftain in the "Iliad" is Tlepolemus, who was driven out by his brother, and joined the Æolians. The probability that Homer was an Asiatic Greek almost amounts to a certainty. The only doubt is whether he was an Ionian or Æolian; and in support of the belief that he was an Æolian, it may be asserted that in his dialect there is as much Æolic as Ionic Greek; that the Trojan war is an Æolian tradition; and that the most circumstantial accounts of his life are evidently based upon Æolian legends.

With respect to the era in which he lived, Mitford[2] places it previous to the Dorian conquest in B.C. 1104; Clinton subsequently to that event, B.C. 962—927; the Arundel Marbles, in B.C. 907. But, according to Herodotus,[3] he flourished about four hundred years before his time. This date is approved by Heyne, and is supported by the opinion generally prevalent in ancient times. Besides these considerations, it will be seen to agree best with the theory of Homer's personality; and for those who deny this, to fix any definite period for the composition of the poems is manifestly groundless and visionary.

There are many lives of Homer, all of which, whatever truth is mixed up with them, derive their materials from early legendary history. Two of these are attributed to Plutarch, and one—by far the most circumstantial—is ascribed to Herodotus. The great historian, as is evident from passages in his work,[4] took great pains to collect information respecting the divine poet, and therefore the following biography has been compiled from his, with the addition of a few traditions recorded by Suidas, in his short compilation.[5] The legend followed by Herodotus is evidently of Æolian origin.

Melanopus, a Magnesian, was one of the early settlers in the

---

[1] See Clinton, vol. i., Appendix.   [2] Mitford, i. 140.
[3] Herod. Eut. 53.   [4] Ibid. lib. ii. and iv.   [5] Suidas s. v.

Æolian town of Cyme. At his death, he left his daughter, Critheïs, to the guardianship of Cleanax. He, finding that she was pregnant, consigned her to the care of Ismenias, who was one of the founders of Smyrna. On the banks of the Meles she gave birth to a son, who was therefore named Melesigenes; and afterwards, because he was given as an hostage to the Colophonians, he was surnamed ὅμηϛος (Homer). The supposed date of his birth, according to Herodotus, was four hundred years before his own time.

In very early youth he exhibited considerable talent, and a Leucadian merchant, named Mentes—whose name the poet has handed down to posterity in the "Odyssey"—struck with his genius, took him with him to sea. On this occasion he visited Ithaca, and there collected the materials for the "Odyssey." Thence he went to Colophon, where he became blind—a tradition doubtless derived from his name, Homer, which, according to another etymology, signified the blind man (ὁ μὴ ὁϛῶν). Later researches[1] have discovered that the name, Homer, was first given to the author of the "Iliad" and "Odyssey," by Xenophanes of Colophon. Smyrna, Cyme, Phocæa, Chios, successively became the place of his abode. At one period of his wanderings he became tutor to the son of a very wealthy man named Chiros, and at that time composed his comic poems. Another account says that he wrote them in order to amuse the children of the master of the shepherd, Glaucus. The "Iliad" and "Odyssey" were composed during the period of his residence at Chios. He married Aresiphane, a Chian, who bore him one daughter and two sons, named Erephon and Theolaus.

On his way to Greece he landed sick on the island of Irus. Some fishermen's boys, who were engaged in an employment, not of a very cleanly kind, asked him the riddle—

Ἅσσ᾽ ἕλομεν, λιπόμεσθα, ἃ δ᾽ οὐχ ἕλομεν, φερόμεσθα.

"What we caught we left, what we could not catch we carried with us."

On this Suidas gravely remarks that he did not die of vexation, because he could not guess the riddle, but of the disease under which he labored when he landed. He lived to a good old age,

[1] Welcker, Ep. Cycl., p. 186.

and was buried in the island. The inhabitants inscribed on his tomb the following elegy—

> Ἐνθάδε τήν ἱεραν κεφαλὴν κατὰ γαῖα καλύπτει,
> Ἀνδρῶν ἡρώων κοσμήτορα θεῖον Ὅμηρον.

> "Here his sacred head in Earth's dark bosom reposes,
>   Homer the poet divine who heroes adorns with his praises."

Dioscorides asserts that Homer's great object was to enforce upon the young the duty of temperance, and quotes many passages from his poems, in which he describes regal banquets, marriage-feasts, and public entertainments as consisting of the simplest fare. Suidas bears testimony to the purity of his life, and mentions a tradition to the effect that his reputed blindness typified his freedom from the power of desire which holds sway through the eyes. And no one can read the poems of Homer without being struck with one noble quality which distinguishes him not only amongst heathen but even amongst Christian poets, namely, that there is scarcely a passage or a thought throughout them which would give offence to the purest and most delicate mind. Horace wisely remarks, in his epistle to Lollius,[1] that the contrast between virtue and vice is more instructively painted in the Homeric poems than in the lectures of philosophers. The terrible evils of ungoverned passions — the prevailing sins of heroic natures—are - put forward as a stern moral lesson in the "Iliad," whilst the self-indulgent luxury and licentious riot of the suitors, the patience and resistance to temptation displayed by Ulysses, enforce the same moral lessons in the "Odyssey."

Such, then, in its general features, is the legendary biography of Homer. How much of truth is contained in it cannot of course be determined. Probably, as in most other cases, there is a groundwork of truth on which has been built up the superstructure of fable. But even a life, the principal part of which rests on no better authority than popular tradition, becomes, in the case of Homer, exceedingly valuable. It proves that the testimony of an age perhaps not far distant from the period at which the Homeric poems were written, believed in the personal existence of their author ; a belief which, as is well known, has

---

[1] Horace, Epistles, i. 2.

been attacked in later times with all the ingenuity of argument and the resources of learning. It is necessary, therefore, to a certain extent, to enter upon the much-vexed question of the origin of the Homeric poems.

No doubt was ever entertained by the ancients respecting the personality of Homer. Pindar,[1] Plato,[2] Aristotle,[3] and others all assumed this fact; nor did they even doubt that the " Iliad" and "Odyssey," were the work of one mind.

The genuineness of the lesser Homeric poems was denied by Herodotus;[4] and all works bearing his name, except the "Iliad" and " Odyssey," were rejected by Aristotle;[5] but the authorship of these remained undoubted.

The difference between these two poems did not escape the critical notice of the ancients, but it never appeared to them so great as to demand such an hypothesis in order to account for it as the supposing that they proceeded from two authors. The one was compared to the sun in its noon-day splendor; the other to that luminary when it sets, shorn of its beams;[6] but they would as readily have doubted the identity of the mid-day and evening sun as that of their greatest bard. Longinus even sees so intimate a connection between the " Iliad" and the " Odyssey," that he considers the latter as the ἐπίλογος, or proper conclusion, of the former poem, a relation which implies such an unity of design as marks the work of a single author.

This, however, was the side on which the ancient creed was first assailed. Some of the Alexandrian grammarians, of no great reputation, asserted, on account of some slight and not unnatural inconsistencies in language and mythology, that the "Iliad" and " Odyssey" belonged to different ages, and were the works of different authors; they were hence called οἱ χωρίζοντες, or the separators. They did not, however, succeed in overthrowing the popular belief. Their theory was looked upon as an ingenious paradox; it gradually died away, and was forgotten. Nor can it be a matter of astonishment that their speculations met with so little support, to those who know, from experience,

[1] Nem. viii. 29.   [2] Plato, Repub. iii. iv. vii.

[3] Nic. Ethics, ix. 10.   [4] Herod. ii. 117; iv. 117.

[5] Arist. Poet.   [6] Longinus.

how different are the works of the same poets at different periods
of their lives, and who know as a fact that the "Paradise Lost"
and "Paradise Regained" are the works of one and the same
Milton.   The doctrine of the Chorizontes was revived by Payne
Knight, who attempted to show inexplicable discrepancies between
events related in the two poems.   Nitzsch defended the theory
on the ground that there was a marked difference between the
theology of the "Iliad" and "Odyssey;" but as he asserts that
the attributes of deity, in the latter poem, are far holier and
purer, the difference may be accounted for by supposing that as
the poet advanced in years his ideas respecting the divine nature
reached a higher standard.

CHAPTER IV.

THEORY OF HEDELIN AND PERRAULT.—HEYNE.—BENTLEY'S SEQUEL.—WOOD'S ESSAY
ON HOMER.—WOLF'S PROLEGOMENA.—THE GROUNDS OF WOLF'S THEORY.—OBSERVA-
TIONS OF NITZSCH IN OPPOSITION TO WOLF'S ARGUMENTS.—HOW FAR HE AGREES WITH
HIS OPPONENT.—ARGUMENT FROM THE STATE OF THE LANGUAGE.—POWER OF MEM-
ORY.—THE QUESTION CAN ONLY BE DECIDED BY INTERNAL EVIDENCE.—WOLF DENIES
THE POETICAL UNITY OF THE POEMS.—INTERPOLATIONS AND ALTERATIONS HIGHLY
PROBABLE. — THE MATERIALS OF THE POEMS. — ANCIENT LAYS. — OBJECTION TO
HEYNE'S HYPOTHESIS.—LACHMANN'S HYPOTHESIS.

SCEPTICISM went no further than this attempt to deny that
the "Iliad" and the "Odyssey" were the works of the same
author, until the end of the seventeenth century. At that time
two French critics, Hedelin and Perrault, asserted that the
Homeric poems were compilations of various lays, the works of
different poets, all having the same subject, namely, the Trojan
war. This theory was adopted by the learned Heyne, who put
it into a more scholar-like form, and supported it with his wonted
learning and ingenuity. Still, however, the principal argument
of any value on which it rests for confirmation is, that so long a
poem, composed previous to the invention of the art of writing,
could scarcely have been the work of one mind. In the early
part of the eighteenth century, Bentley[1] proposed a new solution
of the difficulty. He assumed that, although these poems were
the work of one author, yet still, that he wrote a sequel or series
of songs to sing at festivals, as was the custom with the bards of
the heroic age ; and he accounted for the difference between the
stirring, warlike tone of the "Iliad," and the quiet, peaceful
scenes of the "Odyssey," by saying that the former was composed for men, the latter for women. He supposed that these
lays or songs were transmitted from generation to generation,
thus separate from each other, and that they were not collected
together until after an interval of five hundred years.

[1] " Letter to N. N. by Phileleuth."

In 1770, Wood published an essay on the original genius of Homer, in which he proposed the question, whether the Homeric poems were originally written? This suggested to Wolf the thorough and complete investigation of the subject, and in 1795 the "Prolegomena," or preface to Homer, appeared, the object of which was to prove, that the "Iliad" and "Odyssey" were a collection of separate lays, arranged and put together for the first time during the tyranny and by the order of Pisistratus. The grounds on which Wolf rested his theory were (1), that the art of writing was not sufficiently advanced, or writing material sufficiently convenient, to allow of the belief that the Homeric poems were written ; and (2), that, therefore, as they must have been orally recited, it is not probable that a poem would have been composed longer than could have been recited on a single occasion. The premises from which he deduces his first argument are, (a) that, although the Ionians used skins of sheep and goats[1] for writing on, as early as the first Olympiad, B. C. 776, the Greeks could not have had materials suitable for the transcription of long poems until the time of Amasis, who reigned between B. C. 570 and B. C. 525: (b) that the laws of Zaleucus were the earliest documents committed to writing, and that their probable date is the year B. C. 664. (c) A statement made by Josephus,[2] that Homer did not leave his poems in writing, but that they were handed down.from memory in songs, and afterwards put together and arranged. He confesses, indeed, that his arguments do not go so far as to prove that the art of writing was totally unknown at so early a period as that in which the Homeric poems were composed, but only that it could not possibly have been applied to literary productions. He considers that his view derives support from the internal evidence of the poems themselves, for from two passages in the "Iliad," and one in the "Odyssey," he draws the same. conclusion. The first of these is in the seventh "Iliad:"—

> Throughout all the host,
> To every chief and potentate of Greece,
> From right to left, the herald bore the lot

---

[1] Herod. v. 58.   [2] Apion, i. 2.

> By all disowned ; but when at length he reached
> The inscriber of the lot, who cast it in,
> Illustrious Ajax, in his open palm
> The herald placed it, standing by his side ;
> He conscious with heroic joy, the lot
> Cast at his foot, and thus exclaimed aloud.
>
> *Il.* vii. 183 (Cowper).

Here he conjectures, that if the mark had been written characters, the herald would himself have deciphered it. (2) In the
following passage :—

> Him therefore he dismissed
> To Lycia, charged with tales of dire import,
> Written in tablets, which he bade him show,
> That he might perish, to Anteia's sire.
>
> *Il.* vi. 168 (Cowper).

He asserts that the σήματα λυγρά were not words, but a species
of picture-writing. (3) Lastly, from the " Odyssey," viii. 163,
he infers that the captain remembers the contents of the ship,
instead of having an inventory of it, and, therefore, assumes that
the art of writing could not possibly have been in use at that
time.

Wolf's great opponent, G. W. Nitzsch, has denied that there
is any weight in these arguments. He asserts not only that the
use of wooden tablets and hides was introduced by the Phœnicians
into Ionia as early as the first Olympiad, but that even papyrus
was used long before the reign of Amasis ; that even the laws of
Lycurgus were not orally transmitted, although they preceded
those of Zaleucus ; and that the passage quoted from Josephus,
originated in his misunderstanding the sentiments of the grammarians on this point, who attributed the various readings of Homer
to the rhapsodists. But although, according to his theory, writing was in general use as early as the first Olympiad, it does not
affect the question, whether the Homeric poems were originally
written, unless the Homeric age is supposed to have been nearly
a century later than that fixed by the testimony of antiquity.

It is remarkable, however, that these two great opponents
approach near to one another's views ; for Wolf, after all, admits
that the art of writing was known in Ionia and Magna Græcia in

the seventh and eighth centuries B. C., and was used by Archilochus, Alcman, Pisander, and others, as early as the first Olympiad; and Nitzsch asserts that Homer probably flourished not much before the age of Lycurgus, as determined by Thucydides, and that if he lived earlier (which it is almost certain that he did), it is impossible to maintain that his poems were written.

With respect to the materials out of which the "Iliad" and "Odyssey" were compiled, Nitzsch, as well as another German critic (Ritschl), contended that the author was indebted to earlier bards, that his taste selected legends from a vast number of traditional epics, and his genius combined them into one whole. These were then handed down, orally, by such poets as the Homeridæ, and having become, by lapse of time, separated and dispersed, though not forgotten, were again collected and arranged by Pisistratus.

The most satisfactory method, however, of arriving at a probable solution of this difficult question is, a critical examination of the language in which the Homeric poems themselves are written; and the opinion which is every day gaining more supporters amongst scholars, is that, according to the known laws which regulate the progress and formation of language, the advanced state of the dialect, and the perfection of the metre, unanswerably prove that the poems must have been sung or recited long before they were committed to writing. Porson, for example, observed, that when the poems were composed the digamma must have been pronounced, and yet no trace of it is discovered in any manuscript, however ancient. It is also plain that the slight difference between the language of Homer and later Greek, when compared with the rapid changes observable in other languages, presents a philological anomaly very difficult of explanation, unless on the hypothesis that the poems were subjected to much revision, and adaptation to the language of a more advanced period of literature.

But although it is impossible to avoid making this admission, further considerations and an examination of Wolf's second position will show that it is of no importance towards settling the question at issue, but that it must be decided by the internal evidence of the poems themselves, and by that alone.

Accustomed as we are to all that assistance to literary composition which the art of writing supplies, and, what is still more important, to the substitute for memory itself, which the power of committing our thoughts to paper furnishes, it is scarcely possible to form any idea of the natural powers of the memory when obliged to depend upon its own resources. We are, indeed, acquainted practically with the aid which metre and rhythm furnish; and the importance of this aid was so appreciated by the ancient Greeks, that they symbolized it in the belief that the Muses were daughters of Mnemosyne. It is not, therefore, so impossible a thing as it may at first sight appear, to conceive a poem of many thousand lines composed and arranged as a perfect whole, by an effort of memory, and then so perfectly retained in the mind as to be capable of recitation. Instances are not unknown of the wonderful power of memory when it is compelled to exert itself. Plutarch mentions the astonishing memories which the Greeks possessed. It is said also, that in modern times, the rude Calmucks have a national epic of three hundred and sixty cantos, each fully as long as a book of the "Iliad," and that their bards are in the habit of reciting twenty at one time.

Nor is it difficult to conceive that occasions of festivity might occur, in which the fervid imagination of the Greeks would listen with unwearied rapture to the recitation of the whole "Iliad" within the space of a few days. "If," says K. O. Müller,[1] "the Athenians could at one festival hear in succession nine tragedies, three satiric dramas, and as many comedies, without ever thinking that it might be better to distribute this enjoyment over the whole year, why should not the Greeks of earlier times have been able to listen to the 'Iliad' and 'Odyssey,' and perhaps other poems at the same festival?" Such occasions we know did occur at the Panionian festival,[2] where poetical contests of the bards were held; at Sicyon,[3] during the contests of the rhapsodists in the time of Clisthenes; and also in many other parts of Greece. Besides it is not inconsistent with the theory, that each of these poems was composed with an unity of subject and design, to suppose that some of the parts or episodes might have been

---

[1] Literature of Greece, p. 62.
Heyne, Ex. viii. p. 796. [3] Herod. v. 67.

5

recited separately; that the plan of the whole and the gradual unfolding of the story should be so well known, from familiarity with it, that the hearers could delight in the recitation of a part, and their imaginations readily place and arrange it in the framework which fully occupied their minds. In later times it was essential to the idea of Greek tragedy that the histories which the poets developed should be well known to the audience, and this, probably, was the case with the legends of the Trojan war, which were the original foundation of the "Iliad" and "Odyssey."

Again, to refer, by way of illustration, to the habits of modern times, the popularity of those romances, which are periodically published in parts, shows that even with long intervals between the publication of the parts, it is possible to sustain the interest of a tale and to keep awake the attention of the reader. In the same manner, those who listened to the divine poems of Homer, might have delighted to receive, book by book, his inspired strains.

All these considerations go far to remove two difficulties suggested by Wolf's second argument, but independently of them there are inconsistencies in his theory which cannot be reconciled with one another.

It cannot, however, be too strongly, or too constantly insisted on, that the decision of the question respecting the personality of Homer, is not affected by the fact, which must be admitted, that the poems were composed, recited, and transmitted for a long period without the use of writing. It really depends upon the internal evidence, on an examination of the structure of the poems themselves. If they bear evident, unanswerable marks of unity of design, this fact is strong enough to overthrow all objections, however subtle or ingenious they may be; for it would be more difficult to imagine that oneness of design was the result of accident, or of the piercing and cementing together the works of many different minds, than to admit all the other objections, however incapable of explanation.

This the acute mind of Wolf perceived; and, therefore, as his third argument, he denied the poetical unity of the poems. It is unnecessary to state the steps by which he endeavored to establish this position ; it will be far better to show in the history of this controversy how satisfactorily others have proved their unity. In doing this it must be admitted, that, as the natural result of that transmission, many alterations must have taken place, and many interpolations been introduced; that, although at first a complete whole, they became broken up and separated by the reciters, whether rhapsodists or others ; and that the dismembered parts were rejoined, the dispersed fragments collected, and the poems reconstructed in their present form by command of Pisistratus; but not then for the first time.

It must also be allowed that Homer drew largely upon ancient lays and legends of the ballad kind. The early existence of poetry in those ages, which are termed mythical, the unbounded fruitfulness of Greek genius, the interest which would invest the exploits attributed by tradition to the respective heroes of those races which formed the Greek nation, must have given birth to something like a ballad literature. An epic poet would naturally take advantage of this mass of popular legends. It would be a rich mine from which to draw materials likely to be acceptable to his hearers, and he might thus build up an "Iliad" or an "Odyssey," as authors of more modern times constructed the poem of the "Cid," or the "Niebelungen Lied." This opinion is perfectly consistent with a belief in a single author of the great Homeric poems, and in that unity of design which Aristotle observed and admired both in the "Iliad" and "Odyssey."

. The existence of these various legends and poems, from which the mind of a single poet compiled one consistent and harmonious whole, is perfectly conceivable without going so far as to assert the hypothesis of Heyne,[1] that there existed some older "Iliad" and "Odyssey" from which several bards compiled the different rhapsodies now composing the poems entitled the "Iliad" and "Odyssey." This hypothesis only places the difficulty a step farther back, without furnishing any solution of it ; and it may be asked, is it probable that these numerous poets should each have composed only a single episode, and that on one limited and narrow subject; or, if they composed other pieces, that not one of the rest should have been rescued from oblivion ?

[1] Opusc. vol. vi.

Whatever the external historical evidence may be, it is power-less to overthrow that which is derived from the structure of the poems themselves. Unity of plan is an unanswerable proof of any poem being the work of one mind. This truth was so clearly seen by Lachmann, the most sagacious of modern critics who have assailed the existence of Homer, that he felt that all argument was useless until the unity of the Homeric poems was disproved. He has, therefore, attempted to prove, by a series of apparent incongruities, that the boasted unity which has been the theme of critics from Aristotle downwards, and which was held up as a model by that great master of poetical criticism, does not exist. His theory is, that the "Iliad" is made up of no less than eighteen different and totally distinct lays, easily separable from one another.

CHAPTER V.

I. LANGUAGE, STYLE, AND TASTE OF THE ILIAD.—HOMERIC VERSE.—SIMILE.—DRAMATIC POWER.—OTHER POINTS OF RESEMBLANCE.—LANGUAGE, VERSIFICATION, ETC., OF THE ODYSSEY.—STYLE OF THE ILIAD AND ODYSSEY COMPARED.—II. PLAN OF THE ILIAD AND ODYSSEY.—EPITOMES OF BOTH.—GENERAL OBSERVATIONS.

In order to prove from internal evidence that the Homeric poems are the works of one author, it is necessary to establish three points. I. General similarity of style, taste, and feeling. II. Unity of plan. III. Consistency in the characters.

I. To enter into a critical examination of the style and language of Homer would be inconsistent with the plan of this work; it must suffice, therefore, to state the results which seem to arise out of an accurate study of the text. The language of the "Iliad" is throughout evidently that of one period; it does not exhibit so much variation as might be supposed to take place during the course of two successive generations; but more than this, the propriety of expression, the adaptation of the descriptions to the things described, bear such marks of undesigned and natural resemblance, that it is scarcely possible to imagine them to have proceeded from more than one mind. Such, it must be confessed, is the general impression produced upon the reader, unless biassed and inclined towards the contrary belief by other arguments and considerations. The same words, the same phrases, the same modes of illustration, are constantly recurring. Some favorite similes, e. g. such as those of the lion and the boar, are frequently used. Their details are sufficiently similar to show probable identity of authorship, without wearying by too much repetition. The same musical rhythm and metrical arrangement are preserved throughout. The Homeric verse is *sui generis*—it can be compared to that of no other poet in any age. And this phenomenon, be it remembered, occurred when the laws of metre must have been simply the suggestions of a delicately organized ear and a naturally refined taste. They could not have been reduced to rule in so remote an age, and, therefore, there were no means of attaining resemblance to one great and perfect model by study and imitation.

There is a characteristic of the Homeric poetry which, in the manner of its treatment, is without parallel, although it has been intimated by countless poets since his time : that is, the Simile. It is, evidently, the favorite figure of the bard, full of knowledge gathered from observation of nature, animate and inanimate. He delighted thus to illustrate his subject, and at the same time make the illustration itself a perfect and independent picture, by painting it in the most striking and interesting colors. Apposite as the Homeric similes are, it is not that quality which strikes the reader as constituting their especial beauty ; we almost lose sight of its intention to illustrate, in the profusion and variety of the images presented to us. We should be pleased even if the illustration were scarcely applicable. This is not the case with the similes of any author, except where they are palpable imitations of those of Homer. As no poet ever possessed the same graphic power, so none could venture, without danger of producing weariness, to introduce this figure so frequently. Every part of the "Iliad" abounds with them, except the commencement and conclusion of the poem ; and this fact is to be accounted for by the busy character of these portions : the rapid succession of events left no room for illustration. It will be sufficient to refer to a few of the most characteristic, and at the same time most beautiful Homeric similes, in order to prove that their features are unlike those found in the works of any other poets except his imitators.

> So in some spacious marsh the poplar falls,
> Smooth-skinned with boughs unladen, save aloft,
> Some chariot-builder, with his axe, the trunk
> Severs, that he may warp it to a wheel
> Of shapely form, meantime, exposed it lies
> To parching airs beside the running stream.
>> *Il.* iv. 482 (COWPER).

As a winter flood

The buttressed bridge checks not its sudden force ;
The firm enclosure of vine-planted fields,
Luxuriant, falls before it ; finished works
Of youthful hinds, once pleasant to the eye,
Now levelled, after ceaseless rain from Jove.
So drove Tydides into sudden flight
The Trojans.

Il. v. 87 (COWPER).

As in the garden with the weight surcharged,
Of his own fruit, and drenched by vernal rains,
The poppy falls oblique ; so he his head
Hung languid, by his helmet's weight oppress'd.

Il. viii. 306 (COWPER).

As when the watch-dogs and assembled swains
Have driven a tawny lion from the stalls ;
Then, interdicting him his wished repast,
Watch all the night, he famished, yet again
Come, furious on, but speeds not; kept aloof
By frequent spears from daring hands, but more
By flashing torches, which, though fierce, he dreads,
Till at the dawn he sullen stalks away ;
So from before the Trojans Ajax stalked,
Sullen and with reluctance slow retired,
His brave heart trembling for the fleet of Greece.

Il. xi. 547 (COWPER).

     As the feathery snows
Fall frequent on some wintry day, when Jove
Hath risen to shed them on the race of man,
And show his arrowy stores, he lulls the winds,
Then shakes them down continual, covering thick
Mountain-tops, promontories, flowery meads,
And cultured valleys rich, the ports and shores
Receives it also of the hoary deep ;
But there the waves bound it, while all beside
Lies whelmed beneath Jove's fast descending shower.
So, thick from side to side, by Trojans hurled
Against the Greeks, and by the Greeks returned,
The stormy volleys flew.

Il. xii. 278 (COWPER).

     As wolves that gorge
The prey yet panting terrible in force ;
When on the mountains wild they have devoured
An antlered stag new slain with bloody jaws,
Troop all at once to some clear fountain, there

To lap with slender tongues the brimming wave;
No fears have they, but at their ease eject,
From full maws flatulent, the clotted gore
Such seemed the Myrmidon heroic chiefs.

Il. xvi. 156 (Cowper).

As the luxuriant olive, by a swain
Reared in some solitude, where rills abound,
Puts forth her buds, and fanned by genial airs,
On all sides hangs her boughs with whitest flowers;
But by a sudden whirlwind, from its trench,
Upturned it lies, extended on the field:
Such Panthus' warlike son, Euphorbus, seemed.

Il. xvii. 53 (Cowper).

Again, dramatic power pervades the whole poem. Every character describes himself and tells his own story. The poet is never seen, his sentiments are never known but through the medium of his actors: he is never subjective, he seems to forget himself. Although he is describing his own feelings, and enforcing his own sentiments, he never personally appears upon the stage, but leaves it to his characters to express his thoughts; and this is not only the case sometimes, but universally. Is it probable, then, that more than one poet, in one age, should have possessed this dramatic faculty in so eminent a degree?

Uniformity on other points of this nature seems to stamp the poem as the work of one mind.

Stories the most different from one another are told precisely in the same way; conversations and councils are carried on after the same plan. The sentiments on all important subjects, whether religious, political, or social, are uniform and without variation. One high tone of moral principle and willing obedience to law, both human and divine, pervades the whole work.

It is, doubtless, possible to conceive that a school of poets, such as the bards of the Homeric age must have been, venerated for their inspiration, and respected for their moral and religious worth, would have resembled each other in mental culture, taste, and sentiments; but they could not have been equal in that mental power, which would have been necessary to produce the uniformity in these points observable in the Homeric poems. Throughout the "Iliad," no more inequality of talent is to be discerned than in great works which are known to have had but one author—at any rate no more than would result from inter-polations and additions, the introduction of which, to a certain extent, it is impossible to deny.

The language of the "Odyssey" is, throughout the whole poem, as uniform in its structure and its principles as that of the "Iliad." The versification never varies, it has always the same mechanical structure and the same harmonious flow, which is so difficult to arrive at, without betraying a palpable attempt at imitation. There can be traced also from beginning to end, a consistent moral and religious principle, dramatic power, fidelity in describing, and taste in appreciating the beauties of nature, and lastly, spirit and picturesqueness in the use of similes and illustrations.

These considerations are in favor of the hypothesis that the "Odyssey" had but one author, and was not formed by collecting together lays and episodes by different poets. It now remains to inquire, whether the confessed discrepancies in language, taste, and sentiment, which exist between the "Iliad" and "Odyssey," are too great to warrant the belief that one poet was the author of both.

As regards language, the "Odyssey" undoubtedly exhibits, in a few instances, alterations in the form of words, which implies some slight advance. The forms in the "Odyssey," for example, are shorter than those in the "Iliad." The manifest tendency of the Greek language having been towards contraction and sim-plification of orthography, it is plain that this difference proves that the date of the "Odyssey" is subsequent to that of the "Iliad." But, on the other hand, as the grammatical construc-tion has undergone no change, it is probable that the difference of time was not greater than that of a single life.

Again, words are introduced in the "Odyssey" which are not found in the "Iliad." But this was absolutely required by the subject of the poem. Ideas were to be expressed in the former, which find no place in the latter, and therefore demanded new terms. A nomenclature was wanted to describe the manners and customs of domestic life, and the various wonders met with in the voyages and wanderings of Odysseus, different from that which represented the warlike exploits of heroes absent from their hearths and homes, although the poet was depicting one social period.

It cannot be denied that the "Odyssey" does not show the same sublimity and grandeur, the same fervid enthusiasm, and torrent-like eloquence as the "Iliad;" but it does not follow for that reason that it is an inferior work. It displays equal genius, but less imagination. The calmness of wisdom supersedes the storms of passion, and gives a general coloring to the whole, as different from that of the "Iliad" as the wrathful hero of the Trojan war differs from the prudent Odysseus. There is a contrast not only between the subjects, but the objects, of the two poems, sufficient to account for difference of style. The subject of the "Odyssey" is human life in all its varied points of view, its strange vicissitudes of fortune; the object is to inculcate, by precept and example, lessons of moral and political wisdom.

Doubtless, Homer was older when he wrote the "Odyssey," but he shows no marks, as Longinus would have us suppose, of decaying and declining genius. The subject was one suited to the riper and calmer judgment of maturer years, but it is treated skilfully and appropriately. The language, imagery, and poetical ornament are as suitable to its gentler nature, as fire and impetuosity are to the stirring scenes of the "Iliad." Wherever sublimity is appropriate, the "Odyssey" rises to as great a height as the "Iliad." If the awful contest of the elements is described, there is no deficiency in animation; if the terror, inspired by the unexpected presence of Odysseus, and the glories of his triumph over vice and profligacy are painted, the language is as majestic and dignified as that which narrates a battle in the "Iliad." The religious and almost devotional feeling which pervades the second poem, is far more awful and sublime than the mythological attributes with which the poet of the "Iliad" invests the Divine nature. Everywhere there are points of unequalled excellence which mark the world's poet. In moral power, in wise instruction, in tranquil reflection, in simplicity of historical narrative, in pathos, and in comic liveliness, the "Odyssey" is even superior to the grander poem.

If there is any difference observable between the metrical character of the "Iliad" and "Odyssey," it is simply this, that there is greater gravity and sedateness in that of the latter, more rapidity and energy in that of the former.[1] In the "Iliad" dactyles are more abundant; but in both, the versification, like the diction, is that which is best suited to the poet's intention, and leaves nothing in either case to be desired.

The dissimilarity of style, feeling, and sentiment in the "Iliad" and "Odyssey," furnishes but slight grounds for disbelieving the identity of authorship. The same ocean is at one time tossed by storms, at another smooth and tranquil as a lake. The same mind which is at one time agitated by the violence of passion, is at another calm as that of a child. The "Iliad" has its intervals of tranquillity and rest, but the variety of its action, the powerful interest with which it hurries us from scene to scene, and from episode to episode; the tumult of emotion which the descriptions of human passion excite in the breasts of those who sympathize with the varied fortunes of its heroes, remind us of a wild ocean across which sweep furious tempests, but which is occasionally lighted up by transient gleams of sunshine. The "Odyssey" by its peaceful beauty reminds us of voyages on the mirror-like surface of a summer sea, sparkling in the bright and cheerful sun-beam, broken only by a gentle ripple. In these two divine poems we see the same mind, the same creative imagination under two different aspects; and when we remember that vigor and passion are the characteristics of youth and of mature age, whilst a sadder and more serious calmness marks a later period of life, we may well assent to the theory of Longinus so far as to attribute the "Iliad" to the manhood, and the "Odyssey" to the old age of the great poet, although we cannot admit that his intellectual vigor had declined. In the one, doubtless, we are dazzled by his genius in its noonday splendor; in the other we admire its setting glories, less brilliant indeed, but not less beautiful.

II. The unity of plan and natural connection of the principal events will best be shown by a short epitome of the "Iliad" and "Odyssey;" and it will be plainly seen that as the plot of the latter poem is more intricate and complex than that of the former, so the skill displayed in the construction of it is more remarkable.

---

[1] See Coleridge, Introduction, p. 171.

ARGUMENT OF THE ILIAD.

The poet proposes to sing of Achilles' wrath and its terrible consequences to the Greeks. When the poem opens, more than eight years of the war are supposed to have passed away.[1] Chryseïs, who has been allotted to Agamemnon as his portion of the Theban spoil, is the daughter of a priest of Apollo; her father proposes to ransom her, but is refused. Apollo, in order to avenge the cause of his servant, afflicts the army with pestilence. Achilles calls a council, at which Agamemnon consents to restore Chryseïs, but declares that he will take in her place Briseïs, the favorite of Achilles. Hence a fierce quarrel arises between the heroes, and Achilles refuses to take part in the war. He then entreats Thetis to prevail on Zeus to avenge his wrongs: she accedes to this request of her son, and her prayer is granted.

Zeus, mindful of his promise to Thetis, deceives Agamemnon in a dream.[2] A council of war is called, in which Thersites attacks Agamemnon for his conduct towards Achilles: a battle is determined upon. This furnishes an opportunity for enumerating the forces both of the Greeks and Trojans.

The armies now meet, and Paris challenges Menelaus: Helen is to be the prize of the victor.[3] Menelaus is victorious, but Paris is rescued by Aphrodite, and conveyed to the apartments of Helen. Agamemnon then demands the fulfilment of the conditions.

Zeus sends Athene to renew hostilities by causing some one to violate the truce.[4] In the disguise of Laodocus she persuades Pandarus to shoot at Menelaus: he is wounded, and the battle begins.

The battle continues, and Diomede is the hero of it.[5] Wounded at first by Pandarus, he afterwards slays him. He pursues Aphrodite, and wounds her in the wrist; afterwards he attacks Ares, whom he drives from the field.

As Athene is the patroness of the invincible warrior Diomede, the augur Helenus sends Hector to Troy to advise a procession

[1] Il. i.   [2] Ibid. ii.   [3] Ibid. iii.
[4] Ibid. iv.   [5] Ibid. v.

to the temple of the goddess.[1] This gives him an opportunity of visiting Paris, and of exhorting him to return to the battle, and also of having an interview with his wife, Andromache.

Another single combat is proposed, and this time Hector is the challenger.[2] Ajax is selected by lot as the Greek champion. They fight, and night coming on, the heralds separate them. A council is held at Troy, in which Antenor advises the surrender of Helen, but Paris will not consent. The Greeks fortify their camp.

Zeus forbids the gods to interfere; and taking his seat on Ida, he weighs in a balance the fates of the two nations, and by his decree fortune favors the Trojans.[3] They assault the Greek camp. Heré and Athene set off in disobedience to the divine command, but are stopped by a message from Zeus. Night puts an end to the assault, but Hector prepares for a renewal of it in the morning.

Agamemnon calls a council, and complains of the false promises of Zeus; in his despair he proposes to return to Greece.[4] Nestor advises him to conciliate Achilles by restoring Briseïs: consequently Odysseus, Phœnix, and Ajax are sent to the tent of Achilles, but their proposals are treated with scorn.

The son of Atreus cannot sleep; he resolves, therefore, to seek counsel from Nestor and Menelaus.[5] During the same night Diomede and Odysseus make an expedition to the Trojan camp, slay a spy named Dolon, and afterwards the Thracian chieftain Rhesus, whose chariot and horses they capture.

Morning breaks, and Discord excites the Greeks to battle.[6] Atrides has pre-eminently distinguished himself. Diomede, Odysseus, and the physician Machaon, are all wounded and retire from the field. Achilles, who, notwithstanding his wrath, feels for the Greeks, sends Patroclus to inquire who is wounded. Nestor urges him to intercede with Achilles, and to persuade him to return; or if not, to entreat that he will send Patroclus disguised in his own armor.

The evil fortune of the Greeks still continues. Hector assaults their fortified camp, and succeeds in forcing an entrance.[7] The Greeks fly in confusion to their ships.

[1] Il. vi.   [2] Ibid. vii.   [3] Ibid. viii.   [4] Ibid. ix.
[5] Ibid. x.   [6] Ibid. xi.   [7] Ibid. xii.

Poseidon, disobeying the command of Zeus, disguised as Cal-
chas, sides with the Greeks ; Zeus still supports the Trojans.[1]
Many heroes are slain.   Hector still leads the assault, upbraids
Paris with his effeminacy, and hurls defiance at Ajax.

Nestor, who had been sitting drinking with the wounded Machaon, goes forth to view the bloody field.[2]   There he meets Odysseus, Diomede, and Agamemnon, who rebuke him for forsaking
the battle.   Heré borrows the cestus of Aphrodite, and, vanquished by love, Zeus sleeps.   Poseidon takes advantage of his
slumbers to help and encourage the Greeks.

The Greeks rally and rout the Trojans.[3]   Zeus awakes, reproaches Heré, and sends Iris to warn Poseidon from the field of
battle.   He declares the Greeks shall suffer until the wrath of
Achilles is appeased.   Apollo then, armed with the ægis, puts
the Greeks to flight.   Hector calls for fire to burn their fleet, but
all that come Ajax receives on his spear's point, till at length
twelve fall by his single arm.

Achilles arrays Patroclus in his armor,[4] gives him the command of the Myrmidons, and sends him to the relief of the camp.
The Trojans, thinking that it is Achilles, fly.   Patroclus pursues them, and performs wonderful feats of valor.   At length
Apollo smites him on the back, his head grows dizzy, his armor
falls from him, he is wounded by Euphorbus, and then run
through the back by Hector.   The dying words of the young
warrior foretell the death of his conqueror by the hands of
Achilles.

Menelaus bravely defends the body of Patroclus.[5]   Hector overtakes the bearers of Achilles' arms and puts them on.   Zeus
declares, that, though successful for a while, he shall never return
in them to Troy.   Zeus now relents, and sends Athene, in the
form of Phœnix, to assist the Greeks.   Menelaus bids Antilochus
carry the tidings of Patroclus' death to Achilles, and then, with
Meriones, bears the body from the field.

The groans of Achilles at his friend's death alarm Thetis in
the depths of ocean.[6]   She hastens to comfort him, and promises
that Hephæstus shall furnish him with new armor.   Iris, sent

---

[1] Il. xiii.   [2] Ibid. xiv.   [3] Ibid. xv.
[4] Ibid. xvi.   [5] Ibid. xvii.   [6] Ibid. xviii.

by Heré, bids him seek the fight. He obeys, stands by the entrenchment, and, at his very shout, confusion seizes the Trojans. Polydamas proposes that they should at once retire within the walls of Troy, but Hector wrathfully refuses. Hephæstus forges the armor, and the shield is described.

Achilles is reconciled with Agamemnon and generously exacts no conditions, but the latter voluntarily restores Briseïs.[1] Achilles arrays himself in his armor, mounts his chariot, and drives forth to battle.

Zeus now permits the gods to engage in the battle.[2] Æneas meets Achilles and is rescued by Poseidon, and afterwards Hector is saved by Apollo.

Achilles takes twelve youths prisoners, as offerings to the manes of Patroclus.[3] The river god endeavors to overwhelm him with his waters, but Athene and Poseidon appear, and tell him that this foe shall soon be conquered. The fire god prevails over the deity of the stream. The deities engage in the hottest of the battle.

Priam urges Hector not to remain and brave the fury of so dread a warrior as Achilles.[4] They meet and fight. Zeus weighs their doom in his golden balance; down sinks the lot of Hector, and his patron Apollo leaves his side. He falls transfixed by the spear of his adversary, who strips him of his armor, and drags his corpse at his chariot wheels.

The funeral rites of Patroclus are performed,[5] the twelve human victims sacrificed, and games are celebrated in his honor.

Achilles still wreaks his vengeance on the corpse of Hector; and Apollo, in compassion, preserves it from mutilation and decay.[6] The aged Priam, at the command of Zeus, begs his son's body, and Achilles, by the advice of Thetis, accepts the ransom. The funeral of Hector concludes the poem.

ARGUMENT OF THE ODYSSEY.

Odysseus being detained in the island of Calypso, a council of the gods is held, at which his return to Ithaca is resolved upon.[7]

[1] Il. xix.   [2] Ibid. xx.   [3] Ibid. xxi.   [4] Ibid. xxii.
[5] Ibid. xxiii.   [6] Ibid. xxiv.   [7] Odys. i.

Athene, in the likeness of Mentes, appears to Telemachus, and bids him dismiss the suitors of Penelope. She upbraids their wastefulness and extravagance, and commands Telemachus to summon a council, and prepare an expedition to Pylos and Sparta, in search of his father.

Telemachus obeys the instructions of the goddess, but, through the influence of the suitors, a ship is refused him, and the council hastily dissolved.[1] Athene, in the form of Mentor, provides him with a ship manned by volunteers, and his nurse, Euryclea, supplies him with provisions. He sails at sunset, accompanied by Athene, without his mother's knowledge.

The voyagers arrive at Pylos, and are hospitably received by Nestor, who tells them all that he knows respecting the Greeks since they left Troy.[2] Nestor then advises Telemachus to go to Menelaus, in order to learn tidings of Ulysses. The goddess soars to heaven, and is recognized by Nestor. Telemachus departs for Sparta, accompanied by Nestor's son Pisistratus, and at night they are entertained at Pheræ by Diocles.

They arrive at " the Hollow Lacedæmon," and Menelaus informs them that Odysseus is in the island of Calypso.[3] The scene now shifts to Ithaca, and the suitors are represented as engaged in sports before the palace-gates. One of them, Antinous, undertakes to attack Telemachus on his voyage home. Penelope being distressed with anxiety for her son, Athene appears to her in a dream to comfort her, in the form of her sister Iphthima.

Zeus sends Hermes to Calypso, commanding her to send away Odysseus.[4] She reluctantly obeys, and enables him to build a raft. He sets sail, but the angry Neptune, who was now returning from Æthiopia, raises a violent tempest and wrecks his raft. An ocean nymph gives him a magic zone, and tells him, without fear, to swim to Phæacia. After much suffering he arrives in safety.

Odysseus, oppressed with fatigue, sleeps.[5] Meanwhile Athene, in a dream, commands Nausicaa, the daughter of Alcinous, King of Phæacia, to go to the river and wash her garments for her approaching marriage. The princess, after her task is done,

[1] Odys. ii.   [2] Ibid. iii.   [3] Ibid. iv.
[4] Ibid. v.   [5] Ibid. vi.

plays at ball with her maidens, and the ball falling in the water wakes Odysseus. Nausicaa declares who she is, gives him food and wine and raiment, and leads him to her father's city.

Athene, in the form of a maiden bearing a pitcher, conducts Odysseus to the magnificent palace and gardens of Alcinous.[1] He, as a suppliant, begs the protection of Areta the queen, is hospitably received, and promised a safe return to Ithaca. He relates the story of his wanderings.

A council is held, and a galley prepared for the departure of Odysseus.[2] A banquet follows in his honor, and games are celebrated. The court bard Demodocus sings in joyous strains the loves of Ares and Aphrodite. Next, inspired by Apollo, he sings of the Trojan horse, and draws tears from the eyes of the stranger. Alcinous thereupon inquires who he is, and why he weeps.

Odysseus tells the tale of his adventures; he relates his victory over the Ciconians;[3] his visit to the Lotophagi; his imprisonment in the cave of the Cyclops Polyphemus; his arrival at the island of Æolus;[4] the destruction of his fleet by the Læstrygonians; his year's sojourn in the palace of the enchantress Circe; and his determination to visit the realms of Hades, in order to consult the spirit of Tiresias.

He proceeds to relate his descent to Hades; his interview with Tiresias, who prophesies the difficulties of his voyage home;[5] how that he conversed with his mother's shade, and many persons famed in legendary story, and witnessed the torments of Tityus, Tantalus, and Sisyphus.

He describes his adventures subsequent to his return from Hades;[6] his escape from the Sirens, and from Scylla and Charybdis, with the loss of six of his companions; how his friends, urged by the pangs of hunger, slew the oxen of the Sun; how his ship was wrecked in a storm, and himself alone saved on the fragments of his vessel.

The Phæacians load him with presents.[7] He sails, and in a deep sleep is conveyed to Ithaca. He wakes unconscious that he is in his native land. His ship is changed into a rock by Nep-

[1] Odys. vii.　　[2] Ibid. viii.　　[3] Ibid. ix.　　[4] Ibid. x.
[5] Ibid. xi.　　[6] Ibid. xii.　　[7] Ibid. xiii.

6

tunc.   Athene appears to him as a youthful shepherd, and tells him he is in Ithaca.   They consult how to assail the suitors ; he hides his treasures in a cave, and is changed into an aged wrinkled beggar by Athene.

He is hospitably received in the house of a noble swineherd named Eumæus.[1]   He tells his host a feigned story, and declares that Odysseus will soon return home.

Meanwhile, Athene has visited Lacedæmon, in order to summon Telemachus home.[2]   As he is offering up prayers and libations before setting sail, Theoclymenus, an Argive prophet, who has slain one of his countrymen, begs to be taken on board.   The scene shifts to Ithaca, and Eumæus tells his story to Odysseus. Telemachus arrives at Ithaca.   He commits Theoclymenus to the charge of Piræus, and landing, proceeds to the dwelling of Eumæus.

Eumæus is sent to Penelope to announce the return of Telemachus.[3]   At the command of Athene, Odysseus makes himself known to his son.   The suitors, who had gone in vain to intercept Telemachus, return to the city.

Telemachus tells his mother the history of his expedition.[4] Odysseus, led by Eumæus, arrives at the palace, and is recognized by his dog Argus.   Eumæus first enters the banquet hall, and Odysseus after him.   He is treated with such insult by Antinous, that even his profligate companions rebuke him for violating the laws of hospitality.   Penelope sends for the stranger, but he entreats permission to wait until the departure of the suitors.   Eumæus leaves him and returns home.

The beggar Irus, who is a favorite with the suitors, insults Ulysses, who severely chastises him, although supported in his insolence by his patrons.[5]   The extravagance and debauchery of the suitors continue, but Amphinomus, who in the sixteenth book had opposed the design upon the life of Telemachus, shows himself less wicked than the rest.   Penelope receives the suitor's gifts, but refuses compliance with their wishes.   Odysseus upbraids Melantho, the wanton mistress of Eurymachus, and is taunted and insulted by her and her paramour.

[1] Odys. xiv.   [2] Ibid. xv.   [3] Ibid. xvi.
[4] Ibid. xvii.   [5] Ibid. xviii.

Ulysses and Telemachus remove the arms from the armory.[1] The former tells Penelope that he has seen her husband, and that he will soon return. She describes to him the web by which she deceives the suitors. Euryclea, attending on Ulysses while bathing, discovers who he is, by a scar on his leg. The accident which caused it is described.

Ulysses, passing the night in the porch of the palace, is witness to the licentious conduct of the women.[2] A feast is celebrated in honor of Apollo, and the debauchery of the suitors continues. The suitors urge the assassination of Telemachus, but Amphinomus, warned by an omen, declares that he is under the divine protection. Theoclymenus, the Hyperesian seer, beholds, as in a vision, the awful punishment which awaits the suitors.

Penelope promises to marry the suitor, who shall bend the bow of Ulysses, and shoot between twelve axes placed in a line.[3] The bow is brought forward, but no one can bend it. Odysseus discovers himself to Eumæus and Philætius; bends the bow, and shoots between all the axes; and, as he shoots, thunder and lightning burst from heaven.

Ulysses discovers himself, and all the suitors, with the exception of Melanthius, Medon the bard, and Phemius the herald, are slain; the latter two are spared because they were in secret faithful to Ulysses.[4] Melanthius is then bound, and afterwards cut to pieces. The suitor's paramours are condemned to clear away the dead, and are then hung.

Euryclea informs Penelope that her husband is returned, and the suitors slain.[5] She will not believe the news, but at length she is convinced, and is transported with tenderness and love. They discourse of all that has happened to them since they separated. They retire to rest, and next morning Ulysses and his friends leave the city to visit Laertes.

Hermes conducts the souls of the suitors to Hades.[6] Odysseus discovers himself to his father, Laertes. A rebellion breaks out in which Eupithes, the father of the suitor Antinous, is the ringleader. Eupithes is slain by Laertes, and the rebels defeated.

[1] Odys. xix.　　[2] Ibid. xx.　　[3] Ibid. xxi.
[4] Ibid. xxii.　　[5] Ibid. xxiii.　　[6] Ibid. xxiv.

By the mediation of Athene, Odysseus grants peace to his offend-
ing but now submissive subjects.

A mere cursory perusal of these epitomes is sufficient to show
that there is in both poems that unity of plot which Aristotle
pointed out and admired. Events follow each other in natural
succession; they do not bear marks of having been forced into
their places; the subsidiary narratives, or episodes, are suggested
and ever after rendered necessary by the regular course of the
action.   And these are the results of the poet's taste, and not of
technical and artificial contrivance.

In the "Iliad," the one great event proposed by the poet as
the subject of his song, is the wrath of Achilles; and, with the
exception of a few passages, which may be considered as interpolations, the development of this idea, with all its terrible and
widely extended consequences, forms the web and texture of the
plot from the commencement to the catastrophe.   The disastrous
consequences are represented of two kinds, (1) Those which the
insult and injustice, of which the Greeks had been guilty towards
Achilles, brought upon themselves, and, (2) those which sprang
from Achilles' indulgence of his own angry feelings, and his
determined refusal to abstain from the contest.

Both these combine to invest with a powerful interest the
character of Achilles, and to make him, amongst the many heroes
of the poem, the noblest, the most heroic of them all, and to claim
for him and for his wrongs, the largest amount of the reader's
sympathy.   The first produces this effect by representing him
as undeservedly injured; the second, by showing his superiority
to the other Greek chieftains, and their incapacity as compared
with his warlike prowess.   As, therefore, there is one hero to
whom the rest are subordinate, the interest, however divided,
concentrates itself on this one point; and although we gladly accompany the poet in his delightful digressions, we feel that there
is in reality one hero, the course of whose adventures we are
pursuing.

The unity of the plan consists in this, that all its events group
themselves round Achilles.   Nor is this unity broken by the
action being continued after the wrath of Achilles has been paci-

fied, and the death of his friend avenged. This might, perhaps, at first sight appear the most natural catastrophe, were it not for the strong feeling which existed amongst the Greeks respecting the rites of sepulture. Not even the funeral games of Patroclus would have been sufficient to leave that impression upon the minds and feelings of his hearers, which a humane and religious poet would consider desirable. The vengeance taken by the exasperated hero on the senseless corpse of his enemy, was too horrible an idea to be left in possession of the mind, at the conclusion of the poem, without counteraction. This would have been carrying vengeance too far, and in an age which, though rude and warlike, had much true refinement, would, perhaps, have destroyed the admiration felt for the hero.

Ferocious as in some of its features the warrior character was, as typified in Achilles, it was humanized and softened by a noble and compassionate nature. The poet had an excellent opportunity for exhibiting the brighter side of the heroic character, by representing Achilles as sympathizing with the bitter grief of a bereaved father, and granting to his earnest supplications the only comfort of which he was capable. For this reason the present conclusion appears to be an integral part of the "Iliad," and absolutely necessary to the full completeness of the poet's design.

[In the "Odyssey," the unity of the plot, notwithstanding its greater complexity, is still more evident, if viewed according to the same principle; here the interest is still more decidedly concentrated upon the fortunes of an individual. He is engaged in a greater variety of adventures than the hero of the "Iliad" could possibly be, because the latter holds himself aloof from all the exploits which constitute the main substance of the poem; the hero of the "Iliad," on the contrary, is personally engaged in most of them. Hence there are in the "Odyssey," longer narratives and more numerous digressions from the main order of events; but all converge to the same point. The variety of interest, the rapid change of scene, are absolutely required by the conditions which the poet has imposed upon himself. He was bound to give a long series of interesting adventures, and the only method of doing this was by thus interweaving them with a plot of the dimensions suited to epic poetry.]

The " Odyssey" has been supposed naturally to terminate with
the recognition of Ulysses.   This is, doubtless, the denouement ;
but the moral object of the poem would not have been accomplished without the restoration of the legitimate monarch to his
throne, and to his proper place in the hearts and affections of his
people.   Nor is it easy to believe that the meeting of Odysseus
with his father Laertes is unnecessary to satisfy the interest of
the poem, or that any poet besides the author of the whole, could
have described it in such exquisitely touching terms.   It is
therefore probable that the present conclusion formed part of the
poet's design.

With regard to the circumstances attending the vengeance
taken upon the suitors, it must be ' confessed that the justice of
the case, the belief that such shameless vice demanded the sever-
est punishment, is the only defence which can be made for the
savage mutilation of Melanthius; it is so utterly inconsistent
with the general character of Odysseus, that if this portion of
the poem is genuine, it must be intended to represent him, not as
gratifying a brutal vengeance, but acting as the appointed minister of inexorable unrelenting justice.   The genuineness, however, of the second Necyia, or the descent of the suitors to
Hades, cannot be defended : it is superfluous and unnecessary ;
it is so palpable an imitation that it may safely be pronounced an
interpolation by a subsequent and not very skilful hand.

CHAPTER VI.

III. The well-known authority of Horace laid down, that consistency of character is essential to epic excellence. His axiom—

"———— servetur ad imum
Qualis ab incepto processerit, et sibi constet,"[1]

was founded upon a study of Homer, nor has the character of the great poet, on this point, ever been successfully impugned. Very brief observations therefore will be necessary.

In his heroes, the poet evidently intended to typify some striking phase of the heroic character. They all have their points of resemblance, but the points of contrast are more fully dwelt upon. Each is a representative man: standing out, therefore, thus in bold relief, the slightest inconsistency would be at once detected. So strong was the poet's impression of the distinct individuality of his heroes, that frequently the same distinctive epithet is applied to each, on the majority of occasions, throughout his whole career. Opposite as are the traits which mark the character of Achilles, they are all, vices as well as virtues, such as may be found united in noble and impetuous natures. Revengeful as he is, even to ferocity, his warm and passionate heart can sympathize with deep sorrow, and feel compassion for the vanquished. He is haughty and reserved, and yet a devoted and

[1] Horace, Art. Poet. 126.

affectionate friend, unrelenting under a sense of injustice, yet, when satisfaction is offered, he is generously and unconditionally forgiving.

Agamemnon has all the regard for his subjects, which marks the sovereign of a free people, but his generosity proceeds from impulse rather than principle, and therefore he is generally dignified, but sometimes vacillating. *weak*

Menelaus, though not kingly, possesses the virtues of royal race, he is brave and gentle, and has an unfeigned respect for the regal authority.

Nestor is an old man, and an experienced statesman, he has all the garrulity of the one, and the long-sighted wisdom of the other. He is too cheerful to betray much of the querulousness of age, although he cannot forbear comparing the virtues of former days with the degeneracy of the present generation.

Ajax and Diomede are thorough soldiers. The former has all the physical strength and animal courage which fit a man for the perils of war; the latter, the moral firmness and well-disciplined coolness which render him fit either to command or obey.

Odysseus possesses every qualification, bodily as well as mental, for influencing men's minds; he is of noble figure and graceful bearing, sound judging and discreet; an accurate observer of men and things. His intimate knowledge of the human heart and its crooked ways, causes the policy, which is his favorite weapon, to appear at times crafty and dishonest, but it is only appearance, for he is benevolent, and has a strong sense of justice.

Hector unites moral with physical courage, but his warlike spirit sometimes degenerates into rashness. He is domestic and affectionate, and shows that tenderness towards women and children which characterizes true bravery.

Priam is an Oriental sovereign, whose yielding yet amiable temper allows things to take their own course. He is too careless and self-indulgent to have any high moral principle, and yet he has strong affections and impulses towards good. At length the depth of his despair awakens his energy, and in his old age, for the first time, he acts with vigor and heroism.

Paris is an effeminate and conceited fop, but brave notwithstanding, as those often are who have been brought up in refinement and luxury.

Helen, though a light wanton, who has left her husband and child for an adulterer, is full of fascination. She is neither bold nor depraved; she can admire chastity, she feels remorse for her sin; to her seducer she is tender and faithful; but even when restored to her husband there remains that voluptuous self-indulgence which perhaps paved the way to her weakness and her fall.

Hecuba is a woman of strong passions, whose ferocity is increased and not softened by affliction; she never can look on Helen in any other light than as the cause of all her sorrows, and of course her revengeful temper can never forgive her.

Andromache, the affectionate wife and mother, has not a spark of selfishness in her character. In his life-time she was wrapped up in her husband, and after his death, though overwhelmed with the weight of her sorrows, she thinks more of her husband's fame, her child's irreparable loss, and the ruin of her country.

Such are the principal characters of the "Iliad." Those who play an important part in the "Odyssey," are very few. Helen and Odysseus have been already described, and in the luxurious matron restored to her place in society, and the patient strong-willed voyager struggling with adverse fortune, the same points of character which were depicted in the "Iliad" are plainly discoverable, modified, as they necessarily must be, by change of circumstances.

Telemachus is a modest, ingenuous, and promising youth, full of consideration for his mother, and although not yet able to act for himself, willing to act with decision and energy at the suggestion of a wise counsellor, and with a strong sense of filial duty and obedience to his father's will.

Penelope appears to possess the cool diplomatic policy which distinguishes her husband, alloyed with somewhat of duplicity. Exposed as she is to the solicitations of the suitors, she has doubtless a difficult part to play; but the false hopes with which she deceives them, and the stratagem with which she puts off the fulfilment of her promise, whilst she permits their riot and extravagance, are scarcely consistent with a high tone of morality. She remains, however, faithful to her husband, even when his return scarcely seems probable; and when her fidelity is rewarded by his return, her coldness gradually melts, her caution gives way to conviction, at length all her calculating shrewdness vanishes. The mask and restraint under which she had so long lived are removed, and her true woman's nature shines forth at once in all its tenderness and affection. Such a change, at first sight may appear inconsistent, but the skilful and gradual manner in which it is managed by the poet renders it perfectly natural.

Euryclea is a model nurse; she continues the same attention to Telemachus when he is a youth which she paid to him in infancy; nor is her kindness unreturned by her foster-child, for she it is to whom he applies in his difficulty when a ship is refused him by the suitors.

The elegant and unaffected simplicity of Nausicaa is most charming, and the noble swineherd, Eumæus, the keeper of the king's swine, the principal wealth of his rocky isle, presents an inimitable picture of that sturdy yeoman-like independence which is fostered and nurtured by the pursuits of rural life.

Such is the internal evidence in favor of both the great Homeric poems having been the works of one mind, and to this evidence may be added the following considerations. It is not too much to assert that the conditions requisite for denying the personality of Homer have never been fulfilled in any nation or in any times. The separators of the "Iliad" from the "Odyssey" require the belief that, during a period extending over no very wide space, there should have lived two poets, whose talents and genius were of so high an order and so nearly equal, as to have produced these two great poems. And yet the history of the world proves that no nation, during the whole period of its existence, has ever possessed more than one great epic poet. Rome had one Virgil, modern Italy one Dante, England one Milton.

If the separators demand that which is improbable, those who attribute the poems to a large number of original bards, argue in favor of a moral impossibility. To adopt their view, implies the belief that at a period when all the rest of the world was destitute of literature, except the Semitic nations inhabiting Palestine, Greece and her colonies were so fruitful in poets, as to give birth, almost simultaneously, to a vast number; that this phenomenon never occurred in that country, either before or since; that they all chose for their theme different parts of the same subject; and that these, by accident or design, were so portioned out amongst them, as to be capable of being welded together into one harmonious whole.   This whole was so complete, as to contain all that so acute a critic as Aristotle, and many scholars of the most accomplished taste since his time, deemed essential to an epic poem. Moreover, those who arranged and set in order these separate poems, whether we call them Rhapsodi or Diasceuastæ, must have possessed such exquisite skill and judgment, that the places where they are joined together never present the appearance of abrupt transition from one part to another.   And as this union could not have been effected without the composition of some fresh passages, they must have been poets and imitators nearly equal to the original composers themselves.

The most probable conclusion to be arrived at from balancing and comparing together these discordant views, is the following: At some period beyond the reach of history, a long and difficult struggle took place on the coast of Asia Minor between the natives and the Hellenic inhabitants of the opposite continent, which ended in the success of the latter.   Hence arose in a poetic age a multitude of lays and legends, which were constantly sung and recited on all public and private occasions, and took a strong hold on the taste and affections of the conquering people. These lays celebrated the exploits of heroes supposed to have been engaged in this war, whose names were well known and popular, and lived in the memory of posterity.

Legends of the gods and mythological traditions, which gradually assumed an uniform and systematic form, were mingled with the deeds of men, and thus the formation of the Greek mythology came to be attributed to the author of the Homeric poems.   At length there arose one master mind, the grasp of whose intellect could conceive a framework into which it was possible to weave these various traditions, so as to form one epic story.   The time when this took place is unknown, but as the state of society, of government, of the arts, correspond somewhat with those of Orientals, as described in Sacred History at the time of the

Jewish monarchy, the period at which this poet flourished, may have been that fixed by Herodotus. He was a Greek, certainly an Asiatic, probably an Ionian; what his name was matters not, after ages have called him Homer. In those traditions of a warlike nature, he found the materials for a poem, which he called the "Iliad," the central subject from which all the events and episodes diverged, being the wrath of Achilles. From those lays which sing of the arts of peace and the wonders of foreign lands, which he enriched by his own knowledge and observation, he framed the skeleton of the "Odyssey." Probably he did not write them, but if he had known how to write, and had done so, few would have been able to read his poems. The art of writing may have been invented, but it must have been in its infancy, and known to few, and the materials for writing must have been scarce and inconvenient.

Literature was addressed to the ear. At every social meeting, every gathering for joy or for sorrow, the bard was a welcome guest. Possessing the strong powers of memory which belong to one absorbed in the subject of his inspiration, he sang parts of his tale to an audience which listened with rapt attention. After he had passed away, his poems still lived in the affections of his countrymen. Multitudes of admirers (Homeridæ), schools of poets, like the schools of the prophets, of whom mention is made in the Old Testament, recited or imitated his strains, and wandered as minstrels from place to place, some reciting portions of Homer, others original poems, afterwards called Cyclic, the themes of which were connected with the Trojan war.

These wandering minstrels are frequently designated by the name of Rhapsodists, respecting the meaning of which word there is much doubt and difficulty, and nothing is for certain known. Some have derived it from the ῥάβδος, or *wand*, which the bard carried as the insignia of his office. Others from ῥάπτειν, *to sew*, because they joined, or, as it were, stitched together the various lays into one large poem. Pindar[1] alludes to both etymologies.

Thus the poems got broken up, dispersed, and separated. Their popularity prevented them from being forgotten; but when

[1] See Dict. of Antiq., ii. 506.

the art of writing so advanced, as to provide the means of preserving them, they existed only in an unconnected form. Solon,[1]
according to Diogenes Laertius, was the first to perceive that the
unconnected poems and episodes which the bards and minstrels
were accustomed to recite, were parts of a whole, and under his
direction some attempt was made at arrangement and order.
Then arose Pisistratus, famed like the rest who bear the misap-
plied name of tyrants, for their patronage of learning and literature.   He saw that the first step to cultivate Athenian taste was
to collect together into one these Homeric fragments, the " dis-
jeeta membra poetæ."   Part, probably, already existed in writing, and from these imperfect copies, but still more from oral
traditions, the Homeric poems were arranged by poets employed
under the direction of Pisistratus, and assumed the form which
they now possess.   Thus they became the fixed and recognized
standard of Greek poetic taste, and the foundation of their national literature.

This was an age ready to admire with enthusiasm rather than
to criticize.   The age of cold criticism did not commence in
Greece until the fire of Hellenic genius was well nigh extinct.
Hence much was accepted as genuine and Homeric which was
in reality the work of imitators—poems which the Homerids and
Rhapsodists had themselves written.   Not only perfect works
were attributed to Homer which modern critical taste has with
reason pronounced deficient in the stamp of his genius, but interpolations were introduced by those who are commonly called
Diasccuastæ into the genuine poems.

To the first undoubtedly belong those poems which are classed
under the appellation of Cyclic, the Hymns, or Proemia, as the
ancients termed them; and the comic and satiric poems, the
"Margites" and the "Batrachomyomachia," or Battle of Frogs
and Mice.

Easy as it is to determine the spurious poems of Homer from
their immeasurable inferiority to the " Iliad" and " Odyssey," it
is not so easy to point out the interpolations, so skilfully are
they interwoven with the original web of the story.

Discrepancies and inconsistencies do not furnish sufficient

[1] Diog. Laert., i. 57.

grounds for determining a passage to be spurious, since in so long a poem, especially if retained in the memory without the help of writing, it is not only probable but certain that the poet would fall into errors of this kind. Horace knew human nature well when he said—

"Aliquando bonus dormitat Homerus."

Nor can it be asserted that all passages or episodes are interpolated which could be safely omitted without injury to the plot, or breaking the thread of the narrative. If all those parts were interpolations which have in turn been held to be so by successive critics, very little of the "Iliad" would be left, except the first book; and that portion which commences with the thirteenth and ends with the eighteenth. Many of the most beautiful scenes would be eliminated—such as the speech of Andromache to Hector,[1] and the description of the shield of Achilles,[2] and other passages which have always justly been considered as best representing the mind and genius of Homer. The arguments, however, most deserving of consideration, are those which have been brought against the genuineness of the following passages; but even many of these arguments, although the most plausible, are far from satisfactory.

I. The catalogue of the ships has been condemned,[3] simply because it may be omitted without injury; but it may be answered, (1.) that such an enumeration, setting forth, as it does, the glory of Greece, gave the poet an opportunity of kindling a feeling of enthusiasm in his audience which no poet would willingly have passed over. (2.) That there is not throughout this long description the slightest inconsistency with any other part of the poem. (3.) That the accuracy of the descriptive epithets attached to each locality exhibits that felicitous power of observing and depicting the most striking natural features which is discernible throughout the Homeric poems.

II. The single combat between Menelaus and Paris has been considered spurious, on the ground of inconsistency with what follows.

---

[1] Il. iii.   [2] Ibid. xviii.   [3] Ibid. ii.

III. The scene on the walls of the city between Priam and Helen[1] is said by Heyne to be an interpolation.

IV. The Aristea of Diomede,[2] which forms the subject of the fifth and sixth books, has been thought by Heyne, with some probability, to be a separate poem.

V. The expedition of Diomede and Odysseus[3] by night, commonly called the Dolonea, where they kill Rhesus, the Thracian chieftain.

VI. All the conclusion of the poem subsequent to the death of Hector. This assertion bears some appearance of probability, because there is no doubt that the death of Hector is the true catastrophe of the poem. But it must not be forgotten how deep a reverence the ancient Greeks entertained for the dead, nor would this reverence have been satisfied had not Achilles fully avenged his friend's death, and performed his funeral obsequies. This same reverence probably caused the poet not to consider his work perfect until the mutilated and insulted corpse of the brave Trojan was restored to his mourning father, and the last sacred offices were performed even to the enemy of his country.

Such are some of the alleged interpolations in the "Iliad." In the "Odyssey" they are by no means so numerous.

I. The song of Demodocus, the Phæacian bard,[4] has been pronounced spurious, chiefly on the ground that there is a manifest discrepancy in the mythology. Venus being here represented as the wife of Vulcan, instead of one of the Graces. Mure has well observed,[5] (1.) that the legend is represented as that of a Phæacian bard, and therefore need not be in accordance with the Homeric mythology; (2.) that the adultery and divorce of Venus reconcile the apparent opposition.

II. The Alexandrians, Aristophanes, and Aristarchus, considered that the "Odyssey" terminated with the 296th line of the twenty-third book. The recognition of Ulysses and Penelope is, doubtless, the proper catastrophe, and the second Necyia,[6] or descent to Hades, has so many points of resemblance to the first that it is scarcely possible to conceive such unnecessary repeti-

---

[1] Il. iii.   [2] Ibid. v. vi.   [3] Ibid. x.
[4] Od. viii. ·   [5] Mure, ii. xviii. 5.   [6] Od. xxiv.

tion, especially in a poem, the construction of which is so artificial, and the unity of design so carefully maintained throughout
as it is in the " Odyssey."

That there are interpolations and corruptions it would be idle
to deny, but so skilfully have they been introduced that no critic
can point them out with certainty, nor is there one of those
which are best supported, so contradictory of the Homeric spirit
as to offend the taste of the most fastidious admirer.

Even Wolf himself was scarcely converted by his own arguments:[1] "So often," says he, " as I withdraw my mind from the
historical arguments, and observe in Homer's poems one coloring,
the adaptation of the events to the times, and the times to the
events, the consistency and agreement of the allusions, the same-
ness of character preserved in the heroes, I am angry with myself, and blame my own diligence and boldness, and look on all
which we read in Homer as Homeric, and in them admire the
skill of Homer alone."

One more question still remains for consideration, and that an
important one, on which scholars have entertained great variety
of opinions. Were the events recorded in the Homeric poems
purely fabulous, and the productions of the poet's imagination,
or was there some substratum of historical truths on which they
were founded?

It is an historical-fact that an Hellenic race, called Æolians,
had settlements at some early period on the coasts of Asia Minor.
It is plain, also, that they were not Asiatics; that they differed
from the inhabitants of Asia, and from all Orientals in their
language, their habits and customs, their religious faith and worship. It is also probable, from the internal evidence of poems
written by one who was himself one of cognate race with them,
that they were inferior to the Asiatics in the arts, luxuries, and
refinements of civilized life. And, lastly, as the Europeans with
whom they were evidently connected by blood, were celebrated
not only in mythical times, but also in those ages which are
within the reach of history, for their valor and warlike prowess,
it is not too much to assume that they were superior to the generality of Orientals as warriors. Greeks, in historical times, were

[1] Wolf, Preface to Homer, p. xxii.

successful in their struggles against the people of Asia; it is probable, therefore, that it would have been so in those ages of which there are only traditions, and no trustworthy records.

Now it is not probable that the Æolians should have obtained a settlement in the Troad without a struggle; that the inhabitants should have tamely and unresistingly evacuated a territory consisting of a fertile and well-watered plain, possessing forests of timber fit for building ships, an extensive sea-coast, and a beautiful climate. The settlement must have been made by conquests, and not by a simple act of migration, such as takes place to uninhabited countries.

The legends of the conquering people furnish precisely such a narrative as would account for their settlement in Asia Minor. Stripped of all their romantic detail, of the fabulous matter which gradually grew amidst them in the national lays and ballads, they relate that a confederate army of Greeks invaded the Troad, maintained a long and difficult struggle with the inhabitants, and were eventually successful. This is a tale the parallel of which may be found in the history of all nations, a tale which is not only antecedently credible, but which alone would account for the subsequent state of that portion of Asia Minor. It is not, therefore, sufficient to say that the traditions of the Trojan war, which, dispersed in different lays and legends, furnished Homer with the materials for his poems, may possibly have originated in some such struggle, but it may be asserted that no other hypothesis will satisfactorily account for the historical fact that an Æolian migration into the coast-country of Asia Minor took place in pre-historic times.

It may even be added, in further support of this view, that legends so numerous, so similar in their details, so uniform in their character, could scarcely have existed unless they had their origin in substantial truth. So deep a root had they taken in the Greek mind, so absorbing was their interest to the exclusion of any poetical topics which did not claim kindred with them, so early did a firm belief exist in their general truthfulness, so wide was their influence over the whole field of Greek literature—not in one age only, but during centuries —that the only plausible mode of accounting for the phenome-

7

non is by assuming the hypothesis of their being founded on fact. Every other method would be not only difficult, but unnatural.

If we argued that the probable and improbable parts of the legend rest on the same evidence, and therefore that if we believe in a Trojan war at all, we must on the same grounds receive as true all the mythological and miraculous machinery, the answer is that we do not believe in the Trojan war only because it is the production of the legend, but because that bare framework, which imagination afterwards clothed with poetical and mythical ornament, is absolutely necessary in order to account for what rests on actual historical evidence—namely, the occupation of the Troad by Æolians.

CHAPTER VII.

THE HOMERIC AGE.—DIVISION OF THE SUBJECT.—VALDE OF HOMERIC TESTIMONY.—
RELIGION.—ZEUS AND THE OTHER DEITIES —WORSHIP.—NO HERO-WORSHIP.—DIVINA-
TION.—DREAMS.—FUTURE STATE.—GOVERNMENT.—KINGLY POWER HEREDITARY AND
LIMITED.—ADMINISTRATION OF JUSTICE.—SOCIAL HABITS AND INSTITUTIONS.—HOSPI-
TALITY.—BARBARISM IN WAR.—INSECURE STATE OF SOCIETY.—LOVE.—THE CONDI-
TION OF THE FEMALE SEX.—FEMALE EMPLOYMENTS.—HOUSEHOLDS.—MARRIAGE.—OLD
AGE.—DEATH.—SCIENCE.—ASTRONOMY.—GEOGRAPHY.—MEDICINE.—ARITHMETIC.—
POETRY.—ORATORY.—MUSIC.—STATUARY.—PAINTING. — ORNAMENTAL ARTS.—USE-
FUL ARTS.—ART OF WAR.

THE Homeric poems contain so many particulars respecting
the age and state of society which they profess to describe, that
it will be interesting to examine the details of the picture presented to our view. These points shall be treated of in the following order :—religion, government, social habits and institutions, science and art.

On these points the authority of the Homeric poems ought to
be allowed great weight. The poet, as he is evidently describing
scenery with which he himself is frequently familiar, is also
depicting a state of society either such as prevailed in his own
times or was not far removed from them. Tradition furnished
him with his story and his heroes, but personal observation, and
such testimony as did not extend so far backward as to be out of
the sphere of truth and probability, provided him with the scenes
in which they moved, and the manner of life which they led, as
well domestic as political. The trust reposed in Homer as an
historian by ancient authors, such as Thucydides and Strabo,[1] is
far greater than is thus claimed for him. They felt strongly
that he was their only authority, that if they deserted him they
had nothing to trust to, and therefore they clung to him, not
only as a faithful delineator of life and manners and principles,
but as a truthful and credible historian.

[1] Strabo, Geogr., l. i.

It has often been remarked that the state of society which the Homeric poems depict, is a patriarchal one, and points of resemblance have been pointed out between it and that patriarchal period which is described in sacred literature. Doubtless the Homeric age is patriarchal in its character : it is the intermediate period between barbarism and refinement ; it has all the delightful simplicity of patriarchal times without the affectation of more advanced social cultivation. But with this simplicity, the descriptions given by Homer combine an intercourse with the world by means of extended commerce, and consequently a state of art, science, and general civilization, in advance of the patriarchal stage of society.

There will not, therefore, be found a very close parallelism. The patriarch of a pastoral tribe, summoned from his native land into a new country, living in tents, his riches principally consisting in flocks and herds, and asses, and camels, and servants, would naturally differ much from the chieftains, or kings, of races inhabiting Western Asia and Europe—living in cities, in the enjoyment of wealth and luxury, raising armies, and going, for the sake of conquest, on distant expeditions. The period of the Jewish monarchy will furnish points of resemblance to the Homeric age, not to be found in patriarchal times.

It is probable that the earliest form of religion in Greece was monotheism. It has been already observed, on the authority of Herodotus,[1] that the Pelasgians worshipped gods which had neither name nor surname. The only way in which the fact of their knowing no distinguishing appellations for different deities can be accounted for, is by supposing that they were the worshippers of one god. But, with so imaginative a people as the Greeks, this belief did not continue long ; they soon peopled heaven and earth, and the sea, and the regions under the earth, with deities. Men of heroic character were, by an admiring posterity, admitted into the peaceful orders of the gods after death, and the transition to polytheism must have been early and rapid. As these deities were the creations of a poetic imagination, and as the development and moulding into form of those traditions which owed their birth and their origin to the popular mind, was the

[1] Herod. ii. 52.

work of the early poets, Herodotus tells us that Homer and Hesiod were the framers of the Greek theogony. It cannot be supposed that the names given by Homer to the gods, were for the first time made known through the medium of his poems, or that the pedigrees of Hesiod were unheard of before. That Homer first described these persons, marked out more definitely the sphere of their respective authorities, and assigned to each more clearly their specific attributes, is highly probable; and thus, without being entirely the authors, Homer and Hesiod may be considered the framers and systematizers of the popular religious belief.

The mythology of Homer doubtless embodies those ideas of deity, which, in a more vague and uncertain form, had pervaded Greece long before, and the generations of Hesiod are figurative personifications of the order of creation as imagined by some old philosophy. "The way," says Thirlwall,[1] "in which Hesiod treats his subject, suggests a strong suspicion that his theogony or cosmogony was not the fruit of his own invention; and that, although to us it breathes the first lispings of Greek philosophy, they are only the faint echoes of an earlier and deeper strain."

The chief of the Olympian deities is Zeus; as he originally established the laws of Nature, so he constantly directs and controls all their operations. He rules over the rest of the gods as a king, or rather as the father of a royal race. His word and nod are law. His wisdom is surpassingly great, but his principal attribute is strength rather than wisdom; he is neither omniscient, omnipresent, nor all-powerful. He holds the balance which decides human destinies, but still Fate is an independent and co-ordinate power. Sometimes his will coincides with the decrees of Fate, sometimes he struggles in vain to resist its decisions. He can delay or hasten that which is pre-ordained, but he cannot change it.

Although an abstract principle, Destiny seems to represent the natural idea of Providence and the First Cause, whereas Zeus and the other deities constitute the personal machinery by which the fixed ordinances of this mysterious principle are carried

[1] Thirlwall, vol. i. c. 6.

into effect. This is the universal belief of Homer's gods and men. Heré says that all which shall happen to a man is allotted at his birth.[1] Athene declares that even the gods are powerless to save, when Fate summons a man.[2] Poseidon determines to rescue Æneas, because it is fated that he shall escape,[3] and Hector comforts Andromache with the assurance that no man can slay him until the appointed time. Zeus is subject to human weaknesses and wants, such as hunger and thirst. He "sleeps, and must be awakened." Nor is he free from such passions as agitate the human breast. He is not free from the emotions either of anger or desire. Limited only by Destiny, he controls the affairs of men with strict impartiality. By him kings rule with justice; the sacred rites of hospitality are under his protection. He defends the cause of the widow and the orphan; no suppliant addresses him in vain. He hears prayer and he especially punishes perjury, adultery, and the neglect of duty to parents, and the principal instruments of his vengeance are the pestilence and the thunderbolt.

The other deities are as inferior to him in their moral attributes as they are in power. They fear and stand in awe of their sovereign ruler, but frequently thwart his inclinations, and endeavor to resist or overreach him. Amongst themselves strife, and envy, and jealousy prevail, as they might amongst the members of an earthly court. The petty disputes and quarrels, the loves and caprices of the Olympian family constitute some of the few portions of the Homeric poems, in which an almost comic vein supersedes their grave stateliness and serious dignity. Zeus, supremely good and great, is often called upon to quell the factions and curb the humors of his quarrelsome courtiers, and to threaten expulsion from Olympus in case of disobedience to his will.[4]

A perfect analogy is maintained between the nature of gods and men. As in the veins of man flows the principle of life, so in their veins flow the divine ichor, the principle of immortality, and their frames require the support of nectar and ambrosia, as men need that of earthly food.

Although Zeus was generally the rewarder and protector of

[1] Il. xx. 128.   [2] Od. iii. 237.   [3] Il. xx. 300.   [4] Ibid. viii. 13.

truth and virtue, the inferior deities in their intercourse with men exercised a species of favoritism. This led them to violate the well-known principles and sanctions of morality. Minerva[1] advises Pandarus to bribe Apollo to aid in the murder of Menelaus, and even Zeus approves the treacherous deed. Hence the sin of the deepest dye was not to offend against the immutable principles of natural justice, but to neglect or offend a deity; and the sum and substance of religion consisted in averting their anger and propitiating their favor by prayer and by expensive offerings and sacrifices.

The executors of vengeance on the wicked were the Furies, whose abode was the darkness of the unseen world; they were unerring, implacable. According to Hesiod, they could punish gods as well as men;[2] and, therefore, they were as much dreaded by them as by mortals.

The religion of the heroic age was free from any taint of idolatry. No mention is made of any visible representation of Deity, excepting the statue of Athene in the citadel of Troy. The funeral rites of Patroclus, however, prove that it was not unpolluted by that darker stain, the offering of human sacrifices. This, however, is reprobated by Homer,[3] and perhaps introduced as characteristic of his hero's fierce temper and implacable resentment. Temples were not common. Mention is made of the oracular shrine of Delphi, and in the midst of the Phæacian market-place stood one in honor of Poseidon. They offered sacrifices beneath the open vault of heaven, and, like the nations of Canaan, in high places and sacred groves.

As in patriarchal ages, the patriarch was priest of his tribe, or family and household, so in the Homeric, the priestly office was united with that of the king. Not that we are to suppose that the kings were priests in the sense in which we generally understand the term, but that it was one of the functions of the king to offer sacrifice in behalf of his people. There were besides, priests, like Chryses, who were dedicated to the worship of some particular deity, and attached to some locality where the worship of that deity was established.

Earthly and sensual in their nature although the Homeric

---

[1] Il. iv. 101. [2] Theog. ii. 21. [3] Il. xxiv.

deities were, still they formed a race of beings perfectly distinct from mortals. No notion yet prevailed of elevating a mortal to the rank of a god. Those of distinguished virtue might, like Hercules and Ganymede, be admitted into the society of the gods, or endowed with immortality and perpetual youth, as Calypso wished Odysseus to be,[1] but this was all: hero-worship had not as yet appeared in Greece. The first dawn of this worship appears in Hesiod, where the spirits of the mighty dead are spoken of as tutelary deities, or guardian angels, watching over the conduct and the fortunes of men.

The desire of examining into futurity had not yet attained its highest development. Individuals, like the seer Calchas,[2] were believed to be inspired by Apollo, and to possess the gift of prophecy. The oracles of Dodona and Delphi had already become celebrated.[3] Natural phenomena, the appearance of the heavenly bodies, and the flight of birds of good or ill omen, were considered as prognosticating future events; but human energy was deemed superior to them all, and there was a lofty confidence felt in the justice and holiness of a righteous cause. "The best of omens is," says Hector, "to fight in one's country's defence."[4] In the Homeric age, too, it was not customary to divine future events by examining the entrails of the victim. Dreams were thought to be direct revelations from Zeus to man. It was thus that Agamemnon was induced to give battle to the Trojans, and Achilles urged to celebrate the funeral of Patroclus.[5]

One of the most important subjects for examination connected with religion is the belief respecting the condition of man after death. Homer evidently entertained some vague notion of the impossibility of the soul existing in a state of activity unless united to some immortal body. "In the house of Hades," says Achilles,[6] "the soul and image (ψυχὴ καὶ εἴδωλον) exist, but they have no vitals (φρένες)." The blood of a slaughtered victim is the device resorted to in order to supply that bodily vigor which is necessary to the activity of the spiritual principle. The separate existence of the soul appeared to him to imply a sad and melancholy immortality: it was an unreal shade in the midst of

[1] Od. v. 136.   [2] Il. i. 70.   [3] Od. xiv. 327 ; Il. ix. 404.
[4] Il. xii. 243.   [5] Ibid. ii. 8 ; xxiii. 65.   [6] Ibid. xxiii. 103.

a dark world of shadows. The indistinctness of his ideas causes them also to be inconsistent; for, imperfect as the existence appears to be which he describes, yet Odysseus not only sees, but converses with the shades of his mother, Hercules, and Achilles. The very administration of retributive justice in the courts below seems like a phantasmagoria—an unreal scene enacted in imitation of the realities of the visible world. In that system, punishment occupies a much more definite position than reward; the happiness of the blest was but a cheerless one after all, whilst the tortures of the wicked are painted in language calculated to convey lessons of terrible warning. The disembodied spirit could enjoy no rest in the regions of the invisible, until the funeral rites were performed. Hence it was that an enemy's vengeance pursued his foe after death, and delighted to mutilate the senseless corpse, and leave it a prey to dogs and birds; and hence the self-abasing agony with which the aged Priam implores that the mangled corpse of his warrior son may be restored for burial.

The form of government universal throughout Greece in the Homeric age was a limited hereditary monarchy. The monarch reigned by divine right, and from Zeus derived his authority.[1] But, nevertheless, the wisdom, the personal strength, stature and beauty with which Homer invests monarchs, implies that in some way or other personal merit contributed much to ensure the permanent possession of the throne. Agamemnon is hereditary monarch of Argos and the right of Telemachus to inherit his father's throne is recognized, yet still circumstances are considered possible which might exclude him from it. "Many chieftains," he says, "there are in Ithaca, of whom any one might be king."[2] When the aged Laertes and Odysseus become unfit for the cares of royalty, they abdicate in favor of their more vigorous sons.[3]

A council of state assisted the deliberations of the monarch. In Phæacia, the members of it are represented as bearing, like the king himself, the title of βασίλεις, or kings; and, therefore, are in reality his peers. Priam's council is described as meeting at the gates of the palace, a custom recorded in sacred history;

[1] Il. ii. 197; ii. 204. Theog. 96.   [2] Od. i. 394.   [3] Ibid. xi. 493.

and in the same place Nestor sat to administer justice. On important occasions a popular assembly was also convened. Telemachus, for example, appeals to the assembled people against the lawlessness of the suitors ; and Alcinous is represented as calling an assembly of the people to provide a ship and stores for Odysseus. In fact the governments of this age were, as described by Thucydides, πάτριαι βασίλειαι ἐπὶ ῥητοῖς γέρασι, hereditary monarchies, with defined privileges. The king deliberated with his council, and then referred the matter to the people. The ensign of regal power was a sceptre, but not a crown. One instance, and one alone, is mentioned by Homer, of a female sovereign. Andromache relates to Hector that when her father died, her mother became queen of Hypoplacia.[1]

Laws are mentioned in the "Iliad,"[2] but they vere rather traditional principles (θέμιστες) than enactments (νόμοι). Constitutional rights were unknown. The liberties of the subject and the administration of justice depended on the wisdom of the king and his councillors. Murder was considered a private rather than a public wrong. The family of the murdered man pursued with vengeance the murderer, unless he made compensation, or fled to a foreign land.[3] Sometimes the question of this compensation was decided by arbitration. Public wrongs were punished rarely, and then by the people themselves rather than by a public executioner ; and, as amongst the Israelites, the usual capital punishment was stoning to death.

The right of every stranger to demand the offices of hospitality was recognized as sacred.   "Be not forgetfu to entertain strangers," said St. Paul,[4] alluding to the incidents of patriarchal times, "for thereby some have entertained angels unawares." And, similarly, we are told in the "Odyssey" that the gods sometimes visit the dwellings of mankind in the shape of strangers.[5] It mattered not whether he was friend or foe, merchant or pirate,[6] if he but asked the shelter of a roof it was granted, and a participation in all that it contained, with ungrudging generosity. No questions were asked until the unknown guest had

[1] Il. vi. 425.   [2] Ibid. ii. 204.   [3] Od. xi. 493.
[4] Heb. xiii. 2.   [5] Od. vi. 208, xvii. 485.   [6] Ibid. xv. 373 ; xvii. 475.

received a hearty welcome.[1] Iobates did not ask to see the cre-
dentials of Bellerophon until he had entertained him during nine
days, nor did Nector inquire who Telemachus and Mentor were
until the feast was concluded, and the usual libation offered.

The domestic manners of the Homeric age were marked by
mingled refinement and barbarism, by moral purity, and yet by
a freedom almost approaching to indelicacy, by humanity almost
chivalrous, and a ferocity scarcely consistent with civilized life.
The song and the dance, the notes of the lyre, the recitation of
the bard, enlivened their social banquets, which were not dis-
graced by intemperance. But once, and that in the case of the
centaur Eurytion,[2] is intoxication described, and then attended
with such fearful consequences, as plainly prove the popular ab-
horrence of the vice, and how undeserved the expression of Horace,

"Laudibus arguitur vini vinosus Homerus."[3]

The tables of the great were covered with simple but plenteous
fare, which was enjoyed by guests of every rank; the libation in
honor of the gods preceded the enjoyment of the wine-cup.

Distinguished as Homer's heroes are for many noble and generous qualities, war was carried on with all the horrors which disgrace even barbarous tribes. In battle no quarter was given.
The only motive which induced the victor to spare the life of his
fallen foe, was the hope of obtaining ransom. Agamemnon reproaches Menelaus for listening to the entreaties for quarter of a
noble Trojan.[4] "Let none of them," he says, "escape deep destruction, no, not even the child in the mother's womb." " Thus
he spoke," remarks the poet, " and with justice, and he turned
his brother's mind." The bodies of the slain were stripped and
spoiled of their arms, and then insulted, mutilated, and thrown to
be mangled by birds and dogs.

Thus Hector spoils the dead body of Patroclus,[5] and seeks still
further to gratify his savage vengeance by depriving his foe of
that burial which was necessary for his future happiness, and
giving him to be devoured by the dogs of Troy. And the noble-

[1] Il. vi. 176; Od. iii. 69; Thuc. i. 5.   [2] Od. xxi. 295.
[3] Ep. i. xix. 6.   [4] Il. vi. 57.   [5] Ibid. xvii. 125.

minded Achilles imagined that the vengeance which he inflicted
on the body of Hector, was an offering of duty to his departed
friend, and on this ground alone hesitates to restore the corpse to
the mournful entreaties of the bereaved father.[1]

When a nation or a city was conquered, there was no mercy
for the vanquished.[2]   Such is the description given by Priam of
the evils of war, " My sons are slain, my daughters dragged into
captivity, the chambers of my palace violated, the infant children
dashed to the ground."

The wife of Meleager[3] is represented as recounting to her
husband the evils which fall upon those whose city is taken.
"They slay the men, the fire reduces the city to ashes, others
drag the women and children into slavery."   Such was the ferocity which was considered not unbecoming the Homeric hero in
war, a ferocity which marks even the rude and savage language
which warriors habitually address to each other, when they meet
as foemen on the field of battle.

The habits and manners of the age in time of peace, argue an
insecure state of society.   Legitimate commerce must have been
liable to constant danger and interruption from the prevalence
of piracy, which was as common as among the Norsemen and
sea-kings of later times.   As in a similar condition of society
in modern Europe, when the right of the stranger was recognized, the raids of the Highland chieftain, or the robberies of
the German baron, were deemed no disgrace; so the pirate in
the Homeric age was thought to atone for the cruelty and injustice of his outrages by their brilliance and gallantry.[4]   Notwithstanding the protection afforded to the domestic circle by the
holy ties of guest and host, and the sacred rites of hospitality,
it was often violated by the licentious ravisher.   Such deeds as,
according to the legend, led to the Trojan war itself, were probably too common, and the rape of Helen was by no means an
isolated event in the history of the Heroic Age.

We meet with little to justify the belief that the passion of
love was invested with that purity which belongs to the more
chivalrous manners of modern times.   The influence of Christi-

[1] Il. xxiv. 592.   [2] Ibid. xxii. 60.
[3] Ibid. ix. 590.   [4] Thucyd. and Odys.

anity alone added this element to mere sensual passion, in the
same way that it first moderated the vindictiveness of the warrior, and produced a generous spirit of mutual consideration
even between the bitterest enemies. The female sex, however,
enjoyed a much higher position than they did in a more advanced
period of Greek civilization. Oriental habits so far prevailed,
that their chambers, like the Eastern harem, were separate from
those of the men, and, as a general rule, the sexes lived distinct
from one another, but the occasional intercourse between them
was, to a certain extent, free and unrestrained.

Helen and Andromache, in the "Iliad," and Penelope in the
"Odyssey," enjoy a freedom somewhat approaching to that of
modern times. This freedom implies that they were considered
as the companions for the serious hours, and not as mere toys
for the amusement of man's lighter moments. Hence the behavior of Homer's greatest heroes towards women is marked by
politeness and tenderness, and even by a respect, which shows
that they recognized and did homage to the moral superiority of the weaker sex. The delicacy with which they regarded
maiden modesty, and the confidence consequently felt by woman
in the safety of her honor, were such, that offices were innocently
performed by women, which the greater refinement of modern
manners would consider inconsistent with maidenly modesty.

Telemachus, at the court of the Pylian monarch,[1] was attended
at his toilet and his bath by the virgin Polycaste, and the same
attention was offered by Penelope to Ulysses, when he returned
an unknown wanderer to his home.[2]

For the honorable position which women occupied, they were
well fitted by their virtue and accomplishments. The conjugal
devotion of Andromache, and the constancy of Penelope, were
probably not mere imaginary pictures. Even those of the highest
rank and the greatest refinement did not consider the humblest
domestic duties unworthy. Nestor's royal spouse prepares his
couch,[3] and the Princess Nausicaa washes her clothes in the river,
and tramples on them with her naked feet, like a Highland
maiden. The mistress superintended her maidens, and engaged

[1] Od. iii.   [2] Ibid. xix. 317.   [3] Ibid. iii. 403.

with them in their daily tasks, and then relieved her toil with the more elegant and graceful employment of the loom.

The members of a chieftain's household were very numerous.[1] They were slaves, generally prisoners of war, and were treated with kindness and consideration. Most domestic duties were performed by women, but the banquet was sometimes attended by young and pampered servitors, with glossy curls and fair faces.[2]

Young princes were assigned to the care of a private tutor, who, if we may judge from the address of Phœnix to Achilles,[3] performed also the duties of a nurse to their young charge; and nurses, on the other hand, if Euryclea is a specimen, attended on their foster-children even when they arrived at maturity.

Although female captives lived with the Homeric heroes as concubines, and their children were treated as though they were legitimate, polygamy did not exist amongst them. Priam was an Asiatic, and had many wives, according to Oriental custom. Children did not generally marry without the consent of their parents. Achilles refuses to marry the daughter of Agamemnon,[4] because Peleus will give him a wife if he returns home in safety. In the "Odyssey," also, the suitors consider Penelope bound to consult her father, and Nausicaa blames any maiden who would marry contrary to her parents' will. When a marriage was concluded, the bridegroom gave presents to the bride, and she, in her turn, was usually suitably portioned. It was not considered right that widows should marry whilst their children were so young as to require a mother's care.[5]

Active in his habits, and warlike in his pursuits, the hero looked upon old age as burdensome, and as rendering him incapable of the chief enjoyments of life, but, nevertheless, the aged were always treated with the greatest respect, their experience valued, and their counsel sought, in circumstances of difficulty. The dead were lamented with dirges and wailings, the surviving relatives mourned in dust and ashes.[6] Games and feasts were celebrated at the funeral of departed heroes,[7] their bodies were

[1] Od. xxii. 441. [2] Ibid. xv. 30. [3] Il. ix. 481.
[4] Ibid. ix. 388. [5] Od. xix. 594. [6] Il. xviii. 24.
[7] Il. xxiv. ; and Od. xxiv.

burnt upon a pile, frequently with their armor,[1] the ashes collected in an urn and buried. A mound, a stone, a tree, or, as in the case of Elpenor, some symbol of his pursuits during life, formed the simple memorial of the dead.[2]

Science was yet in its infancy, but although the Homeric poems contain but little scientific knowledge, they nevertheless display much careful and accurate observation of physical phenomena. The wonders of the starry heavens naturally engaged, in early times, the attention of the thoughtful and inquisitive mind. Homer had not arrived at the sublime idea which Job conceived, when he said, "God hangeth the earth upon nothing, He stretcheth the north over the empty space," but he saw from the coast of Asia that the sun, which rose and set in the ocean, shot its first beams across the island of Syros in different places at different seasons of the year.[3] He observed the fact of the solstices, although the reason was unknown in his days, and he naturally described that island as the place where were situated the tropics of the sun (ὅθι τροπαὶ ἠελίοιο). The difference between stars and planets was not yet known, but one brilliant star, the planet Venus, from its different position with relation to the sun, was denominated sometimes Hesperus, sometimes Phosphorus, the morning or the evening star. That both these were but one planet had not yet been discovered. The fixed stars had already begun to be arranged in groups, but the only constellations which as yet had received names, were the Great Bear, which he describes as always turning round and watching the mighty hunter Orion; the Pleiads, but not the Bull in which they are situated; the Hyads, Boötes, and Orion. Of these, the Bear alone bathes not in the waters of the ocean, i. e., is alone within the circle of perpetual apparition. Boötes he distinguishes by the epithet "late-setting" (ὀψὲ δύοντα),[4] implying that this constellation scarcely sets at all; in fact, on the coast of Asia Minor, only part of it ever sinks beneath the horizon. The brilliant track of light[5] which he describes as running by the dwelling of the gods, is probably the Milky Way. Orion's dog is probably Sirius,[6] for he speaks of its splendor in autumn, and its fatal influence

[1] Il. vi. 418.   [2] Od. xii. 16.   [3] Ibid. xv. 403.
[4] Ibid. v. 272.   [5] Ibid. vi. 45.   [6] Il. xxii. 29.

on the health of men. The rainbow which he, taught by some vague traditions of the truth, believed to have been placed in the cloud by Zeus as a sign to mortals,[1] he personifies as the heavenly messenger, this idea having probably grown out of the notion that it was the path bridging the space between earth and heaven.

The fact, of which the most practical use was then made, was, that when a star was visible on the horizon just before sunrise, or just after sunset, a particular season of the year was defined. By this phenomenon the agriculturist marked the proper period for his regularly recurring labors, and the mariner was taught to avoid the perils of a stormy sea.

Commercial intercourse had already contributed something to geographical knowledge ; even the manners of the northern nations were not unknown. Homer speaks of the Scythians, who live on milk, especially that of mares, and who have their households in wagons,

$$\text{Σκυθὰς ἱππημόλγους, Γλακτοφαγῶν, ἀκηναῖς αἴκι ἐχόντων,}$$

thus attributing to them a mode of life like those of the nomad Tartar tribes in modern times. The ocean[2] he believed to be a vast river, the source of all other streams, flowing entirely round the earth. The geographical knowledge of Homer extends westward, and not to the east, or to the interior of the Asiatic continent; hence he was familiar with the commerce of Phœnicia and Sidon, but not of Tyre, for, as Sir I. Newton observed, the Tyrians traded in the Red Sea and Persian Gulf, the Sidonians in the Mediterranean.

His geographical accuracy is very remarkable. Each epithet in the catalogue of the ships catches the characteristic features of the country which it describes. The topography of Ithaca has been carefully examined and verified by modern travellers,[3] the numerous cities and various languages of Crete[4] exactly agrees with the history of its colonization. Some of his apparent inaccuracies may be accounted for. Pharos, for example, he describes as distant a day's voyage from the coast; doubtless the alluvium of the Nile during the lapse of centuries caused this

[1] Il. xi. 27.   [2] Ibid. xxi. 196 ; Od. xi. 156.
[3] Gell and Dodwell.   [4] Od. xix. 172.

distance to be diminished; and his omitting to mention the vol-
canoes of Ætna and Vesuvius, though he speaks of the Italian
and Sicilian coasts, is explicable on the hypothesis that no erup-
tions had taken place during his memory. Surgery was the only
branch practiced of the science of medicine. Disease was
inflicted by the vengeance of heaven, and no human skill was
able to arrest the blow. Wounds which were the work of human
weapons, were able to be treated by man. The surgeon was
held in the highest esteem. He knew, however, only the mere
rudiments of anatomy, and the treatment which he prescribed
was very simple. The wound was dressed with herbs, and the
hemorrhage was stopped by the rust of a brazen spear.

The only notice of arithmetical science found in the Homeric
poems is a passage in the "Odyssey,"[1] which shows that as yet
it had not advanced beyond the simple plan of enumerating large
sums on the fingers. Proteus is represented as counting his
phocæ by fives—πεμπάσσεται. Evidently, therefore, the more
convenient method of a decimal notation was unknown.

Commercial intercourse with the wealthy and luxurious nations
of Asia furnished the means at once for indulging and cultivating the natural taste for the beautiful which distinguished the
Ionian race. Hence, although science was in its infancy, and
society in an intermediate condition between barbarism and refinement, art, nevertheless, was in a remarkably flourishing state.

In no race of mankind were the faculties of mind and body
more harmoniously proportioned, or the appreciation of the sensible more nicely blended with that of the spiritual, than in the
Ionian. None, therefore, had greater natural capabilities, as
well as greater external advantages for the cultivation of art.
The Homeric poems themselves, and the place which the bard
occupied in public estimation, are an evidence of their love for
poetry of the highest order. The numerous speeches contained
in the "Iliad" and "Odyssey" prove the cultivation of even the
graces of oratory, and the practice of reciting poems to the
accompaniment of the harp, shows that, although the science of
harmony was not yet understood, music as an art was commonly
known. Musical instruments were, of course, very simple, and

[1] Od. iv. 412.

consisted of the flute or pipe (αὐλός or σῦριγξ), and the harp (φόρμιγξ, κίθαρα). Of the construction of the former there is no description, but the latter was strung with seven strings of gut,[1] each sounding a musical note at a proper interval (σύμφωνοι), and therefore, as its compass was seven notes, it must have been capable of producing some variety of harmony.

Statuary was but little known—sculpture in marble not at all, for, besides the statue of Athene at Troy, mention is only made of figures holding lights in the palace of Alcinous, and dogs at the gates, executed in gold and silver, the work of Hephæstus. It is probable, therefore, that such statues as did exist were wrought and graven in metal.

No traces, also, are to be found of the existence of painting. Color was only used to decorate the productions of the inferior arts. Wools of different dyes were woven in patterns, or used with gold and silver threads in embroidering, and the figure-heads of ships and ivory horse-trappings were stained in crimson and purple. In fact, epic poetry itself created and developed those faculties which afterwards produced the higher arts of sculpture and painting. Poetry did not borrow from art, but art from poetry. The poet's fancy conceived ideal forms, and embodied them in graphic and picturesque language; the artist realized these descriptions, and presented their results in a form to be apprehended by the external senses. Even in the lower mechanical arts it is scarcely possible that then anything existed completely corresponding with the Homeric descriptions; they were founded in fact, and doubtless accurate enough not to strike his hearers as unnatural impossibilities, but they had not their exact counterparts. Even modern genius, with all the appliances of modern art, cannot realize the endless variety of the Homeric shield. It must not, therefore, be supposed, that ancient plastic art could execute in all its fulness what the rich and vivid fancy of Homer could imagine.

Nevertheless, it may be repeated, art flourished and its productions were both ingenious and beautiful. However much the description may have surpassed the reality, the poet's eye, as well as that of his hearers, must have been accustomed to splen-

[1] Od. xxi. 408.

dor and magnificence, or else he could neither have described nor they have understood the palaces of Priam[1] and Odysseus,[2] or the house and gardens of Alcinous,[3] with all their rich architecture and luxurious furniture.

It may be assumed, therefore, that the works of the famed Sidonian looms, said to have been imported to Troy by Paris,[4] were well known to the Greeks; that furniture had somewhat of the elegance of Odysseus' bed,[5] the tripods described in the Iliad,[6] and the ivory work spoken of in the "Odyssey."[7] Armor was richly ornamented, like that of Agamemnon and Æneas; and articles of dress, both male and female, embroidered with tasteful designs, like that of Odysseus, and that presented by Antinous to Penelope.

Nor were the useful arts less understood than the ornamental. Their lands were skilfully and industriously cultivated—they ploughed with mules and oxen,[8] and, like the Israelites, used oxen to tread out the corn.[9] The grain was ground in handmills by women, as it was in Palestine in our Saviour's days, or pounded with a pestle and mortar.[10] Polyphemus made cheese, and separated the curd from the whey by means of the acid juice of figs.[11] They melted metals in furnaces, and increased the heat with bellows.[12] They fished with net and line, although fish was not esteemed as an article of food. Their tools used by the shipbuilder, the wheelwright, and the carpenter, comprise all the common tools now in use, except the saw; and, lastly, the probability is that the art of writing, which had long been practiced by the most civilized nations of the East, was also to the Greeks not entirely unknown.

Such were the arts of peace in the Homeric age. Their art of war scarcely deserves the name. There were no tactics, no regular line-of-battle, no evolutions by which an army could be manœuvred as if it were one body. The general-in-chief was but first in council; the inferior generals only chieftains, each of his own people. They thought more of prowess as soldiers, than

[1] Il. vi. 243.   [2] Od. xxiii.   [3] Ibid. vii. 86.
[4] Il. vi. 289.   [5] Ibid. xxiii. 195.   [6] Ibid. xviii. 374.
[7] Od. viii. 404.   [8] Il. xx. 495.   [9] Deut. xx. 4.
[10] Il. x. 353.   [11] Od. ix. 219.   [12] Il. xviii. 470.

of their skill as officers.   They were champions provoking each other to single combat, and exciting the troops to bravery by their example, rather than directing by their experience.

In the Homeric army chariots supplied the place of cavalry, and these were so small and light that Diomede entertained the idea of carrying off the field the chariot of Rhesus whom he had slain.   It was essential to a chieftain to have a loud voice in order to lead the war-cry efficiently, hence "good in the battle-cry," ἀγαθὸς βοήν, is a favorite epithet of the Homeric heroes. This shout seems to have been the only mode of cheering the troops to the onset, for although the trumpet is introduced in simile it is never made use of in a Homeric battle.[1]

Military service appears to have been compulsory.   Odysseus feigns madness, Achilles disguises himself in order to avoid it, and Echepolus offers a present to Agamemnon in order to purchase immunity.

Their cities were strongly fortified, for in architecture, or at least in masonry, they had made great advances, as they had in other civil arts; but little military skill was required to defend them against assailants who in engineering were rude and inexperienced.

Their fleets consisted of transports rather than ships of war. They were without decks, suited only for coasting voyages, and were capable of containing from fifty to one hundred and twenty men.[2]

Such is briefly the state of society in the heroic age, so far as it can be discovered from the only records which exist, namely, the Homeric poems; and though it is impossible not to be struck with the mixture of ferocity and urbanity, of rudeness and civilization, the seed can be discovered of that pre-eminence which Greece in after ages so long maintained.

[1] Il. xviii. 219.   [2] Thuc. i. 10.

CHAPTER VIII.

HOMERIC HYMNS AND MINOR POEMS.—PROOF THAT THEY ARE SPURIOUS.—THE HYMN
PRELUDES.—BATTLE OF FROGS AND MICE.—MARGITES.—HESIOD.—CLIMATE OF BŒO-
TIA AS COMPARED WITH THAT OF THE ASIATIC COAST.—DULNESS ATTRIBUTED TO
THE BŒOTIANS.—CAUSES OF IT.—PARALLEL DRAWN BETWEEN BŒOTIA AND GER-
MANY.—CHARACTERISTIC FEATURES OF THE HESIODIC POETRY.—THE AGE OF HESIOD
SUBSEQUENT TO THAT OF HOMER.—PROOF OF THIS FROM LANGUAGE, PHILOSOPHY,
AND GEOGRAPHY.—IMITATIONS OF HOMER.—NOTICES OF HESIOD CONTAINED IN HIS
WORKS —WORKS AND DAYS.—THEOGONY.—EŒÆ.—CYCLIC POETS.

As certain hymns, which were known and admired in a more
advanced literary period, were ascribed to the mythical bards,
such as Olen, Orpheus, Linus, and Musæus, so many minor
poems consisting of hymns and humorous effusions, have been
attributed to the author of the " Iliad" and the " Odyssey."
The whole number of these amounts to nearly fifty ; there are six
longer and twenty-seven shorter hymns, besides those poems
which, like " The Battle of the Frogs and Mice," are of a ludicrous and burlesque character, and a few short addresses to cities
or private persons which have been entitled Epigrams.   Although
the genuineness of many of these has been supported by fair
authority, and hymns, termed Homeric, are sometimes spoken of
by ancient writers—and even the careful Thucydides[1] quotes a
passage from the "Hymn to Apollo," as if it were a Homeric
production—there is no doubt that they are spurious.

They were not admitted as genuine by the Alexandrian grammarians ; their spirit and style bear no closer resemblance to those
of the authentic poems than might have been attained by a school
of admirers and imitators.   There is nothing in the "Iliad" and
" Odyssey" exactly parallel to them, except the song of Demodocus, which may have been an interpolation.   In the hymn
quoted by Thucydides, Homer is made to speak of himself, which

[1] Thuc. iii. 104.

is directly opposed to the purely objective spirit of his poetry. Words occur in the minor poems, such as λύρα[1] for a harp, δίλτός[2] for a writing tablet, and πλῆκτρον,[3] an instrument for playing on the lyre, which are not found in the "Iliad" or "Odyssey," and which argue a different period of art.

Strabo[4] tells us that Homer never applies the name of Samos to the island properly so called, but only to Cephallenia and Samothrace; but the Samos, on the Ionian coast, is mentioned in the "Hymn to Apollo." Cnidus, also, which is there spoken of, was not founded in the time of Homer.

Whoever were the authors of the Homeric hymns and minor poems, or to whatever age they belong, it is not improbable that the popular admiration excited in favor of Homer in the time of Pisistratus, led to an unfounded claim being made in their favor.

From the title of Procemia, or preludes, given them by the ancients, they had, doubtless, been usually sung by the bards and rhapsodists, as introductions to their recitations of the true Homeric poems; it is therefore easy to conceive how the belief might have rapidly arisen that they were the works of the same author.

Of the mock-heroic and ludicrous poems, the "Batrachomyo-machia," or Battle of the Frogs and Mice, and the "Margites," are the most celebrated. The first of these is a parody of the "Iliad," and has been ascribed, without sufficient foundation, to a humor-ous poet named Pigres; but the free and bold attacks contained in it on the popular mythology, and the satiric spirit, almost like that of Aristophanes, which pervades the whole, points to an age of philosophical scepticism for the period of its composition, and to some Athenian wit for its author. The "Margites" is a per-sonal satire, and therefore it is utterly inconceivable that a pro-duction should have belonged to the heroic age which, according to all the acknowledged facts and principles of literary history, marks an age when manners and habits have become artificial; when poetical inspiration has lost its freshness, and the critical powers of the human mind have become sharpened and matured.

---

[1] "Hymn to Apollo."   [2] Batrach. v. 3.
[3] "Hymn to Apollo," 185.   [4] Strabo, x. 457; Mure, ii. 320.

HESIOD.

From its sunny father-land in Ionia, epic poetry now migrated to a severer climate; its new home was Ascra, in the mountainous regions of Bœotia.   The founder of the new school of poetry was Hesiod; by descent he was an Asiatic Greek, for his father was a native of Cyma, an Æolian town, not far from Smyrna. Commercial pursuits led him to take up his abode in Bœotia: life, there, was evidently a hard struggle.   The care of making provision for the daily wants of life, whether by commerce or agriculture, pressed heavily upon the inhabitants: poverty and necessity produced a deadening effect upon their genius.   The Bœotians had not the sensibility of the Ionian Greek, the epigrammatic terseness and shrewd moral discernment of the Dorian, or the elegant taste of the Athenian.   This fact, though universally admitted, was generally attributed to the effect produced by the atmosphere upon the human mind; it was considered thick and heavy, weighing down the spirits, and adverse to liveliness and brilliancy of imagination.   The same effect was also attributed to the atmosphere of other mountainous regions, such as Arcadia and Acarnania; and it is probable that narrow circumstances, and the difficulty of gaining subsistence, exercised the same influence upon the Arcadian and Acarnanian mind which it did upon the Bœotian. That, to the poet accustomed in his earlier years to the softness of an Asiatic clime, that of Bœotia appeared rough and ungenial, is plain from his powerful description of winter,[1] and from the expressions which he uses with regard to his adopted home. " Ascra," he says, "is bad in winter, unpleasant in summer;"[2] and if the poetry of Homer is compared with that of Hesiod, it seems as though the former poet scarcely knew what winter was, whilst the latter speaks of. its severity in language almost as strong as would be used by one accustomed to the winters of England or of Germany.

The same sadness and gloom which distinguish the climate of Ascra from that of the coast of Asia, mark the poetry of Hesiod. The romantic ideal of the heroic age, the regal splendor, the ori-

[1] Works and Days, 501.   [2] Ibid. 640.

ental luxury, give place to the stern realities of common life and daily duty. His description of the lot of humanity is less brilliant, but more true. He feels, from sad experience, that man is born to trouble. He laments that the age in which he lives is one of iron. The anger of the gods has inflicted upon him a daily routine of toil and sorrow. The gifts of nature are sparingly and grudgingly afforded. The human race has become morally degenerate, as the soil which he inhabits has become physically inferior.

Impressed with the sense of these social evils, the object of the Hesiodic poetry is to apply a remedy, its scope and purpose is didactic and moral. He labors, therefore, to instruct his hearers in commerce, and especially in agriculture. He brings to bear upon the precepts which he enforces, all his own knowledge and personal experience respecting the nature of the soil and climate; and so judicious are his rules and instructions—so well adapted to the circumstances of the locality, that modern travellers in Greece inform us, that the agricultural principles laid down by Hesiod are still recognized and observed by the descendants of those to whom he addressed them.[1]

It appears somewhat strange, that Greek legend should have placed the favorite haunts of the Muses in Bœotia, a country rich, indeed, and fertile, but inhabited by a race of men devoted to rude, hard agricultural labor, and having the unenviable reputation of dulness rather than of poetic talent. It has been remarked, that, in this district of Greece, Phœnician names are very prevalent; whatever, therefore, is the credibility of the story respecting Hesiod's settlement there, it is most probable that at some time or other, there took place a migration of Eastern civilization, and with it, of poetical inspiration. But though Bœotia became the residence of poets, poetry did not take deep and permanent root there. The list of Bœotian poets is but a short one: it comprises but the names of Hesiod, Pindar, and Corinna.

But, perhaps, although Bœotia was not fruitful in poets, the want of genius attributed to it was exaggerated. There was, probably, a difference of national talent between the Bœotians and the other Greeks, rather than an absence of it. If so, it is natu-

[1] Ampère, p. 34.

ral to expect that the lively imagination of the Athenians, with whom the calumny originated, could not understand or appreciate a character of intellect totally different from their own. If the intellect of the Bœotian was grave and solid, it may have been too profound for the vivacity of an Athenian to value it as it deserved. A modern German[1] has discovered a physical resemblance between the plain country of Bœotia and his own native country. May there not, therefore, exist also a moral resemblance between the inhabitants? The German character is distinguished by a thoughtful gravity, which livelier imaginations often mistake for dulness and heaviness. It was long before the rest of Europe valued as they deserved either their painting, their music, or their poetry; but now no one doubts of their excellence and their pure classical taste, although their characteristics differ from those of the painting, music, and poetry of the rest of the world.

The epic of Hesiod, except so far as its dialect and hexametrical form is concerned, is totally different from that of Homer. The latter is heroic and mythic. His plots exhibit a complete plan, tending to one great end, and aiming at poetical unity. His characters are all in all; they are called into existence, as it were, by a creative power of the poet's mind, which seems totally unconscious of its own existence; it is scarcely a narrative, it is almost a drama of action, and hence, Homer has been called the Father of Tragedy. The poetry of Hesiod is rather didactic and ethical. There is no convergence of the whole interest on one point—no attempt to make all the parts tend to bring about one great catastrophe. The poet speaks in his own person, and his existence is always kept before the reader's eyes. His subjects, too, are of a totally different kind from those of Homer, and the treatment of them is simple, calm, without enthusiasm, without the ornament of that glorious imagery which elevates the thoughts above this every-day world.

The object of Hesiod is, as that of every poet ought to be, to elevate and purify the feelings;[2] but he endeavors to effect this object, not by scenes which speak to the passions, or the sympathies, but by teaching us that we are men, and not of heroic

[1] Ulrichs.   [2] Aristot. Poet.

mould; that we are subject to the influence of the gods; that to them we must look with religious reverence and awe; that the lot of man is to labor, and that his sphere of duty is in the routine of ordinary life. Forming a humble estimate of man's condition, he considers a dependence upon the gods as more becoming to him than self-reliance. Together with the spirit and sentiment of religious awe, which pervades his principal poem, are plentifully intermingled moral truths, uncompromisingly stated, and maxims full of practical wisdom, and accurate observation of the human heart, and calculated to elevate human nature and to improve man's social condition.

In determining the age of Hesiod, there is no more light to guide the inquirer than there is in the case of Homer. Herodotus believes them to have been contemporaries, and the chronological investigations of Sir Isaac Newton led him to adopt a similar conclusion, and to fix their era about B.C. 870. Cicero[1] considers Homer the elder of the two, and Clinton[2] believes him to have flourished about a century after Homer, and four hundred years before Herodotus. Many considerations, drawn from the internal evidence of the Hesiodic poems, tend to establish the belief, that the age of Hesiod was subsequent, although not far removed from that of Homer. Differences in language, new ideas on philosophical subjects, a wider range of geographical knowledge, point to a later and more mature period, and many passages of Hesiod are manifest imitations of the Homeric poetry.

Θέμις, for example, is always used by Homer, to signify law, and the more modern term νόμος never has this meaning; whilst Hesiod, in two passages,[3] makes use of νόμος to express this idea. Eros, or Love, is not mentioned by Homer, but in the poems of Hesiod the word occurs in the sense in which it is used by the earliest mythical philosophers, as a primeval cause of the universe. The views respecting a future state are better defined by Hesiod, and are of a less gloomy and melancholy character. The month is divided into three portions or *decades*, a practice, which, as is well known, was adopted by the Athenians. The river Eridanus,[4] as also the Ister and the Phasis, are mentioned by Hesiod; and

---

[1] De Senect.   [2] Fasti Hellenici, i. 381.
[3] Works and Days, Theog. 66.   [4] Theog. 338.

the river of Egypt is by Homer termed Ægyptus—by Hesiod, the Nile.

Many passages might be cited from the works of Hesiod which are imitations of Homer. The description of the Happy Islands given to Menelaus, by Proteus, has its counterpart in the "Works and Days;"[1] the "Shield of Heracles" is a copy, though an inferior one, of that of Achilles ; sometimes the same incidents are introduced. The marriage rites and the festive banquet[2] are represented on both; on both the women assist in the defence of a besieged city.[3] In the description of the Chimeræ, Hesiod borrows two lines, word for word, from the "Iliad."[4] Hesiod's "War of the Titans," and Homer's "Battle of the Gods," are so parallel that one must be an imitation of the other, and here two lines are exactly alike, with the exception of a single word. Hesiod says of a poet, "his voice flows sweet" (γλυκερή ῥέει αὐδή); Homer, of an orator, "his voice flowed sweeter than honey" (μέλιτος γλυκίων ῥέεν αὐδή). The dignity of Hesiod's Zeus is, as it were, a reflection from the awful majesty which invests the Father of Gods in the "Iliad." Hesiod borrows a thought from Homer, and amplifies and exaggerates, as, for example, when he makes the anvil occupy nine days in falling from heaven to earth, whilst Homer's Hephæstus falls in one day from Olympus to Lemnos, as our own Milton says:—

> From morn
> To noon he fell, from noon to dewy eve,
> A summer's day ; and with the setting sun
> Dropt from the zenith, like a fallen star
> On Lemnos, the Ægean isle.

The works of Hesiod are our only sure guide to the history of his life, and to the circumstances of his native country.

Bœotia had originally been a country of heroic legends, the race of the Theban Cadmus had furnished many a lay, and many a warlike tradition; but its subsequent inhabitants, the Æolic Bœotians, were a rural, pastoral race, without the chivalrous spirit of the warrior, absorbed, as has been already stated, in the cares of life, and in providing for their daily necessities.

[1] Works and Days, 168.
[2] Hes. Shield, 273 ; Il. xviii. 491.
[3] Shield, 242 ; Il. xviii. 514.
[4] Il. vi. 181 ; Theog. 323.

A native[1] of the obscure mountain village of Ascra, the child of a humble emigrant, was watching his father's flock at the foot of Mount Helicon. Whilst thus engaged the Muses appeared to him, conferred on him the gift of poetical inspiration, together with a wand of laurel, as symbolical of his new profession. At the funeral of Amphidamas of Chalcis he entered the lists with other poets, and was successful. His prize he dedicated to his divine patronesses.[2] His brother, Perses, defrauded him of his inheritance, but afterwards reduced to poverty, was obliged to sue for pardon and assistance from the brother whom he injured. This is all that he tells us respecting himself. The pretended lives which are extant are evidently fabulous and legendary; but although so little is known, it is highly probable that Hesiod was a real person, that there was a Bœotian poet of that name, and that he was the author of some of the poems now attributed to him. The only work which, with the exception of interpolated passages, has universally and without dispute been attributed to him is the "Works and Days" ("Εϱγα ϰαὶ 'Ημέϱαι). Its leading subject is the various occupations and duties of life, in its several relations, with a conclusion consisting of a calendar for the use of agriculturists and navigators, and a number of cautions principally against the violation of common decency. It is probable, therefore, that the original title was simply 'Εϱγα, and that the calendar was added sometime subsequently, and the title then altered to suit this addition. The unconnected nature of Hesiod's poetry, and the absence of a regular plot, easily admit of interpolation and additions.

The "Theogony" contains a history of the origin of the world, and the genealogies of the gods. It is an important and interesting work, because Herodotus ascribes to Hesiod, conjointly with Homer, the settlement of the Greek theogony. But although Aristarchus, the Alexandrian grammarian, considered it genuine, this was not the opinion of the Bœotians themselves. On his system of the universe were built up many theories of the Greek physical philosophers, who imagined they saw in them the germ of all their speculations. Homer's simple idea of creation contains no physical philosophy,[3] which makes it probable, as was stated

---

[1] Theog. 20; Works and Days, 650.   [2] Ibid. 27.   [3] Il. xiv. 200.

before, that the Hesiodic poem belongs to an age subsequent to that of Homer, an age farther advanced in philosophical studies. The conclusion of this poem is a catalogue of heroes, born of mortal mothers to the deities of Olympus. This forms the connecting link between the "Theogony" and the "Eœœ," which is a history of the favorites of the gods, who thus became the mothers of heroes. Its title is derived from two Greek words ἢ οἵη ("or such as were"), a formula with which many of the descriptions are introduced.

The "Eœœ" has been by some considered as the same with another Hesiodic poem entitled "The Catalogues of Women," but the probability is, that the scope of the latter was more extensive than that of the former, comprehending the genealogies not only of the favorites of heaven, but of other celebrated women of the heroic age. The "Shield of Heracles" has generally been considered as either wholly or in part genuine, but it is almost certain that the introductory verses originally formed part of the "Eœœ."

Such are the principal Hesiodic poems, of which there are many, and they constitute, perhaps, the oldest specimens of what has been termed the gnomic and genealogical epics of Greek literature.

A brief notice only is necessary of the remaining poets, which were comprised in the so-called Epic Cycle. This title was given to a collection of epic writers made by the Alexandrian grammarians, in the second century before the Christian era. They comprised the "Iliad" and "Odyssey," and all those epic poems which were of the Homeric form, as contrasted with those which were composed after the Hesiodic mould. The principal writers of this school were Arctinus of Miletus, Lesches of Lesbos, Agias of Trœzen, Eumelus of Corinth, Stasinus of Cyprus, and Eugammon of Cyrene. The number of epics belonging to this cycle, which are no longer extant, amounts to thirty. Of these, five related to the war with Troy; one to the return of the chiefs after that expedition; one, the Telegonia, was a continuation of the "Odyssey;" the subjects of two were Theban history, and two celebrated the exploits of Hercules. The title, therefore, of cyclic poet by no means originally implied any disparagement, but afterwards it was used to designate the inferior poets of this class, to the exclusion of the Homeric poems; and hence the use of the term by Horace in his satirical description of an inferior poet.[1]

[1] Art. Poet. 136.

CHAPTER IX.

ELEGIES AND IAMBICS THE LITERATURE OF FREE INSTITUTIONS.—ELEGY SOFT AS WELL
AS PATRIOTIC.—ITS MUSICAL ACCOMPANIMENT.—ITS METRE COMPARED WITH THE
EPIC.—CALLINUS.—TYRTÆUS.—ARCHILOCHUS.—SIMONIDES.—MIMNERMUS.—SOLON.—
THEOGNIS. — XENOPHANES OF ELEA. — PHOCYLIDES. — IAMBICS. — ARCHILOCHUS OF
PAROS.—HE INVENTED THE EPODE.—SIMONIDES OF AMORGOS AND SOLON.—HIPPONAX.
—CHOLIAMBIC METRE.—HESIOD'S FABLE THE OLDEST.—ARCHILOCHUS AND STESI-
CHORUS.—ÆSOP—HIS LIFE.

SUCH was the poetry—in fact the only literature—of the age
distinguished by the monarchical principle; an age in which,
although the duties of the sovereign as the father and pastor of
his people in peace and their leader in war were strictly limited
and defined, still his divine right and his god-like authority were
devoutly acknowledged. But the rise of freer institutions gave
birth to freer expressions of thoughts and developed a new kind
of poetical literature—the Elegiac and the Iambic. These, like
the epic of Homer, owe their origin to the lively spirit and sus-
ceptible imagination of Ionian poets, natives of Asia Minor and
the adjacent archipelago.

The original signification of the word elegy was the same as
that in which it is used in modern times. Whether its etymology
is, as has been supposed, from ἐελέγειν, it originally signified a
song of sorrow; but afterwards it was applied to all strains,
whether of joy or sorrow, which were composed in the metre at
first devoted to the voice of lamentation. Cheerfulness, for example, mingles with mourning in the elegies of Archilochus of
Paros,[1] the inventor of the iambic verse and of personal satire;
narratives of political struggles, expressed in the language of a
patriotic and martial spirit, unite with strains of sorrow and com-
miseration for the subjugation of Ionia to the Lydian satrap, in
those of Mimnermus ;[2] whom Horace[3] praises even above his admired Callimachus, as the first of elegiac poets.

---

[1] B. C. 720.   [2] B. C. 594.   [3] Horace, Ep. II. ii. 100.

There can be no doubt that although commerce had brought to Greece a greater love of independence, it had also brought with it in its train a love of luxury and greater softness of character. The growth of national independence and of free institutions had led the poet to forsake the celebration of some great chieftain's ancestors, and the enlivening his banquet by recording the heroic exploits of his family, and the genealogy of his race ; and to substitute regrets for lost national glory, or gratulations on the rising freedom of his father-land. Still his strains were poured forth not only in the language of patriotism, but in the plaintive accents of the softer passions.

The musical accompaniment was in accordance with this new species of poetry. · No longer did the bard sweep the heart-stirring chords of the harp, but the soft notes of the Phrygian flute imitated the emotions of the elegiac poet.

The metre which he adopted differed from that of the epic poetry. In the latter the same measure recurred in every line throughout the whole poem ; and thus the narrative could be continned, until complete, without break or interruption. In the former, a shorter line was subjoined to the old epic hexameter, and thus formed a couplet, at the termination of which the thought expressed might naturally be brought to a close.

How the deviation of the second line of the elegiac stanza from the heroic hexameter was first suggested to the ear, or why the poet deemed it more suitable to express his new state of feeling, it is difficult to say. It seems, however, to have been the first transition from the continuous rhythm to the periodic in poetry; a sign of an advance in the art, although not in the national inspiration of poetry. A change analogous to this is observable in the Greek prose writing, from the loose style (λεξις εἰρομένη) of the Ionic historian, Herodotus, to the periodic style (λεξις κατεστραμμένη) of the Attic Thucydides.

From this peculiarity in the elegiac metre, it was used in monumental and other inscriptions (ἐπιγράμματα) wherever brevity of expression required terseness and conciseness: and hence the term epigram has been since applied to all poetical compositions the characteristic of which is that the thoughts are expressed briefly and pointedly. As the earliest idea of the epigram was simply that of an inscription, brevity, neatness, elegance, and the seizing in a few words all the characteristic features of the thing described, were all that was required. It was reserved for later times to add the condition of an unexpected turn of thought and expression.

The first of the elegiac poets, and the inventor of the metre, was Callinus, of Ephesus.[1] He flourished during the period in which the Cimmerian hordes invaded Asia Minor and destroyed Magnesia ;[2] and again, after an interval of nearly fifty years, took Sardis, and attacked the poet's native city.[3] Hence his poetry breathes a warlike and patriotic spirit. He exhorts his countrymen to break the enervating chains of oriental luxury, and to resist the inroads of their barbarian enemy. But one specimen of his poetry has been preserved by Stobæus ; and even of this Müller[4] doubts whether the conclusion may not be part of a poem by his contemporary, Tyrtæus.

The age of Tyrtæus is synchronous with the second Messenian war, and the usual date ascribed to this war (B. C. 685). Tradition reports that he was a lame schoolmaster of Athens ;[5] that the Spartans were commanded, by an oracle, to seek a leader from the Athenians; and that they, in mockery, sent Tyrtæus. Matthiæ thinks that the designation, schoolmaster, arose from his profession being that of a rhapsodist. However this may be, that which Athens intended as mockery proved the safety of Sparta ; for the animating strains of the lame bard—his urgent appeals to the love of country—his descriptions of firmness and resolution in the field—his enlivening anapæsts ($\dot{\epsilon}\mu\beta\alpha\tau\acute{\eta}\rho\iota\alpha\ \mu\acute{\epsilon}\lambda\eta$) to cheer and encourage the troops on their long and dreary marches—produced a striking effect upon the true-hearted Spartans, and contributed more to victory than the profoundest tactics of a skilful general would have done.

Nor were his political admonitions in his "Eunomia" less valuable, at a period when the old Dorian aristocratic institutions of Sparta were menaced by some of her own citizens, who, discontented at the devastation of their estates in Messenia by the insurgents, were demanding an agrarian law.[6]

[1] Gaisford's Poetæ Minores, i. 426.
[2] B. C. 727.
[3] About B. C. 678.
[4] Müller, p. 110.
[5] Matthiæ, History of Literature.
[6] Plutarch.

9

The poetry of Archilochus of Paros, and Simonides of Amorgos, was of two kinds—iambic and elegiac. At present we will confine our attention to the latter only. Archilochus is commonly said to have lived about B. C. 720,[1] and Suidas places the date of Simonides about B. C. 780; but it is more probable that the date assigned by Eusebius to Simonides (B. C. 664) is the correct one, and that Archilochus was his contemporary. Respecting the subjects treated of in the elegies of Simonides, nothing is known. Those of Archilochus (although some are melancholy) are the earliest specimens extant of the symposiac kind. Their subjects are those which are in modern times called Anacreontic, and celebrate the delights of wine and revelry. They mark the decay of a warlike and patriotic spirit in the Asiatic Ionian race, the growing softness of manners derived from their oriental neighbors, destined first to corrupt and debase them, and then to deprive them of their independence.

In the latter part of the seventh century before the Christian ara, flourished Mimnermus of Smyrna. In his days the sad catastrophe fell upon Ionia,[2] Gyges took Colophon, and Smyrna surrendered to the arms of Halyattes. The old twofold nature of the elegy, that of sad pathos and warlike spirit, mingled well in the strains of Mimnermus. He bewailed that the native independence of Ionia was now lost, her sun set, her military glory ruined, as it seemed, for ever, and yet there burst forth strains of enthusiasm when he speaks of the bygone valor and ancient exploits of his degenerate countrymen.

Both before and after the legislative measures of Solon, which rendered his archonship, in B. C. 594, so celebrated, this great lawgiver distinguished himself as an elegiac poet. The fragments of his poetry which are extant consist chiefly of maxims (γνῶμαι) both moral and poetical, and hence he is considered one of the gnomic poets. In them are found noble thoughts on the use and abuse of riches, such as we might expect from one who, like him, sympathized with the sorrows of the poor, and one great object of whose legislature was to relieve them from the grinding oppression of the wealthier classes.

Another object to which he devoted his muse was the recovery

---

[1] Matthiæ.   [2] Herod. i. 16.

of Salamis from the Megarians, and, on this occasion, tradition
furnishes us with an example of the power of song upon the sus-
ceptible Athenians.   Habited as an herald, and feigning frenzy,
which was then considered akin to inspiration, he recited an
appeal to the sympathies of the assembled people in behalf of
that beautiful island.   The enthusiasm thus kindled, spread far
and wide, and with one voice an expedition was voted against
the Megarians, which was successful in wresting Salamis from
their power.

We learn from an inscription on a tripod, preserved by Pausanias,[1] that Echembrotus, an Arcadian, sang elegies to the accompaniment of the flute at the Pythian games, B. C. 586, and on
that occasion the prize was awarded to him.   But the substitu-
tion of singing with a musical accompaniment for simple recitation, was considered unsuited to the solemnity of the festival,
and was consequently forbidden.

The Dorian[2] colonies in Sicily were numerous and celebrated
in very early times, and in that island Megara in Attica founded
a colony bearing the same name, which appears to have kept up
continual communication with the parent state.   Theognis was a
native of the Sicilian Megara, but resided at the Attic city, and
took a deep and personal interest in the political convulsions
which disturbed Greece during the era of the Tyrants.   He was
the poet of the old aristocracy of birth, which was now beginning
to crumble away before the growing power of the wealthier commons, led by some popular and influential citizen, who was commonly called in Greece a tyrant (τύραννος).

The Dorian συσσίτια, or public tables, which had their most
perfect development in the leading Dorian state of Sparta, and
which, like all their other institutions, were attributed to Lycurgus, were social bonds of union, which kept up the old hereditary
aristocratic feeling amongst the members of them.   We can
easily conceive the influence and popularity of such elegies as
those of Theognis if sung at these friendly meetings.   They
would produce an effect similar to that of our after-dinner
speeches, and songs expressive of party-feeling delivered and
sung at the political reunions of our own day.   Theognis

---

[1] Paus. x. 7, 3.   [2] Müller's Dorians, i. 6, 10.

flourished about B. C. 548, and more fragments are extant of his elegies than of any other elegiac poet.

The elegies of Kenophanes of Elea, the founder of the Eleatic school of philosophy, who flourished about B. C. 540, were also suited to be sung at public entertainments. His contemporary, Phocylides of Miletus, is said, by Müller,[1] to have written principally in hexameters, but Matthiæ[2] considers the ποίημα νουθετικόν, in that metre which bears his name, to have been spurious, and the work of some Christian author. All his compositions are introduced by the words, "And this, too, is Phocylides's." One epigrammatic and paradoxical distich preserved, has been wittily paraphrased by our own Porson.[3]

> Καὶ τόδε Φωκυλίδεω· Λέριοι κακοί· οὐχ ὁ μὲν, ὃς δ' οὐ,
> Πάντες πλὴν Προκλέους, καὶ Προκλέης Λέριος.

"This, too, is Phocylides's; the Lerians are rogues, not one a rogue and another not, but all except Procles, and Procles is a Lerian."

> The Germans in Greek
> Are sadly to seek:
> Not five in five score,
> But ninety-five more,
> All but friend Hermann;
> And Hermann's a German.

Contemporary with the invention of the elegy was that of iambic poetry by Archilochus of Paros. The head-quarters of the mystical worship of Demeter (the Roman Ceres) was at Eleusis, but the epic hymn to Demeter informs us that the place next in importance, where her mysteries were celebrated, was Paros, of which Archilochus was a native. The worship of Demeter was nearly allied to that of Dionysus, and, like it, gave full scope to the initiated to indulge in frolic, jest, and bantering raillery.

Now, one characteristic of the iambic metre, as opposed to the stateliness of the epic and the epigrammatic terseness of elegiac verse, is rapidity. It is evidently well suited to express the quickness of repartee, and the sharpness of satire. Moreover, its facility and the similarity of its rhythm to that of conversational prose, rendered it suitable for giving utterance to effusions

---

[1] Müller, p. 120.		[2] Matthiæ, History of Literature, part i. (ee).
[3] Gaisford, Poetæ Minores, fr. 5.

which were originally, and probably still continued to be in some instances, extemporaneous.

The expressions of Horace,

"Archilochum proprio rabies armavit iambo;"

and again,

" In *celeres* iambos misit furentem,"

as well as that of Cicero, "Archilochia edicta,"[1] recognize the object and adaptation of this metre, and hence the very word passed into a proverb, for to rail at any one was expressed in Greek by the word ἰαμβίζειν. With regard to the etymology of the word, it is probably, like elegy, one of those which were derived from sound, that its root is the shout of joy ἰή, just as αἰάζειν is from αἰ, ὀτοτύζειν from ὀτότοι, and so forth.

The iambic metre, as is evident from its forming one of the two elements of the Attic drama, was as peculiarly belonging to the Ionian race, as the lyric or choral poetry belonged to the Dorian.

Archilochus himself was an Ionian Greek, and either he himself, or his father, Telesicles, was the leader of a colony to Thasos. His ancestors had held the priesthood of Demeter, and were therefore nobles. He flourished about B. C. 720, and, consequently, was one of the oldest of the Ionian poets.

The admiration with which Archilochus was regarded by the ancients, both Greek and Roman, proves that his poems could not have conveyed mere licentious raillery. When we find Plato[2] speaking of him as the wisest of poets, Horace[3] professing to imitate him, and Quinctilian[4] eulogizing his brief yet thrilling sentences (*breves vibrantesque sententiæ*), full of life and vigor, we can scarcely doubt the truthfulness as well as the power of his satire.

When we speak of Archilochus as an iambic poet, it must not be supposed that his poetical effusions were either entirely, or even chiefly, confined to that metre. His name is connected with it as its inventor, and as the poet who applied it to an especial purpose, that of personal satire; but the vast number of metres in which his poems are written, show that Greek

---

[1] Ep. ad Att. ii. 21.   [2] Plato, Republ. ii. 365.

[3] Horace, Ep. i. xix. 23.   [4] Quinct. x. 1, § 60.

metre had already attained that variety which rendered it capable of expressing every conceivable feeling and emotion.

Besides employing all the existing metres, he was also the inventor of the ἰπφδός, a metre imitated by Horace in that book of his "Odes" which is distinguished by this title. The epode is a short verse subjoined to a longer one. Whether the poet had any object in view in introducing this metre beyond mere variety, it is impossible to determine; but although we cannot, the delicately attuned ear of the Greek might probably have recognized a peculiar appropriateness to the subject treated in this metrical combination.

Simonides of Amorgos, and Solon, were also iambic poets. A specimen of the iambics of the former is preserved by Stobæus; and some fragments of Solon's in Gaisford's collection.[1]

Simonides of Amorgos must be carefully distinguished from the celebrated lyric poet of that name. They have often been confounded one with the other, both in ancient and modern times, and their poems have been mixed indiscriminately in one collection. It is not, however, difficult to separate them, for the probability is, that only the iambic fragments belong to Simonides of Amorgos, and that almost all the lyric and the elegiac verses are the productions of the Cean poet. His poems were of two kinds, gnomic and satirical, and the bitter irony which distinguishes the latter, is fully equalled by the knowledge of human nature which marks the former. Of the latter, the most celebrated is his satire on woman. In it he represents the various shades of female character by the following allegories:—1. The swine; 2. the fox; 3. the dog; 4. the earth; 5. the sea; 6. the ass; 7. the weasel; 8. the mare; 9. the ape; 10. the bee. Suidas[2] informs us that he was a native of Samos, and the leader of a colony to Amorgos, one of the Cyclades, where he founded three cities. The period at which he flourished was most probably about Ol. xxix. B. C. 665 or B. C. 662.[3]

In a philological point of view, the fragments of Simonides are invaluable as specimens of the Ionic dialect in its oldest form.

But the iambics of the Ephesian Hipponax, beyond all others,

---

[1] Gaisford, No. 28.   [2] Suid. s. v.   [3] Clint. Fest. Hell. in annis.

not excepting even those of Archilochus himself, deserve the epithets given to this metre, on account of their bitterness and severity. He flourished at the time when the empire of Crœsus was destroyed by Cyrus, a period when Ionic softness and self-indulgent luxury had reached its zenith, and his indignation did not spare their degeneracy. He is said to have invented the choliambic or lame iambic, the last foot of which was a spondee instead of an iambus; a metre afterwards much used by the writers of fables.

That the fable was not indigenous in Greece, or its colonies, is certain, but whence it derived its origin it is impossible to determine. It bears the strongest resemblance to the parabolic symbolism of Oriental nations. Many of these fables, which have found their way into all the languages of the civilized world, can be traced to the East, and if the fables ascribed to Æsop are really his, the introduction in such early times of such animals as peacocks, monkeys, and panthers, seem to point to an Indian original. But still all nations of Europe, however independent their existence, have their fables, and some were traditionally known in the early ages of Greek literature by the name of Libyan, as though there were no doubt of their African origin.

The oldest fable which we meet with in Greek literature is that well-known one of Hesiod,[1] "The Hawk and the Nightingale."

Archilochus, and the Sicilian lyric poet, Stesichorus, both wrote fables. That of "The Horse, the Man, and the Stag" was written by the latter, in order to warn the people of Himera against the designs of the tyrant Phalaris;[2] but the name which modern times always connects with fable is that of Æsop.

As the traditional author of compositions orally handed down and afterwards versified by subsequent writers, Æsop demands a place amongst the authors of Greek literature. His very existence, like that of Homer himself, has been doubted; but mentioned as he is by Aristophanes, Plato, Aristotle, and others, it is hard to believe that he was a mere imaginary person. It is probable that many fables were attributed to him which were not his, just as all the Hesiodic poems were attributed to Hesiod; but the

[1] Works and Days, 202.　　　　　　[2] Arist. Rhet. ii. 20.

opinion of Bentley is probably the correct one, that he was the author of fables which he related orally, although he did not leave any written works.

On the authority of Eugeon, a Samian historian, quoted by Suidas,[2] we are informed that Æsop was a native of Mesembria in Thrace, although Sardis, Samos, and Phrygia, claimed the honor of being his birth-place. He was the slave of a Lydian, named Xanthus, and afterwards of Iadmon, who emancipated him. He subsequently lived at the court of Crœsus.

Herodotus[3] tells us of a fellow-slave of Æsop, named Rhodopis, who lived in the time of Amasis, King of Egypt. Plutarch, whose authority is of little value, relates that he was sent by Crœsus to distribute a gratuity among the citizens of Delphi, and that a dispute arising they threw him from a precipice and killed him.

[1] Dis. Fables of Æsop.   [2] Suidas, s. v. Αἴσωπος.
[3] Herod. ii. 134.

CHAPTER X.

GREEK MUSIC.—TERPANDER THE INVENTOR OF MUSICAL SCIENCE.—THE GREEKS DID NOT
UNDERSTAND HARMONY.—DEFINITION OF ἁρμονία —THE THREE GENERA.—IMPROVE-
MENTS INTRODUCED BY TERPANDER.—THE COLORS.—MODES —THE DORIAN MODE THE
OLDEST.—CHARACTER OF DORIAN MUSIC.—CONSERVATIVE PRINCIPLES OF THE DORI-
ANS.—ELEVEN-STRINGED LYRE OF TIMOTHEUS.—OLYMPUS OF PHRYGIA.—THALETAS
OF CRETE.

WE have now arrived at the period of lyric poetry, a style more subjective than any which preceded it, which gave utterance to the language of deep and fervent passion, and was inseparably connected with music, both vocal and instrumental. It will, therefore, be necessary to prefix to this portion of the subject a few general remarks on the musical theory of the Greeks.

The sense or appreciation of melody must always have been possessed by that people in a very high degree. The ear, which was so nicely tuned as to enjoy the varied metres of Greek poetry, must have possessed a national music as an art, long be-fore it was reduced to system and became a science; and the bards of Pieria, and the minstrels of whom we hear in the mythical age, were doubtless, as far as the mere art is concerned, practised and accomplished musicians.

Owing to the connection between music and lyric poetry, the first inventor of musical science was not only a musician, but a poet likewise. This was Terpander, a native of Antissa, in Les-bos. He flourished about B. C. 648. He was the first who adapted melodies to the national lays of the Lacedæmonians (μέλος πρῶτος περιέθηκε τοῖς ποιήμασι, καὶ τοὺς Λακεδαιμονίων νόμους ἐμελοποίησε).[1]

The musical science of the Greeks comprehended only the laws of melody, and the principles of harmony were not understood by them. The only approach to harmony with which they were

[1] Müller's Dorians, i. 309; ii. 333. Clem. Alex.

acquainted was that of two voices singing at the interval of an octave. Of this simplest form of musical concord they could not possibly have been ignorant, because, as the pitch of male and female voices differ by an octave, it would become known to them as soon as they were accustomed to make use of a chorus of men and women. This species of concord was technically termed μαγαδίζειν, and as the constitution of the Greek musical scale was peculiarly unfitted for harmonies we are driven to interpret all passages which speak of concord, and of two instruments played simultaneously in different moods, as alluding to this simple kind of harmony.

The term ἀςμονική (harmony), therefore, as used by the Greeks only signified the science of melody. This is evident by the definition of it given by Euclid. "Harmony is the theoretical and practical science of the nature of tune, and tune is composed of notes and intervals arranged in a certain order."

Another fact, which shows the imperfect nature of Greek music, is that the instrument to which, until the time of Terpander, the Greek theory was adapted was the tetrachord. The scale, therefore, only consisted of four notes, and the two extreme notes of the scale were at an interval of a fourth. The arrangement of the intermediate intervals determined what the Greeks designated the genus to which the scale belonged. There were three genera.— 1. The diatonic, in which the intervals between the four notes were semitone, tone, tone. 2. The chromatic, the intervals of which were semitone, semitone, tone and a half. 3. The enharmonic, which, as is evident from its nature, was the most artificial and pedantic, and consequently most difficult. The intervals in this genus were quarter-tone, quarter-tone, two tones.

The improvement introduced by Terpander was to increase the compass of the instrument, and consequently of the scale, to an octave by the addition of three strings. This compass was called a diapason (διὰ πασῶν). But it must be remarked, that, although the compass was increased, the fundamental system still remained unaltered: it was not one octave but two tetrachords, with the interval of a tone between them. The third string was omitted in this new arrangement in order to make the number of notes in the octave seven.   ʎ'

Certain modifications of the intervals in each genus were technically termed χρόαι (colors), and constituted species. The diatonic
admitted two χρόαι, the chromatic three. The enharmonic only
one, making six in all.

Other arrangements of the intervals, combined also with difference of musical pitch, determined the different modes, τόνοι.
These in the earliest state of the science, when the tetrachord
alone was known, were three in number, the Lydian, Phrygian,
and the Dorian. In these modes, the Lydian was the highest,
and the Dorian the lowest. As musical science advanced, these
modes were gradually increased in number, until at last they
amounted to fifteen, of which the Hyper-Lydian was the highest,
and the Hypo-Dorian the lowest.

The subject of Greek music is one of great obscurity; and this
obscurity is increased by the subject of concord and discord
being treated of so differently from the way in which they are
treated in the modern system. For example, the third, which is
our easiest and most natural concord, was not considered a conso-
nant interval at all. It is plain, therefore, that in the method
of tuning the scale adopted by the ancient Greeks, the major third
did not exist at all.

It is a remarkable fact, that the tetrachord remained as the
fundamental principle of the scale until Gregory, the composer
of the chaunt which still bears his name, substituted the octave,
and thus laid the foundation for the modern theory.[1]

The Dorian mode was most probably the oldest, and in fact
the only genuine Greek style of music. The Lydian and Phrygian were introduced subsequently by the Æolians of Lesbos.
These, from their geographical position, had constant communication with Greece on the one hand, and the musical schools of Asia
Minor on the other; and hence the two newer modes were soon
combined with the Dorian and formed one national system. As
the Dorian music resembled in its style the peculiar features of
the national character, and was marked with sobriety and severity,
it acquired refinement from the introduction of the Lydian and
Phrygian measures. This stern race, strongly impressed with
the important influence which music exercises over the moral

[1] Burney's Hist. Music.

character of a people, and therefore cultivating it as an integral part of education, were naturally careful that music should express that sentiment and principle which so strongly marked all their institutions. "The ancients," says Müller,[1] "who were infinitely quicker in discovering the moral character of music than can be the case in modern times, attributed to it something solemn, firm, and manly, calculated to inspire fortitude in supporting misfortunes and hardships, and to strengthen the mind against the attacks of passion. They discovered in it a calm sublimity, and a simple grandeur which bordered on severity, equally opposed to inconstancy and enthusiasm; and this is precisely the character which we find so strongly impressed on the religion, arts, and manners of the Dorians. We are thus enabled to draw a distinction between the Greeks of Asia and those sprung from the mountains in the north of Greece, who, proud of their lofty nature and vigor of mind, had acquired but little refinement from contact with strangers." (

The Dorian race of Sparta, eminently conservative in all the principles which it professed, slowly and unwillingly admitted improvements in anything, and thus Terpander, when he increased the gamut to seven notes, was obliged to obtain the sanction of a law to legalize the introduction of his invention into Sparta. But if there is any truth in the Spartan enactment respecting the eleven-stringed lyre of Timotheus,[2] the Dorian attachment to antiquity would not permit progress to go further. It decreed, that Timotheus should be censured as introducing effeminate music, and compelled to restore his lyre to the original compass of seven notes.[3] Doubtful although the authenticity of this document is, it proves that an opinion has been long entertained of the strictness with which the Spartans were anxious to maintain the severity of their musical style.

Terpander then may fairly be considered the founder of Greek musical science. He invented also some system of musical notation, and his written melodies, adapted and arranged for the cithara, were known in Greece by the title of νόμοι. A Phrygian musician, named Olympus, whose whole story is mythical, is said

---

[1] Müller's Dorians, iv. 6.   Mus. Crit. i. 506.
[2] Müller's Dorians, iv. 6, 3.

to have been the inventor of flute music, and to have composed in a wild and noisy style, suited to the orgiastic rites of the **Phrygian** deity.

Attached to the worship of Zeus, as the fabulous Olympus is said to have been to that of the mother of the gods, was a native of Crete, named Thaletas. He flourished about B.C. 620, and devoted himself to the improvement of the music used at the religious festivals. The music attributed to Olympus formed the foundation of his system, and the improvements which he made upon it he introduced into Sparta, and, by engrafting them upon the system of Terpander, became the second founder of that science which was afterwards so ably cultivated by a long series of professors.

CHAPTER XI.

GREEK lyric poetry is the development of the national feeling with respect to religious worship, and all the stirring or interesting events of public and private life. It was peculiarly the poetry of that race, of which the Æolians and Dorians formed the two branches, and the subjects to which it was devoted, the dialects in which it was written, and the characters and moral and intellectual features of those two branches will serve to distinguish the schools to which the poets, who were its authors, respectively belonged.

The solemn ceremonials of religion at once inspired the serious temper and elevated mind of the Dorian, and decided the form in which he should pour forth strains, expressive of awe and veneration for the deities of his race. The dignified march of the priests and their attendants, the more cheerful dance of the assistant band of youths and virgins, suggested that with them lyric poetry should assume the form of stateliness, and yet at the same time be adapted by variety for the many-voiced chorus. The deep religious feelings, and the grave character which marked the race, found expression in the sonorous effect and open, long-sustained vowel-sounds of the pure Doric dialect; its very harshness prevented expressions of cheerfulness from conveying any idea of lightness or frivolity.

The choral lyric of the Dorians was eminently fitted for solemn and sacred subjects, whilst the Æolian measures and dialect, participating, to a certain extent, in Asiatic softness, was suitable to the expression of human sentiment and passion. The influence of Asia is plainly visible in the lyric poetry of the Æolians. Alcman was a native of Sardis; Callinus, of Ephesus; Mimnermus, of Smyrna. The islands in its immediate neighborhood, Teos, Paros, and Ceos, could each boast of its lyric poet, and Lesbos was the native country of Terpander, Alcæus, and Sappho. The choral lyric is always marked by solemnity and not by passion. If ever it descended from heaven to earth, it was in order to celebrate the glories of heroes, who, by their exploits, appeared to partake almost of a divine nature, or to call forth sympathy on those solemn occasions, which partake most of a religious nature, that is, marriages and funerals. These are events of human life, but they are blessed and consecrated by the especial invocation of deity.

The lyric poetry of the Æolian school, on the other hand,—although some of it, like the hymeneal of Sappho and the choral poetry of Corinna, resembled the Dorian in its object and purpose,—was all passion and feeling. It sympathized with man rather than endeavored to elevate the soul to the contemplation of, and communion with deity. Lyric poetry is the outpouring of the human heart, when inspired either by religion or love. The former characterizes the lyric of the Dorians, the latter that of the Æolians; in this aspect it viewed all the subjects which it celebrated.

If the Lesbian poets touched upon the events of political life, it was not in a spirit of grave and sober reflection on the high and noble destinies or the sad fortunes of men, but in a strain of vehemently excited feeling. But, though passionate and voluptuous, they did not give utterance to self-indulgent feelings only; they laid bare their own sentiments, but they expressed sympathy with those of others. If they sang of love, self seemed forgotten in their devotion to the object of their affections; if of the joys of the banquet, their theme was the social enjoyment which accompanies the wine cup, and not the mere gratification of the appetite.

The deities in whose honor choral odes, accompanied with music and dancing, were sung, were Apollo and Dionysus. The earliest choral song was the Pæan, sung in praise of the former god, as the averter of evil; but although the pæan properly belonged to the worship of Apollo, the term was sometimes applied to poems sung in honor of other deities.[1]   It was essentially a song of joy, as is evidenced by the exclamation ἰή, which always formed part of its burden.   When evil was anticipated, it implied hope; when danger was past, it expressed confidence and gratitude.   Homer[2] represents a pæan as being sung in honor of Apollo, when the Achæans were suffering from the wrath of that deity.   When the Dorian armies marched to battle, the pæan cheered and awoke their warlike spirit; and when the victory was won a similar strain expressed their triumph over their foes. Müller[3] attributes the origin of the Dorian religious music and poetry to the ancient Phrygian inhabitants of Crete, who celebrated the worship of the mother of the gods.   He states, on the authority of Athenæus,[4] that the pæan, as well as the nome and the hyporcheme, were known in Crete in the earliest times, and that the two last were in that island connected with cyclic dances.   The other choral songs were nomes, hyporchemes, parthenia, prosodia, and dithyrambs.

The nomes (νόμοι)[5] were lyric hymns in honor of Apollo, set to written tunes; the hyporchemes (ὑπορχήματα) were songs subordinate to the music, and accompanying the pantomimic dance which bore the same name.[6]   The musical accompaniment was that of the flute, and, therefore, the hyporcheme properly belonged to the worship of Dionysus, for the flute was his instrument, as the cithara was that of Apollo.   A hyporcheme of Pratinas is preserved by Athenæus,[7] in which he complains that music is usurping an undue supremacy over poetry.   The parthenia (παρθένια) were grave and modest songs, sung by young virgins; the prosodia (προσοδία) were hymns sung as the procession of priests marched up towards the altar; and the dithyramb was a characteristic poem in honor of Dionysus.

The dithyramb was the germ of the choral element in the Attic tragedy.   It was a hymn sung to the flute, whilst the rest

[1] Hellen. iv. 7 ; Anab. iii. 2.   [2] Il. i. 473.
[3] Müller's Dorians, iv. 6, 5.   [4] Athen. iv. p. 181, B.
[5] Nitzsch, Hist. Hom. p. 40.   [6] Æschyl. Choeph. v. 1013.
[7] Athenæus, xiv.

of the chorus danced in a circle round the altar of the god. From this circumstance the dithyrambic choruses were called Cyclian. It is probable, however, that in the earliest ages this form was not peculiar to the dithyrambic chorus alone, if the etymology of Hesychius[1] is to be trusted, who makes κόρος equivalent to κύκλος, or στέφανος; thus connecting it with the Latin word *corona*, which signifies a band arranged in a circular form.

At what period the dithyramb was first used is unknown; it is said, however, that it was first introduced and exhibited in regular choral form by Arion, in the city of Corinth.[2] He is also said to have added to the mere choral element, the recitation of verses by actors, representing satyrs, thus, in fact, investing it with a rude dramatic form; and from this modification it gradually became more dramatic and less choral. The sentiments uttered by such characters as satyrs would, of course, be of a joyous if not of a jocose[3] kind, and hence there were two kinds of dithyrambs, the one such as we have just described, the other of a grave, solemn, and tragic kind, celebrating the sorrows and dangers of Dionysus in his varied adventures.

The meaning and etymology of the word dithyrambus have been the subject of much investigation, but are still involved in obscurity. Bloomfield[4] was the first to observe the undoubted connection between the words διθύραμβος, ἴαμβος, θρίαμβος (the Latin word *triumphus*). It is equally certain that it is allied to the Greek words θρίον and θύρσος.[5] Now θρίον signifies (1) a fig-leaf,[6] (2) something wrapped in fig-leaves,[7] and the thyrsus,[8] which was emblematic of the infant Dionysus wrapped in ivy, was sometimes a spear terminated by a cone and wreathed with ivy-leaves, sometimes a simple shaft without ivy, surmounted by a θρίον instead of a cone. If, then, this connection is to be considered as established, the dithyrambus Δι-θύρ-αμβος would imply the iambic or wild satyric strain sung to that god, whose symbol is the thyrsus. If it be objected that the syllable Δι points to Zeus rather than Dionysus, it may be answered that the transition from the Cretan

---

[1] Hesych. in loco.
[2] Pindar, Ol. xiii. 18.
[3] Hor. Art. Poet.
[4] Mus. Crit. ii. 70.
[5] Liddell and Scott, Lex. in loco.
[6] Aristoph. Vesp. 436.
[7] Aristoph. Ran. 134, &c.
[8] Don. Theat. of Greeks, p. 18.

10

worship of Zeus to the Dorian worship of Apollo, and the subsequent connection of the worship of Apollo with that of Dionysus, is sufficient to account for this element of the word.[1]
Moreover, the signification of the word Dionysus (the god of Ny-
sos) proves that some word of which Δι or Δις was the root, was
as much the generic name of deity, as the cognate word *deus* was
in Latin.

Such were the forms of lyric poetry, which formed part of the
religious worship of the Dorian race. But although they partly
entered into the ceremonials of the Dionysiac worship, the principal deities of the Dorians were Apollo and Diana, and not
Dionysus. In all their settlements their worship may be traced
so universally, that its presence is a proof that the people amongst
whom it prevails is of Doric origin. Müller[2] affirms that Apollo
was a deity worshipped only by races of Hellenic descent,
and was not a national deity of the Pelasgic race. Owing to
successive Dorian migrations this worship first pervaded Delphi
and Delos, and the other seats of this worship on the continent
and islands of the Ægean, next it spread over the coasts of Asia
Minor, and lastly was introduced into the Peloponnese.

The simplicity which marked the whole character of the Dorians, was originally visible in their religious belief. They did
not, at first, people every spot with supernatural beings, or fill
Olympus with deities, like the more imaginative Ionians. The
only two male deities whom they recognized were Zeus and Apollo.
Zeus, it was believed, held communication with man, through
Apollo; he is sometimes called his son,[3] and is the bearer of his
commands and revelations.

In the Homeric hymns, as well as in the " Iliad," he is represented as the bearer to men of the divine blessings and divine
vengeance. He is always the author of evil which is justly deserved; not of evil abstractedly. In the " Iliad"[4] he is represented as the inflicter of pestilence, only to be cured by appeasing
his wrath through priestly interposition. His weapons of vengeance are, from their swiftness and unseen nature, represented
as arrows ; and the archer himself is called the far-darting one.

But though the minister of divine vengeance, his names of

---

[1] Plato, de Leg. iii. 700.   [2] Müller's Dorians, 228.
[3] Ἔκατός Διὸς υἱός, Alcman, Hephæst. Gaisf. p. 61.   [4] Il. i.

Apollo and Fæan imply that he was a protecting and a healing power. The former was, according to its oldest orthography, 'Aπίλλων, the averter (of ill), a title synonymous with the other epithets applied to him of ἀλεξίκακος and ἀποτρόπαιος. The latter from παίω, *to heal*, was applied to him as the only deity who could heal the wounds which he had himself inflicted. It is probable that the connection between Apollo and ἀπόλλυμι, *to destroy*, and between Pæan and παίω, *to strike*, is only accidental; and that the use of the epithets in these senses is an instance of that play upon words which was universally admired by the Greek poets.

The goddess Diana, who was associated with Apollo as an object of Dorian worship, was represented as his sister. These two constituted the male and female development of the same idea of deity—they symbolized the sources of light; they were personifications of the two principal heavenly bodies, the sun and moon.

The belief that Apollo was the sun-god, harmonizes with all the attributes ascribed to him. The rays of the sun might be poetically symbolized by the arrows of the god. The distance of the sun from the earth would procure for Apollo the title of the "Far-darter"—the baneful effects of the solar heat on the one hand, or its healthful influence on the other, would cause him to be looked upon as the inflicter of fever and pestilence, as well as the healing power. Lastly, as the source of physical light and heat, he would naturally be worshipped as the author of poetical and prophetical enthusiasm, and as bearing the messages of intellectual light and knowledge from God to man; as the divine illuminator of man's mental darkness.

The worship of Apollo and Diana was afterwards superseded by that of Dionysus, and the pæan gave place to the dithyramb. How this came to pass, history does not inform us; we know only that the former worship was peculiarly Hellenic, whilst the latter was of foreign origin. It is plain that the Dionysiac worship was a degenerate and less spiritual one.

Instead of the refinements of poetry and music being consecrated to the service of heavenly beings, they were devoted to that of deities who dwelt amongst men, who made earth their abiding place. Apollo and Diana had symbolized the heavenly causes of production; Dionysus represented the fertility of earth. A link lower down in the chain of causes was thus substituted as an object of adoration for that which had previously been regarded as the first cause. But the Dorian choral lyric was national and patriotic, as well as religious, and hence possesses an historical value.

The political events and circumstances of the times entered very largely into the writings of the lyric poets; and from the personal knowledge which Alcman, Thaletas, and Tyrtæus possessed of the people of Sparta, reliance can safely be placed on their authority. In fact, to them are we indebted for all that is authentic in the history of the first and second Messenian wars, since the other romantic incidents contained in the narratives of Plutarch, are only based upon family legends and popular traditions.

The distinction between the two schools cannot be maintained when treating of the convivial poetry of the Greeks, for poems of this class were written both by Æolians and Dorians. The most popular of these lyric compositions were the Scolia. The guests at a banquet passed a branch of myrtle from one side to the other of the table, and each in turn, as he held it, was called upon to sing a few verses. The connection of metre and subject was preserved throughout the whole series of singers, and the whole poem thus sung was termed σκόλιον. These compositions did not, as might be expected, merely celebrate the pleasures and enjoyments of social life, but were frequently vehicles of sage and wise reflections, or of free and patriotic sentiments.

Grave and solemn as was the natural temper of the Dorians, their lyric poetry permitted the introduction of light and secular subjects. The songs which enlivened the banquet did not always speak the words of wisdom; they were sometimes, as might be expected, during hours of unrestrained freedom and social relaxation, joyous and voluptuous, as those of the Æolians, and not unfrequently coarse and licentious.

The following scolia, by Pittacus, Simonides, and Callistratus, will exhibit the general scope and tendency of these compositions:—

Συνετῶν ἐστὶν ἀνδρῶν
Πρὶν γενέσθαι τὰ δυσχερῆ

Προνοῆσαι ὅπως μὴ γένηται·
Ἀνδρείων δὲ, γενόμενα εὖ ϶έσθαι.

Against each ill provides the prudent breast:
The brave man feels whatever is is best.

Ὑγιαίνειν μὲν ἄριστον ἀνδρὶ ϶νατῷ·
Δεύτερον δὲ, καλὸν φυὰν γενέσθαι·
Τὸ τρίτον δὲ, πλουτεῖν ἀδόλως·
Καὶ τὸ τέταρτον, ἡβᾶν μετὰ τῶν φίλων.

Of mortal joys the first is health;
The second gift is beauty's charm;
The next to these is guileless wealth;
Then youth if blessed with friendship warm.

Ἐν μύρτου κλαδὶ τὸ ξίφος φορήσω,   κ. τ. λ.

I'll wreathe my sword in myrtle bough—
The sword that laid the tyrant low,
When patriots, burning to be free,
To Athens gave equality.

Harmodius, hail! though 'reft of breath,
Thou ne'er shalt feel the stroke of death;
The heroes' Happy Isles shall be
The bright abodes allotted thee.

I'll wreathe my sword in myrtle bough—
The sword that laid Hipparchus low;
When at Minerva's adverse fane
He knelt, and never rose again.

While freedom's name is understood,
You shall delight the wise and good;
You dared to set your country free,
And gave her laws equality.

There were also other songs (παροίνια), which were purely convivial; κῶμοι, or songs accompanied with dances on occasions of
domestic rejoicings; and ἰπιθαλάμια, sung at marriages in honor of
the bride.

The following were the principal lyric poets who flourished
during this, its first period:—

EUMELUS, (about) B.C. 768.

Eumelus,[1] a native of Corinth, who lived in the early Olym-

[1] See Matthiæ, Hist. of Lit.

piads. He was the author of epic poems, and also an historical poem, the subject of which was Corinth. The lyrical production for which he is known, is a prosodion in honor of Apollo; and whilst doubt rests upon the genuineness of the other poems which are ascribed to him, this was considered by Pausanias as his work.[1] He is not placed by the Alexandrian grammarians in their canon of nine lyric poets. These were Alcman, Alcæus, Sappho, Stesichorus, Ibycus, Anacreon, Simonides, Bacchylides, and Pindar.

ALCMAN, (about) B. C. 671.

Alcman, whom tradition hands down as the greatest lyric poet of whom Sparta could boast, was a native of Sardis; brought to Sparta as a slave, he was emancipated, and naturalized as a citizen. He lived, according to Suidas, about B. C. 671. Müller says that he was a child at the close of the reign of Ardys, B. C. 629. The period of his poetical career at Sparta was that immediately succeeding the second Messenian war. Probably, the high reputation which he enjoyed was owing to the fact, that his adopted countrymen had now, for the first time, leisure to devote themselves to the refinements of poetry, as the fragments which have come down to us, scarcely warrant the estimation in which they were held, or the title awarded to him of the principal lyric poet. His poems comprehend all the species of lyric composition above mentioned, and his love songs, of which style of poetry he is said·by Suidas to have been the inventor, are distinguished by a voluptuousness, which forms a marked contrast to the severity of the Dorian character.

The poems for which he was most famed were parthenia. These were choruses, sung by bands of virgins, and accompanied by music, in which science he was a proficient. They were of a solemn kind, and their subjects were of a religious character.

ARION, (about) B. C. 628.

Arion, who is said to have been the inventor of the dithyrambus, was also a lyric poet; he was a native of Lesbos, and a

---

[1] Paus. iv. 4, § 1.

friend of Periander of Corinth, and therefore lived about B. C. 635. The following legend is told respecting him, by Herodotus, on the authority of the Corinthians and Lesbians.

Having made a voyage to Italy, and earned a large sum of money, he hired a Corinthian vessel at Tarentum, in order to return to the court of Periander. The sailors, tempted by his wealth, determined to throw him overboard, but he, discovering their intention, entreated them to take his money, but spare his life. His prayers were ineffectual, for they only gave him the alternative, of either killing himself, in order that he might obtain the rites of burial, or leaping into the sea. Arion then besought the sailors, that they would permit him to stand in the stern of the vessel and sing. Delighted at the prospect of hearing him, they consented. Taking therefore his cithara, he sang the Orthian nome, and when his strain was ended, he leaped into the sea, and a dolphin bore him safe to Tænarus. A monument at Tænarus commemorated this legend in the days of Herodotus, and, in after ages, the poet and his harp were immortalized among the constellations.

ALCÆUS, (about) B. C. 610.

Alcæus was also a Lesbian, a native of Mitylene, whose patriotism shone forth in his military prowess,[1] as well as in his impassioned poetry.[3] At the very commencement of his political career, B. C. 610, his native country was distracted by those contests between the aristocratic and democratic parties, which were the curse of every Greek state at some period of its history. Alcæus was noble, and therefore supported the aristocratic faction. The success of democracy led as usual to the establishment of a tyranny, and Alcæus and his brother were exiled. After a time he returned, and headed an unsuccessful attempt to restore the aristocratic party to power.

On this occasion, the celebrated Pittacus was elected tyrannus by the people. His moderation led him to pardon Alcæus and the exiled nobles, notwithstanding the literary provocations with which the poet had assailed him, magnanimously saying that for-

[1] Herod. i. 24. [3] Hor. Od. i. iii. 2; ii. xiii. 28.
[3] Quinct. xi. 63.

givencss is better than revenge. He then became a wanderer from his native land, and died in exile.

His poems are especially interesting, as having furnished to Horace, not only a metrical model, but also the subject-matter, of some of his most beautiful odes. They may be divided into three classes. 1. Hymns, some of which relate, in simple and graceful verse, some favorite legend of the deity to whom they were addressed; for example, the adventures of Mercury, imitated by Horace.[1]

2. Odes, which sing the praises of love and wine, of which the most beautiful are those which he addressed to the object of his admiration, even more than of his love, the poetess Sappho.[2] Müller observes, that his drinking songs were not invitations to mere sensual enjoyment, but universally connected with reflections on the circumstances of the times, or upon man's destiny in general.

3. But it is in the third class of his poems that the peculiar features of the mind of Alcæus are especially exhibited, viz., his zeal as a political partisan, and his hearty devotion to the principles of his party. These poems were called διχοσταοιαστικά, or party poems. One of them is imitated by Horace,[3] in that ode in which he describes the state, during times of civil commotion, as a tempest-tossed vessel, the sport of the wind and waves; a metaphor which has been adopted by poets and orators in every age. There is another, also imitated by Horace,[4] in which, transported with joy at the liberation of his country from the tyranny of Myrsilus, he exclaims, Now is the time for drinking, since Myrsilus is dead.

SAPPHO, (about) B. C. 610.

Contemporary with Alcæus, and perhaps even more admired, was the much calumniated Sappho. She was a woman of the liveliest fancy, and the most ardent passions. Warm-hearted, and endowed with more than common tenderness of disposition, openness, and candor, which made it impossible for her to conceal her inmost thoughts, or to veil her feelings in words less warm than

[1] Hor. Od. i. 10.   [2] Arist. Rhet. i. 9.
[3] Hor. Od. i. 14.   [4] Ibid. i. 37.

the feelings themselves, have caused her character to be maligned, and her motives misinterpreted.[1] Müller remarks, "That the strict morality with which she reproves the licentiousness of her brother Charaxus, fully acquits her of levity of character, inasmuch as her reproof would have been her own condemnation." It is not, of course, to be supposed that Sappho was purer-minded than other women of her age, but there is no evidence for believing that she was inferior to them in morality. She was the native of a country in which little restraint was put upon the indulgence of the softer passions, whose poets were accustomed to express their amatory feelings in the warmest language. She, therefore, as a poet, would naturally pour forth her feelings in similar strains, she would forget her sex in the enthusiasm of inspiration, but it by no means follows that in her conduct she would forget her sex's modesty. It must be remembered that Sappho was an Æolian, and therefore enjoyed far more liberty and public intercourse with general society than Ionian women, who lived in a retirement and seclusion almost like that of Orientals, with the sole exception that they were actively employed in the management of domestic concerns. Hence the Athenians were likely to consider the openness with which Sappho expressed those feelings which women instinctively conceal, as unmaidenly, nay, even as unfeminine. It is true that she does not hesitate to pour forth her passionate accents in the most glowing language, but then in her case, it was thinking aloud; nor did she know the duty of concealment. She seems to have instinctively felt that poets have a right[2] to dare anything. Nor was there a calumny breathed against her for generations after her death. The Athenian comic poets were the first to slander her, and to attack her, as they were wont to attack the female sex generally. Their accusations, moreover, were addressed to an audience from which women were excluded, and at a period when the virtuous of the sex were denied that education which would have fitted them to be companions of men of refinement, and thus were degraded from their proper place in society. Sappho's reputation was first assailed when accomplishments were possessed by the licentious

[1] On this subject see Welcker, Sappho befreit, &c. Gütt. 1816.
[2] Hor. Art. Poet.

alone of the female sex, and the mere fact of being a poetess would have been sufficient to create a prejudice against her.

Her poems were principally epithalamia and hymns, and as, among the Latin poets, Horace delighted to imitate Alcæus, in his nobler odes, and adopted the metre of Sappho in his lighter and softer poems; so the sweetest and most poetical of them all, Catullus,[1] often appropriated the impassioned thoughts, and nature-loving imagery of Sappho—the brightest of those bright female minds which throw a lustre over Greek lyric poetry.[2]   Of one of her poems, the wise Solon is said to have exclaimed, that he would not be content to die, until he had committed it to memory.   And it is a matter of the deepest regret that so few fragments of her compositions are preserved.   The following are faithful translations of two, which have always been admired for their singular beauty :—

> Blest as the immortal gods is he,
> The youth who fondly sits by thee,
> And hears and sees thee all the while
> Softly speak, and sweetly smile.
>
> 'Twas this deprived my soul of rest,
> And raised such tumults in my breast;
> For while I gazed, in transport tost,
> My breath was gone, my voice was lost.
>
> My bosom glowed; the subtle flame
> Ran quick through all my vital frame;
> O'er my dim eyes a darkness hung,
> My ears with hollow murmurs rung.
>
> In dewy damps my limbs were chilled;
> My blood with gentle horrors thrilled,
> My feeble pulse forgot to play,
> I fainted, sank, and died away.
>
> AMBROSE PHILLIPS.

AD LESBIAM.

> Ille mî par esse deo videtur,
> Ille, si fas est, superare divos,
> Qui sedens adversus identidem te
>   Spectat, et audit.

---

[1] See Catul. LI.   [2] Stobæus, xxix. 28.

Dulce ridentem; misero quod omnis
Eripit sensus mihi ; nam simul te,
Lesbia, aspexi, nihil est super mi
                  Voce loquendum.

Lingua sed torpet ; tenues sub artus
Flamma dimanat ; sonitu suopte
Tinniunt aures ; gemina teguntur
                Lumina nocte.
                        CATULLUS.

HYMN TO VENUS.

O Venus, beauty of the skies,
To whom a thousand temples rise,
Gaily false in gentle smiles,
Full of love-perplexing wiles ;
O goddess, from my heart remove,
The wasting cares and pains of love !

If ever thou hast kindly heard
A song in soft distress preferred,
Propitious to my tuneful vow,
O, gentle goddess! hear me now ;
Descend, thou bright immortal guest,
In all thy radiant charms confess'd.

Thou once didst leave almighty Jove,
And all the golden roof above ;
The car, thy wanton sparrows drew,
Hovering in air they lightly flew ;
As to my bower they wing'd their way,
I saw their quivering pinions play.

The birds dismissed (while you remain),
Bore back their empty car again ;
Then you with looks divinely mild,
In every heavenly feature smiled,
And asked what new complaints I made,
And why I call'd you to my aid.

What frenzy in my bosom raged,
And by what cure to be assuaged ;
What gentle youth I would allure,
Whom in my artful toils secure.
Who does thy tender heart subdue—
Tell me, my Sappho—tell me who ?

Though now he shuns thy longing arms,
He soon shall court thy slighted charms ;
Though now thy offerings he despise,
He soon to thee shall sacrifice.
Though now he freeze, he soon shall burn,
And be thy victim in his turn.

Celestial visitant, once more,
Thy needful presence I implore !
In pity come and case my grief,
Bring my distempered soul relief ;
Favor thy suppliant's hidden fires,
And give me all my heart desires.

AMBROSE PHILLIPS.

Respecting her biography but little is known ; the principal authorities are the Parian marble, and the traditions contained in Ovid's epistle of Sappho[1] to the imaginary Phaon. She was born either at Eresos or Mitylene, about the forty-second Olympiad, and was therefore a contemporary of Alcæus, Stesichorus, and Pittacus. Her father's home has been variously stated, and he died when she was six years old. Her mother's name was Cleis. She had three brothers, Larychus, Charaxus, and Eurygius. She married an Andrian, named Cercolas, by whom she had one daughter, who was named after her mother Cleis. Her life, like that of many other Lesbian women of talent and refinement, was passed in literary pursuits, in the midst of a circle of female friends and pupils of her own sex, to whom she was devotedly attached. Amongst them are preserved the names of Anagora of Miletus, Goggyla of Colophon, and Eunice of Salamis,[2] and from the epithet γεραιτέρα, which she applies to herself, it is evident she lived beyond the prime of life. Besides elegies, iambics, and monodies, she wrote nine books of lyric poems, and is said to have invented the plectrum.[3]

The whole romantic story of Sappho's love for Phaon, and her leap, in the despair of disappointed love, from the Leucadian promontory, are legendary. That Sappho, in her amatory poems, delighted to sing of the loves of Aphrodite and Adonis, is very probable, and hence, the last line of the Sapphic stanza was termed by the grammarians, an Adonian. Hesiod[4] also states that a

---

[1] Heroid. xv.   [2] Fr. 20.   [3] Suidas, s. v.   [4] Theog. 986.

child named Phaethon was carried away by Aphrodite. This name may perhaps have become corrupted into Phaon, and substituted, in the legend, for that of Adonis ; and if made the subject of any of Sappho's odes, may have come to be considered as the name of a lover of her own.[1] A similar account may be given of the Leucadian rock, since a legend of the same kind forms part of the love-tale of Adonis and Aphrodite. Perhaps, as has been suggested, the whole legend originated in the poets having spoken of a violent passion, as one which could only be cured by a leap from the Leucadian promontory. The rhythm of her poems, with some slight variations, is essentially the same as that of her fellow-countryman Alcæus. The following neatly-turned epigram is extant in honor of the admired poetess :—

> Ἐννέα τὰς Μούσας φασίν τινες· ὡς ὀλιγώρως·
> Ἠνίδε καὶ Σαπφὼ Λεσβόθεν ἡ δεκάτη.

Some count the Muses nine ; how careless ! when
Sappho of Lesbos makes the number ten.

ERINNA, (about) B.C. 610.

Erinna, the young Rhodian poetess, as she was the friend of Sappho, may be mentioned here, although her poems were of the epic class. Her principal work, "The Distaff" (Ἠλακάτη), consisted of only three hundred lines ; but short as they were, they have been thought worthy of comparison even with Homer. The four lines which remain, furnish no opportunity of judging of her merit. Great, however, must have been the genius of a maiden who, cut off at the early age of nineteen, left such fame behind her, and such reason to lament her untimely fate.

[1] Müller, 174–5.

CHAPTER XII.

STESICHORUS. — BIOGRAPHY. — LEGENDS. — CHARACTERISTICS OF HIS POETRY.—THE
IMPROVER OF BUCOLIC POETRY.—IBYCUS. — THE CRANES OF IBYCUS — ANACREON.
—THE POEMS ATTRIBUTED TO HIM SPURIOUS.—BIOGRAPHY.—HIS ASSOCIATES ESPE-
CIALLY MIMNERMUS. — STORY OF HIS DEATH. — SIMONIDES. — HIS LIFE. — LEGEND
RESPECTING HIM.—EPITAPH ON ARCHEDICE. — BACCHYLIDES. — PINDAR.—CHARAC-
TERISTIC FEATURES OF HIS AGE.—RISE AND PROGRESS OF BŒOTIAN POETRY.—BIO-
GRAPHY.—STYLE OF PINDAR'S POETRY.—EPINICIAN ODES.—HIS MODE OF PRODUCING
VARIETY. — ADVICE OF CORINNA. — RELIGIOUS CHARACTER OF PINDAR'S MIND. —
TESTIMONY OF HORACE.—PINDARIC METRES.

STESICHORUS, B. C. 632—560.

CONTEMPORARY with Sappho and Alcæus, was Stesichorus, of
Himera in Sicily; the friend, as it is said, of Phalaris,[1] tyrant
of Agrigentum.   He was born B. C. 632, and died B. C. 560.[2]
There is a tradition that he was the son of Hesiod.   This of
course involves an anachronism, but the origin of it has been
satisfactorily accounted for,[3] by connecting it with another account, which states that his family lived at Metaurus, a Locrian
colony in Italy.   Among the Ozolian Locrians there lived a line
of bards, admirers and followers of Hesiod, who, like the Homerides, affected the title of sons of that poet.[4]   One of these
families probably migrated to Metaurus, and from them Stesichorus descended.   Snidas[5] informs us that his original name was
Tisias, and that he was called Stesichorus, ὅτι πρῶτος κιθαρῳδίᾳ χορὸν
ἴστησεν.   The meaning of this is that he introduced in choruses
the epode in addition to the strophe and antistrophe, during the
recital of which the chorus remained stationary.   Greek legends
tell of miraculous events connected with his life.   When an infant,
a nightingale sat and sang upon his lips.   In after life he was
struck blind after writing an attack on Helen, and when he wrote
a recantation was restored to sight.   He had two brothers—

---

[1] Phalaris, Ep.   [2] Rhet. ii. 20.   [3] Müller.
[4] Clinton, Fasti Hellenici.   [5] Suidas, s. v.

Mamertinus and Helianax—the one celebrated as a geometrician, the other as a legislator.

The distinguishing characteristic of Stesichorus' poetry is, that he adapted epic subjects to lyric verse. The difficulty of such a task as this, the poetic skill which it must have required, is acknowledged by Quinctilian,[1] who, whilst he finds fault with him for diffuseness, nevertheless compares him to Homer, and says that "he supported the weight of epic poetry with his lyre."[2]

Müller seems to think a successful union of these two styles impossible.[3] Doubtless to embody in a lyric poem, with all its usual accompaniments, an epic narrative, or even a single episode —especially one in the Hesiodic style, from which school of poetry Stesichorus borrowed—would be a vain attempt; but to touch lightly on and narrate briefly some striking exploits of popular and favorite heroes, or some scenes of marvellous or pathetic interest, such as Horace occasionally introduces in his most beautiful odes, would be perfectly appropriate: and in this, as far as we can judge from the fragments extant, the art of Stesichorus consisted. He thus recalled the old reminiscences of the ancient bards, and adorned them with all the modern graces of the voice, the instrument, and the dance.

As the spirit which pervaded Greek lyric poetry gave expression to the affections and interests of private life, we owe, as might be expected, the position which the Bucolic, or Pastoral, occupies in Greek poetry to a Dorian lyric poet. Stesichorus was the first to invest it with a classical character. With this species of poetry we are familiar in the pastorals of Theocritus, who belongs to a far later age of Greek literature, and to the delightful eclogues of his imitator, Virgil. It is not a favorite in the present day, but there was a period in the history of English literature when the imitation of the ancients was highly valued, and when this species of poetry was much admired.

It is difficult to arrive at a satisfactory theory of the origin of bucolic poetry. Epicharmus, the Sicilian, celebrates the βουκολιασμοί of the Italian and Sicilian shepherds,[4] and describes them as songs accompanied with dancing. It is probable, therefore, that the

---

[1] Quinct. i. 62.   [2] Ibid. i. 62.   [3] Müller, p. 200.

[4] Athenæus, xiv.; Hesych.; Etym. M.

Pastoral was the native poetry of the Siculi, the aboriginal inhabitants of Italy, who having been driven from their native country
by a conquering race, formed new settlements in Sicily, and gave
their name to the island. They were a simple and pastoral race,
and the original Bucolic doubtless presented a real picture of
habits and manners—related the joys and cares, and loves of this
shepherd people, the pleasures and anxieties of rural life. The
early connection established between Dorian colonists and the
aboriginal Siculi, soon caused the Bucolic to put on a Doric dress,
and adopt the Dorian dialect, to be grafted as a new branch of
the Dorian literature. It was also in its origin, like the Dorian
choral lyric, consecrated to the service of religion; pastoral poetry
formed part of the worship of the Siculan rural deity, Pales, from
which the Romans derived their festival of Palilia, and hymns of
a similar character were sung in honor of Diana by the shepherd
inhabitants of the upland pastures and mountainous districts in
the Peloponnesus.[1] Many traces of its Siculan origin may be
discovered in the bucolic poetry itself. The frequently recurring
name of Tityrus was used by the Dorians of Italy to designate
the goat which was "Father of the herd," and thence was transferred to the goatherd himself. The earliest pastoral is said to have
been sung by a Sicilian cowherd named Diomus,[2] and the shepherd Daphnis, the hero of Theocritus' "Idylls," is represented
as pouring forth his laments for his mistress's jealousy, and his
loss of sight, of which she was the cruel cause, in the neighborhood of the Sicilian Himera.

IBYCUS, (about) B. C. 540.

Ibycus was a native of Rhegium,[3] descended from a Messenian
family, who migrated thither after the second Messenian war.
Suidas says that he flourished about B. C. 560; but if, as is generally believed, he was the friend of Polycrates of Samos, his era
must be placed about B. C. 540. The warmth of his amatory
poems obtained for him the epithet of *love-maddened* (ἐρωτομανέ-
στατος); but some of his poems were of a loftier and more epic
character.

---

[1] Servius, ad Virg. Ecl.   [2] Müller, Hist. Literature.
[3] Suidas; Cic. Tusc. Quæst. iv. 33.

A miraculous legend is related of him, which gave rise to the proverbial expression "the cranes of Ibycus." As he was travelling he was attacked by robbers and murdered. In his dying moments he called upon some cranes which were flying over his head to avenge his death. Suddenly in the Corinthian theatre the cranes appeared to the assembled audience, and hovered over its roofless walls. One of the murderers, who was present, exclaimed, "Behold the avengers of Ibycus," and thus involuntarily convicted himself of the crime.

ANACREON, (about) B. C. 540.

Those who have admired, in their school days, the graceful odes which bear the name of Anacreon may be surprised to find that they are not the works of this poet, but belong to an age probably as late as the Christian era. Beautiful as these little effusions are, we in vain look for the glowing warmth and poetical enthusiasm which characterize the muse of Greece in its most flourishing lyric period, and which are visible in the very few genuine fragments remaining to us. He was born at Teos, and thence migrated to Abdera, B. C. 542,[1] but his great patron was Polycrates, who, like most of the τύραννοι, was a great encourager of literature, and all the arts of civilized life. Tradition represents his poetry as being entirely of that class which is still called Anacreontic. It celebrated the joys of love and wine. His life, too, is said to have been in accordance with the spirit of his poetry.

After the death of Polycrates he attached himself to a band of contemporary poets, who lived at the court of Hipparchus, and were joyous, jovial, and voluptuous, devoted heart and soul to the sensual enjoyment of life. Mimnermus, of whom mention has been already made among the elegiac poets, formed the only exception in the society to which, as well as Anacreon, he belonged. He was no less a sensualist than they were, nor had he more moral principle, or strength of mind, to restrain his appetite; but his refinement was greater, and his temperament naturally melancholy. He saw the hollowness of mere selfish enjoyment, and

---

[1] Matthiæ, History of Literature, s. v.

11

he gave utterance to his glowing spirit in lamentations on the shortness and sorrows of life. Anacreon was probably a man of strong passions, and possessed one of those vigorous and healthy physical constitutions which even debauchery and self-indulgence fail to destroy. At any rate he is said to have attained the age of eighty-five years, and even then (about B. C. 480) to have died not of disease, but by accidentally swallowing a grape-stone.

This legend, however, bears so much the appearance of having been invented, because such a death was not inappropriate to á lover of conviviality, that it is scarcely deserving of credit. He was buried in his native country ; and his friend Simonides wrote two epitaphs to his memory. Another, also, is preserved in the Greek "Anthology," of which the following is a translation by an anonymous author :—

Θάλλοι τετραχόρυμβος, χ. τ. λ.

> This tomb be thine, Anacreon ; all around
> Let ivy wreathe, let flow'rets deck the ground,
> And from its earth enriched with such a prize,
> Let wells of milk and streams of wine arise ;
> So will thine ashes yet a pleasure know,
> If any pleasure reach the shades below.

SIMONIDES, born B. C. 556.

Simonides[1] was born in the island of Ceos, Ol. lvi. i. (B. C. 556). His family was connected with the Dionysiac worship, and the part which he himself, when a boy, is said to have taken in this poetical worship probably fostered his natural genius for poetry. The principal part of his life was spent at Athens, at the court of Hipparchus. How long after the expulsion of the tyrants he remained at Athens is uncertain, but he next removed to Thessaly, where he enjoyed the patronage of two families, the Aleuadæ and Scopadæ.

A legend is told by Cicero,[2] relating to the life of the poet in Thessaly. In a triumphal ode in which he had sung the praises of Scopas, he introduced also those of Castor and Pollux. Scopas, therefore, asserted that the two heroes should fairly pay half the promised premium for his poem. During the banquet, it was told

---

[1] Matthiæ, History of Literature.   [2] Cicero, de Nat. ii. 86.

Simonides that two young men were at the door who wished to speak with him. He obeyed the summons, but found no one there; and in his absence the banqueting-room fell and crushed Scopas and his friends. After this event the heaven-protected poet returned to Athens, where, in his eightieth year, he gained, for the fifty-sixth time, the prize in the dithyrambic chorus. The . last years of his long life were spent at the court of Hiero. Amongst all the eminent literary men whom the taste and munificence of the tyrant attracted to Syracuse, Simonides was his chief favorite. He was a more worldly-minded man than the high-souled Pindar, and could far more easily adapt himself to the manners of a court, and the society of a prince.

Simonides was also, to a certain extent, a philosopher, as well as a poet. He possessed stores of moral and political wisdom, which rendered him a valuable counsellor to Hiero, as well as an agreeable companion. As a lyric poet he was inferior to Pindar; his style is not adorned with that sublime beauty, that variety of imagery and illustration. But though surpassed in lyric power by him who brought the ode to 'perfection, he stands unrivalled in the neatness and elegance of his epigrams, and the mournful and affectionate strains of his elegiac poetry. As he was the first to use the elegiac metre for funeral songs and monumental inscriptions, so in the skill and force with which he used it, he has never been equalled. The simple epitaph on Archedice, the daughter of Hippias, Ἀνδρὸς ἀριστεύσαντος, κ. τ. λ. is well known to every reader of Thucydides, and the following quaint yet faithful translation will give some idea of its neatness to the English reader:—

> Archedice, the daughter of King Hippias,
>   Who in his time
> Of all the potentates of Greece was prime,
>   This dust doth hide,
> Daughter, wife, sister, mother, unto kings she was,
>   Yet free from pride.
>   HOBBES.

Many a touching epitaph may be read in the "Anthologia," written by him in honor of the patriot warriors of Greece, who fell in the Persian war at Salamis, and Artemisium, and Thermopylæ, and Marathon. With the elegy written in honor of those who fell at the last-mentioned of these glorious occasions, he vanquished Æschylus himself.[1]   Probably the terrible and majestic style of the great tragic poet was ill adapted to inspire tenderness and sympathy.

BACCHYLIDES.

Bacchylides belonged to a family in which, as was so often the case, poetry was followed as an hereditary profession.   He was the nephew of Simonides.   Nothing is known respecting his life, except that he was born at Ceos, that he lived with Simonides and Pindar at the court of Hiero, and was a rival of Pindar, although it can scarcely be believed that he was a worthy one.

As far as a judgment can be formed from the few relics extant of his numerous and various poems, they exhibit polish, correctness, delicacy, and ornament, but not the fire or fervor of Pindar. His excellence was the result of education rather than of natural poetic inspiration.   The emperor Julian is said to have drawn from the lyrics of Bacchylides rules for the conduct of life, so highly did he appreciate their ethical value.[2]   The following epigram will furnish a specimen of the sentiments frequently found in the poetry of Bacchylides :—

> Λυδία μὲν γὰρ λίθος
> Μανύει χρυσόν·
> Ἀνδρῶν δ' ἀρετὰν
> Σοφίαν τε παγχρατὴς
> Ἐλέγχει ἀγήθεια.

"The touchstone tries the purity of gold,
 And by all-conquering truth man's worth and wit is told."

PINDAR, born B. C. 517.

Pindar flourished on the confines of the two great literary periods. Æschylus was his contemporary; and therefore the Attic drama was attaining perfection at the very time when assembled Greece listened with rapt attention to the inspired effusions of his lyric muse. His genius, however, was totally independent of Attic taste, and had nothing in common with it; and

[1] Ol. lxxii. 3.　　　　　　　　　[2] Pearce's Longinus.

although his earliest composition was probably written but three years before Æschylus exhibited his first tragedy, their walks were perfectly distinct; they arrived at eminence by two parallel but different paths: they belonged to different schools of art and different ages of poetry.

With Pindar the independent existence of Dorian lyric poetry ceased, whilst Æschylus was the founder of the drama strictly so called, which only incorporated lyric odes as adjuncts, and assigned them a place, which gradually became more and more subordinate. But whilst Pindar is considered as belonging to the earlier period of Greek literary history, it must not be forgotten that the era in which he flourished was pre-eminently fitted for the development of his genius. The germ of Greek national talent was just unfolding itself. At the festivals where Pindar sang his songs of triumph, assembled Greece was now beginning to feel, for the first time, her greatness as one united nation. The Greeks were now ready to act in concert in any great enterprise; they were already animated by that oneness of spirit which, notwithstanding occasional defections and treacherous desertions from the national cause, enabled them successfully to resist the power of Persia. Pindar, though a Dorian, could regard Ionian Athens without jealousy as the centre of that union around which the rest of Greece was grouped and clustered; and in the presence of Greeks of every race and blood congregated at their games, which were the symbols of union, he could extol her praises without fearing to excite Dorian jealousy. The ground on which Pindar took his stand was a neutral one, in which all Greeks could meet without any worse feelings than a spirit of generous rivalry.

Pindar, the greatest of all Greek lyric poets, was born at Cynoscephalæ, a Theban village in the native country of Hesiod and Corinna. The date of his birth is, according to Matthiæ, Ol. lxv. 3, B. C. 517, but Clinton places it one year earlier, and Müller in B. C. 522.

The Persian war, whilst it concentrated the warlike spirit of Greece in one united effort, and thus assured her safe position amongst the nations of the world, gave strength and vigor and enthusiasm to the poetic faculty. Still, however, poetry was the wild outpourings of inspiration; it disdained the rules of art; it could not be criticized according to any principles of taste. But when the war was over, and tranquillity ensured, and the ascendancy of Athens established, and thus itself elevated to the rank of a capital of Greece, it became a school of poetry, and the art did not depend upon the independent taste of each individual poet, but seemed to recognize some general scientific principles.

It has already been said, that the literary and poetic talent of Bœotia, as exhibited in Hesiod and his school, was not indigenous, but was introduced from foreign climes. A band of settlers from Asia formed a settlement in her fertile plains, and the pastoral valleys hidden in the recesses of her mountains. The Theban Cadmus, the literary civilizer of Greece, is fabled to have come from Tyre. The Phœnician colonists, together with letters, introduced poetry, and sowed those seeds which afterwards brought forth fruit in their adopted country. The poetry of those Semitic nations from which they came, contained, as we see in the sacred writings, every species of composition, with the exception of the dramatic alone. The worship of Dionysus probably prevailed in early ages in this land of grapes and vineyards, and, together with its wild dithyrambic poetry, was soon naturalized in Thebes and its territory. His worship was a rural worship, and its rites and ceremonies were naturally adapted to the rural habits of the Bœotian agriculturists and herdsmen. The music of the flute, the favorite instrument of Dionysiac worship, soon began to be heard, where hitherto had only been heard the harp of the Ismenian Apollo. The worship of the Sun God and the Wine God became amalgamated; and soon the wilder and more licentious foreign rites supplanted the purer worship of their older deity in the affections of a rude and coarse-minded people. This is a brief sketch of the probable origin of that Bœotian poetry which Pindar and his fair instructors and rivals, Myrtis and Corinna, brought to perfection. The epic poetry of Hesiod and his school had taken its external form from that which was prevalent in Ionia. This school had now ceased for centuries, and in the choral worship of Dionysus originated the wild ode of Pindar.

The worship of Dionysus was joyous and exhilarating, like the wine of which he was the patron. The shrill accompaniment of the flute was therefore better adapted to its romping dances than the stately lyre. The early Greek flute was like the fife; its tones sharp, lively, thrilling, and it produced that inspiriting effect which renders the fife so suitable to martial music. This kind, therefore, of instrumental music was much cultivated in Bœotia, and the father of Pindar, whose name is said to have been Dai-phantus, was a flute-player; but Pindar's genius disdained to confine itself to his paternal profession. He went to Athens, and became a pupil of Lasus, the dithyrambic poet, to learn the laws of metrical arrangement, so far as they were then understood, and the theory of adapting poetry to the necessary accompaniments of music and dancing. It is probable, however, that Pindar had not much education, for he reproaches Simonides and his nephew, Bacchylides, with being μάθοντις, as though he felt the truth of the proverb, that man must be born a poet, but cannot be made one.

At an early age, B. C. 502, he wrote his tenth Pythian, in honor of a noble Thessalian, named Hippocles. His reputation soon spread throughout Greece and her colonies, and even all those countries of Europe which were accustomed to send their distinguished natives as competitors at the games.

No nation ever felt a more ardent thirst for fame and distinction than the Greeks, they lived upon praise, they were eminently social, and therefore nothing was so valuable to them as the position which they occupied in the eyes of others. They felt that the aid of such a poet as Pindar was essential to the attainment of this end; and, therefore, every tribute of affection and respect was universally lavished upon the Bœotian bard. All felt that on his tribute of praise depended immortality. Athens appointed him her resident πρόξινος, or consul, at Thebes, and presented him with ten thousand drachmæ, and, after his death, honored him with a statue.[1] But the most generous of all his patrons was Hiero of Syracuse. This munificent promoter of literature, as we have seen, occupied in Sicily a place similar to that of Pisistratus

---

[1] Isocr. Περί 'Αντιδ. Pausan. i. 8.

at Athens.   At his refined and polished court all literary men
found kindness and protection.

Four years he resided at the court of Hiero, but his usual residence was Thebes.   He was not made to be a courtier; his was a
noble, truthful, independent spirit, which could praise, but not
flatter.   Politics and public affairs, which were alien to the subjects of his poetry, had no interest for him; but he was always
ready to use his influence as a poet to quell those factious disputes
which even then distracted Thebes, and his heart was ever open
to sympathize with the sorrows of his countrymen, as well as to
celebrate their triumphs and victories.   The time of his death is
as uncertain as that of his birth, but he is said to have attained
the age of eighty years.   The style of his poetry was as varied as
his metrical harmonies.   He wrote dithyrambs, odes to be sung at
processions and by female choruses, encomiums, dirges, scolia, hyporchemes, and epinician, or triumphal odes.   With the exception
of fragments and quotations, none are preserved except the epini-
cia, but the care with which these have been handed down from
generation to generation justifies the assumption that they are the
most valuable of his works.

The odes of Pindar cannot be classed in point of style with any
other species of poetry, although parts of them resemble and partake of the nature of all kinds.   The mythological epic, the mournful elegy, the didactic nome, the triumphal dithyramb, the sacred
pæan, have all and each of them their counterparts in his poems,
but still these poems form a species by themselves.   Hence ancient
critics applied to them the title of εἴδη, a term which implies specific
poems coming under no certain designation.

The epinician odes were composed in honor of the victor at
the four great games of Greece, and therefore are arranged in
four divisions, the Olympian, Pythian, Nemean, and Isthmian.
Amongst them, however, are found a few in honor of conquerors
at other subordinate festivals.

The return of a victor at the games to his native city, was an
event celebrated with public rejoicings and solemn religious thanks-
givings.   A procession welcomed the successful hero, and attended
him to the temple, sacrifices were offered, and the banquet which
usually accompanied sacrifices followed.   The triumphal ode, the

principal feature in the solemnity, was sung, partly like the stro-
phes and antistrophes of the dramatic chorus, as the procession
moved along, partly like the stasima and epodes during intervals
of rest. The festival was prolonged to a late hour, and ended
with a joyous revel, which was called κῶμος. At this revel the
praises of the victor were again sung, and the poem which celebrated them was, from its being sung in the comus, termed an
encomium.

Besides his general merit as a poet, the peculiar skill which
Pindar exhibited was the interweaving other cognate incidents
with the immediate subject of his poem. The praise of the steeds
and their owner, the merits of the athlete and the musician, would
not have afforded sufficient variety; and therefore digressions,
suggested by their names and persons, formed the staple materials
of his odes.

Plutarch asserts that Corinna recommended him to produce
variety of effect by embodying in his odes mythological traditions,
and if this be true, to her first he may have been indebted for his
peculiar artifice.

These mythical traditions form a large portion of many odes,
but they are never out of place, they are always suggested by the
subject; and though at times they are so long as to deserve the
reproof with which Corinna qualified her instruction, "one ought
to sow with the hand, not with the whole bag," they are not introduced without reason. At one time an apophthegm containing
a mythical allusion, leads him to subjoin the whole legend in an
expanded form; at another, the descent of the victor from heroic
ancestors, naturally leads to the celebration of their exploits; at
another, he connects the hero's family history with the ancient
legends of the country to which he belongs. This was a fruitful
source of imagery. The glory of the individual was considered
as reflecting credit on his country, the personal interest of the
Greek was absorbed and merged in that of his native land, and
his victory was considered a national triumph. Hence every glorious recollection of ancient times adapted to display national
greatness, became a topic for the poet, certain of being acceptable
to his hearers.

In the odes of Pindar are visible the true majesty and grandeur of religious poetry, and the religious character of his mind, as well as his firm belief in a superintending providence, would not permit him to connect success with mere human causes.   He always represents the gods as the givers of victory, and speaks of piety, and the fulfilment of relative duties, as the causes which recommend the conqueror to their favor.

Nor did he neglect to warn the victor of the dangers of success, and the temptations which it offers to overweening pride.   Humility, gratitude, and moderation in victory, are to him subjects of praise, and of the moral lessons which he teaches to those whose victories he is at the same time celebrating.

The above are a few of the most striking characteristics of Pindar's poetry.   It is not surprising that this proneness to digress and to depart far from his main subject, to which allusion has been made, and the overflowing stream of imagery which the analogical power of his mind supplied, render his plan confused, and his style full of obscurity.   Like one hurried down the rapids of a river, and whirled round in its numerous eddies, the reader's head gets confused and loses sight of the poet's ideas from their very number and the rapidity with which he passes by them.

The great feature of his mind was rapidity in seeing analogies and resemblances; one idea leads to another connected with it, and the poet is insensibly led away by a long train and succession of ideas, in which a connection can always be traced, although he saw them far more quickly than the reader can hope to follow him.

The criticism of Horace accurately describes this characteristic of the Pindaric ode.

> Monte decurrens velut amnis, imbres
> Quem super notas aluêre ripas
> Fervet, immensusque ruit profundo
>   Pindarus ore.
>   HOR. *Od.* IV. ii.

The just and discriminating taste of the same Latin poet pronounced a judgment, the truth of which has been proved by the experience of every succeeding generation, namely, that his powers defy imitation or rivalry.

Pindarum quisquis studet æmulari,
Iule, ceratis ope Dædalea
Nititur pennis, vitreo daturus
        Nomina ponto.
                HOR. *Od.* IV. ii.

The rhythm of Pindar's metres appears to be, more than those
of any other ancient poet, under the influence of music; and the
imperfect knowledge of Greek music which we possess, renders
his metrical harmonies so difficult to analyze and explain.

So much, however, as this is clear, that there was a recognized
inseparable connection between music and poetry, and that certain metres were considered as especially suited to each of the
different modes.   Now, originally, there were only three modes,
the Lydian, Phrygian, and Dorian.   Afterwards, two more were
introduced, the Ionian below, the Æolian above the Phrygian in
musical pitch.   The Ionian was a modification of the Phrygian,
the Æolian of the Lydian.   The graver and more stately metres
were considered as more suitable to that mode of which the pitch
was lower, whilst more appropriate expression was supposed to
be given to rapid and lively measures by that higher pitch which
is always allowed to impart greater brilliancy of tone.   If, then,
the assumption be correct that the epinician odes of Pindar can
be divided into Dorian, Æolian, and Lydian, according to the
musical mode for which they are best adapted, the metre can be
our only guide in this classification.   The Dorian odes will be
those of which the style is most epic in character, the systems
generally dactylic, and in which the structure of the verse
approaches most nearly to the hexametrical rhythm.   As the
rhythm became lighter and more rapid, we should be inclined to
consider that the musical accompaniment would be of a higher
pitch, and so long as they were of an intermediate or mixed character, they might be classed as Æolian.   Lastly, the brilliant
Lydian mode must be confined to those odes which abound in the
tripping, dancing trochees, the liveliest and gayest of all the
Greek metrical systems.   It may be still a matter of question
whether there are sufficient grounds for this arbitrary arrangement of the odes of Pindar.

CHAPTER XIII.

POETRY NATURALLY PRECEDES PROSE COMPOSITION.—CAUSES WHICH PROBABLY LED TO
THE INTRODUCTION OF PROSE WRITING.—THE CHANGE GRADUAL —INFLUENCE OF PO-
LITICAL CIRCUMSTANCES.—THE ERA OF THE SEVEN SAGES —PERIANDER.—PITTACUS.
—THALES.—SOLON.—CLEOBULUS —BIAS.—CHILON —SACERDOTAL AND ORPHIC LITE-
RATURE —IONIA THE PARENT OF PROSE LITERATURE AS WELL AS OF POETRY.—THE
LOGOGRAPHI.—THE CHARACTER OF THEIR WORKS.—THEIR AUTHORITY —CADMUS.
—ACUSILAUS.—HECATÆUS.

POETRY being the natural and spontaneous language of the
emotions, constitutes, as is evident, the only literature in that
period of mingled rudeness and refinement which lies between
barbarism and advanced civilization. It is the natural outpouring and overflow of the feelings—it recognizes no artificial limita-
tions except the laws of metrical harmony and the metaphysical
principles of grammar which the human mind, from its natural
constitution, cannot disregard. It is the language of the imagination, and therefore of the creative and perceptive powers ; but
it makes little demand upon the logical and reflective faculties.
Prose writing, on the contrary, implies that all the intellectual
powers are in a higher state of advancement, and more equally
balanced: it is an effort not merely of genius, but of reason.
Hence many changes take place in the subjects on which the
human intellect is employed before any alteration takes place
in the outward form. Even the apparently uncongenial subjects
of moral, physical, and political philosophy, enter into a national
literature before it throws off the trammels of metre, and appears
in the plainer, but unusual, and less popular garb of prose composition. The introduction of prose literature was at first, probably, a matter of necessity, and afterwards of convenience. The
increased extent of human experience, the wider field of knowledge and practical wisdom which began to be gradually explored,
absolutely demanded the unrestrained freedom of prose. Either

investigation must have been retarded or even stopped in its career, or some freer form substituted for the communication of ideas. Increased facility, moreover, in the art of writing, would have a tendency to produce the same result. The rapidity of human thought was unwilling to submit to unnecessary restraint when writing materials of a more convenient form furnished readier means of expression. But, notwithstanding the necessities of the case, the change was slow and gradual.

In that epoch which is commonly called the era of the "Seven Wise Men of Greece," no complete separation had taken place between philosophy and poetry. These great men, whose names have been handed down to succeeding ages as the luminaries of their age, stand, as it were, upon the debatable land between the poetical and philosophical ages; they were not undistinguished as poets, but, nevertheless, they owe their reputation principally to their moral, political, and philosophical wisdom. The subjects of contemplation which interested the Greek mind were now in a transition state. The motives and principles of human conduct were beginning to be examined and analyzed in a more philosophical spirit; but the results of observation, whether moral or political, were expressed in verse even more frequently than in prose. The political state of Greece, moreover, at this period, caused legislative wisdom and an ability to deal with great social questions to be more highly valued than they had hitherto been, and the title of σοφός, or *sage*, was conferred on him who benefited his fellow-creatures by his practical knowledge, and illustrated his intellectual pre-eminence by his moral virtues.

Revolutions were now taking place throughout the different Grecian states. The limited hereditary monarchies (πατρίκαι βασιλίαι ἐπὶ ῥητοῖς γέρασι [1]) were decaying; the aristocracies of birth were crumbling away. The scenes of bloodshed, the rendering asunder of civil society necessarily preceding the introduction of free institutions among communities which had conceived a desire for them, but were not as yet sufficiently prepared to receive them, set men thinking on political subjects. The exigencies of the times turned the attention of deep and serious thinkers, who in the previous age would have been the poets of their times, to

[1] Thucyd. i.

subjects of practical interest, to devise means for remedying these social evils. But the legislator, the popular leader, and the tyrant, who devoted themselves to these studies, wrote in hexameters or elegiacs their practical precepts and wise admonitions; nay, even the laws which they enacted for the benefit of the state. The laws of Charondas were, according to Hermippus, written in verse, and even sung at banquets;[1] and hence, probably, the application of the same term, νόμος, both to a law and a metrical composition.[2] The ancient Roman laws were likewise written in verse, and it is also said that the Turdetani in Spain had metrical laws.

To this distinguished body belonged Zaleucus, the lawgiver of the Epizephyrian Locrians; Charondas, the Catanian; and Epimenides of Crete, whose skill in ceremonies of purification caused him to be called in to purify Athens (B. C. 598) from the guilt and pollution which were considered as attaching to it, from the massacre of Cylon and his followers (B. C. 612). But his fame is built upon a more stable foundation, namely, that he was the friend and assistant of Solon in framing his code of laws. Thus they addressed themselves to the feelings and old literary prejudices of the people; and even the guests at the social board listened to the words of wisdom, instead of mere legends and heroic lays. These sages, because of the practical tendency of their compositions, deserved the title of, and prepared the way for, that class of writers which were afterwards called Gnomic poets, as well as for those who, like Æsop, veiled their words of wisdom and rules of life under the enigmatical form of apologues, or fables (ἀπόλογοι, μῦθοι), and still later for prose composition generally and the laborious investigations of the great philosophical schools, Asia and Greece.

When speaking of the Seven Sages, it must be remembered, that this number is a mere arbitrary one; different names have been given, of those who were to be admitted into this body; by some the number has been increased to eleven, or even more, whilst Plutarch and others mention only five.

The four universally recognized, are Thales, Bias, Pittacus, and

---

[1] Athenæus, xiv. 3.   [2] Arist. Prob. xix.

Solon ; and the number is usually completed by the addition of Cleobulus, Chilo, and Periander.

The list authorized by Plato[1] is identical with that given above, with the exception of substituting Myson, a native of the obscure village of Chenæ, of whose claims history is silent, in the place of Periander.

According to Demetrius Phalereus, and all the best authorities, the epoch at which the Seven Wise Men were so named, was the archonship of Damasias, B. C. 586.

The following legendary tale is told respecting them. A golden tripod was found in the nets of some Milesian fishermen, and the Delphian oracle being asked whose it should be, decreed that it should be given to the wisest man. The fishermen naturally thought of their distinguished countrymen Thales. He, however, modestly declined it, and offered it to Bias of Priene. Thus it passed through the hands of the seven in succession, and Solon, who received it last, dedicated it to Apollo, as alone worthy to be called "the wise."

These sages lived between the years B. C. 665 and B. C. 540.

Periander, the earliest of them, succeeded Cypselus as tyrant of Corinth, about B. C. 625. His public and private character have both been vehemently assailed, but only by those whose political principles rendered them his bitterest enemies. The times in which he ruled made severe measures necessary, and these were easily misrepresented as tyrannical. The vigor with which he suppressed the aristocratic institutions of the Dorians, proves him to have been a friend to free and popular ones.[2] In all respects, he appears to have been a wise politician, a maintainer of public morality, a friend to commerce, and a munificent patron of art and literature.[3] The duration of his tyranny, and therefore the time of his death, are uncertain. It is not improbable that he owes his place amongst the Wise Men of Greece, rather to his political position than his literary eminence. A friend of wise men, and a promoter of learning, he displayed those qualifications for which the Greek τύραννοι were universally distinguished, the cultivation of wisdom and virtue, but he seems to have been a patron rather than a philosopher.[4]

---

[1] Protag. p. 343.   [2] Müller, i. 8, 3.   [3] Arist. Pol.   [4] Thucyd. vi.

Pittacus was born at Mytilene, B. C. 652.[1] His father is said to have been a Thracian, his mother a Lesbian. In the revolution in B. C. 612, he, with Alcæus, joined the aristocratic faction. Six years later, he distinguished himself in a battle with the Athenians, in which Alcæus, like his imitator Horace at Philippi, left his shield, and fled from the field of battle. After a succession of τύραννοι, Pittacus was at length chosen chief ruler of the state, αἰσυμνήτης, a jurisdiction which he successfully administered during ten years, and then resigned it, at the request of the Lesbians.

Aristotle,[2] on the authority of the poet Alcæus, asserts that Pittacus was a tyrant in the modern sense of the term, but the general testimony of antiquity is in favor of his virtue and patriotism. His character is usually described as consistent with two of his remarkable sayings, "A victory should be gained without bloodshed," and "Speak not evil of friends or even of enemies."

He died B. C. 569, having written six hundred elegiac verses, and a prose work in defence of his laws.

Thales, the most distinguished of the number, the founder of the Ionian philosophy, was born at Miletus, about B. C. 635.[3] In addition to the practical wisdom which obtained for him a place among the Seven Sages, his scientific investigations caused him to be regarded by Aristotle,[4] as the first discoverer of mathematical and physical philosophy. He is said to have calculated the solar eclipse which took place B. C. 609, and his engineering skill was exhibited in turning the course of the Halys, at the command of Crœsus.[5]

Solon, the celebrated Athenian archon and legislator, was born about B. C. 638. The date of his archonship was B. C. 594. He was related maternally to the family of Pisistratus. His practical wisdom was the result of personal experience, and acquired during foreign travel, in the capacity of a merchant, an occupation which the extravagance of his father had rendered necessary.

To enter upon the subject of Solon's institutions, which form

[1] Suidas, s. v.
[2] Pol. iii. 10.
[3] Diog. Laert. i. 37 ; Clinton, p. 7.
[4] Arist. Metaph.
[5] Herod. i. 75.

the most interesting subject connected with his life, would be beside the purpose of this history.   His poems, which were almost
entirely moral and political, are more distinguished for their wisdom than for any poetical power ; their characteristics are simplicity and energy.

His philosophical acquirements must have been of a high order,
since Athens was indebted to him for the improvement and cor-
rection of the calendar, and the establishment of the trieteris,
or cycle, which was completed at the termination of every two
years.

Cleobulus was a citizen of Lindus, in Rhodes, and a contemporary of Solon.   His influence as a legislator has obtained for him
the reputation of having been τύραννος, or, like Pittacus, αἰσυμνήτης,
of his native city.   Egyptian physical philosophy was by this time
beginning to find its way into Greece, and Cleobulus is said to
have been one of its professors ; hence some have supposed that
he travelled to Egypt, and there became instructed in the principles of natural science.   His fame rests, however, on his moral
apophthegms, and not on his scientific discoveries.   His daughter
Cleobulina is frequently celebrated by the ancients for her elegant accomplishments and amiable hospitality.[1]

Bias[2] was a native of the Ionian town of Priene, and flourished
about B. C. 550.   Little is recorded of him, except a few maxims
of practical wisdom and proverbial sayings, and the fact related
by Diogenes Laertius, that, after having pleaded a cause successfully, he died suddenly at a good old age.

Chilon was a native of Sparta, and filled the important office
of ephor.   He flourished about B. C. 596.   Herodotus[3] mentions
that when Hippocrates was sacrificing at the Olympic festival,
the caldrons boiled over without fire.   Chilon being present, and
thinking that this prodigy boded ill, advised him not to marry a
woman likely to have children ; if already married, to divorce his
wife, and if he had a son, to disown him.   Notwithstanding this
advice, Hippocrates had a son.   This was Pisistratus, the head
of the revolutionary party, and afterwards tyrant of Athens.   He

[1] Clem. Alex. Strom. iv. 19.
[2] Herod. i. 27 ; Arist. Rhet. ii. 13 ; Cic. de Am. 16.
[3] Herod. i. 59.

12

is the reputed author of the celebrated maxim γνῶθι σέαυτον (know thyself), and is said to have died of joy on his son being proclaimed victor in the Olympic games.

A religious belief existed at this epoch, which exercised no slight influence upon literature.[1]

The doctrine of a future state and an unseen world had led the poets, in their theogonies, to people the dark regions beneath the earth with their own peculiar deities, the χθόνιοι θέοι. The worship of these deities was of a mysterious nature; the doctrines taught, as connected with the immortality of the soul, were kept as invisible secrets, except for the initiated. Amongst these mysteries, the Eleusinian were deemed the most awful; they were celebrated in honor of Demeter, the mother of Persephone, queen of the unseen world, who, every year snatched away from earth, was every year supposed to return in pristine beauty. By this myth was typified death, and the descent of the body into the grave, and the restoration of the soul to life and immortality. But besides these, there were other mysteries in honor of a Dionysus, who, according to some post-Homeric theogony, was considered a Chthonian deity.[2] Those who were initiated in them, professed to be dedicated to the mythic poet Orpheus, and, instead of attaching an idea of secrecy to their revelations, embodied them in the form of odes and hymns, which are known by the name of Orphic poems. Thus, then, in the devotees of this worship, is visible the mixed character of priest and poet. They did not keep their doctrines secret, like the mysterious worshippers of Demeter; their enthusiasm, developed in poetry, extended beyond the inner circle of their own disciples, and influenced the popular creed. Hence they became invested with supernatural functions; the knowledge of the divine will and a spirit of prophecy were attributed to them, and they were believed to possess the power of influencing and propitiating the gods themselves.

Amongst these sacerdotal poets, were Epimenides, whose priestly character has already been alluded to, Pherecydes of Syros, and Abaris, who is commonly called the Hyperborean.

The lives of these sacerdotal authors belong to tradition rather

---

[1] Müller's Hist. Greek Literature, 233, &c.
[2] Herod. ix. 81.

than history, and in them there is consequently a large admixture of fabulous legend.

EPIMENIDES.

Epimenides[1] is said to have been the son of a nymph of Crete, and a story is told of him which has found its way into the literature of other countries. It is said, that, overcome by the heat of the sun, he fell asleep in a cave, and so remained for fifty-seven years. Whilst he retained his youth, he found to his surprise, on his return home, that his brother had become an old man. Many works on ceremonial and genealogical subjects are attributed to him, but it is probable that scarcely any of them are genuine. Cicero[2] gives Epimenides the title of *propheta*, and St. Paul, who, from passages in his writings,[3] appears to have been well versed in Greek literature, quotes a line from his writings, in the Epistle to Titus.[4]

" One of themselves, even a prophet of their own, said, ' The Cretians are alway liars, evil beasts, slow bellies.' "

PHERECYDES.

Pherecydes,[5] although the period at which he flourished is uncertain, probably lived about B. C. 548. He is said to have been the first prose writer on philosophical subjects; but even if this be the case, he can scarcely be termed a philosopher. Philosophical investigation did not as yet exist, and although speculations on subjects of a philosophical nature were doubtless now paving the way for legitimate inquiry, they were, nevertheless, imitations and adaptations of the doctrines taught by the poets of the Hesiodic and Orphic schools. That he taught the doctrine of the metempsychosis, perhaps led to the prevalent belief that from him Pythagoras derived this portion of his system. But in his sacerdotal and prophetical character Pherecydes was more celebrated than as a poet and a philosopher.

ABARIS.

To relate the various traditions respecting Abaris would be

---

[1] Diog. Laert. i. 109.
[2] De Divin.
[3] See 1 Cor. xv. 33 ; Acts xvii. 28.
[4] Tit. i. 12.
[5] Suidas ; Cic. Tusc. i. 16.

beyond the compass of this work.   He is called a Hyperborean,[1] which implies that he was devoted to the worship of Apollo ; the unknown regions north of the Caucasus being considered as under the protection of that deity.   He cured diseases, lived without food, and was supposed to be the author of a theogony in prose.[2] The best authorities fix the time at which he flourished about B. C. 570.   Such was the literature of the period which immediately preceded and introduced prose composition.

Although the Muse of Greece had her European dwelling-place amongst the Pierians in the valleys of Parnassus and Helicon, and was nurtured there by Hesiod and his countrymen, it was in Ionia that she attained her maturity and perfection.   Moreover, on tracing the gradual progress and development of Greek litera- ture, it is evident that Ionia was not only the nurse of early epic poetry, and its protector from the influence of Dorian rudeness, but that, with few exceptions, literature of every kind was the offspring of the Ionian mind.   The influence of Ionian genius is visible in the satire of the iambic metre, the plaintive sadness and martial enthusiasm or the terse neatness of the elegy, the wisdom of didactic poetry, and the wit of parody and fable, and, in later times, the peculiar characteristic part of the Greek drama, both tragedy and comedy, is due to the Attic branch of the Ionian race.   The Ionian Greeks also were the earliest authors of prose as well as of poetry.

In investigating the origin of prose literature, it must be remembered that the object of Greek poetry was recitation.   Pre- vious to the invention of writing it was necessarily confined to this ; and even after this epoch the scarcity and inconvenience of materials for writing caused authors to compose their works for hearers and not for readers.   The time for recitation, too, was the hours of relaxation, the banquet, and the symposium, and when the art of music was cultivated, and a species of poetry introduced adapted to singing instead of recitation, the cheering notes of the harp or flute accompanied the inspiration of the lyric bard.

Poetry was, therefore, as has been observed, on all these accounts, the appropriate vehicle of thought, and even when a more philo- sophical and observant age demanded a more exact and perspicu-

[1] Herod. iv. 36.   [2] Lobeck's Aglaoph.

ous method of communicating knowledge, poetry for some time furnished the source from which the prose writers drew their stores. The logographi, as they were called, took the theogonies, the genealogies, and the vague philosophical speculations of their predecessors, the epic poets, translated them, as it were, into unmetrical and unadorned language, and invested legendary tales, mythological fables, traditional pedigrees, or the physical hypotheses of a poetical imagination, with earnestness, reality, and truthfulness.

The fact that the latter epic poetry wore more of a didactic garb, and exhibited more reflectiveness and more intimate acquaintance with the human heart and with the springs of moral action, prepares us to expect that when thought once indulged in the unrestrained freedom of prose, it would also devote itself to historical and philosophical inquiry. This proves to be the case; but an examination of what is known respecting the earliest historical writers will show that, in these rude beginnings, there was no logical connection between the events narrated, scarcely even any historical order. No distinction was made between real and fictitious accounts, probably because, in the absence of personal observation and historical investigation, all were esteemed of equal value. Thucydides[1] tells us that popular traditions were generally received without inquiry as to their authenticity, and that people took little trouble to search after truth. The logographers collected together the traditions of the principal cities, and interspersed them with legends of gods and heroes, derived from poetical sources. They cared more for amusement than instruction; they compiled their accounts not so much with a view to truth, as to give pleasure to their hearers.[2] The principle on which they generally endeavored to arrange their materials was a geographical one. This plan of arrangement indicates that the leading ideas which had possession of their minds were rather those of a poet than of an historian. They were derived from the wonders of mythology and tradition, and from the picturesque features of countries which had become known to them by hearsay or observation. These they would describe in a plain and simple style, and then, with all the artlessness of children, relate the

[1] Thucyd. Hist. ii. 134.   [2] Ibid. i. 21.

wonderful tales and traditions connected with them.[1]   Such topics
as these were full of interest for their hearers.   They would sit
for hours listening with breathless attention to the marvels of
foreign lands, some of which were familiar to them, others only
known by report, in the same way that the Italian will listen to
the story-teller of modern times.

Traces of this principle of connection may be found at a more
advanced epoch of historical literature, in the digressions of the
later and better arranged histories of Herodotus.   Small as must
have been their real value, as vehicles of historic truth, the works
of these logographi were looked upon as possessing some authority by the geographer Strabo and the historian Dionysius of
Halicarnassus.

It is evident from the above description, which is as specific as
the sources from which our information is derived, that, although
these writings are termed historical, there was nothing in them,
excepting, perhaps, those of Hecatæus, approaching to historical
records or annals.   The Greeks, perhaps from want of union
amongst themselves, and the consequent jealousy which existed
between the different states into which Greece was divided, or from
there being amongst them no single individual whose personal
vanity, like that of Eastern monarchs, would seek for monumental
records of his exploits, had no national *fasti;* they seemed, in
fact—until Herodotus, by the brilliance and liveliness of his
talents, gave a living interest to those scenes in which Greece had
played so heroic a part—to undervalue the exploits of their own
immediate ancestors, whilst absorbed in those of the heroic age.
We look in vain, therefore, for such records as the pictorial
inscriptions which enable us to determine and arrange the
dynasties of Egypt, and the ancient cuneiform characters which
promise hereafter to throw such light upon the histories of
Assyria, Nineveh, and Babylon.   The deficiency under which
Greek history labors, in this respect, stands out in still stronger
contrast to the accurate, because inspired, literary records of the
Jewish people.   The theocracy amongst the Jews, and the monarchies of other Eastern nations, by different methods, produced
similar historical results.   God's immediate government of his

---

[1] Dion. Hal. vi. 819; Cic. de Or. ii. 12; Thucyd. i. 21.

chosen people has enriched us with a history of his dealings with man, authenticated by the infallibility of inspiration; and respect for a monarch, or the spirit of flattery, or personal vanity, has stored up in sculpture and painting almost imperishable chronicles of the Oriental and Egyptian dynasties. These are the true materials of history, but they are not found in the first logographic literature of Greece.

The earliest of these quasi-historians, who belong to that period of literary history, which is contained in this book, were Cadmus and Hecatæus of Miletus, and Acusilaus of Argos. Pherccydes, of the island of Leros, belongs to the second or flourishing period of Greek literature.

CADMUS, (about) B. C. 540.

Cadmus is evidently confounded by Suidas with the Cadmus of mythical tradition, for he speaks of him as the introducer into Greece of the Phœnician alphabet. Josephus[1] states that he flourished soon after the Persian invasion, but the common opinion is, that he lived and wrote about B. C. 540.[2] Tradition speaks of him as the author of an historical work, on the foundation of Miletus and colonization of Ionia (κτίσεις Μιλήτου καὶ Ἰωνίας). In what way he treated the subject, it is impossible to say, for it has perished; and Dionysius pronounces the work bearing his name, which was extant in the Augustine age, to be a forgery.

ACUSILAUS.

Although Acusilaus was a native of Argos, he forms no exception to the statement already made, that Ionia was the nurse of the earliest historical literature of Greece; for so imbued was his mind with Ionic taste and intellectual cultivation, that the dialect in which he wrote was the Ionian. What traces we possess of him prove, that his works consisted of a transcript in prose of the legends belonging to the mythical era, and some genealogies translated from Hesiod. Suidas[3] was not acquainted with any writings of Acusilaus, but only asserts that he compiled some genealogies from brazen plates, discovered by his father. The

---

[1] Josephus, c. Apion, i. 2.   [2] Müller, Hist. Greek Lit.
[3] Suidas; Fragm. Acus. Museum Crit. i. 216; Plato, Symp.

time when he flourished is uncertain, but it was, probably, soon after the age of Cadmus.

HECATÆUS, (about) B. C. 540.

Hecatæus is well known to us, through the history of Herodotus, not only as a celebrated historian (λογόποιος), but also as taking a part in the political affairs of his country.   When Aristagoras was persuading the Ionians to revolt, he endeavored, though unsuccessfully, to dissuade them from the attempt.[1]   Again, on the invasion of Ionia by the Persian satrap Artaphernes, he recommended Aristagoras, as a temporary measure, to fortify and occupy the island of Leros.[2]   In this case, also, his prudent counsels were disregarded.   Both Müller and Suidas place the epoch at which he wrote, earlier than these times of national difficulties.   The former B. C. 540, the latter B. C. 520.   If the testimony borne to his character is to be depended upon, the statesmanlike views exhibited in his public career are sufficient proof that he was fitted for discharging the duty of an historian, and the account we have of his love of foreign travel bears similar testimony to his probable faithfulness as a geographer.[3] His historical work was genealogical, and the sources from which he drew his materials were similar to those of his contemporaries: but still, unlike them, he appears to have applied a critical and philosophical spirit to the separation of that which appeared to be true, from that which was evidently traditional.

He was, however, like other logographers, infected with a belief in mythical genealogies, for Herodotus[4] tells us, that he boasted, in the presence of the Egyptian priests, that he was the sixteenth in descent from a god.   They are said to have completely refuted him, by the superior antiquity of their genealogical records.   On his authority, the same historian rests his account of the early Pelasgian history.[5]   He was, evidently, far in advance of his age, and Herodotus had, doubtless, carefully studied his writings; but he had compared them with the results of his own observation, and, therefore, did not place undue confidence

[1] Herod. v. 36.   [2] Ibid. v. 124.   [3] Ibid. v. 24.
[4] Ibid. ii. 143.   [5] Ibid. vi. 137.

in him, and was not misled by his errors. Hence the unsparing
ridicule which he casts upon his theory of the disc-like form of
the earth,[1] the causes which led to the inundation of the Nile,
and his romantic story of the sunny island of the Hyperboreans.[2]
His geographical work bears marks of careful personal investigation, it is descriptive and interspersed with historical notices; in
connection with his geographical knowledge, it must be remembered, that when Aristagoras visited Cleomenes, king of Sparta,
in order to invite him to take part in the Ionian revolt, he is
said to have taken with him a map of the country.[3] From the
intimate relation in which Hecatæus stood to Aristagoras, it is
probable that this was his work. At any rate, it is the earliest
occasion on which this species of geographical illustration is mentioned, and it coincides with the era of Hecatæus. The map
spoken of by Herodotus was probably founded on the system of
this eminent geographer. Such progress had the Greek language
already made, that the Ionic of Hecatæus is said to have been
even purer than that of Herodotus.

[1] Herod. ii. 21.   [2] Ibid. iv. 13, 33.   [3] Ibid. v. 49.

CHAPTER XIV.

GREEK PHILOSOPHY OWED ITS ORIGIN TO THE GREEK MIND, AND NOT TO FOREIGN INFLU-
ENCES.—INFLUENCE OF RELIGION, POETRY, AND POLITICS.—PHERECYDES OF SYROS
FIRST TREATED OF PHILOSOPHICAL SUBJECTS.—THERE WAS, HOWEVER, AS YET NO
PHILOSOPHICAL SYSTEM.—THALES THE FIRST PHYSICAL PHILOSOPHER.—THE EARLI-
EST PHILOSOPHICAL DOCTRINES DIFFICULT TO DISCOVER.—THE ORIENTAL ORIGIN OF
GREEK PHILOSOPHY INSISTED ON BY COMPARATIVELY MODERN AUTHORITIES.—ARGU-
MENTS AGAINST THIS THEORY.—PERIOD AT WHICH ORIENTAL DOCTRINES WERE FIRST
INFUSED INTO GREEK PHILOSOPHY.—POINT OF RESEMBLANCE BETWEEN THE PHILO-
SOPHICAL AND POETICAL LITERATURE OF GREECE.—PHILOSOPHY FOLLOWED THE SUB-
DIVISIONS OF THE GREEK NATION.—THE IONIAN AND DORIAN SCHOOLS.—THE ELEATIC
SCHOOL.—ITS RELATION TO THE OTHER TWO.

As philosophy is the expression of human thought, a history
of Greek philosophy must necessarily obtain a place in the history of Greek literature. It has already been seen how in the
intellectual progress of the Greek nation the subjects treated of in
poetry became more philosophical in their character. The warlike adventures of the heroic age, which delight us in the Homeric
poems, gave place to the theogonies and cosmogonies of Hesiod;
physical and metaphysical theories and speculations—not, indeed,
as yet founded on induction and observation, but as baseless and
fanciful as the most imaginative poetical effusions—were expressed
in the same metrical language to which alone the popular ear and
taste were as yet accustomed.

It is commonly assumed that the philosophy of Greece was of
Oriental origin, but with this theory it is impossible to reconcile
the phenomenon that different systems sprang up, and opposing
schools were formed simultaneously and independently of each
other.

If then the spirit of philosophical investigation, which was developed so early in the Greek nation, owed its beginnings to the
Greek mind itself and not to foreign influences, the question arises,
to what influences are we indebted for these invaluable treasures
of intellectual power ?

The three subjects which exercised the greatest influence in forming the Greek mind, and in directing its speculation, were religion, poetry, and politics. Impressed with a strong and lively sentiment of veneration for Deity, the Greek, when he began to think, was not long in perceiving how abhorrent to all pure and high views were the doctrines of the popular mythology. Again, when he turned his thoughts inward and contemplated his own nature, he naturally concluded that so far as man could form a conception of a Divine nature, it must be of a Being bearing some resemblance to the noblest part of himself, namely, his intellect. The same inquiring spirit, therefore, which aspired to investigate the laws of the universe, and the nature of that one Being or principle by which the order and operations of nature were governed, would also seek to trace the operations of mind, and the laws which governed the intellect. Whilst the germ of philosophy may be thus traced even in the very mythical superstitions of Greek popular religion, a symbolical connection between the powers and processes of nature and the ceremonials of public worship was maintained by those mysteries which were revealed only to the initiated few. The popular religion recognized an indwelling of the Divine presence in every natural phenomenon and every visible created thing, and so far recognized also laws of nature, and therefore a subject for philosophical inquiry. The religion inculcated by the mysteries taught that the ceremonies, blindly and ignorantly performed, were symbolical of certain natural phenomena, and therefore prepared the initiated worshippers to contemplate not only the phenomena but the laws according to which the operations of nature were carried on.

The religion of Greece, as well mystical as popular, taught that Nature worked in obedience to the Divine laws, and therefore the mind of Greece was thus prepared to inquire into and speculate upon the laws themselves.

Again, the poetical sentiment led to similar results. The devotional and poetical feelings are closely connected, and religious sentiments recognize in poetry, or in the outpourings of a fervid imagination, their appropriate vehicle of expression.

None felt more deeply than the Greek this close connection which unites the literature of speculative thought so closely with that of the imagination. Verse was the language of inspiration even in ages when prose writing had become common; the revelations of Deity were in verse; a holiness invested the character of the poet as the favored of heaven, and as owing his power to influence men's minds to direct inspiration. Poetry deals with the ideal, the immaterial; it has to do with imagery; its subjects are the creations of the mind. It invests things which have no real existence with a reality, so far as mental conceptions are concerned. Hence the same faculties which are devoted to the cultivation of poetry are easily diverted to the speculations of metaphysics, or even to that imaginative system of natural science which occupied the minds of the early philosophers.

Lastly, the established relations of society and the institutions of a state arise out of a conception of the moral relations which men bear to one another, and, in their turn, exercise a reciprocal influence upon the notions which individuals form of these relations. Free institutions, such as those which distinguished the Ionian race, imply a jealousy, regard to right and justice, first as regards ourselves, next as regards any interference with the rights of others. It is easy, therefore, to see the influence which politics must have had upon the high and noble tone which pervades Greek moral philosophy.

Pherecydes of Syros, who lived in the era of the Seven Sages, about the 58th or 59th Olympiad,[1] is said to have first attempted to treat in prose of those subjects which may be considered philosophical, and Herodotus[2] relates that he was one of the earliest who wrote on parchment, an invention ascribed to the Ionians.

Living, as he did, in the infancy of philosophy, his speculations, though generally termed philosophical, were rather theological and mythical. "He stands, as it were," says Aristotle, " on the boundary line between mythical poetry and philosophy."[3] Early traditions assert that he derived his knowledge from the Egyptians and Chaldeans, and hence he gained the reputation of a soothsayer and diviner; but there is no better authority for these statements than the theory which attributes to Oriental sources the origin of Greek philosophy. A belief in the metempsychosis

---

[1] Matthiæ, History of Greek Literature; Suidas, s. v.
[2] Herod. v. 58.   [3] Aristotle, Met. xiv. 4.

is also attributed to him, and he is said to have taught this doctrine to Pythagoras.

The passage[1] quoted by O. Müller from the fragments of Pherecydes is the best adapted of any which can be adduced to show the nature of these early speculations. " Zeus," he writes, " Chronos and Chthonia existed from eternity. Chthonia was called Ge, since Zeus endowed her with honor." He next relates how Zeus transformed himself into Eros, the god of love, wishing to form the world from the original materials made by Chronos and Chthonia. " Zeus makes a large and beautiful garment; upon it he paints Earth and Ogenos (Ocean), and the horses of Ogenos, and he spreads the garment over a winged oak." This is evidently poetry, although expressed in prose; assertion, and not speculation; the germ from which philosophy was developed, but not philosophy. There is here no observation of natural phenomena, no attempt to investigate the connection between cause and effect; and yet these are both absolutely necessary to constitute a system of physical science. Again, in the mythical traditions of Greek religion transmitted by the poets, originated many of the earliest so called philosophical dogmas. When Homer taught that Oceanus and Tethys were the progenitors of gods and men, he furnished the germ of the physical assumption that all things are in a perpetual flux. When Hesiod sang of Chaos and Eros as the parents of all existing things, he separated and distinguished matter from the creative cause, a doctrine afterwards adopted by the Ionic school.

As the habit of thought, which led to the speculations of physical philosophy, grew gradually out of the mystical fables of religion and the fantastic creations of the poets, so the principles of moral philosophy may first be traced in the isolated apophthegms and proverbs of moralists and politicians, like the Seven Sages. Observation of human character and motives; of man's political and social relations made amidst the difficult and turbulent circumstances of Greek public life, rather than thought out in solitude, led these great men to embody the results in short and terse sentences, which might make an impression by their novelty, and by their brevity be retained in the memory. These enunci-

[1] Müller, p. 241.

atiens of condensed wisdom were not confined to a few, like the obscure reasoning and speculations of systematic philosophy, but were understood and appreciated by the people generally, and exercised a great influence over the popular mind.

But great as was the reputation which the authors of these moral axioms enjoyed as wise and shrewd thinkers and sagacious observers of human nature, their isolated and unconnected apophthegms were as far from constituting a system of moral philosophy as the beautiful but fanciful fables, already spoken of, were from embodying the true principles of physical investigation. Philosophy implies system, and system implies not merely a collection of independent dicta, however wise and true and well founded they may be, but a logical sequence of cause and effect, a chain of propositions deduced in regular order from first principles, a mutual dependence of the several parts so close that the falsity of one shakes and endangers the safety of the whole.

It is evident that, so far as the progress of the Greek mind has as yet been traced, no philosophical system, either physical or moral, is discoverable. The Hesiodic poets introduced into their poems subjects of a philosophic character, but they treated them as poets, and not as philosophers. The Orphic poems merely related the legendary wonders of mythical religion, although, as they professed, like Hesiod, to give an account of what they believed to be the history of creation, they gave their poetry a philosophical appearance. The gnomic poets and the political sages merely expressed the results of their observation of human character in isolated axioms.

Thales alone forms an exception to this assertion respecting the absence of philosophical system amongst the Greek poets and prose writers who were his predecessors and contemporaries. He was not only a statesman and a moralist, and therefore reckoned among the Seven Sages, but he was also the first physical philosopher, and may be considered as the founder of the Ionian school.

There are many difficulties in the way of arriving at an accurate perception of the doctrines and theories taught by the earliest philosophers. They not only lie scattered up and down the works of various writers, but when their supposed speculations are collected together and arranged, it is impossible to be certain that they are genuine. They may be quoted with particular objects in order to defend some favorite thesis; they may be wilfully misrepresented or accidentally misunderstood ; and lastly, in the later philosophical writers in which they are found most plentifully, the sources from which the information has been derived are frequently spurious and supposititious treatises.

It is on the authority of authors of comparatively modern date, that the Oriental origin of Greek philosophy has been so much insisted on, whilst in the works of the oldest philosophical writers themselves, and of ancient historians, there is little or no evidence of that intercourse between them and Oriental philosophers which would be sufficient to account for their deriving their theories from such foreign sources. The doctrines of India, Persia, and Egypt are doubtless discovered in the philosophy of Greece, but the resemblance is rather general than exact, nor is it greater than might be expected to arise from the human intellect being applied to the investigation of the same subjects.

The antecedent probability of such resemblance being discovered is still farther increased by the ethnical connection which subsists between the different races of mankind. Knowing, as we do, that in the inhabitants of Greece were united two elements, from one of which the Persians derived their origin—from the other the civilized races of Northern India—we are prepared to expect that many of the philosophical doctrines held in their different countries would be found to be identical. It is not necessary to suppose intercourse between the founders of Greek philosophy and the Brachmans of India, or the Magi of Persia, in order to account for similarity of philosophical ideas developed from similarly constituted minds. Had there been any strong resemblance in points of detail, we might infer an historical connection, because it is in details, rather than in vague and general principles, that instruction and tradition exercise their principal influence ; but in details and subordinate parts, even of a most important kind, the similarity vanishes, and in the practical results and the application to human conduct and physical phenomena the greatest possible difference is discernible.

A priori, therefore, that degree of resemblance which may

doubtless be traced between Oriental and Greek philosophy, furnishes no grounds for supposing that the latter derives its origin from the former.

Nor is there reason to suppose that Greek philosophy was partly derived from the East, partly the offspring of national intellect. If this were the case, there would be want of unity, if not absolute inconsistency; but this is not the case.

In the speculations of the earliest Greek philosophers, so far as an opinion can be formed from the fragments which remain, and from the dogmas quoted and referred to by other subsequent writers, there is no trace of that want of connection which would necessarily result from the introduction of a foreign element. The sequence of ideas from the principles assumed, however false they may themselves be, is simple and logical, and such as might naturally result from the employment of acute and subtle reasoning powers, unaided by any help but the natural energy of a philosophical and inquiring spirit.

There are likewise some deficiencies observable in the Greek philosophy, which would not have existed had intercourse with the East, and an acquaintance with Oriental systems exercised an influence on its doctrines. Eastern philosophy would have taught Greece more perfect notions respecting the personality of the Deity; would have accustomed the Greek mind to contemplate the divine power as creative, and as present and active in its influence over the phenomena of nature; would have defined more clearly the dealings of God with man as a moral governor of the universe, and probably would have suggested the authority of external revelation. These subjects did not form a part of Greek philosophy. Deity was little more than an abstract principle of reason. Matter was as eternal as God. Revelation was looked upon as a mythical fable. God did not interfere in the concerns or interests of man. Whatever appearance is to be found of dependence upon divine help and support, it proceeds from the natural instinct which recognizes the need of supernatural assistance, and which yearns for fellowship and communion with the Supreme Being. Moreover, when the historical evidence on which the assumption is based is accurately investigated, it appears to be wholly inadequate to establish the truth of such a theory.

It is, in fact, derived from the authority of authors who flourished in too late a period to be of any value—a period subsequent to a time when an Oriental influence on philosophy had doubtless begun to be established. Accordingly, doctrines which were introduced after the decay of Greek philosophy had commenced, were erroneously referred to an age antecedent to its flourishing era; and principles, which were afterwards infused, were mistaken for the original sources from which the whole system was derived. It is not here contended that there is no connection between Greek and Oriental philosophy, but that the latter is not the parent in any sense of the former; that they were independent of one another; that the spirit of Greek philosophy is essentially Greek; and that Oriental doctrines were a subsequent and late admixture and infusion. The period fixed by Ritter,[1] with great appearance of probability, for the first infusion of Oriental doctrines into Greek philosophy synchronizes with the decay of the Socratic schools.

In investigating the history of Greek philosophical literature, a striking point of resemblance is observable between it and their poetical literature, a resemblance arising out of the national character itself. If history, and not mere mythical tradition, is taken as a guide, it is clear that, although the Greek boasted of a common national existence, and the Hellenic name was a national title used in a collective sense, and opposed to that of barbarian; yet that this national whole was made up of several separate tribes. These tribes, as they were distinct in dialect, so they differed widely in feelings, principles, tastes, interests, and politics; almost so widely as sometimes to preclude the possibility of amalgamation. They yearned, indeed, for unity. They possessed institutions, the object of which was to be a bond of union, and to keep up an undying remembrance of their common name, and sometimes under extreme pressure and danger externally, that unity was attained—temporarily, indeed, but still sufficiently for warranting the assertion that Greece was one nation, though divided by opposite principles and conflicting interests.

Similar to their national character was also, as we have seen, their national literature. Its several parts originated in different

[1] Ritter, p. 160.

18

localities, they were the produce of differently constituted minds, and it was long before the several parts united in one whole, harmonious, indeed, but still exhibiting the characteristic differences of its original elements, and forming that peculiarly national species of composition, the Attic drama.

The epic poem resulted from the liveliness, energy, and exquisite taste of the Ionian Greek. When transplanted into the ruder country of Hesiod it lost its heroic character, and became depressed to a human level, by depicting the cares, the sorrows, the difficulties of human life; but though it lost much of its superhuman grandeur, it gained in moral dignity and instructive power. Grave sternness characterized the lyric muse of the Dorians, effeminate softness and passionate transport inspired the Æolian poets of Lesbos; but all these different elements make up a literature, possessing characteristics common to all; some of its features are peculiar to itself, unlike those of any other original national literature, and evidently the developments of one nation's mind.

Similar to this also, was the progressive formation of Greek philosophy. It was first cultivated in separate schools, professing different principles, and, to a certain extent, pursuing different subjects of inquiry. The localities of these schools of philosophy were originally as distinct as those of the schools of poetry, nor was it until the age of Socrates that one universal home of Greek philosophy was established in that centre of nationality, of literature, and of science, Athens.

So long as the schools of Socrates, Plato, and Aristotle were maintained, there may be said to have existed, notwithstanding the differences which subsisted between them, a period of philosophical unity in Greece; but this unity it was as impossible to maintain, as it was to keep up their wished-for unity as a nation; with corruption came division, and philosophy, though still bearing the name of Greece, was no longer the uniform expression of Greek intellect.

Philosophy, like poetry, followed the subdivisions of the Greek nation. The Ionians had their school in Asia Minor, which devoted itself principally to the investigation of physical phenomena, and only incidentally pursued the science of morals. The Dorian school, which, from its great founder, was termed the Pythagorean, flourished in the colonies of southern Italy, and this school, even when it examined the phenomena of nature, applied to them the principles and reasonings of ethical philosophy. This difference is precisely what might be expected from the lively sensibility of the Ionian mind to the marvels and beauties of nature, which is so universally manifested in their poetical literature, and from the strict sense of duty which led the Dorian to view every subject in an ethical aspect, to refer everything to a standard of moral fitness. Thus, to them the identity of moral and natural laws was perfectly familiar, and thus, whilst the Ionians, in their enthusiastic admiration of the beauties of nature, forgot the Divine author, the Dorian referred all the laws by which these phenomena were regulated to a manifestation of the attributes and perfections of the Deity.

It is clear from what has been stated, that in philosophy, as well as in literature, the Ionian race maintained its superiority. The method of investigation pursued by this school was far more philosophical than that of the Dorians; it was inductive, and endeavored to discover the facts, the ὅτι, as it was termed, rather than to investigate the διότι, *i.e.*, to account for the phenomena on certain preconceived notions of moral fitness and propriety. Throughout its whole existence the school of Ionia enjoyed a reputation worthy of a succession of philosophers, which began with Thales, and ended with Socrates.

Besides these two earliest schools, there arose another, somewhat later in point of time, but afterwards becoming more widely influential than either of the other two. The Pythagoreans viewed the phenomena of nature under a moral aspect, the Ionians under a physical one, but a third school sprang up also at Elea, the characteristic of which was logical and metaphysical analysis.

Genealogically, the Eleatic school was Ionian, for the place from which it derived its name, the modern Velia in Italy, was an Ionian colony, and the founder of the sect was Xenophanes, an Ionian,[1] but, geographically, it came within the influence of the Pythagorean schools.

It was, indeed, related to both, and yet, in the method of investigation which it pursued, independent of either. There will, in

[1] Ol. lx., b. c. 540.

fact, be found to have existed a principle of antagonism between the Eleatic philosophy and the two other systems. It did not pretend to the original investigation of natural phenomena, but it professed to examine, according to the principles of human reason, the logical conclusiveness of the arguments adduced. Refutation of error, therefore, was its province, rather than the investigation of new truths.

CHAPTER XV.

TWO SYSTEMS IN THE IONIAN SCHOOL, THE DYNAMICAL AND MECHANICAL.—THE PHILO-
SOPHY OF THALES.—ANAXIMANDER.—ANAXIMENES.—HERACLITUS.—PYTHAGORAS.—
HIS DOCTRINES OF NUMBER AND HARMONY —HIS THEORY OF THE HUMAN SOUL.—
HIS BELIEF IN THE SUPERIORITY OF INTELLECTUAL ACTIVITY TO CORPOREAL ORGANI-
ZATION.—THE ELEATIC SCHOOL.—ITS ORIGIN.—XENOPHANES.—HIS HISTORY AND DOC-
TRINES.

THE Ionian school of philosophy embraced two distinct systems,
the dynamical and mechanical. The former supposes an innate
force and energy in nature, the spontaneous changes and developments or generations of which, without the operation of any external influence, constitute the visible phenomena. The latter assumes the existence of immutable elements, incapable of development or alteration of form, and the phenomena are produced by
the different combinations of these elements set in motion, either
by an internal power or an external influence. The dynamical
theory was supported by Thales, Anaximenes, Diogenes of Apollonia, and Heraclitus; the mechanical by Anaximander, Anaxagoras, and his disciple Archelaus, the teacher of Socrates. Of
these Thales, Anaximenes, Anaximander, and Heraclitus belong
to the period of Greek literature which is treated of in this book.

THALES.

A biography of Thales has already been inserted amongst those
of the Seven Sages; it will therefore only be necessary here to
give some account of his philosophical system. False as his theories are, they deserve the title of philosophical, because they are
founded on observation and analogy, and so far widely differ from
the mere assertions of poetry. He may, therefore, be considered
as the founder of Greek philosophy. He observed first the natural process by which the life of vegetation is developed, from a

germ or seed,[1] and second, that moisture generates warmth, and warmth is the cause of nutrition and production. Hence his two leading doctrines, that the whole world was a living being, matured and produced from a seed, in which the phenomena were contained, although as yet latent and imperfect; and that the origin of all things was the element of moisture, or water.

Cicero[2] informs us that he believed in an intelligent First Cause, and asserted that out of water the Divine mind created all things.[3] That the Deity was without beginning and the soul of man immortal, are mentioned as articles of his creed. Doctrines are also attributed to him, which argue remarkable progress in astronomy and geometry. He is said to have been the first to calculate and predict a solar eclipse;[3] to have taught that the moon shone by reflected light, and to have discovered that the angle inscribed in a semicircle is a right angle.

ANAXIMANDER.

Anaximander, in order to preserve the chronological arrangement, must be placed next to Thales, although, as has been stated, he was a mechanical philosopher. He was a native of Miletus, was born in the third year of the forty-third Olympiad, and died shortly after the fifty-eighth Olympiad.[4] Tradition informs us that his earliest labors were devoted to subjects of practical utility. Strabo[5] ascribes to him the first map; Diogenes[6] the use, if not the invention, of the sun-dial. He taught that the Deity pervaded the universe; and, therefore, that all the heavenly bodies were divine, as being the dwelling-places of the divine essence.

The absence of resemblance between his philosophy and that of Thales, renders the statement of Strabo, that he was the pupil of the latter, highly improbable; indeed, the succession and mutual relation of the philosophers in the Ionian school, appear to be arbitrarily assumed. According to Anaximander, then, the principle (ἀςχή) of all nature was the infinite (τὸ ἄπειςον), i. e., a mixture (μίγμα) of elements from which substances were evolved by separation (διαχςισίς), the homogeneous parts being attracted

---

[1] Arist. Metaph. i. 3.   [2] De Nat. Deor. i. 10.   [3] Cic. de Div. i. 49.
[4] B. C. 609.   [5] Strabo, i. 1.   [6] Diog. Laert. ii. 1.

to each other.[1]   The external cause which produced this effect mechanically, was motion, and this was eternal; into the infinite all things were again dissolved.   The difference between the dynamical and mechanical theory, is at once made clear by this example.   The elements evidently possess no internal power of change, but an external force impressed upon them produces new combinations.   According to the system of Anaximander, the earth was cylindrical, and was situated in the centre of the Universe, where it was kept motionless by its equi-distance from all the forces and motions which surrounded it.   The heavenly bodies moved round the earth, each on a material orbit, or sphere. The cold elements, which had been separated by motion from the hot, arranged themselves in the centre, the hot elements in the circumference of the universe.   The solar heat, acting upon the moister parts of the earth, produced animated beings by a process of fermentation, the last created of which was man.

ANAXIMENES.

Anaximenes was also a native of Miletus, who flourished about the sixtieth Olympiad.   There is a general resemblance discoverable between his fundamental doctrines and those of Thales, taking into consideration that the primary element of Thales was water, that of Anaximenes, air.   From air he supposed that all things were produced; and, like Anaximander, he believed that into air all were finally resolved.   This was the undying principle of vitality which pervaded the world; it was the breath of life which caused man to be a living soul.   The modifications of this element, by which all things were generated, were effected by rarefaction and condensation (ὑπὸ μανότητος καὶ πυκνότητος), and hence originated the four simple bodies, the four elements, as they still continued to be termed popularly, earth, air, fire, water. Both Anaximander and Anaximenes have been accused of atheism, although both held the eternity and agency of an intelligent First Cause.   Their atheism consisted in attributing, like the rest of the Ionic school, physical effects to physical causes, instead of accounting for their existence on the principles of my-

[1] Arist. Metaph. xii. 2.

thology. Their real belief was pantheism, the belief in all pervading mind, and not a personal Deity. As from the epic tradition, that ocean flowed around the earth, was developed the Thaletic idea that the earth, like a broad island, floated on water; so this philosopher held that the earth, flat like a leaf, was supported on the air. From the earth were produced all the heavenly bodies, and these, in form and substance, resemble their parent.

HERACLITUS.

Heraclitus was born at Ephesus about the sixty-ninth Olympiad.[1] Owing to the early state of the Greek language, the infancy of prose composition at the period when he wrote, and its consequent inapplicability to the expression of philosophical thought, he is notorious for the difficulty of his style, and the figurative form in which he enunciated his doctrines. He has therefore been surnamed σκοτεινός, or the *obscure.*

The fragments which have been preserved and collected by the indefatigable industry of Schleiermacher,[2] bear witness to the justness of this epithet, by the obscurity of their diction, and their archaic style. Aristotle, in his " Rhetoric,"[3] mentions this defect in his composition, as an example of style difficult to punctuate. Prose was just growing out of poetry, its language was rather metaphorical than exact, and the ideas of the philosopher had not as yet found any corresponding terms; and hence, it is difficult to comprehend what his doctrines are, because of the figurative language in which they are conveyed. He is said by Aristotle[4] to have taught, that all things were in motion except one power, by which all were moulded. This power was fate (εἱμαρμένη), fixed and determined by the will of the Divine mind.

Melancholy in temperament, and aristocratic in his prejudices, he separated himself from the stirring pursuits of active life, refused the government of his native city,[5] and devoted himself to retirement and contemplation, and to mourning over the sin and misery of man. Who his instructor was is doubtful, but disin-

---

[1] B.C. 504.   [2] Museum der Alterthumswiss.   [3] Rhet. iii. 5.
[4] De Cœlo, iii. 1.   [5] Diog. Laert.

clined by temper to learn from others,[1] it is probable that he drew upon the resources of his own mind for his doctrines, and that his theories were the result of observation rather than erudition. There is an important feature which distinguishes the philosophy of Heraclitus from that of the other philosophers of the Ionian school, namely, that the agency of the Deity as the great First Cause, is more prominently brought forward. Although they all believed in the Divine intelligence, the laws of nature were to them the great object of investigation, but he considered them as the instruments of the Divine will, the expositions of the Divine wisdom. According to him even the reason of man is not part of his nature, but is due to the inspiration of heavenly influence, and this influence is the cause of consciousness.[2] This infusion of divinity extended to all nature, and hence his celebrated dictum, "Enter, for here too are gods." His faith, however, was pantheistic, rather than a belief in a personal deity; but this was the theological creed of the whole Ionic school.[3]

The original element of Heraclitus was fire, which was the vital principle in the universe, and also in man. The various transmutations of this element were ascribed by him to a self-existing motion. Harmony, he says, is the cause and preserver of all things, but it is a harmony of antagonism; an agreement of contraries. This idea probably arose from illustrating physical science by moral considerations; for example, sickness makes health pleasant, and labor rest.

As fire is the element out of which all things were produced, so it is that into which all will be resolved, and this composition and resolution will recur continually in certain cycles. Heraclitus also taught the imperfection of the external senses as the means of acquiring knowledge, the germ from which were afterwards developed doctrines, exercising an important influence upon Greek philosophy.

PYTHAGORAS.

So much of fabulous legend is mixed up with the history of Pythagoras,[4] that not only is there great uncertainty respecting

---

[1] Eth. vii. 5.
[2] Diog. Laert. ix. 10.
[3] Arist. de Part. An. i. 5.
[4] Herod. iv. 95.

the period at which he flourished, but also respecting the principal circumstances of his life.[1]

The Dorian and Achæan states of that part of Italy, which, owing to its being colonized by Greek settlers, was named Magna Græcia, turned their attention to subjects of philosophical inquiry, almost contemporaneously with the establishment of the Ionian schools : and whilst the opulence of commerce was fitting the cities of Ionia to become the nursing-mothers of philosophy, Grecian enterprise was providing for intellectual efforts another home in the west, in the luxurious and refined settlements of the now wild and desolate Calabria. The celebrated legislation of Charondas of Catana, as well as that of the Locrian Zaleucus, proves that social questions had thus early engaged the attention of powerful minds, in that part of the European continent. At Crotona, a colony of the Achæans, a school flourished, devoted to the study of medicine, the existence of which probably attracted Pythagoras, after he had completed his travels, to found his philosophical school in that city, about the sixtieth Olympiad, B. C. 540.

He is said by the best authorities to have been born at Samos, in the forty-ninth Olympiad, and to have traced his pedigree to the Tyrrhenian Pelasgians. Nothing is known of his early history, except that he visited the greater part of the civilized world, to gratify his love of observation and his taste for philosophical inquiry; and tradition points to him as the first who called himself a philosopher, φιλόσοφος, i. e, a *lover of wisdom*, whilst others assumed to themselves the less modest title of σόφοι, or *wise men*.

His political principles were evidently aristocratic, for he was diametrically opposed to the government of τύραννοι, who were, as has been already stated, the temporary patrons and leaders of the growing democratic interests. The influence also of himself, and his followers, was sufficiently powerful to impose an aristocratic constitution on Crotona and the neighboring states.   The league which he established, although it was a religious and philosophical fraternity, admission into which was accompanied by mystical rites of initiation, constituted also a political bond of union, and its object was to propagate aristocratic principles.

---

[1] Porphyry and Iamblichus, Life of Pythagoras.

Hence it was a political tumult, originating with the popular party, which led to its suppression, and the consequent persecution of the Pythagoreans. The revolution which succeeded, and which pervaded all the states of Magna Græcia, whilst it made the Pythagorean sect the great object of attack, was in fact a struggle between the two great opposing political factions, and led to the ascendancy of Achæan over Dorian political principles, the utter subversion of aristocracy, and the final establishment of democratical constitutions. In this revolution, Pythagoras sought safety in flight, but in vain. The principles, and therefore the influence, of his enemies extended far and wide, and he was put to death at Metapontum,[1] whilst Crotona, which had rejected his wise counsels, sank into decay as rapidly as it had risen to prosperity.

The views which have been generally entertained respecting the Pythagorean philosophy have been derived, not from an examination of ancient authorities, and those fragments of Pythagorean writers which are probably genuine, but from writers who lived since the commencement of the Christian era. These authors accepted as genuine a vast number of works which bore the title of Pythagorean, but which are unquestionably spurious, and also made no difference between the Pythagoreanism of ancient and of modern times. The inconsistencies, therefore, of those who misunderstood the precepts of their master, were incorporated in a system with which it was impossible that they could be reconciled.

It is difficult to form a clear conception of the relation which number bore to the Pythagorean philosophy, even generally; in particular cases it is impossible. Probably in some of its applications, no clear ideas existed in the minds of these philosophers themselves. At one time, the term number is used as though it merely signified the arithmetical proportion in which elements are combined, so as to produce different phenomena. Again, in discussing the theory of musical harmony, and that theory of harmony or music of the spheres which he applied to his astronomical system, number simply expresses the ratio which strings, producing musical tones, bear to one another, and of that relation

[1] Cic. de Fin. v. 2.

of the several parts of the universe, which constitutes order, regularity, and stability. In these cases, number is only used as representing, symbolically, the mutual relation of things which have an existence independent of it.

At another time, when the monad or unity is spoken of as the principle of all being, it appears as though the perception which he formed of it was that of something real and material.

Upon the whole, however, it appears probable that the symbolical sense of the term, was the one adopted by Pythagoras himself, and that, by a forced analogy, number was afterwards made use of by his followers to account for phenomena to which it was totally incapable of being applied. They committed the common error of confounding the symbol with the thing signified. Instead of being content with affirming that harmony depended on the proportion of the parts to one another, and that therefore this proportion was the law, according to which the operations of nature were carried on, the followers of Pythagoras carried his theory further, and considered that which was in reality only its symbolical representative, the material and efficient cause of all things. Harmony seems to have been the foundation of the Pythagorean system; the leading idea which at first got possession of his mind. Music had now begun to exercise an influence over poetry, it was but a step to introduce it into the domain of philosophy. Its application to account for the order and regularity which reigned among the heavenly bodies, naturally suggested itself to an astronomer, whose studies had been directed to it in the abstract, and who, even in his medical studies, was led to make observations on its influence upon the human frame.

Nor is number an unnatural symbol of the rules which govern the various relations and offices of moral conduct. There seems to have been a tendency in the human mind, to connect mysterious ideas with abstract numbers. No one can satisfactorily explain the almost reverential feeling with which the numbers three and seven have been universally regarded, and yet the fact is nevertheless undoubted. The application of number as the measure of all quantity; the relation which the principles of geometry were soon found to bear, not only to extension and space, but to all science; the capability which it has of symbolically representing even the abstract operations of the human mind itself, will go far to illustrate this tendency, but not to explain it.

The Pythagorean axiom, in which are embodied the two significations of the term number, before alluded to, is as follows:— Number is the essence (οὐσία) and principle (ἀρχή) of all things. Now, what is contended for is, that so far as essence was considered as only identical in meaning with principle or first cause (ἀρχή), the doctrine which the Pythagorean philosophy intended to convey is clear and intelligible, but when it is used[1] to signify the substance of things (ὕλη), language, which was intended to be symbolical, is applied by a false analogy to subjects to which it is inapplicable.

A passage in the "Metaphysics" of Aristotle[2] seems to imply that the studies of the Pythagoreans being mathematical, they assumed that the principles of mathematics were those of all other things. Now, number is the first of these, and in natural phenomena many numerical analogies are observable. Again, the properties of harmony are represented by number. The false conclusion drawn from these premises was not that the laws of the natural universe were harmony, and represented by number, but that the universe itself was number and harmony; probably, all that Pythagoras contended for was, that in all works, human and divine, harmony and proportion, and therefore number is discernible as the regulating principle. Had the Pythagoreans been acquainted with the modern theory of chemical equivalents, they would have seen in it the most perfect illustration of their system.

This theory of number, as the first principle in nature, is rendered obscure by those who, like Ritter, considered the co-ordinate series alluded to by Aristotle,[3] as a table of primal elements, whereas the object of this catalogue was totally different; the parallel columns representing a series of goods, with their corresponding contraries, and among these is reckoned the unit, the primal element, the representative or symbol of perfection.

From these considerations it is clear that the Pythagorean theory of number was reasonable, so far as it resolved all the

---

[1] Arist. Metaph. i. 5.   [2] Ibid.   [3] Eth. i. 4.

relations, whether of space or time, into those of number or proportion, and asserted that the order of the universe was maintained
by the laws of harmony; but that it became arbitrary, mere
words without meaning, when it assumed that mathematical
quantities and ideas were not symbols of things, but the things
themselves, the elements out of which material essences originated, and that even virtue, justice, and all other moral qualities
were defined by certain fixed and determined numbers.

The same mysticism and obscurity, which pervaded the doctrines already spoken of, enter also into the investigations of the
Pythagoreans respecting the spiritual nature of man. The human
soul, they believed to be an emanation from the Deity, eternal,
personal, dwelling in other bodies successively, and punished or
rewarded in its future state of being, able to energize only by
means of its union with the body, the senses of which are its
instruments and organs. They divided it into two parts, the
rational and irrational: the governing part, the peculiar property
of man; the other the seat of the passions and instincts, common
to man, together with the lower animals.

After all, the most important feature of the Pythagorean philosophy was, that it had for its principal objects the enunciation
of one great truth, the superiority of intellectual activity to
corporeal organization. Arbitrary as its theory of numbers may
have been, nevertheless in teaching that all knowledge was resolva-
ble into that of mathematical relations, it referred its origin not to
the operations of the bodily senses, but of pure intellect. Even
in musical harmony the effects and phenomena alone are apprehended and appreciated by the ear; the theory and the principles
of harmony must be investigated by the logical powers. Thus the
intellect was made the judge of truth of every kind, without any
necessary dependence upon the deceptive tendencies of the external senses. It was, doubtless, a yearning after this result, so
seductive to contemplative minds, which led Pythagoras and his
followers into the unsound applications and illogical developments
of a theory which, in its simplicity, appeared to rest upon no
unreasonable foundation.

THE ELEATIC SCHOOL.

In this school philosophical investigation was pursued on more strictly logical principles than have been hitherto observable. The founders of it recognized, in existent systems, a mixture of what they considered truth and error ; they perceived that all contained many arbitrary assumptions and inconsequential reasonings, and, as a first step, they applied themselves not to fresh investigation, but to examining the theories already existing. They brought the truth or falsehood of each theory to the test of a strict logical analysis. It is evident that the introduction of this principle into philosophical studies forms an era infinitely more important than one merely distinguished for an advance in original inquiry.

The following is a brief history of the rise of the Eleatic school. The original founders of the Greek colonies carried with them not only commercial enterprise and spirit, but also that desire of intellectual advancement, which so strongly marks the national character. Hence, the little colony of Elea, in Magna Græcia, soon grew into eminence for its patronage of science and learning. About the sixtieth Olympiad, although the date is somewhat uncertain, there flourished in the Ionian city of Colophon, which had been previously celebrated as the native town of Mimnermus,[1] an elegiac poet named Xenophanes. Political troubles, probably the attack by the monarch of Persia upon the liberties of Ionia, drove him from his native land. He travelled through Sicily and Southern Italy, supporting himself as a wandering minstrel, by the recitation of his poems, and finally settled at Elea.

Notwithstanding the assertion of Plato,[2] that the Eleatic doctrines existed previous to the time of Xenophanes, no doubt exists that the wandering and exiled rhapsodist turned his thoughts to philosophy, and became the founder of the celebrated philosophical school in his adopted city. Various opinions have been held on the question, as to who was his philosophical instructor, but as the characteristic of his didactic poetry is a determined opposition to the vicious polytheism of the epic poets, there is

[1] Hor. Epist. ii. ii. 100.　　　　[2] Soph. p. 242.

nothing in his system which might not have been the work of an original thinker, placing himself in direct antagonism to immoral doctrines.[1]   Out of the negation of the prevailing superstitions, his positive doctrines respecting the Deity naturally arose.   He denied a plurality of gods.   He ridiculed the attributing human forms to the deities.   He directed the bitterest attacks against the impiety of representing the gods as guilty of disgraceful crimes, such as are found constantly in the poems of Homer and Hesiod.

His positive doctrines were that God is omnipotent and all-wise, without beginning or end ; that a plurality of gods is inconsistent with and contradictory to the attributes of Deity, for two all-powerful beings could not exist together.   It has been doubted whether the monotheism of Xenophanes was not in reality pantheism.   He asserts that God was the same as the universe, but he also asserts the existence of a material world.   Whether, therefore, his idea of God was a spiritual essence pervading the material universe, it is impossible to determine, but pure pantheism is totally inconsistent with the belief, which he undoubtedly entertained, that God had a personal existence, and that he was the all-wise governor of the universe.   According to the natural system of Xenophanes, the four elements were the original principles of all things.   In the midst of all his hypotheses, this philosopher appears to have been deeply impressed with the imperfection of all human knowledge.   He saw that the nature of the Deity and all existing things was beyond the sphere as well of the intellectual powers as the corporeal senses of man.

Although the positions laid down by the Eleatic school were rather negative than positive, they, nevertheless, marked a great and important advance in philosophical speculation ; first, in asserting the unity of the Deity; and secondly, in referring the conclusions of other systems to the test of reason.

[1] Ritter ; Diog. Laert. and Sext. Empir.

BOOK II.

CHAPTER I.

AGE OF PISISTRATUS.—ESTABLISHMENT OF TYRANNIES IN GREECE.—PATRONAGE OF LITERATURE BY PISISTRATUS.—THE DRAMA.—DRAMATIC TASTE OF THE IONIAN RACE. —NATURE OF DRAMATIC POETRY.—RELIGIOUS CHARACTER OF THE ATTIC DRAMA.— RELIGIOUS DRAMA OF THE ROMISH CHURCH.—THE RELIGION OF GREECE NOT UNFA- VORABLE TO THE DRAMA, OR TO ITS FORMING A PART OF AN ACT OF WORSHIP.—THE LUDICROUS ELEMENT NATURAL TO THE DIONYSIAC WORSHIP. —SOME NATIONS DES- TITUTE OF DRAMATIC LITERATURE — THE TWO ELEMENTS OF THE DRAMA, THE CHORUS AND THE DIALOGUE.—THE CHORUS IS (1) THE RELIGIOUS AND MORAL ELE- MENT, AND (2) THE REPRESENTATION OF THE SPECTATORS.—THE ESSENCE OF THE DRAMA IS THE DIALOGUE.—LYRICAL COMEDY AND TRAGEDY.

THE period at which Greece began to have a fixed and established national literature was that of Pisistratus, commonly called the tyrant (τύραννος) of Athens.

Almost every Greek state, except Argos and Sparta, was, at some period of its existence, under the government of a τύραννος. The period of his sway was the transition state through which each little republic passed in its progress towards liberty.

The tyrants were in fact the regenerators of Greece. Absolute monarchy had given way to an aristocracy of birth, this had degenerated into an oppressive oligarchy; the people increasing in commercial wealth and that intelligence which accompanies it, had gained sufficient strength to throw off the yoke, but not enough to govern and act for themselves. The dominion of a τύραννος was therefore necessarily preparatory to the establishment of free constitutions. The era of these provisional governments was an era of progress; their policy was, owing to the cir-

14

cumstances which raised them to power, favorable to the improvement and cultivation of the national character.

When, therefore, we read that Sparta and Argos were the uncompromising enemies of tyranny, we must remember that this implies that they were the bitterest opponents of liberty. They were Dorians, and therefore, by the prejudices of race and blood, aristocratic; to oppose tyrants would, therefore, be to oppose the overthrow of their own political system.

The Ionian race, on the other hand, was by nature enterprising, restless, fond of foreign travel, and of intercourse with other nations, commercial, and zealously attached to free institutions. Amongst the Ionian states, therefore, the tyrants flourished. Whether the tyrannies were succeeded by a free constitutional government, or by the evils of unbridled democracy, depended on the following alternative, whether or not at the time when the tyrant was overthrown the people were sufficiently advanced and educated to govern themselves.

In Athens, the capital of the most advanced section of the Ionian race, in the days of the great legislator, and great patron of freedom, Solon, a relation of Solon was the leader of the anti-aristocratic party.[1] This was Pisistratus. He was himself, as is so often the case with popular leaders, a member of an illustrious family; he was a descendant of the house of Codrus, the ancient royal family of Athens. His munificent disposition, his personal beauty and bravery, his shining abilities and powerful eloquence, all contributed to increase and establish his influence,[2] and he used his influence to improve and cultivate the taste and intellect of his countrymen. He restored the great Panathenaic festival, in all its splendor; under his patronage the literary contests of the rhapsodists flourished, the immortal poems of Homer were collected and arranged, and thus became fixed and recognized standards of Attic taste, as they had been previously national favorites.

But his enlightened and cultivated mind not only encouraged a love for the ancient literature of Ionian Greece, but fostered and matured that branch of it which afterwards possessed the

[1] Herod. i. 59, κ. τ. λ.   [2] Plutarch, vit. Sol.; Cic. de Orat. iii.

greatest influence over Greece, both morally and politically, that a national literature has ever before or since exercised.

In his ten years of power, the drama made its first appearance at Athens,[1] rude, indeed, and in its infancy, but still giving promise of its future greatness, growing, like all other poetry, out of religious feeling, and now consecrated by this wise ruler to the service of religion.

From what has been already said of the Ionian character, it is evident, that it was of that peculiar kind, which, à priori, we should expect would be devotedly and passionately attached to dramatic performances. The whole essence of the drama is, as A. V. Schlegel[2] has observed, activity and energy; it is not enough to describe it as a poem, in which the characters speak and not the poet, for this is the case in mere dialogue, and dialogue is not dramatic unless there is some end or object to look forward to with interest, some effect to be produced, some catastrophe to be brought about. In epic poetry, we never forget that the characters belong to another age, one, perhaps, long gone by; we feel an interest in what they do, and what they suffer, but only such an interest as we should take in historical characters. The train of incidents follow one another, in calm, quiet, and regular order; the action stops at intervals, in order that the scene and the locality may be described; the attention is divided, so to speak, between animate and inanimate nature. But in dramatic poetry, the spectator throws himself into the midst of the events which are represented before his eyes; he makes one of the characters; he seems to have a share of their fortunes, just as he would in real life; he cannot believe that it is not a reality; the scene, the dresses, the human voices, the gestures, all combine to realize it to him, hence he actively sympathizes, instead of being merely passively moved.

The great secret of all poetry is what the ancients called πρὸ ὀμμάτων ποιεῖν,[3] that is, picturesqueness, the realization of the thing described; now dramatic poetry possesses all the requisites which can be imagined for attaining this end. The dramatist has at his immediate disposal resources which the writer of epic

[1] B. c. 535, Clinton's Fasti Hellenici.   [2] Lect. I.
[3] Arist. Rhet.

poetry would seek for in vain. We can, therefore, easily understand the absorbing interest with which the lively, energetic Ionian would witness a dramatic exhibition; we can picture to ourselves the enormous theatre crowded with all classes, sitting with breathless attention to hear even a whole tetralogy, although many hours must have passed during the representation.

There are two characteristic features of the Attic drama which cannot be too constantly kept in mind when investigating its nature and history. The first is, its religious character; the second, the actual participation of the audience in the action of the play. The old cyclic chorus was part of a religious ceremony, and derived its name (κύκλιος) from its circling dance around the altar of Dionysus. And so the drama, the oldest element of which was the choral, was an act of worship addressed to the same deity. The theatre was a temple consecrated to him. The θυμέλη, on which the chief member of the chorus stood, when he took a part in the dialogue with the actors on the stage, was an altar. And hence, it must have been with a seriousness approaching to religious awe, that an Athenian audience beheld illustrated, in the fortunes of the great houses of mythical antiquity, the struggle of man's free-will with the omnipotent power of Destiny, a power to which gods as well as men were supposed subject, and which even the divine will (Numen, Αἶσα) was impotent to resist.

This contemplation of the struggle with the irresistible decrees of Fate, which the best and most virtuous had constantly to maintain, and which is the essence of Greek tragic story, naturally led to melancholy views of human life, and passages abound in the Greek tragedians in accordance with the solemn lamentation of Job, that "Man is born to misery as the sparks fly upwards;" and with the words of the inspired Preacher,[1] "Wherefore I praised the dead which are already dead, more than the living which are yet alive. Yea, better is he than both they, which hath not yet been, who hath not seen the evil work that is done under the sun." The tragic poet would have sympathized with the sentiments of Isaiah, "The righteous is taken away from the evil to come."[2]

[1] Eccles. iv. 2, 3.　　[2] Isai. lvii. 1.

In the "Œdipus Coloneus"[1] the woes of Œdipus suggest an
entire chorus on the vanity of life :—

> One only healing hour remains,
> When Death, man's comforter and friend,
> Appears his weary course to end ;
> Of all the dreams of bliss there are,
> Not to be born is best by far ;
> Next best, by far the best for man,
> To speed as fast as speed he can.   ANSTICE.

So Euripides exclaims,[2] that

> "All mortal things are but a shadow ;"

and that

> "Tis not in mortal nature to be happy."

And even the comic poet[3] tells the same tale, and has brought
together many of the expressions which either Homer or the
tragedians have used to describe man's misery.

"Mortals living in darkness; like to the generations of leaves;
feeble; moulded of clay; creatures fleeing, as it were a shadow,
never continuing in one stay; unfledged; ephemeral; wretched;
like a dream that is gone."

The believers in a pure faith can scarcely understand a reli-
gions element in dramatic exhibitions.   They who know that God
is a spirit, and that they who worship him must worship him in
spirit and in truth, feel that his attributes are too awful to permit
any ideas connected with Deity to be brought into contact with
the exhibition of human passions.   Religious poetry of any kind,
except that which is inspired, has seldom been the work of minds
sufficiently heavenly and spiritual to be perfectly successful in
attaining the end of poetry, namely, the elevation of the thoughts
to a level with the subject.   It brings God down to man instead
of raising man to him.   It causes that which is most offensive to
religious feeling and even good taste, irreverent familiarity with
subjects which cannot be contemplated without awe.   But a religious drama would be, to those who realize to their own minds
the spirituality of God, nothing less than anthropomorphism and
idolatry.

Christians of a less advanced age, and believers in a more sen-

---

[1] Verse 1218.   [2] Eurip. Med. 1193.   [3] Aristoph. Aves, 685.

suous creed, were able to view with pleasure the mystery-plays in which the gravest truths of the Gospel were dramatically represented; nay, more, just as the ancient Athenians could look even upon their gross and licentious comedy, as forming part of a religious ceremony, so could Christians imagine a religious element in profane dramas, which represented, in a ludicrous light, subjects of the most holy character.   So closely was the drama connected with religion,[1] that it has been said, that even the plays of our own Shakspeare were reproductions of the prose romances of the day without the monkish religious element.

But the imaginative Greek did not experience this difficulty. His gods were either the creatures of his own fancy, or they were human beings like himself, who had, while alive, attained the heroic standard, and after death had been deified.   They possessed the same properties, feelings, passions and moral imperfections as himself; even the Supreme ruler of them all was not omnipotent.   His own native land was theirs, they were like his fellow-countrymen.   He could bathe in the river, or drink of the fountain, or seek shade in the grove, or climb the hill which were pervaded by the influence, and consecrated by the presence, of deity.   Parnassus, where the Muses, the authors of all inspiration, resided, was close at hand.   The mighty Olympus, the dwelling-place of Zeus himself, he might behold with his own eyes.

That dramatic representations should enter into the ceremonial of public worship, is quite consistent with the nature of the Greek religious belief.   If it consisted in a deification of the powers of nature, it follows that the works of nature, the visible manifestations of these powers, were symbols and representations of their deities.   The Greeks, therefore, became at once accustomed to connect the mimetic art with worship, and to accompany the choral ode with imitative dances, performed by characters representing the gods in whose honor they were performed, together with their train of attendant deities.   Although we might expect that these would be of a solemn nature, as, in fact, they were in the earliest species of choral poetry, namely, the dithyrambic, which symbolized the story of the birth of Dionysus, we can easily conceive the rapid introduction of the ludicrous

[1] Don. Greek Theatre.

element also. Dionysus was the god and giver of wine, which gladdens and cheers man's heart. How natural then it was, that the early symbolizing and expressing the sentiments connected with his worship, should be by means of comedy, even before his dramatic worship took the form of tragedy, and that the origin of the former should be even prior, in point of time, to that of the latter.

We must now proceed to distinguish the original elements out of which the Attic drama sprung. They are two, the chorus and the dialogue. The language itself, in which each of these is written, shows that the former is the Doric, the latter the Ionic element. Not that the choruses in an Attic tragedy are written strictly in the Doric dialect, but that important peculiarity of it, which so singularly adapts it for musical accompaniment, namely, the broad or open pronunciation of the "a" sound being invariably retained, sufficiently demonstrates its Doric origin.

When we consider how absorbing is the interest connected with theatrical amusements, it seems surprising that there should have been nations totally ignorant of them. The Semitic races had no drama. The Chevalier Bunsen[1] says, "The drama or the combination of the lyric and epic elements, and the complete representation of the eternal laws of human destiny in political society, is entirely unknown to the Semite. It is exclusively the creation of the Hellenic mind, feebly imitated by the Romans, reproduced with originality by the Germanic race. But Iranian India is not entirely wanting in this last of the three species of poetical composition."

Hebrew poetry, although it exhibits every variety of composition, is destitute of the dramatic element. The sublime and Homeric Isaiah celebrates in a triumphant epinician the glories of Israel.[2] The mournful and affectionate *threni* of Jeremiah reminds us of the elegies of Simonides; one-seventh of the Psalms are elegies;[3] the book of Job abounds in them; the songs of Miriam and Deborah, the prophecy of Balaam, the numerous Psalms which sing the praises of the Most High, are grander odes and hymns than can be found throughout the whole range of classic

---

[1] Brit. Assoc. Report, 1847.   [2] Isai. xiv.   [3] Lowth, De Sac. Po.

poetry.   The Proverbs of Solomon contain a collection of didactic poetry, in comparison with which the wisest gnomes of the Greeks sink into insignificance : Ezekiel is, in his ideas and language, as tragic as Æschylus, but he did not write tragedies.   Even those portions of Holy Scripture which most resemble dramatic compositions, are not dramas.   The sixty-third chapter of Isaiah is simply a dialogue maintained between a chorus and the Messiah. The song of Solomon has no fable, no action.   The story of Job has no change of fortune.   All these, therefore, whilst they possess some of the qualities, are destitute of the essentials of dramatic compositions.

Egypt, Arabia, Persia, however rich their national literature may have been, did not, as far as we have any evidence, possess any.   Dramatic performances have existed in India from very early times, and hence, perhaps, the Greeks, as an Indo-Germanic race, were likewise distinguished by a taste for this kind of literature.   But it was only in one division of the Greek nation that dramatic literature arrived at perfection.   The drama was of Attic growth, and all the great dramatic writers were Attic, and the beautiful language in which they wrote was Attic likewise.

It has already been shown, when treating of lyric poetry, that choral poetry is essentially Doric; that although the poets were not native Dorians, yet they adopted that dialect, and addressed themselves to the feelings and sympathies of that race.

It was the choral element which gave the religious tone to the drama; which kept up the connection between it and public worship.   If pious and moral sentiments were to be enforced, and reflections made upon the action of the play, it was the duty of the chorus to sustain the part of the religious and moral instructor.   Who can read the choruses of the three great tragedians, without being forcibly impressed with the high moral tone, the deep religious fervor, the true wisdom, the virtuous indignation, the sympathy with all that is pure, and wise, and holy, which breathes in them?   We can never forget that they are Dorian in sentiment, as well as in the outward form of rhythm and language.

Besides the religious and moral importance of the chorus, there is another object which must be kept in mind.   That is, the realization of the audience. The chorus represented the spectators; the connection which subsisted between it and the actors in the dialogue, symbolized, as it were, the sympathy which is taken for granted, between the feelings of the spectators and the fortunes of those upon the stage.

The θυμίλη, or altar, on which the chief choreutes stood, when, in the name of the rest, he took part in the dialogue, was the central part of the circle in which the audience sat; in him, therefore, they might be supposed to be concentrated, and therefore personified.

The choral element, then, of the Grecian drama, developed these two essential points, the religious character of the performance, and the realization of the audience. 1. The character of the drama was religious, because the chorus was originally a solemn dance, and sacred hymn, and it preserved that character by means of the sentiments to which it gave utterance, being always full of sympathy with virtue and goodness, of indignation against vice and injustice, teaching submission to the divine will, and fortitude under the terrible fiat of a destiny which it would be in vain to resist, and therefore unmanly to bewail.

2. The chorus represented the spectator; it was therefore the link by which he was connected with and, as it were, made one of the characters on the stage. He was thus supposed to enter into their feelings and fortunes, and the sentiments of the chorus are the echoes of his own, the expression of his own sympathies.

It thus fulfilled that important office, which Horace attributes to it, of being a public instructor.[1] It kept the sympathies of the audience in a right direction, and caused them to be given to right objects.

But, although the chorus was an important element in the Greek tragic drama, and to the sacred choral songs and dances the drama owed its origin, still it is the dialogue, and not the chorus, which constitutes the essence of the drama. The chorus was doubtless mimetic, for the gymnopædic, hyporchematic, and pyrrhic dances, which are said to have corresponded to the tragic, comic, and satyric choruses respectively, were all mimetic, but it could not be dramatic.

[1] Hor. Art. Poet.

Previous to the date which is generally assigned to the first invention of tragedy, there are said to have existed performances both tragic and comic, but of a non-dramatic kind. These have been termed, by modern scholars, the lyrical comedy and tragedy, because the choruses and recitations were accompanied by the lyre, instead of the flute, which was the case in the dithyrambi. In these, the only actors were the members of the chorus, and hence Diogenes Laertius[1] asserts that the chorus alone enacted the whole διεδραμάτιζε. If we apply the term dramatic, simply to mimetic action, this word is correctly used; if to that which is commonly understood by it, this species of performance was not dramatic.

The Orchomenian inscriptions, the oldest of which is supposed by Böckh to be earlier than B. C. 220, mentions both tragic and comic performances, long before the time of Thespis. When, therefore, the invention of comedy is claimed for the Sicilian Epicharmus, lyric comedy is implied; and in like manner, tragedy, which is said to have existed before the time of Thespis, was not dramatic, but lyric tragedy.

[1] Diog. Laert. iii. 56.

CHAPTER. II.

ORIGIN OF THE DIALOGUE.—ACCOUNT GIVEN BY ARISTOTLE.—ORIGIN OF THE TERMS τραγῳδία AND κωμῳδία.—TWOFOLD NATURE OF THE DIONYSIAC WORSHIP.—ITS HISTORY AND INTRODUCTION INTO GREECE —AMALGAMATION OF IT WITH THE ELEUSINIAN WORSHIP OF IACCHUS.—THE PROGRESSIVE ADVANCE OF THE TRAGIC DRAMA TRACED. —INTRODUCTION OF SATYRS.—ARION.—THESPIS.—PHRYNICHUS.—CHŒRILUS.—PRA-TINAS.—ATHENIAN POLITICAL AND DRAMATIC GREATNESS CONTEMPORANEOUS.

THE subject now to be examined is, how the dialogue came to be connected with the original chorus. Aristotle informs us that tragedy (that is, the new element which distinguished the τραγικος τρόπος from the old chorus) was the first extemporaneous narrative delivered by the ἐξάρχοντες. These were the chief performers in the dance and the directors of the rest of the dancers,[1] and were the principal executors of the mimetic action; they performed, in fact, the united functions of a ballet-master and coryphæus, and as these extemporaneous effusions gave birth to tragedy, so in the licentious and unrestrained phallic dance they were the original germ of comedy.

That these narratives at first were confined to legends connected with the birth and subsequent adventures of Dionysus there can be no doubt, and probably the reciter, habited in goat-skins, represented one of his attendant deities, the satyrs. Hence the name given to this entertainment τραγῳδία, or the *goat-ode;* and, on a similar principle, comedy was designated as κωμῳδία, the *ode of the revellers.* And hence, when in later times the adventures of other gods or heroes were introduced into these narratives or episodes, the people, disappointed of their favorite and familiar legend, or struck with the inconsistency of any other plots unconnected with the subject of the festival which they were celebrating, would express their disapprobation, and exclaim οὐδὲν πρὸς Διόνυσον, "this has nothing to do with Dionysus."

[1] Il. xviii. 605.

The introduction of subjects not connected with the history of Dionysus is attributed to Thespis, who is therefore considered the inventor of tragedy, and the proverb above mentioned is said to have been first used with reference to his dramas when exhibited at Athens.　Plutarch,[1] however, assigns the origin and first use of this proverb to the time of Phrynichus and Æschylus.

The feelings which accompanied the worship of Dionysus were of a mixed nature.　The death and birth of the god symbolized the decay of Nature, and its revival in the spring; the latter the cause of joy and gladness, the former of grief and sorrow; hence the subjects of tragedy might be at one time mournful and another cheerful, and, consequently, it was not until tragedy was severed from this limited range of subjects and adopted other adventures, that it limited itself in its choice to pathetic histories, which are now considered essential to the idea of tragedy.

To trace through its numerous forms the worship of Dionysus is a work of no common difficulty.　The title "god of many names," given him by Sophocles, implies, of course, numerous attributes, and, therefore, numerous phases in which he has been presented to the imagination.

The voice of tradition points to India as the birth-place of the god, and antiquity[2] asserts his identity with the Egyptian Osiris, whilst it makes Orus, the son of Osiris, the same as the Greek Apollo.　The similarity existing between some rites observed in the worship of the Indian Bacchus and those of Dionysus, render it probable that they were originally one and the same deity.　Herodotus asserts that this worship came to Greece from Egypt and Phœnicia.

Now, from the ports of Phœnicia all the commerce of the East flowed to Greece, and, therefore, whatever customs, civil or religious, were introduced from that coast of the Mediterranean, would be said to come from that country.　The testimony of Holy Scripture informs us not only that the merchants of Phœnicia were the richest and most celebrated in the world, but that the neighboring land of Canaan was one of remarkable fertility.　It is described as a land flowing with milk and honey, the glory of all lands.　It is said to have abounded in fine vineyards, and to

[1] Plutarch. Symp. i. 5.　　　　[2] Herod. ii. 42, 144.

have produced the finest grapes.[1] The spies who went first to inspect the promised land, "cut down a branch with one cluster of grapes, and they bare it between two on a staff." Strabo and Pliny both speak of bunches growing in Palestine of an extraordinary size. The numerous passages in which the labors of the vintage and the fruit of the vine furnish metaphorical expressions to the sacred writers, proves to what an extent the cultivation of the vine prevailed. It is highly probable, therefore, that the idolatrous Canaanites held vintage festivals in honor of a god of wine, and that from them the Dionysiac worship travelled into Greece.

Mr. Mitchell remarks,[2] that some allusion to a Dionysiac worship is found in the devil-worship of the Gentiles. In two places, the original word translated "Devils," is שְׂעִירִים, to which word Gesenius affixes the following signification, "Hairy, rough, a buck, a he-goat; plural, inhabitants of solitary places, perhaps wild men in the form of he-goats, similar to the Greek satyrs."

The prevalence, moreover, of the Dionysiac worship in Crete is easy of explanation, on the supposition of its existence among the Canaanitish tribes. It has been disputed, whether Crete was colonized from Canaan, or the reverse; but a connection between Crete and Canaan is generally allowed. This island, from its situation, seems to have been in very early times a mark for colonization, and from the variety of nations which inhabited it, and the different religious faiths professed by them, the Dionysiac worship in Crete became mixed up with other traditions.[3] If a Canaanitish colony settled in Crete, their new abode would well compensate for that which they had left; its fair climate, its general fertility, and above all, its fitness for cultivating the vine, would point it out as a place peculiarly adapted for establishing the worship of their patron deity.

If we trace the Dionysiac worship still further northward, to the barbarian regions of Thrace, we see rites of cruelty and bloodshed superadded to the lawless indulgence of sensual passions. The female Bacchantes lose their feminine nature; they are no longer mere creatures of sensual passion, but are maddened with the fury of drunken fiends. Inebriation leads to

---

[1] Numb. xiii. 22. [2] Introd. to Frogs, p. 51.
[3] See Odys. xix. 172.

bloodshed, and tradition represents the Bacchanals, as rending asunder the mangled limbs of the Thracian Orpheus.

The worship of Dionysus was evidently, in all its developments, licentious and depraved. But there existed in Greece, another worship of a purer kind. Earth, the mother of all things, was to the Greeks the object of mysterious adoration, under the title of Demeter (Γῆ μήτης). Mythology represented her as the mother of two children, Iacchus, who symbolized the joyous youthful principle of nascent and reviving nature; and Proserpine, inhabiting the regions of gloom and darkness, and symbolizing the death and decay which succeed to the bright and cheerful seasons of the year. This mythical faith had a moral as well as a natural signification. It represented man's sorrow and despair at being cast out from the favor of heaven, on account of sin, and the joy which he experiences when he is forgiven and reconciled. Such were the truths symbolized in the Eleusinian mysteries, which taught also the immortality of the soul, and a future state of rewards and punishments. And when their annual festival took place, its ceremonies commenced with expiatory and propitiatory rites, and ended with gay processions, in honor of Iacchus, and scenes of joy and revelry.

The Eleusinian rites then, and the views which they inculcated, were chaste, pure, and solemn; the worship of Dionysus, on the other hand, was licentious, and encouraged the indulgence of sensual passion; but there was some similarity between the truths symbolized in so different a manner. There was sufficient affinity to admit of amalgamation, and the purifying of the one by the influence of the other.

At some period or other, it is uncertain when, this amalgamation took place, and the two worships were united together. Hence the chorus in the "Antigone,"[1] addresses Bacchus as ruling in the united mysteries of Demeter and Dionysus. It is probable that a more enlightened age perceived the licentious abuses to which the Dionysiac worship led, and that its wild debauchery was sobered by this combination with a purer ceremonial.

If Greek tragedy is traced from its first origin, the following

[1] Verse 1106.

will be found to have been the progressive steps by which it advanced to perfection.

The village Dionysiac festival gave rise to rude extemporaneous poetry, in which the sorrows and triumphs of the patron deity were celebrated. Then succeeded the cyclian chorus, which was composed of fifty practised performers, and their hymns were composed by the dithyrambic poet. Even in this early stage, it might be expected that the performers would adopt a theatrical costume. The dance, the song, the music, were all imitative, and dress and disguise would realize the subject and heighten the illusion. The simplest garb which they would adopt, would be that of the companions of Dionysus, in peace and war, in sorrow and triumph, in toil and festivity. These were the supernatural inhabitants of wood, and cave, and fountain; the satyrs, grotesque to our ideas, but still partners with the god in scenes of tragic interest, according to the popular mythology.

The first step to the introduction of costume was to attire these imaginary beings in the skins of goats. Their songs and dances were sportive as well as serious; the varied adventures of Dionysus had both these aspects; there is therefore no more inconsistency in the union of the comic and tragic elements in one piece, than there is in the introduction of comic characters and comic scenes in the plays of Shakspeare.

Afterwards, when tragedy assumed a serious and grave form, and dignity and pathos were recognized as its characteristics, the satyrs were banished from it, to a drama of their own, and as the farce follows the tragedy, so a satyric drama formed the fourth in every tragic tetralogy.

It is said that Arion[1] was not only the inventor of the dithyrambic poetry,[2] but also attired the singers in the garb of satyrs. If this be the case, theatrical costume, in its simplest form, dates as far back as the times of Periander, tyrant of Corinth.

In the age of Thespis,[3] a native of Icaria, a village near Athens, this banishment of the satyrs from tragedy had not taken place. The choreutæ still, generally speaking, represented satyrs, but between their songs he introduced a performer, who recited some mythological legend relating to Dionysus. The performer wore

---

[1] Herod. i. 24.   [2] Ibid. v. 67.   [3] B. C. 536.

an appropriate mask and costume, and accompanied his recitation with suitable action. He was therefore an actor, and consequently Thespis is properly considered as having invented the dramatic form of tragedy; but at this period, there was no plot, nor was there any dialogue, except between the actors and the chorus. Between these, however, a dialogue was maintained, and from this circumstance, an actor derived his name ὑποκριτης, i. e., respondent to the chorus.

In this condition tragedy remained until the time of Phrynichus, who exhibited his first tragedy, B. C. 511. The subjects of tragedy were now no longer confined to the adventures of Dionysus. The single actor recited such events, historical or mythological, as were calculated to move the feelings of the spectators. The chorus represented characters illustrating the recitation. In one play they were the daughters of Danaus; in another they were Phœnician women whom war had deprived of their fathers, brothers, or husbands; in a third they were Milesian captives. Respecting this play, Herodotus[1] informs us that its pathos was so great that the whole audience burst into tears, and the Athenian people sentenced the poet to pay a fine of one thousand drachmæ for representing the calamities of a people with whose woes they sympathized. Suidas enumerates ten tragedies, written by Phrynichus; but he omits that of the Phœnicians. It is evident, from the anecdote just related, that he possessed dramatic and pathetic talent of a very high order; and, probably, the introduction of female characters, which is attributed to him, was owing to his skill in moving the softer passion of pity, rather than the other dramatic passion of terror.[2] He appears also to have been celebrated for the gracefulness of the dances which he invented, and for the beautiful, although archaic, taste of his lyric odes.[3] It is clear that in the tragedies of Phrynichus, the separation of the tragic from the satiric element, must have taken place. His contemporary, Chœrilus, B. C. 523,[4] may be considered as having probably developed the satyric dramas, if we may place any confidence in the following verse of an anonymous poet:—

Ἡνίκα μὲν βασιλεὺς ἦν Χοιρίλος ἐν Σατύροις,

---

[1] Herod. vi. 21.   [2] Vide Arist. Poet.
[3] Suidas; Plat. Symp. iii.; Aves, 750; Ranæ, 908. [4] Suidas.

which attributes to him pre-eminence in this kind of composition. During forty years Chœrilus[1] continued an exhibition of tragedies ; and, during that time, produced one hundred and fifty tragedies, and gained thirteen victories.

The tradition that Chœrilus excelled in the satiric drama, and the undoubted fact that a satiric chorus could not possibly have harmonized with the affecting tragedies of Phrynichus, constitute fair grounds for assuming that the separation of the tragic and satiric dramas commenced with him. The grammarians, however, attribute the first introduction of pure satiric dramas to Pratinas,[2] a native of Phlius, resident at Athens, who did not exhibit until more than twenty years later than Chœrilus.[3] The probability, however, is that he completed the separation which had already been begun, and then devoted his talents to perfecting that drama which he had assisted in founding. He wrote, also, hyporchematic lyric poems,[4] which were probably introduced by way of choruses in his satiric dramas. Chœrilus also appears to have stoutly maintained the superior importance of poetry as compared with music, and to have opposed the encroachments of the latter, when there appeared danger lest the instrumental accompaniment should drown the voice of the singer, and music become predominant instead of auxiliary.

Pratinas was a Phlian, and therefore a Dorian. After him tragedy became exclusively Athenian. It had already, since the days of Pisistratus, become naturalized in that capital, but Dorian influences had been the strongest, and the lyric element in which the drama originated prevailed. From this period it became gradually less important, and the tendency, which had already begun to show itself slightly even in the plays of Thespis, to less of a lyric and more of the dramatic element, is now plainly visible ; it also now began to satisfy those conditions which modern taste considers essentially dramatic, and to display those inimitable excellencies which distinguish it in its best period.

The era of Athenian political greatness, and that in which Athenian tragedy flourished, exactly coincide. The first dramatic contest of Æschylus, in which he contended with Chœrilus and

---

[1] Suidas.
[2] Ibid. s. v.
[3] B. c. 500.
[4] Athenæus, xiv. 617.

15

Pratinas, took place B. C. 499, and the years in which were fought the battles of Arginusæ and Ægospotamos[1] were marked by the deaths of Euripides and Sophocles.[2]

During this period many tragic writers lived; such were Aristarchus of Tegea (B. C. 454); Achæus of Eretria (B. C. 447); Xenocles, who was victorious over Euripides (B. C. 415); Agathon (B. C. 416); and Euphorion, the son of Æschylus himself. Each of these must have composed and exhibited a vast number of tragedies; nevertheless, with the exception of a few fragments, none remain to us. Many of those which have perished were probably of great beauty, because Æschylus, Sophocles, and Euripides were all occasionally beaten by competitors, and even the "Œdipus Rex" and the "Medea" were unsuccessful. Making, therefore, all allowances for popular caprice, the testimony of success would of itself prove that some of their compositions would bear comparison with those which we now admire. Still, the fact that so many plays of Æschylus, Sophocles, and Euripides have survived, whilst all the rest have perished, may well make us feel satisfied, that, upon the whole, we possess the finest specimens of the Greek dramatic writings, and that although occasionally a play may have pleased more, the public voice of Athens assigned the palm to the three great tragedians. On this point, we can appeal to the comic poet[1] who, although in his love and admiration for antiquity he does not refuse praise to the older dramatists, admits none of them as candidates for the tragic throne.

[1] B. C. 406.   [2] B. C. 405.
[3] Aristoph. Batrach.

CHAPTER III.

HOMERIC SPIRIT OF THE THREE GREAT TRAGIC POETS.—THEIR RELIGIOUS BELIEF AND MYTHOLOGY COMPARED WITH THOSE OF HOMER.—SUCCESSIVE ERAS OF POETRY AND RELIGIOUS BELIEF.—ÆSCHYLUS, HIS LIFE.—OBSERVATIONS UPON THE STYLE AND LANGUAGE OF ÆSCHYLUS.—HIS EXTANT TRAGEDIES.—THE PERSIANS.—THE SEVEN AGAINST THEBES.—THE SUPPLIANTS.—THE PROMETHEUS BOUND.—THE ORESTEAN TRILOGY, AGAMEMNON, CHOEPHORI, AND EUMENIDES.—SYMBOLISM OF THIS TRILOGY. —POLITICAL OBJECT OF THE EUMENIDES.—QUOTATIONS.

ALTHOUGH the revival of a taste for epic poetry, by the exertions of Pisistratus, gave a fresh impulse to literature; still, in the long interval which had elapsed between the time of Homer and the rise of Athenian tragedy, Greek intellect had made great advances. The language, the tone of thought, the numerous Homerisms of Æschylus, and even of Sophocles, show that the three great dramatists were imbued with the Homeric spirit, and Æschylus modestly termed his tragedies only slices from the mighty feasts of Homer;[1] but still this spirit was modified by that of their own age.

They were as creative as Homer was, but their liberty of creating was confined within certain bounds, and limited by the recognized laws of human action. Heroic as were their characters, they must act according to the moral principles which govern man. The pure and awful conception which philosophic Greece now formed of the divine nature, would not permit it to be defiled by mean or petty passions, or swayed by unworthy motives. . The whole religious creed of Æschylus, Sophocles, and Euripides was totally different from that of Homer, except the mere names of the deities, and the machinery of mythology. Homer's gods were, as we have seen, rather partisans, than impartial protectors of the human race carrying out in their government the eternal principles of immutable justice. The peace of Olympus was dis-

[1] Athenæus, viii. 39.

turbed by petty quarrels and unworthy jealousies; their every-day life was sensual, their characters were marked with the lowest immorality. They were able to be bribed by their worship-pers. Sacrifice was a mere price for favor, not an offering of atonement or propitiation. Deceit and fraud were unscrupulously used. Zeus himself, the father of gods and men, was often treated with disrespect, and was, like man, subject to an irresisti-ble Destiny.

The supreme being of Æschylus and Sophocles is purer, loving righteousness and hating iniquity, all-seeing, omnipresent, subject neither to sleep nor age. Destiny still existed, still ruled man-kind, but its power was subordinate to the supreme will of God (αἶσα), the divine command, and the eternal principles of justice.

The mythological features and traditions which remain, are those which, in the histories of the great tragic families, describe the undying vengeance of a pure God exercised against the sinner; the punishment which pursues unceasingly the violator of the house of life, the perjurer, the adulterer, the violator of hospitali-ty, until he is penitent, purified, and reconciled.

As Homer, Pindar, Æschylus, Sophocles, and Euripides may be considered as the representatives of successive poetical eras, so their poetry may be said to embody different phases of Greek religious belief. Homer represents the popular, Pindar the priest-ly creed; Æschylus and Sophocles that mysterious need of com-fort and support from on high, and riddance of the burden of sin,, of which the human heart is naturally conscious; Euripides, that philosophical belief which fast degenerates, first into scepticism, and next into infidelity.

ÆSCHYLUS, born B. C. 525.

Æschylus was the son of Euphorion, born at Eleusis in Attica, B. C. 525,[1] and therefore a native Athenian. His father is sup-posed to have been employed in the mystical worship of Demeter, and from those awful rites in which he is said to have been initi-ated may have been derived that supernatural grandeur and reli-gions solemnity which pervade his tragedies. At an early age he

---

[1] Olym. lxiii. 4.

devoted himself to poetry. Pausanias[1] relates, that being employed when a boy in a vineyard, he dreamed that Dionysus
appeared to him and commanded him to write tragedy ; he obeyed
the vision. He first contended for the tragic prize against Pratinas
and Chœrilus, B. C. 499.   But he was not a successful competitor
until B. C. 484, a year signalized by the birth of Herodotus.   His
" Persians," the earliest of his dramas which have come down to
us, was exhibited with the " Phineus," "Glaucus Potnieus," and
the satiric play entitled " Prometheus, the Fire-bearer," B. C. 472.
Four years afterwards he was vanquished by Sophocles, and vexed
at his defeat retired from Athens to the court of Hiero,[2] who received him with his usual kindness and hospitality.   Suidas[3] attributes
his exile to the fall of the wooden benches in the theatre, an
accident for which the dramatic poet was held partially responsible.
The most probable cause, however, of his exile was religious persecution on account of his philosophical opinions, and the unpopularity of his political sentiments.   He was a Pythagorean,[4] and
therefore too enlightened to believe the fictions of the popular
mythology ; and Aristotle[5] tells us that a charge of impiety had
been brought against him, with reference to the Eleusinian mystery.   The "Eumenides" shows that he was deeply attached to
the old aristocratical institutions of his country, and that he did
not think it consistent with his duty as a public instructor to
shrink from supporting them against the innovations of the democratic party.   Not that the "Eumenides" had as yet been exhibited, for the Orestean trilogy was not acted until B. C. 458.
But as immediately after that event he a second time retired to
Sicily, it is probable that his former visit may have been caused
by similar unacceptable sentiments having appeared in some of
his former dramas.   In the decision of the prize, however, it is
not probable that politics had any share, for Cimon[6] was one of
the judges who decided in favor of his young competitor.
Æschylus was a warrior[7] as well as a poet; the field of Marathon witnessed his prowess as well as that of his brothers, Amin-
ias, and Cynægirus,[8] of whom the former opened the attack at

[1] Paus. i. 21-2.   [2] Plutarch. Cim. 8.   [3] Suidas, s. v.
[4] Cic. Tusc. ii. 10.   [5] Eth. Nic. iii. 1.   [6] Plutarch. vit. Cim.
[7] Suidas, s. v.   [8] Herod. vi. 114.

Salamis.[1] Accident was the cause of his death, in the sixty-ninth year of his age, B. C. 456, at Gela, the place of his exile: an eagle let fall a tortoise on the poet's bald head, mistaking it for a stone, and thus he died, as an oracle is said to have foretold, by a stroke from heaven. The Gelans instituted public games in his honor, and inscribed on his tomb an epitaph which he himself had written; in which, as Athenæus[2] observes, he shows that he values his fame as a warrior far higher than his reputation as a poet.

$$\text{Ἀλκὴν δ' εὐδόκιμον Μαραθώνιον ἄλσος ἀν εἴποι.}$$
$$\text{Καὶ βαθυχαιτήεις Μῆδος ἐπιστάμενος.}$$

To have been one of those distinguished by the title Μαραθωνόμαχοι was his highest glory. In his " Persians," in the descriptions of Grecian triumph and Persian ruin, no one can fail to see that the language is inspired by the enthusiasm of one who was an actor in the scenes which he paints so vividly; and we sympathize with the saying of Gorgias, that when he wrote that play, Mars, and not Dionysus, was the author of his inspiration. When the dramatic prize was awarded to Sophocles, Æschylus felt conscious that it had been voted unjustly, and appealed to the judgment of posterity. The confidence which he reposed in posterity was responded to by his immediate successors; for no sooner was he dead than money was granted from the public treasury to defray the cost of exhibiting his tragedies, and four prizes were awarded to his son, Euphorion, for tragedies exhibited by him, but written by his father.

Every critic, from Quinctilian[3] downwards (and we learn from Aristophanes that an example of this criticism was set by his own countrymen), has been in the habit of condemning the style of Æschylus as bombastic and exaggerated. But in this criticism they have too much lost sight of the subjects which his dramas embodied, and the characters which gave utterance to his gigantic words ;—they were vast, supernatural, sketched in rough, obscure, and vague outlines; they stand forth in dreamy proportions, figures of another world, leaving much to be filled up by the imagination. Of the two tragic passions he felt and excited

[1] Herod. viii. 48.   [2] Athen. xiv. 23.
[3] Quinct. Inst. Or. x. 1.   [4] Vide Ranæ.

terror rather than pity, and he called forth terror by veiling his characters in an awful gloominess, as though conscious that sublimity would be destroyed if their forms were accurately delineated and brought out into the broad daylight. Terror is nurtured and enhanced by concealment, whilst pity is the result of sympathy, and sympathy requires that the object in whose behalf it is invited, should be plainly depicted and accurately known.

In objects of supernatural terror, the exhibition should be somewhat of the nature of a phantasmagoria, like the shadowy shapes which flit before the eyes of Cassandra in her prophetic vision;[1] too much reality dispels the illusion, and changes that which would be sublime into the ridiculous. Æschylus always avoids this error: we never see his supernatural machinery. The same conception of the true nature of the sublime which suggested his subjects, inspired his language likewise; his metaphors, sometimes harsh, sometimes even confused; his rugged compounds have just that degree of obscurity which produces instead of injuring sublime effect. The quick sensibilities of his audience, who could follow him with ease through a difficult figure, and that facility of composition which is a distinguishing feature of the Greek language, and which no modern language possesses, except the German, tempted him to indulge his imagination without limit.

The language of Æschylus is the language of gods and of heroes; it is as appropriate to the sentiments which it embodies and the characters which give it utterance, as the mask and the *cothurnus* which he invented, and the costume which he improved in magnificence, were calculated to give dignity, and as the scene-painting which he introduced was powerful in assisting the illusion.

The non-existence of grammatical science is another cause of the obscurity of his style, for which he is not responsible. There was no regular syntax to curb his abruptness, or to create an artificial connection between one idea and the next in a series. The principle which regulated language was then, and even as late as the time of Thucydides, rather attraction than government; and even this early principle was, in the time of Æschylus, deficient in power. His style is, like his thought, grand as an

---

[1] Æsch. Agam.

Egyptian temple, or the Cyclopian edifices of the Pelasgians ; or, to use the words of Müller, "like a temple built of huge rectangular blocks of polished marble."[1]

But the stately and sublime Æschylus does not hesitate to descend to the homeliest details, if he thinks that it will make the picture more graphic and the character more true to life. The nurse in the "Choephori"[2] specifies the minutest details with the garrulity and absence of delicacy which mark the old attached domestic, who knows no other way of describing her affection than by enumerating the little offices which she performed for her charge in infancy; and the contrast is put in a strong light between the little cares which she then bore patiently, and her overwhelming sufferings at his loss, and the ruin of the house of Agamemnon.

Æschylus is said to have composed seventy tragedies; according to Suidas,[3] ninety, in a space of forty-four years, and to have gained either eighteen or thirteen victories. Besides these he wrote elegies, and his satiric dramas are said to have possessed merit equal to that of his tragedies.

Seven tragedies are still extant, which all formed parts of connected trilogies; for Sophocles was the first who exhibited as a trilogy three tragedies, which had no connection.

The earliest of these dramas is the "Persians," exhibited B.C. 472.[4] It formed the second tragedy in a trilogy, of which the "Phineas" was the first, and the "Glaucus Pontius" was the third. It is the only historical play which we possess, and its subject was the triumph of Greece over the power of Persia.

"The Seven against Thebes" stands next in chronological order. It connects the destinies of Thebes with the terrible curse pronounced by Œdipus on "Eteocles and Polynices," and fulfilled in their unnatural and deadly strife. It is the second in a trilogy of which the third was the "Eleusinians," and the first is unknown. There is nothing, perhaps, which so strikingly proves the pathetic superiority of Sophocles to Æschylus as a comparison of the Antigone of this drama with the heroine of Sophocles.

---

[1] Müller's Hist. of Lit. p. 335. [2] Choeph. 721.
[3] Suidas, s. v. and Vit. Æsch. [4] Clinton's Fasti Hellenici.

The next trilogy embodied the history of the house of Danaus. The first and last plays are lost, but the second was the extant play of the "Suppliants." Although deficient in dramatic interest, its choral odes are of great beauty.

In the "Prometheus Bound" a tritagonistes is introduced, an improvement which is due to Sophocles; this, therefore, marks it as one of Æschylus's latest compositions. The first of this trilogy was the "Prometheus, the Fire-bringer," the third the "Prometheus Unbound."

It is difficult to reconcile the plot of this drama with the religious submission and devotion to the will of the Supreme Being, which characterizes Æschylus. It appeals to our sympathies more pathetically than any other of his tragedies, and yet they are against Zeus and on the side of his victim. Terror is excited by the fearful punishment which has overtaken stubborn resistance and defiance of Zeus, and is heightened by the Salvator Rosa-like scenery which is so sublimely described; but pity is also awakened in behalf of the friend of man, who suffers because of his benevolence.

Prometheus the Titan, who represents man's inventive intellect, has doubtless, in the opening drama, blessed man with the gift of fire and all those arts of life which would accompany such a gift, as well as those blessings of which fire may be considered a mythical representation; but intellectual eminence, unchecked and uncontrolled, has led to arrogance, presumption, and impiety.

In the second play, Prometheus' punishment has commenced. He is chained to the bare scathed rocks of Caucasus. Though severe, his punishment is deserved; he has sinned, and will not make submission. The reasonings and persuasions of Oceanus and his daughters, even of the god Hermes himself, are all in vain; he still daringly braves the wrathful thunderbolts of Zeus.

Still his strong will and his dauntless and unbending spirit command our respect, and produce a conviction that his sin is not such as to awaken indignation, but the error of a great mind. Hence the skill with which Æschylus has combined his religious lesson with the dramatic interest which must be on the side of suffering. We sympathize with the resolution of Prometheus, although we feel that he is in error, and at the same time we are convinced that the authority of Zeus must, at all risks, be maintained.

The last three plays which are extant fortunately form a complete trilogy. It is the last which he exhibited; the date of it is B. C. 458.[1] The legend which it embodies is that of Orestes, and the three dramas which form it are "Agamemnon," "Choephori," and "Eumenides."

The subject of the "Agamemnon" is the sin and punishment of that monarch. His sin is ambition, his punishment ruin and death in the moment of triumph and prosperity. In the furtherance of his ambitious views, he has been regardless of human life (πολύκτονος),[2] and has, by the sacrifice of his daughter Iphigenia, shown himself insensible to natural affection. Hence, in this play contrast is the chief beauty. The splendor of his conquest, the wealth of the royal house to which he belongs, are painted in glowing colors,[3] in order to make his fall appear more striking and terrible. But besides his own sin, ancestral guilt presses heavily upon him. Cassandra, in her prophetic vision, beholds the shades of the murdered children of Thyestes, and connects this tale of horror with the approaching catastrophe. Ægisthus, too, according to the laws of blood-guilt, is the appropriate avenger, for he is a son of Thyestes.

Although the sins of Agamemnon are sufficient to vindicate the justice of heaven, there is nothing to palliate the horrible crime of Clytemnestra. We cannot sympathize with her first jealousy of Cassandra, for, as an adulteress, she has forfeited all title to sympathy, and we know that this is not her real motive, but that the deed was premeditated long before, as the line of telegraphic signals had been posted by her orders.

Clytemnestra has nothing feminine in her character—we scarcely remember that she is woman. She is a compound of the worst vices, lust, cruelty and subtlety. She murders her husband under the mask of conjugal love, and, when the deed is done, her moral sense is so depraved, that she defends the act by cunning sophistry.

In the "Choephori," remorse begins at length to exert its

[1] Clinton's Fasti Hellenici.   [2] Verse 460.
[3] Agam. 934, 1010.; also Choeph. 788.

power. Like Lady Macbeth, Clytemnestra is tortured by horrible dreams, and seeks to appease the manes of her murdered
husband by offerings at his tomb. She dreams that she has
given birth to a serpent, and suckled it with her blood. Orestes,
at the command of Apollo, and threatened, if disobedient, with
the furies of his father, enters the palace in disguise, pretending
to bring the news that he is dead. Ægisthus is first slain, and
Orestes then meets Clytemnestra, his sword still recking with the
blood of her paramour. The ensuing scene is deeply affecting;
she appeals to him by a mother's love; he hesitates—but only
for a moment. They disappear: soon the palace doors open, and,
behold, the guilty pair sleep side by side, the sleep of death.
They have kept their oath—in death they are not divided.

God's slow and sure revenge against murder most unnatural,
has taken effect, and its terrible nature is enhanced by the twofold character in which Orestes appears, as his father's avenger,
and his mother's murderer.

Firmly persuaded, as Orestes is, that he is acting in obedience
to the command of Loxias, he cannot still the remorseful voice
of conscience, until the unnatural bloodshed is expiated and
atoned for.[1] Visions of the angry "hounds" of his mother flit
around him, invisible to other eyes. They weep tears of blood,
and seem so numerous as to fill all space. They drive him from
his native land, and force him to be an exile until he has obtained
purification.

This catastrophe prepares us for the opening of the "Eumenides;" it is the link which connects the action of the two plays
with one another.

The "Eumenides" opens with the appearance of the terrified
Pythoness, who announces[2] that the holy shrine is occupied by a
suppliant, whose head and sword drop blood, and that female
forms, like Gorgons and Harpies, black, and distilling from their
eyes loathsome rheum, are slumbering around him. The shade
of Clytemnestra appears, and awakes them, and they find, that
whilst they slept, their victim has, under the protection of
Apollo, and guidance of Hermes, escaped to Athens.

The scene now changes to the temple of Pallas, in the Athe-

<hr/>

[1] Cheoph. 1043.   [2] Verse 34, κ. τ. λ.

nian Acropolis. The judges are set; the cause is pleaded; the ballot taken; Pallas establishes the principle of Athenian law, that if the votes are equal, the defendant is acquitted. The result is equality, and Pallas, by one white ball, acquits the defendant. Orestes then departs with expressions of gratitude to Pallas, Loxias, and Zeus Soter, and promises everlasting respect and friendship between Argos and Athens.

The calm wisdom of Pallas appeases the frantic wrath of the Furies. She promises they shall be henceforth worshipped at Athens, under the milder name of Eumenides, or the gracious deities, and they declare that they will bless the land which owns her for its patron.

This trilogy is full of symbolism. The power of faith, and of the consciousness of obedience to a divine command, to lull for a time the strings of an uneasy conscience, is represented by the Furies slumbering, for a time, in the sacred shrine of Apollo, just as the Furies themselves symbolize the remorseful terrors of a guilty conscience, which pursue the sinner who has not made his peace with God and man. But this calm is temporary and imperfect; conscience will awaken, nor can there be perfect peace, unless there is a sense of acquittal, justification, and reconciliation with God. Whence Æschylus derived this sublime philosophy, it is impossible to say. Cicero asserts that he was a Pythagorean; probably these truths which speak so naturally to the conscious promptings of the human heart, were drawn from a much wider study of Greek philosophy than merely one system, and from a still deeper, and more comprehensive study, that of human nature itself.

Again, does not the remorse of Orestes teach the poet's belief, that where the Deity has implanted in man moral instincts and natural affections, this evidence of his will cannot be violated with impunity under any circumstances? Revelation and nature constitute equal obligations. Happy are we, who are taught to find, not only no antagonism, but a strict accordance between these two laws, which proceed from one and the same great Author.

The ballot of Pallas symbolizes the principle of mercy; mercy, not from man alone, but from God. Where man cannot decide, the voice of Heaven interferes, and declares that Heaven forgives, and therefore man must pardon also.

But it is universally allowed, that this trilogy, and especially the concluding tragedy, had a political object. Æschylus felt it a sacred duty to support the ancient institutions of his country, as of divine origin, and therefore of divine right. He was aristocratic and conservative, as Sophocles was attached to the cause of freedom and progress.

The court of Areopagus was not only venerable for its antiquity, and the solemn nature of those causes which were taken cognizance of by this tribunal; but from its constitution, although much altered, it was still the stronghold of the aristocratic party. Hence it presented a great obstacle to the liberal policy of Pericles. Shortly before the time when this trilogy was exhibited (Ol. lxxx. 2), Ephialtes, an eminent general and statesman of his party, proposed a bill, the provisions of which struck a death-blow to this court of judicature. The result of it would have been, according to Cicero,[1] to render absolute the political power of the Ecclesia. Before this bill (ψήφισμα) became ratified by law (νόμος), Æschylus exhibited this trilogy, in order, if possible, to stem the tide of democracy. Party spirit raged high, and although the opposition was ineffectual, and the measure was ultimately carried, the proposer himself was assassinated, and the murderers were never discovered. This opposition on the part of Æschylus is perfectly in accordance with his general political principles. In an earlier period of his life, he had been a supporter of Aristides, and an opponent of Themistocles, at the time when they were at the head of the two opposite parties, afterwards led by Cimon and Pericles. Agreeably to these political sentiments, he extols, in the "Persians," the exploits of Aristides, as compared with those of Themistocles,[2] whilst Herodotus,[3] whose political bias was evidently towards the democratical party, gives a somewhat different coloring to the transaction.

Such was the primary political object of the "Eumenides;" it also had two others, secondary and subordinate. The promise of Orestes to maintain inviolable friendship with Athens, implied a

---

[1] Cic. de Rep. i. 27.   [2] See Müller's Eum.; Pers. 439, &c.
[3] Herod. viii. 95.

recommendation on the part of the poet to cement a union and alliance between Athens and Argus, and the speech of Pallas (v. 375) is an attempt to rest on mythological grounds the claim of the Athenians to the disputed territory of the Troad.

The passages of which the following are translations, will serve as specimens of the innumerable noble sentiments and beautiful ideas which delight the reader of the Æschylean tragedy.

In the first chorus of the Agamemnon, he speaks of the struggle between the duties of the chieftain and the affection of a father:—

> An evil lot is mine to choose,
> Hard fate obedience to refuse,
>   Hard fate to slay my child !
> My home's bright ornament and pride;
> 'Twere hard if at the altar's side
> A father's hand were crimson-dyed !—
>   With virgin gore defiled.
> Still to whichever part I lean,
> Is sorrow's threatening aspect seen;
> How may I leave my true allies?
>   How quit the host I lead?
>
>   *Agam.* 199 (ANSTICE).

A few verses further on he describes the behavior of the victim.

> Her pleading eyes shot Pity's dart,
> To rankle in each murderer's heart;
> Like form by painter's fancy dreamed,
> So pale, so fair, so still she seemed.
>
>   *Agam.* 239 (ANSTICE).

The purity of divine justice, and the certainty of retribution, are favorite topics.

> For vainly wealth's proud bulwarks tower,
> When man, in insolence of power,
> Justice, thy law disdains to know,
> And dares, with impious foot, thine altar overthrow.
>
>   *   *   *   *   *
>
> Yet treasured long, the meed of crime
> Shall whelm the wretch in after time. .
>
>   *Agam.* 360 (ANSTICE).

Bow down to Justice—mortal man, attend!
Low at her spotless altar bend,
Nor spurn with impious foot, allured by gain,
  Her holy shrine. For retribution's day,
Fraught with the bitter certain meed of pain,
  Waits but its time the guilty to repay.
Eumen. 488 (ANSTICE).

  Falsely, I ween, the sages told,
  In parables they framed of old,
  That glad success and future high,
  Beget a fatal progeny.

   *   *   *

  *   *   *   *

  For ne'er to righteous halls,
  Though wealth adorn their master's lot,
    Such evil offspring falls ;
  'Tis guilt alone that teems with sorrow.
Agam. 710 (ANSTICE).

'Tis true that Justice oft is found
The smoke-dimmed cottage walls around,
  Shedding her purest light.
In gilded palaces, where gain
Leaves on its master's hand a stain,
  She speeds her holy flight,
    Disdainful stalking by,
    In sullen majesty,
Nor smiles on wealth that bears thy stamp, Iniquity !
Agam. 750 (ANSTICE).

The following are descriptions of Menelaus' regrets and Helen's eauty:—

  Nor now delighted will he trace
  Her statue's imitative grace ;
  The dull cold stone may ill supply
  The living richness of her eye ;
  The dream, with fancy's coloring warm,
  Departs an unsubstantial form,
  Glides through the arms that fain would clasp,
  And mocks the lover's eager grasp,
  Then spreads aloft its airy wings,
  That wait on slumber's wanderings.
Agam. 409 (ANSTICE).

The fable of the lion's cub, gentle and playful at first, afterwards displaying its natural instinct for blood, introduces subjoined description of Helen:—

> Bride of Paris, such art thou,
> To Ilium when thy venturous prow,
> First bore thee o'er the ocean brine,
> What melting loveliness was thine?
> A spirit like the breathless calm
> When summer's gentle air is balm;
> Eyes darting many a tender glance,
> An unassuming elegance;
> Whose quiet charms new beauty lent
> To grace each costly ornament.
> Love's very flower whose bloom invites,
> Yet stings the gazer it delights.
>
> *Agam.* 700.

CHAPTER IV.

SOPHOCLES, born B. C. 495.

SOPHOCLES COMPARED WITH ÆSCHYLUS.—HIS BIRTH, PARENTAGE, AND EDUCATION.—
DRAMATIC SUCCESS.—APPOINTED ONE OF THE TEN GENERALS.—UNFITNESS FOR THE
OFFICE.—HIS POLITICAL SENTIMENTS AND CONDUCT.—THE UNNATURAL CONDUCT OF
HIS SON IOPHON.—CHORUS IN THE ŒDIPUS COLONEUS.—HIS DEATH.—EPIGRAMS OF
SIMONIDES AND SIMMIAS.—CHARACTER OF HIS POETRY.—THE ETHICAL CHARACTER
OF THE SOPHOCLEAN DRAMA.—HIS DRAMATIC REFORMS.—THE NUMBER OF HIS COM-
POSITIONS.—THE CHRONOLOGICAL ORDER OF THOSE EXTANT.—ANTIGONE.—ELECTRA.
—THE GRANDEUR OF ÆSCHYLUS CONTRASTED WITH THE BEAUTY OF SOPHOCLES.

ALTHOUGH in the grand and lofty conceptions of genius
Æschylus was never surpassed, there are other points of excellence in which his successor Sophocles proved himself a worthy
competitor.   Sophocles had not the same lyrical power, but he
had more harmony and sweetness.   His characters have not that
awful and superhuman vastness, but they are more interesting,
and appeal more to our sympathies and affections, and in the
construction of his plots he displays more dramatic skill, and
approaches more nearly to that complex nature which is, perhaps,
the only point in which modern tragedy is superior to that of
Greece.   He gave a finish and polish both to the language and
poetry of the drama, without lowering the moral standard or
impairing the dignity with which it was invested by Æschylus.

Sophocles,[1] for a history of whose life there exist few authentic
data, was an Athenian citizen, a native of the bright and cheerful
suburban village of Colonus,[2] the natural beauty of which he himself has immortalized.   According to Suidas, he was born about
the seventy-third Olympiad ; according to the "Parian Chronicle," in B. C. 496.[3]   But the date usually received is B. C. 495,

---

[1] Suidas, s. v.   [2] Œdip. Colon.   [3] Olym. 71, 2.

16

thirty years subsequent to the birth of Æschylus. He was the son of Sophilus, who is said to have been a smith or a sword-cutler. If so, the liberal education which Sophocles received, and the high military command with which he was entrusted, prove that the commercial spirit of the Athenian republic did not despise the social position of the manufacturer, and, probably, in the case of Sophilus, as in that of the father of Demosthenes, it was a path which led to wealth. The beauty and gracefulness of his person equalled the elegance of his mind,[1] and he received a liberal education, including dancing and music. In the latter of these two accomplishments he was instructed, when very young, by Lamprus, a celebrated musician. In the public rejoicings which took place after the victory of Salamis, Sophocles was chosen, for his skill in these two arts, to lead the band of beautiful youths who danced around the trophy, and he himself sang the pæan to the accompaniment of his lyre. He was then but fifteen; so young did he become the servant of the Muses.

At the age of twenty-seven he first came forward as a tragic poet, and contested the prize with Æschylus, who had now maintained his superiority for thirty-one years. The successful play is said to have been the "Triptolemus." It has perished, and therefore we have no opportunity of determining its merits; the decision, however, might have been a fair one, although Æschylus considered it as unjust, for Cimon, whom the archon appointed as umpire, would, from his political bias, and, possibly, from the literary tastes in which he had been brought up, have been inclined to admire Æschylus.

For twenty-eight years nothing is heard of him, but it may be assumed, that during this period he was never vanquished in a dramatic contest; for although his young rival, Euripides, gained his first victory B. C. 441, yet it does not appear that his adversary was Sophocles.

In B. C. 440, he exhibited the most beautiful of his extant tragedies, the "Antigone." So delighted were the Athenians, not only with its dramatic excellence, but its political principles, that they elected him one of the ten generals for the year. This

[1] Athen. i. 37.

proved by no means a suitable reward for the great poet.[1] The active business of military command was distasteful to one who was of a social and self-indulgent temper, and who enjoyed the calm repose of literary leisure. It is related in a passage of Athenæus, that his colleague, Pericles, declared him to be a good poet, but a bad general: and the same anecdote, which paints in lively colors the sallies of his wit, hints that he was as unfitted for the diplomatic and civil functions attached to the office of strategus; for that as a politician he was neither sagacious nor energetic, but one of your simple, honest Athenians. Plutarch also relates that he modestly confessed his own inferiority, and that when, in a council of war, he was asked for his opinion before Nicias, he replied, "I am oldest in age, but you in wisdom."

It was during the expedition against the aristocratical party in Samos, a war so congenial to his principles, as well as to those of Pericles, that he formed his intimacy with the Athenian-minded Herodotus, who, in his admiration for the literature of his adopted country, seems so especially imbued with the spirit of Sophocles.

He was a steady supporter of liberal principles, and the only instance of apparent inconsistency discoverable in his character is when during the revolutionary period he was instrumental in establishing the Council of Four Hundred.[2] But it may be easily conceived, that in those times of fearful anarchy he thought such a measure, though abstractedly unconstitutional, was rendered necessary by the exigency of the crisis, and the only one likely to arrest the progress of affairs to a bloody revolution. Numerous sentiments in his plays bear witness to his attachment to the cause of freedom, and his whole life is one continued proof of his patriotism. He could not, as many other poets did in seasons of trouble, seek the protection of foreign despots, and live dependent on the favor and patronage of tyrants. From his birth to his death, he never left his country, except in the public service. The last work of his old age sang the praises of his native village, and is evidently dictated by a warm affection for his country.

---

[1] Athen. xiii. 81.   [2] Thuc. vii. 1; Arist. Rhet. iii. 18.

An affecting episode saddens the conclusion of the aged poet's life.

Iophon was the eldest of his five sons; and he, jealous of a son of his brother Ariston, who bore the poet's name, and fearing that Sophocles would bequeath to him a large share of his property, accused his aged father of mental imbecility. The only answer which the poet made to this unnatural charge was the recitation of the beautiful chorus in the " Œdipus Coloneus," which he had but lately written. His judges, struck with admiration, unanimously gave their verdict in his favor, and the poet returned to his home in triumph.

It is impossible to read this truthful ode without realizing the language[1] in which the aged poet describes the loveliness of his birth-place ;—one can imagine the triumphant answer which its recitation formed to the slander of his undutiful son. It seems as though when we read we walked with Sophocles in this fair spot, the fairest round Athens, and doubtless his favorite haunt. We are inclined to exclaim with Horace :—

> Auditis ? an me ludit amabilis
> Insania ? audire et videor pios
> Errare per lucos, amœnæ
> Quos et aquæ subeunt et auræ.

We seem to hear the tuneful yet sad voice of the nightingale hidden in the dark green ivy and the clustering vine purpled with fruit, beneath whose shade sports the young Dionysus, surrounded by a revel rout of nymphs, his young nurses. Our feet press the crocus and the narcissus, and our ears are soothed by the murmurs of the glassy Cephisus.

How must the patriotic feelings of the Athenians have been moved when in the very sight of that hill where the contest took place between their divine benefactors and tutelary deities,[2] and of this sea which was the source of their glory and their wealth, and which enabled them to enjoy the fruits of all countries as though they were their own,[3] the chorus poured forth its concluding strain :—

[1] Œdip. Col. 694. [2] Ovid. Met. vi. 70.
[3] Thucyd. i.

Son of Saturn old, whose sway
Stormy winds and waves obey,
Thine be honor's well-earned meed,
Tamer of the champing steed ;
First he wore on Attic plain
Bit of steel and curbing rein ;
Oft too o'er the waters blue,
Athens strain thy laboring crew,
Practiced hands the bark are plying,
Oars are bending, spray is flying,
Sunny waves beneath them glancing,
Sportive naiads round them dancing,
With their hundred feet in motion,
Twinkling 'mid the foam of ocean.

Œdip. Col. v. 712 (Anstice).

Of his death there are different traditions ; some say, and this legend is recorded in the following epigram of Simonides,[1]

'Εσβέσθης, γηραιὲ Σοφόκλεες, ἄνθος ἀοιδῶν,
Οἰνωπὸν Βάκχου βότρυν ἐρεπτόμενος,

Anthol. vii. 20,

that he was killed by swallowing a grape stone ; others that he expired whilst publicly reciting his " Antigone ;" others that he died of joy on gaining a dramatic victory.[2] These are poetic legends ; but, as all agree in connecting his death with his career as a poet, he probably died when his intellect and poetical talent were still unimpaired, in the exercises of his beloved art, in extreme old age, without disease and without suffering.

Καλῶς ἐτελεύτησ' οὐδὲν ὑπομείνας κακόν.

Phrynichus.

A beautiful epigram by Simmias, the Theban, is preserved in the Greek Anthology, of which the following translation is well known :—

'Ηρέμ' ὑπὲρ τύμβοιο, κ. τ. λ.

Wind, gentle evergreen, to form a shade
Around the tomb where Sophocles is laid ;
Sweet ivy, wind thy boughs and intertwine
With blushing roses and the clustering vine ;
Thus will thy lasting leaves with beauties hung,
Prove grateful emblems of the lays he sung,
Whose soul exalted by the god of wit,
Among the Muses and the Graces writ.

---

[1] Simonides, Anth. Gr. vii. 20. [2] Vit. Anonym.

In the tragedies of Sophocles is seen the perfection of the Greek drama; for although Aristotle pronounces Euripides to be the most tragic of poets;[1] and Longinus[2] pronounces him to have been unequalled in his tragic representations of love and madness, yet no tragic poet equalled Sophocles in combining dignity, purity, pathos, and piety with the most refined genius and the highest poetical talent. The sweetness of his language obtained for him the appellation of the " Bee."[3] In the due proportion of the choral part to the dramatic, in the artificial construction of his plots, in metrical harmony and in polished diction, Sophocles developed and perfected the excellences of Æschylus; he so moulded dramatic poetry, and accommodated it to human feelings, as to produce the greatest possible effect on the heart, and to afford the purest possible delight to a refined taste. Inferior to Æschylus in boldness of conception, his softer pictures are more soothing to the imagination. The thrilling supernatural interest of Æschylus was adapted to enthral the mind of Greece in the infancy of dramatic literature, just as the unreal wonders of the fairy tale and the romance delight childhood; but a more educated and manly mind is better satisfied with scenes which have an air of reality, and may have their counterpart in actual life. We admire and stand in awe of the heroes of Æschylus: we sympathize with, and feel for, those of Sophocles.

In order to pity or sympathize, Aristotle ingeniously observes, we ought to be able to imagine that the case which appeals to our feelings may possibly be our own. This condition is necessary in order to enable us fully to realize it to ourselves in all its features.

The characters of Æschylus are of too superhuman a mould for this; we can never look upon them even when they are mortals, as standing in any relation to ourselves. They are either above man in excellence, or below him in wickedness.

But it is not so with those of Sophocles. We can realize to ourselves an Œdipus struggling with a fate, which is at last too strong for him. We can feel for him, although his own faults and his own actions contribute their part to the fulfilment of the

[1] Arist. Poet. xxvi.   [2] Long. xv. 3.   [3] Suidas, s. v.

prophecies.   Even his curse, which works such woe on his undutiful sons, like that of Shakspeare's Lear, is not inconsistent with
the ungovernable wildness of human passion.   The calm and
dignified submission to the will of Heaven, with which Œdipus
meets his fate, is that of a good and pious man, but it is not
beyond the reach of human virtue.   We can feel for the timidity
of Ismene, and the unselfish heroism of Antigone; great as it is,
it is not too high for the hope of successful imitation.   In like
manner, all can sympathize with the patience and endurance of
Philoctetes, his hoping against hope in his desert solitude, with
the jealous affections of Deianira, and the honest but mistaken
pride of Ajax.

In neither of the tragedians do morals hold a higher place than
in Sophocles.   He is essentially ethical.   Interesting as his plots
are, the interest forms but a small part of their merit.   In every
one, he sets before his eyes the holy object of instilling a veneration for the will of heaven, and a respect for the laws and sanctions
of immutable justice.

Sophocles[1] applied the powers of mind to the technical detail
of his art, and therefore comes forward as a dramatic reformer,
as well as a poet.   He introduced the third actor; he increased
the number of the chorus from twelve to fifteen, and thus rendered it more effective, whilst by shortening the choral odes he
diminished the interruptions to the dramatic action; at the same
time he lengthened the dramatic portion.   The standard length
of tragedies had, at the time when Sophocles flourished, become
considerably greater.   The only extant play of Æschylus which
is of the same length as those of Sophocles, is the "Agamemnon."
This alteration in length is attributed by Suidas[2] to Aristarchus,
who first exhibited about the middle of the fifth century before
Christ.

Sophocles is said to have written a prose essay on the chorus,
in answer to the theories of Thespis and Chœrilus.   He was evidently the first to see, that in reality choruses should only be
considered as periods of rest and repose to refresh the attention
of the audience; for in his latter dramas his choruses begin to
have far less reference to the immediate action of the play, and

---

[1] Antig. 449.   [2] Suidas, s. v.

are simply beautiful specimens of lyric poetry. The number of dramas, including tragedies and satiric dramas, which he wrote and exhibited was a hundred and thirteen, of which seven remain, comprehending most probably his finest compositions. With respect to the order in which they were produced, nothing certain is known, except that the date of the "Philoctetes" is B. C. 409, and that of the "Œdipus Coloneus" B. c. 401; this play having been exhibited by the younger Sophocles as a posthumous work of his father's. The date of the "Antigone," which is probably the earliest of the extant tragedies, is placed by Clinton and others B. c. 440. The following chronological order has been suggested by O. Müller,[1]—"Antigone," "Electra," "Trachiniæ," "Œdipus Rex," "Ajax," "Philoctetes," "Œdipus Coloneus."

The two leading ideas which pervade the beautiful tragedy of the "Antigone," are the supremacy of law and the sacredness of that affection which binds families together. These two ideas are painted in the strongest colors. The duties arising from these principles are represented in the play as in direct antagonism to one another; it seems scarcely possible to fulfil the just claims of both without violating the natural dictates of conscience. There appears to be no middle course open between insubordination and impiety. The moral lesson then, which the poet deduces from these conflicting difficulties is, that great as both these principles are, human ordinances must not press their claims upon the conscience to an extreme. The claims of the state to the obedience of its citizens must be kept in subordination to the law of natural justice, or else it becomes tyranny, and as such, subject to divine vengeance. He who, like Antigone, firmly determines never to swerve from obedience to God's will written in the heart, which alone gives force and sanction to human laws, must be ready to suffer martyrdom for these high principles, and submit to earthly sorrow and suffering in the cause of religion. The fate of Antigone is not a punishment, it is the penalty which, by God's appointment, awaits those who have bravery and faith enough to prefer God to man, when they come in competition. The lesson it teaches is, that such is the fiery trial of virtue, that often we cannot choose whom we will

[1] Müller's Hist. Greek Lit. xxiv. 3.

serve, without being prepared to suffer for our moral consistency. The fate of Cleon, on the other hand, is punishment; it falls heavily on his guilty head, as retribution almost invariably does in this life, and, as is generally the case, it involves in one common destruction the innocent and the guilty.

In the "Antigone" the tie of family affection is exhibited in its most sacred form. Reverence for the dead, and the duties resulting from this reverence, formed, it is well known, an important part of Greek religion.

The instinctive belief in a future state, and in a higher and more perfect condition of being than was enjoyed on earth, elevated the departed hero, or even the manes of a beloved relative, almost to the rank of a deity. The long, perhaps the eternal communion with each other, to be enjoyed by the departed, connects Antigone with a far stronger tie to her lost brother, than to all that remain on earth. "Far longer," she exclaims, "shall I have to please those below, than those here."

The poets were deeply impressed with a feeling of the duties due to the dead; it was this impression probably which induced Homer in his "Iliad," and Sophocles in his "Ajax," to prolong their respective poems beyond that which otherwise would naturally have been the true and appropriate catastrophe. The character of Antigone may be thought in parts harsh, severe, unfeminine; but conscious heroism, when disappointed of meeting with sympathy where it has a right to expect it, is naturally, on the first impulse, severe; and no one can read the sad and affecting lament of Antigone, when led on her last path to death, her touching appeals, her sense of unpitied loveliness, and not trace therein all the tenderest feelings of woman's nature.

The beauty of the "Electra" consists in the concentration of the entire interest in the person of the heroine. She is the point to which all the rays converge, the principal figure round which all the others are grouped. It is impossible to forget her for a moment, she can never be absent from the thoughts of the reader. The grand idea which had possession of the mind of Æschylus, in his corresponding play, was divine vengeance, consummated by the deaths of Æschylus and Clytemnestra. This view was necessary to maintaining the connection of events in the Orestean tri-

logy. Sophocles was not fettered by such necessity, he had introduced the custom of exhibiting three unconnected plays, instead of
a connected trilogy. He was therefore at liberty to view in an independent light the legend which furnished him, as well as Æschylus, with a subject for tragedy. Although, therefore, the scene
in which the body of Clytemnestra is shown to Ægisthus, and he
finds, to his horror, that it is his paramour, and not Orestes, is,
without exception, the finest, and the most elaborately worked up,
of any which he wrote, the death of Clytemnestra is not the great
object to which the reader looks with interest. He is absorbed
in the contemplation of Electra's character, and the effect which
the action of the play will produce upon her mind. He watches
the workings of her mind, her strong and irrepressible impulses
of hatred against the sin of her mother, and therefore against her
mother also, excited to the utmost pitch, by the insults heaped
upon her by the murderess and the usurper. The analysis, so to
speak, of her nature, agitated by these strong emotions, forms
the subject which the poet proposed to himself to paint, and which
he has delineated so minutely and exactly. The first origin, as
well as all the consequent motives to the terrible deed of vengeance, proceed from her. She it was who saved her infant brother
Orestes from death, and from her unextinguishable hatred of the
murderer, and unwearied devotion to the holy cause of avenging
her beloved father's death, and consequently her continual exhor-
tations to her brother to return, all the incidents of the tragedy
are developed. Like Antigone, Electra is a model of constancy
in her purpose, though, unlike the constancy of Antigone, hers
proceeds from impulse, rather than from a sense of duty; both
are high-minded, but Electra, from having all her life so much responsibility thrown upon her, is less feminine. These observations
on two of the Sophoclean tragedies will furnish the reader with
a general idea of the mode in which this poet generally treats his
subjects, and the analysis already given of the tragedies of Æschylus affords a sufficient specimen of the model after which a Greek
tragedy was usually constructed.

In minor points it is easy to contrast the serene beauty of
Sophocles' mind with the terrible grandeur of Æschylus. In
both the "Choephori" and the "Electra," Clytemnestra is warned

by a dream; but in the former, she imagines that she has brought forth a serpent, and suckled it with her blood; in the latter, the sceptre of Agamemnon, again restored to life, is planted on the domestic hearth, gives forth buds and blossoms, and becomes a great tree, which fills the whole land. Æschylus paints throughout, the progress and completion of God's vengeance upon the murderers; Sophocles traces the transition of Electra's mind from grief and despair, to joy and thankfulness, at her unexpected reunion to her lost brother. In the "Choephori," Clytemnestra only appeals to a mother's love, in order to deprecate the avenger's wrath; in the "Electra," the mother's feelings at first burst forth, and stifle, though only for a moment, the exultations of triumphant ambition, when she hears the son is dead for whom she felt a mother's pains. Even the trifling circumstance that Chrysothemis, the gentle unresisting daughter, is employed by her mother to bring the offerings of the murderess to the tomb of the murdered hero, rather than Electra, who loathes her wickedness, shows that Sophocles avoided those strong contrasts which shock, because they are scarcely natural.

CHAPTER V.

EURIPIDES, born B. C. 480.

THE THREE TRAGIC POETS FORM SUCCESSIVE ERAS IN LITERARY TASTE.—THESE ARE
ANALOGOUS TO THE PROGRESS MADE BY THE INDIVIDUAL MIND.—EURIPIDES, HIS LIFE
AND CHARACTER.—RELIGIOUS, POLITICAL AND PHILOSOPHICAL SENTIMENTS UNPOPU-
LAR.—UNJUSTLY SLANDERED.—HIS SUPPOSED HATRED OF THE FEMALE SEX.—STORY
OF HIS MARRIAGES AND DIVORCES.—HIS EXILE, DEATH, AND EPITAPH.—THE AGE OF
EURIPIDES A PHILOSOPHICAL ERA.—THE EFFECTS OF THIS ON HIS POETRY.—WAS
EURIPIDES THE MOST TRAGIC OF POETS?—HIS PROLOGUES.—THE REAL OBJECTIONS
TO THEM.—THE USE WHICH HE MAKES OF DIVINE INTERPOSITION.—HIS POLITICAL
PRINCIPLES.—HIS FONDNESS FOR SPECIAL PLEADING.—HIS LYRIC POWER.—MONODIES.
—CHRONOLOGICAL LIST OF PLAYS.—ALCESTIS.—MEDEA.—HECUBA.—ELECTRA.—CY-
CLOPS.—PASSAGES FROM THE TRAGEDIES OF EURIPIDES.—ION.—ACHÆUS —AGATHON.
—EUPHORION.—IOPHON.—THE YOUNGER SOPHOCLES AND EURIPIDES.—CHÆREMON.—
THEODECTES.

So great are the absolute excellences of Euripides, and yet so
manifest his defects, as compared with Æschylus and Sophocles,
that it is difficult to determine whether his dramas show an
advance or decline in tragic poetry. Thus much at least is plain,
that the characteristic features of his writings mark a new era in
the public taste, whilst an independent boldness of thought which
pervades them, proves that he was not one to imitate even the
beauties and perfections of others, or to belong to a school, but
able and determined to strike out a new line for himself.

The natural law of progress in literary taste may be traced in
the works of the three great tragic poets. They seem, as the
leading minds of their age succeeding each other at such intervals
as to occupy amongst them the period of three generations, to be
the representatives and directors of popular taste in its gradual
growth and development. The mysterious and supernatural
wonders of Æschylus are succeeded by the dignified and heroic,
but nevertheless natural, characters of Sophocles; and these, in
their turn, give place to the romance of private every-day life,

the unexaggerated picture of manners, in which the human heart
and the affections which influence it in its domestic relations,
constitute the leading subject. A view of human nature is
exhibited, which shocks us at first as embodying a low standard,
but which is in fact not below reality. In it one of the great
moving springs of action is sexual love; it unites tenderness with
weakness—the pathos of the tragic with the wit of the comic
poet, and is seasoned with a shrewd and subtile knowledge of
human nature. It is not even averse to the brilliant sophisms
of a selfish and worldly philosophy. These are the principal
features of the Euripidean drama, which distinguish it from
that of Æschylus and Sophocles. Sophocles, it has been said,
represented men as they ought to be, Euripides as they really
are.[1] The judgment which would prefer Euripides to Æschylus
and Sophocles may be a degenerate one, but it is clear that such
is the usual progress of national literary taste, through its three
phases of unreal mysticism, historic truth, and romantic fiction.
The individual mind exhibits the same phenomena in the growth
and unfolding of the imaginative powers, which are, of course,
those cultivated by poetry. The child delights first in the supernatural wonders of the fairy tale, next he descends from the
beings of another world, and takes an interest in the heroes, and
kings, and princes, as recorded in biography and history; and it
requires time before he can take interest in the love scenes and
every-day occurrences of a novel.

The birth of Euripides took place in troubled but glorious
times. When the Persian invasion threatened Greece, Themistocles advised his countrymen to leave their native city, and to
trust to their fleet for protection.[2] Amongst the exiles the
parents of Euripides, Mnesarchus and Clito, left their home in
Attica and fled to Salamis. They had previously, according to
Suidas,[3] migrated from Bœotia. The bitter satire of Aristophanes,[4] who hated the degenerate taste and false philosophy of
Euripides, accused his mother of being an herb-woman of bad
character, but there is no foundation for this slander. On the
contrary, the probability is that his parents were persons of rank

[1] Arist. Poet. xxv.   [2] Herod. vii. 143.
[3] Suidas, s. v.   [4] Aves, Eq. 19, et passim.

and consideration. He is said to have been born on the same day on which the battle of Salamis was fought. If so, a remarkable coincidence links together the three great poets, for Æschylus, as has been stated, a warrior in the prime of life, distinguished himself on that glorious day, and Sophocles, then a youth of great personal beauty, took part in the public rejoicings with which the victory was celebrated.

In early life he was a painter, and received a complete philosophical education. Prodicus instructed him in rhetoric, Socrates in morals, and Anaxagoras in physics. To this he owed the acuteness of his mind, and the pleasure which he took in indulging his taste for subtile disputation. Although he did not gain a prize until b. c. 441, he is said to have devoted himself to tragic poetry at a very early age, and to have exhibited the "Peliades," in his own name, when he was twenty-five years old.[1]

Few men have suffered more from slander than Euripides. He was of an austere and ascetic temper, and this may have rendered him unpopular with the light-hearted and social Athenians; and his attachment to the new philosophy and the modern system of education, which Aristophanes attacked with all his bitterness, and never failed to bring on all occasions before the public notice, exposed him to hatred and suspicion. We know that party spirit was very violent against him. His belief in the physical system of Anaxagoras, and his consequent rejection of the mythological absurdities of the popular creed, would render him, like his great master Socrates, liable to the vague but easy accusation of impiety.

His political sentiments were likewise unacceptable to the Athenian populace, who were, in fact, the judges of a dramatic poet's capacity, and no sin was visited by them so severely as opposition to the will of the sovereign people. His well-known sentiment,—

'Η γλῶσσ' ὀμώμοχ' ἡ δὲ φρὴν ἀνώμοτος,

"My tongue has sworn, but my mind is unsworn,"[2]

which he may have derived from the sophistical rhetoric of Prodicus, subjected him to a public prosecution. The effect of this

---

[1] Vit. anon.   [2] Hippol. 608; Arist. Rhet. iii. 15.

unpopularity continued during after ages, and Athenæus unjustly stigmatizes him as a man of grossly immoral character. The imputation of his having been an implacable hater of the female sex has also no foundation to rest upon, except the fact, that he attributes so many terrible consequences to the uncontrolled violence of female passion.

His enemies have forgotten and lost sight of the devoted affection of his Antigone and Alcestis, and have pointed to the fearful terms in which he so often depicts female depravity. Unfortunately, the legendary field which furnished subjects for Greek tragedy, was too fruitful in examples of blood-thirsty and profligate females. Perhaps he need not have selected instances of female rather than of male immorality ; but it must be remembered, that it was new to the Greek drama to make love the point on which the interest turned, and, therefore, his attention was directed, more than that of his predecessors, to study the different phases, either bad or good, of female character.

So many inconsistencies occur in the accounts given of his marriages, the infidelities and consequent divorces of his wives, that no dependence can be placed upon them. The common story is, that he first married Chœrilla, who bore him three sons ; that, on her proving unfaithful, he divorced her, and married Melitto, in which connection he was equally unfortunate.

Party feeling drove Euripides (B. c. 408), as it had already driven Æschylus, from Athens, and he sought an asylum at the court of Archelaus, King of Macedon, who treated him with the greatest kindness and respect.

He escaped public odium only to fall a victim to private jealousy. In Macedonia he provoked the envy of two poets, Arrhidæus and Crateuas, and they let loose upon him some savage hounds belonging to the king, who tore him to pieces, at the advanced age of seventy-five,[1] in the year of the disastrous battle of Arginusæ. Another account deals out to him poetical retribution, as a woman-hater, and asserts that he was torn to pieces by women. Archelaus caused him to be buried at Pella. The number of his dramas is said by some to have been seventy-five, by others ninety-two.

[1] B. c. 405, Olym. 93, 3.

The following elegant epigram to his memory, by an anonymous author, is preserved in the "Anthology,"[1] and it has been imitated by Ben Jonson, on Drayton's tomb in Westminster Abbey.

Οὐ σὸν μνῆμα τόδ' ἔστ', Εὐριπίδη, ἀλλὰ σὺ τοῦδε,
Τῇ σῇ γὰρ δόξῃ μνῆμα τόδ' ἀμπέχεται.

> Divine Euripides, this tomb we see
> So fair, is not a monument for thee,
> So much as thou for it; since all will own,
> Thy name and lasting praise adorn the stone.

Such was the life of one who, although during the greater part of his career the contemporary of Sóphocles, belongs, as has already been partially shown, to a new generation, and represents a new phase of thè Athenian mind. The age in which he flourished was one of philosophy rather than of poetry. The warmth of genius was now succeeded by the cold calculations and ingenious subtleties of speculative criticism, and Euripides, whether his was a master mind which led the public taste, or his plays merely an indication of what was the state of the Athenian mind, evidently delighted in the nice distinctions of a sophistical philosophy in brilliant and sharp antitheses, startling paradoxes, hairsplitting arguments, a dexterous use of language, like that of the Athenian law courts, and an affectation of pedantic ornament which Aristophanes considers as characteristic of his style.[2]

An amusing instance of Euripides' love for speculative philosophy is found in the "Menalippe." Menalippe bore two children to Neptune, and hid them in a cow-house. Her father discovered them, and ordered them to be burnt as monsters. She accordingly argues, according to the physical principles of Anaxagoras, that they might be natural, and thus pleads for their preservation.

The philosophical innovations which he introduced, however objectionable, prove him at any rate to have been a man of independent thought and fearless courage. It is said, that, on one occasion, the audience clamorously demanded that a sentiment, in the play which they were witnessing, should be expunged, but the poet came forward, and boldly told them that it was his duty to teach them, not theirs to teach him. Foreigners could

---

[1] Anthol. vii. 46.   [2] Κομψευριπικῶς, Aristoph. Equit. 18.

appreciate the sweetness of his poetry, to which his own country-men were at times insensible, for the suffering relics of Nicias' army in Sicily were released from their bondage, because they recited some verses from his tragedies.

Genius invests its heroes in the brightest colors; it delights to paint them of heroic mould, and to measure them by a higher moral standard than that of ordinary human nature. It forms to itself a chivalrous ideal of characters belonging to historical or mythical ages. Their passions and feelings, though called by the same names, are nobler and more sublime than those which agitate the breasts of those with whom we are in daily intercourse. The philosopher sees that this view is an untruthful one, and therefore curbs his genius and confines himself to the result of his observation and experience. This is the reason for the common-place, unromantic view which Euripides takes of human nature. He does not transport himself into the world of ideal heroism, but brings down gods and heroes to a level with Athenian citizens, with the very auditory which fills the theatre, and witnesses the dramas which he represents.

In the tragedies of Euripides, there is more truth and less poetry. They probably present a fair and just picture of Athe-nian life and manners and modes of thinking. He did not trans-gress the custom of deriving his plots from the usual heroic and mythical sources, but his heroes were no longer the same, except in name, with those of Homer and Æschylus and Sophocles; they argued, disputed, conversed, like Athenian citizens, who had re-ceived their theoretical education in the schools of the philoso-phers, and their practical training in the law courts and the ecclesia. His dramas were unnatural, inasmuch as they did vio-lence to the traditional belief, with which the Athenian mind was imbued, and represented characters, with which they had been familiar from time immemorial, in a different moral garb to that which they had hitherto worn. They were natural, inasmuch as they represented men and women, such as were met with in the intercourse of daily life, in the places of public resort in Athens.

The low moral position which woman so often occupies in the Euripidean tragedy; the proverbial sayings respecting the frailty of the sex; the terrible crimes which he paints, as resulting from

17

lawless love, are consistent with the state of Athenian society; they are indications of woman's social position. The seclusion in which Athenian women of character lived, narrowed their minds; the domestic duties, which alone were supposed to belong to them, rendered a refined education unnecessary. When we find Demosthenes describing the only object of marriage, as being "to have legitimate children, and a trustworthy guardian of one's property," we see at once that an Athenian did not look upon a wife as a companion. A virtuous woman was almost secluded from the occupations and amusements of Athenian life. Those with whom men associated, were of loose morals, violent passions, shrewd intellect, and elegant accomplishments. They were such as Euripides so often describes. His audience were almost entirely men, and therefore they would not only recognize the truth of the picture, but also their vanity would be gratified, by the superiority ascribed by the poet to their own sex.

No one observed these two leading characteristics of Euripides more keenly than Aristophanes. He saw in him the representative and supporter of the new and now fashionable system of education, which attributed the highest possible importance to the skilful use of words; the patron of a loose morality, the introducer of an artificial and affected rhetoric, inimical to the true principles of pathos and tragic effect. He saw that he lowered the dignity of tragic subjects; that he depressed gods and heroes to the level of men, and even made them beggars, and garbed them in all the outward attire of poverty, of "looped and windowed raggedness," in order to excite sympathy.

Is there then any truth in the criticism of Aristotle, that Euripides is the most tragic of poets? Schlegel[1] has reconciled this opinion with the many defects of Euripides, and his manifest inferiority in so many points to Æschylus and Sophocles, by supposing that Aristotle alluded to the fact of all his dramas ending unhappily. This may have been one element in his criticism, but not the whole. Doubtless, if in his conception of heroic characters, Euripides presented a true picture of Athenian everyday life, seasoned with that polished wit which Greek critics termed ἀστειότης, he deserves the epithet of comic rather than

[1] Lect. v.

tragic; but still he has great power over the feelings. His
softness charms, although he is deficient in moral earnestness
and severe grandeur. We are more ready to sympathize with
his characters, even from the very fact of their being on a level
with ourselves.

With regard to the structure of the Euripidean tragedy, Aristophanes and other succeeding critics have found fault with the
prologue. The feature, although not unusual, was not an essential portion of the Athenian drama; in fact Æschylus has
prefixed prologues to but few of his plays, Sophocles to none.
Euripides, on the other hand, has made use of prologues in all
cases, and evidently piqued himself on his skill in their composition. The principal objection brought against the Euripidean
prologue is, that it not only made the audience acquainted with all
that it was necessary for them to know previous to the time when
the action is supposed to commence, but also anticipated the events,
and, therefore, the interest of the play. This was, doubtless, in
some instances the case; as, for example, in the "Hecuba,"
the "Ion," and the "Troades." But it must be remembered,
that, owing to the well-known sources from which tragic plots
were derived, this was not so great an evil as we should imagine.
An Athenian audience could witness with the greatest delight,
the representation of a play, the plot of which was almost the
same as those of many former tragedies, and which was founded
on incidents with which they had been familiar from childhood.
In the same way (if it is allowable to compare small things with
great), the unaltered representation of the well-known adventures
of Punch, is always witnessed with delight by spectators who
can anticipate every scene, and are well acquainted with every
incident.

From the mode in which Aristophanes attacks the prologues of
Euripides in the "Frogs," this does not appear to have been the
objection which struck his mind. It is far more probable that the
reasons which rendered them offensive to Athenian taste were,
firstly, that it was an unartistic and clumsily contrived method
of bringing about a denouement; which ought, according to all
the rules and precedents of classic art, to have been effected by
the regular and natural action of the play itself; and secondly,

that the constant and uniform indulgence in this habit struck the nice and discriminating taste of an Athenian audience as stupid and monotonous;—their fickle and volatile nature looked for variety and novelty of construction, as they could not expect much novelty of plot. This, as far as it can be understood, appears to be the point to which Aristophanes directs his sarcasm. —"Look," says Æschylus, in his controversy with Euripides for the tragic throne, "I will destroy all your prologues with a bottle."[1] He then proceeds to show, by quotations, that all the wondrous adventures which each prologizer so garrulously narrates are wound up by the loss of a bottle.

For example, he commences with the prologue to the "Archelaus."—:

> Ægyptus, as the legend tells,
> And fifty daughters, at the Argive coast,
> Arrived with plashing oars, and—lost a bottle!

The same deficiency in artistic skill led to his so frequently unravelling any complication in the plots, and extricating the characters from any involved situation, by the intervention of a deity. But the feeling with which Euripides contemplates the power of deity, differs totally from that of Sophocles and Æschylus. He neither invests them with that supernatural awfulness, nor bows in their presence with that solemn veneration which is so discernible in Æschylus, and even in Sophocles. The gods are to him evidently not objects of belief, but the machinery of the poet, a machinery of the most powerful kind, because venerated by the people. He deferred to the popular theology, although the philosophical system which he professed, whose aim was ingenious sophistry, did not stop short of entire scepticism.

As in the plays of his two great predecessors, we can, in the Euripidean tragedy, trace his political bias, and discern occasions on which he made the sentiments uttered by his characters the vehicle for political instruction. Bitter as was the hatred of Aristophanes towards Euripides, as the introducer of a new and degenerate taste in poetry, and the supporter of the modern superficial and sophistical system of education, in one point at least they were entirely agreed.

[1] Ranæ, 1165.

They both equally hated a demagogue, and saw the evils resulting to their country from the pernicious influence of this class
of men. They are attacked in the "Hecuba," under the person
of Ulysses, and in the "Orestes," still more openly. He was a
friend to the agricultural rather than to the commercial interest,
which he now saw was becoming too powerful. He attacked, in
no measured terms, the maritime class,[1] which, although originally
the source of freedom and wealth and national glory, had now
become the promoter of anarchy and insubordination. But though
he saw the destructive tendency of ochlocratic influence, he was
a friend to true liberty, and diametrically opposed to oligarchal
principles: in the "Andromache," for example, he controverts
the principles of the Lacedæmonian constitution, and his hostility
to the Dorians and their political system is openly displayed in
the "Heraclidæ," the whole object of which is political. He was,
in fact, a moderate man, who saw that safety and good order were
inconsistent with either extreme; that neither demagogues, like
Cleon and their followers on the one hand, nor rich profligates
like Alcibiades, on the other, were likely to maintain inviolate
their national institutions. He considered, that in the prosperity
of the middle classes was bound up the welfare of a community.
Of his fondness for what is popularly termed "special pleading,"
and for introducing into the theatre the language of the law courts,
little need be said, every play is full of examples of this litigious
disputation. It is sufficient to mention the scenes between Adme-
tus and his father, in the "Alcestis;" between Hecuba and Ulysses,
between Orestes and Tyndarus, and between Peleus and Menelaus, in the "Andromache." From a poet, whose great art was
the exciting the softer emotions, whose plays are, strictly speaking, plays of the passions, we should naturally expect softness
and beauty in his lyrical poetry. Nor is the reader disappointed;
for his choral odes and lyric pieces are the most tender, and, at
the same time, the sweetest of his compositions ; and his monodies,
or solo passages recited by the principal *dramatis personæ*, are
unrivalled. In his day, the chorus had evidently lost the high
and dignified position in tragedy, which it had formerly enjoyed.
The odes are fewer, the subjects of the choral songs less connected

[1] Hecuba, 610.

with the dramatic action.   Many more lyric pieces were recited by the persons of the drama than was usual in the older tragedies. One cannot help thinking, that the chorus now began to be employed, rather in deference to prejudice and established custom, than as an essential part of the tragedy.   Beautiful as the choruses of Euripides undoubtedly are, many of them might be omitted without detriment, which never could be the case with those of the two other tragic poets.

The following is a list of the extant dramas of Euripides, with the dates of their representations :—

	B. C.
Alcestis	438
Medea	431
Hippolytus	428
Hecuba	423
Heraclidæ	421 ?
Supplices	
Ion	
Hercules Furens	Uncertain,
Andromache	
Iphigenia at Tauris	
Troades	415
Electra (about)	415
Helena	
Iphigenia at Aulis	
Bacchæ	Uncertain.
Phœnissæ	
Cyclops (Satyric)	
Orestes	408

The first of these, the "Alcestis," is a melo-drama, as the comic scenes which it contains disqualify it for the appellation of a tragedy; and notwithstanding its tragic subject, it is said to have been exhibited in the place of the usual satiric drama at the conclusion of a tragic trilogy.

Above all the other plays, the "Medea" contains the true elements of tragedy.   The contest between parental affection and the pangs of jealousy which agitates the heart of Medea, is inferior to nothing in Æschylus and Sophocles.   Nor is the "Hecuba" much inferior in pathetic power.   How tenderly and touchingly depicted is the resignation of Polyxena—how deep the affliction of the bereaved mother—how terrible the resolution with which she rises superior to her overwhelming sorrows, and lays her plans for the gratification of her vengeance!

In the " Electra," however, we most clearly discover the inferiority of Euripides. Each of the three tragic poets has selected the same subject, and, therefore, the methods in which they have treated it may thus be subjected to a strict comparison. In these tragedies the leading features of the authors are strikingly illustrated.

In the " Choephori," terror is the chief characteristic; in the " Electra" of Sophocles, tenderness; in that of Euripides, homeliness.

The " Cyclops," is a most interesting and important relic of antiquity, for in it we have the only example of the satiric drama which has been handed down to modern times. Inferior as Euripides is to Æschylus and Sophocles in art and taste, he has, in this case, been happy in the choice of a subject singularly suitable to the purpose, and has adorned it with all the graces of elegant simplicity. The language and thought, which might have been thought too homely for tragedy, are here not out of place, amidst rural occupations and the scenes of pastoral life. The passage, of which the following is a translation, is a pleasing specimen of the poetry which adorned the ancient satiric drama:—

In yon trench, by yonder cave,
Slake your thirst, your fleeces lave;
Or if ye must wander still,
Seek at least the dewy hill:
Must a pebble bring you back,
Flung across your wilful track;
Hie thee, horned one, back again
To the shepherd Cyclops' den;
See, the porter stands before
His rustic master's rocky door:
Mothers, hear your sucklings bleating,
For their evening meal entreating;
Penned, the livelong day they lie,
Now give them food and lullaby.
Will ye never, never learn
From the grassy mead to turn;
Never rest, when day grows dim,
In Ætna's grot, each weary limb.

Cyclops, 41 (ANSTICE).

The beautiful choruses, of which the following passages form part, have always been admired by scholars, and are well calculated to exemplify the lyrical power of Euripides:—

> The fatal hour was midnight's calm,
> When the feast was done, and sleep like balm
>   Was shed on every eye.
> Hush'd was the choral symphony,
>   The sacrifice was o'er,
> My lord to rest his limbs had flung,
> His idle spear in its place was hung,
>   He dreamed of foes no more.
> And I, while I lost my lifeless gaze,
> In the depth of the golden mirror's blaze;
>   That my last light task was aiding,
> Was wreathing with fillets my tresses' maize,
>   And with playful fingers braiding.
> Then came a shout;
> Through the noiseless city the cry rang out,
> "Your homes are won, if ye scale the tower,
> Sons of the Greeks! is it not the hour?"
>   *Hec.* 886 (ANSTICE).

> We will not look on her burial sod,
>   As the cell of sepulchral sleep:
> It shall be as the shrine of a radiant God,
> And the pilgrim shall visit that blest abode,
>   To worship, and not to weep.
> And as he turns his steps aside,
>   Thus shall he breathe his vow—
> Here slept a self-devoted bride
> Of old, to save her lord she died,
>   She is a spirit now.   *Alc.* 1010 (ANSTICE).

The most celebrated contemporaries and competitors of Æschylus, Sophocles, and Euripides, were Ion, Achæus, and Agathon.

ION.

Ion was a native of Chios, who at an early age became a resident at Athens. He possessed great versatility of talent, for, besides tragedies, he wrote a history in the Ionic dialect, several lyric, elegiac, and dithyrambic poems, and forty fables. After the death of Æschylus, he became a competitor for the prize of tragedy, and was once successful. The titles of some of his tragedies, together with a few fragments of considerable beauty, are still extant. He is said[1] to have been surnamed "The Eastern Star," because he died whilst writing an ode which began with these words. The beauty and excellence of his poetry consisted rather in the absence of faults than the presence of sublime ideas. Longinus says he wrote with polish, correctness, and graceful ornament, but without the fire and enthusiasm of Sophocles. "No one,"[2] he asserts, "would hesitate to prefer the 'Œdipus Tyrannus' to all that Ion has ever written." He was one of the five canonical tragic poets of the Alexandrian grammarians.

ACHÆUS.

Achæus was born at Eretria, B. C. 484. Although he exhibited many tragedies, he only once gained the prize. His principal merit seems to have been as an author of satiric dramas. Some fragments, as well as seventeen titles of his tragedies, are still preserved. He was also admitted into the Alexandrian canon.

AGATHON.

Agathon was a rich Athenian, of good family and handsome person. His accomplishments, cheerfulness, and conversational powers, caused him to move in the fashionable literary society of the day. The "Symposium" of Plato is represented as having been given at his house, on the occasion of his gaining the prize for the first time in the dramatic contest. The date of this victory is B. C. 416, in which year the poet was about thirty years of age. A congenial taste, both in philosophy and poetry, united him in friendship with Euripides, for, like him, he delighted in the ingenuity of the sophistical philosophy. The foppery and effeminacy in which his personal beauty tempted him to indulge, appear to have affected his poetry, for although his style is celebrated for exquisite polish and softness,[3] it is disfigured by affectation.[4] The introduction of choral odes not intimately connected with the subject of the tragedy, has already been noticed in the case of Euripides. This was carried to so great an extent by Agathon,

---

[1] Vide Pearce's Longinus.
[2] Longinus, xxxiii.
[3] Plat. Symp.
[4] Aristoph. Thesm. v. 190.

that Aristotle[1] attributes to him this alteration in the structure of the tragic drama. The most celebrated of his works bore the title of Ἄνθος, the "Flower," but the titles of only four of his tragedies are extant.

After the deaths of the three great tragic poets, a taste and talent for poetry continued hereditary in their families; but it is clear that their descendants, although they wrote and exhibited tragedies for a few generations, were only poets by profession, and not from the enthusiasm of inspiration. Nothing which they produced has stood the test of time, although whilst they lived they enjoyed some reputation and gained some distinction. Euphorion, the son of Æschylus, was a successful competitor against Sophocles and Euripides. Iophon, the son of Sophocles, and Sophocles the younger, his grandson, were considered worthy of obtaining the tragic wreath. A nephew of Euripides, who bore the same name as his illustrious relative, is also mentioned as a tragic poet.

Chæremon,[2] who lived B. C. 380, possessed some excellencies, but his tragedies had more of the epic than the dramatic element in their composition.

Theodectes, who exhibited about B. C. 356, was an orator and a philosopher by inclination, a tragic poet by profession; and his tragedies, as well as those of his contemporaries, although they suited the corrupt taste of the times, were displays of rhetoric rather than poetry.

[1] Poet. xviii. 12.   [2] Arist. Poet. i.

CHAPTER VI.

SITUATION AND CONSTRUCTION OF THE THEATRE OF DIONYSUS.—DATE OF ITS BUILDING.—SEATS. — THYMELE. — STAGE. — SCENERY. — PARTLY ARCHITECTURAL, PARTLY PAINTED.—CURTAIN.—LOGEION.—THE EFFECT PRODUCED BY THE GROUPING.—SIZE OF THEATRE.—CONTRIVANCES TO REMEDY THE INCONVENIENCE OF DISTANCE.—THE THEATRE ROOFLESS, AND THEREFORE NATURAL AND ARTIFICIAL SCENERY WAS COMBINED.—THE GREEKS LIVED IN THE OPEN AIR.—MACHINERY.—THE ECCYCLEMA, AND THE OCCASIONS ON WHICH IT WAS USED.—INSTRUMENTAL MUSIC.—DECORATIONS OF THE ORCHESTRA AND THYMELE.—PURPOSES FOR WHICH THE THEATRE WAS USED.—THE FOUR DIONYSIA.—LITURGIES AND THEORIC FUND.—NUMBER AND ARRANGEMENT OF TRAGIC CHORUS.—COSTUME.—DISTRIBUTION OF PARTS AMONGST THE ACTORS.—GREEK TRAGEDY NOT LIKE MODERN OPERA.

IN order to understand the Greek drama and the method of its representation, it is necessary to describe the theatre itself, the means of producing stage effect, the arrangements of the scenery, the theatrical costume, and the distribution of the parts among the actors.

The knowledge which we at present possess on these subjects is derived from the remains of theatres which have been discovered, from the internal evidence of the plays themselves, and from the descriptions of Vitruvius, which were doubtless based upon the great stone theatre at Athens, situated near the temple of Dionysus.[1] This theatre was begun Ol. lxx. 1, B.C. 500, the year preceding that in which Æschylus first exhibited tragedy. It was probably soon sufficiently completed to allow of dramatic representations taking place in it, but it was not entirely finished until about Ol. 100, during the financial administration of Lycurgus.

The situation of the theatre of Dionysus was surpassingly beautiful. The architect had taken advantage of a sloping ascent, which saved him the necessity of much expensive masonry, and the architectural effect was increased by the buildings of the

[1] Müller, Diss. on Eum.

Acropolis, which overlooked the whole.   It commanded beautiful and extensive views of the surrounding country.

Immediately opposite to the audience, and visible to all those who occupied the upper benches, was the stadium, a place of such absorbing interest to the Greek, and hence the numerous passages in the Attic drama, in which allusions are made to it and to its exciting contests,[1] as the visible presence of the arena in which the scenes described may be supposed to have occurred, added force and life to the illustration.

The theatre was surrounded by an open arcade adorned with numerous statues.   From this the benches descended like semi-circular steps, intersected by staircases, to the orchestra, an open area bounded by the seats, the wall of the theatre, and the stage. The lower seats were appropriated to those who had performed eminent public services, to the principal magistrates and members of the Senate, or βουλή, and was, therefore, called the βουλευτικόν.

The right of occupying these reserved seats was termed πϱοεδϱία, and was highly esteemed.   A separate part was also assigned to the young men, ἔφηβοι, and hence termed the ἐφηβικόν.[2] In the centre of the orchestra stood the θυμέλη, an altar sacred to Dionysus, and therefore symbolical of the religious object of the spectacle.   It was the place on which the chorus stood when not performing its solemn dance and song, and the leader of the chorus took his stand there when joining in the dialogue on the stage.

The thymele was the central point of the whole building; the sacrifice, therefore, offered upon it represented the united adoration of all present as worshippers, converging to this point, as the chorus, which made it their centre of action, symbolized ideally the spectators themselves.

The stage was on a level with the lowest range of seats, and therefore twelve feet above the orchestra; the part of it which projected into the orchestra was the λογεῖον, so called because the actors stood there whilst speaking.   It was of wood, in order that its reverberation might assist the voice, whilst the other part

---

[1] Choeph. 1011; Antig. 291; Med. 1151; Elect. 825, &c.
[2] Aristoph. Aves, 794; and Schol. 699.

of the stage (προσκήνιον) was of stone. A double flight of stairs led from the stage to the orchestra. The scenery was almost entirely architectural. Massive stone erections along the back and sides of the proscenium represented the columned front of a palace or temple with three entrances. From the centre or royal doorway (βασίλειον), the principal character in the play always made his entrance. The character next in importance made his appearance from the portal on the right, and the inferior persons of the drama came on the stage through the left entrance. There were also entrances (είσοδοι) on each side of the orchestra; that on the right was supposed to lead into the country, that on the left into the town.

Besides these means of exit and entrance, there were concealed beneath the seats of the spectators the Stairs of Charon and the two anapiesmata, one of which was a trap-door in the orchestra, the other in the logeion. Through these the ghosts of the dead, and the other inhabitants of the lower world, appeared and disappeared. The scenic buildings extended across the extreme breadth of the theatre, and screened the rooms and chambers necessary for the actors and machinery.

The scenic buildings, assisted by certain mechanical contrivances to be described hereafter, were admirably suited to the representation of most tragedies, for the action generally took place in front of a palace, or, as, for example, in the "Eumenides," in the court of a temple, and therefore the scene in tragedy was rarely changed. This was more frequently necessary in comedy. In that case a curtain was drawn up from below to screen the proscenium from the spectators, and, meanwhile, painted scenery of wood and canvas was arranged in front of the architectural erections. Such pains were taken to produce natural effects, that Gemelli imagines that even real trees were sometimes introduced for that purpose.

It is plain that, although architectural scenery was in most cases suitable, there were some in which landscape painting was necessary. In the "Philoctetes" the scene represented the rocky caverns of a desert island, in the "Prometheus" the wild ravines of Caucasus. One scene of the "Œdipus Coloneus" is laid in a grove, one in the "Ajax Flagellifer" in an encampment.

In the early period of the drama the curtain was probably only used when a change of scene was required. In all the plays extant of Æschylus and Sophocles, with the exception perhaps of the "Œdipus Tyrannus," the stage was empty at the commencement and the conclusion. But in many plays of Euripides a curtain must have been used at the commencement, because at the very opening, some of the characters must have been discovered grouped upon the stage.

The narrowness of the logeion caused a picturesque effect, different from that to which we are accustomed in modern times. The modern idea of scenic representation is, that the deeper and more distant the perspective the greater the effect. But the beauty of perspective is one especial department in which the moderns have far surpassed the ancients, and the simple severity of Greek taste led them to value a mode of grouping which, as Schlegel says, resembles the clear order of *basso relievo*, rather than the more intricate and confused arrangement of a picture. Moreover, depth of perspective, and breadth of light and shade, imply an advanced era of art, at which the ancients never arrived. The pictures of the earliest masters, however bright, clear, and well defined, have not many distances. A comparison of the pictures which Raphael painted in his earlier style, with the masterpieces of his later years, exhibit advances in a knowledge of the principles of the picturesque in this respect, which he made in a few years, but which are generally the work of centuries.

The theatres of the Greeks were of vast dimensions. As the performances took place only during a few days in the spring, they attracted to them not only the native population, but foreigners from all parts, to participate in the enjoyments of this religious festival. Day after day the same individuals crowded to the spectacle and filled the building, unwearied and delighted, from morning till the dusk of evening. Hence the theatre was constructed to contain these vast assemblies.[1] That at Athens is said to have contained no fewer than thirty thousand. But this is asserted by Cockerell, after personal examination and measurement, to be an exaggeration. The probability is, that it would have contained about half that number.

[1] Plato, Symp.

The inconvenience of distance in so large a building was reme-died by the cothurnus, or buskin, which gave additional height to the figure, and by the mask, which not only enlarged the features and rendered them visible in all parts of the theatre, but by the construction of the mouth on the principle of a speaking-trumpet, caused the voice to be distinctly heard. Besides this, great atten-tion was paid to the principles of acoustics, and Vitruvius informs us that reverberators for the voice were constructed in different parts of the edifice.

The theatre had no roof, no artificial lighting, the cheerful sky and transparent atmosphere of their sunny climate were over the heads of the spectators, and the position of the theatre was so chosen that the natural objects which surrounded them were visi-ble from the benches, and enhanced the effect, and, as it were, formed a portion of the artificial scenery.

There can be no doubt that the ancient dramatists took advan-tage of this union of the fictitious and the real, and combined them together, in order to assist the illusion. The Stairs of Charon, situated almost amongst the audience themselves, the entrances not on the stage, but in the walls of the theatre, are proofs of it. Schlegel[1] remarks that, in the "Eumenides," the spectators are twice addressed, as if they formed part of the *dramatis per-sonæ*, once by the Pythoness, as the Greeks assembled in front of the Delphic temple, and again by Pallas, as the Athenian people in the court of the Areopagus, and on the same principle, in v. 658, the Acropolis is pointed out as really before the eyes of the spectators. The addresses to the spectators in all the Attic come-dies are too numerous to mention. So when the powers of heaven, and the eternal source of light are appealed to (as is so often the case, for example, in the "Antigone," vv. 802 and 879), the actor doubtless raised his hands and eyes to the real heaven, and apos-trophized the rising or the setting sun. This practice of pressing Nature into the service of Art has been blamed as destructive of illusion. Schlegel defends it on the following principle, that if a picture aims not only at being an imitation, but at producing illu-sion, the frame or edge must be concealed, and it must be viewed through an aperture. In dramatic scenery you cannot conceal

[1] Lect. iii.

the frame, and therefore it is better not to endeavor to hide it, but to transgress the strict rules of imitation, and permit this imperfect blending of reality with fiction.   In some places of outdoor popular amusement in this country the scenic effect is produced in a similar manner, by the combination of paintings, arranged on the principles of perspective, with the natural landscape.

This exposure to the open air was no inconvenience.   In the early spring, when the principal performances took place at Athens, the sun's rays were not so powerful or the storms so frequent and violent as to interfere with the spectacle; and in the rural festivals and the less important exhibitions in the city, the audience were, in case of bad weather, forced to submit to the disappointment of having their amusement stopped.   In the case of a sudden storm, the spectators sought shelter in the spacious arcades which surrounded the theatre.

From the out-door nature of theatrical representations, and the important use made of the natural scenery, the scene was always laid out of doors, and interiors, when necessary, were exhibited by mechanical contrivance.

But this to the Greek did not appear unnatural.   The Athenian was accustomed to out-door life.   The softness of the climate enabled him to enjoy the open air, and the incommodious size of the generality of private dwellings, did not tempt him to forego this cheerful mode of existence.   He gossipped and heard the news in the agora—he attended the lectures of the philosopher, if his taste led him in that direction, in some garden or grove or portico.   The great national deliberative body of which he was a member met in the Pnyx in the open air.   Some of the courts, in which he served as a dicast, or juryman, were held in the open air also.   When in the country he delighted in outdoor occupations and amusements.   Nothing seems to have annoyed or vexed him so much as the being cramped or confined. Hence the awning introduced by the Romans to screen them in the theatre from the sun and rain was not thought of by the Greeks,—in fact, they would not have considered it a luxury to be thus deprived of the fresh air and bright sunshine.

To have represented the female characters as conversing in public would have been inconsistent with the retired life led by the women of Ionian race. The stage, therefore, represented the court of the palace or temple, and had for its boundary the principal edifice.

There was likewise ingenious and well contrived machinery calculated to aid the illusion, and to render the dramatic effect perfect. Machines and ropes, and suspended platforms, concealed by clouds for the descent and appearance of gods and heroes, and for the ascent of persons from earth to heaven; a thunder chamber below the stage, and another above, from which flashed artificial lightning.

The eccyclema was a contrivance peculiar to the Greek stage. It was a semicircular machine, representing an interior, and when the great central doors of the scene were thrown open, it was exposed to view, or, as some think, wheeled forward through the opening. The latter opinion is most probably the correct one, as it is most in accordance with the term ἐκκύκλημα, or ἐξώστρα, as it is sometimes called, and also with the verbs ἐκκυκλεῖν and εἰσκυκλεῖν, which describe the mode of using the machine.

The following instances are cited by Müller from the tragedies of Æschylus, Sophocles, and Euripides, in which the eccyclema was evidently employed. It may be observed, that they are all cases in which the action represented would take place within doors—they are all scenes in which deeds of bloodshed and murder have been committed, for the principles of correct taste forbade that such scenes should take place in the presence of the spectators.[1] When the eccyclema was made use of, the characters were arranged as *tableaux vivans,* so as to produce the best effects of picturesque grouping in sculpture and painting.

ÆSCHYLUS.

1. In the "Agamemnon," v. 1345, the eccyclema represented the apartment containing the bath, the murdered hero, and Clytemnestra, with the weapon in her hand reeking with blood.

2. In the "Choephori," v. 967, the chamber as before. Orestes standing over the corpses of Clytemnestra and Ægisthus.

[1] Hor. Art. Poet.

18

SOPHOCLES.

3. In the "Electra," v. 1450, a covered corpse is rolled upon the stage in an eccyclema, which Ægis thus supposes is Orestes. He unveils it, and behold it is Clytemnestra.

4. In the "Antigone," v. 1293, the corpse of Eurydice is thus exhibited after her suicide.

5. In the "Ajax," v. 346, the interior of the tent is thus thrown open to the view of the assembled people.

6. In the "Œdipus Tyrannus," v. 1297, the self-blinded monarch is thus shown for the first time after his terrible catastrophe.

EURIPIDES.

7. In the "Hercules Furens," v. 1030, Hercules is thus discovered bound to a pillar and surrounded by the dead bodies of his wife and children.

8. In the "Hippolytus," v. 818, the doors of the palace are thrown open, and the corpse of Phædra is seen after her suicide.

There is every probability that as art improved and popular taste became less severe, instrumental music gradually became a more important element in the Greek theatre, and thus the orchestra came to be used not only for the choral dances, as the name implies, but for the musicians (auletæ and citharœdi) who played the accompaniments.[1] The thymele, which stood in the centre, represented, as has been stated, the Dionysiac altar, round which the cyclic or dithyrambic choruses performed their dances. As the chorus occupied the orchestra, and the leader (ἡγέμων) the thymele, there can be no doubt that both were decorated as occasion required, so as to harmonize with the action of the play, and the decorations of the stage.

In the "Choephori" and the "Persæ," for example, it is the opinion of Gemelli that the thymele represented in the one case the tomb of Agamemnon, in the other that of Darius. In the "Eumenides," Müller[2] imagines that the orchestra represented

---

[1] See Suidas, and Etym. Mag. v. σκηνή.
[2] Müller, Diss. on Eumen.

the court in front of the temple, in which the central altar had on it the statues of Gaia, Themis, Phœbe, and Apollo.

In the "Suppliants" the orchestra represented the place of public meeting in the city of Argos, and was adorned with the altars and statues of Zeus, Helios, Apollo, Poseidon, and Hermes, the Argive ἀγώνιοι, or ἀγοραῖοι ϑεοί; that is, the deities who presided over the place of meeting (ἀγορα), or the meeting itself (ἀγων).

In the "Agamemnon" the scene represented the palace of the Atridæ. Along its front were ranged statues of gods, fronting the east (δαίμονες ἀντήλιοι) and fronting the main, or royal, entrance, the statue of the tutelary god Apollo, 'Αγυιεύς.[1] The orchestra was the Argive agora, in which stood, as in the "Choephori," the ἀγοραῖοι ϑεοί, and on the thymele was placed a statue of Zeus, to which the chorus addresses its invocation in the stasimon.

The theatre of Dionysus was not only used as a temple of the god, or as a place sacred to the Muses.[2] Advantage was also taken of its vast size, and of the multitudes assembled there, in order to confer public honors on distinguished citizens.[3] Sometimes, too, the storm of political excitement raged within its consecrated precincts. In that terrible revolution which preceded only by a few years the complete downfall of the Athenian power, an assembly was appointed to be held there in order to arrange matters for proclaiming the authority of the Five Thousand; and it was only prevented by the panic at the tidings which arrived, informing them that the enemy were in sight off Salamis.

Theatrical representations only took place at certain seasons of the year. As they were in honor of Dionysus, they were only held at his festivals. The number of these (the Dionysia) in Attica are stated by some authorities to have been four, by others three.[5] In the latter case the Lenæa and Anthesteria are reckoned as one and the same festival. That four is the correct number is now almost universally admitted.

The rural Dionysia, the oldest of them all, were celebrated throughout Attica as a vintage festival in the sixth month of the

[1] Klausen, v. 1051.　　　　　　　　[2] Schöm. Ant.
[3] Demos. de Cor. p. 264.　　　　　　[4] B.C. 411.
[5] Museum Crit. ii. 75; Clinton, Fasti Hellenici, ii. 332.

Attic year (Poseideon), which corresponded to December. This may appear late in the year, but it must be remembered that the rejoicing did not take place until all the labors of the vintage were entirely concluded, and the grapes had been mellowed by drying in the sun and air, in the same way in which they are prepared for the rich sweet wines of Hungary.

The Lenæa, or feast of the wine press (ληνός), was celebrated in the seventh month (Gamelion). It was held at the temple of Dionysus in Limnæ, a district formerly a marsh, situated on the south side of the theatre of Dionysus. The choice of such a situation for Dionysiac temples appears to have been customary. That at Sparta stood, also, in a marshy locality.[1] Probably the convenience of having water close at hand to mix with the wine, led to the selection, so that, as Athenæus[2] expresses it, " the blood of the wine-god might mingle with the tears of the Naiads." This part of Athens was called the Lenæa, because tradition assigned to that spot the erection of the first wine-press.

The Anthesteria, which continued three days, derived its name from the month Anthesterion,[3] in which it was held, the eighth month in the Attic calendar. The first day was called πιθοιγία, the opening of the cask ; the second, χόες, on which the wine was tasted. On this day each of those present, and taking part in the festival, had a separate cup. This custom is said to have originated in the legend of Orestes, who, when he came to Athens, before he was purified from blood-guiltiness, was placed at a separate table, and no one would eat or drink with him.[4] The great Dionysia was celebrated at Athens, as the name implies (τὰ ἐν ἄστει), in the ninth Attic month (Elaphebolion).

Dramatic representations took place at all of these festivals, but all new plays were performed in the capital, and consequently only at the great Dionysia. At the Anthesteria only comedies were exhibited, and rehearsals held in preparation for the great Dionysia. At the time of the great Dionysia, Athens was crowded with a vast concourse of strangers, as all representatives of the dependent states came at that season to Athens to pay their tribute.[5]

---

[1] Strabo, viii. 250.   [2] Athen. p. 465.   [3] Thuc. ii. 15.
[4] Iphig. Taur. 947; Müller, Eum. ₰ 50; Schol. Acharn. 960.
[5] Aristoph. Ach. 477; Æsch. c. Ctes.

The Attic drama was a national affair, and formed a large item of the national expenditure. The splendor with which all festivals and public ceremonies, including theatrical exhibitions, were celebrated, caused the expense to be very considerable ; and of this, part was defrayed by the richer citizens, on whom the λιιτουργίαι devolved, and part by the treasury of the state.

The accidents which were constantly occurring, owing to the crowds who took advantage of free admission to the old wooden theatre, especially on one occasion when part of the scaffolding fell down, caused a small payment to be required.[1] This fee, which was two *oboli*, 3¼*d.* was afterwards, in consequence of a law passed by Pericles, given to the poorer citizens by the state on their application in the assembly. To such an amount did this grant at last arrive that Boech[2] reckons it at from twenty-five to thirty talents annually.

So popular was the theoric fund that, although at length it exhausted all that was left in the treasury after providing for the civil expenditure, Eubulus, in order to court the favor of the populace, procured a law to be passed which rendered it capital to propose any other application of the fund. Demosthenes,[3] by an ingenious evasion of this law, succeeded in getting it repealed at that critical period when all the resources of Athens were needed to repel the aggressions of Philip. But whilst the means of admission to the spectacle were thus furnished to all the poorer citizens from the public resources, taxation of another kind provided the means of representation. On all persons whose property exceeded three talents devolved the regular liturgies (ἐγχύχλιαι λιιτουργίαι), one of which was to furnish, at his own expense, to the dramatic poet a chorus and actors. He had also to find a χοροδιδάσχαλος to instruct the chorus, for the poet's post was only to teach the actors.

It is evident that the progress of art had now entirely altered the nature of dramatic exhibitions considered as solemn acts of religious worship. Originally the chorus was the whole population of some Dorian state celebrating the god with songs and accompanying dances on some high festival. Now the honor of the god was merged in the delight of the worshipper. The poet's

---

[1] B. C. 500.   [2] Pub. Econ. i. 241.   [3] Olynth. i.

skill was pressed into the service of religion, but it required paid professional talent to give effect to the outpourings of his imagination. Thus it was also in the public worship of the Christian church; the hymn of praise first burst forth in simple music, which all could execute—rudely, perhaps, but heartily—in honor of God. Afterwards, as Christian art progressed, the paid professional choir did that, as deputies, which the congregation did before, and the refinements of music were purchased at the expense of the united adoration of the multitude.

We are indebted to K. O. Müller, in his dissertation on the "Eumenides," for the most satisfactory theory respecting the number and arrangement of the tragic chorus; and the system followed out and illustrated by him in the tetralogy, to which the "Eumenides" belongs, is probably, with such slight modifications as might be necessary, the one pursued in all other tragedies.

The number of the dithyrambic chorus, in which the tragic originated, was fifty, and that of the tragic chorus, furnished at the expense of the choragus, and granted by the state to the poet, was probably the same; this would supply forty-eight choreutæ and two actors. Now an examination of the tragedies of Æschylus proves that he almost always introduces two choruses in each play, the one subordinate to the other in importance; and there can be no doubt that the primary chorus in one play became the secondary chorus in another.

In the "Agamemnon," the principal chorus represents the supreme council, consisting of twelve old men; and this number seems to have been the favorite one with Æschylus, as fifteen was with Sophocles, although he sometimes adopted twelve, as for instance, probably, in the "Antigone." The only case in which a chorus of fourteen appears to have been introduced, is in the "Suppliants" of Euripides. If, then, fifteen were allotted to the chorus, both in the "Choephori" and "Eumenides," eight would remain for the satiric drama.

The arrangement in the trilogy, as proposed by Müller, is as follows:—

	AGAMEM.	CHOEPH.	EUMENIDES.
Primary Chorus,	Old Men.	Women.	Furies,
Secondary do. {	Women from Choephori.	Furies from Eumenides.	{ Old men from Agamem. Women from Choeph.

The term *lochus*, applied by Æschylus to the chorus, proves that it was drawn up in rank (κατὰ ζυγά) and file (κατὰ στίχους). The choreutæ always marched three abreast, and either four or five deep, and entered by the door on the left of the audience.

Of the odes which they recited, the first was called the parode, the others the stasima; these were sung by the whole chorus, and the stasima served to form pauses in the action, and to divide the tragedy into acts, but there were no fixed number of acts, as in later times.[1] The odes, which were sung partly by the actors and partly by the chorus, were called (κομμοί) *commi*, because lamentations for the dead were frequently sung in that form.

Of those parts which fell to the lot of the *dramatis personæ*, the odes sung by them alone were called monodies: the first speech, the prologue; the last, when not succeeded by a chorus, the exode; and all between the choral odes were termed episodes. Such were the technical divisions both of the lyric and dramatic portions of Greek tragedy.

An examination of the Greek tragedies will show that, as the drama advanced, the choral parts diminished in length, and the dialogue became proportionally extended.

The connection of the drama with the Dionysiac festival was maintained even in the costume of the actors.[2] Slightly modified, in order that it might not be discordant with the dramatic action, it was nevertheless the gorgeous dress worn in the processions in honor of the god. Many colored tunics (ποικίλαι χιτῶνες), girt round the waist with embroidered girdles (μασχαλιστῆρες), and mantles decorated with gold. To these were added the cothurnus and the mask, the illusion of which was heightened by an artificial head-dress. There was little difference in the male and female garb—except where the male chlamys was substituted for

---

[1] Hor. Art. Poet.   [2] On this subject see Müller, Diss. on Eum.

the female peplus.   The male characters frequently wore swords, otherwise the mask was the principal mark of distinction.

Each character, however, was distinguished by some small but striking mark of difference.   In the "Eumenides," for example, Orestes would bear the ἱκετήριος κλαδός, an olive branch bound round with woollen fillets;[1] Pallas would be known by the ægis and helmet; Apollo would always be represented with a bow; and Hermes with his heraldic baton.

This slight difference in costume was a convenient arrangement, as, from the number of actors employed, each in his time played many parts.   The origin of the drama was, as has been stated, a simple recitation between the choral odes and dances.   Æschylus first introduced dialogue, and therefore added a second actor. He who played the principal parts was termed πρωταγονιστής, the subordinate actor was entitled δευτεραγονιστής.   The improvements introduced subsequently by Sophocles, included a third actor, τριταγονιστής.   Æschylus, as might be expected, took advantage of this innovation, and we find three actors in the "Prometheus," "Agamemnon," "Choephori," and "Eumenides.'   The rule which forbade four actors, and which is alluded to by Horace in the line,

"Nec quarta loqui persona laboret,"[2]

was never at any time infringed.   The following is Müller's idea of the distribution of the parts in the Oresteian trilogy, which may serve as a specimen of the usual practice.

I. AGAMEMNON.

1st Actor.   Watchman.   Herald.   Agamemnon.
2d.   Clytemnestra.
3d.   Cassandra.   Ægisthus.

II. CHOEPHORI.

1st Actor.   Orestes.
2d.   Clytemnestra.   Nurse (?).
3d.   Electra.   Ægisthus.   Domestic.   Pylades.

---

[1] Choeph. 1024.   [2] Hor. Art. Poet. 192.

III. EUMENIDES.

1st Actor.   Orestes.
2d.   Pythoness.   Clytemnestra.   Minerva.
3d.   Apollo.

It is obvious that great skill was requisite on the part of the poet, in order to arrange the several parts, so that more than one might be supported by the same actor.

The resemblance which has sometimes been imagined to exist between Greek tragedy and modern epera, conveys an incorrect idea respecting the nature of the former. In the first place, the whole of the play, except the choral odes, was declaimed, and not sung in recitative; and, secondly, in the opera, the music is the first consideration, whilst the *libretto* is confessedly subordinate. Hence an opera bears the name of the musical composer. But even in the Greek drama, the musical portion was under the direction of the poet, and its excellence assisted in enhancing his reputation. The poetical merit was the first thing considered, and any attempt on the part of the musician to invade this supremacy, was jealously watched and strictly controlled.

CHAPTER VII.

THE law of blood-guilt is a subject of which it is necessary to
make some brief mention, because it so completely pervades the
Greek tragic drama, and exercises so great an influence on its
tone of thought and feeling.

To execute vengeance upon the murderer was recognized as a
duty immediately devolving upon the relatives of the murdered
man, amongst all nations, from the earliest times. " Whoso
sheddeth man's blood, by man shall his blood be shed,"[1] is one
of the oldest revelations of God's will to man, and the appointment of cities of refuge to which he should flee "who had killed
his neighbor ignorantly . . . . lest the avenger of blood pursue
the slayer, while his heart is hot,"[2] shows that so strong was the
feeling on this subject that even the unintentional manslayer required this protection.

Even the public authority of the State could not relieve the
kinsman from this duty, for if a man was guilty of wilful murder, the elders of the city were to "deliver him into the hands of
the avenger of blood."[3]

This duty of making the kinsmen of the deceased the proper
prosecutors, and every prosecution illegal, unless the prosecutors
attested their relationship on oath, was incorporated into the

---

[1] Gen. ix. 6.   [2] Deut. xix. 4, 6.   [3] Ibid. xix. 12.

Athenian code.[1] Nor could the kinsman evade this duty unless the dying man forgave his murderer.

Cases of wilful murder were tried by the court of the Areopagus, those of manslaughter by the ephetæ. When the murderer was convicted, it was the duty of the State to carry the sentence into execution, and if he escaped by flight his exile was perpetual (φυγὴν ἀειφυγίαν). In cases of manslaughter, the criminal fled his country, and it rested with the relatives of his victim to permit him to return after performing ceremonies of purification, and not till then did the duty of seeking vengeance cease.

Passages in the " Iliad" and "Odyssey"[2] show that the law of custom, respecting murder and manslaughter, in the heroic age, was equally severe, and that it rested with the relatives alone to determine the degree of guilt, and to assess the penalty to be exacted. The state did not interfere unless the payment was refused.[3] Pollution clung to the person of the murderer until he was purified ; he must not dare to enter a consecrated place, or even a political assembly, and the avenger of blood was under the immediate protection of Apollo.[4]

The awful nature of blood-guiltiness,[5] and the sacred duty of vengeance as incumbent upon the nearest relatives, were maintained by the tragic poets, but more especially by Æschylus. In the " Choephori" and "Eumenides," Orestes is justified in his parricide ; he will not repent of his deed, or admit his guilt, even before the Areopagus.[6] Clytemnestra was not only a murderess, but she had dared to profane holy things by offerings at her husband's tomb.

Although the deed of Orestes is parricidal, no human power can take vengeance upon him, because he is the avenger of blood ; his mother's furies can alone pursue him, and even they are powerless, when he has visited the shrine of Delphi as a suppliant for purification (προστρόπαιος), and received it at the hands of the god, and been made fit for intercourse with his fellow-men, and for communion in the offices of religion.

With respect to the ceremonies themselves, they consisted of

[1] Demos. c. Mac. 1069.
[2] See Od. ii. 278; Il. ix. 64, 632; xxiii. 88.
[3] Il. xviii. 499.
[4] Herod. 87 ; Eum. 625.
[5] Choeph. 511.
[6] Eumen. 566.

two kinds; gods and men were both to be appeased. Zeus would not pass over injustice, especially the violation of the laws of hospitality, or of the marriage tie.[1] Ate was the minister of divine vengeance, who pursued the guilty with a moral insanity, a judicial blindness, which led the victim unawares into a course inevitably ending in ruin and perdition; hence the gods must be appeased by repentant prayers (λιταί) and lustral waters (καθαρμοί). But the manslayer could not participate in these rites, unless the man whom he had injured was appeased likewise. He must, therefore, perform sacrifices of atonement (ἱλασμοι) to the dead, he must propitiate the favor not only of the powers below (χθονιοι θεοί), but also the manes of the murdered man.

A question naturally suggests itself, why Greek tragedy invariably sought for its subjects in the popular mythology. Many causes may have contributed to establish this rule.

1. The drama was, as we have seen, invested with a sacred character; it was, perhaps, too solemn to be mixed up with matters of personal interest and every-day life. Mythology was made up of those national traditions to which the Greeks looked back with a feeling of respect almost akin to religious veneration; the families which supplied the largest number of tragic subjects were those from which the patriarchs of their race descended. Mythology seemed to blend with religion. Its characters were of the heroic stamp and mould; not so perfect as to remove them beyond the reach of human sympathies, but still approaching in their perfection to gods, or at least to demigods. The Greek mind was essentially inclined to hero-worship, and in the admiration excited by tragedy, this aspiration was gratified. As the period of mythology was one in which the imagination enjoyed full liberty, unrestrained by the fetters of historic truth, there was room for those supernatural incidents which elevate the hero above the ordinary race of mortal men, and, therefore, was especially suitable to the nature of tragedy. The spectacle of a noble nature struggling with an irresistible fate—suffering, not from his own fault, but from a power which was too strong for mortal energies, a spectacle which, Seneca said, even gods might look on with pleasure, seemed more naturally to belong to a re-

[1] Eumen. 204.

mote period, tinged with the bright and gorgeous coloring of poetry, than to the quiet simple daylight of the poet's own times.

Nor did Athenian love of liberty, and attachment to democratic institutions, interfere with this reverence for the ancient monarchs of Greece, or prevent sympathy with their struggles and misfortunes. A noble and unselfish parental regard distinguishes those of royal race for whom the tragedians claim admiration ; they stand forth not as tyrants, but as champions and defenders of their people against oppression. If any one, like Creon, violates the universal law written in the human heart as the guide of life, retribution overtakes him, and he is held up as an object of detestation.

2. It seems to have been a recognized principle in the Greek drama, that the spectators should be acquainted with the general features of the plot; at least, that it should not be entirely unfamiliar to them. The Greeks do not appear to have thought that this anticipation of the interest diminished it in any way. Hence the popular knowledge of the national mythology, and the familiarity of the audience with the crimes and misfortunes of the Labdacidæ and Pelopidæ, led the poet to select his materials from these sources, quite as much as the fact that they furnished him with the greatest number of subjects suitable for tragedy.

3. Awful and terrible as the subjects in themselves were, they belonged to a period in which the audience had no immediate personal interest ; they could contemplate them at such a distance, that their feelings of pity and terror were not harrowed or excited so violently, as to prevent them from enjoying the spectacle. The principles of Athenian taste, their excitable temperament, and warm sensibility were directly opposed to unnecessarily torturing the feelings. In common conversation they could not bear to speak of death, except in a euphemistic way. In tragedy itself, deeds of horror were never represented on the stage. The object of tragedy was not to overwhelm with anguish, but to purify the passions.[1] They could not bear to witness even the imitation of sorrows which affected them too intimately. Of this we have direct proof. There are only two ex-

[1] Arist. Poet.

ceptions to the rule now under consideration, one the "Persians" of Æschylus, the other, the "Taking of Miletus," by Phryni-chus. It has already been stated that the verdict of the Athenian people on the latter of these tragedies, decreed that it was too painfully interesting. The disastrous events of their own days affected them so deeply, that they inflicted a fine on the poet, although they could not but confess the beauty and excellence of his production.

It must not be supposed, however, that they neglected to take advantage of matters of present public interest. The nature of tragedy was too didactic, the tragic poet had too keen a sense of his high mission as a public instructor to deprive himself of this vantage ground. Such instructions, not only moral, but political, as he thought the circumstances of the times required, found its way into the speeches of the characters or the songs of the chorus. The manners and sentiments were an important part of tragedy : according to Aristotle, it was by means of this that the persons of the drama became examples and models, and the office of moral instruction was always recognized as the especial province of the chorus. This duty Horace recognized,

> Ille bonis faveatque, et consilietur amicis ;
> Et regat iratos, et amet peccare timentes :
> Ille dapes laudet mensæ brevis ; ille salubrem
> Justitiam legesque et apertis otia portis :
> Ille tegat commissa, deosque precetur et oret,
> Ut redeat miseris, abeat fortuna superbis.
>
> De Art. Poet. 196.

The tragic poets gave their advice earnestly to their fellow-citizens on matters of modern interest, although it was through the medium of ancient tradition and heroic legend.

Mythology supplied subjects peculiarly suited to the tragic drama, but, nevertheless, history and politics exercised an influence over their treatment and coloring. It was, for example, fresh in the recollections of the Athenian audience, who witnessed the representation of the "Eumenides," that their formidable enemies, the Persians, had encamped on the eastern slope of the Areopagus, and therefore on that spot Æschylus skilfully places the imaginary encampment of the Amazons.[1]

[1] Eumen. 655.

No one can doubt that the politics of the day suggested to Æschylus the whole design of the "Eumenides," that his wish was, as has been shown, to uphold the principles of the old aristocracy and the reverence due to old institutions;[1] that he wished, also, to recommend an alliance with Argos, now the leading democratical State in the Peloponnesus, and the bitter and irreconcilable enemy to Sparta,[2] and to advocate the right of Athens to that part of the Troad around Sigeum which they were then disputing with the Lesbians.[3]

This mode of conveying political instruction is also discernible in other tragedies. The same recommendation of a favorable feeling towards Argos is manifest in the "Suppliants," and as that play was exhibited about the time of the expedition into Egypt (Ol. lxxix. 3), the corn-and-wine-fed Athenians are encouraged in it not to fear the Egyptians, whose food is papyrus, and whose drink is barley-wine, in the same ironical spirit in which Hogarth contrasts the roast beef of Old England with the frog-diet of France.

But this adaptation of old legend to modern political purposes, is more visible in Euripides. He, being professedly a dramatic reformer, did not feel himself so fettered by the solemn dignity of mythology, and made his heroes and even deities descend from their high estate, and converse like mere polished and educated and philosophical Athenians.

In his tragedy of the "Suppliants," he, like Æschylus, recommended fraternization with Argos, whilst in the "Heraclidæ," it is plain that the same people is regarded unfavorably. The welcome of Medea at Athens has been thought to advise symbolically an alliance with Corcyra.

Nor did he refrain from holding up well-known characters to popular odium, if it be true, as has been supposed, that Ulysses, in the "Hecuba," represents the demagogue Cleon, and Paris, in the "Troades," the fascinating but profligate Alcibiades.

[1] Eumen. 179, 639.   [2] Ibid. 734.
[3] Ibid. 375.   See Müller, Eum. § 42.

CHAPTER VIII.

THE DESCRIPTIVE ACCURACY AND GENERAL TRUTHFULNESS OF GREEK LITERATURE.—
IN ESTIMATING THIS, TWO CONSIDERATIONS NECESSARY—1, THE CHANGES WHICH
HAVE TAKEN PLACE IN THE FACE OF THE COUNTRY,—2, LOVE FOR THE SOFTER
BEAUTIES OF NATURE.—WHY THE GREEKS DO NOT DESCRIBE LANDSCAPES.—THE
POETS DID NOT ACT DISINGENUOUSLY IN SELECTING PARTICULAR FEATURES FOR
DESCRIPTION.—PLACE WHICH THE SEA OCCUPIES IN GREEK POETRY.—WHENEVER
TRUTH IS WANTED THE GREEK POETS ARE ALWAYS TRUTHFUL.—INSTANCES OF
HOMERIC ACCURACY.—THIS ACCURACY MADE USE OF AS AN ARGUMENT AGAINST
HOMER'S PERSONALITY.—SUCH OBJECTIONS ANSWERED.—SIMILAR ACCURACY IN ÆS-
CHYLUS, SOPHOCLES, AND EURIPIDES.—TRUTHFULNESS THE CHARACTERISTIC OF
GREEK LITERATURE.—IRONY.—LITOTES.—ÆSCHYLUS.—ARISTOPHANES.

It would be giving but an imperfect idea of Greek genius, if a
few observations were not made on a most striking feature in the
writings of the Greek poets.   That is, their descriptive accuracy
and general truthfulness.   In forming an estimate of their descriptive accuracy, two considerations must be kept in view.

Firstly, that although the general physical features of the country are unaltered, yet still changes have taken place, not only
such as are due to political and social revolutions, but also to
those effects which time invariably produces on the face of a
country.

Devastation spread over the land by barbarian foes—the degeneracy of the inhabitants themselves, and the consequent neglect
of culture and improvement—the destruction of civilization and
liberty for so many centuries, succeeded by ignorance and a condition little better than slavery—have combined to make modern
Greece, as has been beautifully described, "the skeleton of ancient
Greece, enveloped in a mantle of recollections."[1]

" 'Tis Greece, but living Greece no more."

The Nemean forest is an open and barren plain; the green

[1] Ampère, p. 5.

pastures of Cithæron have become a desert. The verdant turf which bordered the Ilissus has given place to a dry and dusty beach. The stream of the Cephisus is so scanty that it is left almost constantly dry.

Secondly, that as descriptions of scenery were introduced by the poets for the purposes of embellishment, their patriotic enthusiasm led them to overlook the defects, and see in their brightest colors all the beautiful features which distinguished their native land. Their euphemism, which, in the intercourse of social life, caused them to shrink from speaking of unpleasant subjects in such terms as could give offence to the most refined taste, pervaded the whole of their literature, and thus affected not only the moral but also the descriptive character of their poetry. Generally speaking, the sublime and terrible scenes of nature had far less charms for them than the softer beauties. Rocks, mountains, precipices, awoke a series of painful images, only appropriate to emergencies in which such scenery was absolutely indispensable. The ravines of the inhospitable Caucasus were suitable to the tortures of Prometheus—the bare gray cliffs of Mycenæ to the Pelopid tragedies—the savage wildness of Cithæron to the unnatural exposure of Œdipus. The crystal rivulet, the soft and verdant turf, inviting repose—the shade of the broad plane-tree—were scenes in which their imagination took far more delight. Picturesque grandeur did not affect the Greek mind with pleasure, as it does the minds of those who inhabit the more northern parts of Europe, and who are accustomed to the sterner and severer beauties of nature, as they are to the rigors of more inhospitable climates. Often does Homer, who would devote a long description to some scene of genial beauty—who paints the sunny coasts of Ionia, the lovely kingdom of the Phæacians, the marvellous gardens of Alcinous, with all the varied tints of his luxuriant fancy—pass over, with the mere distinction of an epithet, scenes of rude and gloomy beauty.

Perhaps it is for this reason that the Greek poets do not describe extensive general views, what the moderns term landscapes, but that their descriptive poetry deals in details. Greece was, in its general features, wild and mountainous. Its rockbound coasts, although washed by the waters of the ever-varying

19

sea, indented by many a beautiful creek and bay, and many a cheerful and populous harbor, teeming with activity and life, presented generally an escarped and rugged aspect. But embosomed in the recesses of these wilds were spots of excessive beauty, green oases, as it were, in the desert, which promised that personal and sensuous enjoyment which in so many instances appears connected with Greek ideas of beauty.

Greek landscape, therefore, was necessarily of a severe character,—a more northern taste would have appreciated it, but it would not appeal to the sensibilities of an Ionian. The poet, therefore, who was the guide of national taste, as being the more perfect representative of the national mind, would not think it inconsistent with faithfulness to pass this over, and to devote his talents to those especial features which were calculated to call forth the sympathies of his hearers.

To paint the loveliness, and pass over the rudeness of nature, might have been disingenuous in a geographer, who professed as his sole object to describe impartially the faults as well as the beauties of a country, but a poet was perfectly justified in selecting beauty, and passing over what he considered deformity, just as the kindred art of the sculptor endeavors to represent not the average of human nature, but the perfection of ideal beauty.

This tendency of the Greek poets to seize on whatever they considered as the beautiful is also exemplified in the large proportionate space which the sea occupies in their works, the delight with which they dwell upon all ideas connected with it. The chief beauty of Greece is its sea. Almost encircled and girdled by it as an island, Attica, as its ancient name implied, is all shore. From every high ground, from the principal parts of Athens itself, the sea is visible; nor could any one look to sea-ward and not observe that bright and transparent atmosphere by which the climate is characterized. And not only by its natural beauties, but by the benefits which it conferred upon Greece, the sea appealed to the national sympathies. The inhabitant of the Ionian colonies of Asia Minor could not but remember that when his ancestors sailed across it from the west they brought with them those liberties and institutions, which rendered him immeasurably superior to his Oriental neighbors, and constituted the difference between Greek and

Barbarian. He felt every day that the same waves wafted to him the wealth and civilization which were the means of maintaining that superiority. Although the scene of the "Iliad" is laid on shore, the passages in it which refer to the sea are numerous, and the adventures narrated in the "Odyssey" are almost exclusively maritime.

If we carry our thoughts onwards to later times; to the glorious naval engagements between Greece and Persia ; to the time when Themistocles, fortified by the voice of the oracle, bade Greece look for protection to her wooden walls; and, lastly, to the supremacy essentially naval which Athens maintained in the Peloponnesian war, we find that the sea was the source of national greatness, and must have reminded the Greek patriot, whenever he looked upon it, of the high destinies of his race. The love with which the Greek regarded the sea, the gratitude which he felt towards it as the source of his national greatness and prosperity, is represented by the numerous maritime descriptions and metaphors and illustrations which are used as ornaments in Greek poetry universally, and are especially to be remarked in the writings of the tragic poets.

Although, therefore, the views of the Greek poets in the descriptions which they gave of their country were perhaps one-sided, they were not for that reason untrue. Their inaccuracy is due to the emissions of those who thought themselves at liberty to select such features as were best fitted to embellish and adorn the picture which they were representing.

But whenever fidelity and accuracy are to be expected, whenever truth is necessary to the consistency of the narrative, and geographical position and physical descriptions would illustrate the story, the ancient Greek poets do not fail. So accurate, for example, is Homer in this respect, that the internal evidence furnished by his geographical descriptions goes far, as has already been shown, to determine the country of which he was a native. Ample testimony has been borne to the fidelity of Homer's descriptions by geographers both of ancient and modern times. Strabo constantly appeals to his authority. Wood, in his "Essay on the Genius of Homer," shows the correspondence between Homer's descriptions, and the results of his own travels, and Colonel

Leake finds in the Homeric poems a topographical guide which seldom fails in accuracy.

The long and snow-capped ridge of Olympus strikes the travel-ler as deserving these epithets more than any of the neighboring mountains.[1] Phthia, nourisher of men, forms in the present day the most fertile portion of Thessaly. In the fat Bœotia the harvest is often plenteous when it fails in the rest of Greece; and the plain of Thebes is especially famed for its fertility; Scyros is, as Homer described it, the escarped; Aulis, the rocky; Lacedæ-mon, the hollow. The confessed beauty of the plain of Sparta still renders it deserving of Homer's epithet of lovely. Both Dodonas have their severe winters; Pyrasos its flowery meads; Epidaurus its vineyards. The Cyclopean remains of Pelasgic architecture, which mark the sites of Tyrins and Mycenæ, prove that these cities well deserved the Homeric epithet of well-built.

Even the apparent misrepresentations of Homer are capable of satisfactory explanation. In the "Iliad," for example, he describes Neptune as seated on the island of Samothrace, survey-ing the plains of Troy. It might be supposed that he neglected the fact, that Imbros, by its position between these two localities, would intercept the view. But in reality, viewed from the Straits of the Dardanelles, the steep rocks of Samothrace are seen to elevate themselves far above the comparatively low lands of Imbros. Still, low as Imbros lies, its rocky coast is steep and escarped, and deserves the Homeric epithet παιπαλόεσσα, compared with the still more level shores of the neighboring island Lesbos.

It has been doubted, without any reason, whether the Ithaca of Homer was identical with the island which now bears that name. The testimony of eye-witnesses, Dodwell and Leake, proves that the description exactly agrees with the present appearance: the ports and approaches remind the traveller of the "Odyssey," and its mountains answer the Homeric description. There is but one single exception, and that one easily accounted for. The mountain slopes are no longer covered with the dark forests which concealed from view the herds of Eumæus.

This remarkable and universal accuracy has been recognized, and made use of as an argument by the opposers of the personality

[1] See Ampère.

of Homer. To describe places so numerous and so distant from each other with the fidelity of an eye-witness appears to them an utter impossibility. Rejecting any other explanation, they assume that as one man could not have visited all these places the descriptive passages must have been the work of several minds.

But, if the theory is adopted that the author of the Homeric poems had his mind deeply imbued with the traditions of his race, and his memory stored with the popular lays and legends in which these traditions were conveyed, a natural solution of the difficulty is at once furnished. In cases where Homer had not himself visited the scene described, each poet or each popular legend supplied the description, and the retentive memory and vivid imagination of the Ionian bard embodied them as occasion required in his own poems.

Such is the truthfulness of the Homeric poetry. Similar exactness, also, characterizes the Attic poets, in that period, when the national poetic talent had arrived at its most perfect and mature development.

Whoever reads the course of the Beacons in the "Agamemnon" of Æschylus, will appreciate the justice of this assertion, and admire the minute geographical accuracy with which it is described. The scenery in the neighborhood of Athens, as depicted by Sophocles in the "Œdipus Coloneus," must have struck every one of the spectators as a living portrait of a locality with which they were familiar from infancy. The following testimony to its fidelity is borne by a modern traveller:—

"All the images in that exquisite chorus of Sophocles, where he dilates with rapture upon the beauties of his native place, may still be verified. The crocus, the narcissus, and a thousand flowers, still mingle their various dyes, and impregnate the atmosphere with odors. The descendants of those ancient olives, on which the eye of Morian Jupiter was fixed in vigilant care, still spread their broad arms, and form a shade impervious to the sun. In the opening of the year the whole grove is vocal with the melody of the nightingale, and at its close the purple clusters, the glory of Bacchus, hang around the trellis work with which the numerous cottages and villas are adorned."[1]

[1] Hughes, Travels in Greece, vol. i.

It is scarcely too much to say, that a selection of descriptive passages from the Greek poets would form a guide-book to the topography of Greece.

Strabo constantly bears witness to the descriptive accuracy of Sophocles and Euripides. He points out, as an example, a passage in which the latter contrasts the principal features of Laconia and Messenia, "the first abounding in valleys, fenced in with steep mountains, and difficult of access to an invading enemy; the other fertile, watered by a thousand springs, adorned with verdant pastures, neither chilled by the rigorous blasts of winter, nor parched by the excessive heats of summer."[1]

But faithfulness in description is a quality which might be expected from Greek love of truth, and hatred of exaggeration. Truthfulness is the essence of Greek literature in every period and in every age. Even in those departments of poetry, where fiction is essential, nothing would satisfy Greek taste but the closest resemblance to truth, the highest degree of verisimilitude.

In their philosophical researches, although the mind had just escaped from the dominion of the imagination, truth, so far as the human mind could reach it, was the object at which they aimed. The honesty with which they pursued this holy object could not indeed curb the speculations of the Ionian Greeks, but still they recognized its authority, and the moral duty of devoting their powers to its attainment.

In history, although its great father eagerly received, with all the wonder-loving zeal of an Ionian, the marvels which he collected from various sources for the delight of his auditors, still he received them from authorities which he thought he had grounds for believing; and when he took his accounts upon trust, he rigidly observed the rule of stating the authority on which he depended. In philosophical history, Thucydides elicited his political principles from the facts which he detailed with the most scrupulous regard to truth, and the most exact impartiality.

Nothing was so offensive to Greek taste, nothing so vulgar in their estimation, as exaggeration. In argument, there was nothing which more called forth their admiration than that art which they termed irony ($\varepsilon \iota \varrho \omega \nu \varepsilon \iota a$), which was the opposite to arrogance

---

[1] Ampère, p. 21.

and love of show or parade, the dissembling the whole strength of argument which you could bring forward, the learning and the personal qualifications which you might happen to possess.

In style, no figure was so common or so great a favorite as that which the grammarians called Litotes, which understates everything rather than incur the risk of being suspected of going beyond the truth. It may be said that understatement is not absolute truthfulness; this doubtless, strictly speaking, is the case; but, nevertheless, understatement indicates a delicate and sensitive regard to truthfulness, it is the tendency of a truthful mind, whereas exaggeration is the characteristic of a disposition which is the precise contrary. Where the mean is so difficult to hit, understatement, if a fault, is a fault in the right direction.

With respect to the materials of which the poets made use, we may observe that the legends which form the foundation of all tragedy are reproduced with the same exactness in their details by all the great dramatic poets in succession. The historic events to which allusions are occasionally made are given with the fidelity of an historian, and national triumphs are not exaggerated even to that extent which might be thought a pardonable sacrifice to national vanity. The narrative of Herodotus, truthful although it is, appears far more romantic and wonderful than any part of Æschylus' "Persæ." The grave importance of the old aristocratic institutions and the high court of Areopagus, are not supported in his "Eumenides" in a spirit of partisanship, but with calm and dignified impartiality, worthy of one who would not sacrifice truth, although firmly persuaded of the righteousness of the cause which he espoused.

Even the allowed licentiousness of comedy did not tempt Aristophanes to go beyond the truth in his sad descriptions of Athenian society. Not a picture which he draws of public moral degeneracy, of political corruption, of unreformed abuses, of fashionable follies, of philosophical absurdity, of private vices, is not borne out by contemporary historical authority.

CHAPTER IX.

COMEDY, ITS ORIGIN.—ETYMOLOGY.—FIRST EXHIBITED IN ICARIA BY SUSARION.—EPI-
CHARMUS, HIS LIFE, AND CHARACTER OF HIS COMEDIES.—PHORMIS.—DINOLOCHUS.—
ATTIC COMEDY, ITS THREEFOLD DIVISION.—CHARACTER OF THE OLD COMEDY, AS TRACED
IN THAT OF ARISTOPHANES.—ITS REFINEMENT, ITS ELEGANCE, AND ITS GROSSNESS.—
ITS EFFECTS FOR GOOD AND FOR EVIL.—ITS IMPARTIALITY.—LAWS BY WHICH IT WAS
PROHIBITED.—THE PARABASIS.

THE origin of the Greek comedy was similar to that of tragedy.
As the latter was the development of the dithyrambic chorus, so
the former grew out of the phallic songs.   At the rural festivals,
in which the country-loving Greeks took such intense delight,
when the harvest or the vintage was over, a band of jovial revellers (κῶμος) formed dances and processions, bearing aloft in triumphant merriment the emblem of fertility and increase (φαλλός),
so prominent not only in Greek, but also in Egyptian and Asiatic
worship.   Their leader sang such a song as that in the "Acharnians" of Aristophanes,[1] whilst the rest joined in a rude and
boisterous chorus.   In these rustic rejoicings is discernible the
first gleam both of the dramatic and choral portions, and hence
the custom of the song and the dance accompanying the revel-
ler, and the etymology of the term comedy, the song or ode of
the Comus.   Comedy, Aristotle informs us,[2] was at first, like
tragedy, entirely extempore; rude and biting jests, indecent and
licentious songs, such as might be expected from the nature of
the phallic ceremony, accompanied by gestures, like those of
mountebanks or morrice-dancers, delighted the admiring crowd.
This amusement first assumed a tangible form in Icaria, one of
the demi of Attica, and the inhabitants of this district first incorporated it with the worship of Dionysus, which they are said to
have introduced into Greece.

[1] Aristoph. Ach. 232.   [2] Aristotle, Poet. iv.

We learn from a Chronicle preserved amongst the Marmora Oxoniensia, as filled up and interpreted by Bentley, that Susarion, a Megarean, who lived about the time of Solon, amused the Icarians by carrying from place to place in carts his company of buffoons, whose faces, instead of being concealed by masks, were smeared with the lees of wine. Hence his actors were called τρυγῳδοί, or *lee-singers*, and comedy acquired the name of τρυγῳδία, or the *lee-song*.

From his example Thespis, who lived soon after, conveyed in a similar way his itinerant tragic company, like the strolling players who frequent our village fairs. To this custom Horace alludes in his "Epistle to the Pisos."

> " Ignotum tragicæ genus invenisse camenæ
> Dicitur, et plaustris vexisse poemata Thespis."

Still, however, comedy consisted only of extemporary effusions; and it was not until the time of Epicharmus that it assumed a written form. He was the first, as Posidippus was the last, in a series of one hundred and four comic poets, who flourished during a period of two hundred and fifty years. Epicharmus was born in the island of Cos, about B. C. 540, and both his father and himself were physicians.[1] He resided some little time at Megara in Sicily, which was a colony from Megara on the Isthmus of Corinth, and the native country of Susarion. There he probably had an opportunity of witnessing the comic performances of Susarion's company. He soon after became a resident at the court of Hiero. He studied philosophy under Pythagoras, and many traces of this training are to be found in the moral axioms or gnomes which abound in his writings, and the philosophical discussions which frequently give a serious complexion to the extant fragments of his comedies.

If there be any truth in the assertion of Horace, that Plautus imitated him,[2] and in the tradition that he founded his "Menæchmi" on a comedy of Epicharmus, he must have been far in advance of his age in the construction of a plot; and, if so, it is probable that the expression of Aristotle (τὸ μύθους ποιεῖν)[3]

---

[1] Müller, Dorians, ii. 8. 5 ; iv. 7. 2.   [2] Hor. Ep. ii. i. 58.
[3] Arist. Poet. 6.

refers to this talent, and not (as it is often interpreted) to the circumstance that his comedies were generally on mythological subjects. Many of the titles of his plays, which are preserved, are doubtless mythological, but it is known that he wrote on other subjects likewise. The titles of thirty-five of his comedies are known, twenty-six of which are preserved by Athenæus. He died, according to Diogenes Laertius, at the age of ninety; according to Lucian, at ninety-seven.[1]

For the above reasons, comedy is said to have been of Sicilian origin, and Epicharmus has been considered its inventor. The assertion of Plato[2] is perfectly consistent with truth, that Epicharmus and Homer were the first founders (ἄρχοι), the former of comedy, the latter of tragedy.

Although Epicharmus was the earliest author of written comedy as cultivated amongst the Dorians, it is probable that Phormis was his contemporary. He was a native of Arcadia, but subsequently joined the brilliant literary circle which adorned the court of Syracuse. Suidas[3] informs us that he first attired his actors in costume, and adorned the stage with purple curtains. The eight titles of his comedies, which are still extant, show that his subjects were principally mythological, that is, they were burlesque parodies on popular heroic legends.

The last of the Dorian comic writers was Dinolochus, the pupil of Epicharmus, a native of Agrigentum or Syracuse; he is said to have written fourteen comedies, but nothing remains of his works except some of their titles. Almost simultaneously with the Dorian comedy in Sicily, a drama, having the same origin, and nearly resembling it in character, was making rapid progress in Attica. This was what is technically termed the old Attic comedy, the principal writers of which were Chionides and Magnes.

As in the Attic drama, there can plainly be traced various stages of progress before it arrived at that which, in modern times, is considered the true form of comedy, namely, the comedy of character or manners, it has been customary to divide it into three species, which are termed the old, middle, and new come-

---

[1] B. c. 450–43.　　　[2] Plato, Theat. 152.　　　[3] Suidas, s. v.

dy.[1] These divisions are of course arbitrary, and as the advance from one stage to another took place gradually, it is somewhat difficult to determine accurately the epoch when each species gave place to the succeeding one. The middle comedy, however, is usually said to commence about the xcviiith or xcixth Olympiad, and to continue until about the cxiith, when Philemon and Menander, the authors of the new comedy, began to exhibit.

The characteristic feature of the old comedy is personality, that of the middle comedy philosophical and literary criticism, and an attack upon the follies of classes, rather than of individuals. The new comedy is the comedy of manners, and in all respects resembles that of Plautus and Terence, as well as that of modern times.

As the comedies of Aristophanes are the only specimens of the old comedy which have been preserved in a sufficiently perfect state, all our ideas respecting its nature must be founded on a study of his plays.

In order to form a correct estimate of its nature, it is necessary to divest the mind of all notions which have been derived from comedies of the present day. The tragic principle is the same in all ages, and hence between ancient and modern tragedy there are many points of resemblance, together with much dissimilarity, but the old Attic comedy is totally unlike its modern namesake. It is quite *sui generis*—there is nothing with which it can be compared. In its loose and unconnected structure, the incompleteness and want of uniformity in its plot, it somewhat resembles a modern pantomime. Like pantomime, it consists of numerous independent scenes and ludicrous situations, satirical attacks on the vices, and sparkling allusions to the prevalent follies of the day, and much of the humor consists in practical jokes, as well as in the smartness of the dialogue and repartee. It also indulged in the most unrestrained personalities. Real personages were exhibited on the stage, the shafts of the poet's ridicule were fearlessly directed against them. These gross attacks were not confined to public characters only, who might be considered fair marks for censure as well as praise, but the secrets of domestic life were laid open, its sanctity violated, the

[1] See Clinton's Fasti Hellenici, vol. ii. Introd. p. 36.

faults of private characters held up to odium or ridicule, and even virtuous and patriotic conduct sometimes misrepresented and ridiculed.

Nothing was safe from the virulence of the comic poet. The most serious business of life was caricatured, the most time-honored political institutions unsparingly criticized—the whole public administration, educational, legal, financial, and executive remorselessly attacked. Besides this, the poet assumed to himself the functions of a literary censor; he aspired to lead the public taste and direct the critical judgment of the Athenian people on all literary and philosophical questions. All this abuse and slander, and caricature and criticism, was conveyed in the most exquisite and polished style; it was recommended by all the re-finements of taste and the graces of poetry. It was because of this exquisite elegance and purity which distinguished the style of the Attic comic writing, as well as its energetic power, that Quinc-tilian recommends an orator to study, as the best model next to Homer, the writings of the old Attic comedy. Doubtless it abounded in grossness and obscenity, such as would not be tolerated in dramatic exhibitions of the present day. But an age in which man was not softened by the influence of good female society, in which the virtuous of the female sex were not educated so as to fit them for being companions of the men, whilst the vicious applied themselves to the task of making the leisure hours of the male sex pass agreeably by all the accomplishments and elegances of a finished education, was necessarily a gross one. The comic poet, therefore, was not the corrupter of his country-men. The worst that can be said against him is, that, with all his taste and talent and education, he was not in advance of his age in this point—that he did not stem the tide of corruption—that he pandered to a degraded popular taste instead of using his best endeavors to mould it to a higher standard.

The old comedy was to the Athenians the representative of many influences which exist in the present day. It was the news-paper—the review—the satire—the pamphlet—the caricature—the pantomime of Athens.

Addressed to the thousands who flocked to the theatre to wit-ness the representation of a new comedy, most of whom were keenly alive to every witty allusion and stroke of satire, and who took a deep interest in everything of a public nature, because each individual was personally engaged in the administration of state affairs, the old comedy must have been a powerful engine for good or for evil. There can be little doubt that, scurrilous and immoral as it often was, the good, nevertheless, predominated. Gross and depraved as the Athenians were already, notwithstanding their refinement, it is not likely that comedy corrupted their morals in this respect. The vices which prevailed would have existed without it, and were neither increased nor fostered by it.

But the comic poet seems, generally speaking, to have been on the side of that which was good in taste—in education—in politics. Fostered as the free satire of comedy was by the unbounded license of a democracy, and owing its vigor, as well as its existence, to the patronage of a sovereign people, it neither spared the vices nor flattered the follies of its patrons. Like those of the court fool in the Middle Ages, its most biting jests were received with good humor, and welcomed as acceptable by its supporters, although they themselves were the objects of them.

Notwithstanding the favor with which it was viewed by the people, its extreme personality sometimes provoked the interference of the law.

In B. c. 440, a law was passed, either prohibiting it altogether, or forbidding the representation or mentioning the names of real persons on the stage.[1] During the period when this remained in force, as Horace tells us, the comic chorus—

Turpiter obticuit, sublato jure nocendi.

Hor. *Art. Poet.*

It was again re-enacted about B. c. 415, through the influence of Alcibiades, whose vanity, ambition, and ostentation, attachment to the war party, and support of the new systems of philosophy and education had drawn upon him the enmity of the comic poet. Whenever liberty was crushed, whether in the revolution of B. c. 411, or under the tyranny of the Thirty, the spirit of comedy was paralyzed, and the succeeding century, in which Athenian liberty

[1] See Clinton's Fasti Hellenici, vol. ii. Introd. p. 56.

received its death-blow and gradually wasted and declined, soon witnessed the change from the bold personalities of the old to the more vague generalities of the middle comedy.

The parabasis is a remarkable feature in the old comedy. In it the ideal nature of the representation was neglected: the poet himself, or the chorus as his representative, together with the audience, were identified with the action of the play; the poet, in his own person, addressed the audience, as is the case in the modern prologue. Its introduction was almost universal, but not absolutely essential; for the "Ecclesiazusæ," "Lysistrata," and "Plutus" have no parabasis.

It is probable that it originated in some traditional custom connected with comedy in its earliest phase. Perhaps when, as in tragedy, some written recitations succeeded the extemporaneous effusions of the comus, the poet accompanied and directed the chorus and exercised the privilege of speaking his mind to the people.

The grammarians assumed no less than six technical divisions of the parabasis. The principal part was written in anapæstic, sometimes trochaic verse, and ended with a succession of short lines to be repeated in a breath, and this was called πνῖγος, because the rapidity of utterance produced the effect of choking.

In the parabasis the subject of the play might be totally neglected: it was not necessary to make a single allusion to it. The poet considered himself at liberty to call the attention of the audience to any matters of public interest, or to circumstances which concerned himself individually; he might bring forward either seriously or in jest any measures for reforming state abuses, or he might sing his own praises, or purge himself from any malignant slanders or accusations. The unconnected nature of the plot prevented this from being considered an interruption, and it never struck the Athenian people, whom every novelty amused, that it destroyed the dramatic effect, or prevented them from realizing to themselves the events which took place upon the stage.

CHAPTER X.

CHIONIDES.

CHIONIDES was the oldest Athenian comic writer. Suidas calls him the protagonist of the old comedy. He fixes the period at which he first exhibited eight years before the Persian war. Others, on the authority of Aristotle,[1] assert, that he flourished more than twenty years later. There are, however, strong grounds for disputing the genuineness of this passage in the "Poetics." Of his comedies nothing remains, except three titles and two quotations. He was followed in a few years by Magnes, of whom mention is made in the " Knights" of Aristophanes.[2]

> Could it 'scape observing sight what was Magnes' wretched plight,
>   When his hairs and his temples were hoary,
> Yet who battled with more zeal or more trophies left to tell,
>   Of his former achievements and glory ?
> He came piping, dancing, tapping, figgnatting and wind-clapping,
>   Frog-besmeared, and with Lydian grimaces ;
> Yet he, too, had his date, nor could wit nor merit great
>   Preserve him unchanged in your graces.
> Youth passed brilliantly and bright, when his head was old and white,
>   Strange reverse and hard fortune confronted.
> What boots taste or tact, forsooth, if they 've lost their nicest truth,
>   Or a whit where the edge has grown blunted ?
>   MITCHELL.

---

[1] Arist. Poet. iii.   [2] Aristoph. Eq. v. 520.

From this passage it appears that he arrived at an advanced age, and outlived his popularity; that with his physical vigor he lost his humor and powers of amusement. His victories, his versatility of talent, and ingenuity in imitations, evidenced by the varied titles of his plays, were forgotten by the fickle multitude, and they deserted their old favorite for more lively competitors. Nine plays and two victories are attributed to him, but the testimony of Aristophanes seems to point to far more than these. Only a few lines now remain of the comedies of Magnes.

CRATINUS.

Amongst the numerous poets of the old comedy, Horace[1] and Quinctilian have accustomed us to consider Cratinus, Eupolis, and Aristophanes as the chief. Although they succeeded one another in the above order, they were contemporaries and rivals. Cratinus was a native of Attica, and was born 'about B. C. 519. Little is known of his life, and that little rests upon doubtful authority. We are told, for example, on the one hand,[2] that he never gained a dramatic victory until he was more than eighty years old; on the other,[3] that he began to exhibit at about sixty-five years of age. The historical evidence is in favor of this latter statement. Like Magnes, he outlived his popularity, which commenced so late in life. He was as great a lover of conviviality as Aristophanes, and was celebrated for the genial and bacchanalian spirit which warmed his poetry, and which rendered it certain that they could not have been the productions of a water drinker, to whom no one was a bitterer foe than Cratinus. Horace, who was a thorough believer in the poetical inspiration of wine, supports his opinion by the authority of Cratinus in the following lines:—

> Prisco si credis, Mæcenas docte, Cratino,
> Nulla placere diu nec vivere carmina possunt,
> Quæ scribuntur aquæ potoribus.
> > HOR. *Ep.* I. xix. 1.

Probably, therefore, there is some truth in the accusation of Suidas, that he carried his love of social enjoyment to a vicious

---

[1] Hor. Sat. I. iv. 1.   [2] Vit. Anon.   [3] Euseb. Chron.

excess, and that he deserved the epithet which was given him of "Philpot" (Φιλοπότης). His poetry appears to have been full of spirit and energy, his language highly figurative, his metre so bold and grand, especially the lyrical portion, as to have been considered equal to those of the tragedians. He wrote twenty-one comedies, none of which have survived; and gained nine victories, in one of which he vanquished Aristophanes himself. His great rival was fully aware of his fervid imagination, and of his impetuous and torrent-like eloquence. In the same passage[1] in which he describes his desertion by his fickle and ungrateful admirers, he speaks of the high place which he ought to occupy in the public estimation, although he could not refrain from indulging his love of humor and satire:—

> Who Cratinus may forget, or the storm of whim and wit
>   Which shook theatres under his guiding?
> When Panegyric's song poured her flood of praise along,
>   Who but he on the top wave was riding?
> Foe nor rival might him meet, plane and oak ta'en by the feet,
>   Did him instant and humble prostration;
> For his step was as the tread of a flood that leaves its bed,
>   And his march it was rude desolation.
>
>   *   *   *   *   *
>
> Thus in glory was he seen while his years as yet were green;
>   But now that his dotage is on him,
> God help him! for no eye of all those who pass him by
>   Throws a look of compassion upon him.
> 'Tis a conch, but with the loss of its garnish and its gloss;
>   'Tis a harp that hath lost all its crowning;
> 'Tis a pipe where deftest hand may the stops no more command,
>   Nor on it divisions be running.
>
>   *   *   *   *   *
>
> Oh, if ever yet a bard waited, page-like, high reward,
>   Former exploits and just reputation,
> By an emphasis of right, some had earned this noble wight,
>   In the hall a most constant potation:
> And in theatre's high station there a mark for admiration
>   To anchor her aspect and face on;
> In his honor he should sit, nor serve triflers in the pit
>   As an object their rude jests to pass on.
>   MITCHELL.

---

[1] Aristoph. Eq. 532.

20

EUPOLIS.

Eupolis was not more than two years older than Aristophanes, and was, therefore, probably born about B. C. 446. Suidas informs us that he was seventeen years old when he exhibited his first comedy. This event, therefore, must have taken place about B. C. 429. An improbable story is told of his having been thrown overboard by Alcibiades and drowned, when on his way to Sicily, because of a personal attack in one of his comedies. The more likely account is[1] that he fell in a naval engagement in the Hellespont, perhaps at the battle of Ægospotami.

As Cratinus was celebrated for the bitterness of his satire, Eupolis, though probably no less personal in his caricature, was distinguished for his broad humor, and the ingenuity of his *doubles entendres*. Aristophanes was not only a rival, but an imitator, of Eupolis, and the latter accuses him, in his "Baptæ," of direct plagiarism.

This charge Aristophanes[2] retorts upon Eupolis in the "Clouds," and seems very sore at Eupolis having joked him on the subject of his baldness.[3]

Suidas attributes to him seventeen comedies, of which modern critics have asserted that fifteen are genuine, and of these the titles are preserved.

CRATES.

The name of Crates must not be passed over. He was a contemporary of Cratinus, but somewhat younger. He commenced as an actor in the comedies of Cratinus, and afterwards wrote plays remarkable for their broad humor and drollery. He is said to have been the first Attic poet bold enough to follow the example of Epicharmus, and introduce drunken characters on the stage. Fourteen plays have been attributed to him, and of eight of these a few fragments remain; the most beautiful amongst them has been thus translated by Cumberland:—

"These shrivelled sinews, and this bending frame,
　The workmanship of Time's strong hand proclaim;
Skilled to reverse whate'er the gods create,
　And make that crooked which they fashion straight.

---

[1] Suidas, s. v.　　　[2] Aristoph. Clouds, 549.　　　[3] Ibid. 530.

> Hard choice for men to die—or else to be
> That tottering, wretched, wrinkling thing you see!
> Age, then, we all prefer, for age we pray,
> And travel on to life's last lingering day,
> Then sinking slowly down from worse to worse,
> Find heaven's ecstatic boon our greatest curse."

Aristophanes tells us that Crates was, like his predecessors, in his turn a victim to the fickleness of the Athenian people.[1]

> I spare myself the toil to record the buffets vile,
>   The affronts, and the contumelies hateful,
> Which on Crates frequent fell; yet I dare you, sirs, to tell
>   Where was caterer more pleasing or grateful?
> Who knew better how to lay *soup piquant* and *entremets*,
>   Dainty patties and little side dishes?
> Where, with all your bards, a muse cooked more delicate *ragouts*,
>   Or hashed sentiment so to your wishes?
>
>   MITCHELL.

ARISTOPHANES.

Aristophanes was, as he himself tells us, a native of the Attic borough Cydathene. The precise date of his birth is unknown,[2] but as he was very nearly the same age as Eupolis, and almost a youth (σχεδὸν μειϱακίσκος) when, during the time of the plague at Athens, he exhibited his first comedy B. C. 427, the probability is that he was born about B. C. 445. He possessed some property in Ægina, and hence some accounts assert that he was born in that island. His father's name was Philip, and, according to Athenian custom, one of his three sons also bore that name. In early life he was a pupil of Prodicus, and thus became acquainted with that sophistical system of education which he afterwards attacked so violently in his comedies. His stature was tall, his frame powerful, his temper social and convivial. The demagogue Cleon, whose enmity he had provoked by his unsparing satire, brought an action against him to deprive him of his rights as a citizen, but a verdict was given in his favor. So popular was he,[3] that a crown of olive was publicly decreed to him, and his wit and genius, added to the social qualities of a perfect man of the

[1] Aristoph. Knights, 550.　　　[2] Clinton's Fasti Hellenici.
[3] Plutarch.

world, rendered him an acceptable friend and associate of Plato and the other distinguished men who were his contemporaries. His last comedy was exhibited B. C. 388, and he died at the advanced age of seventy years, having been the author of fifty-four plays,[1] of which eleven are extant.

The following epigram in honor of him is preserved in the "Anthologia."

Αἱ Χάριτες τέμενός τι λαβεῖν, ὕπερ οὐχὶ πησεῖται,
Ζητοῦσαι, ψυχὴν εὕρον Ἀριστοφάνους.

"Once did the Graces wish for a shrine which never should perish,
And as they sought, they the soul found of Aristophanes."

BANQUETERS.

His earliest comedy was the "Banqueters" (Δαιταλεῖς), which he exhibited under the name of "Philomedes," since, until he exhibited the "Knights," he was below the age at which it was legal to compete for a prize.

What the legal age was at which a dramatic poet was admissible as a competitor, it is impossible to determine.   The scholiast on Aristophanes fixes it at thirty years, but it is well known that Æschylus, Sophocles, and Euripides, all exhibited tragedies before they had arrived at that age.   Clinton[2] has satisfactorily proved that the law of which the scholiast speaks, referred, not to dramatic poets, but to the ten ῥήτορες, or public orators, who were elected by lot to plead state causes in the senate or ecclesia.   Nothing more can be stated with certainty, than that there was some restriction as to age, or else Aristophanes would have been able to exhibit the "Banqueters" in his own name, as he did the "Knights" five years subsequently.   Young as he was when he brought out his maiden comedy, the second prize was awarded to him.

The subject of this play is an attack upon the modern system of education introduced by the sophists.   Aristophanes was a man of the old school, and a great admirer of the old Athenian educational theory, in which the culture of body and mind went hand in hand.   He believed in the utility of the play-ground as well as the school-room; he thought that gymnastics, as well as

---

[1] Suidas, s. v.   [2] Clinton, vol. ii. Introd. p. 56.

literature, were essential, in order to develope the manly vigor of a nation. Under the modern system, he saw that the study of a sophistical rhetoric and of the flippant and subtle arts which fitted the student for the ecclesia or the law-court, so absorbed the thoughts of the youthful citizens, that the hardy exercises of the palæstra were neglected. This produced an effeminate mode of life, as well as a foppish tone of mind, amongst the young fashionable Athenians, destructive of public morals. The very cleverness and shrewdness and command of language, which their education gave them, fostered self-conceit and disrespect for lawful authority, and young Athens bade fair, puffed up with superficial showy accomplishments, to despise their more sober-minded and simple elders as old-fashioned, and to ridicule the generation for which the poet himself, though but a boy, felt the highest respect and admiration.

This comedy has been likewise supposed to have had a sanitary object. The terrible plague was now raging at Athens, and the poet thought that the gymnastic exercises, which formed an integral part of the old education, would be advantageous to the health of the people.

ACHARNIANS.

The "Acharnians" was the earliest of his extant plays, and was exhibited in the sixth year of the Peloponnesian war. In it the poet paints the sad evils of war, the miseries to which the necessary policy of Pericles had subjected the country-loving Athenians. Consequently, in it the poet ludicrously attributes the war itself to a personal insult offered to Pericles. It was a theme likely to be popular. The Athenians delighted in the freedom of rural life, they missed their farms and their villas, they could not bear to see them year after year devastated by the Lacedæmonian armies, whilst they were confined in a close, and stifling, and pestilential city. Acharnæ was the largest and richest borough of Attica, and was the first to suffer from the Spartan invasion. Dicæopolis, a native of that demus, is represented as making a separate peace for himself and his family, and enjoying all the amusements and festivities and plenty and good cheer, which constitute the blessings of quiet times. He can command every delicacy which could whet the appetite of an Athenian epicure. Dicæopolis is a free-trader, and rejoices that, as far as he himself is concerned, the war restrictions on commerce are removed, and that the opening of the Bœotian markets supplies him with all the foreign luxuries which he wants, and of which the war has so long deprived him, in the quiet retirement of his farm.

He and his family celebrate the rural Dionysia with all its attendant ceremonies and gay processions. In the midst of these enjoyments, Lamachus, as the representative of the war-party, sends his servant to beg permission to purchase a few thrushes and eels; a spirited dialogue ensues, in which are contrasted the enjoyments of peace and the hardships of war.

Lamachus soon returns from his campaign, and wounds and disasters, and almost death, put a finishing stroke to the exploits of the ill-fated and vainglorious general, whilst, as the play concludes, the song of victory proclaims the jovial triumph of the peace-loving Dicæopolis.

KNIGHTS.

The next of his extant plays was the "Knights;" it was exhibited B. C. 424, and gained the first prize. The vulgar and arrogant demagogue, Cleon, was now at the height of his power and popularity, it therefore required no small amount of courage to attack him. But the young poet was a fearless patriot. No artist could be found willing to model a mask representing the well-known coarse features of the popular leader. Callistratus, the best comic actor of the day, shrunk from personating the character. But Aristophanes would not be disappointed of his purpose. He smeared his face with wine lees, and acted the part himself, and, enlisting in his cause the knights who held the second place in rank and fortune amongst the Athenian citizens, and whose military exploits gave them a high claim to respect and consideration, he proceeded, as he beforehand threatened, to cut him up into soles for shoes.

Personifying the Athenian people as Demus, in the same way that the people of England are represented as John Bull, he faithfully represents in this character all the vices and follies, public and private, of his countrymen. This ill-tempered, cross-grained, jealous-pated, self-indulgent, old gentleman, has just bought a new Paphlagonian slave, by trade a tanner. This slave is Cleon, who appeals to the superstitious feelings of Demus by flattering oracles, and to his selfishness, by supplying his table with his favorite dainties; and by his noisy tongue and disgusting subservience, gains a complete ascendancy over his confiding master.

Nicias and Demosthenes, the leaders of the aristocratic party, are slaves in the same household, and determine to rid themselves of the overbearing tyranny of the new steward, by raising up a formidable rival, who can beat him with his own weapons. This is a sausage-seller, more vulgar, low, arrogant, and a greater adept in the art of a popular leader and of those demagogues, whom Aristophanes hated mortally, than even Cleon himself. The plot succeeds, the sausage-seller becomes a reformed character, and Demus, boiled in a magic caldron, turns out a genuine Athenian of the olden time, a worthy descendant of the heroes who fought at Marathon.

CLOUDS.

The " Clouds," which was exhibited B. C. 423, is the most important of all his comedies. And though it was unsuccessful in the contest for the prize, owing to the strong party excited against it by Alcibiades, it must certainly be ranked as the best of the author's productions. In it the modern school of subtle and sophistical philosophy was the object of the poet's attack. The genius of the old Attic comedy was powerless, unless it indulged in personality; it demanded the representation of an individual, even when it attacked a class. Personality was its essence. The whole race of demagogues was personified by Cleon; the war-party by Lamachus; the philosophy of the day was represented by Socrates. Why, then, was a philosopher, whose opinions differed so materially from those attacked, selected as the representative of them?

The sophists professed, at a certain price, to make their pupils men of the world; to teach them how to get on in life; to be skilful *speakers* (λιστικοί), good *men of business* (πρακτικοί), *full of resource* (μηχανικοί), *ready debaters* (δημηγορικοί), *sharp practi-*

tioners (δικανικοί).   These were the ends which they proposed to themselves, but they were unscrupulous as to the means.

Socrates, on the other hand, without fee or reward, devoted himself to the task of regenerating Athenian society; his object was to make the youth of Athens high-principled, honorable gentlemen (καλοὶ κ' ἀγαθοὶ).

But in looking about for a type of the philosopher, Aristophanes naturally fixed upon the one who attracted the largest share of the public attention; who, from the tenor of his life and teaching, had made himself the greatest number of enemies; and who, for his eccentricities, laid himself most open to comic ridicule.   All these conditions were fulfilled in Socrates.

He was the most notorious of all who professed to be public instructors.   He did not deliver his lectures to a select class of friends and pupils, but was always ready to converse and dispute in public with persons of every degree of intellect and rank and station.   Few, the comic poet amongst the number, had any intimate knowledge of his sentiments or doctrines, or cared strictly to investigate them.   The general notion prevailed, that he assented to, rather than believed in the popular mythology; all knew that he was a philosopher, and, therefore, without further inquiry, assumed that his philosophy was that which Aristophanes denounced as the cause of the prevalent moral corruption.   Besides, he was an admirable subject for caricature; his ugly face, which was even copied in pottery and earthenware; his absent manners, which caused him at Potidæa to stand stock-still a whole day;[1] his wild stare to the right and left as he walked;[2] his bare feet and careless dress and disregard of the common practices of Athenian polite life, pointed him out as the very man to represent the professors of that μετεωροσοφία, or *soaring wisdom*, which disdained the common concerns of life, which only cared

"To tread the air, and contemplate the sun."

It would have been expecting too much to hope that the keen wit of Aristophanes could have foregone an opportunity thus spontaneously presented to him.   Everybody in Athens knew him, and the moment his representative appeared on the stage

[1] Symp. p. 462.   [2] Ibid. p. 464.

would recognize him. He was too fair a mark to be passed over. It is commonly said that a satirical temper will sacrifice a friend for the sake of a jest, and to make a butt of the philosopher was an irresistible temptation to Aristophanes. Probably he did not wish to injure him, nor, in fact, did he. The assertion that the attack in the "Clouds" was instrumental in causing the death of Socrates so many years after, is too groundless to dwell upon for an instant. Nor can any one read this comedy without perceiving that, although the satire is pungent, it is good-natured, and that the effect likely to be produced by it was not a hostile feeling, but a hearty laugh at the absurdities and follies of a mistaken old man.

WASPS.

In the "Wasps" the object of the poet is to attack the well-known litigiousness of the Athenian people. Philocleon (*lover of Cleon*), a name doubtless adopted in order to strike a second blow against that object of his deserved detestation, is represented as a victim of this absorbing passion. His son Bdelycleon (*abominator of Cleon*) tries to cure him of his taste. In order to wean him from attending the courts, he establishes a court of justice in his own house, and brings the house-dog before this august tribunal for stealing a Sicilian cheese. So simple is the plot, and the whole life of the play rests upon its broad humor and the buffoonery of Philocleon.

But its object was a most important one: nothing could be worse than the administration of justice at Athens; the small fee paid to the dicasts, or jurymen, caused the mass of the people to look to this employment as one of their means of living. Bribery was by no means uncommon; the power which an unscrupulous dicast necessarily wielded puffed up the pride of the populace and rendered them formidable enemies, and the temptation was a strong one to replenish the public treasury by fines and confiscations, because not only the state but individuals participated in its wealth. Sycophancy, or false accusations by common informers, became a complete scourge; and no man's life or property was safe from an accusation of treason against the sovereign people. This comedy furnished a model to Racine for his only comedy "Les Plaideurs," which, though a copy, and inferior, perhaps, in breadth of humor, far surpasses the original in the skill and art with which the plot is constructed.

PEACE.

The "Peace" has the same end in view as the "Acharnians," namely, to show what the author had so much at heart—the miseries and privations attendant upon a long-protracted war.

Trygæus, an Athenian citizen, rides to heaven on a beetle, in order to see whether he can persuade the gods to put an end to the war. He finds that Zeus and the gods are from home, and that War has thrown Peace into a well, whilst he and Tumult are pounding the Greek states in a mortar—the generals being the pestles which he uses for that purpose. Trygæus succeeds, with the assistance of a band of rustics, who of course, as representing the Athenian country party, are on his side, in liberating Peace, and brings her with triumph and rejoicing to Athens.

LYSISTRATA.

In the "Lysistrata," on the plot of which it is impossible to dwell, as it is one of the coarsest of the Aristophanic dramas, the evils of war are again brought forward, and peace is made by the influence of Lysistrata and her female associates.

THESMOPHORIAZUSÆ.

The title of the "Thesmophoriazusæ" originates in the Thesmophoria, or feast of Ceres and Proserpine, at which women alone were present. It is a bitter attack upon the vices prevalent amongst the female sex. The poet makes it a medium for attacking and parodying the tragedies of Euripides. His rhetorical style and sophistical philosophy were hateful to Aristophanes. He was deeply impressed with the idea that Euripides had substituted mere dialectical ingenuity for the straightforward wisdom enunciated in the gnomes of Æschylus and Sophocles. He grieved over the probable destruction, by this means, of national vigor and manly discipline. The following is the simple plot of this play. Euripides, informed that the women will take advantage of their assembling at the festival to avenge themselves on him for his misogynous temper, disguises his brother-in-law Mnesilochus as a woman, and sends him to plead in his behalf.

The women discover the deceit, and Euripides, in order to effect the rescue of his relative, assumes a number of characters. This gives occasion to many clever and amusing parodies of scenes in the Euripidean tragedy.

ECCLESIAZUSÆ.

In the Ecclesiazusæ, or the "Female Members of Parliament," a play which is; like the "Lysistrata," full of grossness and obscenity, some discontented women disguise themselves in male attire, and vote in the assembly that the supreme political power should be transferred from the men to themselves. Its subject is purely political. The Utopian theories of Plato, and the institutions of the great rival of Athens, Sparta, which were the object of that great philosopher's admiration, were the mark at which the comic poet aimed the shafts of his ridicule; but this was not all, the purpose of comedy would not have been attained if he had not struck nearer home. It was also intended as a warning addressed to all restless innovators, to beware how they endangered by fanciful reforms the integrity of the Athenian institution.

FROGS.

The "Frogs" continues the attack upon the Euripidean tragedy, which was begun in the "Thesmophoriazusæ." All the great tragic poets were now dead, and Greek tragedy had arrived at its period of decay. Dionysus, therefore, the god of tragedy, descends to the infernal regions in search of a poet. Æschylus and Euripides contend for the honor of returning to earth. A most amusing contest ensues, in which the peculiar merits and defects of each poet are exhibited, compared, and criticized. The question is for a long time undecided, but at last Euripides is ruined by his dishonest sophistry. He suffers a double defeat, for not only is Æschylus selected to return to earth, but Sophocles is, during his absence, installed in the tragic throne below.

The comedy of the "Frogs" is distinguished for the beauty of its choral odes, as all the Aristophanic comedies are for the Attic purity of their style. These sweet and graceful poems satisfactorily prove that, whilst the author of them surpassed in wit all those writers who were eminent in his own walk of literature, he equalled in elegance of language and lyric talent the tragic poets themselves.

The "Birds," which was acted B. C. 414, and gained the second prize, is pronounced by Süvern, in his elaborate essay, to be the most ingenious of all the poet's works. This very ingenuity renders it extremely difficult to discover the poet's object, and the facts which he has allegorically represented. Schlegel considers it as a piece of farcical buffoonery, of which the mechanism is like that of a fairy-tale, but not without some philosophical purpose. The more probable interpretation given of it by Süvern is, that Aristophanes wished to exhibit the corrupt and unhealthy state of Athenian society, and to prove to them that there was no hope of amelioration, except by a thorough moral reform and entire reconstruction of their social system. He had also in his mind's eye, as a secondary object, the unfortunate Sicilian expedition, the folly of which he incidentally makes the subject of his humorous satire.

The plot of the play is as follows:—Peisthetærus, an Athenian of a sophistical turn, and his friend Euelpides, whose temper, as his name implies, is of that light-hearted and sanguine kind which characterized the Athenian people, are disgusted with the state of things at Athens. At the suggestion of an oracle, they visit Tereus, who had been changed into a hoopoe, and propose to .him a scheme for building a city, by which the birds shall regain universal dominion, and this new dynasty shall be the authors of unspeakable blessings to mankind.

The proposal is favorably received by an assembly of the birds, convened for the purpose of discussion by the hoopoe, and a city is built called Nephelococcygia, or Cloud-cuckoo-town. Situated between earth and heaven, it cuts off all communication between gods and men, and starves the latter into conceding the supreme sovereignty of the world to the birds, and Zeus gives Peisthetærus his daughter in marriage. If, as has been stated, there is in this comedy an allusion to the Sicilian expedition, the founding of Cloud-cuckoo-town would represent the attempt to establish Athenian supremacy in the Mediterranean, cut off the communication between Sparta and her allies in Sicily and Magna Græcia, as the imaginary city prevented all intercourse between gods and men, and thus reduce the pretensions of the Lacedæmonians.

In support of this theory it may be urged, that, according to Thucydides, the Athenians did in reality entertain these ulterior designs. He states that the reason why Alcibiades so warmly advocated the Sicilian expedition, contrary to the advice of Nicias, was that he hoped by means of it to gain possession not only of Sicily but Carthage likewise.[1] And when, on his traitorous desertion to Sparta, he endeavors to persuade the Spartans to enter into the Syracusan quarrel,[2] he does not hesitate to say that the ambitious design of the Athenians was to subdue first Sicily, then Italy, next to invade Carthage, then to increase their army by the enlistment of Iberian mercenaries, and to reinforce their fleet by means of the timber of the Italian forests, thus invest the Peloponnese by sea and land, and finally extend their supremacy (ἀρχή) over the whole Greek nation.

PLUTUS.

The "Plutus' which had, in another form, been represented twenty years before, furnishes a specimen of the middle comedy. It was an allegorical satire upon a class, not upon individuals: and, as Addison[3] has already observed, it conveyed two moral lessons. In the first place, it vindicated the conduct of Providence in the distribution of wealth; and in the next, it showed the tendency of riches to corrupt the morals of those who possessed them.

Plutus was struck blind by Zeus, because he declared that he would grant wealth only to the virtuous. Chremylus, a good old man, but poor, falls in with him, and persuades him to accompany him home. His old intimate, Poverty, refuses to turn out, and reads him a good lecture in political economy, telling him that she was the mother of the arts, and that if every one were rich, there would be no producers of the luxuries which wealth purchases. She is, however, at last ejected. Plutus is then restored to sight by Æsculapius, and immediately commences the course which he had intended in early life. At length Hermes enters and com-

---

[1] Thuc. vi. 15.   [2] Ibid. vi. 90.   [3] Addison, Spect. No. 464.

plains, that, now that good men are rich, the gods get no sacrifices, and the priests are starved. Even the good old Chremylus becomes corrupted by wealth, and forsaking his trust in Providence, proposes to set up Plutus in the temple of Zeus.

Such was the old Attic comedy, as learned from the comedies of Aristophanes. The following is the chronological order in which, according to Clinton, the extant comedies of Aristophanes were exhibited:—

B. C. 425.	"Acharnians."	B. C. 411.	"Lysistrata."
424.	"Knights."	411.	"Thesmophoriazusæ."
422.	"Clouds."	405.	"Frogs."
422.	"Wasps."	392.	"Ecclesiazusæ."
421.	"Peace."	388.	"Plutus."
414.	"Birds."		

The remaining poets of the old and middle comedy[1] constitute a long list of names, but the few fragments which remain of their works render any notice of them uninteresting and unnecessary. The poets of the new comedy flourished subsequently to the period comprehended in this history.

[1] See Clinton, Fasti Hellenici, Introd. p. 36.

CHAPTER XI.

WHY HISTORY WAS CULTIVATED EARLIER AMONG THE SEMITIC NATIONS THAN AMONG THE GREEKS.—PHERECYDES OF LEROS.—HIS WORKS.—CHARON OF LAMPSACUS.—HELLANICUS.—HERODORUS OF HERACLEA.—HERODOTUS.—THE IMPROVEMENTS WHICH HE INTRODUCED INTO HISTORY.—HIS BIRTH, PARENTAGE, NATIVE CITY.—HIS SOURCES OF INFORMATION.—HIS TRAVELS.—THE TRADITION THAT HE RECITED HIS HISTORY AT THE OLYMPIC GAMES.—HIS RESIDENCE AT SAMOS, ATHENS, AND THURII.—HE DID NOT TRAVEL MUCH IN ITALY.—SOME OF HIS IDEAS TAKEN FROM SOPHOCLES.—HIS POETIC TALENTS.—METHOD IN WHICH HE INTRODUCES HIS DIGRESSIONS.—HIS AUTHORITY AS AN HISTORIAN.—HIS STYLE OF WRITING.—HIS RELIGIOUS SENTIMENTS.—THE GEOGRAPHY OF HERODOTUS.

FOR many centuries, whilst the literature of Greece was limited to poetry, the Egyptians and Semitic nations had been the possessors of genuine and authentic historical records. These not only contain narratives of events, but are also of inestimable chronological value, and the investigation of them is adding every year fresh stores of information to the history of the ancient world.

The hieroglyphics on Egyptian monuments, the arrow-headed inscriptions of Assyria, the sculptures of Nineveh, are all so many historical works, and by the light which they mutually throw on one another are capable of furnishing a trustworthy account of the length of dynasties, the duration of empires, the lives and conquests of kings, the natural productions and state of civilization in different nations, the habits and manners of both the conquering and the conquered people. The Jews, also, from their peculiar condition as the chosen people of the Most High, possessed historical writings still more ancient and more perfect than any other nation.

The Greeks, on the other hand, had no history, properly so called, until the period on which we are now entering. A taste for history had been formed at the time when Cadmus and Acusilaus and Hecatæus flourished, but they had neither the power.nor the materials for satisfying that taste.   There were no annals or registers previously existing which they could consult, or which could teach them the habits of historical inquiry and inves- tigation.   They had not yet begun to chronicle and register con- temporaneous records and memorials, and thus to collect materials for future historians.   The names of victors in the national games, with the dates of their triumphs, and interpolated lists of priest- esses of Heré at Argos, constituted almost all their early annals.

Such is the difference which exists on this point between the Greeks and the Semitic nations.   The reason for this difference is to be found in their respective political and social conditions. The nations of the East were under the sway of despotic monarchs, and had established hierarchies.   Both of these institutions are favorable to the storing up and preservation of historical records. The Greeks had neither priestly castes nor hereditary despotisms. Under an absolute monarchy, a nation exists only in the name of its sovereign ; everything centres in him : the glory of his people becomes his glory.   Historical records are the monarch's private diary.   It is his personal interest that nothing should be forgotten of his wars, progresses, victories, and extensions of dominion.   The walls of palaces and temples are made, by means of inscriptions and sculptures and paintings, to minister to his vanity, and to hand down imperishable records of his fame to posterity.   All the learned men in the empire would naturally be found at his court, and would take his exploits for their theme.

Again, it is the tendency of a priesthood religiously to preserve all historical documents.   The Jewish priesthood were appointed to this important office by divine authority.   The Egyptian priests were the recognized sources of information to whom Herodotus always applied.   In the Assyrian sculptures and inscriptions may be found many traces of priestly influence.   The colleges of priests and augurs at Rome were the depositaries of the national annals.   The monks of the Middle Ages were at once the pre- servers of literature and the historians of their times.

• Amongst the Greeks all these encouragements and aids to his- tory were wanting ; there was no central point round which all the events of former times would group themselves, or to which the whole interest would converge. . But besides, the glory of

Greece as one nation did not commence until their struggle for independence in the Persian war, and it was this very war which taught them the need of history, and immediately that the need was felt, supplied it, by producing an historian. The only previous occasion on which Greece was supposed to have fought as one united people, namely, in the Trojan war, was at a period so distant as necessarily to belong to mythology and poetry.

PHERECYDES OF LEROS.

The first historian of the flourishing era of Greek literature, Pherecydes, had scarcely emancipated himself from the mythical taste of his predecessors. He was born in the little island of Leros ; the date of his birth is unknown, but he flourished during the Persian war. As he took up his residence at Athens, he is called both a Lerian and an Athenian. Lucian places him amongst his examples of longevity, and he is said to have lived to the age of eighty-five. His traditional history, in ten books, consists of family records of the ancient Athenian houses, and connects them with the gods and heroes of the mythical period. The only portion of his works which is valuable, in an historical point of view, is an account of Darius's Scythian Expedition.

CHARON.

Charon of Lampsacus is thought by some to have been one of the existing historical authorities consulted by Herodotus. At any rate, the extant fragments of his works show that he compiled the annals of the Persian war. The time at which he flourished is very uncertain. Passow, on insufficient grounds, places his era as early as Ol. lxvii., Matthiæ as late as Ol. lxxv. Probably the era at which he wrote and flourished was, during the time when Herodotus was pursuing his travels,[1] and, therefore, a little prior to the composition of his great work. He wrote on Æthiopian, Persian, Grecian, Libyan, and Lampsacenian history,[2] and thus followed in the steps of his predecessor Hecatæus ; but he derived much of his knowledge from popular and traditional sources, rather than from personal observation and inquiry. He was a chronicler (ὡρόγραφος) rather than an historian.

[1] Dahlman, a. s. Buche s. Leben.   [2] Suidas, s. v.

21

HELLANICUS, born about B. C. 496.

Hellanicus was the most celebrated amongst the predecessors and contemporaries of Herodotus: he was born at Mitylene, about B. C. 496.   War, which in his old age desolated his native country, drove him as an exile into Asia Minor, where he died, according to Lucian, at the advanced age of eighty-five.   His works were numerous and varied, on genealogy, history, and chronology, but nothing now remains of them but fragments. His style was simple and unadorned, but he was careless as to the sources from which he derived his statements, and, according to Thucydides, inaccurate in his chronology.   His indolence in the investigation of truth led him to accept, without sufficient examination, popular legends and traditions, provided they were striking and amusing.   Dahlman[1] remarks, that Hellanicus, more than any other historian, overlaid Italian history with Greek tradition, and threw it into that confused state which has cost modern scholars so much toil and labor.

HERODORUS OF HERACLEA.

The name of one more prose writer belonging to the same era must be mentioned, Heredorus of Heraclea.   His works were of a mythological character; one of them treated of legends relating to Hercules, the other of the Argonautic Expedition; they are said to have contained some geographical and historical information, but probably of no value or authority.

HERODOTUS, born B. C. 484.

It has already been stated, that the necessity of the case called forth the historian, and that all materials previous to the Persian war, possessing any interest for the Greeks, belonged to the ages of tradition and legend.   But the struggle between a brave people in defence of their national existence and the aggressions of despotism furnished just such a subject as would have inspired a poet, if the events had been so long past as to be capable of ideal treatment.   As it was, they required being set forth in all the

[1] Life of Herod. vi.

array of truthfulness, and set before the eyes of those who eagerly looked for the real facts with faithfulness and accuracy. These requirements exercised a powerful influence in turning the abilities of Herodotus into the channel in which they flowed.

Although attempts of an historical nature had been made in former periods, by the records of oral tradition preserved by Herodotus of Heraclea, and the historical but ill-arranged summaries of Hellanicus, alluded to by Thucydides,[1] Herodotus was the first who attached to history the necessary aids of geography and chronology, without which, it has been said by Strabo, that history is a blind guide. For this reason, although others had written on the same subjects as himself, and even on the Persian war,[2] he is rightly termed the Father of History, as well as because he was the first to show that facts might be highly interesting without the aid of fiction. It is on account of this lively interest with which he invests his subject, that Müller terms him the Homer of history.

Almost the only authorities for the circumstances known respecting Herodotus, are the short biographical memoir of Suidas, and the scattered notices contained in his own work. He was a native of Halicarnassus, of good family; his parents' names were Lyxes and Dryo, and he had a brother named Theodorus. His native city was the capital of six confederate Dorian states; subsequently, like other Greek colonies, it was conquered by Crœsus, and at length became tributary to Persia. Of its queen Artemisía, Herodotus,[3] when enumerating the Persian forces of Darius, expresses the highest admiration, on account of her spirit and bravery. Xerxes also highly valued her wisdom, and the Athenians were so annoyed that a woman should make war against Athens, as to offer ten thousand drachmæ to any one who would take her alive.[4] To her care Dahlman[5] attributes the preservation of her kingdom in this unsuccessful campaign, and probably also the safety of the family of Herodotus, and adds, that he passed his youth in a peaceful home, because Halicarnassus did not join the Athenian confederacy until many years had passed away.

Respecting the time of his birth, as well as of his early youth

[1] Thucyd. i. 97.   [2] Herod. vi. 55.   [3] Ibid. vii. 99.
[4] Ibid. viii. 93, 103.   [5] Dahlman.

and education, we have little information; the date of the former is usually given as B. C. 484 (Ol. lxxiv. 1). Aulus Gellius,[1] on the authority of Pamphila, who wrote in the reign of Nero, states that the historians Hellanicus, Herodotus, and Thucydides, were almost contemporaries, and that at the commencement of the Peloponnesian war Hellanicus was sixty-five years old, Herodotus fifty-three, and Thucydides forty. Darius, therefore, had just died, and the disastrous attempt of the Asiatic Greeks to achieve independence had taken place ten years previously, when Herodotus was born; and we know that he was well acquainted with the works of the logographers as well as with the poetical literature of Greece. He was evidently thoroughly imbued with the spirit of Homer and Hesiod, whose era he fixed at about four centuries before his own time; for their poems he felt an enthusiastic admiration, and attributed to them the formation of the Greek theogony. This, doubtless, is overstated, as these poets must have done no more than systematize and expand the traditions of popular mythology.

The information given by Herodotus was collected by himself from local sources, and from personal intercourse with natives of those countries whose history he relates. To his own observation, likewise, is owing his geographical knowledge, which, notwithstanding some inaccuracies, displays habits of careful and diligent observation.[2] It is evident, from his works, that his travels were extensive, and occupied a large portion of his life. Probably from B. C. 464 to 444, that is, from the twentieth to the fortieth year of his age. Twenty of the best and most vigorous years of his life, and doubtless the whole of his fortune, did this enterprising man devote to foreign travel and to storing up materials for his history.

The order of his travels it is impossible to determine, for it must be remembered that his work is a history illustrated by local knowledge, and not a book of travels illustrated by history. It was from an historical point of view that he viewed every place which he visited; the objects of historical interest attracted him; and when in his leisure and retirement, whether at Samos,[3] or Halicarnassus,[4] or Thurii[5] (for so various are the statements re-

---

[1] Noct. Att. xv. 23.   [2] Herod. i. 170.   [3] Suidas.
[4] Lucian.   [5] Pliny.

specting the place where he wrote), he digested and arranged the materials which he had collected, he enriched his history with the fruits of many years' diligent toil.

There are various statements respecting the place at which his work was written. Suidas confers that honor on Samos, Lucian on Halicarnassus, Pliny on Thurii; but as there can be no doubt that the principal part of his travels was completed before he wrote his book, the probability is that he wrote it at Thurii.

If the nine books which he wrote are examined in order, it will be found that he must have travelled to the following parts of the world.

He must have been well acquainted with the islands of the Ægean,[1] the coast of Asia Minor,[2] and all the places in the neighborhood of his native city, whose skies he pronounces to be the brightest, and whose seasons the most genial in the world,[3] and he must have extended his survey as far as Lydia.[4] He must have seen Tyre and the Holy Land, where he found columns erected during the expedition of Sesostris.[5] When there he became acquainted with the rite of circumcision,[6] although he inaccurately attributes to the Egyptians its introduction amongst the Syrians in Palestine. He also visited Jerusalem, which he calls Cadytis,[7] a name evidently connected with the Arabic word El-kedesh (the holy), and mentions the defeat and death of Josiah at Megiddo,[8] and the march of the conqueror, Pharaoh Necho, to Jerusalem. He visited Mesopotamia, and its rivers Tigris and Euphrates, the city of Babylon, and the site of the still more ancient city of Nineveh.[9] This site he places on the Tigris, which accords with modern discoveries, whether we assume with Layard that Nimrûd is within the limits of the ancient Nineveh, or with Rawlinson, that the real site of Nineveh is the mound which is said to contain the tomb of Jonah. With respect to Babylon, he appeals to the testimony of his own eyes in support of his description of its surprising fertility in corn and barrenness of trees. He describes Ecbatana, the capital of Media, with all the accuracy of one whose own eyes had seen its walls, and compares them with

[1] Herod. i. 24. [2] Ibid. ii. 44. [3] Ibid. i. 142.
[4] Ibid. iii. 5. [5] Ibid. ii. 106. [6] Ibid. ii. 104.
[7] Ibid. ii. 159. [8] 2 Kings, xxii. [9] Herod. i. 193.

the circuit of the walls of Athens.[1]   He likewise penetrated into
Asia as far east as Susa, and saw the royal road which stretched
from Ephesus to Susa, and which was traversed over in three
months and three days.[2]   And at some time or other he travelled
westward to the towns of Magna Græcia, and the islands of the
Mediterranean.

Egypt, both Upper and Lower, and the course of the Nile as
far as Elephantine,[3] Arabia, to the east of that river, and Cyrene[4]
to the west, he doubtless saw with his own eyes, although the
names and descriptions of the nomad tribes of Libya, and his information respecting Carthage, were probably derived from the
testimony of others.   Thrace and Scythia are described with the
fidelity of an eye-witness, as also the Euxine and the Propontis,
and from thence he caught a glimpse of the Palus Mæotis.
Lastly, in Greece itself, and the islands to the west, he was personally acquainted with every place of historical interest, whether
within or without the Peloponnesus, its oracular seats and sacred
temples, its battle-fields and illustrious cities.[5]

The time necessarily occupied in these travels, and the certainty
that the historian's great work was not written until they were
finished, throw discredit on the story told by Lucian, that Herodotus read his history to the assembled Greek nation at the
Olympic festival, and that Thucydides, then a boy, was present,
and so affected with the narrative as to burst into tears.   The
Olympic festival, which would synchronize with the boyhood of
Thucydides, is Ol. lxxxi., B. C. 456, and in that year Herodotus
could only have been thirty-two years of age.   Many arguments
have been brought forward on both sides of the question, but the
balance of them appears to be against the credibility of this reci-
tatien.   The time and place, however, were well imagined, and
the idea ingeniously conceived by one who professes only to write
for amusement, and makes scarcely any pretensions to historical
authority.

If there is any part of his work which it is probable that he
recited at this great national festival of the Greeks, it is the
history of their struggles and triumphs over Persia.   This por-

---

[1] Herod. i. 98 ; v. 89.   [2] Ibid. v. 52.   [3] Ibid. ii. 74.
[4] Ibid. iv. 181.   [5] Ibid. i. 14, 20 ; ii. 5, 52.

tion may have excited the enthusiasm to which the tradition alludes, and have been the original story with which he afterwards interwove all the various knowledge resulting from his long and active life. An examination of his work proves that he intended this for his great object, and that everything else is subordinate to this end. A love of Greece and her free institutions was the prevailing feature of his mind. This feeling seems to have been fostered and strengthened by a comparison of Greek customs, laws, and constitutions, with those of all other countries which he visited. Although he could appreciate excellence wherever he discovered it, still Greece had no rival in his affections, and his admiration for Greek political principles, especially those of Athens, subjected him to the unfounded charge of one-sided prejudice in its favor. This accusation is found in a treatise which is attributed, though probably incorrectly, to Plutarch ;[1] but this, like other calumnies brought against him, is now disregarded, whilst modern researches and investigations tend to establish on a firmer basis his character for impartiality, and his authority as an historian.

One can easily beheve that some episodes or portions of his history were at times related by the author himself to a choice circle of admiring hearers. His simple and natural truthfulness, and, at the same time, his flowing garrulity; the negligent carelessness with which he breaks off the thread of his main story, and runs off into a digression, remind one of the old story-tellers. We can readily picture to our imagination an old man, full of his story, amusing a congregation of listeners, just as a storyteller in Italy in the present day will gather around him a little band, who will hang upon his lips with mute attention ; but it is plain that this is perfectly consistent with the idea that the work, as a whole, was composed in the later years of his life, when he had sought rest from the weariness of voyages by sea and land.

Then he delighted to look back into the past, to call to remembrance the wonders he had seen, and to draw upon these copious stores of a retentive memory in order to perfect that work which would bear his name down to posterity.

[1] De malig. Her.

Passages have been quoted[1] to prove the probability that his
work was completed at least in Magna Græcia. He illustrates
the figure of the Crimea by comparing it with Iapygia. The
history of the physician Democedes he must have learned in Italy;
and, lastly, when Clisthenes, King of Sicyon, invited all the most
distinguished Greeks to compete for the honor of his daughter's
hand, Herodotus mentions first the candidate who came from
Sybaris.

During the early part of his life, probably for more than thirty
years, the fixed residence of Herodotus, when not engaged in
travelling, was at Halicarnassus. When his uncle, Panyasis,
the epic poet, was put to death by Lygdamis, the tyrant of that
city, Herodotus fled to Samos.[2] He thus, from residing in the
country which received him as an exile, became an Ionian, and
learned the dialect in which he wrote. His attachment to Athens,
which is so observable in his writings, arose from the constant
intercourse subsisting between Samos and that city, but more especially from his friendship with Sophocles. Sophocles (B. C. 440)
was appointed strategus, and sent with Pericles to carry on the
Samian war, and is said to have composed an ode to Herodotus
whilst engaged in that campaign. In this war the political bias
of Herodotus would be entirely on the side of the Athenians, and
the liberal politicians, Pericles and Sophocles. The Samian war
was a war of opinion, and the Athenian forces were supporting
the cause of democracy against the aristocratic party.

It is probable that, after the taking of Samos,[3] Herodotus left
that island, and returned to Halicarnassus, where he was one of
those who succeeded in liberating his native city from the tyranny of Lygdamis. His sympathy with Athenian politics, which
were now in the ascendancy, owing to the influence of Pericles,
led him to migrate to Athens; for, according to his own testimony, he was probably there at the beginning of the Peloponnesian war.[4] There he resided as a μέτοικος, honored and respected,
until, at the commencement of the Peloponnesian war, he joined
the party of colonists which migrated to Thurii.

It is not probable that after this period he travelled much, for

---

[1] Dahlman, iii.; iv. 15, 99; iii. 131, 137; v. 44; vi. 21, 127.
[2] Suidas, s. v.   [3] B. C. 439.   [4] Herod v. 77.

his knowledge of the geography of Western Europe is far less accurate than that which was acquired in his Oriental travels. For example, he asserts that Sardinia is the greatest of all islands, an error into which he would not have fallen had he himself visited it.

A clear proof, also, that he did not travel in Italy far from home, is, that not only he does not mention any of the principal states which now began to be of importance in Roman history, but he appears ignorant of the existence of Rome itself, although her power was already widely established amongst the nations of Italy. That Herodotus was deeply imbued with the poetic literature of Greece, has been already stated; and the resemblance which has been traced in many places to passages in the tragedies of Sophocles, has caused it to be a general opinion that the dramatic poet derived some of his sentiments from the historian. Mr. Donaldson,[1] however, has incontestably proved that, instead of this being the case, the admiration which Herodotus felt for Greece and Greek literature, led him to adopt the thoughts of Sophocles, and that the prose of the former is a paraphrase of the poetry of the latter. The passages in which these parallelisms occur are precisely those in which it is far more probable that the historian would have copied the poet, than the poet have borrowed from the historian.[2] They are, in most cases, gnomic or proverbial sentences, which are characteristic of Greek poetry generally, and especially of a dramatic poet who felt that his mission was to be a moral instructor; and poetry is the natural language of the proverb, prose its paraphrase. The numerous Greek proverbial sayings which are scattered throughout the works of Herodotus,[3] prove that he drew largely from the copious stores of moral and political wisdom contained in the gnomic poets; it is, therefore, far more probable that he borrowed from Sophocles likewise, than that Sophocles should have versified his prose,[4] and thus have formed the only exception. They, moreover, occur in those incidents which are of more than doubtful histori-

---

[1] See Philol. Soc. Trans. p. 163.
[2] See Antig. 930; Herod. iii. 119.
[3] See ex. gr. i. 8, 86; i. 207; iii. 38, 72, 127; iv. 149.
[4] See vi. 1; vii. 9, 10, 46; viii. 3, 6, &c.

cal accuracy, but which are introduced as embellishments, to give
a romantic interest to the general narrative. They are cases in
which he combines the skill of the poet with the spirit of the historian, and gives a life and reality to his scenes, by introducing
in his details that verisimilitude which is often more natural and
credible than truth itself.

Throughout the whole of the history of Herodotus, the poetic
talent is clearly visible, which makes us forget that he is not a
native Ionian, but that this nurse of the picturesque in art and
literature was only the country of his adoption. His work is a
complete epic in its structure; its subject, one complete and harmonious whole—the triumph of Greece over Persia. All its
other parts are, historically considered, digressions; but, poetically, episodes. They do not appear interruptions, but illustrations, and resting places for the mind, from which it returns with
fresh ardor to the original thread of the story. They are sometimes like the houses of entertainment which a traveller meets
with in his journey, and in which he falls in with the natives of
other lands, ready to communicate their knowledge, and to enliven
him with their stock of anecdotes and information. At other
times, they resemble objects of interest and curiosity, or prospects
of striking beauty, which tempt him gladly to leave for a time
the road which he is pursuing, although, after having wandered
for a time, he is by no means indisposed to return and pursue his
journey. Few could have read these nine books, so appropriately
distinguished by the names of the Muses, without being delighted
with his digressions, and being struck with the natural way in
which he introduces them.

The following sketch of the method which he pursues, will be
sufficient to prove this assertion.[1] He assumes the traditional
existence of bitter hostility between Europe and Asia in the earliest times. The stories of Io, Medea, and Helen are examples of
this feud in the mythical period. It was first manifested in historical times by Crœsus, King of Lydia. A history, therefore,
of this kingdom is necessary to his plan. But Lydia was conquered by Cyrus, King of Persia. He is thus led to trace the
successive dynasties of Assyria, Media, and Persia, the steps by

[1] See Smith's Dict. s. v.

like this only its principal features can be noticed, and that in a brief and cursory manner.

In examining it, we must not expect to find a regular system. He was an historian, and not a geographer. He was conscious of the indispensable necessity of geography, in order to render history intelligible ; but still it is subsidiary, and therefore subordinate to his historical investigations. Besides this, it must be remembered that the science of geography was unknown, that his accounts are the earliest on record, and that, in the absence of the art of surveying, all his conclusions respecting form, distance, relative position, and magnitude, are derived from the experience and evidence of the unassisted external senses.   Hence, with some few exceptions, his geography consists of the positions which different countries occupy with relation to each other, without any attempt to determine accurately distances or dimensions. Yet, wonderful to say, Ptolemy, who flourished six centuries later, knew little more than he did.   In some instances his knowledge surpasses that of Strabo and Pliny, and in many, notwithstanding his errors, modern discovery has tended to establish his character for accuracy.

The following was his theory of the distribution of land and water on the surface of the earth.   Rejecting as absurd the idea that the land was a round disc, as from the lathe of the turner,[1] as well as the Homeric and Platonic belief, that the ocean was a river,[2] he asserted that the land (ἡ γῆ) is one vast continent, the shores of which are washed by the ocean,[3] on the west by the Atlantic, which forms one with the Southern or Red Sea; and on the north by the Northern Sea.   It must be remembered, that by the term Red Sea he does not designate the Arabian Gulf, but the whole sea on the south of Asia and south-east of Africa ; whilst by the Atlantic he understood the whole expanse of ocean outside the Pillars of Hercules.   Whether Europe is bounded by the sea along its entire northern limit, and on its eastern boundary, and what forms the eastern boundary of India, he does not profess to know for certain.[4]   All beyond India to the east is waste.   This world-wide continent is divided into the three which

[1] Herod. iv. 36.   [2] Ibid. ii. 23.

[3] Ibid. i. 202.   [4] Ibid. iv. 45.

are each commonly called by that name, *viz.* Europe, Asia and Africa.[1] The Phasis he makes the boundary between Europe and Asia, rather than the Tanais ; whilst Africa is divided from Asia, not by the Isthmus of Suez, but by the river Nile. He believed that Europe extended across all the northern portion of the earth from east to west, and was therefore larger than Asia and Africa together. In this error he was followed by subsequent geographers.

The comparative dimensions of the three continents, according to Pliny, are still more incorrect, and a nearer approach to the truth was not made until the time of Ptolemy. The consequence of thus cramping the dimensions of Asia is, that he makes Asia Minor and the peninsula of Arabia far too narrow. It is remarkable that he knew the Caspian Sea to be a lake, whilst so long afterwards, at the period of Alexander's visit to its shores, the observations made arrived at a different result, and determined that it was a gulf of the Northern Ocean. The land farthest to the west with which he was acquainted was the coast of Cornwall; he speaks of it as abounding in tin mines, and as forming a portion of the group now called the Scilly Isles, which he includes with it under the general title of Cassiterides, or Tin-Islands.[2]

As his observation led him erroneously to imagine that Europe nearly balanced Asia and Libya, he assumed a similar analogy to exist between the Danube and the Nile. He imagined that the former was equal in length to the latter,[3] and that the one divided Europe down the middle, as the other divided Libya,[4] and that the mouths of both were on the same meridian of longitude.[5] He believed also that the sea of Azof is nearly as large as the Euxine,[6] and that its north-west coast ran in a due northerly direction from the Bosphorus ;[7] nor was he acquainted with the fact that the Crimea is a peninsula.[8] Of India and its extent his ideas were vague and indistinct. The peninsular portion of it is probably alluded to, where he speaks of a country inhabited by blacks stretching very far to the south of Persia.

[1] Herod. iv. 45. [2] Ibid. iii. 115. [3] Ibid. ii. 33.
[4] Ibid. iv. 49. [5] Ibid. ii. 34. [6] Ibid. i. 86.
[7] Ibid. i. 99. [8] Ibid. iv. 99.

Of Africa the knowledge of Herodotus was greater than that of Ptolemy, far greater than that of Strabo. He had heard from the natives of Cyrenaica that a great river existed in the interior, running from west to east, which some, with whom he was inclined to agree, supposed to be a portion of the Nile.[1] This was doubtless the Niger; and although, from the ascertained elevation of the intermediate country, modern science has decided that any connection between the Nile and the Niger is improbable, yet the question has even yet not been completely determined. He knew also that Africa had been circumnavigated, and that it stretched far to the south of the Niger and the Nile.[2] He derived this knowledge from the testimony, first, of the Phœnicians, and next of the Carthagenian navigators. The former proved the correctness of their story, and the fact of their having crossed the equator by their declaration that they had the sun on their right hand. Herodotus confesses that he cannot give credit to this tale. In fact, the state of science did not enable him to understand the phenomenon.

Such was the geographical knowledge which the father of history derived from his limited opportunities. Credulous as to what was told him, his veracity, wherever his own observation is concerned, is unimpeachable. His errors are not those of culpahle ignorance, but the unavoidable result of his age being one in which science was in its infancy. For this reason he was ignorant that snow was found at high elevations in warm climates.[3] He attempted to account for the overflow of the Nile on grounds which are philosophically untenable,[4] and could not understand how the circumnavigators of Africa had the sun on their right hand. It is not improbable that when he stated that the sun in India is vertical before midday, he may have been recording the fact communicated to him by others, that when tho sun reaches the meridian in India,[5] it is not yet noon in the countries to the westward.

[1] Herod. ii. 28.   [2] Ibid. iv. 42, 43.   [3] Ibid. ii. 22.
[4] Ibid. ii. 24.   [5] Ibid. iii. 104.

CHAPTER XII.

THUCYDIDES, born about B. C. 471.

PHILOSOPHICAL HISTORY. — THUCYDIDES ITS INVENTOR. — HIS LIFE. — EXTENT OF HIS
HISTORY.—THE AUTHENTICITY OF THE EIGHTH BOOK EXAMINED.—SUMMARY OF GREEK
HISTORY IN THE FIRST BOOK.—STORY OF HARMODIUS AND ARISTOGITON —THE PLAN
OF HIS HISTORY.—DIGRESSIONS.—CHRONOLOGICAL ARRANGEMENT.—THE ADVANTAGE
OF HIS BEING A CONTEMPORARY HISTORIAN.—THE SPEECHES OF THUCYDIDES.—THEIR
VALUE. — THEIR STYLE. — TRUTHFULNESS IN HIS GENERAL NARRATIVE. — GRAPHIC
POWER.—HIS CHIEF INTELLECTUAL QUALITIES.—HERODOTUS AND THUCYDIDES COM-
PARED.

WE have now arrived at the period in which history has assumed a more advanced and accomplished form. Its aim is now
no longer simple amusement, but instruction.[1] Its incidents are
viewed as conveying lessons of practical wisdom to the statesman,
when commented on and grouped together under certain general
heads by the comprehensive mind and generalizing powers of the
philosopher. They are considered as developments of the principles of moral action, and as illustrating man's social and political relations. This is the highest and noblest task of history,
and worthily was it performed by the thoughtful inventor of
philosophical history, Thucydides. In modern times, his example
has been wisely followed; philosophical history is appreciated as
it deserves. The mere annalist is no longer considered as fulfilling the whole duty of the historian. But it must be confessed
that for the two invaluable qualities of thoughtfulness and suggestiveness, no historian has ever surpassed Thucydides. The
intrinsic value of his great work, which he modestly styles a
compilation (συγγραφή), fully accounts for its being imperishable;
and the verdict of posterity has stamped it as that which he intended it to be—an everlasting possession (κτῆμα ἰς ἀιί).

Thucydides was an Athenian citizen, the son of Olorus,[2] belong-

---

[1] Thucyd. i. 22.   [2] Ibid. i. 1; iv. 104.

ing to the Attic borough Halimus. The date of his birth is not quite certain, but it was probably B. C. 471,[1] or B. C. 472.[2] Whether he was a pupil of the orator Antiphon, is doubtful, but the assertion is made by Suidas, and supported by other authorities.[3] In the year B. C. 424, he was entrusted with the command of the Athenian fleet at Thesos, and whilst there was summoned to the relief of Amphipolis against the Spartan general, Brasidas. Unfortunately, he did not arrive until too late. Amphipolis had surrendered on the very day, in the evening of which he arrived at the mouth of the Strymon.[4] The Athenians frequently visited ill-success on the part of their generals as severely as they would incompetence. The demagogue, Cleon, was now at the zenith of his popularity, and being both politically and personally hostile to Thucydides, took advantage of this occasion to excite the popular feeling against him. Thucydides, therefore, went into voluntary exile,[5] and resided in places where he was safe, owing to the ascendancy of oligarchal and Peloponnesian influence, during a period of twenty years.

Every year of this eventful period—the most important which Greece has ever known[6]—was probably occupied in chronicling each incident as it occurred, and whilst it was fresh in his memory, and produced the most vivid impressions. His exile in Thrace probably furnished him with the opportunity of digesting his materials, and to this episode in his life we owe his history; for the arrangement of his materials and the composition of part of it were doubtless the employment of his long banishment. It was not, however, completed until the war was finished; for he mentions the duration of it, although his history is broken off before he could complete his original design.

There are many conflicting statements respecting his return to his native country and his death. But the probability is, that, when peace was concluded with Lacedæmon, B. C. 404, a decree was passed to permit the return of all exiles, and that shortly after this Thucydides came back to Athens. Pausanias tells us

[1] Clinton's Fasti Hellenici ; Suidas, s. v. Antiph.
[2] Aul. Gell. xv. 23, quoted by Clinton.
[3] Matthiæ, History of Literature.   [4] Thuc. iv. 102.
[5] Ibid. v. 26.   [6] Ibid. i. 21.

22

that he died by the hand of an assassin, and this event is placed by one authority as early as B. C. 401,[1] by another as late as Ol. xcvii. 2 (B. C. 391).[2]

The anonymous life of him states that he died of disease, and was buried in Cœle near Athens, and that a simple pillar marks the spot with this inscription—

"Here lies Thucydides, son of Olorus the Halimusian."

The history of Thucydides, which was designed to comprise a complete account of this important war, is only continued as far as the middle of the twenty-first year (B. C. 411). The words with which it concludes, seem to imply that it was not abruptly interrupted, but that from some cause or other he voluntarily brought it to a termination. "When," he says, "the winter after this summer ends, the twenty-first year will be complete."

The eighth, or concluding book, is distinguished from the preceding ones by the absence of speeches—those reflections of the historian's mind which form so valuable and interesting a portion of his great work. This circumstance, coupled with an imaginary inferiority in point of style, has led to much doubt being cast upon its genuineness. Some have ignorantly ascribed it to Xenophon, whose style is totally different from that of this book; others to a daughter, who, together with the son named Timotheus, survived him. There is, however, no external evidence against its genuineness, whilst the internal evidence is in its favor. The style of language and the tone of thought are as vigorous as in the rest of his work; the instances of carelessness are scarcely more frequent than every reader of Thucydides is accustomed to expect, and if they were, this would only prove that less elaborate care was bestowed on the concluding portion of a work, for the non-completion of which we can imagine no other cause than want of time and opportunity. The same haste will account for the absence of speeches, which are evidently the most thoughtful and most highly-wrought portions of his other books. But even of these some germs are discernible, which most probably, if time had allowed, would have been worked out and perfected.[3]

[1] Krüger, ü. d. Leben des Thuk.
[2] Matthiæ, History of Literature.
[3] See Thucyd. c. 27, 45, 46, 76.

There is nothing in the whole range of Greek literature so important to the historical student as the brief summary of early Greek history contained in the first book. Although not free entirely from the trammels of mythological tradition, the author gives its deserved value to poetical testimony, and prepares the way for a more philosophical interpretation quite consistent with subsequent theories and discoveries. These few chapters are eminently suggestive; they are a text for the philosophical historian to expand and dilate upon; they furnish the materials and ground-work for the construction of all sound views respecting the origin and progress of Greek civilization. A remarkable specimen of the able manner in which he handles popular traditions and recollections, is furnished in the discussion respecting the story of Harmodius and Aristogiton. It is a masterly piece of historical criticism.

Like Herodotus, Thucydides considers his subject as one complete whole. Hence, after the introduction to which allusion has been made, the Peloponnesian war is one subject which employs his thoughts and his pen. To this narrative the digressions which are necessary to illustrate it form episodes. One is the treachery of Pausanias,[1] which led to the appointment of the Athenians, by the unanimous voice of the allies, to the high position of ἑλληνοταμίαι, or *treasures of Greece;* another, the rise and progress of the Athenian supremacy.

The arrangement of his history is somewhat singular; not only is it chronological, but the successive events are accurately assigned to the summer or winter half-year in which they occurred. The only inconvenience resulting from this is, that the scene is continually shifting, and thus the interest is divided and the mind sometimes feels distracted by the variety of subjects to which it is compelled in succession to give its attention.

There are, on the other hand, manifest advantages connected with this method of chronological computation. Each campaign in this war generally took place in the summer, and therefore the periods of action and rest were thus distinguished. It was, too, the only plan which could be equally suitable to all Greece, because the names of the months differed in the different states

---

[1] Thucyd. i. 128–134.   [2] Ibid. i. 89–117.

of Greece. Computation by Olympiads was not yet adopted, for although Thucydides[1] and Xenophon[2] each in two instances define an event by the Olympiad in which it took place, the first historian who introduced this practice was Timæus, of Sicily, B. C. 264, from which time his example was generally followed.

Thucydides lived during the period of which he related the history, and this is sometimes considered objectionable, because of the danger which exists lest the historian should be influenced by his own political bias, and by the party prejudices of his times. This was especially to be feared in the historian of a war such as the Peloponnesian. It was essentially a war of race, and therefore of political principle.

Whatever the overt causes were which led to it, Thucydides expressly informs us, it arose from the jealousy felt by Lacedæmon of the overweening power of Athens. The liberty of Greece and the tyranny of Athens were the Spartan war-cry. It was a contest between Ionian and Dorian, those ancient and implacable foes; between oligarchy and democracy; between the maintenance of things as they were, and progress. But the impartiality of Thucydides was uninfluenced by this state of things. He does not conceal his political sentiments. He honestly avows them, but he does not swerve from historic truth. From all this strife of opinions he stands aloof; he seems to occupy an eminence from which he can calmly and coolly survey the opposing parties, whilst his own feelings are beyond the reach of the storm which rages beneath his feet. He saw, as every wise and philosophical man must have seen, the fearful evils of unbridled democracy, and, therefore, his bias was on the side of putting some rational limit to progress; but he could, nevertheless, admire the policy of Pericles, and candidly express his approbation. He believed that this great statesman was a friend only to constitutional liberty; that he knew what were the passions of an Athenian mob, and, therefore, never became a demagogue; that he owed his influence not to pandering to their passions, but to his uprightness and wisdom.

The authority, then, of Thucydides is invaluable, because he possessed all the knowledge which personal observation could

---

[1] Thucyd. iii. 8; v. 49.   [2] Hell. i. 2; ii. 3.

alone supply, and that honesty which could not be corrupted, or even blinded, by party politics, or superficial and prejudiced views.

The most striking feature of the history of Thucydides consists in the speeches which he attributes to the principal characters. In what light they are to be regarded as historical documents will best be seen from his own words:—"As to the speeches of each individual, either before the war, or when engaged in it, it would have been difficult to remember accurately, either what I myself heard, or what others reported to me. I have, therefore, reported their speeches according as I thought most suitable to the speaker and to the occasion, keeping, however, as closely as possible to the general sense of what they actually said."[1]

However nearly, therefore, the speeches of Thucydides may have represented the sentiments of those who are supposed to have delivered them, there can be little doubt that the historian made them the occasion of conveying his own views, or the views of the two great opposing parties, respecting the political complexion of affairs.

Allowing himself, therefore, the freedom which he claims, it is scarcely possible to conceive that his own views, or the prevalent ideas of the times, would not be introduced in them; for this reason they are so valuable, we have in them a just picture of the politics of the day, together with a commentary on them, by a sound-judging and impartial mind. And what a strange and yet faithful picture is drawn in many of them of Athenian inconsistency! We see vanity and self-conceit, side by side with noble-minded liberality, and absence of all jealousy against foreigners; cringing submission to demagogues, joined with a power of appreciating statesman-like wisdom; firm attachment to liberty, and cruel tyranny towards their subject states; utter disregard for the principles of justice, if they interfered with selfish aggrandizement, and yet a patriotic anxiety for the honor of their native country.

Cicero says,[2] respecting the speeches of Thucydides, " They contain so many obscure and recondite sentiments, that they can with difficulty be understood." This very obscurity arises from their deep philosophical character. The historian's copiousness of ideas far exceeds that of his language, and the rapidity with

---

[1] Thucyd. i. 22. [2] Cic. Orat. ix.

which his thoughts succeed one another, surpasses his power of expressing them. Containing as they do, in many instances, the germs of thought, rather than its lucid and perfect development, they are more suited for the calm and deliberate study of a reader than for delivery, as it would have been almost impossible to have followed his involved arguments and subtle reasoning. They contain little of rhetorical embellishment; here and there a striking and poetical metaphor adds beauty to the style as well as point to the argument. Antithesis is the figure which he most frequently uses, as may be expected in the case of an author whose principal characteristic is conciseness and brevity, but even in these there is not much variety. One for example, namely, that between λόγος and ἔργον (*word* and *deed*) is repeated almost incessantly.

According to the theory laid down by Aristotle, the proof from argument holds the chief and most prominent place; his object is conviction rather than persuasion, and thus his speeches, consistently with the tenor of his whole work, perform the promise which he holds out in the introduction, namely, that his work is composed as an everlasting possession for future ages, rather than a mere prize composition intended for the gratification of the moment.

Written before oratory was reduced to an art, they nevertheless furnish the most copious illustrations of all the rules of art. They are strictly artistic without being artificial. A comparison of them with Aristotle's " Treatise on Rhetoric" will show that almost every one of the principles which he lays down, may be illustrated by an example drawn from the speeches of Thueydides.

As they are the orations of statesmen and generals, they are, with very few exceptions, of the deliberative kind; one, the funeral oration pronounced by Pericles over those who fell in the first year of the war, is a specimen of demonstrative oratory or panegyric;[1] and the speeches of Cleon and Diodotus, on the condemnation of the Mityleneans, are partly of the judicial kind, although the question is principally argued as one of political expediency.

[1] Thucyd. ii. 35–46.

The style, moreover, is to a certain extent varied according to circumstances; for example, when a Spartan is represented as speaking, the concise mode of expression is retained, which is characteristic of that people; but, nevertheless, though graphic and characteristic, the style of Thucydides himself may still be recognized.

Throughout the historical narrative, a strict love of truth is visible, together with habits of patient and laborious investigation. It is clear that he omitted no means of ascertaining the truth of what was said, and that, when aware of the facts, he would not garble or misrepresent them, but only array them in an interesting garb by his skilful treatment.

"What I have written,"[1] he says, "is founded not on mere reports or notions of my own, but on a personal knowledge, wherever it was possible, and in other cases on a laborious and accurate examination of the testimony of others." The fact that he was the first historian who paid attention to chronological arrangement, shows the high value which he set on historical accuracy; and the unaffected brevity of his style proves that all he cared for was to state what he saw, or heard, or thought, without embellishment of language or unnecessary amplification.

And yet this brevity and conciseness did not proceed, in his case, from a deficiency in descriptive, or graphic power; he possessed enough of imaginative power to have invested dry bare facts with the most thrilling interest. But his minute exactness produces as much effect as the most highly colored and poetical description. The details of the plague at Athens, with all its sad moral and physical results, are as affecting as a poem, and have furnished materials for poems. His talents for description are again remarkably exhibited in his delineations of the operations during the siege of Platæa,[2] and the methods taken by the besieged to effect their escape; and the same talent is observable perhaps to a still greater extent, in his narrative of the disastrous Sicilian expedition.

But the intellectual qualities, in which he has seldom been equalled, are moral wisdom and political sagacity. His know-

[1] Thucyd. i. 22.   [2] Ibid. ii. 75.

ledge of human nature; his intelligent quickness, similar to that which he describes as being possessed by Themistocles; his intuitive perception of the motives which actuate either individuals or bodies of men; his keen observation of the different shades of party feeling, and the principles of Greek politics, render his work full of instruction for the moral and political student in all ages. This union of moral and political wisdom with descriptive power, renders the pictures which he draws of the demoralization which prevailed in Greek society so dark and tragical. With what a masterly hand he traces step by step this downward course[1] when the plague devastated Athens! The imminent danger which threatened all, concentrated all men's thoughts upon themselves; every other tie was forgotten; the nearest and dearest relatives died deserted and unassisted; even the reverence for the dead, which exercised so strong an influence over the Greek mind, existed no longer; the sentiment of veneration in so important a form once destroyed, the fear of God soon ceased, and the principle upon which all acted was, "Let us eat and drink, for to-morrow we die."

In describing the Corcyrean sedition,[2] he is not content with relating the horrible atrocities which took place in this bloody conflict between the oligarchal and democratical parties, his philosophical mind discerned the causes which produced it; the breaking up of moral principle which had already taken place throughout Greece, and which afterwards, in other states, produced similar atrocities. In the true spirit of a philosopher, he points out the indications which even language presented of this social disorganization: "The common acceptation of words,"[3] he says, "was arbitrarily altered; inconsiderate rashness was considered manliness and *esprit-de-corps*; prudent caution a mere cloak for cowardice; calm judgment nothing else but idleness; mad violence was accounted spirit; to concert measures with caution, and without committing oneself, was thought to be a mere fair excuse for tergiversation."

His far-seeing mind was aware how deeply rooted, and widely extended, social and political mischief had become; that the ties of party, and of political partisanship, were held to be stronger

---

[1] Thucyd. ii. 52–53.   [2] Ibid. iii. 81.   [3] Ibid. iii. 82, 83.

than those of kindred; faction had taken the place of patriotism; to revenge an injury was thought sweeter than not to have suffered one; oaths were binding only so long as suited the convenience of those who swore them; knavery was called cleverness, and honesty simplicity; and hence men became proud of the latter and ashamed of the former. Thus moral corruption in every form prevailed, and sincerity, which is the principal qualities of noble natures, was first ridiculed, and then disappeared.

It is worthy of remark that Thucydides strictly confines himself to his subject; absorbed in the war without, he gives us but little information of the state of things within the walls of Athens, except such matters of public interest as were connected with external history. But during this period, many important moral influences were being brought to bear upon the Athenian mind. Socrates was daily teaching his lessons of moral wisdom in the public thoroughfares and places of resort, throughout the crowded city; not, like the sophists, only to the rich and noble, but to the masses of the people. The tragic poets were annually fulfilling their office of public instruction, and thus furnishing matter for reflection and conversation to their countrymen during the rest of the year; and comedy, like the periodical literature of our own day, was lashing the follies and vices of individuals, exposing corruption and abuse in the public administration, guiding the public taste in literature and philosophy.

But these matters did not occupy the mind of the historian. His idea, as well as that of his countrymen, evidently was that the history of a country implied its relation to the rest of the world; whether Greek or barbarian, internal history was only important so far as it was connected with this; its reputation was advanced by warlike exploits, and triumphs, and successes; war, therefore, with its various successes and reverses, was the subject naturally chosen, and formed the groundwork for his philosophical reflections.

In comparing together the two great historians, it is plain that the mind and talents of both were admirably suited to the work which they took in hand. The extensive field in which Herodotus labored, the abundance and variety of materials with which his habits of investigation furnished him, afforded an opportunity for embellishing and illustrating his history with the marvels of foreign lands[1]; he collected such accounts as would please and delight the reader, and invested them with the peculiar charm of his simple and attractive style.

The glorious exploits of a great and free people stemming a tide of barbarian invaders, who appeared by their very numbers likely to overwhelm them, and finally triumphing completely over them; the features of the earth which we inhabit, hitherto unknown, or misrepresented by fable, and enveloped in mystery; the customs and histories of the barbarians with whom they had been at war, and of all other nations whose names were connected with Persia, either by lineage or conquest, were subjects which required the talents of a simple narrator, who had such love of truth as not wilfully to exaggerate, and such judgment as to select what was best worthy of attention.

Thucydides had a narrower field. The mind of Greece was the subject of his study, as displayed in a single war, which was in its rise, progress, and consequences the most important which Greece had ever seen. It did not in itself possess that heart-stirring interest which characterizes the Persian war. In it united Greece was not struggling for her liberties against a foreign foe, animated by one common patriotism, inspired by an enthusiastic love of liberty; but it presented the sad spectacle of Greece divided against herself, torn by the jealousies of race, and distracted by the animosities of faction. The task of Thucydides was that of studying the warring passions and antagonistic workings of one mind. It was one, therefore, which, in order to become interesting and profitable, demanded that there should be brought to bear upon it the powers of a keen analytical intellect. To separate history from the traditions and falsehoods with which it had been overlaid, and to give the early history of Greece in its most truthful form; to trace Athenian supremacy from its rise to its ruin, the growing jealousy of other states, whether inferiors or rivals, to which that supremacy gave rise; to show its connection with the enmities of race, and the oppositions of politics; to point out what causes led to such wide results; how the insatiable ambition of Athens, gratifying itself in direct disobedience to the advice

of their wise statesman, Pericles, led step by step to their ultimate ruin, required not a mere narrator of events, however
brilliant, but a moral philosopher and a statesman. Such was
Thucydides. Although his work shows an advance in the science
of historical composition over that of Herodotus, and his mind
is of a higher, because of a more thoughtful order, yet his fame
by no means obscures the glory which belongs to the father of
history. They appear both to have attained that important wisdom which knows

> Quid ferre recusent
> Quid valeant humeri,—(HOR. *Art. Poet.*),

and each to have chosen the method of treatment best adapted
for their subject-matter. Their walks are different; they can
never be considered as rivals, and therefore neither can claim
superiority.

Herodotus is almost as objective as Homer; there is little or
nothing of self in his writings; all his thoughts are absorbed in
telling his story. His narrative embodies the spirit of the times
in which he lived. Thucydides is subjective; he values facts as
illustrations of the principles which are deeply rooted in his own
mind; he gives a complete delineation of his own sentiments; he
is fitted to lead and direct public opinion, and his judgment on
passing events and human conduct is far in advance of his age,
and far more comprehensive and philosophical than that of his
contemporaries.

CHAPTER XIII.

XENOPHON, born B. C. 447.

XENOPHON was the son of Gryllus, a native Athenian. The
time of his birth is variously stated. Matthiæ places it Ol. lxxxiii.
2, B. C. 447.[1] Clinton supposes him to have been about forty-two
at the time of the "Anabasis," and consequently to have been
born about B. C. 443.[2] He began life as a soldier, and, in B. C.
424, fought at the battle of Delium.[3] In the flight from that
disastrous field, he fell from his horse, and owed his safety to the
broad shoulders of the philosopher Socrates. This was the commencement of a firm and lasting friendship between these distinguished men. To whatever other instructors he owed any part
of his education, it is certain that he derived all his moral and
philosophical principles from Socrates.

Nothing worthy of mention is known respecting him until B. C.
401, when he joined as a volunteer, without any military appointment, the expedition of Cyrus the younger against Artaxerxes
Mnemon. For a knowledge of his conduct on this occasion, and
the motives which led to it, we are indebted to his own history.[4]
Proxenus, a young man of great ambition, but upright principle,
was a native of Thebes, and having come to Athens to study under
Gorgias, formed a friendship with Xenophon.[5] He subsequently

---

[1] Matthiæ, History of Literature.
[2] Fasti Hellenici, ii. 89.   [3] Thucyd. iv. 96.
[4] Anab. iii. I.   [5] Ibid. ii. 6.

entered the service of Cyrus, and invited his Athenian friend to follow his example. The love of enterprise so natural to one who was at heart a thorough soldier, together with the political troubles which distracted his native land, tempted him to accept an invitation which scarcely appears consistent with Athenian patriotism. Before he decided, he asked the advice of Socrates. He, strange to say, made no objection, but recommended him to consult the Delphian oracle. Xenophon had determined to go, and only asked the oracle to what gods he should sacrifice in order to insure success. Xenophon then went to Sardis, and arrived in time to join the expedition.

The army of Cyrus crossed the Taurus and the Euphrates, and met the Persians at Cunaxa, near Babylon. The Greeks were successful, but Cyrus fell; and as soon as his death was known, the Orientals fled, and left the ten thousand Greeks in the plains of Mesopotamia. By the treachery of Tissaphernes, the Greek generals were thrown into captivity, and afterwards put to death. It was at this desperate crisis that the qualifications of Xenophon pointed him out as the one to rescue them from their difficulties. Impressed, like his great master, with the idea that man's counsels are under divine direction, he dreamed a dream which determined him to persuade the officers of Proxenus to put themselves at the head of his countrymen and lead them home. This memorable retreat stamps forever the character of Xenophon as a man of patient endurance, gentle temper, cool resolution, and firm determination. His conduct presents a striking instance of the force of circumstances to call forth talents which have been latent only because no opportunities have before occurred of exhibiting them. He showed a natural fitness for stations of command, and, above all, that important qualification of an officer —sympathy with the soldier. This was Xenophon's philosophy; he was not endowed with acute analytical powers; he was not capable of deep original observation ; his views of philosophy were even what might be termed popular and superficial. But as no one has surpassed him in his power of apprehending and appreciating the practical bearing of any philosophical question, so his conduct on this trying occasion proved that his philosophy had a practical effect upon his character.   His philosophy was not so much of the head as of the heart.

As the retreat itself exhibits Xenophon as a great commander, so his history entitles him to rank much higher as an historian than as a theoretical philosopher, and for this reason he more appropriately finds a place in this chapter.   His simple and natural descriptions of the countries which lay on the line of march, are doubtless unimaginative, and have none of the glowing fervor and gorgeous coloring of a poetic mind inspired with the natural beauties which his eyes beheld for the first time; but they pretend to nothing more than a simple and faithful delineation of nature, and are for that reason delightful.   His narrative may be unpoetic, but it is never prosy.   His graphic power has been compared to that of the Flemish painters; and few are insensible to the pleasure of contemplating their art— so true to nature—even of those who may not be able to soar so high as to appreciate fully the divine creations of a Michael Angelo or a Raphael.   His interesting account of the troubles and difficulties and varied adventures which the Greeks met with on their long march; of the invincible perseverance with which they fought their way, sword in hand, through the territories of hostile tribes not inferior to themselves in valor; carries, as it were, the reader with him through the very scenes which he describes; and the story of the return is enlivened and illustrated by amusing pictures of native manners and customs, almost equal to those of Herodotus himself.

The difficulties of the march furnished the historian with a subject worthy of his pen.[1]   Rapid rivers were crossed, and a passage successfully forced through the dangerous defiles and rocky fastnesses of Taurus, garrisoned by the warlike Carduchi. Now the climate suddenly changed.   Relaxed and enervated by the burning sun of Mesopotamia, they had rapidly ascended to the elevated table-land of Armenia.

The snow fell and buried all beneath it, a bitter wind swept over this trackless waste of snow, and, maimed and mutilated by the frost-bite, many died of cold and starvation.   At length, after severe suffering, the army was toiling up the sloping sides

[1] Anab. iv.

of Mount Thcsbes, the front ranks had just reached the ridge, when a shout of joy arose, which was re-echoed from rank to rank until it reached the rear. They had seen the sea, the broad waters of the Euxine lay stretched at their feet. At first Xenophon and the rear guard were alarmed, thinking that they were attacked by the enemy; soon, however, they heard the words, θάλαττα, θάλαττα (*the sea, the sea*), and men and officers threw themselves into each other's arms with tears of joy. The soldiers spontaneously collected stones, and raised a huge mound as a memorial of their safety. In two days more they arrived at Trapezus, the modern Trebizond, and thence the main army proceeded to Cerasus, and found that out of the ten thousand, eight thousand six hundred survived. When their perils were over, the unanimous voice of the army wished to make Xenophon sole general, but he prudently declined the honor, fearing the jealousy of the Spartans. Chirisophus was consequently chosen.

After a succession of events, which are related in the "Anabasis,"[1] Xenophon recruited his exhausted resources by a raid in Lydia, the object of which was to plunder a Persian named Aridates. It is sad to contemplate the narrow-minded principle which actuated the Greeks in their conduct towards barbarians, and which could even justify to a man of piety and virtue like Xenophon, and one who so often in his writings expresses a contempt for wealth, an act of downright robbery. This unworthy exploit seems not to have disturbed his conscience; the only circumstance in it which redounds to his credit is, that he saw in it an opportunity of doing good to others.

During this expedition the army had marched 34,255 stadia (more than 4000 miles), and the time consumed in it was one year and three months.

It was never the good fortune of Xenophon to return to Athens. Whilst he was in Asia a sentence of banishment was passed upon him. The causes which led to the enmity of his fellow-citizens, were probably, 1. The knowledge that his political principles were the same as those of his beloved preceptor Socrates ; 2. His attachment to Sparta ; for Xenophon was with Agesilaus in his Persian campaign (B. C. 396), and he fought on the side of Sparta

[1] Anab. viii. 8.

against the Athenians at the battle of Coroneia. The grateful
Spartans granted him an estate at Scillus near Olympia. In
this secluded retreat he passed his time in literary leisure, in
horticulture, in the management of his household property, in
social enjoyments, and active field-sports ; in fact, he led the life
of a country gentleman. His employments, says Diogenes Laertius, were hunting, entertaining his friends, and writing his histories.

The excitements of war and the chase are naturally allied
to each other, the one as a serious occupation, the other as a
pastime. It is not surprising that the retired soldier became a
sportsman. The same hearty devotion to his work, which gives
such life and spirit to the details of the " Anabasis," imparts a
similar charm to his lighter compositions. Horses and hunting
were to him a passion, and as much pleasure is derived from his
description of a coursing meeting, as from that of a mountain
bivouac in the snow, and as much practical wisdom on the subject is conveyed in his advice to the purchaser of a horse, or the
trainer of a hound, as a general would acquire from a study of
his campaigns.

His great historical work is his Greek history, or " Hellenica."
Valuable as this is for the exact and truthful narrative of events
which it contains, and pleasing from the graceful and simple
style which universally distinguishes the works of him whose
Greek is the purest Attic that ever was written, it is dry and
uninteresting as compared with the " Return of the Ten Thousand." He was peculiarly fitted for the work of continuing the
history of Thucydides in the same spirit as the author of it would
have done, if the tradition related by Diogenes be true, that he
was the editor of that work ; but we miss the vigorous, thoughtful,
and philosophical mind of the older historian. The " Hellenica"
continue the history of Thucydides as far as the battle of Man-
tineia (B. c. 362).

The intimate knowledge which he had an opportunity of gaining
respecting Cyrus, and the admiration which he entertained for his
character, led him to write the "Cyropædia," an historical or
philosophical romance founded on the real events of the early life
of that prince. It may be considered as embodying his views as

to what ought to be the education of a youth born to high rank and station; of the sentiments, moral and religious, which shed a lustre over an ingenuous mind, and of the political principles which he considered best adapted to ensure the well-being of a state. It is evident that he admired a well-regulated monarchy; nor can this be wondered at, when it is known what were the evils in his day, as well of licentious democracy, as of tyrannical oligarchy. But the institutions which he describes were not those which really existed in Persia at the time when he wrote, but were constructed after an ideal model, and almost as unreal as those in the "Republic" of his fellow-pupil Plato.

The treatise entitled the "Memorabilia" of Socrates, is a view of the practical side of the Socratic philosophy. The life of Xenophon had, from his youth, been one of action rather than of rigid thought and severe contemplation; the circumstances into which he was thrown led him to independent action on his own responsibility, rather than to look to the views or opinions of others. When he thought, it was with reference to immediately acting upon his convictions, and therefore his mind was habitually occupied on particular cases and emergencies, and not on general principles. Hence he thought rapidly rather than deeply. Had he been a moral philosopher, he would have taken the casuistical side of moral philosophy. The deficiency which Plato left, Xenophon supplied. His mind was not suited for analyzing the depths and developing all the intricacies of Socratic reasoning, but it was sufficiently acute to trace it and follow it to its practical results. The "Memorabilia," therefore, is in fact a defence of the tendency of the Socratic teaching, and the teaching itself is only developed incidentally, and with reference to this end, and therefore unsystematically, and in the form of detached sayings and conversations; a subject is not thoroughly worked out as it is in the dialogues of Plato.

On the subject of morals, there was a complete identity of sentiment between Plato and Socrates, and although the philosophy of Plato penetrated far deeper than that of Socrates, yet the whole mind of the latter was contained in that of the former. Still there is reason to believe that Xenophon was a more faithful reporter of the actual Socratic sayings than Plato. The writings

23

of Plato present a vivid picture of his great master, but his Socrates is an imaginary character, whilst everything which the plain and honest soldier-philosopher gives in the "Memorabilia," is not merely Socratic, but actually a sentiment expressed in the very words of Socrates.

If, therefore, the "Memorabilia" presents a picture of the method of instruction which Socrates pursued, and of the practical tendency of the doctrines which he taught, it is such an one as would be delineated by a mind which could remember and retain his words, but was incapable of following him through all the subtleties of metaphysical reasoning. It is the work of a man of good common sense, who was so far a philosopher as to have culled from the conversations of Socrates all that had a practical bearing upon human life and conduct. It is the offering of a religious and affectionate heart, who, in the retirement of his age, devoted some portion of his time to rescue the memory of an injured man from the undeserved imputations of immorality and irreligion.

Two other works of Xenophon are devoted to the memory of Socrates :—1. The "Apology," which professes to contain the substance of his address to his judges. 2. The "Symposium," in which a festive meeting, at the house of Callias, a rich Athenian, at which Socrates is present, furnishes an occasion for exhibiting the most striking features of the philosopher's character.

In the dialogue entitled "Œconomicus," Socrates is also represented as one of the characters, and thus gives a sanction to the views of Xenophon on the cultivation of a garden and a farm, the regulation of a household, the relative duties of wife and husband, and their respective offices as rulers and directors of the domestic economy.

Two treatises on the Spartan and Athenian constitutions, and a treatise on Athenian ways and means, prove him to have been as prudent in the science of government and political economy, as he was in the regulation of a family and in the economy of domestic life ; and in an imaginary conversation between Hiero of Syracuse and Simonides, he shows himself fully impressed with the dangers and responsibilities of high station.

A panegyric on his friend Agesilaus king of Sparta, a military work on the duties of a cavalry officer, and his books on horses and hunting, to which allusion has been already made, complete the list of works which bear the name of this accomplished man. All are characterized by good sense, clear intellect, a capacity for governing others and influencing men's minds, cheerful activity, undaunted spirit, refined taste, unaffected simplicity, and, above all, devoted piety. He was too business-like to be a poet, too much a citizen of the world to be a patriot, too practical to be a deep philosopher.

CTESIAS, flourished about B. C. 400.

Ctesias occupies the last place amongst the Greek historical writers belonging to this period of literary history. Nothing remains of his works but abridgments, together with a few fragments, preserved by Plutarch, Athenæus, and others. He was a native of Cnidus, a contemporary of Thucydides and Xenophon, and lived some time at the court of Persia as domestic physician to Artaxerxes. This gave him an opportunity of access to the archives of the kingdom, and from these materials he composed, in the Ionian dialect, a history of the Assyrian and Persian monarchies, comprised in twenty-three books, and extending to the year B. C. 398.[1] So far as it is possible to trace parts of his narrative in the works of other authors, it must have been of but little historical value.

The accounts contained in the documents and state papers, from which he derived his information, were probably highly colored, and exaggerated by national vanity, and therefore presented as untrue a picture as those Greek accounts which Ctesias professed to correct. Statements, differing from those usually received, are made by him, and hence by some who place implicit confidence in Herodotus, he has been accused of wilful falsehood. But Herodotus was credulous as well as truthful; he may, therefore, have been misled in his estimate of Persian grandeur and Greek valor, by the partiality of his countrymen. And Ctesias, in like manner, without prejudice to his honesty, may have placed too great confidence in the truthfulness of the Persian records which he consulted.

[1] Strabo, xiv.

The history of the ancient Assyrian monarchy, contained in the first six books of his principal work, has met with more credit than it deserves, as it has been accepted by the majority of historians both in ancient and modern times. Nevertheless, it is perfectly irreconcilable with the chronology of Herodotus, and with the notices contained in the sacred Scriptures. He is the author of the mythical story that the Assyrian empire, during a period of thirteen centuries, was reigned over by a dynasty of thirty kings, of whom Ninus was the first; and that Sardanapalus, the last of them, whose effeminate and luxurious character was the type of them all, set fire to his palace, and thus burnt himself and all his wealth (B. C. 876). This is entirely fable—a legend of the succeeding victorious dynasty. According to the chronology of the Old Testament, the Assyrian monarch Sennacherib did not die until B. C. 711, and this event was immediately followed by the revolt of the Medes. Neither Ninus nor the death of Sardanapalus is mentioned by Herodotus, who also reckons that the empire had lasted five hundred and twenty years at the time of the Median revolt, and fixed the final destruction of Nineveh by Cyaxares, in B. C. 606. Modern discovery will probably still more satisfactorily establish how undeserving of the reputation which it has hitherto held is the Assyrian and Persian history of Ctesias.

He left another shorter work on the natural history of India, of which, as well as of his oriental history, an analysis is extant, by Photius the Byzantine. It is of little or no value, being derived from Persian records and traditions, and not from original researches; and thus truth and fable are mingled together. . He was also the author of other treatises, of which nothing but the names remain.

CHAPTER XIV.

ELOQUENCE A FEATURE OF GREEK LITERATURE.—EXAMPLES.—SICILIAN SCHOOLS OF
ELOQUENCE.—TISIAS AND CORAX.—GREEK PROSE IMPROVED BY THE SOPHISTS.—
FIRST SCHOOL OF RHETORIC AT ATHENS ESTABLISHED BY GORGIAS.—RIVALRY BE-
TWEEN THE ORATORS AND PHILOSOPHERS.—ORATORY ABUSED DURING PELOPONNE-
SIAN WAR.—CONSTITUTION AND CHARACTER OF THE ATHENIAN ECCLESIA.—EXAM-
PLES.—THE EXTERNALS OF ORATORY MOST APPRECIATED BY THE ATHENIANS.—CARE
TAKEN IN THE COMPOSITION OF ORATIONS.—NECESSARY QUALIFICATIONS OF AN
ORATOR.—THE INFLUENCE OF FREE INSTITUTIONS ON ORATORY.

ELOQUENCE is one of the principal characteristics of Greek
literature, whether poetical, historical, or philosophical.[1] The
heroes of Homer are all orators. The very philosophers, who despised eloquence, and were the rivals of the orators, could not help
being eloquent; and Cicero[2] observes that, what he most admired
when reading the " Gorgias" was, that Plato, whilst deriding orators, showed himself the most consummate and accomplished orator
of them all. Eloquence gives a charm to the romantic narratives
of Herodotus, the philosophical history of Thucydides, and the
soldier-like annals of Xenophon. Doubtless, also, the traditions
of Solon, Pisistratus, Clisthenes, Pericles, Alcibiades, inspired the
orators of the flourishing period, and their skill was nurtured by
the necessities of a free constitution.

But Greek eloquence, in its perfection, owes a large debt of
gratitude to Thucydides. Cicero,[3] indeed, denies that any rhetorician drew the principles of his art from the speeches of
Thucydides. He affirms that they contain so many obscure and
recondite sentiments that they can scarcely be understood. But
this very obscurity arises from that condensation of thought
which distinguishes Greek orators from the more diffuse and easy
style of Roman or modern eloquence. If to the closely-packed
thought of Thucydides be added the elaborate polish which marks

[1] De Orat. ii. 13, 14.   [2] Ibid. i. x.   [3] Cic. Orat. 9.

the style of the Greek orators universally, the result exhibits all the qualities which command our admiration. The style of Thucydides is exactly that which is best fitted to educate an orator in the severe principles of his art, because it is at once suggestive of thought and an aid to reflection. The tradition is by no means an improbable one, that Demosthenes transcribed his history eight times; and a comparison of the speeches of Thucydides with the principles laid down in the "Rhetoric" of Aristotle, is a complete answer to the assertion of Cicero.

But although the Greeks were by nature orators, as they were by nature poets, oratory, as an art, was of Sicilian origin. At an early period eloquence had been cultivated in those states of Sicily which, after the expulsion of their tyrants, had become democratic.[1] Regular schools of rhetoric had been founded by Tisias and Corax,[2] and their teaching had begun to assume a systematic form. From Sicily rhetorical science found its way to Athens, which had then become the home of learning and philosophy. Greece, by this time, was prepared for its reception; for although the literature of the age was still tinged with a poetic coloring, prose had already attained a high degree of perfection.

For whatever errors the sophists were responsible, however superficial their philosophy may have been, the praise is, at least, due to them of having imparted a beauty and finish to prose composition, which it did not possess before.

The first school of rhetoric at Athens was established by Gorgias of Leontium.[3] He was the inventor of the periodic style, and analyzed the principles of rhetorical rhythm, which is said to have been first employed by Thrasymachus of Chalcedon.[4] Amongst those who attended his instructions were Critias and Alcibiades, both of whom were celebrated for their powers of oratory. Two declamations ascribed to him are still extant, the titles of which are Ἑλένης ἐγκώμιον and Παλαμήδους ἀπολογία.[5] They are mere rhetorical exercises intended to illustrate the principles of the science which he taught. The other sophists of that

[1] B. C. 472–465.
[2] Cic. de Orat. i. 20.
[3] Matthiæ, History of Literature.
[4] Cic. Or. 52.
[5] Reiske, Orat. viii.

period, who were most celebrated as rhetorical teachers, were Protagoras of Abdera, Thrasymachus of Chalcedon, Prodicus of Ceos, and Hippias of Elis.

It was in consequence of all the rhetorical teaching being in the hands of the sophists, that the irreconcilable rivalry subsisted between them and their bitter enemies, the philosophers, and that prejudice which was properly due only to their ostentatious and superficial philosophy was directed against eloquence itself. "The philosophers," writes Cicero, "despised eloquence—the orators wisdom;" but notwithstanding this opposition, eloquence was so congenial to Athenian tastes, and so adapted to the wants of their democratic constitution, that it rapidly advanced to maturity both in practice and theory.

Among those who were celebrated for eloquence, Cicero[1] enumerates Solon, Pisistratus, Clisthenes, Pericles, Critias, Theramenes, and Alcibiades, to whose oratorical powers Demosthenes[2] also bears testimony. The characteristic features of their style, he describes as subtlety, acuteness, and brevity, copiousness of ideas rather than of words. Respecting the accuracy of this criticism we have no means of judging, for the specimens which have come down to us in history are but the probable sentiments of the speaker expressed in the language of the historian.

Oratory, upon the whole, appears to have been most abused during the Peloponnesian war. Pericles, indeed, possessed the three oratorical qualifications—honesty, talent, and patriotism.[3] His moral qualities, therefore, prevented him from abusing the ability with which he influenced the popular will. His successors, Cleon and Hyperbolus, were men of talent, but mere mob-orators; their eloquence was of that noisy and vulgar kind which carries with it the feelings of a mixed multitude; but they were grovelling, self-interested, unprincipled. Alcibiades, whose brilliant eloquence was of a totally different stamp—that of a polished and well-educated Athenian gentleman—had, nevertheless, no more honesty than the baser demagogues, for he cared only to gratify his ostentatious ambition. And Cleophon, who next came upon the public stage, was worse than all; for not only had he no honesty and patriotism, but his oratorical powers

[1] De Clar. Or. 7; De Orat. ii. 22.   [2] Dem. c. Mid.   [3] Arist. Rhet. i.

were inferior likewise ; he was made what he was, not by his own abilities, but by the circumstances of the times.

In order to form an idea of Athenian oratory, it is necessary to consider what was the principal field for its exercise. The constitution of the Athenian ecclesia was a very remarkable one. More than six thousand citizens, possessed of irresponsible political power, to whom all those entrusted with the administration of public affairs were responsible, were met together to decide some question which involved their most important interests, perhaps their national existence. They were prepared to listen with breathless attention if the orator was skilful enough to gain the ear of the assembly; or, on the other hand, to interrupt, with noise and clamor, if his arguments or recommendations were unpalatable. Its numbers prevented it from bearing the remotest resemblance to the calm, business-like, deliberative bodies of modern times ; and yet, except in point of numbers, it was unlike a mob, for it was composed of totally different elements. Every one of these six thousand Athenian citizens prided himself on being a gentleman by birth, station, and occupation. He was, to a certain extent, a man of education, and taste, and refined pursuits. He was accustomed to weigh evidence, as a dicast in the courts of law ; he was capable of enjoying the beauties of literature, as set before him in his· favorite amusement—the drama. He was accustomed to exercise his taste in literary criticism. He could enjoy the tragic grandeur of Æschylus, and Sophocles, and Euripides, and the racy wit of Aristophanes. He was, therefore, quite as capable of criticizing the arguments and the literary powers of the orator.

Moreover, the Athenian governed himself, and not only himself, but the allies over whom he claimed an imperial supremacy. He could form a judgment upon all the bearings, and could enter into all the merits of each political question, foreign and domestic, whether of war, or peace, or commerce, or finance, and knew that on his decision rested the welfare of his country and his own personal prosperity. And, besides all this, not a few of this remarkable people took the same interest in abstract philosophical questions which they did in the stirring transactions of real life ; to many of them philosophical studies were the amusements of their leisure hours. These, then, were prepared to weigh the arguments of the orator in a calm philosophical spirit; they were not likely to be led away by mere appeals to passion and prejudice, or by logical fallacies, however artfully concealed, and whilst they were qualified to admire the true beauties of oratory, they would not be pleased by bad taste or meretricious ornament.

The Athenian δῆμος, in fact, combined the good and bad points in the character of a populace, with the distinguishing features of an educated deliberative assembly. It appreciated, as the populace of all nations usually does, strong and manly common sense, an earnestness such as inspires the hearer with confidence in the sincerity of the orator, and the reality of his views. It admired boldness in grappling with difficulties, fearless devotion to the cause of liberty, and talent for forcible and homely illustrations. At the same time it was easily persuaded, was quick at taking offence, and was readily led away by the grossest flattery. The history of the upright and truthful Thucydides abounds in passages which assert that too often the popular speakers and demagogues thought much more of what would give immediate pleasure to their hearers, than of what would advance the best interests of the commonwealth. Isocrates asserts that those demagogues who were the worst morally, and the most contemptible intellectually, were the most popular. And Aristophanes[1] declares that the office of a popular leader is suited neither for an educated nor a moral man, but only for an illiterate scoundrel. These strong expressions may, perhaps, be the exaggerations in which a popular rhetorician and a comic writer would be likely to indulge, but still the examples with which history furnishes us prove that they are, in the main, true.

It cannot be doubted that the Athenian demus was liable to be swayed by all the worst passions which have influenced the populace of any nation either ancient or modern. Pericles, in his funeral oration, feared to praise in a direct manner those who had sacrificed their lives in the cause of their country, lest he should provoke the mean and petty jealousy of the sovereign people. He felt it necessary to flatter the national pride, and when he had thus excited their sentiments of approbation, skil-

[1] Aristoph. de Pace, v. i.; Equ. 188.

fully to divert them from their course towards those whom he wished to eulogize; and even in those speeches in which he exhibits such a comprehensive acquaintance with all the details of public business, he condescends to recommend his statesman-like views by extolling the glories of Athenian supremacy. The hollow and selfish arguments of Cleon, in the case of the Mityleneans, prove how easily the Athenian people was misled by fallacies when they were on the side of self-interest. The still more savage decree against the ill-fated Melians is a stronger proof that it was almost destitute of moral principles and human sympathies. The jealousy with which the theatrical funds were guarded, by attaching the penalty of death to the mere proposal of their repeal, is a proof that Athenian patriotism would always give way when the question was the loss of any favorite gratification. However stern and pressing the necessities of the case might be, the Athenian citizen would not resign, for his country's sake, the accustomed feast, or the favorite spectacle.

Even the maintenance of their naval supremacy, on which their proud national position was founded, was nothing in comparison with the risk of curtailing the daily fee which the dicasts received for attendance in the courts of law as jurymen.

> *Agor.* Put case,—a brace of orators arose,
> And one thus uttered him—'Tis fit we manned
> A fleet. The other—Sirs, the dicasts must not
> Curtail them of their fee—how went the issue?
> Mark! the ship-advocate is quashed anon—
> Look to the fee-commander—he hath gained
> His cause, and gone about his business presently.
>
> Arist. *Knights*, v. 2 (MITCHELL).

The levity and fickleness with which the demus would change their favorites, according as one outbid the other in the contest for popular favor, is graphically described in another scene of the same comedy,[1] too long for quotation here. One offers to steal bread, and give it to Demus, to provide him with a soft cushion to sit on, and to buy him a pair of shoes; the other, by trade a tanner, throws around his shoulders a cloak, which Demus indignantly refuses, because it smells so strong of leather, and

---

[1] Aristoph. Knights, 742.

follows it up with the offer of a dish of fees as a reward for—doing nothing. Alternate bribes follow in rapid succession ; a box of salve for his poor shins, bruised by kicking and squeezing in the ecclesia; a hare's tail to wipe the rheum from his dear little eyes—a useful present where so many of the population, owing to the dust and dazzling whiteness of the soil, suffered from ophthalmia. Cleon then is anxious to pull out his gray hairs, and make him young again, and both vying with each other in servility, are eager that he should use the hair of their heads for a purpose by no means agreeable. The dark side of the Athenian character laid them open to the deceitful flatteries of designing men, and at the same time tempted and encouraged the orator to become a demagogue, and the man of talent, who was ambitious of influence, to pursue crooked and dishonest paths to popularity. Nor did they only make use of the common arts of rhetoric, but put in action every legislative enactment and form of transacting public business which would assist them in gaining their ends. The intriguing Alcibiades, on one occasion,[1] persuaded the Lacedæmonian ambassadors to deny that they had plenipotentiary powers, in contradiction of their former assertions, in order that the assembly might suspect them of insincerity. Thus an alliance was concluded with Argos, in opposition to the views of the judicious Nicias. Cleon, in the case of Mityleneans,[2] and Nicias, on the question of the Sicilian expedition,[3] did not hesitate to propose the reversal of the vote which the assembly had already passed, although such a proposal was irregular and informal. And that wise statesman and prudent general, when he sent from Sicily requesting a reinforcement or the recall of the army, was so alive to the danger that the fidelity of his messengers might be tampered with, or themselves puzzled and abashed by the cross-examining of adverse orators, and thus fail of giving a correct account of his views, forwarded his dispatch in writing; a proceeding which, by Thucydides mentioning it,[4] we may presume to have been unusual.

An orator would even be guilty of mean and dishonest subterfuges; he would cause the terms of a decree to be altered so as to

---

[1] Thucyd. v. 45.   [2] Ibid. iii. 37.

[3] Ibid. vi. 14.   [4] Ibid. vii. 8.

suit his purpose,[1] or one part to be read by the clerk in court, and the other omitted ; he would deceive the ecclesia as to the real object of a measure proposed for consideration, or keep it in entire ignorance as to its purport, by not having the bill read by the proper officer.

Whilst such were the bad points which laid snares for the honesty of a popular orator, and tempted him to go astray from the strict path of duty, and such the practices which custom sanctioned, the orator had also to bear in mind those circumstances favorable to a better style of oratory, which have already been mentioned. He could not forget that he was addressing an audience, many of whom were possessed of a sound, vigorous, and cultivated intellect; that there were many who could detect and expose a sophism; who were morally competent to admire and applaud uncompromising attachment to truth and justice, as well as intellectually fitted to appreciate logical acuteness, correctness of taste, elegance of style, and all the graces of the most finished eloquence.

In every stage of Athenian oratory, whenever an opportunity is afforded of forming an estimate of the orator's character, we are unavoidably struck with the fact that men of such opposite qualities could command a hearing. At that period, when the influence of demagogues was especially triumphant, the same people which could vote at the will of the vulgar and vain-glorious Cleon, listened also with respect to the finished oratory and statesman-like policy of Pericles, and saw in him a true friend of popular liberty. They could be pleased with the narrow-minded flattery of the former, and yet were not insensible to the liberal views of the latter. They could assent to the ambitious proposals of the intriguing Alcibiades, and yet consider calmly the wise and prudent measures of the far-sighted Nicias.

It is evident that the Athenians not only attended the ecclesia, with a view to public business, or to make up their minds on the question before them, and to vote according to their convictions, but that they took pleasure in the strife of words; they looked upon the debate as a contest in which the combatants were striv-

[1] See Note in Mitch. Aristoph. Equit. 734.

ing for victory, and they did not care sufficiently whether or no victory was on the side of truth.

But it is also evident, from the instructions of the earlier rhetoricians, and from the care which Aristotle took to uphold the importance of argumentative proof, that the Athenian people derived their principal pleasure from - the externals of oratory, the grace of delivery, and the charms of language and style. The Greek ear was probably more sensitive than that of any other nation. The same appreciation of time and tune which could distinguish the most delicate modulations of metrical poetry, could trace the rise and fall of a prose sentence, and according as the clauses were well-balanced or the reverse, be pleased or offended.

The rules which Aristotle lays down in his " Rhetoric,"[1] shows how critical and well-tuned was the Athenian ear. Even false antitheses, in which sound entirely took the place of sense, were considered by that consummate critic as not altogether deficient in oratorical beauty. Longinus quotes a sentence from an oration of Demosthenes,[2] the rhythm of which he considers so perfect, that the mere omission or transposition of a word would destroy its cadence. Ignorant as we are of the accent and pronunciation, it is impossible to discover the principles on which this assertion is founded, but it may be affirmed that there is no sentence in any modern orator of which the structure might not be so slightly altered without diminution of effect or beauty.

We can scarcely understand the patient study and elaborate care with which the Athenian orators worked up their speeches. With us a speech is more effective in proportion as it bears marks of being *ex tempore;* natural and unstudied simplicity, a burst of passionate eloquence which seems to come from the heart, is more captivating and convincing than the most polished periods ; nor is the effect diminished by that degree of roughness which distinguishes nature from art. Many of the most prac- tised speakers of modern times owe their persuasiveness, not so much to what are called the graces of oratory, as to the business- like character which pervades their addresses. A modern orator studies his subject, and makes himself master of all its bearings ;

[1] Rhetoric, book iii.   [2] Demos. de Subl. § 39.

he furnishes himself with arguments, and examples, and facts, and illustrations, but he generally trusts to his own powers to find language when the occasion arrives, or, at most, only prepares some passages to serve as resting-places, or a comprehensive summary of his arguments to serve as a peroration.

The Greek orator, or rather, it should be said, the Athenian orator, for oratory flourished only in Athens, composed and wrote his speech in private, before he delivered it in public ; he bestowed the same care on it which he would on an essay intended for publication. Some of the orations which have come down to us were written as rhetorical exercises, and never spoken at all; others were written by one man and delivered by another. This is the case with some of the orations of Isocrates, in which are displayed the most exquisite graces of style and the greatest perfection of composition. "That great orator," says Cicero,[1] "and perfect teacher nursed his talents within the walls of his house; the light of the forum shone not on his glory."

From the mixed character of the audience which the Athenian orator was called upon to influence in the public assembly, it is clear that he needed many high qualifications. Quickness and tact in observing the state of feeling which pervaded the assembly, and in adapting and accommodating himself to it, a comprehensive and retentive memory, a perfect knowledge of human nature, a command over the powerful resources of the Greek language, and a wide range of political and historical information. The various subjects enumerated by Cicero[2] as necessary for an accomplished orator, were studied by the Greek orators with the utmost diligence, and it is clear, from the summary enumeration of topics in the "Rhetoric" of Aristotle, that not only a sound liberal education, but a long course of preparatory study, was deemed necessary in order to qualify an orator for his profession.

Nor can it be a matter of surprise that such intense devotion to this art or science prevailed. In a republic in which the people were all in all, and every measure was to be submitted to their approbation, there was but this one road to civil eminence. To influence the masses and lead their will in whatever direction

---

[1] Cic. de Claris Orat. viii.   [2] Cic. de Orat. i. 34.

he pleased, was necessarily the great ambition of every able Athenian. The experience of the statesman, the wisdom of the legislator, the cultivation even of the mere man of literary taste were useless and powerless unless recommended by eloquence. Moreover, eloquence was not only in civil life the avenue to distinction, but, to a certain extent, it was also indispensable to the military man. The general was chosen by his fellow-citizens, and therefore owed his position not only to his reputation as a warrior, but to the influence which he exercised over the ecclesia. The harangues of military commanders, to be met with in the pages of history, prove that the success of a campaign depended not only upon the maintenance of discipline as a matter of military command, but on kindling the ardor of the soldiery by eloquent appeals to their enthusiasm and patriotism.

In the council of war he had to deal with officers who were almost on an equality with himself, subordinate, indeed, professionally, but nevertheless quite his equals as Athenian citizens. The persuasiveness, therefore, and skill of the orator were on all accounts of no small importance to enforce his authority as a general.

Greek eloquence arose and flourished during the period of Greek liberty. It did not entirely decay until Athenian independence was utterly crushed. Both died together. Freedom has always been favorable to the growth and cultivation of oratory. It finds no place under tyranny or absolutism, for there are none to whom to address the language either of persuasion or conviction; it languishes unless encouraged by the approbation of numbers, or excited by the antagonism of debate. Hence, whilst oratory flourished under the protection of Athenian democracy, Sparta never produced an orator; and that terse and vigorous, but ungraceful and unadorned style of speech, the name of which has passed into a proverb, was alone congenial to the oligarchal system of Lacedæmon.

CHAPTER XV.

EARLIEST WRITTEN ORATIONS.—ANTIPHON.—HIS LIFE AND OCCUPATION.—RESEMBLANCE OF HIS STYLE TO THAT OF THUCYDIDES.—ANDOCIDES.—HIS LIFE, POLITICS, AND DATES OF HIS EXTANT ORATIONS.—HIS TROUBLES AND EXILE.—VALUE OF HIS ORA TIONS.—LYSIAS.—MIGRATES TO THURII.—IS EXILED, AND RETURNS TO ATHENS.— ASSISTS THRASYBULUS AND HIS PARTY.—HIS STYLE.—INFLUENCE OF HERODOTUS ON IT.—INFLUENCE OF ISOCRATES ON ORATORY.—VARIOUS CRITICISMS ON HIS STYLE.— HIS LIFE AND SUICIDE.—ISÆUS.—LITTLE KNOWN OF HIS LIFE.—HE WAS A PUPIL OF LYSIAS AND ISOCRATES, AND INSTRUCTOR OF DEMOSTHENES.

THE first orators who are said to have composed and delivered written orations are Aristophon, Cleophon, Callistratus, and Phæax,[1] but no fragments of their works remain. The earliest speeches which are now extant are fifteen by Antiphon, and four by Andocides.

ANTIPHON, born B. C. 479.

Antiphon was a native of the Attic borough Rhamnus. His father was Sophilus, a sophist; and to him he owed the principal part of his education. He was rather a teacher of rhetoric, and composer of orations, than an orator. The great object which he proposed to himself as an instructor, was to substitute a practical, searching, and argumentative style of speaking for that showy and ornate oratory, which was taught by the sophists; in this, therefore, he was their rival; and the effect of his teaching may be seen in the terse and logical speeches interspersed throughout the history of his pupil, Thucydides.

In the revolutionary period (B. C. 411),[2] which preceded the reign of terror at Athens, the influence of Antiphon was directed to the establishment of the Four hundred. When the power of his party was overthrown, he was accused of treason, and, after an able defence[3] (the only oration which he ever delivered), was

[1] Matthiæ, History of Literature.   [2] Thucyd. viii. 68.
[3] Cic. Brut. i. 12.

condemned to death, his property confiscated, and his children pronounced infamous (ἄτιμοι).

Of the fifteen orations extant composed by him, three were written for clients, and twelve are merely rhetorical exercises, composed for the sake of practical instruction. They are arranged in three tetralogies; the cases to which they relate are imaginary, and all have the supposed commission of murder for their subject.

The custom of professional orators writing speeches for clients arose from the practice of the Athenian courts, in which the parties to the suit were not represented by counsel, but addressed the dicasts in person. Hence, if not possessed of oratorical talents, they availed themselves of the superior skill of some practised rhetorician. Antiphon is said to have been the first who received a fee for this assistance; but if so, his example was afterwards generally followed. The style of Antiphon is perspicuous, natural, pathetic, and forcible; his reasoning close, logical, and convincing, just such as, making allowance for different minds, we might expect would have given birth to that of Thucydides, and through him to that of Demosthenes. He may be considered the parent of practical oratory, as opposed to that mere ornamental brilliance which the sophists considered its essential quality. The absence of ornament may perhaps produce an effect of hardness and want of grace, but still there is a business-like reality which keeps up a strong interest, and makes it impossible to forget the object which he earnestly and steadily keeps in view.

ANDOCIDES, born b. c. 467.

Andocides was of noble family, and was born at Athens. Like Antiphon, he was attached to the oligarchal party, and his political sentiments involved him in the accusation brought against Alcibiades by the supporters of democracy, of having mutilated the Hermæ. The oration which he delivered in his own defence against this charge, b. c. 415, is one of the four still extant. The following are the titles of the other three, and the dates when they were spoken.

Against Alcibiades, b. c. 416; on his own return to Athens,

24

B. C. 411 ; on peace with Lacedæmon, B. C. 393,[1] or B. C. 391.[2]
His life was chequered by misfortunes, numerous even for the
troubled times in which he lived, but they were principally owing
to his own political insincerity.   Whether an accomplice or not,
in the impiety of Alcibiades, he was sentenced to civil disfran-
chisement, and was obliged to leave Athens.   And when the
establishment of the Four hundred secured the ascendancy of his
own party, he does not appear to have possessed their confidence.
His conduct, during his exile, was suspected even by his friends,
and although he returned to Athens, trusting to their protection,
the oligarchal party brought him to trial, and he only saved his
life by taking sanctuary at the altar.   Four times in all he was
banished from Athens, and at last died in exile.   The orations of
Andocides have little to recommend them in point of style and
oratorical skill, but are invaluable on account of the historical
and political information which they contain.

LYSIAS, born B. C. 458.

Lysias was the son of Cephalus, a Syracusan, who was resident
at Athens.   He was born in that city, and was naturalized, although not admitted to all the privileges of an enfranchised citizen.   He was one of the colonists who, together with Herodotus,
went to Thurii, B. C. 443, where he remained until B. C. 411, and
studied rhetoric under Tisias.   His political principles were
democratical, and when the defeat of the Athenians at Syracuse
caused the ascendancy of Dorian politics in Magna Græcia and
Sicily, he was exiled from Thurii, and returned to Athens.

In the colonies and inferior states, all the partisans of Athens
were democratical, as all the friends of Sparta were oligarchal ;
and hence, when he arrived at Athens, he found a state of things
entirely opposed to his political sentiments.   The revolution took
place, and the reign of the Thirty Tyrants began.   His politics,
therefore, were as unacceptable in Athens as in Thurii.   His property was confiscated, himself imprisoned, and afterwards exiled.
He lived in Megara until the restoration of the constitution in
B. C. 402, which he assisted, by patriotically contributing the relics
of his property in the cause of Thrasybulus and the liberators of

---

[1] Matthiæ, History of Greek Literature.   [2] Clinton.

Athens. He resided at Athens until his death, which took place B. C. 378.[1]

Of two hundred and thirty orations, attributed to Lysias, forty-four are extant, some of which are incomplete. All his orations were written for his clients, with the exception of that against Eratosthenes, which he himself delivered. As his occupation was that of "a chamber counsel," and not of a statesman, the subjects of his orations are of a private nature, and not of political interest, but incidentally they contain valuable information on the Athenian financial system.

The language of Lysias is the purest Attic, and his style combines simplicity with dignity, and elegant ornament with perspicuity. Its principal deficiency is in pathos, and perhaps the criticism of Cicero[2] is correct, which alleges that it is wanting in manly vigor; his sentiments, undoubtedly, are never of an elevated kind. No orator has commanded greater admiration from the ancients, who have in turn attributed to him all the principal qualifications of an accomplished writer. Dionysius[3] praises him for his grace, and for his excellence in the polished style (γλαφυρὸς λόγος), Cicero for subtlety,[4] Quinctilian for truthfulness; and a study of his speeches will show that for elegance, precision, and purity, he has been unequalled by any orator except Isocrates.

It is not improbable that the simplicity which distinguishes the style of Lysias, and which was so remarkable as to be entitled by the ancients ἀφίλης λόγος, was owing, in some degree, to intercourse with Herodotus, and to an admiration for the works of that historian. There were causes naturally tending to bring them together; their political sentiments were in unison. Both were metics, and, like the rest of their class, liberal, and attached to democratic principles, and both joined the Athenian colony which migrated to Thurii.

ISOCRATES, born B. C. 436.

To Isocrates Athenian eloquence is most deeply indebted. He was the founder of the most flourishing school of rhetoric, and numbered the most distinguished orators amongst his pupils.

---

[1] Matthiæ, History of Literature.
[3] Dion. Lys. 10.
[2] Cic. de Orat. i. 54.
[4] Cic. de Orat. iii. 7.

"From his school," says Cicero,[1] "as from the Trojan horse, princes only proceeded . . . . Such were Demosthenes, Hyperides, Lycurgus, Æschines, and Dinarchus." He appears to have been the first who took a comprehensive view of the proper end and object of eloquence, and his pure and refined taste accurately distinguished between its use and abuse. He despised those subtleties with which the artificial system of the sophists had overlaid practical eloquence, and saw how far ornament might be employed without danger to clearness. The criticism of Quinctilian[2] is rather too severe; although his style is highly figurative, the frigidity of excessive ornament can scarcely be laid to the charge of Isocrates; the only fault, perhaps, which he has, is that the rhythm of his periods produces upon the ear the effect of poetry, and the melodious similarity of his cadences is sometimes monotonous. In that passage in which Cicero[3] expresses in a single word the characteristic merit of each Greek orator, and attributes subtlety to Lysias, acuteness to Hyperides, sound to Æschynes, and force to Demosthenes, he attributes, with his usual accuracy of taste and judgment, sweetness to Isocrates.

Care and time in polishing and elaborating their orations are characteristic of the Greek orators universally, but in this Isocrates surpassed them all. It is even said that he spent ten years in completing his celebrated panegyric oration; the exordium of which, after all his pains bestowed upon it, provoked the criticism of Longinus, that it is an example of disgraceful puerility and ambitious exaggeration.[4]

There are few circumstances of interest in his life. Physical weakness and a timid temper indisposed him to take part in active political life, or to deliver the orations which he composed so skilfully;[5] he therefore devoted himself to the work of an instructor, and to the composition of speeches for others. The profession which he had chosen was a profitable one, his pupils paid him large sums, and the fees which he received from his clients were considerable. He was a native of Athens, and his father's name was Theodorus. He established his first school at Chios, in consequence of having lost his inheritance in calamitous and disturbed

---

[1] Cic. de Orat. ii. 22.   [2] Quinct. § 13.   [3] Cic. de Orat. iii. 7.
[4] Quinct. x. 4.   [5] Cic. de Orat. ii. 3.

times; afterwards he opened one at Athens. Although quiet and retiring, his patriotism was fervent and affectionate; for when the fatal battle of Chæronea put an end to Greek independence, so severely did he feel the blow that he died by his own hand, in the ninety-ninth year of his age.

ISÆUS.

Scarcely anything is known respecting the life of Isæus. His father was named Diagoras, and he flourished between the conclusion of the Peloponnesian war and the accession of Philip of Macedon. Whether the place of his birth was Chalcis or Athens is uncertain. His instructors in oratory were Lysias and Isocrates, and a marked resemblance may be traced between his style and that of the former. In one point, however, he was decidedly inferior to his teacher, namely, that, through affectation of ornament, he lost that simplicity which gives such a charm to the oratory of Lysias. Artifice, also, is so plainly visible as to appear the result of effort, and is therefore destructive of the natural ease which must veil and conceal art, if persuasive and pleasing. Demosthenes was his most distinguished pupil. According to Suidas, he taught him without charge; but Plutarch states (and his account is more in agreement with the custom prevalent at that time), that he received for his instructions ten thousand drachmæ or £400.

Eleven speeches out of fifty, which were considered genuine, are now extant, all of which relate to causes connected with the Athenian law of inheritance. Valuable, therefore, as they are, with reference to this part of Athenian jurisprudence, they are necessarily uninteresting.

CHAPTER XVI.

DEMOSTHENES, born B. C. 385.

It was not merely the perfection of art or the instruction of schools, however accurate and skilful, which gave to oratory its consummate finish, and raised eloquence to the highest degree of perfection. Athenian oratory was finally developed by national dangers, political difficulties, and the death-struggles of Grecian independence. Study and art, and attention to the principles of style and the graces of language did much to form the eloquence of Demosthenes ; but it was the combination of vigor with grace that constituted the superiority of Athenian eloquence, as repre-sented in his person.

During the period of Athenian supremacy, when every citizen was inspired by one spirit of patriotism, and all politics, however different in principle, were absorbed in the promotion of national ascendancy, oratory exhibited itself in the practical wisdom of the statesman, or the sophistical flattery of the demagogue. But the case was totally altered by the party strife which prevailed in the time of Philip of Macedon. The object of the orator was no longer to enforce his views, whether right or wrong, of political expediency. In the midst of Athens there was now a party to whom anxiety for the welfare of their country was no longer a motive to which the orator could appeal, with any hope or prospect of success. Patriotism was dead in the bosoms of those who composed this party: they were actually in the interest of their country's enemy. It was not simply party arrayed against party, each animated by different views, but both sincere. It was not the old opposition between aristocratic and democratic principles. But the traitor was now fighting front to front with the patriotic lover of his country. The spirit, therefore, which animated the strife of words was like that which pervaded the field of battle. This, then, it was which caused those noble bursts of honest indignation, that ardent love of right and hatred of wrong, which abound in the orations of Demosthenes, and which, although assisted by all the force and varied expression of the Attic tongue, command our admiration far more than the language in which they are expressed.

In the Attic borough of Pæania lived a wealthy sword-cutler, named Demosthenes. He died, leaving a son, aged seven years, who bore his name, and a daughter, two years younger. There is great difficulty in determining the exact date of Demosthenes' birth,[1] but the generally received opinion is that he was born in the archonship of Dexitheus. He bequeathed the care of his family, and the administration of his property, which amounted to fourteen talents—a handsome inheritance in the little state of Athens—to three guardians.[2] Such was the dishonesty and extravagance of these men, that only seventy *minæ* (£280) remained when Demosthenes came of age. He immediately called his guardians to account for their mal-administration, but his experienced adversaries put in force against him all the subtleties and delays of Athenian law; and notwithstanding two decisions in his favor, protracted the suit during three years. At length a verdict was given against them, with ten talents (£2,400) damages.

As in the case of his predecessor Isocrates, the ruin of his fortunes proved the foundation of his fame. He had now only the resources of his own intellect to depend upon, and the cultivation of those talents which would enable him to protect himself

---

[1] Plut. Vit. X. Or. See Phil. Mus. ii. p. 407.   [2] Dem. c. Aphob.

against the dishonesty of his guardians. There is little probability in the statement that he in early life studied oratory under
Isocrates,[1] still less in the assertion that he received no early
education at all. The diligence and perseverance by which he
overcame his natural imperfections are well known. Weakly in
constitution, with an impediment in his speech, so great as to
expose him to the nickname of βάταλος, or " the stammerer," he
prepared himself, by steady practice, to address, fearlessly and
effectively, the stormy assemblage of six thousand Athenians.
In the year B. C. 354, Demosthenes undertook the office of chore-
gus, and discharged the duties of this expensive liturgy in a
most public-spirited manner, and with unusual liberality.

Owing to his attachment to the patriotic party in politics, he
had incurred the hostility of Midias, an influential citizen, the
head of a powerful and unpatriotic faction.[2] Midias assaulted
him, during the Dionysiac festival; and Demosthenes accordingly
brought an action against him; and on that occasion (B. C. 353)
he composed one of his orations, which is still extant. It is,
however, unfinished; for, fearing the popular influence of his adversary, Demosthenes compromised the matter, on receiving as
damages the sum of thirty *minæ* (£120).

He had already displayed his abilities as an orator on various
public occasions, and in the previous year he had opposed the
expedition to Euboea, and had succeeded, by means of his oration,
Περὶ Συμμοριῶν, in preventing the Athenians from engaging in a
war with Persia. The aggressive policy of Philip called forth
his strong will and the energies of his independent and patriotic
character, and stamped him as the leading statesman and orator
of his day. In B. C. 358, the King of Macedon began that attack
upon the northern maritime allies of Athens, the final object of
which was to extinguish the liberties of Greece. In Demosthenes he found an unflinching and unyielding foe, who had the will
and the power to rekindle into a flame the expiring spark of
Athenian patriotism; who could dare to tell his fellow-countrymen the truth, however unacceptable it might be; who would not
condescend to flatter their weakness, or to conceal from them
their danger; who was utterly fearless of personal consequences.

[1] Plut. Vit. X. Or.   [2] Dem. c. Mid.

He did not hesitate, at the peril of his life, to advocate the un-popular measure of diverting, to the purposes of the war against Philip,[1] the funds (θιωριxα) which were annually squandered on public festivals and theatrical representations; and when Philip made his attack upon Byzantium, he actually succeeded in getting his measure passed.

The earnestness with which he pleaded the cause of the un-happy Olynthians (B. C. 349), and supported the prayer of their ambassadors for aid, was responded to by the assembly; but, nevertheless, their measures were not of the decided kind which distinguished Athenian politics in former times; and Olynthus at last fell by treachery. In the next event of his public career, the character of Demosthenes stands out in noble contrast with that of his rival, Æschines, the traitor to his country. Peace with Philip was absolutely necessary, and the far-sighted Demos-thenes plainly saw that the sooner it was concluded the better. Delay in the negotiations would enable Philip to pursue, uninter-rupted, his schemes of aggrandizement. The wilful delay of Æschines, who was sent with an embassy to administer the oaths to the king, gave Philip the time he required. The wretched inhabitants of Phocis were sacrificed; and, notwithstanding the Athenians refused their sanction, Philip was admitted a member of the Amphictyonic league. These events occasioned the orations Ηιρι Ειρηνης (B. C. 346), and that Πιρι Παραπριοβιιας (B. C. 343). In the latter he denounced the treachery of Æschines, but he escaped the punishment which he deserved. His Philippics belong to this period (B. C. 344, 342): the terrible vehemence with which he attacked the ambition of the Macedonian monarch, the truth-ful energy with which he endeavored to impress upon his hearers the necessity of a combined resistance on the part of all Greece, have caused their title to be given to the speeches of Cicero against Antony, and to all orations which consist of a spirited and bitter invective. The orator was unsuccessful, but the event proved that had Greek energy been equal to his, Greece might perhaps have warded off the blow.

Philip's influence in Greece was now so firmly established (B. C. 339), that he was elected general-in-chief of the Amphictyonic

[1] Dem. Olynth. iii.

army. The next year was fought the disastrous battle of Chæronea, which left to Greece only the outward form and name of
liberty. Over those who fell on this field, Demosthenes was
selected to deliver the funeral oration.

The ascendancy of Philip gave fresh strength to his party in
Athens, which was headed by Demosthenes' rival, Æschines.   It
was at this conjuncture that Ctesiphon proposed that a golden
crown should be decreed to Demosthenes in the theatre, at the
Dionysiac festival, as a reward for his patriotism.   Æschines
immediately accused Ctesiphon of having proposed the confer-
ring a reward in an illegal manner and an improper place, but
his principal attack was made against the merits of Demosthenes.   For eight years he deferred prosecuting the charge, and he
was then (B. C. 330) answered by Demosthenes in the oration Περὶ
Στεφάνου. Demosthenes had scarcely finished his speech when
Æschines threw up the cause. He did not obtain one-fifth of
the votes, and, therefore, according to the law of Athens, was
obliged to leave the country.

When the rebel Harpalus fled to Athens, B. C. 325, with some
of the treasure which Alexander had accumulated in his Asiatic
expedition, Demosthenes is said to have been one of those who
were bribed to afford him protection.   There is little authority
for the accusation, and when we consider the uprightness which
always distinguished him, and the generosity with which he once,
at his own expense, sent the Thebans a present of arms, the
charge seems scarcely credible.   The hostility of the Macedonian party is quite sufficient to account for the accusation, and
their influence was strong enough to cause his condemnation and
imprisonment.   He, however, escaped from his prison, and lived
in exile until the death of Alexander (B. C. 323).

This event inspired the Greeks with fresh hopes, which were
raised still higher by the powerful oratory of Demosthenes: his
ungrateful country recognized his value, and he was recalled
from exile, and entered his native city in triumph. The hopes
of Greece, however, were not destined to be realized, for Athens
was left alone by her timid allies, and Antipater marched to
Athens.

Upon this Demosthenes fled to the temple of Poseidon at Calauria, and there swallowed poison, which he was in the habit of carrying about his person.

> Sævus et illum
> Exitus eripuit, quem mirabantur Athenæ
> Torrentem, et pleni moderantem fræna theatri.
> Dîs ille adversis genitus fatoque sinistro,
> Quem pater ardentis massæ fuligine lippus
> A carbone, et forcipibus, gladiosque parante
> Incude, et luteo Vulcano ad rhetora misit.—Juv. x. 126.

> And he too fell whom Athens, wandering, saw
> Her fierce democracy at will o'erawe,
> And fulmine over Greece! Some angry Power
> Scowled with dire influence on his natal hour.

> Bleared with the glowing mass, the ambitious sire,
> From anvils, sledges, bellows, tongs, and fire,
> From tempering swords, his own more safe employ,
> To study rhetoric sent his hopeful boy.
>
> GIFFORD.

The honest truthfulness of his character, the careful study with which he prepared himself for his profession, and the diligence with which he composed his orations, gave an impressiveness, vigor, and a conciseness to his style which have never been equalled. It is not unlike that of Thucydides, but is far superior in perspicuity. Cicero considers him inferior to Lysias and Hyperides in wit (ἀστεῖον, *facetiæ*),[1] and the skill with which he combines grace with vehemence, induces Dionysius to compare him with Lysias in beauty of language.[2] This criticism is not incorrect, for his language is almost always refined, even where it is the most earnest; and wherever his plain-spoken honesty bears the appearance of harshness, no one would willingly exchange the forcible character which this impresses on his oratory for more graceful and polished sentences.

Longinus thus concludes a panegyric upon the majesty and vehemence of his language: "It would be much easier to behold steadfastly the lightning's flash, than to gaze upon his passionate expressions, which so rapidly succeed one another."[3]

Action, manner, and delivery were thought by Demosthenes

---

[1] Cic. Orat. 26. [2] De admir. vi Dicend. Dem.
[3] Longin. Sub. 34.

of greater importance than even matter and style. When asked what was the chief thing in speaking, he gave to delivery, the first, second, and third places in relative importance.[1] His practice, in this respect, agreed with his theory; for when Æschines read to the Rhodians, with unbounded applause, the speech of his rival in favor of Ctesiphon, he exclaimed, "If you had heard him deliver it, how much greater would have been your admiration." He is said to have left sixty-five orations, and of these sixty are extant.

ÆSCHINES, born B. C. 389.

Æschines, the bitter enemy and rival of Demosthenes, is seldom mentioned by Cicero: he translated his orations against Ctesiphon, and Πεϱὶ Παϱαπϱεσβείας, but the translations are lost. The principal characteristic which he ascribes to him is sonorous effect; but this imperfectly describes the beauty and force of his oratory. Little inferior to Demosthenes in thought and language, he was far superior to him in natural gifts and qualifications. Three orations are extant, which prove that intellectually, although not morally, he was a worthy antagonist.

Æschines was a native of Attica. Of his parentage we have little certain information. His adversary, Demosthenes, represents his father as having been a slave, and afterwards a petty schoolmaster,[2] and his mother is said to have been a dancer, of loose character. Æschines, on the contrary, asserts that his father was a man of good family, and his mother a free-born Athenian citizen.[3]

Whatever may have been the true state of the case, his family achieved distinction; for his elder brother, Philochares, was for three years one of the ten Athenian generals, and Aphobetus, his younger brother, was entrusted with a mission to Persia.

The earliest notice which we have respecting Æschines is, that he acted as an assistant in a small school kept by his father, and also in the gymnasium. Like other Athenian youths, he served from his eighteenth to his twentieth year in the πεϱίπολοι,—a body of young men who garrisoned the fortresses on the frontier and coast of Attica. After that he was secretary to the orator Aristo-

---

[1] Cic. de Orat. iii. 56.   [2] Dem. de Coronâ.   [3] De Fals. Leg.

phon, and subsequently to Eubulus, whose democratical sentiments had great influence on the political principles of Æschines. He then made an unsuccessful attempt as an actor, and afterwards served his country as a soldier, in which capacity, having distinguished himself at Mantinea, and other battles, he was, according to his own account, rewarded with a crown.[1]

When he came forward as a speaker in the assembly, his democratic principles, knowledge of public business, and military reputation so recommended him to his countrymen, that he was, on three occasions, employed as ambassador between the Athenians and Philip. Notwithstanding all that has been urged in his defence, there can be little doubt that he was far more zealous in advancing the interests of the Macedonian king, than in promoting the welfare of his country.

On two occasions, B. C. 346 and B. C. 340, Æschines was, by Philip's influence, delegated as pylagoras from Athens to the Amphictyonic council, and his advice led to the utter destruction of the ill-fated Locrians. The first decided blow to the political influence of Æschines was struck by the oration of Demosthenes, Πιρὶ Παζαπζιοβιίας, which was published, but not spoken; the oration, Πιρὶ Στιφάνου, finally decided his fate, and he went into exile to Asia Minor, and afterwards established a school of rhetoric in Rhodes.

He died at Samos B. C. 314, and of the numerous orations which he wrote and delivered, only three were published, and these are all still extant.

HYPERIDES, born B. C. 396 (?).

Little as there is known respecting Hyperides either as a politician or an orator, there can be no doubt that he may justly be compared with his staunch friend Demosthenes for uncompromising and self-denying patriotism. Trained in philosophy by Plato, and educated as an orator in the school of Isocrates, he was distinguished for acute reasoning;[2] and, like Lysias, for that graceful wit (Gr. ἀστιιότης, Lat. facetiæ), the principles of which modern taste finds it so difficult to comprehend, and on the nature of

---

[1] De Fals. Leg.   [2] De Orat. iii. 7 ; Orator, 26.

which Roman and Greek taste differed, as may be seen, by comparing the theory of Aristotle with that of Cicero.[1]

On all occasions he was a firm and strenuous opponent of Philip's party, and when Harpalus came to Athens he was the only man in Athens unsuspected of corruption. The acknowledged uprightness of Hyperides, and the fact that on this occasion he came forward to accuse Demosthenes of having received the money of Harpalus, are the only circumstances which cast the slightest suspicion on the otherwise spotless character of the great orator; but as the motives which actuated the conduct of Demosthenes are entirely unknown, and the friendship which existed between him and Hyperides was only temporarily interrupted, it may fairly be supposed that, although there were sufficient grounds to warrant suspicion, and consequently this breach between the two patriots, the charge was proved groundless, and the fair fame of Demosthenes reestablished to the satisfaction of his friends.

After the battle of Cranon (B. C. 322) when Athens submitted to the disgrace of a Macedonian garrison taking possession of Munychia, Hyperides fled to Ægina. But his invincible hostility to the enemies of his country made him a mark for the vengeance of the conqueror. The soldiers of Antipater pursued him to the place of his exile, and put him to death, after cutting out that tongue whose eloquence had so long denounced Athenian treachery and Macedonian ambition.[2] Out of sixty-one orations known to have been composed by him, only fragments remain,[3] of which the longest is a part of the funeral oration delivered by him in the Ceramicus in honor of Leosthenes, and those who fell in the Lamian war.[4]

The following is the opinion entertained by Longinus respecting the style of this good man and accomplished orator.

"If excellencies are to be estimated by their number, rather than their real quality, Hyperides would altogether surpass Demosthenes, for he has more variety and a greater number of beauties. In all these, he is all but the first; like a competitor in the games who is second in his contests with all the professional combatants, but beats all the amateurs. For Hyperides,

---

[1] Arist. Rhet. ; Cic. de Orat. ii. 62, 63.
[2] B. C. 322.
[3] Stobæi Floril. cxxiv. 36.
[4] Diod. xiii. 13.

besides imitating all the excellencies of Demosthenes in everything except arrangement, has added the beauties and graces of
Lysias. Where simplicity is required, he excels in softness, nor
has he the monotony of Demosthenes. His style is full of character, his expression sweet and harmonious. His wit is inex-
pressibly refined, his irony polished and gentleman-like, his jests
neither far-fetched nor ungraceful. He is skilful in evading an
argument; his satire sportive, yet pungent and well aimed; his
comic humor inimitable.

"His style is touching and full of feeling. Yet, notwithstanding his good points are numerous, they are deficient in grandeur
and spirit; they are ineffective, and do not produce great and
startling emotions in the hearer."[1]

DEMADES.

From the honest patriot we turn to one who rose by the pros-
titution of brilliant natural talents to fraud and treachery. Demades,[2] we are told, was a common sailor; and hence, perhaps,
the metaphor used by Plutarch, when he calls him the shipwreck
of his country. His extraordinary natural powers rendered
him independent of the rules of art, and a ready and sharp
debater;[3] and his effective extempore speaking formed a striking
exception to the practice prevalent amongst his contemporaries
of previously preparing their orations with great study and
diligence.

Unprincipled as a politician, and profligate in his private character,[4] he did not scruple to supply means for his extravagant
pleasures by selling his influence to any one who would purchase
it. Not only, like the rest of his party, did he enrich himself
by Philip's gold, but on one occasion he could so far conquer or
dissemble his hostility to Demosthenes, as to receive a bribe of
five talents on condition of using his influence to rescue him and
his friends when demanded by Alexander.[5] As he rose by
treachery, so he fell by insincerity. Antipater discovered among
the papers of Perdiccas some letters signed by Demades, advis-

[1] Long. de Sub. 34.
[2] Cic. Orat. 26; Brut. 9.
[5] Diod. xvii. 15.
[3] Suidas, s. v.; Quinct. ii. 17.
[4] Ath. ii. 44.

ing him to attack the former. Accordingly he caused him and his son Demeas to be put to death (B. C. 319).

LYCURGUS, born B. C. 408.

Lycurgus[1] was an Athenian citizen of the noble family of the Eteobutadæ. His father, Lycophron, was put to death by the Thirty Tyrants. In his youth a zealous and distinguished pupil of Plato and Isocrates, his manhood was passed in an intimate friendship with the uncompromising and patriotic Demosthenes. Well deserving as he is of the place assigned to him by Plutarch amongst the ten Athenian orators, he is still more celebrated for his administrative talents and his unimpeachable integrity. Three times successively his fellow-citizens elected him minister of finance, and thus for fifteen years he had the control of the public revenue. So successful was his administration, that he raised the revenue to the highest point which it had ever attained, and his employment of the resources thus placed at his disposal was equally judicious. He strengthened the defences of the city, reinforced the fleet, and embellished Athens with many public buildings.

Amongst the many anecdotes recorded of Lycurgus by Plutarch, one bears testimony to the high value which he set upon a moral and virtuous education. When blamed by some one for squandering large sums on the sophists, he is said to have answered that if any one would undertake to make his sons better than himself, he would willingly lavish upon him half his fortune. His sons were probably worthy of his paternal care and high character, for on both himself and his eldest son the high honor of public entertainment in the Prytaneum was conferred as a reward for his public services. At his death[2] he was honored with a public funeral, and a brazen statue was erected to him in the Ceramicus; a reward which he himself had caused to be decreed to the three great tragedians.

Suidas[3] asserts that he left fifteen orations, besides letters and some other minor works. Of these only one entire oration and a few fragments now remain. Without much grace, or power,

---

[1] Plut. Vit. X. Or.; Suidas; Matthiæ, Hist. of Literature.
[2] B. C. 323.   [3] Suidas, s. v.

or elegance, his style is that of a straightforward upright man, of sound practical habits and strict virtuous principles.

DINARCHUS, born B. C. 360.

Dinarchus was the last of the ten orators of Athens, and he owes his celebrity not so much to his own abilities, as to the rapid decline of oratory, which synchronizes with his rise to eminence, and, therefore, left him without rivals. He was born at Corinth, and as his foreign origin disqualified him for the public occupations of an Athenian citizen, he employed his talents in writing speeches for other orators to deliver. His attachment to the Macedonian party rendered him an object of popular suspicion, and having amassed great wealth by his literary works he fled to Chalcis in Eubœa. At length, his instructor, Theophrastus, enabled him, by his influence, to return to his adopted country. Some authorities assert that he composed one hundred and sixty orations, others only sixty, and of these only three are now extant. Although some critics have entertained a high opinion of his oratorical talents, the artificial character of his style stamps him as a skilful imitator of Demosthenes, rather than as possessing genius and originality.

Such were the rise and progress of Greek oratory, and such the principal professors of that art. A study of the specimens which are still extant strikes us with admiration of the varied talents, the diligent study, the extensive knowledge, the accurate acquaintance with human nature, the logical acuteness, the command of language which must have been demanded as the qualifications of an Athenian orator, and which are so abundantly exhibited in their compositions.

25

CHAPTER XVII.

PHILOSOPHY FLOURISHED LATER THAN LITERATURE.—DIOGENES OF APOLLONIA.—HIS PHYSICAL THEORY.—ANAXAGORAS.—HIS CHARACTER, AND PHILOSOPHICAL SYSTEM. —HIS INCONSISTENCIES.—HIS THEORY OF KNOWLEDGE.—HIS SYSTEM COMPARED WITH THAT OF HIS PREDECESSORS.—PARMENIDES.—THE TIME OF HIS BIRTH UNCERTAIN.— CELEBRATED AS A LEGISLATOR.—A MORAL POET RATHER THAN A PHILOSOPHER.—HIS VIEW OF HUMAN NATURE MOURNFUL.—ZENO.—HIS CONNECTION WITH PARMENIDES. —FOUNDER OF DIALECTICS.—HIS FALLACIES.—HIS PHYSICS.—MELISSUS.—HIS SYSTEM A NEGATIVE ONE.—HIS PHYSICS NEARLY THOSE OF THE ELEATIC SCHOOL.—EMPEDO- CLES.—SOME OF HIS DOCTRINES PYTHAGOREAN.—HE IS SAID TO HAVE INVENTED RHETORIC.—FABLE MIXED UP WITH HIS LIFE.—HE REFUSED THE TYRANNY.—HIS DOCTRINE OF THE DEITY.—NECESSITY.—THE ELEMENTS.

THE flourishing period of Greek literature generally, and of Greek philosophical literature, do not exactly coincide. Philosophy, as might be expected from the progress of the human intellect and the development of its powers, is somewhat later in coming to perfection. When the Attic drama was represented by Æschylus, philosophy may be considered to have been still almost in its infancy; it did not arrive at the prime of its existence until the time of Socrates: with him it began to flourish.

DIOGENES OF APOLLONIA, flourished B. C. 498.

The earliest philosopher belonging to the literary era now under consideration was Diogenes. He was a native of Apollonia in Crete,[1] and was attached to the dynamical section of the Ionian school. The strong resemblance of his theories to those of Anaximenes makes it highly probable that he was one of his disciples. If, as is said, he was a contemporary of Anaxagoras, he must have flourished about B. C. 498.

His physical theory was, that all things originated in one First Cause, or elementary principle; that this original essence underwent continual changes, and by the reciprocal influence of the

[1] Diog. Laert. ix.

results onc upon the other, not only new phenomena were developed, but these, in their turn, were again resolved into that which was their common origin. The universe, therefore, contained within itself an inherent and spontaneous vitality. Life was the soul, and from observing the cause of vitality, both animal and vegetable, he concluded that the soul was air.[1] The inseparable property of this living being was consciousness and reason. He evidently, therefore, confuses air, the first cause of motion, with reason, which is the principle of consciousness. He taught that the order which prevailed in the physical universe originates in an intelligent First Cause, because he assumed that order could be the result of intelligence alone.

The advance which philosophy had now made consisted in this, that to the principle of animation held by Anaximenes, and to the simple vital energy maintained by Thales, was now added that of intellect. A soul was attributed to the universe, of precisely the same nature as the human soul. Diogenes had not arrived at the idea of a personal intelligent First Cause, directing the order of Nature, but only at that of a principle of rationality pervading Nature itself. His first principle was air ; this was capable of assuming various forms by an inherent power of spontaneous change. As far as can be determined from the few scattered fragments of his philosophy which remain, the mode by which solid matter was produced was by condensation. The original air was warm,[2] and this, cooled and condensed towards the central point, produced the earth. From his theory that the universe was an animated and rational being, it followed as a corollary that all things possessed intelligence, and that wherever it was not discernible, it nevertheless was present in a latent state. Hence the inferior animals were endowed with a reasonable soul, but external circumstances impeded its exercise. His style of writing is said by Diogenes Laertius to have united dignity with simplicity. Diogenes completes the list of the dynamical philosophers belonging to the Ionian school. We now proceed with the history of the mechanical philosophers.

[1] Arist. de An. i. 2.   [2] Diog. Laert. ix. 57.

ANAXAGORAS, born B. C. 500 (?).

Anaxagoras of Clazomene was born Olymp. lxx. 1,[1] or, according to other authorities, Olymp. lxvii.[2] Early in life he went to
Athens, for the purposes of study, where amongst his distinguished disciples were numbered Pericles and Euripides. So devoted
was he to philosophical investigation, deeming this the only
worthy employment of life,[3] that although wealthy and of high
birth, political life had no charms for him,[4] and he even allowed
his private affairs to fall into confusion. This involved him in
want and poverty in his old age, and when the policy of Pericles
became unpopular, his friendship with that great man exposed
him to persecution, together with the rest who adhered to those
political principles. Like Socrates, he was accused of impiety,
probably because his philosophical theories were necessarily inconsistent with the mythical superstitions of the popular religion,
and because he attempted to account for them by a moral and
allegorical explanation. He was imprisoned, and at length compelled to fly for safety to Lampsacus. He died Olymp. lxxxviii.,
and the Lampsaceni instituted an annual feast in his honor.

His mathematical acquirements, as well as his knowledge of
astronomy, are said to have been sufficient to enable him to make
some approach towards discovering the cause of both solar and
lunar eclipses.

The fundamental principle of his physical theory was, that
there could be no essential change or development of one thing
from another, and no increase or diminution in the number of
things, but that all production was caused by the mixture of the
simple elements, and all destruction by the separation of them.
These simple elements were infinite in number, and infinitely
differing from each other, but the constituent particles of com-
posite essences were homogeneous, and similar to the whole which
was composed of them. They were also not cognizable by the
external senses. The terms by which Anaxagoras designated
them were τὰ ἀόρατα ὁμοιομέρη and ἡμῖν ἀναίσθητα.

The original condition of all things, he maintained, was one of

[1] Diog. Laert. ii.   [2] Wyttenb. Bibl. cr.
[3] Eth. Nic. x. 9.   [4] Cic. Tusc. v. 39.

confusion and disorder, and the order of Nature was due to the existence of a moving force imparting motion, which, deriving his ideas from that of the heavenly bodies, he considered circular. This motive cause was intelligence (νοῦς), and existed from all eternity. By attributing order, and therefore creation, and all that is beautiful and just in morals, to an Intelligent Cause, he at once denied the doctrines of chance and necessity, and when he called necessity (εἱμαςμένη) an empty term (ὄνομα κενόν), he used an argument similar to that by which Butler proved the absurdity of ascribing effects to a power which was but an unreal abstraction. The part of his system most manifestly open to objection is, that by making intellect the only cause of arrangement he contradicts himself, because he must necessarily assume other first causes amongst those elements, to which motion is imparted by intellect. The shrewd and observant mind of Aristotle[1] did not fail to observe this fallacy. When he attempts to carry his general principles into the investigation of the causes which lead to individual phenomena, their inapplicability, and the consequent inconsistency of his philosophical system, become more strikingly manifest. Matter appears then to be separated entirely from influence of mind, and the existence of causes to be arbitrarily assumed.

In addition to these considerations, if the language, in which Anaxagoras speaks of his moving force, is accurately examined, he seems to draw a distinction between the universal mind and the particular mind, which he designates soul (ψυχή), and thus he destroys the unity of that principle which is the fundamental ground of his system.[2]

His theory of sensation, according to which external impressions act upon the mind and set it in motion, also contradicts the independent and absolute existence of mind as the first and original cause, and makes it a force which depends for its activity on corporeal organization.

His theory of the mode by which knowledge is attained by man is in harmony and consistency with his system. As the elementary ὁμοιομέρη are not cognizable by the senses, by the intellect alone we are able to arrive at truth. His view is, that

---

[1] Arist. Met. i. 4.　　　　　　　　[2] Ibid. de An. i. 2.

the idea formed by the senses of sensible objects is an inadequate one, and consequently untrue.   He was not so impractical as to undervalue the importance of impressions upon the senses, but he would only allow that they were helps and aids towards the discovery of truth.   From the observed imperfection of the senses he was deeply impressed with the depth of human ignorance as compared with the vast range of subjects to be known.

Liable as the system of Anaxagoras undoubtedly is to the objections which lie against those of his predecessors, on the ground of arbitrary assumptions and inconsistencies, his conclusions are generally logically drawn, even when his premises are false.   The care with which he endeavors to establish a logical connection between cause and effect renders him deserving of the respect with which his views are generally treated both by Aristotle and Cicero ; and to him Athens is indebted for the first introduction of philosophical study into that city.   The approach, however imperfect, which he made towards a belief in an intelligent First Cause as the author and arranger of the universe, marks an important epoch in the progress of philosophy, as the beauty of his style imparted a new grace to Greek prose composition.

Parmenides, born (about) b. c. 520.

Various accounts are given respecting the period at which Parmenides flourished.   He was a native of Elea and a member of the school established in that city, and, according to Plato and Aristotle,[1] the most celebrated of the Eleatic philosophers.   Aristotle states, that he was said to have been a pupil of Xenophanes.[2]   In order to reconcile this tradition with the statement of Plato, that he came to Athens in the sixty-fifth year of his age, and there met with Socrates, Ritter assumes his birth to have been about Ol. lxv.   Matthiæ, on the authority of Fülleborn, states that he flourished about b. c. 464.

As a legislator he was no less famous than as a philosopher. His code was so highly appreciated by his fellow-citizens that they took an oath every year to observe his laws.

Many fragments of his poem Περὶ Φύσεως, a subject which in-

---

[1] Plat. Theat. ; Arist. Met.   [2] Arist. Met. i. 5.

cludes what in modern times are called metaphysical, as well as physical speculations, have been preserved.[1] It is no easy task to elicit a philosophical system from the metaphorical and allegorical language of poetry, and the didactic mind of the legislator and moral poet is perceptible in the poem, rather than the logical analysis, which characterizes the philosopher. According to Parmenides, that which is, is self-produced, uncreated, and unchangeable; nor is there such a thing as that which is not (τὸ μὴ ὂν). Hence, he denies the existence of a vacuum, as that implies non-existence; and, as motion implies change, that which is, is in a state of complete and eternal rest. The form which he attributes to it is the spherical, as being the most perfect and symmetrical. That which is, and the fulness of it, constitute the intellectual faculty, and its object; for these are one and the same.

Ταὐτὸν δ' ἐστὶ νοεῖν τε καὶ οὕνεκεν ἐστι νόημα (v. 95).

Of that which is, he assumed two opposite species; of one, the properties were light and heat; of the other, cold and darkness. The order of the universe is produced and maintained by the combination or separation of these opposite elements, through the instrumentality of two causes, Love and Discord; of which doctrine he considered the division of the human race into two sexes as typical.

His view of human nature was a mournful one; man is, according to all the philosophers of this school, but a portion of the phenomenal and transitory, not of the eternal; the soul is material, and composed of the four elements, and he is subject to an irresistible necessity.

ZENO, flourished (about) B.C. 464.

Zeno was a member of the Eleatic school, a disciple of Parmenides, at the same time with Empedocles of Agrigentum. He showed his attachment to his instructor by writing a treatise in defence of his metaphysical theories. This work, the object of which was to support the doctrine of one First Cause, enjoyed a high reputation amongst the ancients. He was not only a philosopher, but took an active part in the public affairs of his coun-

---

[1] Fülleb. Beyträgen, vi.

try, and, according to Strabo,[1] assisted Parmenides in his legislation. He engaged in a conspiracy against the tyrant of Elea, and, being discovered, was put to the torture. It is said that he bore his sufferings with the utmost fortitude, and bit off his tongue rather than be tempted to betray his associates.[2]

He is principally interesting to us as the first who arranged his arguments in the form of dialogue, and as the inventor of dialectic science,[3] so far as this, that his conclusions were logically deduced from axioms or principles universally admitted to be true.

In the time of Zeno, science seems already to have assumed the form of amusement and pastime, as well as of serious investigation. The four celebrated arguments by which he endeavored to prove the infinite divisibility of space,[4] and to disprove the reality of motion, are of that paradoxical nature which puzzles whilst it does not convince, and the fallacy of them, though difficult to refute, is so manifest that it can hardly be supposed they were seriously maintained. Ritter[5] explains the fallacy of his reasoning in all these arguments, by stating that whilst Zeno maintains the infinite divisibility of space, he neglects that of time.

The popular fallacy of Achilles and the tortoise, which is the second of these four, is well known, and is exposed by Archbishop Whately in the following manner :—

" Aldrich[6] purposes to remove the difficulty in this sophistical puzzle, by demonstrating that, in a certain given time, Achilles would overtake the tortoise, as if any one had ever doubted that. The very problem proposed is to surmount the difficulty of a seeming demonstration of a thing palpably impossible ; to show that it is palpably impossible is no solution of the problem.

" I have heard the present example adduced as a proof that the pretensions of logic are futile, since (it was said) the most perfect logical demonstration may lead from true premises to an absurd conclusion. The reverse is the truth. The example before us furnishes a confirmation of the utility of an acquaintance

---

[1] Strabo, vi. 1.   [2] Cic. Tusc. ii. 22.   [3] Arist. Top. i. 1.
[4] Ibid. Phys. vi. 9.   [5] Gesch. Phil. v. 4.
[6] Whately's Logic, Append. p. 347.

with the syllogistic form; in which form the pretended demonstration in question cannot possibly be exhibited. An attempt
to do so will evince the utter want of connection between the premises and the conclusion."

In physics the· four elements, the existence of which he assumed, are almost coincident with those usually admitted by the
Eleatic school, namely, *the warm* (θεςμόν), *the cold* (ψυχςόν), *the
dry* (ξηςόν), and *the moist* (ὑγςόν). The moving force was necessity, its two species, love and contention, and of these four elements, combined in various proportions, he held that the human
soul was composed. The divine character of an individual soul
depended upon the predominance of the purer elements in its
composition.

MELISSUS, flourished (about) B. C. 428.

MELISSUS was an Ionian, a native and inhabitant of Samos.
His opinions, therefore, were probably derived from a study of
the works, and not from the personal instructions of the Eleatic
philosophers. He commanded the Samians in a naval battle
against the Athenian fleet under Pericles, Ol. lxxxviii. 1, B.C.
428, and defeated them. The only work which he wrote was in
prose, and its subject was " of Nature and that which Is" (Πεςι
Φύσεως και του Όντος).[1] The views which it contains are those of
Xenophanes on the unity of the First Cause, but more clearly and
perspicuously developed and expressed than was possible in the
figurative language of poetry. But, although his sentiments are
clearly expressed, and it is not difficult to see what his meaning
is, the reasoning by which he deduces his conclusions is vague and
unsatisfactory. It would be uninteresting to examine the fallacy
of his arguments, and therefore it will be sufficient to state the
results at which he arrives. That which is (τὸ ἰόν), the First Cause,
is one, unchangeable, indivisible; there is no vacuum, and therefore no motion. As that which is is indivisible, it must therefore
be incorporeal. It is not cognizable by the senses, because all
things which are the objects of sensuous perception are liable to
change. Hence, as nothing exists except that which is, all that
we perceive by the senses is non-existent.

[1] Brandis, Comm. Eleat.

It is evident that the system of Melissus is a purely negative one, and therefore a characteristic representative of the tendencies of the Eleatic school. He attributed no positive qualities to anything in Nature.[1] As he does not appear to have had any conception of a pure intellectual existence, he cannot be considered as the founder of idealism, but only as having prepared the way for it by denying every other species of existence.

His physical theories nearly coincided with those of the Eleatic school. That which is, is alone infinite, but all else finite. The order of Nature is governed by necessity, subdivided into the two antagonist forces of love and strife, and the elements are the four commonly adopted.

EMPEDOCLES, born (about) B. C. 444.

Empedocles[2] was born about Olymp. lxxxiv., in the Dorian colony of Agrigentum, which was at that time in its most flourishing condition. As was the case with many others, the easy circumstances and high rank of the family to which he belonged furnished him with the leisure to devote himself to philosophical studies. Sufficient traces may be discovered in his fragments of Pythagorean doctrines to prove that he adopted some tenets of that school; but the most trustworthy authorities assert that he was a disciple of Parmenides, and although not precisely identical, his physical theories are evidently derived from those of the Eleatic school.

The title of his work, of which fragments have come down to us, is Περι Φύσεως; and, like the gnomic poems of Parmenides, is written in epic verse. The enthusiasm of poetical language is a bad vehicle for philosophical doctrines, and hence it is not surprising that Aristotle[3] blames him for assertions unsupported by reasoning.

His name has also been connected with the history of oratory. Ritter considers that the tradition of his being the inventor of rhetoric[4] originated in a misunderstanding; or that the assertion was made by Aristotle, because he was the teacher of Gorgias; but it is not improbable that there is in it some foundation of

[1] Ritter, v. 5; see note.   [2] Simpl. Phys.; Diog. Laert.; Suidas.
[3] Arist. Phys. viii. 1.   [4] Cic. Brut. 12, 64; Quinct. iii. 1.

truth. History proves that eloquence and liberty flourish and decline together. Eloquence withers under despotical sway or oligarchal institutions. In the democratic states of Sicily, when Empedocles flourished, it had been for some time cultivated as an art, and when an art is cultivated it is not long before it is systematized and taught as a science. The usual tradition, therefore, that this scientific treatment of rhetoric is to be attributed to Empedocles, as well as to Corax and Tisias, becomes far from improbable. It may easily be imagined that one who, even in a philosophical poem, displayed such elegant taste, power of language, and correctness of ear as Empedocles, would have possessed, not only considerable eloquence, but also an accurate critical judgment respecting the principles of oratory.

With the accounts of his life and character there is a large admixture of fable. In his poem he claims almost divine honors, as possessing supernatural knowledge respecting the operations of Nature, the power of healing disease, and the gift of prophecy; and even in his dress he affected a priestly and sacred character. His superior knowledge doubtless gained for him a reputation higher than he deserved, and just as a knowledge of magical arts was attributed to philosophers in the middle ages, so tradition ascribed to him a miraculous power over the laws of Nature.

It is said[1] that when his fellow-citizens offered him the tyranny of Agrigentum, to which his wealth, worth, and abilities gave him a fair claim, he refused the honor, preferring a life of retirement and study. As the incidents of his life were exaggerated by fable, so many equally fabulous accounts are extant of his death. Timæus gives that which is most probable, namely, that being exiled from his native city, he died somewhere in the Peloponnese.

The Deity, according to Empedocles, is ineffable, incorruptible, incapable of representation; but whilst in this negative aspect of his system he denies form, he also, like the other philosophers of this school—which was in all its tendencies pantheistic—denies personality. Although God is the all-ruling, yet he ascribes the same attribute and divine nature to the uniting and all-pervading

[1] Diog. Laert. viii. 63.

force of love.　In other places Deity is pure abstract intellect, the one First Cause; but truth, the object of intellect, is described in the same terms, and as this unity and perfection are supposed to reside in the central part of the universe, and to be symbolized by a sphere, the ancients supposed the sphere to be the god of Empedocles.　The truth is, his leading idea was that Deity is manifested in his works, and that, though immaterial and not subject to the cognizance of the senses, he is revealed and developed in the material and the sensible.　The laws, or moving forces of love and strife, constitute Necessity, to which all things are subject.

The elements of the material universe are the usual four, of which fire is the purest, and out of these are compounded the phenomena of Nature.　These phenomena are classified as warm and cold, of which the two sexes are symbolical.　One can plainly recognize in his system the idea prevalent in the Eleatic school, of two opposing forces in Nature by which the balance seems to be maintained.　They had a vague notion that combination and equilibrium are the result of antagonism; that the two great forces of Nature are attraction and repulsion.　The same duality which is supposed to exist in the forces of Nature distinguishes also the elements on which they act.　Homogeneous particles are separated and dissolved by the force of strife, and therefore existence and vitality are thus destroyed, whereas love binds these together.　Again, strife has likewise a productive energy, for, by separating heterogeneous particles, it combines them with those that are akin to them.

Such is a brief account of the philosophers of the Eleatic school, and the theories which they maintained.　The two aspects from which they viewed the subjects of human knowledge, sometimes led them into inconsistencies with each other and with themselves, and their tendency to examine the truth and falsehood of preceding theories, rather than to investigate the natural phenomena themselves, invests their philosophy with a negative rather than a positive character.　But nevertheless, this school, as a detecter and exposer of error, marks an important epoch in philosophy, and its very defects and incompetency paved the way for more extensive and interesting investigations.

CHAPTER XVIII.

THE NATURAL PHILOSOPHY OF THE EARLY GREEK SCHOOLS OF NO VALUE.—THIS IS NOT THE CASE WITH MENTAL AND MORAL PHILOSOPHY.—PROGRESS OF THESE BRANCHES OF PHILOSOPHY.—ATHENS NOW THE SEAT OF PHILOSOPHY.—CAUSES WHICH LED TO HER LITERARY AND PHILOSOPHICAL AS WELL AS POLITICAL SUPREMACY.—WHY HISTORY TOOK PRECEDENCE OF PHILOSOPHY AT ATHENS.—REVIEW OF THE STATE OF PHILOSOPHY.—THE SOPHISTS.—THEY IMPROVED GREEK PROSE, AND DIRECTED MAN TO THE STUDY OF HIMSELF. — THE CHARACTER OF THE TIMES AT WHICH THEY FLOURISHED. — STATE OF EDUCATION. — THE SOPHISTS BECAME THE PUBLIC IN-STRUCTORS.—THEIR ABILITIES.—HOW THEY PERFORMED THEIR FUNCTIONS.—EVI-DENCE OF THE EXISTENCE OF "SOPHISTICAL" TEACHING.—THE EXTENT TO WHICH THE PHILOSOPHERS ARE CORRECT IN THEIR ESTIMATE OF THE SOPHISTS.—THE FACT THAT SO LITTLE REMAINS OF THEIR WORKS PROVES THAT THEY WERE OF LITTLE VALUE.

IT is evident from the preceding pages that the natural philo-sophy of the early Greek schools is, scientifically, worthless. It is valuable historically, as a monument of human labor and in-tellectual ingenuity, and as illustrating the active powers of human thought. But the philosopher started in most instances from arbitrary assumptions, unreal hypotheses, and preconceived ideas of fitness; he was misled by imaginary analogies, which were also pressed beyond the bounds of probability, instead of carefully observing natural phenomena. His labors, therefore, were fruitless, although they can never be uninteresting or con-temptible.

Even where a strictly inductive method is pursued, physical science must, from the nature of the case, make slow progress, and theories which appear well grounded and logically deduced, as far as the knowledge of the premises admitted, are liable to be overthrown and superseded by the progress of observation and scientific discovery; and hence, in the investigation of phy-sical truth, each generation must necessarily surpass in knowledge the preceding one.

But the case is different with respect to moral and mental

philosophy. The human mind was as accessible a subject of investigation to the ancient as it is to the modern. Each philosopher who possessed sufficient ability had within himself the subject which he was studying, and therefore by investigating the principles of that nature with which he became acquainted through his own individual consciousness, he could discover its phenomena and the nature of its operation. He could thus become an acute logician and a skilful metaphysician. Again, the same course of study, combined with a practical knowledge of human nature, as exhibited in men's social relations, would enable him to investigate the subject of man's highest good and true happiness, so far at any rate as this life is concerned, and so far as is possible without the aid of Divine revelation. The value, therefore, of Greek mental and moral philosophy must always remain unchangeable; it can never be superseded by modern investigations; and hence all modern systems, the truth and value of which are recognized, are founded upon the principles of the ancient philosophers.

We are now arrived at the period in which we shall have to trace the development and progress to perfection of these branches of philosophy. The seat of science is now transferred from the different provincial schools to the metropolis of Greek national literature and refinement, Athens. When Athens became the political capital of Greece she necessarily became the home and centre of science and literature. The causes which led to her political supremacy led also to her literary and philosophical pre-eminence. The independent spirit which made Greece forget her differences of race and combine as one nation against Persia, was totally inconsistent with long subjection to oligarchal principles. Sparta could not long maintain her ascendancy. Although the Medism of Pausanias was the immediate and overt cause which led to her fall from power, it cannot be supposed that she could have long remained at the head of the Greek confederacy. Her reserved temper shrunk from intercourse with other people. Her institutions were modeled with a view to stability rather than progress. It was therefore evidently the

¹ Thucyd. i.

destiny of Athens to exercise an extensive influence over Greece. She always put herself forward as the champion of Greek liberty, and as the leader of the democratic states, she was herself the representative of freedom. The tendency of the Greek mind was towards progress. Those states which did not manifest this tendency formed the exceptions to the rule; and hence, when the national existence of Greece commences, Athens naturally becomes the centre of national activity, the leader of all that distinguishes Greece as a nation. Even when the disastrous result of the Peloponnesian war hurled Athens from her proud position, she was as great in her adversity as she had been in her prosperity.

Before the Persian war broke out, she had established her literary supremacy. The literature of passion and imagination, and the language which is its natural vehicle, that of music and poetry, had been brought to the highest perfection in the Greek drama, and it soon appeared to be a recognized law that the dialect spoken at Athens should be the language in which prose composition should be universally expressed.

The first prose literature which issued from Athens was historical. This is what might be expected. Historical literature is the result of individual effort and industry; philosophical research has always flourished in what has been termed a school— that is, men associated together for the purposes of mutual aid in the work, either in investigation or education. The first of these objects is essential to a school, the second accidental, but experience has shown that the natural tendency of schools is, to lose sight of their primary object in that which is secondary, and to degenerate into mere places of education instead of study. Athens during the Peloponnesian war, itself almost in a state of blockade, its territory and neighborhood periodically ravaged by the Peloponnesian army, could not become a university of this kind, or invite, to its protection and nurture, learned men seeking a place of refuge, where they could in common pursue their quiet studies. An individual mind of more than common activity, and of a thoughtful and philosophical caste, like that of Thucydides, would naturally be tempted to give a record of the stirring events around him, make them the groundwork of his philosophical reflections, and point to the lessons of political wisdom to be derived from them. He would teach philosophical statesmanship through the medium of history.

But when the war was over, the ancient literary supremacy of Athens seemed to revive, and arise out of the ruins of her political power. All Greece recognized her claim to mental pre-eminence as beyond the reach of the changes and chances of human fortune; and she quickly became the university of Greece, the nursing mother of philosophy.

But, previous to entering upon this brilliant period, during which—whilst philosophy was essentially national, and the development, not of a part, but of the whole of the Greek mind—its home was Athens, and its language Athenian; let us in a few words review the progress which human thought had already made.

In Ionia the dynamical theory of physics or physiology, as founded by Thales, developed by Anaximenes and Diogenes, and finally consummated by Heraclitus, had taught that the universe was an eternal living being, possessing in itself a principle of vitality, which, by spontaneous development, produced all phenomena, whether physical or moral.

The mechanical philosophers denied the existence of any internal power of change, but taught that the eternal immutable elements were acted upon by some natural moving forces, either external or internal, and thus by new combinations were produced new phenomena.

The Dorian idea, as developed by the Pythagoreans, was, that all phenomena must be referred to moral fitness and design, as to a final cause; and they attempted to explain all physical and metaphysical phenomena by mathematical analogies, and the numerical principles of harmony.

The Eleatic school devoted its energies to examining the philosophical views of its predecessors, and bringing them to the test of logical principles, and hence its dogmas are of a negative character. They showed, for example, that the self-developing power of many parts was *not* consistent with the existence of one First Cause. They therefore deduced the doctrine of one God, the all-ruling, omnipresent, eternal; but whilst they denied him the attributes of humanity, they denied him personality likewise, and their notion of Deity became pure pantheism.

Whilst the doctrines of the Ionian and Dorian schools were thus proved to be false, the Eleatic doctrines were confessedly one-sided and inadequate. This shook men's belief in truth itself, and gave rise to the sophistical philosophy.

THE SOPHISTS.

Although it may be said that the sophists have left no fragments, which entitle them to a place in a history of literature; nevertheless, the discussion of their tenets, and a refutation of their errors, occupy so important a part in the literature of their own, and the succeeding period, that such a history would be incomplete without some account of the rise and progress of their system.

Moreover, Greek literature is under great obligations to the sophists for the improvements which they effected in Attic prose. Their skilfulness in the use of words increased the copiousness and richness of the language, and their logical precision, exercising an influence on its structure, improved it in elegance and perspicuity.

Whatever objections, too, may with truth be urged against their philosophical system, this praise must be at least accorded them, that they first directed man to the study of himself. The great value which Socrates afterwards attributed to the consciousness of identity, was first perceived and taught by the sophists. The human mind, and the principles on which its operations were carried on, had not previously been studied. The reflex action of the mind upon itself had been neglected, in the interest felt in investigating the phenomena of external nature. The failure of all former systems, the recklessness of any connection between cause and effect with which favorite theories had been pursued and developed, taught thoughtful men that the true beginning of philosophical study was a more accurate investigation of the principles of reasoning.

Before discussing their history, it will be necessary to review the circumstances of the times in which they flourished.

In the middle of the fifth century before the Christian era,

26

literature was at its zenith, and Athenian taste in the arts and
the sense of the beautiful had attained their highest perfection.
Still there was much of sensuality mingled with this mental culture.   Virtue itself was rather a matter of taste than of sentiment,
and even the admiration of the beautiful tempted the warm temperament and lively imagination of the Greek to seek for pleasure
in sensual gratification.   Athens is an example how far æsthetic
perfection may exist side by side with moral pollution.

Tragedy had applied all its energies, in its character of a popular ethical instructor, to arrest the increasing tendency to moral
degradation, and nobly had it performed its task, not only by the
moral tendency of the plots chosen by the great tragedians, but
by the moral sentiments which they never lost an opportunity of
enforcing at a time when the heart as well as the ear was especially open, and when their lessons were supported by all the
charms of taste and beauty which could engage the attention.

But, notwithstanding the zeal with which the tragic poets
labored to accomplish their mission, the testimony of the historian and the comic poet proves that the tone of public morality
was low and depraved.

This moral contamination appears not to have been confined
to Athens, but to have overspread the whole of Greece; the strife
of faction and revolutionary hatred between classes and parties,
which did not desolate Athens until the termination of the century,
was, year after year, deluging all the little states of Greece in
blood.   Although the historian does not enter at length into
detail, we cannot doubt but that the state of things was as fearful
in Epidamnus and Platæa as he describes it to have been in the
ill-fated island of Corcyra.

Assuming, then, that such was the moral condition, not only
of Athens but of all Greece, it is easy to imagine what views
would be popularly entertained on the subject of education.   The
old Athenian system so much praised by Aristophanes, which
had taught Athenians of the olden time their duties as soldiers
and citizens, would rapidly become unpopular, and be voted out
of date and unsuited to the times, as not calculated to fit the
young Athenian for public life, or for gaining an influence in an
ecclesia, such as Thucydides and Aristophanes describe.   The

public voice would be for substituting a system of education in which moral principle would be neglected for the sake of showy accomplishments.

The sophists threw themselves at once into this false educational system; and, by the influence of their abilities, took the lead in it, and became the public instructors of the higher classes at Athens. It must not be supposed that they were all, without exception, nothing more than shallow pretenders to learning. The education which they gave was superficial, because no more was asked of them, but it does not follow that they knew no more than they were required to teach. All of them were educated and accomplished men, and expert dialecticians. Many of them had a fair acquaintance with various branches of learning and philosophy. Hippias, of Elis, notwithstanding all his vanity and pretension, possessed varied accomplishments and versatility of genius. Democritus was a most ingenious thinker, and most learned in the philosophy of preceding ages. Protagoras had an extensive knowledge of politics and history. Gorgias was an enthusiastic student of natural philosophy, although his dialectic subtlety led him into the grossest absurdities.

It cannot be doubted that the sophists were, generally speaking, men of ability, but the important point for inquiry is what influence they voluntarily exercised on society. To accuse them of having demoralized Athens is unjust, but how far they are responsible for the existing demoralization admits of question. The place which they occupied in the Greek social system, and especially in the Athenian, was that of educators and instructors. How, then, did they fulfil this important function? In the first place, it is plain that they did not, like the philosophers, consider the communication of knowledge to others a duty; profit, and that of an exorbitant kind, was their avowed motive. Protagoras demanded no less a sum than one hundred minæ (four hundred pounds) to complete the education of a finished Athenian gentleman. Hence they came in contact only with the wealthier classes, and the education which they professed to give was such as they required, and such as would fit them for the distinctions to which they aspired. It is easy to see, therefore, that although not chargeable with an intention to corrupt youth, their system would be

one of false display—superficial rather than philosophical—in
mere accordance with the spirit of the age, and not in advance
of it.   They swam with the tide of popular error, instead of at-
tempting to stem it at the risk of losing their popularity.   The
young wealthy Athenian would wish for an education rather
showy than substantial, for learning rather varied and extensive
than deep.   What he would above all things require would be
dialectic skill and rhetorical power : the one would make him
shine in private life as a man of brilliant conversational power ;
the other would distinguish him as a public man, and enable him
to gain the influence which he coveted in the popular assembly.
To give this education, and no more, was the business of the
sophists.   A priori, it might be expected that in order to impart
dialectical skill, they might be tempted to forget that truth is the
real object of dialectic, and its abuse victory and display ; to
argue for the latter rather than the former, and thus encourage
sceptical indifferentism: and as for the fact, there is abundant evidence[1] to prove the existence of a system of instruction, the object of which was to make the worse appear the better reason.
Although Aristophanes put forward Socrates as the object of his
attack, because he was a prominent and well-known character, it
cannot be supposed that he was fighting an unreal shadow, or
that the contest between the two λόγοι, or the ancient and modern
systems of education, had no prototypes in Athenian life.   Had
the comic poet attempted such a thing, the audience would have
hissed and pelted him.[2]   The whole essence of Athenian comedy
was either a just attack on real abuses, or an unjust libel on real
characters ; anything unreal would not have been endured for a
moment by an Athenian audience, until the more quiet times of
the middle comedy, when the national spirit had been almost
crushed by successive misfortunes.   Besides this there are passages in the works of Plato and Aristotle, not only which directly
combat these views, but also which indirectly show the existence
of a prevalent tendency to captious and sophistical objections,
against which it was necessary that a philosopher should be constantly upon his guard.

[1] Arist. Rhet. ii. 24; Plato, Apol. Soc.; Aristoph. Nub.
[2] Athen. vi. 245 ; xiii. 583.

If, then, the system of education which we call sophistical, existed, to whom must its existence be attributed? Not to the philosophers, for of them we can ourselves be judges. They were not only its most conscientious opponents, but were eminent for their devotedness to the cause of truth, of justice, and of virtue. The only other instructors, then, were the sophists. Surely, then, it is not too much to say that their motives were selfish, and that, instead of denouncing a vicious system, they gave a negative encouragement to it, by a species of education which answered their own ends, and hastened the advance of moral and political corruption. To represent the sophists as wilful and designing impostors, whose object was to corrupt the public morality, is going too far. It is enough to say that they professed to qualify the youth of the leading families to shine and become influential in a degenerate state of society, to cultivate those talents and adorn them with those accomplishments which were all that Athenian society, now fast becoming morally corrupt, looked for or valued. They did not consider it their business, as instructors of youth, to teach them to aspire to higher and nobler views, to set before their eyes a purer and more perfect standard, to reform the morals of society. A low moral standard was set up and admitted, and they did not care to elevate it. Hence, although the language used respecting them would have been severe from men of the world, it was not so in the mouths of men whose views were as upright and uncompromising as were those of Plato and Aristotle.

But whatever may be the truth with respect to their dishonesty, there is every reason to believe that, whilst they pretended to much knowledge, they were on many points incompetent and unsound. The vast range of subjects which Hippias[1] professed to teach, of itself argues ostentatious pretension or superficial knowledge. The oratory of Gorgias is universally confessed to have been mere florid bombast and well-balanced antitheses. Theodorus and Thrasymachus wrote treatises on rhetoric, noticed by Quinctilian,[2] but narrow-minded, and deficient in enlarged and philosophical views of the subject; and the latter[3] taught

[1] See Plato, Prot.; and Mag. Hipp. and Min.
[2] Inst. Orat. iii. 3.　　　　　　　　[3] See Plato, Rep.

that the only standard of justice is the will of the governing power, and represented the just men as weak and contemptible, and the unjust as commanding respect. His teaching embodied, as a motive to action, the principle, " So long as thou doest well unto thyself, men will speak well of thee."

Of the philosophers, their adversaries, voluminous works have been preserved as precious treasures, and handed down from generation to generation ; much that they contain deserves to be recorded in letters of gold. Had the teaching of the sophists approached near to that of their opponents in value, their writings would have met with the same immortality. But this has not been the case. Of their teaching little has come down to us ; it is all comprised in a few worthless fragments, neither suggestive of a train of thought nor conveying direct instruction.

The only exception to this is a short essay of Gorgias, which, if it be an average specimen of sophistical teaching, proves all that can be wished respecting their fallacious reasoning and their corrupt scepticism. It is not deficient in ingenuity or specious-ness ; the doctrine deduced in it from the Eleatic philosophy, though based on fallacy, is plausible, but common sense at once refutes his view. Its sum and substance is, that nothing exists ; if anything exists, it cannot be known ; if anything can be known, it cannot be communicated to others.

Without imputing to them the crime of wilfully corrupting public morals, the view held by Plato[1] seems to be the true one ; namely, that if the tone of society is vicious, the teachers of such a society must be vicious also, otherwise their teaching would be rejected or neutralized by pernicious social influences.

[1] Rep. vi. 6, p. 492.

CHAPTER XIX.

SOCRATES, born B. C. 468.

To arrest the progress of this popular demoralization and corrupt mode of thinking, speaking, and acting, there was providentially raised up a teacher of righteousness in the person of Socrates.   He was a philosopher in the highest sense of the term, for he loved that true wisdom which consists in virtue, and what is more important, he was the first who caused the truths of philosophy to exercise a practical influence upon the masses of mankind.   His instruction was based upon a knowledge of the human heart, and upon the dictates of a pure moral sense ; self-knowledge and moral consciousness were to him the great end of study.   He felt that he had a moral, rather than a philosophical mission ; however important physical science might be, he considered the study of human character, and the improvement of the human heart, an all-absorbing duty ; in this sense he drew down philosophy from heaven to earth,[1] and his life set forth and illustrated his doctrine.

He was not the founder of any school, although all the subsequent celebrated schools of Greece were developments of his principles

[1] Tusc. Dis. v. 4, 10.

ciples. He did not profess to have any regular philosophical system; his object was to lead men to a consciousness of error as it arose, and consequently to a confession of it; but his mind was of that true philosophical caste which, in proportion to its higher attainments in virtue, feels its distance from the standard of perfection, and the farther it advances in knowledge is the more conscious of human ignorance. This consciousness was to him the commencement of all wisdom, the first step in obedience to the divine admonition, Γνῶθι σεαυτόν (*know thyself*), which he received from the Delphian deity; self-ignorance he considered as nearly akin to madness.[1]

In the streets and highways of the city, in the midst of these crowds who thronged Athens at that crowded time, when the policy of Pericles had assembled all Attica within the walls, his lessons were delivered as occasion called them forth, and were listened to with enthusiastic attention.

He was born Ol. lxxvii. 4, and was the son of Sophroniscus, a sculptor. Some say that in his youth he followed his father's profession, and a group of the Graces, which proved him to be no mean artist, was shown in the Acropolis as his work. He is said to have naturally had strong passions and an impetuous temper, but to have conquered them by a powerful will and firm moral principles.

The commencement of his philosophical career is thus related by Diogenes.[2] A wealthy Athenian, passing his father's workshop, observed the youthful Socrates practising his art. He had previously seen him attending the lectures of Anaxagoras and Archelaus; and, struck with his zeal, he generously supplied the means for enabling him to pursue his philosophical studies without laboring at his profession of an artist. Diligent as he was in those studies which were pursued in the schools of Athens, he nevertheless, to use the words of Pericles,[3] "pursued philosophy without effeminacy." Study did not distract his attention from his public duties as a soldier and a citizen. For the hardships of a military life, his hardy and robust constitution, which survived the terrible pestilence to which so many fell victims, eminently fitted him. He braved the rigors of a northern winter in the cam-

---

[1] Xen. Memor. iii. 9.　　[2] Ibid. ii. 18.　　[3] Thucyd. ii.

paign of Potidæa, which was one of the overt causes of the Peloponnesian war (B. C. 432), and afterwards served at Delium and
Amphipolis (B. C. 424). In the disastrous flight from the field of
Delium, he saved and bore off in his arms his beloved pupil, Xenophon. But he was deeply impressed with the belief that his
vocation was to reform Athenian morals and to remodel society.
So strong was his conviction, that he believed in the ever present
direction of a heavenly monitor.[1] He thought that a divine voice
first urged him to cultivate that portion of the Muse's art which
included the study of philosophy, and inspired him on each occasion with the words to which he gave utterance. His earnestness
and self-devotion to his work sprang from his belief in a divine
commission.

What Socrates meant, when he professed to act under the
guidance of a dæmon, or genius, has been the subject of much
discussion. Probably impressed with the idea of being called
to the fulfilment of a work almost apostolic, he not only felt the
need of divine direction, but even experienced this support. It
is most probable that one so habituated to self-communion as
Socrates, would be conscious of the providential superintendence
of the Supreme Being.

In his attempt to regenerate society he felt, as all moralists
must feel, that his best prospects of success were with the young,
and with those especially whose talents, cultivated by learning,
were likely to influence their contemporaries. For this reason
the clever, rich, and popular, but profligate Alcibiades, was one
of his earliest pupils, but his volatile and ostentatious disposition
was proof against the wisdom of the philosopher.

With his future biographer, Xenophon, he was successful, as
far as the man himself was concerned, for in Xenophon we see a
perfect reflection of the practical side of his great master's character, as his imaginative qualities are represented in his other
distinguished pupil, Plato; but, political prejudice caused the loss
. of these benefits to his country; a jealousy of his anti-democratical
principles exiled Xenophon from his native land.

The worth and talents of Pericles inspired him with hopes of
giving to Athens a worthy successor in the person of his gallant

---

[1] Plato, Phæd. i.

son; but, although in every way he was full of promise, the philosopher's hopes were disappointed by his condemnation to death amongst the victors at Arginusæ.

The secret voice which he implicitly obeyed had warned him to abstain from public affairs, and to devote himself to the work of the Muses,[1] that is, to literature, science, and philosophy. Hence in busy Athens, where to take an interest in politics was considered a citizen's duty, his neutrality brought upon him the hatred of all political partisans. His earnestness as a social reformer unjustly involved him in that odium with which the sophists were justly regarded. The comic poet, in his play of the " Clouds," exhibited B. C. 423, held him up to public obloquy and ridicule as the leader of the new lights and author of the new and unsound philosophy. His peculiar physiognomy, flat nose, prominent eyes, and corpulent figure; his coarse attire, ill calculated to win the respect of the polished Athenians; his humorous mockery, unsparing scorn and bitter irony; his public manner of teaching; the resistless eloquence and logical power which, notwithstanding all these personal disadvantages, arrested and riveted the attention of every one who heard him, had rendered him a well-known and marked man, and therefore a fit subject for dramatic representation.

We may acquit Aristophanes of any malicious design, or of any further wish than to fix upon the most prominent philosophical reformer as the representative of a new and unpopular system, knowing that the mass of the people would be little able to distinguish him from the sophistical pretenders. Probably he would have been horror-struck at the idea that his sportive mockery had caused the condemnation and death of an innocent and holy man.

The persecution of Socrates was not religious but political. Impiety is a sweeping charge, easily made, and neither admitting nor requiring that definite and exact proof which is expected in other cases. Great men in all ages have fallen by charges preferred under the pretence of religion. It might be supposed that his non-interference in politics would have defended him against this danger, but it must be remembered that neutrality deprives a

---

[1] Plato, Phæd. i.

man of the protection of friends and partisans, and the bias of Socrates towards aristocratic principles could not but have been a matter of notoriety. His love for the younger Pericles, who fell amongst the unpopular generals at Arginusæ; his intimacy with Alcibiades and Critias, who had taken so leading a part in the overthrow of the constitution, rendered him suspected of being opposed to democracy. His judges belonged to that party who, having been exiled by the Thirty Tyrants, had subsequently caused their expulsion. All new views, therefore, either of politics or education, naturally suggested to them obstacles to their policy, which was a return to the old state of things, as embodied in the constitution of Solon. Socrates, therefore, fell a victim to the spirit of party.

On three occasions he departed from his rule of non-interference with the affairs of public life, and on all of them the firmness and nobleness of his character were eminently displayed. When the ten generals who had gained the victory at Arginusæ were brought to their unjust trial, Socrates was one of the prytanes, or presidents of the council, and although the people, excited almost to fury by the demagogues, were determined on their condemnation, and clamored for their blood, Socrates fearlessly withstood their rage, and refused to enroll their infamous decree.[1] Doubtless his feelings were of a mixed nature. He could not contemplate with patience the destruction of his distinguished disciple, the younger Pericles; but this was not his only motive. His endeavors to save them proceeded quite as much from a stern, uncompromising love of justice, and from a wish to save his countrymen from the disgrace of so unjust a verdict.

Again, when Theramenes took sanctuary at the altar of Vesta in the council-hall, we find Socrates again interposing between the popular fury and its intended victim. And, lastly, when, in order to involve him in their guilt, the Thirty chose him with some others to seize Leon of Salamis, an innocent man, and lead him to death, he fearlessly refused to obey their commands.[2]

For twenty-five years or more he undauntedly pursued his blameless course unmolested, but, as in the case of most social reformers, prejudice and unpopularity at length prevailed. In

[1] Xen. Hellen. i.   [2] Plato, Apol.

the year B. C. 399, when his age was threescore years and ten, Melitus, Anytus, and Lycon brought against him, under the law of Diopithes, an accusation consisting of the following counts. "Socrates is guilty, (1.) of not believing in the national deities; (2.) of corrupting the youth." In addition to the motives of a public nature already alluded to, which led to his accusation, it is said, on the authority of Xenophon, that Anytus was instigated by private animosity.[1] Anytus was not only a liberal in politics, but a rich leather-seller, who wished to bring up his son to his own trade. But Socrates, seeing that he was fit for better things, tried to persuade him to study philosophy. Other cases similar to this may have furnished grounds for the charge that he corrupted those whom he professed to educate. His enmity to all moral and political abuse was also probably enhanced by the bitter and satirical vein of irony which ran through his teaching. Men will frequently bear violence, but not ridicule; and Socrates did not hesitate to ridicule, as well as to attack the national institutions.[2] Again, the Greeks regarded the works of their old poets with a reverence due almost to sacred writings. That part, therefore, of the accusation which charged him with corrupting the youth by perverting and misapplying the sentiments of their beloved and venerated poets, was likely to carry along with it the public feeling and sympathy.

But, notwithstanding all the circumstances which were in favor of the accusers, he was found guilty by but a small majority.[3] In a body of dicasts as large as a full attendance in an English House of Commons, two hundred and eighty-one were for his condemnation, and two hundred and seventy-six for his acquittal. To epitomize his defence in a work like this would be unsatisfactory. It is a perfect whole, neither more nor less than what it ought to have been. He sought not to move the pity of his judges, he cared not for acquittal. He was proudly conscious of his innocence; he did not conceal his feeling that he had faithfully discharged his duties, although there is no vain ostentation in the way in which he appeals to this fact. He forms a correct estimate of his own worth, and thus realizes Aristotle's[4] conception of the

[1] Xen. Apol. 29; quoted by Grote.   [2] Xen. Memor. i. 2.
[3] Plato, Apol. 25.   [4] Arist. Eth.

magnanimous character, and exhibits that union of humility and high-mindedness which is observable in none, perhaps, with the exception of St. Paul. There is good reason for believing that had he not disdained all unworthy self-abasement, had he canvassed the compassion of his judges, instead of honestly telling them unpalatable truths, he would either have been acquitted, or, at least, not have been capitally condemned.

The beautiful peroration of his apology has been the admiration of all ages; Cicero translated it from Plato, Steele translated it from Cicero.[1] The last words of it are sublime for their simplicity, and their spirit of pious resignation: "It is time to depart, I to die, you to live; whose lot is the better is known to God alone."

When found guilty, he did not take the means which the Athenian law allowed, to arrest judgment. His accusers had made the charge capital; Socrates might have proposed the infliction of a pecuniary fine; and had it been a severe one, it might have been sufficient to turn the scale in his favor; but he felt that he deserved reward instead of punishment, and was too honest to conceal this feeling. He therefore proposed a fine of thirty minæ, which his friends promised to pay for him; but which was too small to render it probable that it would be accepted. It so chanced that the sacred trireme had sailed for Delos on the day of his condemnation, and as no one could be put to death until its return, Socrates remained for thirty days in prison, and in chains. All offers of means to escape he refused, for, consistent to the last, he would not violate the law.

To this interval we are indebted for that conversation on the immortality of the soul, which Plato has embodied in his "Phædo," and although Plato was not himself present, it is so Socratic, that there can be little doubt that it was faithfully reported by those who were with him at his last moments.

His last words show that, so far was he from being guilty of that which the Athenians would have called impiety, that he even complied with superstitions which he himself disbelieved. "Crito," he said, just before he drank the hemlock, "we owe a cock to Æsculapius, do not neglect to pay it." He felt that

---

[1] Cic. Tusc. i.; Spect. 146.

death was the last and best remedy for all the ills and ailments of life.

Such were the life and death of this great man, who has commanded more admiration and reverence than any individual of ancient or modern times, and whose death has been felt as the greatest of all human examples, not only by his own countrymen, but by the whole civilized world.

The Fathers of the Christian Church vie with heathen moralists, in deservedly extolling the wisdom and self-denying virtue of Socrates; nor can any one read his story, the chief details of which are familiar to us even from childhood, without the deepest veneration for one who testified to the sincerity of his doctrines by his life, and died a martyr not only to truth, but also to the principle óf obedience to the law.

His death was the signal for the voluntary exile and dispersion of his friends. It is said that the Athenians repented of their intolerance, but this is scarcely to be believed of so light-minded and unfeeling a people. The deed they had done probably made no remorseful impression on their consciences, and was speedily banished from their recollections.

In examining the doctrines of the Socratic philosophy, we must not expect to find the regular system which characterizes a school. Socrates, it has already been stated, was neither a member of a school, nor did he profess to be the founder of one. His force of character exercised a greater influence over his hearers, and over posterity, than that of any mere human moral teacher; but he did not aspire to the title of master, or the right to unqualified submission to his dicta on the part of his disciples. His character was that of a moral and political reformer, and a religious missionary. Under all circumstances, in all places, wherever he saw occasion, he was at hand to inculcate noble sentiments of virtue and obedience to law. Although, therefore, owing to the consistency of his views and principles, and the philosophical character of his mind, his doctrines may be reduced to a system, they were not delivered nor taught by himself in a systematic form. The political circumstances of the times in which he lived, did not admit of such a mode of teaching. He could not assemble round him in public a crowd of admirers, listening, day after day, to lessons systematically following one another in an orderly series. With the exception of a few intimates and friends who constantly enjoyed his society, those whom he instructed and questioned, and with whom he disputed on one day, were totally different from those who conversed with him on the next.

*The exigencies of the times required that the seeds of moral virtue should be sown broad-east. His duty was, if we may use the words of Holy Writ, "to cast his bread upon the waters," and no one ever felt more deeply what his duty was than Socrates. The times furnished many valuable opportunities for isolated lessons, for the original outpourings of a full heart, deeply impressed with the necessity there was for his ministrations, but they were not suitable for establishing a school of philosophy. Socrates lived and taught during that disastrous social period, the Peloponnesian war. The disorganized state of society demanded an immediate and severe remedy. The sophists, who were, as we have seen, the recognized teachers of the Athenian youth, were not qualified for leaders in such critical times, because they were only on a par with, and not in advance of, their age. Their object was to lead men in the path of virtue only so far as was consistent with popularity. As their end was profit, they had no idea of self-sacrifice or voluntary submission to personal inconvenience. Hence their teaching was infected with the prevalent low tone of public morals; and in order to rid themselves of intellectual difficulties and moral anxieties, they took refuge in a cold and indifferent scepticism as to all truth.

Socrates, although, from there being no other moral teachers at that time, he must be considered as belonging to the class which bore the name of Sophists (for it must be remembered that the sophists were not a sect, but a profession), was unlike the rest of that profession. His pure mind saw from what a mass of moral impurity his countrymen required to be cleansed; that nothing would be sufficient short of a complete moral regeneration; and he felt that he must apply all his energies to making them good men, and, as a means to this, good citizens.

It is on this account that his moral doctrines so often take a political coloring; he did not think that there were no higher moral sanctions and obligations than those imposed by human laws: but as a practical and popular teacher, he saw that, in many instances, no teaching could be more effectual than to exalt the majesty and supremacy of law, and the political duty of obedience and subordination.

It is plain that to say that this was universally the character of his teaching would be giving only a one-sided view of the mind of Socrates. If his character is contemplated from the opposite points of view taken by his two most distinguished disciples, the Socrates of Plato seems totally different from that of Xenophon; but this apparent dissimilarity is easily explained by considering the different hands by whom his portraiture is drawn. Plato was a philosopher, endued with a poetic imagination, and a mind which delighted in the contemplation of abstract truth, who thought the highest happiness and the highest virtue consisted in such employment; who could scarcely descend to the sober practical business of life, or the application of moral science to men's political and social relation, simply because his system denied the reality of all visible phenomena. Hence, as might be expected, we see in the writings of Plato the theoretic side of Socrates. Xenophon had a philosophical, but, at the same time, a practical mind. An intellect as clear as his beautiful style is lucid. He was a matter-of-fact soldier, who wisely took a common sense view of all that related to human happiness. Hence the aspect from which he contemplated the Socratic character was that which was in accordance with the structure of his own mind. The dicta, which he considered the *memorabilia,* or things worthy to be remembered, of his great master and beloved friend, laid hold at once of his memory and his affections. They were such as had a practical bearing upon the concerns of human life.

Plato caught at and apprehended the lofty aspirations of the free spirit, liberated as it were from fetters which bound her to her temporary tabernacle of the flesh, her earthly prison-house. He beheld him in communion with the invisible world, holding converse with the Deity by prayer, by oracle, by the mysterious voice of his invisible monitor, which ever directed him in the course of his life, and pointed out the line which he was to pursue. He followed him with all his poetic enthusiasm into the world beyond the grave, the region pervaded by the pleroma of the divine nature. Xenophon delighted to see his spirit, which he, no less than Plato, recognized and admired as divine, humbling itself to the things of earth, applying itself to unravel the difficulties of the moral constitution of man, and drawing practical lessons from them, calculated to guide men in the path of virtue and happiness. Plato, as a general rule, is the exponent of his free and unrestrained conversation with his own friends, associates, and disciples, who are morally nearly on a level with him, and whose minds could soar with him to the regions of the invisible: Xenophon is the recorder of his every-day lessons, which produced such an effect upon the awe-struck crowd, that, thoughtless and wicked as they were, hating him so bitterly as at times to insult and even strike him, they stood as though enchanted, and in presence of a superior power.

It is, therefore, from a combination of the two views which are derived from these two authorities that a true conception of Socrates must be formed.

The observations which have been already made will explain the accusation made against Socrates, of undervaluing and despising physical and mathematical science. Doubtless he does at times speak of them in disparaging terms, but it is only in comparison with the importance of moral science and the study of human nature.

The exigencies of the times in which he lived made the investigation of moral science of paramount importance. He had a deep and awful impression that every moment of his valuable existence was lost and wasted which was not devoted to the investigation of moral and social questions, and to the advancement of moral and social reforms. Hence his axiom, which he reverenced as a supernatural revelation, that self-knowledge is the first and the indispensable step to all other science. There was then, on his part, no contempt of mathematical or natural science, but a deep and religious feeling of their secondary importance, as compared with that which alone he thought would make men better, and therefore happier. Besides, no philosopher had as yet appreciated or taught the importance of mathematical and physical studies as a part of mental training. The end which they had in view

27

was simply the knowledge to be acquired. We, in modern times, see in such studies another end—the cultivation of the reasoning faculties. Had Socrates seen this mental, and therefore moral, effect produced by abstract studies, they would have occupied, probably, in his teaching, even a more prominent place. Coupled with the internal conviction that he was under supernatural guidance, and was constrained to pursue one path of duty, his estimate of moral science was something of that kind which leads the Christian teacher, without undervaluing secular knowledge, to estimate still more highly that which makes men wise unto salvation.

Other difficulties which have been found by philosophers to lie in the way of eliciting the Socratic system from the writings of Xenophon and Plato, are the following. First, that Xenophon wrote as his defender, and therefore was, to a certain extent, his panegyrist; whilst Plato was himself a philosopher, an original thinker, whose intellectual powers were equal to those of his great master; and therefore it is difficult to discover how many of his opinions are his own, and how many are due to Socrates. The scattered notices, therefore, which have been found in the writings of Aristotle have been made use of to correct the erroneous inferences likely to be drawn from an examination of the assertions of Xenophon and Plato.

The first great. doctrine which Socrates taught was the real objective existence of truth and morality. In the dawnings of philosophy Nature first arrested man's attention, and in the interesting investigations which thickly crowded upon him, he neglected to turn his thoughts inward upon himself, and to contemplate the moral and intellectual nature with which he was himself endowed. The wide field of research which Nature opened gave room for a vast variety of contradictory theories, one as probable and as capable of support as the other. It is therefore not to be wondered at that a notion gradually arose that there is no such thing as truth, or that when attention began to be turned from physiology to morals, the same false axiom should have obtained there also.

Whatever may be said of the sophists in their favor, there is abundant evidence to show that this was the tendency of their teaching. Socrates was the first to expose the unsoundness of this immoral system. Struck with the unsatisfactory results to which the students of Nature had universally arrived, he promised his disciples that, in the study of their own moral and intellectual nature, they would avoid this uncertainty.

Secondly, his intense feeling of religion led him to see at once the unreasonableness of that atheistic tendency which pervaded the philosophical speculations of his age. This unbelief he attributed to the prevailing scepticism as to everything which was not perceptible to the external senses. The same evidence which he thought conclusive in proving the real existence of truth he applied also to prove the existence of Deity. As our self-consciousness unanswerably proved to us the existence of a divine nature within us, it as plainly spoke of the presence of Deity in the universe. The doctrines of Socrates may be arranged under three heads :—

I. His idea of God.

II. His belief in the immortality of the soul.

III. His moral theory.

I. As causes are often known only by their effects, and the forces of Nature by the phenomena, so the soul—that which we are conscious rules within us—is known only by its operations. Therefore, to refuse belief in Deity because he does not assume such a form and nature as is discernible by the senses is folly, but nevertheless his existence is as clearly known as if he were visible by marks of design and final causes in the universe, but especially by his operations in the intellectual nature of man. He reasoned upwards, by analogy, from the acknowledged existence of a rational ruling principle within us, to a similar mind, supreme over the powers of the universe, from which the human mind, identical in its nature, derived its origin. The subordination of all secondary causes to the great First Cause is illustrated by the mode in which man acts ; hence in this point the explanation is derived from the study of self. Posture, for example, or corporeal action, is referable primarily to muscular activity, but ultimately to the intelligent determination of the will.

To contemplate the attributes of Deity in his relation to man, seemed to Socrates of such infinite importance to his work of moral reform, that he does not seem to have indulged in profitless speculations as to the divine essence. Content with the belief in the existence of an intelligent, omnipresent, omniscient Being, the supreme and intelligent source and ruler of all things, he inquired no further.[1] Although there is no doubt that he rejected all ideas of Deity in human form, and held that the divine (τὸ Ͽεῖον) was one, yet he did not care to disturb the popular notions of polytheism, so that their ideas of the Divine nature were invested with the attributes of an all-wise and all-good Providence. It seems as though his reverential feelings were so deep as to think that even polytheism was less dangerous than atheism, or even than the disbelief in a personal Deity, the author of man's happiness, which is inseparable from pantheism. So little did he deserve the charge of irreligion advanced against him by his accusers.

II. The doctrine of the immortality of the soul followed as a corollary, from the belief that the rational part of man's nature was a portion of the Supreme Mind which governs the universe. Certainty on such a point as this is not to be expected antecedent to divine revelation; nor can we be surprised at finding the strongest hopes and the deepest internal convictions sometimes expressed in wavering and uncertain terms. Of the exact condition of the soul after death, he could assert nothing, whatever his conjectures might be; but that it would be well with the virtuous, and the reverse with the wicked, was evidently his firm persuasion; and, moreover, that when freed from the restraints of the body and the interference of bodily passions, the soul would be able to exert its intellectual energy. The concluding scene of his life, so beautifully narrated by Plato, will show what his belief was; and how, in that belief, a philosopher could die and enter upon the unknown world with pious resignation to the will of that Divine Being, to whose service he had faithfully devoted his talents and his faculties.

III. The cardinal principle of his ethical philosophy harmonized with his view of the relation subsisting between the divine and human nature. If the soul of man is a portion of the Deity, virtue, and therefore happiness, must be sought by endeavoring

---

[1] Xen. Mem. i. 1, &c.

to mould ourselves after the divine image. The practical rule, therefore, would be a negative one. As our resemblance to the Deity consists in our intellectual nature, so that in which we differ from him is our sensual nature. Our duty, therefore, is, to render ourselves independent of sensual wants, to mortify our passions by abstaining from the gratification of them, to culti- vate the intellect, and to restrain and curb the desires of the body. Other lower motives will, of course, be found occasionally intro- duced, as likely to influence those who were inaccessible to the higher and purer considerations ;[1] but all systems of ethics per- mit this practice, without it being deemed necessary that low motives should form a part of the system.

The great end and object of life was, according to Socrates, the perfection of the intellect. Our great moral duty, knowledge; the object of all knowledge, one—truth, the good, the beautiful, the divine reason.

It was here that the carrying out his theory led him beyond the confines of truth. All virtue was thus resolved into know- ledge or scientific wisdom (σοφία); and hence the paradoxical and contradictory doctrine of Socrates, which Aristotle, in his more practical ethical system, thought it so important to refute and counteract. Socrates held that, if all virtue was science (σοφία), no one could knowingly commit sin.[2] For he that knew what was right would do it. Therefore men err from ignorance of what is right, and those who are wicked are so involuntarily. How likely this doctrine was to mislead others, and how capable it was of misrepresentation to the prejudice of its author, is plain. Even if Socrates could have satisfactorily explained it, others would have wrested it to their destruction; and if his pure- minded opposition to the sensuality and immorality of the pcpu- lar mythology subjected him to the charge of impiety, such a doctrine as this might easily be distorted into the vague charge of corrupting the youth.

Out of the reformation in philosophy which Socrates effected, sprang all the great schools of Greece. The public and uncon- nected teaching of the great reformer and moral missionary was succeeded by systematic scholasticism. Aristippus founded the

[1] Xen. Mem. iv. 5.   [2] Ibid. iii. 9.

Cyrenaic school, Antisthenes that of the Cynics. The voluntary exile of his immediate friends after his persecution and death, led to the foundations of those of Megara, Elis, and Eretria. Afterwards, in safer but not less stirring times, Plato gathered around him the disciples of his Academy; and still later, when Athenian liberty had expired, the Peripatetics listened to the doctrines of Aristotle.

A brief notice of the intermediate period will be necessary, before proceeding to that of the times and doctrines of these two great philosophers.

CHAPTER XX.

BIOGRAPHY OF ARISTIPPUS.—THE CYRENAIC SCHOOL THE PARENT OF THE EPICUREAN
PHILOSOPHY.—ITS DOCTRINES DEGENERATE AND CORRUPT.—POINTS OF RESEMBLANCE
BETWEEN THE TEACHING OF ARISTIPPUS AND SOCRATES.—THE CYRENAIC FOURFOLD
DIVISION OF THE SUBJECTS OF SCIENCE.—LIFE OF ANTISTHENES.—NEGATIVE CHARAC-
TER OF THE CYNIC PHILOSOPHY.—THE STYLE OF ANTISTHENES.—HIS TEACHING
GENERALLY ETHICAL.—HIS LOGICS.—THE UNPOPULARITY OF HIS MORAL TEACHING
CAUSED IT TO BE MISREPRESENTED.—EUCLIDES, AND THE SCHOOL OF MEGARA.—THE
DOCTRINES OF EUCLIDES PARTLY ELEATIC, PARTLY SOCRATIC.

ARISTIPPUS, born (about) B. C. 465.

ARISTIPPUS was a native of Cyrene, in Africa, and, from his
residence at the court of the elder Dionysius, as well as his dis-
creditable intimacy with the notorious Laïs, and the relation in
which he stood to Socrates, makes it probable that the date of
his birth was about B. C. 465.[1] Like many other philosophers,
who from this very circumstance had leisure to devote themselves
to liberal studies, he was the son of wealthy parents. Born in a
city of luxury and prosperity, the capital of a rich district, enjoying a delightful climate, and situated in the midst of a beautiful
and fertile plain, the seeds of that self-indulgent voluptuousness
which marks his system, were probably early sown in him, and
fostered by the indulgence of his paternal home. A love of
science, and the fame of Socrates, which had reached his native
city, induced him to visit Athens and enrol himself among his
disciples. With him he remained until his death, although his
selfish pleasure-loving character led him to be absent from the
painful scene of his death.[2] The same inclination which shrank
from any scenes calculated to disturb his habitual serenity, led
him, as he confessed to Socrates, to live in exile rather than mix
in the troubled politics of his native country,[3] to be the flatterer
and companion of the Syracusan tyrant, and to submit con-

---

[1] Diod. xv. 76. [2] Plato, Phæd. [3] Xen. Mem. ii. 1.

tentedly to captivity and insult from the Persian satrap, Arta-phernes.

According to some authorities, Aristippus left behind him no philosophical writings; and if so, his opinions must have been subsequently digested and systematized by the school which he founded. Others give a large catalogue of his works; but Ritter inclines to the supposition that they are not genuine; and some epistles, which bear his name, have been proved by Bentley to be forgeries.

CYRENAIC SCHOOL.

The Cyrenaic school, so called from the birth-place of its founder, Aristippus, was the parent of the Epicurean philosophy, and is said to have been even more sensual than its offspring.[1] That man's chief good and highest happiness consisted in sensual enjoyment, was the leading dogma of its corrupt teaching.[2] Although, therefore, Aristippus professed the profoundest admiration for Socrates, he was a degenerate disciple of his great master. He held that all things were naturally subservient to the use and pleasure of man, and that all man need beware of was, the becoming a slave to them. If he avoided this, all enjoyment was lawful.

This principle of the Cyrenaic school is alluded to by Horace, when he says,

> " Nunc in Aristippi furtim præcepta relabor,
> Et mihi res, non me rebus, subjungere conor."[3]

And the licentious philosopher himself illustrates it in the following saying :—

> Ἔχω τὴν Λαΐδα, οὐκ ἔχομαι ὑπὸ τῆς Λαΐδος.

The corollary which he drew from this doctrine rescues it from entire condemnation, that all circumstances and fortunes alike, prosperity as well as adversity, were capable of ministering to the happiness of man.

> " Omnis Aristippum decuit color et status et res."[4]

The only relation which subsists between the Socratic, teach-

[1] Gesner in Hor.
[2] Cic. de Nat. Deor. 3.
[3] Hor. Epis. I. i. 18.
[4] Ibid. Epis. I. xvii. 23.

ing and the Cyrenaic school is, that owing to Aristippus being a disciple of Socrates, the latter may be said to owe its origin to the former; but so opposite were the characters of the self-indulgent voluptuary and man of the world, and the stern moralist and contemplative philosopher, that little resemblance can be traced between the Socratic and Cyrenaic doctrines.

The first point of resemblance is the superiority which the Cyrenaics attributed to ethical over physical science. The mysteries of the latter they thought beyond the powers of human comprehension, whilst the obvious importance of the former, in a practical point of view, rendered them in their estimation the proper subject of all inquiry. The term, therefore, which they applied to all science, whether logical, physical, or moral, was τὸ ἠθικον, implying by this, that all philosophy was subordinate to this one branch, and could only be usefully studied in this point of view.

To say that they entirely neglected the study of natural phenomena is an exaggeration. It is obvious from the following fivefold division adopted by them of the subjects of science, that the fourth head implies physical, the fifth logical science. 1. *Things chosen and avoided* (τὰ αἱρετα καὶ τὰ φευκτά); 2. *Passions* (τὰ παθή); *Actions* (αἱ πράξεις); 4. *Causes* (αἱ αἰτίαι); 5. *Proofs* (αἱ πίστεις).

The second point of resemblance is to be found in the objects of choice and aversion. Socrates taught that happiness is the chief good, but that men choose sensual pleasure, because they do not know in what true pleasure consists. Both, therefore, agreed in considering pleasure the chief good, although the idea which Socrates formed of it was purer and truer. Aristippus, as has been already stated, taught that man must maintain his authority over pleasure, as over all other things, and must not become its slave. Hence it followed as a corollary that the enjoyment of present pleasure alone was permitted, desire was strictly forbidden, because it coveted that which was beyond man's power, and therefore caused him to be subject instead of to govern. The inculcation of this carelessness and indifference as to the moral quality of actions, was entirely in accordance with the traditional character of the philosopher, who, we are told, on one occasion, when travelling through the Desert of Libya, bade his slaves throw away a rich treasure rather than permit the rapidity of his progress to be impeded.[1]

> " Græcus Aristippus, qui servos projicere aurum
> In mediâ jussit Libyâ, quia tardius ircnt
> Propter onus segnes."[2]

The viciousness of this system is self-evident. It makes prudence a vice instead of a virtue, because prudence implies the sacrifice of present indulgence, prompted by a desire of some future higher, but unseen, and therefore uncertain good. It destroys, as Ritter well observes, the unity of moral purpose.

The second division of the subjects of science had for its object the definition of pleasure and pain, the showing that they were in their nature positive, and affections of the soul, the one a gentle, the other a violent agitation ($\varkappa\iota\nu\eta\sigma\iota\varsigma$) of it. Pleasure was not, as the Epicureans taught, a mere negation of pain, nor pain a negation of pleasure.

The soul, when influenced by pleasure, was said to be like the sea, not glassy as in a dead calm, but gently rippling beneath the breath of the zephyr. When agitated by pain, it was like the sea upheaved and tossed by the violence of a tempest.

Actions were in themselves destitute of moral quality, either good or evil. Nothing determined their quality except human law and custom. The only difference between them was measured by the result. The highest inducement to justice, rather than injustice, was, that "honesty is the best policy."

In physics, or rather metaphysics, the axiom of this school was, that each individual is conscious of the affections ($\pi\alpha\theta\eta$) of his own mind, but not of the causes by which they are produced. To know, therefore, what truth is absolutely is impossible, although each man may know what his sensations are, which are the only avenues to knowledge. Hence men may agree in the use of common terms, but they cannot be sure that there is any identity in the conceptions which they express. How sad was this scepticism when compared with the teaching of Socrates, with his humble estimate of the vastness of human ignorance, and its

---

[1] Diog. Laert. ii. 77.'   [2] Hor. Sat. ii. iii. 100.

inability to grasp infinite truth, and therefore to make assertions dogmatically and arrogantly.

Such were the early doctrines of the Cyrenaic school; for of their logical theory, comprised in the fifth division, there is no information. In the times of Alexander's successors the Cyrenaic doctrines underwent considerable modifications.

ANTISTHÉNES.

Antisthenes was the son of an Athenian father, and, according to Suidas and Diogenes Laertius, of a Thracian mother. He was the disciple, first of the sophist Gorgias, and afterwards of Socrates, and was one of those who were present at the death-bed of his instructor.[1] A warrior in his early years, he fought at the battle of Tanagra, and died at Athens at the age of seventy.

The school which he founded met in the Cynosarges, a gymnasium for Athenians who, like himself, were born of foreign mothers. It is more probable and consistent with analogy, that from this circumstance his followers were called Cynics, than that they owed their designation to their snarling manners and doglike mode of life. His opinions were in direct antagonism to those of the Cyrenaic school. In fact, they took the form rather of a negation of what he considered their errors, than a positive exposition of truth. The knowledge which he thought most important was to unlearn error (τὸ κακὰ ἀπομάθειν). As the founder of the Cyrenaic sect, nursed in the lap of luxury, became easy-tempered, self-indulgent, and indifferent, inclined to make the best of things as he found them, so Antisthenes, born in poverty, and excluded from political rights, as wanting the pure blood of an Athenian citizen, set at defiance the external accidents of fortune. His temper, probably soured by the consciousness of an inferior position in life, gave to his teaching the bitterness of sarcasm and invective, rather than a calm spirit of philosophical inquiry. Probably the vicious luxury which he saw prevalent around him, inspired him with that just moral indignation which was developed in the writers of the old comedy, and under similar circumstances in the noble sentiments of the Roman satirists.

In his outward garb and appearance he was himself a type and

[1] Plato, Phæd.

example of his teaching—not merely teaching a contempt for
external goods, but professing poverty as a duty, austere in practice as in creed.   It was not likely that a philosophy such as this
would be popular in refined and luxurious Athens, especially when
even inquirers were repulsed by the biting sarcasm and ostentatious vanity of the philosopher, a pride which exhibited itself in
mock humility, and which provoked Socrates to tell him that it
was visible through the holes in his robe.   Hence he found few
disciples, and Diogenes, who was most congenial to him, was the
only one who remained with him until his death.   His style is
vehement and powerful, yet pure and elegant.   Amongst the
fragments of his works are two oratorical exercises (μελέται), entitled " Ajax" and " Ulysses," and also an epistle.[1]

Although, like Socrates, he stood forward as a moral reformer,
and, therefore, his philosophy was almost entirely ethical, and his
treatment of the subject generally negative and antagonistic, he
at times soared to the higher regions of metaphysical science.
He asserted, in direct opposition to the popular mythology, that
there was but one God of the natural world, without form, or
likeness to any earthly being.[2]

With respect to the science of mind, or logic, wherever he saw
any difficulty which he could not surmount, he denied the possibility of doing so; for example, he asserted that definition was
impossible, because he saw that correct definition was difficult.
To define essence he held to be impossible, because it consisted in
ascribing a quality which may be seen in the concrete, but which
cannot be seen in the abstract, and was, in fact, only its point of
resemblance to some other things.   For example, we can see man,
the concrete (ἄνθρωπος), but not man-ness the abstract (ἀνθρωπότης);
and again, when we predicate whiteness of silver, we only state
the quality in which it resembles tin.

The unpopularity of his moral teaching has subjected it to much
misrepresentation, so that it is difficult to determine how many of
the doctrines ascribed to him are really his.   It is plain that his
idea of the highest good was a life according to virtue.   Virtue
is sufficient for happiness, and therefore the virtuous man is self-

[1] Winckelman, fragm. Antisth. ; Reiske, vol. viii. ; Orell. Epp. Soc.
[2] Cic. de Nat. Deor. i. 1.

sufficient, and independent of every external good. This doctrine of independence, pushed to a vicious extent, led to a rude contempt for all civil institutions, and even for the decent customs of civilized life; but this unnatural isolation could not overcome the natural tendency of human sympathies, and even Antisthenes was not deaf to the claims of friendship, if the choice of friends was influenced by a regard to virtue. Virtue (he held) is learned by teaching, and consists in practical wisdom (φρόνησίς), united with strength of character (ἰσχυς); of this needful ingredient of manliness he considered Hercules as the symbol, whose temple, as a constant memorial to his disciples, overlooked his gymnasium.

EUCLIDES.

The persecution and death of Socrates dispersed his disciples, and they found in Megara a temporary refuge from popular fury.[1] Amongst the earliest of his followers was Euclides, a native of Megara, which circumstance doubtless determined the rest in choosing their abode.

Previously to his acquaintance with Socrates, he had attached himself to the Eleatic philosophy. His doctrines, therefore, were Eleatic, tinctured with the ethics and logic of Socrates. Although, in temper, mild and gentle, approaching even to indolence and indifference, he was of a dialectical turn of mind, and his inclination for subtle disputations, most of which were fallacies, subjected him to the rebuke of Socrates.

The school which he founded was termed the Megarian. We are told that in reasoning he adopted the elenchthic, or indirect method, that is, the *reductio ad absurdum;* and in this he was followed by his school, the later members of which, on account of their skill in this method of refutation, were sometimes called Eristici or Dialectici. Although he was the author of six dialogues, none of them have been preserved.

---

[1] Diog. Laert. ii. 106; Cic. Acad. ii. 42.

CHAPTER XXI.

BIOGRAPHY OF PLATO.—HIS TRAVELS.—OBJECTS OF HIS THREE JOURNEYS TO SICILY.—
FALSE VIEWS RESPECTING HIS PHILOSOPHY.—TESTIMONY OF ARISTOTLE.—THE BEAU-
TY OF HIS STYLE.—THE DRAMATIC CHARACTER OF THE PLATONIC DIALOGUE.—THE
DIALOGUES ARRANGED IN TRILOGIES AND TETRALOGIES.—SOME ARRANGEMENT NECES-
SARY.—THE DIFFICULTIES AND MODE OF RECONCILING THEM.—HIS SPURIOUS WRIT-
INGS.—POINTS TO WHICH ATTENTION MUST BE PAID IN ARRANGING HIS GENUINE
WORKS.—THE DIALOGUES WHICH ARE THE MOST SOCRATIC NOT NECESSARILY THE
EARLIEST.—THE TRUE TEST OF THEIR ORDER.—SCHLEIERMACHER'S ARRANGEMENT.

PLATO, born B. C. 429.

THE most important events of an author's life often become a
key to his works, and an invaluable assistance to understanding
them. It is, therefore, much to be regretted that there exists so
little trustworthy information respecting the life of Plato, and
especially respecting his travels. The life by Diogenes Laertius
is of little authority, that by Tenneman, prefixed to his system
of the Platonic philosophy, comprehends all the results of modern
investigation.

In the month of May, B. C. 429, Ol. lxxxvii. 4,[1] was born at
Athens, or, as others say, at Ægina, the greatest philosopher
whom the world ever saw. This epoch is marked by the death
of the noble-minded Pericles in the following year, when Athens
lost, in the plague, the flower of her population. The boyhood
of Plato was passed during that period of demoralization and
suffering, the Peloponnesian war. He was of illustrious descent,
both by the father's and mother's side; through the former being
related to Codrus, through the latter to Solon. His real name
was Aristocles, but the name of Plato (from πλατύς, broad) was
given him because of the breadth of his shoulders. Weakness of
voice prevented him from becoming an orator, and therefore, from
taking that active part in political life to which his birth entitled

---

[1] Athenæus, v. p. 217; Clinton, Fasti Hellenici.

him: but being endowed with a pure taste and a love for literature, he devoted himself to poetry: and tradition tells,[1] that
emblematic of the mellifluous sweetness of his style, a swarm of
bees settled upon his infant lips whilst sleeping in his cradle.
There is another legend, which also symbolizes the sweetness of
his eloquence. One night he dreamed that he folded in his arms
a young swan, which, when fully fledged, soared to heaven, singing with inconceivable sweetness.

In his early years he manifested a talent for poetry, which
afterwards influenced his later compositions. He attempted both
epic and tragedy, but, struck with his immeasurable inferiority to
Homer, he burnt his poems, and gave up poetry for ever. He
then commenced the study of philosophy, and when quite a youth,
attended the instructions of Cratylus, and learned from him the
theories of Heraclitus.[2]

At twenty years of age, as he himself tells us,[3] he devoted
himself altogether to philosophy, and became a disciple of Socrates, for whom, to the time of his death, he felt the warmest
attachment which ever existed between tutor and pupil. The
resemblances discovered between some of the Platonic doctrines,
and those of Oriental philosophers, and the notion so long prevalent, that Greek philosophy originated in the East, have caused
many voyages to be attributed to Plato without sufficient authority.

Some writers[4] would have us believe that he visited Phœnicia,
and there learnt from the Hebrews the knowledge of the true
God; and that he was instructed by the Magi and the Assyrians
in their systems of philosophy. Allusions to parts of their systems furnish no proof of this, because acquaintance with them
might, without personal intercourse, have been gained at Athens,
which had now become the home of literature and science. The
travels of Plato, which are supported by the best authority, are
to Italy, Sicily, Cyrene, and Egypt.[5] He evidently returned to
Athens, B. C. 395; for Diogenes Laertius[6] informs us that he
served at Tanagra, Corinth, and Delium; not, of course, the celebrated battles of Tanagra and Delium, but some other engage-

[1] Cic. de Div. i. 36.
[2] Plato, Symp. 187.
[5] Clinton, Fasti Hellenici, ii.
[3] Arist. Met. i. 6.
[4] See Tusc. Disp. iv. 19.
[6] Diog. Laert. iii. 6, 7, 8.

ments in the Corinthian or Theban war. Previously to his more distant travels, he, together with the other friends of Socrates, retired to Megara, where it is probable that some of his dialogues were written. Three times he visited Sicily;[1] once, in order to see the eruption of Ætna, in the reign of the elder Dionysius, when he was in his fortieth year; twice during that of the younger. On his return to Athens, after his first voyage thither, he began to give gratuitous instruction in philosophy, in the groves of the Academy, partly in those dialogues, which, though not the earliest philosophical writings in that form, have never been equalled, partly in more formal lectures. Besides the numbers who crowded to his public instructions, he was daily in the society of a chosen few, who sat at his frugal board, and listened with enthusiasm to the words of wisdom which flowed so eloquently from his lips.[2]

A period of twenty-two years elapsed between his first and second voyages to Sicily. His object on this occasion was to instruct the younger Dionysius, and, together with Dio, to remodel the Syracusan constitution. In this design, however, he failed; Dio was banished by the tyrant, and Plato returned to Athens.

In the object of his third journey, which was to effect a reconciliation between Dio and Dionysius, he was equally unsuccessful. He was now advanced in years, and the rest of his honored life passed peacefully, in literary occupation, and the society of his disciples. He died on his birthday, B. C. 347, at the age of eighty-one, his mental powers unimpaired, and whilst employed in the very act of writing.

The following epigram was written to his memory by Speusippus:—

Σῶμα μὲν ἐν κόλποις κατέχει τόδε γαῖα Πλάτωνος,
Ψυχὴ δ' ἰσοθέων τάξιν ἔχει μακάρων.

"Earth in her friendly bosom the body of Plato embraces,
But his soul immortal holds rank with the gods and the godlike."

Although Socrates was the master under whom Plato studied, and although, in his modest self-abasement and devoted affection, he attributed to his instructions all his philosophical knowledge, it must not be supposed that his enlarged and enlightened mind

[1] Plato, Ep. vii.; Athen. xi.; Diog. Laert. iii. 18.
[2] Athen. i. 7; x. 14.

confined itself to the study of one system, or to the lessons of one instructor, however highly he may have respected him. In his boyhood he studied the philosophy of Heraclitus, in Italy he became acquainted with that of Pythagoras. The probability is, that he examined the whole range of Greek philosophy; for he evidently saw and avoided the falsehood of its two extremes, Ionian materialism, and the pure idealism of the Eleatic school. In fact he may be said to have arranged and moulded into one harmonious whole, the unconnected parts left by the labors of his predecessors.

Schleiermacher observes, that two unfounded opinions have prevailed from very early times respecting Plato and his Dialogues; first, that in them there is no consistency or system, either of thinking or teaching, that his principles are uncertain and contradictory, and that no mutual relation or interdependence between his works can possibly be discovered, because in reality there is none. The labors of modern scholars and philosophers have shown the incorrectness of this view, and proved that it arose from a misunderstanding of Platonism, and an inability to follow out and investigate his train of thought. The fact is, that Plato's system is, perhaps more than any other, the development of one idea. The keystone of his creed is that the human soul has the power of motion residing in itself, that therefore it neither comes into existence nor ceases to exist: that all spiritual essence is the same, including even Deity; that the soul has already known that which really is; and, although it has lost the knowledge, partially recovers it by recollection.

The other prevalent idea is, that there was some secret and more systematic philosophy, never committed to writing, but contained in oral lectures and conversations, transmitted only by tradition; and, therefore, in vain to be looked for in his works. These professed to expound and define more accurately the doctrines contained in the dialogues. *A priori*, this view is just what might be expected to result from the universal admiration and reverence with which Plato has been regarded in all ages of the world, and from the wide field for speculation and expansion furnished by the imaginative and poetical method in which he treats philosophy. The relation in which unauthoritative tradition

28

stands to the written doctrines of the Christian revelation furnishes a case somewhat parallel. But, however strong the temptation may be to indulge in such a view, there are no historical traces of such traditional teaching. It is plain, moreover, that where the ἄγραφα δόγματα differ from the written works, they must be unsafe guides; where they coincide, they are unnecessary.

The testimony of Aristotle on this point, although negative, is most satisfactory. He was for many years a disciple and intimate associate of Plato. The character of his mind was such as readily to reduce to system all that he had heard, as well as read; if there had been any authentic doctrines not contained in Plato's written works, not only would he have been aware of their existence, but he would have made use of them. He, however, although he alludes to traditional teaching,[1] never appeals to its authority, whilst, on the contrary, he is constantly quoting from, or referring to, doctrines which we can trace for ourselves in the genuine Platonic dialogues.

The philosophy of Plato was the first attempt to reconcile and systematize previous discoveries, and in this task he was followed with even greater success by the great master of philosophical system, Aristotle.

Plato, therefore, takes a comprehensive view of all ancient philosophy, and this, which exposed him unfairly to the charge of plagiarism,[2] is of itself sufficient defence against the accusation; for, by the copious details with which he filled up its barren outlines, and the new ideas with which he so richly illustrated them, he made the discoveries which he adopted fairly his own, and invested them with all the charms of novelty and originality.

No language can do justice to the exquisite beauty of his style. Attic prose, the most beautiful of all prose, and most readily appreciated by the English ear, had now reached its zenith of perfection. And as that of his fellow disciple, Xenophon, has never been equalled for simplicity and perspicuity, so that of Plato has no rival for skill and elegance. We discern in it the fervid genius of the poet, combined with the terse accuracy of the philosopher. The playfulness of familiar discourse, which is so necessary to the dramatic truthfulness of dialogue, is always

---

[1] Arist. Phys. iv. 2.   [2] Diog. Laert. iii.

polished and graceful, and never degenerates into coarseness and vulgarity. He possesses all the power which distinguished Socrates, of drawing his illustrations from the most homely objects, and yet he is free from the unseemly coarseness in which his great master so frequently delighted. Cicero, whose critical taste discerned this combination of singular excellencies, said, that if Jupiter talked with men he would converse in the language of Plato. It is said, by his anonymous biographer, that he took for his model the pure Attic phraseology of the Aristophanic comedy; and the same genius which enabled the comic writer to clothe in metrical language the familiar converse of every day Athenian life, taught the philosopher to express in graceful prose the gorgeous ideas of his vivid imagination.

Plato was not the first to throw his discourses into the form of dialogue. The Socratic method of arguing, the object of which was to lead the pupil to discover truth for himself rather than to communicate it dogmatically, and to force an opponent to convict himself of error, had already taught some of his followers to adopt this form. Xenophon, Antisthenes, Euclides, and others, had already composed philosophical dialogues, but in dramatic effect they were all far surpassed by Plato. A dialogue, observes Schlegel,[1] may be philosophical, but not dramatic; and this difference he illustrates by a reference to the dialogues of Plato. No one has ever doubted that the principal charm of the Platonic dialogue is its mimetic and dramatic quality. It is not merely instructive, but entertaining. The interest of the reader is kept alive waiting for the issue, and the effect eventually to be produced on the speakers by their progressive interchange of thought, just as the spectator anxiously watches the progress of the action and expects the completion of his satisfaction in the *dénouement* of the play. The scene seems to pass before the eyes of the reader invested with life and reality. We imagine that we form part of the society, and are present at the conversations. Many of the arguments and objections are just those which we should ourselves be ready to offer: they are fairly put and met, not merely suggested for the sake of being overthrown. The presence of this dramatic character is one test for deter-

[1] Lect. i.

mining the genuineness of those dialogues, respecting which doubts have been entertained; and it seems especially to have struck the earlier commentators. Aristophanes, of Byzantium, the grammarian, actually arranged some of them in trilogies, just as if they had been intended, like the tragedies of the great dramatists, for theatrical representation. In still later times Thrasyllus rearranged them in tetralogies. It is plain, however, that both these arrangements were unwarrantable and arbitrary, and were the result of carrying too far a favorite idea.

The orderly and logical character of Plato's mind, however—which is abundantly evident, notwithstanding his fervid imagination—caused it to be felt that some arrangement was necessary; that, however complete in itself each dialogue might be, there was some connection between them; that they were parts of one great system.

The arrangement, nevertheless, was attended with great difficulty. Supposing that his discoveries and theories developed themselves in the order which might have been naturally expected, some dialogues, which upon the whole contained internal evidence of his early productions, contained also passages which implied more philosophical maturity. The only method of reconciling such difficulties with the order and classification adopted was to suppose, first, that such passages were the expressions of knowledge which Plato had acquired from others; and, secondly, that additions were subsequently made to the works which he wrote in his earlier years.

Amongst the Platonic writings which are now almost universally acknowledged to be spurious, the "Epistles" are, perhaps, the most skilful imitations of his style. The rest, of which it is unnecessary to give a catalogue, differ so much both in composition and matter, that no doubt is entertained upon the subject by modern scholars.

Whilst the universal admiration of Plato, and the respect paid to his authority, led to the "pious fraud" of attributing to him spurious writings and traditional doctrines, modern times are indebted to it for the state of perfection in which the dialogues have been handed down. Whatever works may be lost, there are contained in those extant, ample materials for a complete analysis of his philosophical system. We have the same means of comprehending it as those disciples who attended his lectures and listened to his oral instruction in the academy.

With respect to his genuine works, although Socher has excluded four important ones—"Parmenides," "Sophistes," "Politicus," and "Critias;" Aste still more, including the "Apology," and the "Crito;" and even Schleiermacher, whose arrangement is incomparably the best, rejects the "Hippias Minor"[1] and "Menexenus,"[2] there do not appear to be adequate grounds for the rejection of them. It remains, therefore, to endeavor to arrange them in some such order as will exhibit which were his earlier and which his later compositions.

This order can only be determined by the internal evidence, and the points to which attention must be paid are:—(1) The artistic skill displayed in composition, including gracefulness and polish of style, and dramatic and imitative power. (2) The gradual development of his philosophical system, from its first principles to its most complicated results, and the progressive advance of his intellectual powers.

As there is no doubt that literary skill increases with literary practice, and in proportion to the unfolding of the mental powers; and dramatic and imitative art is improved by a larger and wider experience and intercourse with human nature, and therefore marked inferiority in these points would form a strong objection to assigning any dialogue to Plato's later years, the first of these considerations must not be lightly passed over; but still too much reliance must not be placed on it as an argument, because the probability is that an author of exquisite taste, like Plato, would often recur to his earlier writings, with a view to improving their external form. The prevalent notion that Plato thoroughly revised the whole of his works, is supported by the old tradition that he valued so highly beauty of style as to correct and improve, frequently, the introduction to his great work the "Republic;"[3] and Dionysius also bears testimony to a prevalent notion that he never left off combing and

---

[1] Arist. Met. v. 29.   [2] Ibid. Rhet. iii. 14.
[3] Wolf, Proleg. in Homer. p. 153.

curling (*κτενίζων καὶ βοστρυχίζων*) his dialogues,[1] even till he was eighty years of age. Except in the especial case of Plato, we should expect to find, as we advanced chronologically, more of philosóphy and less of imaginative power; for it is a law of the human mind, that, as the powers of reason and analysis strengthen, those of the imagination decline; but Plato's imagination appears to have been as vivid in his old age as it was in his youth. But even he does not form a complete exception to the general rule, for the "Republic," the "Laws," and the "Timæus," which are acknowledged as his latest works, exhibit the least imaginative and dramatic power.[2]

To determine, therefore, the present question, the principal weight ought to be given to the evidence of intellectual progress. It must not be assumed that those dialogues, which contain pure Socratic doctrines, are for that reason the earliest; because it must be remembered that he studied the philosophy of Heraclitus before he became acquainted with Socrates, and that during the whole time of his intercourse with his great master, he was living in an atmosphere of philosophy, in a city in which various scientific systems were habitually discussed; and therefore he must have had many opportunities of examining them all. The criterion of order must therefore be the development of his own mind, the unfolding and perfecting of that orderly system which can be deduced from his writings. It must be not a mere expansion of the Socratic system, but an inquiry, becoming gradually more and more comprehensive, a progressive widening of the sphere of scientific research by an original mind, formed and imbued with Socratic teaching.

Many arrangements have been proposed, but that of Schleiermacher, although liable to some objections, appears the most probable and most generally admitted.

He arranges the Platonic dialogues in three classes, according to the philosophical progress which they display. In the first he places the "Phædrus," "Protagoras," and "Parmenides," together with some of the smaller dialogues, the subjects of which are in connection with them; and to this period must be referred

---

[1] De Comp. Verb. 25; Quinct. Inst. viii. 6, 64.
[2] Ritter, *in loco.*

the "Apology," the "Crito," and the "Euthyphron," dictated by his attachment to the master he had just lost, the dates of which are universally fixed immediately after the death of Socrates. Ritter assigns the "Gorgias" to this first period, because of its connection with the subject-matter of the "Phædrus" and "Protagoras." Schleiermacher places it in the second class, which belongs to the period when his logical and dialectic philosophy was fully matured. In the second are arranged the "Gorgias," "Theætetus," "Menon," "Euthydemus," "Cratylus," "Sophistes," "Politicus," "Philebus," "Symposium," and "Phædon." In the third, the "Critias," "Politia," "Timæus," and the "Laws." The last three are universally acknowledged to have been his latest dialogues. Such is the nearest satisfactory approximation which has been made to a chronological arrangement of the writings of Plato, and such the grounds and principles on which their order and relative position have been established.

CHAPTER XXII.

BEFORE examining the philosophy of Plato in its several divisions, it is necessary to state what was his idea of philosophy generally. It is then, according to him, the passionate love of wisdom. This love springs from the natural impulse after knowledge which is the property of man's intellectual nature, the consciousness that knowledge is the only satisfaction of our mental wants and necessities.

In obedience to this impulse, and in order to satisfy his intellectual aspirations, the philosopher investigates nature—both external and internal to himself. He endeavors to discover the constitution of the world and of his own mind. His object is not only to make observations, and to collect facts, but to generalize and classify—to discover a law. He sees many phenomena, many effects ; he traces them backwards to their causes ; and, at length, by continuing his analytical process, he ends in the discovery of one fundamental cause—eternal, uniform, pervading all nature. The many—that is the phenomena—are the results and developments of this Unity ; the knowledge of all is contained in the knowledge of the one. As, therefore, Plato by his analysis arrives, through the chain of successive causes, at this one source, from which all diverge; so, when the synthetical process commences, the foundation and starting-point of his system is the comprehensiveness and oneness of absolute science (ἐπιστήμη), and its purely intellectual nature, which embraces within its sphere all truth and all self-consciousness. To investigate the nature and essence of science is the subject of one whole dialogue, the "Theætetus." To determine its definition he entirely fails; nor can he do more than state that there is no standard with which to compare it, except itself; that all terms used in its description involve the term science itself; and that the nearest possible approach to accurate definition is "right opinion, deduced by logical inference." This one, and all-comprehensive science, he designates dialectic. Science, however, though the end of all intellectual energy, is not unpractical; it exercises an irresistible control over man's moral nature. A man who possesses science is constrained to obey the commands imposed by this knowledge of good and evil; so that virtue is inseparable from science, and he who does wrong and is enslaved by his passions, does not in reality possess science. But, he held, such is the imperfection of man that he never attains perfect science any more than perfect virtue. He must place it before him as the aim of all his intellectual energies, even though he cannot attain it. God alone can be wise (σοφός); man can only be a lover of it (φιλόσοφος).[1] Hence, as wisdom is really in its true sense unattainable by man, its representative is learning; and therefore, the love of learning and the love of wisdom are one and the same, τό γε φιλομαθὲς καὶ φιλόσοφον ταὐτόν.[2]

The object of Plato was evidently the noble one of placing before man a high intellectual, and consequently, by implication, a high moral standard as the end and object of his aspirations; to encourage his efforts after the true, the pure, the beautiful, and the virtuous, knowing that the character would be purified in the endeavor, and that the consciousness of the progress made, step by step, would be of itself a reward. The object of science was, as he taught, the true, the eternal, the immutable, that which is; in one alone could these attributes be found united—that is

[1] Phæd. ii. 78, d.   [2] De Rep. ii. 376, b.

God. Man's duty, then, according to the Platonic system, is to know God and his attributes, and to aim at being under the practical influence of this knowledge. This the Christian is taught, but much more simply and plainly, to know God, and Jesus Christ whom he hath sent, and to prepose to himself a perfect standard, to be perfect even as his Father in heaven is perfect, and to look forward, by that help which Plato had no warrant to look for, to attain the perfect measure of the fulness of Christ.

Although Plato believed and taught that man ought to strive after and devote himself to the contemplation of the One, the Eternal, the Infinite, he was humbly conscious that no one could attain to the perfection of such knowledge; that it is too wonderful and excellent for human powers. Man's incapacity for apprehending this knowledge he attributed to his soul, during his present state of existence, being cramped and confined by its earthly tabernacle.

Only when the soul is freed from the impediment of a mortal body, and arrives at its own native heavenly dwelling-place, can it behold science (*i. e.* the objects of science) such as it really is.[1]

But although his enthusiastic and lofty mind placed so high the ideal and the object of pure dialectic science, yet he allowed that there were other subdivisions of science, which had subordinate ends in view besides the true and the eternal. He adored as it were the supreme Good; he confessed man's nothingness as compared to it; he encouraged the intellect to soar as high as was permitted in that direction; but he would also have it applied to physical, arithmetical, and other sciences, in order to store up materials for the pursuit of that master science which comprehends all. None but that is worthy of being the final end of man's present intellectual energies; yet all other sciences, as furnishing *data* of which dialectic teaches the use and application, are necessary, and therefore the pursuit of them praiseworthy.

Nor did he fail to see that he whose mind was thus purified by the application of its intellectual energies, would be better adapted to undertake the practical business of life, than one who had studied details instead of principles, and had been fettered to

[1] Phæd. p. 247, d.; De Rep. vi. 484.

lower and less philosophical views of political, mental, and moral philosophy.

The heads under which the philosophical system of Plato must be divided, are those of Dialectics, Physics, and Ethics. Under Ethics are included Politics, because, in the investigation of moral obligations, man is considered in his social relations, and as a member of a political community.

In considering the first of these, it must not be forgotten that the term dialectic is used in a totally different sense from that in which it is generally applied by the ancient philosophers, *viz.*, as the equivalent of logic. Plato, as we have already seen, uses it in a far wider and more comprehensive sense, as the science of that which is the true, the eternal, the immutable.

Nor is this assertion contradicted by the fact, that he does sometimes use the term in its more common acceptation.[1] The art or science of conversing in the form of dialogue is, according to Plato, identical with that of reasoning, for he considers dialogue as the only correct method of clothing argument in language; and the progress of the mind from one judgment to another (διάνοια) is, he says, the voiceless dialogue which the soul holds with itself.

Nor, on the other hand, must it be considered that this comprehensive sense of dialectic infringes upon the domain of physics, for physical science is the science of phenomena which are (not like thought or self-consciousness) unreal, uncertain, mutable. But still, all these divisions, although separable, are closely interwoven one with another, dialectic being, with Plato, the foundation of all philosophy. We must not, therefore, expect to find them treated of in separate works, as they are by the more systematic Aristotle. We must be content to find that, in different dialogues, one subject will predominate, while the rest occupy subordinate portions. For example, the " Theætetus," " Sophistes," " Politicus," and " Parmenides," are dialectic treatises. The " Timæus" is, upon the whole, physical, and the " Republic" and the " Laws" ethical and political.

[1] De Rep. vii. 540.   [2] Soph. 263.

The learning and industry with which Plato had investigated
the systems of preceding philosophers, had digested and made
his own all that was valuable in their labors, showed him the necessity of preparing the way for building up his own theory, by
levelling the erroneous views which had pre-occupied the ground.
He, therefore, in the dialectic dialogues of the "Theætetus,"
and the "Sophistes," refutes the doctrines of the Heraclitic
school, as developed by Protagoras, and their direct contraries,
as held by the Eleatæ.[1]   He first, then, combats the materialist
assertion of Protagoras, that all knowledge is the result of sensation.   Without tracing the unsatisfactory subtleties by which he
establishes his conclusion, it is sufficient to say that he clearly
saw the consequences to which the admission of such an axiom
leads.   He saw that, if this assertion were true, there could be
no such thing as absolute existence; that each object would be,
relatively to each individual, such as he perceived it to be ;[2] that
even the sentient being who had to pronounce judgment upon
truth, could not always be one and the same, for, with variations
of circumstances, of health for example, the power of sensation
varies also.   Hence there would be nothing real, nothing possessing a nature truly its own.   Moreover, universal propositions are
true, not only as regards the present, but the future ; but sensation has only reference to the present; therefore, according to
the theory of Protagoras, there can be no knowledge, and consequently nothing asserted with truth which will hold good beyond
the present time.

The consequence of the Eleatic theories was the direct opposite
to this, namely, the denial of all knowledge through the medium
of the senses ; but to this erroneous view the philosophy of Plato
was equally opposed.   Notwithstanding his natural tendency to
soar from the regions of sense to that of pure intellectual energy,
and the great gulf which, in his views, separates pure thought
from sensuous perception, he saw the absolute necessity of communion between the senses and the intellect.   Opposed as he was
to the materialist doctrine, he was unwilling to allow the non-

[1] Xen. Mem. i. i. 14.   [2] Theæt. p. 152, d. ; p. 166, b.

existence of anything but pure mind. In fact, he stood firm against the two principal strongholds of all infidelity, the one materialism, which refuses to believe anything but what it sees, the other idealism, which considers nothing as real except the conceptions of each individual mind.

These fundamental errors having been refuted, his own theory of the relation of mind to matter is built up upon the following basis.

Man's nature being composed of soul and body, an intimate communion exists between them. There are two sources of knowledge, the one sensation, the other the reflux action of the mind upon the ideas conveyed to it by the external organs. That which is apprehended by the senses is changeable, that which is apprehended by the intellect is immutable and eternal; and this permanent and invariable alone constitutes essence (οὐσία). The bodily organs and the faculty of sensation being imperfect, are impediments to the intellectual contemplation of unchangeable truth. Nor will the soul arrive at an adequate conception of truth, or see things really as they are, until it is freed from the body.[1] True science, then, is to know intellectually the essence of things absolutely (τὸ αὐτὸ ἕκαστον), which he technically terms the *idea* (ἰδία). This doctrine demands a few words in explanation.[2] A strong conviction of the instability of the sensible appears to have been always present to the mind of Plato. The result of this conviction was, the sensible is in a state of continual change, and consequently the sensible is not the true. He assumed, therefore, that there exist from all eternity in the all-pervading fulness of the Divine Intelligence, of which the human soul was part and portion, certain archetypal forms, which are immutable and absolutely existent. These are incorporeal, apprehended by the intellect alone, the types of which the world and all that it contains are the antitypes. All else which exists, whether physically or metaphysically, is only real so far as it participates in them (μετέχει, κοινωνίαν ἔχει). These forms are called by Plato ideas, and the idea may be defined, " that which makes everything which is, to be what it is," or, " whatever exhibits an eternal truth, which forms the basis of the mutability of the sensible." These were the types (παραδείγ

[1] Phæd. 65.   [2] See the Phædo.

ματα) after which God made all created things, impressing their likeness upon matter (ὕλη), which was itself also eternal and formless, yet fitted to receive form.

From the universal nature of the idea, it follows that there must be ideas of all abstract qualities, such as the good, the beautiful, the evil, health, strength, magnitude, color; also of all sensible objects, such as a horse, a temple, a cup, a man—even of each individual man; e. g., Socrates and Simmias. It is evident that the Platonic idea must not be confounded with *abstract* ideas, which are properties, qualities, and accidents drawn off from objects, and contemplated separately; as, e. g., we may contemplate the scent or color of a flower. Each of these qualities would have, according to the Platonic theory, its corresponding idea; but still, as has been shown, there are other ideas which are not abstract. Nor did Plato teach that the idea is arrived at by abstraction or generalization; he believed that a common term was arrived at by these processes, but he also believed that that for which it stood had a real independent existence. The idea is self-existent, eternal, and becomes known to us in our present life by reminiscence, having been previously apprehended by the intellect in a former state of being. It is plain that the difference between the idealism of Plato and the conceptualism of modern times is as follows: the conceptualist holds that common terms suggest ideas of the classes of things which they verbally represent, and that these ideas exist only in the mind as mental conceptions. Plato held that ideas existed not in the individual mind which apprehended them, but in the Divine and all-pervading Intellect, of which each individual mind formed a portion.

From this doctrine it follows, that every object of science is an idea; that the Platonic theory is equally opposed to the Heraclitic doctrine as reproduced by the sophists, which taught that sensation is the only source of knowledge; and to the Eleatic, which, in its admiration of unity, denied the eternal existence of separate and distinct essences.

The supreme idea is that of God; and as the last and highest idea amongst all objects of knowledge is that of the good, it follows that God and the highest good are identical.[1] A belief in God as a rational and intelligent Being is innate in man, an in-

---

[1] De Rep. vii. 517.

stinctive, irresistible conviction, the result of the intimate relation in which he stands to the Deity, the human soul being a part and portion of the Divine mind. Nor could he explain the invariable order discernible in the universe—which he considered an image, as it were, of Deity—except on the hypothesis of design, the existence of an intelligent cause, a reasoning mind, ruling and regulating the whole course of Nature; and as the order of Nature proves unanswerably the existence of an intelligent First Cause, so the perfect beauty which characterizes it is a proof of the goodness of the Deity.[1]

Upon the whole, in weighing and comparing the passages in which Plato speaks of God, we may come to the conclusion that, although his language was inadequate, and at times such as would imply a belief in a mere abstract rational principle, filling and pervading the universe,—in fact, a belief of a pantheistic nature, still the prevailing practical impression influencing his habits of thought was that of a personal Deity.

Take away from his idea of the human soul all the impediments to its free energy—add to it the attributes of eternity, perfection, goodness, and power, and the result is his conception of the divine nature; and, however inadequately this belief may be stated, it is scarcely possible to conceive it to be any other than a practical conviction of a personal Deity, and not mere abstract mind. Multitudes of passages might be adduced which place this beyond a doubt. He denies that the mere abstractions of perfect wisdom and intellect can exist without a living soul (ψυχή).[2] He describes the Deity just as he would a being possessing attributes, as having no sympathy with the wicked, as not hearing their prayers, or accepting their offerings.[3]

The doctrine of reminiscence is the result of his doctrine of ideas, of his denying the reality and stability of sensible objects. If sensible objects differ in appearance at different times according to the aspect under which they are viewed, the true ideas of which the mind forms conceptions cannot correspond with them; they may be similar, but not identical. Again, the archetypal ideas of the beautiful, the just, the good, are far more perfect than the concrete qualities so called, which are met with in the

[1] De Leg. x. 89, b.　　　[2] Phileb. p. 30.　　　[3] De Leg. x. 905.

domains of sensation. These ideas, then, are not acquired by
observation, although they are drawn out by skilful interrogation
from one who has had no means in this life of acquiring them
before. A system of questioning may be so skilfully framed[1]
that a man may be led to enunciate all the facts of geometry,
from the simplest axioms to the most complicated propositions.
How then did he arrive at this knowledge? The difficulty is
solved by the hypothesis that all learning is the recollection of
things previously known, and for a time dormant and forgotten.
In that previous state of existence, when the human soul was an
inhabitant of the ideal world, and part of the fulness (πλήρωμα) of
Deity, it came in contact with those immutable truths and eternal
ideas of which all earthly forms are mere resemblances. Then
did God reveal all truth to the soul of man, which was a partaker
of his own spiritual nature.[2] At the time of birth, when the pure
rational soul comes in contact with irrational matter, all this is
forgotten, to be recovered and again recognized gradually, but
at the best imperfectly. Such was the theory of reminiscence as
held by Plato and his master Socrates; and it is clear that this
doctrine implies a belief in the immortality of the soul. A philosopher, who held the pre-existence of the soul, its possession of
knowledge in that pre-existent state, its communion with and
participation in the mind of the Deity, would have been guilty
of inconsistency if he had taught that its separation from that
body, to which it had been united only for a time, the connection with which could be traced from the commencement to the
end, would cause its dissolution and death.

PHYSICS.

The best and most systematic statement of Plato's physical
theories is contained in the dialogue entitled "Timæus," and
his inclination towards the physical doctrines of Pythagoras led
him to represent his own system as developed by a Pythagorean.
It was natural that he should hold the inferiority of this science
to dialects, because the object of the former was created and
variable, that of the latter self-existent and eternal, and his view
would derive support from the vagueness and uncertainty which
distinguished early physical investigations, owing to the tendency

---

[1] See the Phædo.   [2] Tim. p. 41.

of the Greek mind to indulge in *à priori* speculations, instead of devoting itself to the observation of phenomena.

The material out of which the universe is formed he describes as always becoming but never actually existing.[1] Form being impressed upon this after the likeness of the archetypal idea by the creative power of God, produced the sensible universe. As, therefore, creation is the result of the operation of an intelligent First Cause, the aim and object of physical science is to investigate the final causes of all phenomena, all secondary causes being subsidiary to these.[2]

The train of argument by which Plato establishes his physical theory is as follows. The universe is sensible, therefore it cannot be eternal, but must have had a beginning. Its production must, therefore, be owing to some cause, and as he always referred the origin of all things to an intelligent First Cause, he arrived at the idea that God was the creator of the universe, which, like the rest of the Greeks, he denominated κοσμός, that is, the visible representative of order. God being the supreme good made the world in the likeness of his own perfection—he endowed it with a living soul, and therefore constituted it a living and rational being. As it is the perfection of the beautiful, its form is the most symmetrical, that of the sphere;[3] its motion is also perfect, having its cause residing in itself: it is uniform, circular, and without error.

This soul of the world he held to be diffused through all bodily forms, and from it all other souls originate and are sustained. The corporeal is subject to perpetual change, and may take the forms of the four elements ; and these he illustrates by the analogy of geometrical figures. Fire he compares to the pyramid, air to the octahedron, water to the icosahedron, earth to the cube, and the universe, which unites them all in itself, to the dodecahedron. It would be unprofitable to trace his system any further through all its groundless and mystical assumptions, as he evidently does not scruple to give mythical descriptions of those difficulties which inductive science had not yet fathomed, and to embody in his philosophy the dreamy conceptions of his own imagination.

[1] Tim. p. 50, c. [2] Ibid. p. 46. [3] Ibid. 34.

29

There is one important part of the physics, or rather the physi-ology or metaphysics, of Plato, and that is his theory respecting the human soul, and its eternal destiny hereafter.

Little progress had as yet been made by the philosophers, his predecessors, towards even a vague and indefinite conception of that life and immortality, which were only brought to light by the Gospel. Hence we are struck with admiration at the hope, the conviction, almost amounting to certainty, which appears instinctively to have been impressed upon the mind of Plato, even whilst the arguments by which he attempts to prove his opinions, are inconclusive and unsatisfactory.

Thales, the founder of the dynamical physics, had held that the principle of life was a spontaneous development; that the soul, in which it resided, had in itself an inherent motive force, and therefore was eternal.[1]

On the authority of Cicero,[2] we learn that Pherecydes was the earliest whose teaching on this point was committed to writing.

Pythagoras taught that, by successive transmigrations, the soul is purified from the defilements of the body, so as to be fit to return to, and be absorbed in, the infinite purity of the Divine mind.

So far as there is an opportunity of forming an opinion, the views of Socrates were identical with those of Plato, although perhaps imperfectly developed.

We will first examine Plato's doctrine respecting the nature of the human soul, and next the arguments on which he grounds his belief in its immortality.

The nature of the human soul is the same as that of the soul of the universe; but as, until death separates them, the human soul is connected with a mortal body it stands in a relation to the sensible or perishable, as well as to the ideal or eternal. So far as it is related to the sensible, it participates in the changeable and transitory properties of the sensible; hence, in the soul, there is a mortal as well as an immortal element;[3] the one is divine and the seat of the reason, the other the seat of the passions. But when subordinate to the Divine reason, keeping the passions in check, delighting in pure aspirations, striving

---

[1] Arist. de An. i. 2.   [2] Tusc. Dis. i. 16.   [3] Tim. p. 70.

after the real and the beautiful, it is the link between the Divine and human nature, both of which are combined in man.

This link between the Divine and the human, the ideal and the sensible, has two antagonist tendencies. That which is in the direction of the Divine is represented by ϑυμός, which, though untranslatable, implies spirit, heart, zeal, courage, love, hope, earnestness,—in a word, what we understand by the term emotions. The tendency towards the objects of sense is represented by ἐπιϑυμία, appetite, or concupiscence, which is capable of control and of right direction. The soul, therefore, may be considered as a state in which the reason or Divine soul is the governing power, and the ϑυμός and ἐπιϑυμία, the subordinate members.[1] When, therefore, the reason does not demand more than its right, or the other parts refuse their due obedience, that constitutional state results which, according to Plato, constitutes virtue.

Immortality is the property of the reasonable soul alone, and the following are the principal Platonic statements and arguments which refer to this great doctrine. Most of these will be found in the "Phædon," a dialogue which has for its principal subject-matter the proof of this doctrine.

1.[2] Whatever comes into existence proceeds from its contrary, and as from life comes death, so from death comes life. Therefore the phenomenon which we call death is the passing into life, and our souls exist in the unseen world ('Αἴδης).

2.[3] It is an invariable law of Nature that nothing perishes; if, therefore, the soul existed previous to its union with the body, it necessarily follows that it is mortal.

3.[4] Nothing can be dissolved or dissipated, unless it be compounded, for dissolution is a return into original elements. Now the soul is simple, uncompounded, not cognizable by the senses, and therefore not capable of dissolution, but endued with properties of existence independent of the body.

4.[5] It is not, as has been held by some, a mere harmonious adjustment of the parts of the body which is destroyed when those parts decay; for harmony cannot co-exist with discord, and

[1] De Rep. iv. p. 436.
[2] Ibid. xxiii.
[3] Ibid. xlii.
[4] Phædo, xv., xvi.
[5] Ibid. xxiv.—xxxiv.

the soul, when deranged by vice, presents an appearance of dis-cord rather than harmony.

5.[1] All knowledge is the recollection of truth which was revealed to us in a former state of being, for there is nothing real but the idea, to which we cannot attain in this life; as, therefore, the soul has lived before, so it will again, after it is set free from the body.

6.[2] The number of immortal beings is a constant quantity; if the living died and remained in that state, a universal death would absorb all Nature.

7.[3] The body is the great cause of error, and experience proves that the more we can abstract ourselves from the influence of it, the more free and powerful are the energies of the soul. This approximation, therefore, or tendency towards a perfect state, proves that the natural state of the soul, that in which it is best fitted for intellectual energy, is one of independence of the body.[4] From this argument, especially, is deduced the great practical object of the "Phædon,"—to enforce the duty of fitting the soul by contemplation, by abstracting it from the weaknesses and im-pediments of the body, by causing it to soar even now into the regions of pure thought as a preparation for its eternal destiny.

In the "Symposium," Plato, by the introduction of the prin-ciple of love, that is, the admiration of the good through the medium of the beautiful, endeavors to unite the immortal to the mortal, to give a sensuous character to spiritual things. Al-though the superiority of philosophical contemplation, as a point of duty and a source of happiness, is never lost sight of, still the enjoyment of life, the enlisting of the sympathies in favor of all that is cheering and beautiful, is brought prominently for-ward in this dialogue. It is an endeavor to show how a being destined for immortality, can delight in the pleasures of this mortal existence. In the "Phædon," on the other hand, the great practical end of the philosopher is, to make us *lovers of wisdom* (φιλόσοφοι), not *lovers of the body* (φιλοσώματοι). To wrest the mind away from the body and the things of the body; to make man act the immortal (ἀπαθανατίζειν) as far as possible; to

---

[1] Phædo, xvii.—xxii.   [2] De Rep. x. p. 611.
[3] Phædo, viii.—xii.   [4] Ibid. lvii.—lxii.

detach the immortal from the mortal, and thus to prepare for the joys of that heavenly region where the occupations of the soul will be pure and spiritual.

It follows from this view of his teaching respecting the soul, that, to Plato, death is a subject, not of dread, but of hepe; not of gloomy, but of cheerful contemplation. He looks upon it as an event on which the mind can dwell without interruption to the duties of life, even as Socrates, in his last moments, could use the poisoned cup to perform the social and religious rites of his last social meal.

The lesson which the philosopher teaches, is to aim at the true and the eternal; to soar to the regions of archetypal forms, where truth alone dwells. He strives to infuse, not only a tranquil and resigned spirit at the approach of death, but an actual wish and desire for death, as the condition of attaining immertality. He labors to inculcate a temper similar to that which dictated the words of St. Paul, "My desire is to depart and to be with Christ." Upon the whole, the arguments which have been stated are in reality only supports and aids to the great groundwork on which evidently rests Plato's internal conviction of the soul's immortality. It is this, that, if knowledge is real; if there is nothing real but the ideal forms; if the soul has the power of attaining and conceiving this, of which our consciousness furnishes unanswerable evidence, the soul must have existed, and therefore be capable of existing, independent of the body. And hence the practical lesson—that philosophy implies to wish for knowledge, to wish to exist in the disembodied state, in fact to wish to die.

Throughout the whole of Plato's system may be traced this inseparable connection between knowledge and immortality. The subjects are investigated side by side, and the theory of the one is brought to perfection simultaneously with that of the other. Hence the result produced upon the mind, by the study of Plato's works, is a firm conviction that he was a believer in immortality; and although some of his arguments are inconclusive, the reader is insensibly led to admit the probability at least of his conclusions.

Cato was persuaded by him that, after death, he should dwell with the immortal gods; and Cicero exclaims, "Mallem cum Platone errare quam cum istis vera sentire."

These philosophical theories respecting the condition of the soul after death, are embellished by mythical representations, and adorned with all the skill of the artist and poet. Beautiful but fanciful descriptions of the unseen world give an inexpressible charm to the "Phædon," the most artistic and poetical of the Platonic dialogues. To the genius of the poet, rather than to the thoughtfulness of the philosopher, must be attributed his theory that the sensual man will, as a restless ghost, visible to mortal eyes, because of the bodily impurities still clinging to and defiling the transparent invisible spirit, haunt his grave, longing to rejoin the body which he loved, with all its propensities and passions. The same luxuriant fancy adopted the doctrine of transmigration, which has taken so universal a hold upon the human mind, as not only to have been believed by Pythagoras and Plato, but by the Egyptians[1] and the Druids[2] in ancient times, and to be received by the Brahmans, Buddhists, and Chinese in the present day.

Lastly, Plato evidently taught that a future state would be one of reward and punishment, of communion or even union with God, and with the spirits of the illustrious dead, to him who is really a philosopher, and who has emancipated himself from the fetters of the body.[3] The scene of this happiness he poetically lays in the regions of some kindred star. To attain this end he believed to be in the power of all. Man is free to choose the good and the evil. God is the author of nothing but good; evil is the result of constitution of body and of education;[4] and although his views are sometimes inconsistent, as has been the case with all investigations into the origin of evil, he holds that if man chooses the evil instead of the good, he is alone to blame (Θεὸς ἀναίτιος), *God is not responsible.*[5]

---

[1] Herod. ii. 123.   [2] Cæs. Bell. Gall. vi. 14.   [3] Tim. p. 42.
[4] Ibid. 86.   [5] De Rep. x. p. 617.

CHAPTER XXIII.

ETHICS.

THERE are few points in which Plato more closely resembled
his great master, Socrates, than in the high importance which he
attributed to ethical studies and their cognate subject, political
science. Not only did he make physical science subordinate to
it, but subservient. The phenomena of Nature appeared to him
to have some great moral end in view. The final cause of each
was the good and the beautiful. All things in Nature were so
constituted as to promote virtue and discourage vice, and to set
forth the Deity as the moral Governor of the universe.[1]

The constitution of man is such that he is capable of working
out the designs of God; but as his will is free, and reason is his
guide, it is in his power to fulfil or not the object of his being.
Whilst he thus connected ethics with physics, especially with that
portion of it which developed the psychological nature of man,
he made moral science also dependent upon dialectics, in that
virtue is science, and science is conversant with the idea, or archetypal form, which alone was the supreme good. Hence ethics
imply three subjects of investigation:—I. The good. II. Virtue.
III. The state. 1st, Because man must be considered not merely
in his individual capacity, but as the member of a social community. 2d, Because he considers the harmony which subsists

[1] De Leg. x. 904.

between the members of a well-regulated state, as a type and representation of virtue in an individual.

I. In the investigation of the supreme good, it was necessary, by way of introduction, to do away with the false notions which existed previously respecting it in such great variety. The most popular of these was, as might naturally be expected, that which considered "the good" as identical with pleasure. This doctrine had been taught by Democritus, and by those popular rhetorical teachers of morality, the sophists; and refutations of it, and discussions respecting the true nature of pleasure and pain, and the distinction to be drawn between true and false pleasures, are to be found scattered throughout all the dialogues, especially the "Protagoras," the "Gorgias," and the "Philebus." In these two latter dialogues the subject is continuously treated, for it is commenced in the "Gorgias," and completed in the "Philebus." A lively and amusing discussion of the subject, in opposition partly to the views of the cynics, will also be found in the "Phædon," illustrated with all the dramatic liveliness which characterizes that dialogue.

It must not be supposed that Plato, in denying that the highest good consisted in pleasure, taught that pleasure was not a good. The classification which he made of true and false, pure and impure pleasures,[1] shows that some were to be wished for and enjoyed. The impure pleasures were those which arose from the satisfaction of debasing passions, and these were invariably accompanied with some admixture of pain. From the pure pleasures, although the highest were those derived from the exercise and satisfaction of the intellect, he did not entirely exclude even some pleasures connected with sense, such as, for instance, those of hearing and smell and sight.

It must not be forgotten that, according to Plato, pleasure was not the good, but was to be pursued for the sake of the good.[2] Many inconsistencies may doubtless be observed in Plato's treatment of this subject, but they are practical rather than theoretical inconsistencies. In theory he was impressed with a firm conviction that man's aim, in his aspirations after the good and beautiful, was to separate his intellectual from his carnal nature. This,

[1] Phileb. p. 50.   [2] Gorg. 506.

practically, he found to be impossible. His substitute, therefore, for the attainment of this unattainable standard of perfection was the harmonizing of the superior with the inferior parts of his psychical constitution in their purest and truest developments. Hence the philosopher descends for a time from the regions of pure thought to contemplate the absolute needs and wants of man's compound nature, and, as a means to an end, enlists pleasure on the side of virtue, and teaches that, by the purification of our desires, we may approach nearer to that resemblance to Deity which we cannot absolutely attain.

It is only by such considerations as these that we can attempt to reconcile the oneness of the good, as viewed in one aspect, with its manifold nature when considered in relation to the phenomena of practical life. The idea of the good is absolute, perfect, incapable of degree; the phenomenal goods are only resemblances of the ideal, and therefore some are nearer, some farther off, from the standard of perfection.[1] Hence, he arranges special goods, which are but the likenesses and antitypes to the archetypal form or idea, in a regular series of classes or gradations—each inferior to the one preceding—commencing with the standard of proportion which measures the fitness of things, and all relative duties ; and ending, although he shrinks from mentioning it, with that pleasure mingled with pain from which the embodied soul cannot be entirely emancipated.[2]

II. This theory of the good leads to the subject which immediately arises out of it, that is—virtue. Virtue, then, is essentially one, and is identical with the science of the highest good. But the difficulty of maintaining this theoretical view, when he comes to apply it to the particulars of human conduct, causes Plato frequently to lose sight of its scientific character. His language, therefore, is vague, inconsistent, and contradictory. Impressed, doubtless, with the true doctrine that the moral value of an act is determined by the principle from which it proceeds, he held that no single virtue apart from the rest is truly virtuous, and that he who possesses one virtue possesses all. He is not always consistent in the term which he applies to this universal virtue ; at one time it is Justice ;[3] at another Prudence ;[4] at an-

[1] Phileb. 66, a.
[2] Gorg. 504.
[3] Ritter, vii. 5.
[4] Phæd. 68.

other Temperance.[1]   The only mode in which his notion of the
ideal unity of virtue is to be reconciled with his view of its
manifold nature, is by the hypothesis that the several divisions of virtue were different phases of it.   The division of
virtue which he usually adopts is fourfold.   *Prudence* (φρόνησις),
the virtue of the intellect; *courage* (ἀνδρεια), that of the emotions; *temperance* (σωφροσύνη), of the sensuous; and that virtue
which regulates the parts of the soul according to their due harmony and proportion, *justice* (δικαιοσύνη).   To these he sometimes
adds *piety* (ὁσιότης), but only when he is treating ethical questions popularly, and not as a formal part of his ethical system.

It is clear, however, that justice, taken in the Platonic sense
—that is, not as a relative duty, but as a well-balanced and harmoniously organized condition of the soul—stands highest in his
list of virtues.   As it governs, arranges, and places in order
man's moral nature, the result of it is necessarily all the other
virtues;[2] without it, their existence is impossible; it is the bond
of union which holds them together; it is the central point, in
which meet all elements of moral culture.   When it exists, every
part of the soul performs its proper office, without invading the
rightful province of the other.

III. Justice, moreover, constitutes the connecting link be-.
tween ethics and politics.   Not only is the analogy perfect between the relative duties of the members of a state to one another,
and the harmonious intercommunion of the parts of the soul;
but also the view taken of man is incomplete and inadequate,
unless he is contemplated in his social as well as his individual
capacity.   A well-governed state resembles the inward constitution of a virtuous man,[3] and so dependent is man on the organization of the state of which he is a member, that neither his
moral nor his intellectual nature can be perfectly developed,
except under favorable political circumstances.[4]   The pressing
this analogy too far led to that state of things which he describes
in his imaginary "Republic;" a state not only unattainable, but
by no means tending, as he supposed, to the happiness of man.
Social harmony, mutual dependence of one member upon another,

[1] Gorg. 504.   [2] De Rep. iv. 443.
[3] Ibid. ii. 368.   [4] Ibid. vi. 496.

and upon the whole body politic, for happiness and prosperity; the idea that all are so intimately bound up and connected with one another, that when one member suffers all the members suffer with it; the surrender of individual free will for the general advantage are, to a certain extent, correct principles in politics; but Plato argues from these principles as though their logical results were the worst species of communism.

However extravagant it doubtless is, Plato's imaginary "Republic" would not have appeared so unnatural to Greeks as it does to us. We look upon the great object of civil government as protection to life and property; we interfere as little as possible with the free will, especially with the domestic life of the individual. The respect we pay to it prevents us from interfering in the great question of education, as involving the sacred rights of a parent over his child. The Greeks were accustomed to the notion of merging the individual in the state, of sacrificing personal freedom to the greatness of the political community. This principle is embodied more especially in the Spartan code; it is the pervading feature of Dorian political institutions, which Plato greatly admired, and in accordance with which he framed his own political theories.

How much more healthy are the judicious sentiments of Thucydides, respecting the personal independence and absence of jealous and inquisitive control over private life, which characterized the Athenian, as compared with the Spartan constitution, than the extravagant tyranny of that model-state which Plato describes as too perfect to be found on earth; as the ideal of perfection, to which we ought to approach as nearly as possible?

A modern communist[1] has endeavored to show that the logical consequence of a community of goods is a community of women. The "Republic" of Plato recognized this. The rights of property were abolished, or allowed only to the lowest classes, as if it were a degrading privilege; the charities of domestic life were snapped asunder; the education of children was taken into the hands of the state. Property, children, and women were held to be common. So far was the happiness of the individual lost sight of in the supposed welfare of the community, that the barbarous

[1] .See Edinb. Rév. 1850.

practice, which was common in Greece, of exposing weakly infants, was recommended and approved,[1] and attention to the sick denied as useless to the community.[2]

The three orders of the state corresponded to the three parts of the individual soul. The governor answered to the intellect; the warrior class to the emotions; the working classes to the sensuous, who, like it, were to be kept in entire control, whilst the warriors were to assist the governor in his task. This analogy was carried even further. Each rank assisted in determining the moral quality of the body politic. Its prudence was due to the ruling class, its courage to the military, its temperance to the craftsman, and its justice to the proper adaptation and harmonious mixture of all the other virtues combined.

The growing evil of unpatriotic selfishness, which, in the disjointed times of Plato, was gnawing at the root of civil liberty, probably led him to rate so highly the importance of sacrificing the individual to the state; and the fact that the one and only object which he recognized in politics, was to make men happier by making them morally better, accounts for the opposition which he assigns to education amongst the duties of a state.

The unity of object and purpose, as well as the rarity of such endowments, as qualify for supreme power, led Plato theoretically to determine that the best constitution is an absolute monarchy; but, as in other cases, this theory is modified; and he practically allows that the best forms of government are mixed forms, such as those of Crete and Sparta, in which the monarchical and free principles are combined.[3]

This modification, however, is found in his treatise on the "Laws," and not in that in which he definitely lays down the principles of his model "Republic." He felt that the relation which the whole of his system presupposes between the ideal and the sensible, held good in this case also, and, therefore, whilst in his ideal sketch he gave full scope to his imagination, in his more practical treatise, he showed how near an approximation might safely be made to his principles, and substituted for the absolute will of the monarch, the safer rule of the supreme majesty of law.

---

[1] De Rep. v. 459.   [2] Ibid. iii. 405.   [3] De Leg.

The influence of the state upon the individual member was developed by education, which was, in fact, its great work and duty. A national system of education was to be established; designed, by moral training, to give the youthful members of the community right notions on the subject of pleasure and pain.[1] Simultaneously the body was to be trained by gymnastics, and the mind by music, which terms included all the elements of a liberal education. These two branches, besides the positive effect which they would produce, he imagined would reciprocally counteract each other's defects. A liberal education would correct the rudeness arising from the simple cultivation of the bodily powers, whilst bodily exercise would prevent a highly cultivated taste from degenerating into effeminacy. He appears to have had a dread of the enervating effect of excessive æsthetic refinement, a fear that taste might lead to selfish luxury, and thus corrupt the severe simplicity of ancient morals. For this reason he recommended restrictive enactments on music and the fine arts; for this reason, although himself endowed with the imagination of a poet, he banished from his model "Republic" epic and dramatic poetry;[2] even lyric poetry he only considered admissible if confined to high and ennobling subjects,—the glory and praises of gods and heroes.

Such then is a brief sketch of the Platonic philosophy: many defects doubtless there are in it, glimpses of heavenly truth obscured by mythical extravagancies; conceptions clear probably to his own mind, conveyed to his hearers and readers in vague and mystical language. But, nevertheless, his pure and holy mind, aspiring to something beyond the regions of sense, yearning after that truth and knowledge of which God was the perfect representative, strenuously combating all low and selfish views, and looking on life as a continual preparation for immortality, is worthy a disciple of the great Socrates.

As Plato's theory of number is so intimately connected with his political system, and as the fullest description and explanation which he gives of it are contained in the "Republic,"[3] a few observations respecting it will not be out of place here. Any

[1] De Leg. ii.
[3] De Rep. p. 546.
[2] De Rep. iii. 398; De Leg. vii. 810.

attempt, however, to arrive at an accurate comprehension of a subject, which Cicero pronounced proverbially obscure,[1] would be hopeless.   Plato evidently entertained two separate and distinct ideas on this subject: 1. That numbers possessed in themselves certain mysterious properties.   2. That just as musical harmonies are produced by exact divisions of a string, and may therefore be represented by numbers, so moral conditions and social relations, being harmonies, may be represented in the same manner. The first of these views, being entirely groundless and visionary, gave rise to formulæ, which were entirely arbitrary ; the second has some appearance of probability, but is equally useless and inconclusive, when applied to the purposes of argument or illustration.

The following examples[2] will be sufficient to exhibit the manner in which number is used in the Platonic philosophy.   The product of the first four numbers 1, 2, 3, 4, multiplied together, was called the tetractys, and was supposed to involve a symbolic mystery, and hence it was assumed that its square, $\overline{10}|^2 = 100$, represented the average duration of human life, and its cube, $\overline{10}|^3 = 1000$, the duration of a political community.

For no better reason, Plato decided that the proper number of citizens to constitute a state was neither more nor less than 5040, which is equal to the continued product of the first seven numbers ; for $1 \times 2 \times 3 \times 4 \times 5 \times 6 \times 7 = 5040$.   Lastly, he calculated that the ratio of the unhappiness of a constitutional ruler to that of a tyrant is represented by $\frac{1}{729}$; for an aristocracy in its purest form, i.e., a perfect state, is third in order from an oligarchy, and an oligarchy third from a tyranny; therefore, their relative positions will be represented by the numbers 1, 3, 9, and their relative unhappiness by the cubes, or by 1, and 729.

THE CRATYLUS.

The "Cratylus" has been a source of difficulty to all those who have endeavored to understand the mind of Plato.[3]   It stands apart, as it were, from the rest of the dialogues, and is the only work which professes to treat of a subject which the sophistical philosophy had rendered so important, namely, the nature of

---

[1] Ep. ad Att. vii. 13.   [2] See Trans. of Philolog. Soc.
[3] Vide Diog. Laert. iii.; Schleierm. Introd.; Stalb. de Cra. Pl.

language; and it is not clear what Plato's own theory respecting the philosophy of language was, or what relation it bears to the rest of his system. Nor is it easy to separate jest from earnest, and determine where he is treating the subject as a matter of serious investigation, and where his plays upon words are merely an amusing and even sophistical discussion. The principal subject of the dialogue is evidently the relation of language to knowledge, and as an important part of this subject, the reader is cautioned against the prevailing popular error that language of itself is sufficient to conduct to real knowledge, and that terms have such power to define and limit ideas as to exclude all possibility of doubt and error.

The principal speaker, after whom the dialogue is named, is Cratylus, a philosopher who followed the system of Heraclitus, which taught that the etymology of terms involves the knowledge of the things represented by them. An intimate relation also subsisted between the Heraclitic and stoic philosophy, and the latter school attributed great importance to grammatical investigation; the introduction, therefore, of the name of Cratylus, as a supporter of one of the opposing views, is very appropriate. The theory which he maintains is, that names are given to things according to certain natural laws, and in conformity with their natural properties. This view is illustrated by examples of proper names, both of men and deities, by the names of the heavenly bodies, the elements, the virtues, and so forth; but in these illustrations jest evidently predominates over seriousness. According to this view of the nature of language, it would, in the process of formation, follow a necessary law, and words, like the objects of sense for which they stand, would be the imitations of archetypal ideas. Words, therefore, to a certain extent, do define the nature of things; they represent the effect produced upon the senses, but do not convey such accurate notions as the contemplations of pure intellect. It follows from this theory of language, that verbal arguments may sometimes be sound and logical. This view, supported by the imaginary Cratylus, is so much in accordance with the Platonic system that it was most probably the opinion of the philosopher himself.

Hermogenes, who had instructed Plato in the Eleatic doctrines, as Cratylus had been his teacher in the system of Heraclitus, is made to maintain the opposite view—that language is a conventional instrument, arbitrarily invented, accidentally developed; that there is no natural (φύσει) correspondence or connection between words and things, but that the adaptation of the one to the other only takes place by mutual consent and arrangement.

The above is necessarily but an imperfect sketch of a few features of that great and comprehensive mind, which fearlessly attacked every subject of human contemplation, which analyzed all preceding philosophy, and left so rich a legacy to posterity, that the deepest thinkers of every age and nation have chosen him for their master and their guide. Owing to his unwearied intellectual energies, philosophy was now firmly established in its home at Athens, and the Academy and Garden, the scene of his labors, descended in regular order to his successors, who, as far as their abilities enabled them, taught in this school the Platonic doctrines. Inferior as the Academics were to their great master, they were sometimes incapable of comprehending his doctrines, and hence, sometimes wilfully, sometimes undesignedly, they misrepresented and modified them.

Speusippus,[1] the nephew and immediate successor of Plato, a wise and good man, but not a distinguished philosopher, left a collection of posthumous works which were purchased by Aristotle for about three talents (£720). He was succeeded after an interval of six years by Xénocrates,[2] a native of Chalcedon.[3] He was an industrious and indefatigable student rather than a profound or original thinker. He died at the age of eighty-two, B.C. 314, and during twenty-five years of his long life he filled the chair of Plato in the Academy. His works were voluminous, but nothing remains of them but their titles. Either the principles of his philosophy were in themselves ill-defined, or the authors, in whose works notices of them occur, failed of apprehending them, and therefore have not conveyed clear conceptions of their purport and character. But too little is handed down respecting him to render any further mention of him necessary in a history of Greek classical literature.

The other academics, Polemo, Crates, and Crantor, contributed nothing of importance or value to the advance and progress of philosophical investigation.

[1] B.C. 348.   [2] B.C. 342.   [3] Cic. Acad. i. 4.

CHAPTER XXIV.

ARISTOTLE, born B. C. 384.

ARISTOTLE.—THE UNCERTAINTY OF HIS BIOGRAPHY.—HIS BIRTH-PLACE AND PARENT-
AGE. — VISITS ATHENS.—BECOMES A PUPIL OF PLATO.— HIS ATTACHMENT TO HIS
TUTOR.—HIS EMBASSY TO THE COURT OF PHILIP.—CONTROVERSY WITH ISOCRATES.—
BECOMES TUTOR TO ALEXANDER THE GREAT.—COURSE OF EDUCATION ADOPTED.—
RETURNS TO ATHENS.—LECTURES IN THE LYCEUM.—HIS MANNER OF TEACHING.—
FALSE CHARGE OF POISONING ALEXANDER.—HIS VOLUMINOUS WORKS.—MUNIFICENCE
OF ALEXANDER.—PERSECUTION OF ARISTOTLE.—FLIES TO CHALCIS.—HIS DEATH.—
APPOINTMENT OF A SUCCESSOR.—HIS APPEARANCE.—HIS STYLE CONTRASTED WITH
THAT OF PLATO.—HIS STYLE INFLUENCED BY THE AGE IN WHICH HE LIVED.—HIS
DEFERENCE FOR AUTHORITY.—THE PRACTICAL CHARACTER OF HIS MIND.—HIS VIEWS
LIMITED TO THIS LIFE.—DIVISION OF HIS WORKS.—MEANING OF ESOTERIC AND EXO-
TERIC.—HIS HABIT OF INDUCTION.—DEFECT IN HIS ETHICS.—HIS PHILOSOPHY CON-
TRASTED WITH THAT OF PLATO.

WHILST, in the academy which Plato founded, philosophy was
falling into decay, his most distinguished disciple was developing
its resources, and extending its frontiers with all the manly vigor
of a systematic and practical mind.

The biographies of the eminent philosophers and literary men
of antiquity are generally scanty. Their tranquil lives are not
fertile in those stirring events which occupy a place in history.
Their works are at once the exploits, picture, and history of their
lives, and through them they live in the thoughts and affections
of posterity. Of the life of Aristotle, on the other hand, a
great many particulars are stated, but, nevertheless, it is difficult
to determine which of them is trustworthy. The accounts given
of him not only abound in discrepancies, but these discrepancies
are contradictory and inconsistent with each other.[1] If some
are true, the others must be absolutely false.

The Greek colony Stagira, in Chalcidice, had the honor of
giving birth to this great philosopher, and the epithet by which

[1] Suidas, s. v.; Aristotle; and Nicomachus; Diog. Laert. v.

he is so generally known. He was born Ol. xci. 1. His father,
Nicomachus, was court physician to Amyntas II., King of Macedon, and the author of works on medicine and natural philosophy.[1] The tastes of the father for these subjects probably
tended to form that of the son. In early boyhood he was introduced at court by his father, and thus made that acquaintance
with Philip which exercised so great an influence over his subsequent life. At seventeen years of age he was left an orphan,
and his guardian, Proxenus, a native of Atarneus, residing at
Stagira, procured him the benefits of a good education. An
ample fortune enabled him, in order to prosecute his philosophical studies, to visit Athens, which was now the school of Greece
and the capital of learning and philosophy, a position to which
it aspired even in the time of Thucydides.[2] The other account,
which states that, during this period, he squandered his patri-
mony, then became a soldier, and afterwards a seller of drugs,
has been satisfactorily refuted.

The absence of Plato in Sicily when Aristotle arrived at
Athens gave him an opportunity of laying the foundation for
that superstructure which Plato afterwards raised upon it, and
forming those habits of learned inquiry and original investigation
for which he was distinguished. The progress he thus made soon
distinguished him among his fellow-disciples for his acquired
learning and well-trained habits of inquiry, as well as for his
zeal and energy. This gained for him the commendation of
Plato, who used to say that Xenocrates required the spur, but
Aristotle the bit.[3] Later authorities add that he gave him the
title of " the reader" (ἀναγνώστης), and the "mind of the school"
(ὁ νοῦς τῆς διατριβῆς). The approbation which he thus obtained
from his instructor is perfectly inconsistent with the calumnious
statement that he was guilty of disrespect and ingratitude.
There might probably have been occasionally philosophical disputes between them, marked by impetuosity on the part of the
young and zealous aspirer after truth, and provoking some aspe-
rity on the part of his older instructor; and these may have
been misunderstood and misinterpreted by those who heard of or
saw them. But such disputes, even if maintained with warmth,

---

[1] Pol. iii. 6, 8 ; vii. 2, 8.   [2] Lib. ii.   [3] Diog. Laert. iv. 6.

are perfectly reconcilable with a good understanding upon the whole between the disputants. Whatever evidence exists tends to show marked respect on the part of Aristotle towards Plato, even when his regard for truth caused him to oppose his views. "When," he says, "the question is between truth and our friends, it is right to prefer truth, although both are dear."[1]

At the time of Plato's death,[2] Aristotle was absent as ambassador from Athens to the court of Philip, after which he left Athens for some time. He had no ties of a private nature to detain him there any longer. The ambitious and aggressive policy of Philip, which now began to develop itself, would perhaps expose one who was on terms of friendly intimacy with the Macedonian monarch to political jealousy and personal danger. His own predilections were rather in favor of the protection afforded by a monarchy than the tyranny of a multitude. Moreover, his ardent curiosity and love of observation would induce him, even more than any other philosopher, to increase the sphere of his knowledge by foreign travel, for which his present position in Athens, both public and private, furnished a favorable opportunity. Before leaving Athens, he had a bitter controversy with Isocrates, the most superficial, but, nevertheless, the most popular rhetorician of his day. Isocrates was the representative of that florid style of oratory which depended for its effect more on ornament and style (λέξις), than on argumentative proof (πίστις). To this false theory the calm and vigorous intellect of Aristotle was diametrically opposed, as may be seen from his "Rhetoric," which was probably written at this period.[3]

In B. C. 342, Aristotle, at the request of Philip, became tutor to Alexander, then thirteen years of age. The influence of Aristotle over Philip[4] led to the rebuilding of his native town, which had fallen in his attack upon the Greek colonies of Thrace. There Philip built for him a grove and school called the Nymphæum, and thither he retired to superintend the education of his distinguished pupil. The branches of education in which he instructed him were poetry, oratory, and philosophy, as well natural as moral and political. With a view to the first,[5] he is

[1] Nic. Eth. i. 6; see also ix. 7. [2] B. C. 347.
[3] Rhet. i. 1. [4] Plut. v.; Alex. vii.
[5] Wolf, Proleg. 183.

said to have prepared a revised copy of the "Iliad," and Strabo[1] asserts that some of the emendations are by the hand of Alexander himself. The influence of Aristotle's teaching on the mind of the future conqueror of the world is displayed in that noble generosity, merciful humanity, and strict love of justice, which are the distinguishing features of his moral character.

In three years Alexander left his tutor, in order to become regent during his father's absence, but he still kept up a constant communication with him; and in B. C. 335, shortly after his accession, Aristotle returned to Athens. There is no authority for the story of his having accompanied Alexander on his Indian expedition.

On his arrival at Athens he found Xenocrates teaching in the academy, and the cynics in the Cynosarges. The state, therefore, assigned to him the Lyceum, in the walks of which (οἱ περίπατοι) he delivered his lessons to a large number of eminent disciples; and hence his school acquired the title of Peripatetic.

The dialogues of Plato present a lively picture of the familiar conversational style in which he delivered his instructions. On the other hand, so many of the works of Aristotle extant are in the form of notes for more expanded lectures, that there can be no doubt of his habit being to teach in courses of lectures, delivered orally in regular order. This habit, too, is the most in accordance with his orderly and systematic mind.

All authorities coincide in the generally received account, that subsequently, when the character of Alexander changed so much for the worse, a coolness and estrangement took place between him and his tutor, although his respect for him continued undiminished. The false charge which implicated Aristotle in the improbable crime of poisoning Alexander, is founded solely on a misunderstanding of a passage in Pliny's "Natural History,"[2] and is still further met by the belief now universally held, that Alexander died, not by poison, but a natural death, hastened by his own intemperance.

Thirteen years did Aristotle pass at Athens, in the tranquil activity of a literary life, engaged in the work of daily instruction, and in the composition of his voluminous works. If the

---

[1] Strabo, xiii. 594.   [2] Hist. Nat. xxx. 53.

account of Diogenes[1] is correct, the number of lines which he wrote were four hundred and forty thousand; and we can thus form some idea of that indefatigable industry, which, in so short a space of time, in the midst of the occupation incident to the life of a public instructor, and, notwithstanding the comparatively inconvenient nature of writing materials, produced no less than thirty octavo volumes, the result of original thought and laborious investigation. Of these, about one-fourth survive.

In his literary labors, he was munificently assisted by his royal pupil, to the amount of eight hundred talents (£192,000), a sum which probably was equivalent to £600,000 in our own days. The collection, moreover, of specimens in natural history, which Alexander's extensive conquests enabled him to transmit to Athens, formed the materials for his "History of Animals," the value of which is daily more and more appreciated by modern naturalists.

The open rupture between Greece and Macedon, which ensued upon the death of Alexander,[2] menaced the safety of one who had been so long connected in friendship with that kingdom. But a religious persecution is always far easier than a political accusation, against one who had so completely estranged himself from public affairs. As in the case of Socrates, his ruin was sought by means of a charge of impiety. He had written a scolia in praise of his old disciple, Hermeas; and this his accusers pretended was a pæan, and therefore an act of blasphemy. Fearing the issue of a trial, and looking upon the fate of Socrates as a warning, he escaped to Chalcis in Eubœa. In his absence he was condemned to death by the court of the Areopagus, and the following year he died, at the age of sixty-two, little more than two months before Demosthenes. Less trustworthy accounts say that he took poison, or drowned himself in the Euripus, disappointed at being unable to discover the cause of its marvellous currents.

It is said that, shortly before his death, he appointed his successor in the following symbolical manner. The choice lay between Theophrastus, a Lesbian, and Menedemus, or rather Eudemus, a Rhodian. Calling for the wines of these two islands,

---

[1] Diog. Laert. v. 27.   [2] B. c. 323.

and tasting them, he said that both were good, but that he preferred the Lesbian.

His personal appearance was disagreeable, his features plain, his figure mean; and these defects he endeavored to remedy by particular attention to dress. His countenance wore a sharp and caustic expression; and though he spoke with a lisp, his eloquence was powerful and convincing. His energy and perseverance overcame the weakness of his bodily frame. His devotion to scientific pursuits was kept in check by a calm and sober spirit, which prevented him from running wild in the regions of imagination and theory.

It is impossible to form a correct estimate either of his literary style or his philosophical method, without contrasting them with those of Plato. Plato was endowed with a highly poetical imagination; his great object was knowledge; his delight was speculation. Absorbed in the contemplation of the ideal, he forgot that world in which he lived and moved. His fervid genius imparted a warmth and earnestness to his teaching, almost resembling inspiration. Philosophy was with Plato that which its name implies, a love, or passion, for wisdom. If his arguments were fanciful and inconclusive, they still entranced and carried away the learner, and demanded from him a faith which, although he could not prove, he could not refuse. His unrestrained fancy eschewed the form of a regular lecture or treatise, and poured forth its thoughts in the simple and unsystematic form of conversational dialogue. His style is the purest and sweetest Attic, and his illustrative imagery nothing less than poetical. Lastly, Plato, though he could speculate, could not criticize. He was a consummate artist, but not a critic. He could feel beauty, whether scientific, moral, or artistic, even though he could not explain its nature, or analyze with precision its principles.

Aristotle, on the other hand, had neither poetry, nor imagination, nor fancy in his composition, but then his calm inquiring spirit never indulged in extravagant speculation. He was eminently a practical man; his great object, as he himself says, was not knowledge (γνῶσις), but practice (πρᾶξις).[1] He could not form a conception of the ideal, he could not look inwards as deeply as

---

[1] Nic. Eth. i.

Plato could, and contemplate the energy of the soul with the same shrewdness with which he analyzed the motives of human moral action, and the phenomena of the natural world. His teaching was argumentative and convincing, his reasoning close, but he never sought to recommend his views, either by the embellishments of poetry, or by rhetorical or exciting appeals to the heart and affections, hence he is cold and unimpressive, but intellectually convincing. He had not that sense of dramatic art which would have enabled him to support the life and spirit of a dialogue; but this defect is more than compensated for by the systematic order which distinguishes his treatises. To arrange the contents of a dialogue of Plato in a tabular form would be impossible, but every treatise of Aristotle, almost every chapter, is capable of being exhibited to the student in that shape; in fact, it scarcely admits of a doubt, that they took that systematic form in his mind, before they were made public in treatises or lectures. He appears always to have taken a comprehensive view of his subject, to have arranged it mentally in such a shape, that he could see both the beginning and the end. Each subject was in that form which he himself would have termed εὐσύνοπτον. His style is often pure, always unaffected, rejecting all the accessories of grace and ornament; and though sometimes deficient in clearness, this defect does not appear to arise from mistiness of conception.

The extreme brevity and abruptness so frequently discernible give one the idea of notes and abstracts intended to be expanded when orally delivered, and to be fully developed by means of copious and apposite illustrations. Aristotle could investigate and understand the principles of artistic beauty and taste, although he neither felt them as an inspiration, nor was possessed by them, nor practised them. He was a critic, but not an artist. There can be little doubt that this is to be attributed to the peculiarity of his mental constitution. Plato had genius, Aristotle learning. Ritter considers that this was the tendency of the age in which he lived, an age in which the Greek mind was beginning to decay, for, in its youth, it loved art more than learning. "He was," says Ritter,[1] "the first philosopher of

[1] Ritter, Gesch. d. Phil. ix. iii. 1.

whom it can be said that learning had taken the place of art, and contributed much to establish the pre-eminence of mere learning, with which the later Greek writers were impressed."

Struck, as one cannot help being, with his unequalled learning, it is impossible not to miss, when reading his works, that exquisite grace which distinguishes the language of Plato. Doubtless, the age in which Aristotle lived is, in some sort, the cause of this inferiority; for Attic Greek prose, which, in its infancy, had been fostered by philosophic thought, and had gradually expanded to meet its requirements, had, in the age of Plato, reached its perfection. It then began to decline. When Plato flourished, the polite language of Athens was still that which adorned the comedies of Aristophanes, on a study of which he is said to have formed his style. There was, too, an analogy between the Platonic unrestrained freedom of speculation, and the political liberty of Athens, which still survived its hard and numerous struggles. In the time of Aristotle, Attic Greek had degenerated; the comedies of Aristophanes had ceased to charm. The vigorous eloquence of Demosthenes, who, whilst by patient study he had made his own all the excellences of the Thucydidean style, had eschewed its faults and errors, was heard only on two occasions after Aristotle had established his school in the Lyceum; the poetical rhetoric of Isocrates, which had formed the taste of so many distinguished orators and writers, had ceased altogether. The great writers whom we now admire had become subjects for critical study. There were none to vie with them, none even to imitate them; Aristotle could do no more than, as in his "Rhetoric" and "Poetics," analyze the principles of taste and beauty, which abounded in their works.

Although the conciseness of Aristotle's style generally gives vigor to his sentences, and one cannot deny to it the praise of unaffected simplicity, still he evidently wrote with a careless rapidity; there is, generally speaking, a total absence of grace and ornament. The high authority of Cicero, who, besides conciseness, attributes to the style of Aristotle eloquence and sweetness, seems at variance with this view; but this opinion may have been formed on a study of his exoteric writings, some extant fragments of which display the polish of a more finished style.

Many of the works which remain to us bear marks of being out-lines of lectures, put together, as helps to the memory, for the use of those who heard them delivered, and the apparent abrupt-ness and want of connection were probably remedied, in the delivery, by the introduction of other passages, and especially by numerous happy illustrations.

A cautious temper is observable in almost all his works. The tutor of a prince was likely, as a philosopher, to be a calm student and admirer of authority rather than an enthusiastic striker-out of new views. He is careful to enumerate all the doubts and difficulties, of which his extensive reading made him aware, as arising out of the opposite and conflicting views maintained by the philosophers who preceded him. This caution in weighing and balancing the opinions of others against his own, is doubt-less valuable, and is characteristic of an honest and impartial mind; we feel that when he does come to a decision, we may follow him as a guide; but, on the other hand, it is often fatal to following out a train of original investigation. Learning, if allowed more than its proper influence, is sometimes destructive of that degree of self-confidence which is absolutely necessary to a philosopher and a teacher. His habitual deference to authority is also manifested in his eagerness to support his own views, by showing how far they coincide with the opinions of others, or at least to win for them a prejudice in their favor. An instance of this is seen in his Nicomachus Ethics.[1] It sometimes, also, leads to confusion in his terminology, for he not unfrequently adopts that of others, even when scarcely adapted to give definite and exact expression to his own doctrines.

One cannot, however, set too high a value on the practical nature of Aristotle's mind. He never forgot the immediate bearing of all philosophy upon the happiness of man, he never lost sight of man's wants or requirements. He saw the inade-quacy of all knowledge, unless he could trace in it a visible prac-tical tendency. But beyond this one single point, he falls griev-ously short of his great master, Plato. All his ideas of man's good are limited to the consideration of this life alone. It is impossible to trace in his writings any belief in a future state or

[1] Book i. c. 8.

immortality. He speaks of the popular views entertained,[1] he balances nicely the various opinions which he considers most worthy of consideration, but even in the treatise in which we might expect the subject to be most completely treated of, he comes to no satisfactory conclusion.[2]

In the Nicomachean Ethics, where the subject is alluded to three times, he is in all these passages speaking only of a prevalent belief, but not asserting either its truth or falsehood.[3] The highest idea which he forms of the human soul is, that it is a fifth element, an entelechia,[4] and that man's reason is identical with, and as eternal as, that of God. It is clear that even if this belief implies immortality, it does not imply personal identity.

The most common division of the writings of Aristotle is into two classes, namely, esoteric, called also acroatic or acroamatic, and exoteric, or encyclic. To the latter of these divisions alone does Aristotle make any allusion in his extant treatises;[5] we may conclude, therefore, that all his works, which have come down to us, belong to the esoteric class. Various explanations of these terms have been given, and amongst them Cicero[6] has proposed one, of the incorrectness of which there can be hardly any doubt.

The following is probably the true distinction to be drawn. The philosophers of antiquity were not only the learned and scientific world of Athens, devoted to increasing the stores of speculation and discovery, but they also filled the office of public instructors, they were the preachers, the professors, the schoolmasters, of their day. As universities in modern times are in their original essence places of study, and therefore accidentally places of education, so it was with the schools of the Greek metropolis.

Hence their hearers were of two classes. One consisting of those who pursued different branches of science in a philosophic spirit; the other, of those who were going through a course, or curriculum, of general study. The esoteric method of teaching was addressed to the former, the exoteric treatises therefore would,

[1] Eth. i.
[2] De An.
[3] Nic. Eth. i. 10, 11; iii. 6.
[4] Cic. Tusc. Disp. i. 17.
[5] See, ex gr. Nic. Eth. i. 13; vi. 4; Pol. iii. 6; vii. 1.
[6] De Fin. v. 5.

generally speaking, embrace the usual subjects of Athenian liberal education; but as the distinction is one depending on the method of treatment rather than on the subject-matter, the same subjects might be treated either esoterically or exoterically, according to circumstances.

The vast extent of erudition for which Aristotle was distinguished evidently comprised within its sphere every branch of philosophy, and each branch we fortunately find represented in his extant works. We find amongst them elaborate treatises on logic, of which he was the perfecter, metaphysics, physical science, physiology, mathematics, ethics, politics, natural history, and, besides these, belles lettres, including rhetoric, poetry, and grammar.

In all these will be found displayed that most striking feature of his mind, namely the habit of observation and induction, of deducing his theories from facts. It must not be supposed that, in the importance which he attributed to phenomena, he systematically neglected to investigate the causes which would account for them. It is only in some cases that he tells us that when we know the fact (τὸ ὅτι) it is unnecessary to seek for the reason (διότι).[1] But no one can be blind to the fact that he considered experience as the principal source of knowledge, and that steadily keeping in view, as the object of his research, that which was within the scope of man's faculties, he preferred the actual to the ideal aspect of philosophy.

The want of this high ideal standard is especially felt in his ethical philosophy. Man instinctively yearns for some ideal model of perfection which he may constantly place before his eyes, and aspire to and strive after, even though he feels that the imperfections of his nature preclude the possibility of attainment. Our conscience, that inward witness, tells us that it is not true that man is not assisted by the contemplation of this ideal. The analogous case which he brings forward of the artist[1] is not true in point of fact. Not only is the artist assisted by the contemplation of the beautiful, but, unless he is thoroughly possessed by this inspiration of art, unless the idea which he wishes to embody has a living existence within him, he will never reach the highest

[1] Nic. Eth. i.

point of even human perfection.   In the same way to deny, as
Aristotle is too much inclined to do, the aid which the ideal furnishes, especially to some mental constitutions, is depriving man
of a great aid to moral improvement.   Aristotle would teach man
to form his moral nature by a regard to the circumstances which
surrounded him.   Plato would have led his disciple to purify
himself, and to nurture within himself an admiration of virtue,
by an habitual contemplation of a divine and perfect model.

To describe the groundwork and method of Aristotle's system
briefly, and to exhibit as concisely as possible its contrast to that
of Plato, the following statement will be sufficient.   Plato considered the sensible as transitory, changeable, and therefore untrue;
it was but an imitation, or, at best, it enjoyed nothing more than
a participation in that which alone had real existence—the ideal
world.   With Aristotle, on the contrary, experience of the sensible is the starting point: from the actual he ascends upwards to
the ideal.   He begins with the impressions made upon the senses
from without, and advances, step by step, through each operation
of consciousness, until he arrives at the highest energy of· the
intellect.

From the fact of his commencing with the external and the
sensible, it follows that the phenomena of each science must be
investigated separately, and each science built up and constructed
as a separate and complete whole.   In itself he cannot consider
them, as Plato does, as so many mutually connected parts of one
harmonious whole, but parallel to and independent of one another.

Hence his method is plain, simple, and uniform.   He first defines accurately the object which he has in view; he then clears
the ground for the edifice which he is about to construct, by a
summary and critical view of pre-existing doctrines, of which he
either admits the truth or proves the falsehood.   Next, he fairly
states and discusses the difficulties and doubts which might naturally suggest themselves to the minds of the student, and then
proceeds to trace the object of his treatise, and develope its parts,
from its simplest and best known principles (γνώριμα, ἀρχαί) to its
most complicated and perfect results.

CHAPTER XXV.

LOGIC.

IN the front of the Aristotelian philosophy must be placed logic, of which, as he was the first systematizer, so he is universally allowed to have been the finisher and perfecter. The science and art of reasoning, although illustrated and expanded by subsequent metaphysicians, was fully developed by him, and has made no progress since his time.

The treatise which stands at the head of his logical works, or "Organon," as they are called, from which Bacon adopted the title of "Novum Organum" for his system of inductive philosophy, is that on the "Categories." These are principles of classification, which he adopted as being naturally the highest genera under which all things could be arranged. They were ten in number—substance, quantity, quality, relation, action, passion, time, place, position, habit, or having.

They were, to Aristotle, aids to systematic thought, at once suggesting lines of argument, and serving as repositories in which arguments might be stored up and preserved for use as occasion required. The tendency of his order-loving mind to seek assistances of this kind is discoverable in many parts of his works. Two examples of this will be sufficient. In the "Ethics,"[1] the difference between absolute and relative (an

[1] Nic. Eth. ii. 5 and 7.

application of the category of relation) often furnishes him with a convenient principle of distinction; and, again, the recognized division of the principles of human nature into capacities, passions, and habits, is the leading and fundamental idea on which he constructs his theory of Virtue.[1]

The "Categories" are followed by the treatise Περὶ Ἑρμηνείας, which consists of an analysis of the proposition, both logical and grammatical, as the "Categories" had for their object the nature and classification of simple terms. The two "Analytics" then succeed, which treat of the whole subject of formal logic, but especially argument, the logical form of which is the syllogism. The book on the "Topics," or common-places, the "Loci" of Cicero, the heads or sources from which may be derived arguments of probability, follow next; and, lastly, an investigation of the subject of fallacies completes the "Organon."

METAPHYSICS.

With the science of logic is closely connected that of metaphysics, which, as it is the science of "that which is," the highest good, the universal, the first principles and causes of things, Aristotle dignifies with the highest titles. He calls metaphysics the first philosophy, or even philosophy absolutely, wisdom, theology. His metaphysical system is not entirely comprehended in the books which bear this title, but wherever the τὸ ὄν, or the nature of the Deity, is discussed, there scattered notices of this system will be found. The title given to this collection of treatises is a mere arbitrary one invented in later times, probably by Andronicus Rhodius, having no relation to the subject-matter of the treatises themselves, but simply stating that, in the collection of the entire works, their place was in order of arrangement next to the physics. They were entitled Τῶν μετὰ τὰ φύσικα, A—N.

As the foundation of his philosophy of mind, Aristotle held that the origin of all knowledge is the perception of the senses. In his ethics as well as his metaphysics, he states that we must begin with that which is known to ourselves (γνώριμα ἡμῖν), and thence advance to that which is known absolutely (γνώριμα ἁπλῶς),[2]

[1] Nic. Eth. ii. 4.   [2] Met. vii. 4; Eth. i. 2.

and that the only right method of investigation is inductive, *i. e.*, to collect facts and thence deduce general principles. After that the intellectual process (διάνοια) commences, which continues until the investigation is completed.[1] The intellect is then at rest,.and science (ἐπιστήμη) is the result.

The difference between the Platonic and Aristotelian theory in this respect is plain. Plato maintained that the human mind, having previously possessed all ideas which constitute knowledge, recovered them by reminiscence, and therefore all branches of science were connected together. Aristotle, on the other hand, taught that each particular sensation is the principle and beginning of a particular chain of thought, and, therefore, that any one branch of science may be pursued separately.

If sensation is the avenue to knowledge, it is necessary to investigate the objects of sensation. Their constituent parts which present themselves to the senses, are *matter* (ὕλη) and *form* (μορφή).[2] The only view in which Aristotle's notion of matter can be presented, is a negative one. If it can be conceived possible to separate, mentally, from any object every conceivable property, accident, or predicable of every kind, the residuum would be matter. It is, therefore, the substratum of essence. It is clear, therefore, that Aristotle did not confine the term matter to the modern signification of it; nay, he expressly distinguishes matter, conceivable by the intellect, from that which is apprehended by the senses. In fact, the distinction is similar to that which we recognize between a mechanical and mathematical point, line, or superficies. Matter, then, being not essence, but the substratum of essence, it implies not " being," but "capability of being," or "potentiality" (δύναμις). Form, on the other hand, implies " actuality" (ἐνέργεια), and, therefore, form expresses more nearly the nature of anything, for essence may more properly be predicated when a thing is actually, than when it is potentially.[3]

The next subject of metaphysical inquiry to matter and form, is motion. Motion is the transition from potentiality to actuality. Now, matter is neither self-producing nor self-moving.[4] Therefore, the moving cause must be external and independent, and as

---

[1] De Part. An. i. 1.   [2] Met. vii. 10.
[3] Phys. ii. 1.   [4] Met. i. 3; iv. 5.

each motion must have a cause, we must at last arrive at a First Cause, which is self-existent and eternal.[1]

We have now mentioned three out of the four necessary causes of phenomena enumerated by Aristotle. Matter and form furnish the material and formal causes, and the third is the moving cause by which matter passes into form. The fourth, of which he maintained the necessity, is the final cause. Everything in Nature is done with some end. Although chance may be said contingently (κατὰ συμβιβηκός) to be a cause, yet absolutely (ἁπλῶς) it is the cause of nothing.[2] Every thing in Nature indicates design, the end to which the operations of Nature are directed is "the good," and this is the noblest subject of philosophical investigation.

In order to understand Aristotle's notion of the Deity, it is necessary to explain the two philosophical terms energy (ἐνέργεια), and entelechy (ἐντελέχεια), the latter of which is one of his own invention. By energy, then, is meant an activity or active state. It is opposed to δύναμις, i. e., capacity or potentiality. Energy implies actual and active existence, not a mere possible and potential one. The term entelechy is not so easy to define, as Aristotle is not very accurate in the use of it. Sometimes he uses it as equivalent to energy; and Ritter maintains that between the two there is no essential difference.[3] This view is supported by the following definition. "Entelechy is the form of that which exists in potentiality."[4] From this it would appear that entelechy bears to potentiality the same relation which form does to matter, and therefore would be equivalent to actuality or energy. The sense, however, in which he most consistently uses the term is, " The highest state of development to which each thing is capable of arriving." So far, therefore, as the active state is the highest state of perfection of which anything is capable, it is identical with energy; but it is obvious that if it be the same it is regarded from a different point of view. Energy is an absolute term, entelechy is a relative one, for the capacity of the object is always taken into consideration.

Now God is the great First Cause, eternal, moving all things,

[1] Phys. v. 1.
[2] Ibid. ii. 5.
[3] Rit. ix. iii. 3.
[4] De An. ii. 4.

himself unmoved.   In his essence he unites potentiality, energy, entelechy.   Aristotle maintained the unity of the Deity, and that God is the governing principle of the universe, for he quotes in support of his view a verse from the "Iliad" in praise of monarchy.[1] He is pure intellect, and as the perfection of intellect is self-conscious activity, God is at once thought, and the object of thought. Lastly, as God is the supreme good he is the highest object of scientific contemplation.   This is the sum and substance of Aristotle's ideas respecting the Supreme Being; and although he invests him with all these attributes, the result is indefinite and unsatisfactory, for it is, after all, impossible to determine whether, according to his philosophy, God and the universe are not identical, and therefore whether his theism is anything more than pantheism.

PHYSICS.

In his treatment of physical, as well as moral science, Aristotle is careful to caution his hearers against expecting the same degree of exactness (ἀχριθεία) which distinguishes metaphysics.[2] The object of the latter is the necessary, eternal, and unchangeable, whilst that of physics is the corporeal and changeable, and that of ethics the contingent.   Owing to the materialist view which Aristotle takes of the human soul, psychology forms a part of physiology.   Intellect, indeed, from its being pure essence, and having a cognate relation to the Divine nature, enters into his metaphysical investigations, but that in which intellect or reason resides comes within the domain of the corporeal.

The soul is the final cause, for the sake of which the body exists,[3] and the bodily organs are but so many mechanical contrivances for assisting and perfecting the energy of the soul.   But notwithstanding this subordination of body to soul, the existence of the body is a condition indispensable to the existence of the soul.

Assuming, then, this necessary connection between the two, and combining it with the principle of perfection, he defines the soul as " the first entelechy of a physical organic body."[4]   By a first entelechy he means the possessing the essence of activity,

---

[1] Met. xii. 10.   [2] Ibid. vi. 1; Nic. Eth. i.
[3] De An. i. 3.   [4] Ibid. ii. 1.

31

even though it may be dormant and inactive.　Although he does not venture to determine whether the soul is only nominally or really divisible,[1] he denies to it that property of magnitude which we term extension.　His division of the soul into parts may be best understood by the following tables, which are founded upon the two views given in the Nicomachean ethics :—

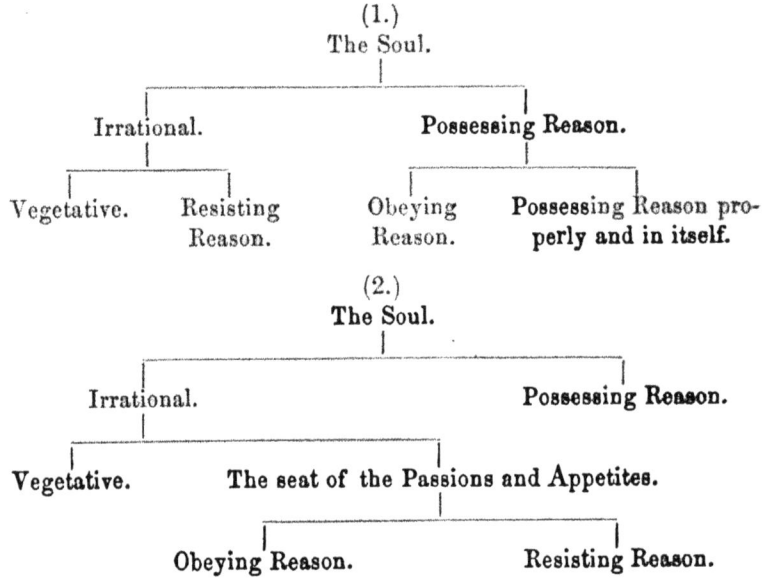

(1.)

The Soul.

Irrational.　　　　　　Possessing Reason.

Vegetative.　　Resisting Reason.　　Obeying Reason.　　Possessing Reason properly and in itself.

(2.)

The Soul.

Irrational.　　　　　　Possessing Reason.

Vegetative.　　The seat of the Passions and Appetites.

Obeying Reason.　　　　Resisting Reason.

The vegetative part of the soul is the principle of growth and reproduction ; that part which possesses reason is the seat of sensation and of the intellectual faculties.

Sensation is like an impression on wax.[2]　The soul receives the form and likeness of the sensible, just as the wax receives the form but not the matter of the seal.　Sensation, then, is the first step to the operations of the intellect.　" Nihil est in intellectu quod non erat in sensu ;" and hence, by a process of development, and mental progress from particulars to universals ($\delta\iota\acute{a}\nu o\iota a$), are produced imagination, and voluntary and involuntary memory.

The Aristotelian system of the universe is derived from his theory of motion.　His reasoning is as follows :—A perpetual motion is the only cause which will account for the continuous change and succession of phenomena which is observable in the

---

[1] Nic. Eth. i. 13.　　　　　　　　[2] De An. ii. 5.

natural order of things, and the only motion which can be per-petual must be circular. From this he deduces that the uni-verse is spherical in form, continually moving in its centre, but having no motion of translation.[1] In the centre of the universe is the earth, because the tendency of the terrestrial is to the centre;[2] round it move the planets, and beyond these lies the orbit of the fixed stars. The four elements are formed by the combinations of the four principles,—*the moist*, or *fluid* (ὑγρόν); *the dry*, or *solid* (ξηρόν) ; *the cold* (ψυχρόν) ; and *the hot* (θερμόν).

It only remains now to devote a few words to his theory of earthly objects. A principle of vitality pervades and animates all things, for even the elements themselves participate in the universal principle of life. Between the highest and lowest states of being there is a gradual transition and progressive advance. Nature proceeds from imperfection to perfection, from inanimate objects to plants, which possess only the life of growth and in-crease.[3] From thence, to the inferior animals, which are distin-guished by indivisible personality and vitality ; and from these she rises to that highest perfection and rational entelechy, the human soul.

We may pass over his anatomical treatises and mechanical problems, and also his historical works, as well as those on natu-ral history ; because, of the first only a few scattered fragments remain, and the latter, though admirable for the accurate obser-vation and erudition which they display, must necessarily be im-perfect and unsatisfactory. His ethical and political philosophy, which must be next considered, forms the most interesting and important portion of Aristotelian literature, perhaps not even excepting his logical works.

In mental and moral philosophy, the subject of study lies within a narrow compass, and is within the reach of the philosopher. His self-consciousness supplies him with all his materials for thought. He analyzes the faculties of his own mind. He contemplates the moral wants and aspirations which he himself experiences, and the moral motives which actuate his conduct. Hence the logical system of Aristotle has never been superseded, and his ethical system is the basis of all sound moral philosophy. The political philosopher,

---

[1] Phys. iv. 5.   [2] De Cœl. ii. 12—14.   [3] Nic. Eth. i. 13.

moreover, has not far to go for his materials. The relations in which he stands to the body politic of which he is a member, supply the *data* upon which he founds his political creed; and although his views may be partial and confined, and inapplicable to the millions of which the giant communities of modern times are composed, they are invaluable illustrations of Greek political modes of thought, and of the views which the wisest and deepest thinkers took respecting national happiness, and the mutual obligations of the governors and governed.

ETHICS.

Aristotle's ethical system is contained in the treatise which has for its title the Nicomachean Ethics. Its authenticity cannot be doubted, although it has been attributed to his son Nicomachus. Two other works are extant upon the same subject. 1. The Eudemean Ethics in seven books, of which three are identical with the fifth, sixth, and seventh books of the Nicomachean Ethics. This treatise is probably a compilation by Eudimus from the lectures of Aristotle. 2. The Great Ethics, which is either the original outline of the complete treatise, or an abstract of it, by some subsequent philosopher. The following is a brief sketch of the Nicomachean Ethics.

Moral science constitutes a subdivision of the more comprehensive science of politics.[1] Man is a social being; that science, therefore, which professes to investigate the subject of human good, will study the nature of man, not only as an individual, but also as a member of a family,[2] and of a state.[3] Aristotle, therefore, divides politics into three parts. Ethics, economics, and politics, strictly so called.

Ethics, or the science of individual good, must be the groundwork of the rest. Families and states are composed of individuals; unless, therefore, the parts be good, the whole cannot be perfect. The development, therefore, of the principles of man's moral nature must necessarily precede an investigation of the principles which regulate human society.

It is plain, from these considerations, that the subject of ethics is entirely practical; it is not therefore necessary to examine

---

[1] Eth. i. 7.   [2] Ibid. vi. 8.   [3] Ibid. i. 2.

into the nature of good abstractedly, but only so far as it relates
to man. So alien to his subject does Aristotle consider any ideal
standard of good, that he considers the knowledge of it useless
to the study of that good, which is attainable by man.[1]

The foundation of Aristotle's ethics is deeply laid on his psychological system. He assumes that we are born with a natural
capacity for receiving virtuous impressions, and for forming virtuous habits :[2] and his conception of the nature of his capacity is so
high a one, that he terms it "natural virtue."[3] Man is endowed
with a moral sense, a perception of moral beauty and excellence,
and with an acuteness[4] on practical subjects which, when cultivated,
is improved into prudence or moral wisdom.[5] Virtue is the law
under which we are born, that law which, if we would attain to
happiness, we are bound to fulfil.

Happiness, in its highest and purest sense, is our "being's end
and aim."[6] It is an energy or activity of the soul, according to
the law of virtue.[7] As man possesses capacities for moral action,
together with a natural taste for that which is morally beautiful,
and a natural disposition or instinct, as it were, to good acts;
virtue and happiness are possible and attainable. Had this not
been the case, all moral instruction would be useless. That for
which Nature had not given man a capacity would have been
beyond his reach; for that which exists by Nature, custom can
never change[8].

But this natural disposition or bias is a mere potentiality
(δύναμις); it is possessed, but not active. In order to become so,
it must be directed by the will, and the will[9] must be directed to
a right end by deliberate preference or moral principle.[10] Aristotle believed in the free agency of man, and therefore in his moral
responsibility.

Man has power over his actions. He can act, or abstain from
acting. By repeated acts, habits are formed, either of virtue or
vice; and therefore man is responsible for his whole character
when formed, as well as for each act which contributes to its
formation.[11]

[1] Eth. i. 6.
[2] Ibid. ii. 1.
[3] Ibid. vi. 13.
[4] Ibid. vi. 10.
[5] Ibid. vi. 5.
[6] Ibid. i. 4, 7.
[7] Ibid. i. 7.
[8] Ibid. ii. 1.
[9] Ibid. iii. 1.
[10] Ibid. iii. 2.
[11] Ibid. iii. 5.

What then is virtue? It is a habit; it is based upon the natural capacities of the human soul; it is formed and established by a voluntary agent acting under the guidance of moral principle. But to these conditions it is also necessary to add what the end or object is at which the habit is to aim. An induction of instances shows that it is a mean, not an absolute, but a relative one; that is, one relative to the internal moral constitution, and to the external circumstances of the agent.[1]

Of this relative mean, each man must judge for himself, under the guidance of his conscience, purified by moral discipline and enlightened by education. The philosopher can only enunciate general principles, the individual must do the rest. The casuist may profess to lay down accurate special rules for conduct, which will meet every case, but his professions will be unfulfilled. He will, from the very nature of the subject, fail of making morals a definite and exact science,[2] like that of mathematics. There must always be something left on which the moral sense may exercise its judicial functions.

The discussion of the virtues or mean states, both moral and intellectual, forms an important portion of the Aristotelian ethics.[3] Amongst them will be found many virtues which belong to man in his political, rather than his individual character; Magnificence, that virtue of the rich, which to an Athenian mind appeared nearly akin to patriotism;[4] the Social qualities,[5] which are not generally raised to the rank of virtues, but which, nevertheless, contribute so much to the happiness of every-day life; Justice,[6] not only that universal justice which implies the doing to every one according to the laws of God and man, and, therefore, is synonymous with virtue; but also that particular justice, which is more especially exercised by administrative or executive authority; and lastly, Friendship,[7] the law of sympathy and love between the virtuous and good, based upon, and originating in, a reasonable self-love, not, indeed, strictly speaking, a virtue, but indispensable to virtue and human happiness.

Friendship is a subject on which the mind of Greece especially

[1] Eth. ii. 2.   [2] Ibid. i. 7.   [3] Ibid. iii. 6, to vi. 13.
[4] Ibid. iv. 2.   [5] Ibid. iv. 6.   [6] Ibid. v.
[7] Ibid. viii. and ix.

loved to dwell.   It pervaded many of her historical and poetical traditions; it was interwoven with many of her best institutions, her holiest recollections.   In one of its forms, that of hospitality, it was a bond which united Greeks in one vast family, even in times of bitter hostility.   A Greek moral philosopher, therefore, would scarcely have accomplished his task, if the discussion of this subject had not formed part of his treatise.   And when we find that Aristotle places friendship so high as to say that its existence would supersede justice, and render it unnecessary, and that the true friend loves his friend for that friend's sake, and for that motive alone, it seems to approach very nearly to the Christian rule of charity, which, based on principle, and not merely on instinct, is said to be "the fulfilling of the law."

Aristotle treats of moral and intellectual virtues separately; but he did not think that they could exist separately.   Moral virtue implies the due regulation of our moral nature with all its appetites, instincts, and passions; these, therefore, must be in subjection to the reason.   Again, the reason does not act with all the vigor of which it is capable, unless the moral nature is in a well-regulated state.   Hence man's moral and intellectual faculties reciprocally act and react upon each other; every good resolution carried into effect, every act of self-control and moral discipline, increases the vigor of the pure reason, and renders it more able to perform its work.[1]

Moreover, the more powerful the reason becomes, the fewer external obstacles to its energies it meets with, the more effectually does it influence the moral nature, and render permanent the moral habits.   Thus continence is gradually improved into temperance;[2] and, if human nature were capable of attaining perfection, man would attain to that ideal standard which Aristotle calls heroic virtue.[3]   But this is above human virtue, just as its opposite, brutality, is never found, so long as human nature continues in its normal condition; but only when bodily mutilation, or moral perversion, or the influence of barbarism, has so far degraded the human being, that he may be considered as having entirely ceased to be a man.[4]

[1] Eth. vi. 13.   [2] Ibid. vii. 8.
[3] Ibid. vii. 1.   [4] Ibid. vii. 5.

Aristotle, in conclusion, proceeds to treat of pleasure. Pleasure had been so interwoven with other moral systems,[1] that it was necessary to define accurately the place which it ought to occupy in the Aristotelian ethical system.

Pleasure, then, had been held by Plato and others to be a motion, or a generation, and therefore of a transitory or transient nature; this Aristotle denies, and affirms it to be a whole, indivisible, complete, perfect, giving a perfection, a finish, as it were, to an energy, being, as he says, what the bloom is to youth.[2]

But, if so, pleasure must be active; it cannot be simply rest; and yet the opinion of mankind appears to be in favor of the notion of its being rest, in some sense or other. These apparent inconsistencies are reconciled in the following manner:—pleasure is rest as regards the body, but energy as regards the mind. It is an activity of the soul,—not a mere animal activity. This marks the difference between true and false pleasures.

Those which are consequent upon the mere activity of our corporeal nature, are low and unreal; those which attend upon the energies of our intellectual nature are true and perfect. Again, pleasure occupies an important place in morals, as a test of our habits, he who feels pleasure in self-denial is really temperate, he who feels uneasiness is not so.[3]

But as happiness is an energy of the soul, according to its highest virtue, contemplative happiness must be superior to every other kind, and must constitute the chief good of man.[4]

If, then, contemplation is the end and object of man—his chief good, his highest happiness—why has Aristotle attributed so much importance to the formation of the moral character? Because, until the moral character is formed, man is unfit not only for enjoying, but also for forming a correct conception of the happiness derived from contemplation. Place before his eyes, in the commencement of his search after happiness, intellectual contemplation, as the end at which he is aiming, and he would neither be able to understand its nature nor estimate its value. It is only by the gradual perfection of our moral nature that the intellect is enabled to act purely and uninterruptedly. The improve-

[1] Eth. x. 2, 3.   [2] Ibid. x. 4.
[3] Ibid. ii. 2.   [4] Ibid. x. 7.

ment of the moral faculties will go on parallel with that of the intellect. If we begin with contemplation, we shall neither find subjects for it of a nature sufficiently exalted to insure real happiness, nor shall we be in a condition to derive happiness from such subjects if suggested to us. Begin with moral training, and we shall attain to higher capacities for intellectual happiness, derived from the contemplation of abstract truth. The Gospel teaches the value of this method of training; that in divine things the improvement of the heart is the way to the cultivation of the understanding: "If any man will do God's will, he shall know of the doctrine, whether it be of God."[1]

Aristotle connects ethics with politics in the following manner.[2] The idea of a state implies a human society formed upon just, moral, or reasonable principles. These principles are developed in its institutions; its object is the greatest good of the body corporate; and, so far as it can be attained consistently with this primary end, the greatest good of each family and individual. Now, on the morality of the individual members, the morality, and therefore the welfare and happiness, of the body depends; for, as in a state, i.e., a free state, the source of power is ultimately the people, on the moral tone of the people the character of the institutions framed by them or their representatives must depend. Hence a state must recognize the moral culture and education of the people as a duty. Private systems of education may, doubtless, possess some advantages, such as their superior capability of being adapted to particular cases, but still they are inferior to a public system in uniformity, and in the power of enforcing their authority.

If, then, morals are the result of education, and education the duty of the state, and if provision is to be made for it by well-regulated public institutions, the science of politics must be investigated or systematized. Besides, in order to secure the advantages of private education, every one who would administer such a system efficiently should study the general political principles of education, and thus endeavor to fit himself for legislating respecting them.

[1] St. John vii. 17.   [2] Eth. x. 9.

CHAPTER XXVI.

ECONOMICS.—SLAVERY.—ANALOGY OF A FAMILY TO A STATE.—POLITICS.—DEFINITION OF A STATE.—TWO SUBJECTS FOR CONSIDERATION.—THREE FORMS OF GOVERNMENT.— THREE DEGENERATE FORMS.—PROPERTY QUALIFICATION A SAFE PRINCIPLE.—THE ANTI-DEMOCRATIC BIAS OF ARISTOTLE.—STATE OF POLITICAL OPINION AT ATHENS.— INFLUENCES ACTING UPON THE OPINIONS OF ARISTOTLE.—HIS HONESTY.—HIS LEADING PRINCIPLE.—INTERNAL ARRANGEMENTS.—PROPERTY.—EDUCATION.—RHETORIC, ITS REAL OBJECT.—ANALYSIS OF THE RHETORIC.—ANALYSIS OF THE POETIC.—CRITICAL SPIRIT OF THE AGE.—CONCLUSION.

ECONOMICS.

IT has been already shown that Aristotle considers ethics, economics, and politics as parts of one great whole, that is—the science of social life. The intermediate link between the individual and the state is the family—the earliest and simplest form of human society, the image and likeness of the political system, the bud from which all political institutions are expanded and developed. The science of economics deals with all the domestic relations, those which subsist between husband and wife, parent and child, master and slave, for holding, as the Greeks always did, the natural right of Greeks over barbarians, Aristotle considers slavery as a natural dispensation. Political freedom is a condition of Hellenic birth—a privilege inseparable from it.[1] These domestic relations he considers as analogous to the political, and illustrates the one by the other. A family resembles a monarchy, in which the father is the sovereign.[2] The relation between the husband and wife is aristocratical, whilst that of brothers is timocratical, or one of political equality. The treatise on this subject, attributed to Aristotle, consists of two books; but of these it is probable that only the first is genuine. The authenticity even of this has been disputed, and it has been ascribed, without reason, to Theophrastus.

[1] Econ. i. 5; Pol. i. 2; Eth. viii.
[2] Ibid. i. i. 3; Eth. viii. 10; Pol. i. 7. •

POLITICS.

A state is a community formed by the union of families for mutual assistance and protection, and the supply of each other's wants. Its objects are mutual benefit, and the establishment of order and virtue, and therefore happiness. The result of this union is independence and self-sufficiency (αὐταρχεία) which cannot be attained in a state of isolation.

The two subjects, the consideration of which Aristotle proposes to himself, are—first, what that highest standard is at which the legislator ought to aim : next, what modification of this it is possible to attain.[1] Of course this latter condition will be determined by the circumstances of the country and the character of the people.

There are three forms of government—monarchy, aristocracy, and free constitutional government, which he names timocracy,[2] or polity. Of these there are three degenerate forms—tyranny, oligarchy, and democracy. This division is not strictly coincident with that given in the "Rhetoric," but it differs only so far as might be expected from the higher degree of scientific accuracy with which the subject is necessarily treated in the "Ethics" and "Politics." Of these constitutions he considers monarchy the best, as it implies a perfectly wise and just sovereign, whose only object is the good of his people ; but its degenerate form, tyranny, he holds to be the worst form possible. On the other hand, timocracy is the worst ; but its corruption, democracy, is less vicious than any of the other degenerate forms. To this conclusion he comes partly from experience, partly from the theoretical idea that the opposition is the greatest between monarchy and tyranny, whilst the difference is but slight between democracy and a free constitution.

In this statement of the Aristotelian doctrine, there are two points especially deserving of observation. First, that Aristotle's view of a free constitution was a safe and constitutional one. The term timocracy, by which he designates it, implies that power is distributed according to a property qualification (ἀπὸ

[1] Pol. iv. 1.   [2] Eth. viii. 10—12; Rhet. i. 8; Pol. iii. 7.

τιμημάτων).[1] This, whilst it is the true principle of free government, is the great safeguard against what he considered the most fearful evil—ochlocracy, or the tyranny of the multitude. On this principle no citizen is excluded from rising to the highest eminence, and enjoying the greatest privileges. The qualification of birth presents an effectual barrier; that of virtue is a standard too indeterminate for man to judge by; but the acquisition of property is open to talent, and perseverance, and industry. It was the principle which distinguished the constitution of Solon, to which admiring Athens had returned after the tyranny of the Thirty. It was the system by which the previously impassable barrier of patrician privilege was broken down, and plebeian rights and liberties, recognized at Rome under the constitution which bears the name of Servius Tullius, and which ever after formed the basis of distinction of ranks, and the distribution of political power in that republic.

The other point is, that the tendency of Aristotle's views is from democratical institutions to monarchy and aristocracy. Even the bias of the Greek mind had now taken this direction. The return to the constitution of Solon, rather than to that of Clisthenes, from which latter is to be dated the firm establishment of Greek freedom, was a retrograde step from that liberty which was overthrown by the "Reign of Terror." One cannot be surprised at this: it is plain that tyranny was, as it always inevitably must be, the first result of anarchy, the fiery trial through which, after a revolutionary period, a nation passes before it regains rational freedom. And at Athens anarchy was the result of the influence of demagogy upon lawless and unbridled liberty.

Greek liberty flourished for one century, and then died. Afterwards it never completely revived again. It recovered, but it was but a sickly plant; its institutions, which had been so long the glory of Greece, had no longer the same hold on the enthusiastic affections of the people. From the period of the Thirty until the days of Aristotle, Athens seems to have been passing through a transition state, gradually preparing her for that quiet submission with which she, like the rest of the world, succumbed

---

[1] Eth. viii. 10.

to the encroachments of the mighty conqueror. If such was the leaning of the Athenian people, still less surprising is it to find in Aristotle an antagonist to popular government. Plato had seen with his own eyes all its worst phases, and would doubtless have used his influence to bias the views and opinions of his disciple. And as for his own independent opinions the circumstances of his life would all tend to form them after the same model. The son of a courtier, patronized by a sovereign prince, entrusted with the education of his heir, his predilections would naturally all be towards monarchy. The tutor of Alexander could not be a democrat. But he was not warped by prejudice or misled by private feelings, or bribed by patronage and favor. His views on politics were, as on other subjects, upright, uncompromising, impartial, and critical ; he was not blind to the fact, that the evils of irresponsible government are even worse than mob rule, and that such a monarchy as he admires, however perfeet in theory, is in practice impossible to realize.

The constitution which appeared attainable to his practical mind was a free one. The great point was to establish the supremacy of the good, whether by the authority of one or many. Hence he thought that the interests to which a legislator should pay chief regard are those of the middle classes,[1] in order that there may be protection against the encroachments of oligarchy on the one hand, and of democracy on the other.

Such are Aristotle's general political principles. The following are the internal arrangements which he recommends. On the subject of property his views were diametrically opposed to those of Plato. A community of goods he held to be equally destructive of private virtue and of public wealth, whilst a community of women, as it put an end to all domestic relations, struck a fatal blow to his fundamental principle, that a body politic is formed by the union of families, and that the political relation is a development of the economical.

So opposed was he to anything like communism that he considered inequality of property a healthy and desirable state of things ; nor was he ignorant of that important principle in poli-

[1] Pol. iii. 15.

tical economy—the division of labor.   The enfranchised citizens
were to have sufficient property and leisure to devote themselves
to public duties, whilst the rest were to be condemned to labor,
and kept distinct, as if inferior to their more fortunate breth-
ren.

But the great duty of the state is, as the conclusion of the
"Ethics" prepares us to expect, education: he felt that the
happiness of a state entirely depends on the physical and moral
excellence of its citizens.   Home education and home influences
were to exert their power until seven years of age,[1] and were
then to be succeeded by a public system.   No mental education
was to commence until the age of seven, although a course of
preparation for it might take place during the two preceding
years.   Judicious as these instructions doubtless are, his views
on the subject of education are narrow and confined.   He includes in it only grammar, drawing, gymnastics, and music;
and though he speaks in high terms of the liberal sciences, he
seems to fear that they may perhaps be carried so far as to be
both physically and morally injurious.[2]   It seems as though he
thought that the very philosophy in which he delighted should
only be pursued by the few, and by no means be used as a means
of education for the many—an inconsistency which, it must be
confessed, appears incapable of explanation.

RHETORIC AND POETIC.

His treatises on the arts of rhetoric and poetry complete the
cycle of Aristotelian literature.

The rhetoric of Aristotle's time, as taught in the school of
Isocrates, was showy and superficial.   Argumentative proof was
considered as subordinate to a polished style and powerful appeals
to the passions.[3]   The art had also fallen into disrepute, because
of the abuse of it, and because its professors often, in a sophistical spirit, used their skill to make the "worse appear the
better reason."   Aristotle undertook not only to rescue it from
this discredit, by showing that abuse is no argument against the
use of any science, but also to prove that all popular systems

[1] Pol. vii. 15—17.   [2] Ibid. viii. 2.   [3] Rhet. i. 1.

had lost sight of the real object of rhetoric, which is primarily
to persuade and convince the intellect, whilst the ornaments of
style and appeals to the passions are only secondary.

No treatise of Aristotle is capable of being exhibited in so
systematic a form as the "Rhetoric."[1] His definition of rhetoric is, "the faculty of understanding the means of persuasion
on any subject." And he describes it as the counterpart of logic,
inasmuch as neither is conversant with any definite science,[2] and
all men, to a certain extent, are able to reason as logicians, or
to accuse and defend as rhetoricians.

The treatise on rhetoric consists of three parts, of which the first
treats of the means of *persuasion* (πίστις), the second of *style*
(λέξις), third of *arrangement* (τάξις). The first and most important
of these occupies the whole of the first two books, nearly three-
fourths of the treatise, whilst style and arrangement are comprised in the third. There are two subdivisions of the means of
persuasion, namely, those which do, and those which do not
belong to an artificial system (ἔντεχνοι καὶ ἄτεχνοι πίστεις). The
ἄτεχνοι are five in number, namely, laws, witnesses, legal instruments, torture, oaths. The ἔντεχνοι are three.

1. The logical, or argumentative proof.

2. The ethical, or the moral character of the speaker as manifested in his speaking.

3. The pathetical, or the appeal to the passions.

The nature of the argumentative proof will differ according to
species of rhetoric in which it is employed. These species are
three in number, namely, the deliberative, the judicial, and the
demonstrative. The end or object of the first is the expedient
and inexpedient; that of the second, the just and the unjust;
that of the third, the honorable and disgraceful. As an aid to
the student, he proceeds to enumerate a large number of common-places, from which arguments may be drawn suitable to the
particular end which he has in view. Such is a brief analysis of
the first book.

The second is principally devoted to a masterly exposition of
the passions, and of the habits and feelings peculiarly belonging

---

[1] Rhet. i. 2.   [2] Ibid. i. 1.

to the periods of youth, maturity, and age, and to those who are endowed with the gifts of nobility, wealth, power, and prosperity. He next enumerates the topics, or common-places, which are common to all the species of oratory as well as the common means of persuasion. Such as examples, maxims, and the elements from which are derived both real and fallacious enthymemes.

Lastly, he lays down two modes of meeting the arguments of an adversary, namely, either by proving the contradictory of his conclusions (ἀντισυλλόγισμος), or by objecting to the matter and form of his reasoning (ἔνστασις).

In analyzing the subject of style, Aristotle first treats of the single words of which it is composed, and next of sentences, their adaptation to please the ear and satisfy the intellect.

The first virtue of style is perspicuity; as far as words are concerned this is accomplished by the use of words in their general acceptation (κύρια), and by words used in their primary sense (οἰκεῖα). Although these words are opposed to metaphors, Aristotle would not by this rule exclude that large class of words which, although metaphorical, have become so naturalized as no longer to produce the effects of ornament and embellishment.

But perspicuity must not be attained at the sacrifice of dignity and beauty. These excellencies will be attained by the use of metaphors, and such words of uncommon use and foreign origin as shall prevent the appearance of homeliness.

The pleasure derived from metaphors and other words, which enhance the beauty of style, is referred by Aristotle[1] to the consciousness of learning or discovery.

Attention must also be paid to beauty in sound as well as in sense. Above all, in obeying these artificial rules, the precept must be remembered that *artis est celare artem.* His sentiment on this subject was that which was afterwards enunciated by Quinctilian,[2] "Ubicumque ars ostentatur veritas abesse videtur."

As appropriateness in the use of words causes beauty, so an exaggerated employment of these elements of beauty produces the contrary effect of frigidity. Excess of ornament causes one

---

[1] Rhet. c. x.   [2] Inst. x. 3.

to observe the want of corresponding ideas, in the same way that (as Archbishop Whately happily illustrates it) an empty fire-place suggests the idea of cold. The infancy of grammatical science rendered it necessary for Aristotle to introduce here, as he does in his "Poetic," certain syntactical rules necessary to ensure purity of style.[1] But whatever attention is paid to these rules of accuracy or good taste, style will fail of producing plea-sure, unless it is expressive of feeling (παθητίκη), and of moral character (ἠθίκη), and is in keeping with the subject-matter. Prose must be rhythmical, but not metrical; but the laws of rhythm which he lays down, dependent as they doubtless are on that combination of accentuation and quantity which is now lost, do not recommend themselves to modern ears, which are unable to appreciate his principles of modulation.[2] It is remarkable that, whilst we cannot admire the cadences of Aristotle, we re-cognize at once with pleasure those recommended by Quinc-tilian.[3]

Aristotle classifies styles under two heads.[4] The loose style (εἰρομίνη), like that of Herodotus, in which the sentence may be terminated at the conclusion of any clause; and the periodic (κατεστραμμίνη), in which the sense and the sentence are completed simultaneously; of the latter Thucydides furnishes the best ex-ample. This style, being more artificial, requires more care, admits of more polish, and is therefore more pleasing. It natu-rally leads to antithesis and alliteration, and an exact balance and equipoise between the clauses which were admired and in-dulged in by the ancients, to an extent which modern taste would consider an affectation.

There are two other subjects[5] which it were to be wished that Aristotle had not so slightly touched upon. The one is the prin-ciple of the picturesque in writing (πρὸ ὀμμάτων ποιεῖν), which is in fact the fundamental principle of vigor and beauty. The other, that of wit and humor, a subject on which there is so great a difference between ancient and modern taste. It is to be regretted that he contented himself with illustrating, by only one species of it, that descriptive liveliness and vivid dramatic power which

---

[1] Rhet. iii. 7.   [2] Ibid. iii. 8.   [3] See Appendix, p. 503.
[4] Rhet. iii. 9.   [5] Ibid. iii. 11.
32

place an action before us as if it were a picture, or rather as a
scene in which the actors themselves seem to live and move, which
enables us to realize the whole to our imaginations, makes us
forget ourselves and all the distracting objects around us, and
transports us into that world of ideas which people the mind of
the poet or the orator.

Again, although it is perfectly intelligible that hyperbole and
puns, and the quaint use of paradox and pleasantries by surprise,
may not be out of place where jest and ridicule are the avowed
object, it is to be regretted that Aristotle has not left us a deeper
analysis of the principles which caused them to be received with
approbation, when used in sober and serious earnestness.   That
such conceits were admired is certain, from the profuse employment of them by both orators and poets, and by the numerous
instances of puns which are met with in the Attic tragedies; but
although our own Shakspeare sometimes indulges in this false
embellishment, modern taste shrinks from the introduction of a
pun in scenes otherwise marked by pathos and sublimity.

Poetry is classed by Aristotle[1] amongst those imitative arts
which produce their imitation by means of rhythm, words, and
melody.   Epic poetry employs the first two, whilst dithyrambic,
nomic, and dramatic poetry, employ all three, either simultaneously or separately. Hence the imitative character is essential
to poetry.   The use of metre does not make a poet, and metrical
compositions, which are merely philosophical or didactic, are not
properly poems.

As the means of imitation differ, so the objects of imitation
differ likewise.[2] Some poets represent men better than they are;
some worse; others exactly in their true character.[3] A third
difference consists in the mode of imitating, whether by narrative
or dramatic action.   These three differences—namely, the means,
objects, and modes of imitation, furnish the principles of classify-
ing the various species of poetry.

The pleasure derived from poetry[4] originates, 1st, in our
natural love of imitation, which causes us to delight even in the
representation of objects in themselves disagreeable.   2d, In the

---

[1] Poet. c. i.   [2] Ibid. c. ii.
[3] Ibid. c. iii.   [4] Ibid. c. iv.

gratification of that desire to learn new facts which all men, as well as philosophers, experience.

A brief inquiry follows into the history and progress of poetry, in which the epic of the old poets is compared to tragedy, and their satirical iambics to the libellous invective of comedy; and the origin of comedy is traced from the phallic songs, and tragedy from the ἰξάζοντες, or *leaders*, of the dithyrambic chorus. The original metre of tragedy, he remarks, was trochaic-tetrameter, the lively nature of which metre proves that the ludicrous element then prevailed in this festive ceremonial of the laughter-loving god. One cannot conceive the superhuman awfulness of Æschylus, or the pathos of Sophocles and Euripides, expressed in metre so dionysiac as the following:—

"Jolly mortals, fill your glasses! let the bumper toast go round."

Naturally, therefore, when the domain of tragedy became that of the passions of pity and terror, the dignified simplicity of the iambus succeeded to the jovial trochee.

The rhythm of the iambic metre is that into which the well-poised periods of polished conversation naturally fall; it is equally adapted to express the most exalted sentiments, and to convey the most familiar ideas. Like our own blank verse, it is the natural language of dramatic action, and must have been as superior to the trochee as blank verse is to the more artificial and more musical rhyme of the French dramatic writers.

Such is the resemblance between the epic and tragedy,[1] that all the elements of the former are contained in the latter; hence an analysis of tragedy will include all the principles of epic poetry.

Tragedy[2] is defined as " an imitation of a serious and perfect action, of suitable extent, tastefully expressed, with all the charms of language, each in its proper place, in the form of action, not narrative, and by exciting pity and terror, causing the purification of these passions." It consists of six parts, decoration, music, diction, character, both intellectual and moral, and lastly, the plot, which is the most important of all.

The requisites of a skilfully constructed plot are—

[1] Poet. c. v.   [2] Ibid. c. vi.

1. Unity,[1] that it should be the imitation of one, not of many parallel actions, and should form so perfect a whole as not to admit of the subtraction or transportation of any of its parts. It may be remarked that this is the only one of the three dramatic unities on which Aristotle insists, although they have been so constantly defended, especially by the French critics on his authority. Once, indeed, he incidentally makes some approach to that of time,[2] when he says that tragedy endeavors to confine itself by one revolution of the sun, or a little more, whilst of the unity of place he makes no mention, and many instances may be adduced in which the two latter are violated in the few extant dramas of the three great tragedians.

2. The poet should relate probable[3] rather than historical events, and this not only because the imagination is his especial province, but because truth is sometimes more improbable than fiction.

3. Its extent[4] should be sufficient to include a revolution of fortune, but not too long to be easily remembered, or to be visible as a whole at one view to the mind's eye without confusion.

The principal and most charming parts of a plot are the revolutions and discoveries.[5] Some poems are distinguished by the former,[6] and others by the latter—for example, the "Iliad" abounds in revolutions and changes of fortune: the "Odyssey" is nothing else but a series of discoveries. Telemachus is discovered to Menelaus, afterwards to Helen; Ulysses to Alcinous. Telemachus to the nurse, the swineherd, Penelope, and Laertes.[7]

Such are the parts of tragedy,[8] when divided according to the category of quality. Its divisions as to quantity are the prologue, episode, exode, parodos, stasima, and commos. On these it is unnecessary to dwell, as they have already been explained in the dramatic portion of this work.

A systematic and practical analysis[9] of all the parts of tragedy already enumerated, and the proper means of exciting the passions of pity and terror, occupy the main body of the treatise;

[1] Poet. c. viii.   [2] Ibid. c. v.   [3] Ibid. c. ix.
[4] Ibid. c. vii.   [5] Ibid. c. vi.   [6] Ibid. c. xxiv.
[7] Od. iv. 150; v. 189; ix. 17; xvi. 206; xix. 545; xxi. 212; xxiii. 211; xxiv. 375.
[8] Poet. c. xii.   [9] Ibid. c. xiii.—xxii.

and under the head of diction he here, as in the "Rhetoric," supplies the want which Greece still continued to feel of a regular grammatical system, by the incidental introduction of such grammatical rules and principles as related to the subject of poetry.

But a small part of the treatise[1] is devoted to discussing the subject of epic poetry separately; firstly, because tragedy contains within itself all the essential qualities belonging to epic poetry; and secondly, because tragedy is so superior in extent, in perspicuity, and in the power of giving pleasure, not only by its literary merit but by the accessory aids of music and decoration. Whatever praise is due to Aristotle for his systematic treatment of this as of other subjects, and for the accuracy of his criticism in matters of taste, it cannot be concealed that, in his admiration for the technical, he loses sight of the natural enthusiasm and inspiration of poetry; that though he could discern the principles of beauty, he was not able to realize to himself the inward life and energy of real poetic genius.

It is a sad example of that cold, critical spirit which seems to have been at this period creeping over the Greek intellect, and chilling the fervor of Athenian imagination, to find a philosopher affirming,[2] that the highest praise which Homer deserves is for his objectivity, and that he will be thought "divine," not because of the inspiration of the poetry, but because he preserved the unity of his plot by confining his poem to one part only of the Trojan war.

With Aristotle the era of Greek classical literature may be considered as having arrived at its close. Poetry had been naturalized at Athens by the patronage and protection of Pisistratus. The drama had risen, flourished, and decayed during the century of Athenian liberty. History had embalmed the exploits of Greek heroism, and the struggles for freedom and independence which were now no more. Oratory had arrived at maturity, and died a natural death when the circumstances of the times were no longer such as to nurture and encourage it. The most powerful intellects had been devoted to philosophical investigations, and had recommended their researches to the popular mind by the embellish-

---

[1] Poet. c. xxiii.—xxvi.   [2] Ibid. c. xxiv.

ments of taste and genius, and the refinements of literary skill. The vast mass of materials which his predecessors had collected, Aristotle had digested, arranged, and systematized.

Already, in his time, the enthusiasm of genius had become cold, and was rapidly being superseded by that spirit which can analyze the principles of art and pass a judgment upon them, but cannot produce the effects which it professes to criticize. The age which succeeded that of Aristotle, and on the confines of which he stands, was one of science rather than of literature ; and of imitation rather than of original genius. The style of Theophrastus,[1] the pupil and successor of Aristotle, was graceful and eloquent,[2] but the little that remains of his numerous works, does not give any high idea of their value, or of any other ability except shrewdness in the discrimination of character.

From the dead level of this uninteresting plain there arise two lofty peaks, whose summits catch the last glowing tints and setting rays of Greek genius and imagination. The wit and wisdom of Menander,[3] the pupil of Theophrastus, live in a few short fragments ; are reflected in the imitations of Lucian, and show what was the spirit of the new comedy, of which he was the most distinguished poet, by the materials which his plays furnished to those of Terence. Theocritus, of Syracuse,[4] delights us with the Doric simplicity of his native bucolic poetry; his truthful pictures of Sicilian rural life.

Lastly, legendary story connects the expiring effort of Greek literature, and the final departure for ever of the divine spirit of poetry, with the death of the comic poet, Philemon,[5] and the fall of Athens. The city and home of the Muses had surrendered to Antigonus, and the aged Philemon, now in his ninetieth year, was on his death-bed. He lifted up his eyes from his last comedy, which he was just finishing, and saw nine maidens leaving the room. They were the Muses. Philemon completed the concluding scene, and immediately expired.[6]

These are bright exceptions ; but amongst their contemporaries and successors, we look in vain for the vigorous thought, the divine wisdom, the fervid eloquence, the graceful wit, the brilliant genius which characterize classical antiquity.

[1] B.C. 321.   [2] Quinct. Inst. xi. 1.   [3] B.C. 312—291.
[4] B.C. 269—214.   [5] B.C. 262.   [6] Suidas.

APPENDIX.

Page 497, line 17.

THERE are few questions connected with the Greek language
and literature more difficult of solution than that of accentuation.
The accents which we now have doubtless did not exist in classical times; but nevertheless, to a certain extent, the principles of
pronunciation did exist, of which they are the signs and symbols.

In prose as well as in poetry, in familiar conversation as well as
in formal oratory, the ancient Greeks pronounced both according
to accent and quantity.   The difficulty of determining the extent
to which they combined these two conditions is principally due
to the utter impossibility of forming an adequate conception of
the exquisitely delicate sensibility which the Athenian ear possessed ; but this difficulty has been increased, firstly, by the vague
and determinate use which we are accustomed to make of the term
accentuation ; secondly, by the fact that, in the English language,
there exists no method of marking that inflexion of the voice
which the Greek accents are designed to point out.   One popular
sense in which the word accent is used, is to denote the modulation
peculiar to the language of the country to which the speaker
belongs, and which becomes especially discernible when he speaks
a foreign language.   Thus we say that a person speaks with a
French, Irish, Scotch, or generally a foreign accent.   Here, then
the word accent implies a general mixture of time, intonation,
and pronunciation of letters ; that certain syllables are unusually
dwelt upon, or slurred over, the voice habitually raised or lowered
in a way to which our ear is not accustomed ; vowels pronounced
as close sounds, which we are in the habit of considering open,
and the contrary.

Again, we use the word accent to denote the syllable which is pronounced with emphasis, whilst the other syllables are pronounced equably and without any distinction. We ask, for example, whether we ought to say córollary, or coróllary. In this case, accent is evidently equivalent to stress, or what the writers on prosody call *ictus*.

Thirdly, accent is used to imply the sentimental expression which is given to words, according to the passion which we wish to exhibit. We speak, for example, of accents of pity, love, gentleness, rage, and so forth.

Fourthly, in music, accent is used to point out that a note is to be executed, either vocally or instrumentally, with a decided energetic expression.

Lastly, in English poetry, we apply the word accent to point out the syllables in the verse on which the stress is laid, and, therefore, it is the sign of quantity, so far as we can be said to have any rules of quantity at all.

Now, in not one of these senses is the word accent used, when applied to the ancient Greek language. The two principles to which the Greeks attended in pronunciation, were time and pitch; we do not mark pitch of voice at all, but only time and emphasis, and these are with us identical, for we have no idea of time, unless emphasis accompanies it. Now Time is equivalent to Quantity, Accent is that affection of the voice which gives a musical note, or vocal sound its proper pitch, whether high or low, and the Greek accents are external visible signs, which point out when the vocal intonation is to be high or sharp, and when low or grave.

In time, or quantity, only two species were recognized by the ancients; the one double of the other in duration. The time in which a short syllable was supposed to be pronounced, was called a *mora*; that in which a long one, two *moræ*. This difference of time took place, first, in the case of the long vowels, which were considered as equivalent to two short ones, for example $\eta = \epsilon\epsilon$, and $\omega = oo$, and the syllable was then said to be long by nature. Secondly, when a short vowel was followed by two or more consonants, as τίτυμμαι, the vowel contained in such a syllable was called long by position. There can be no doubt that in such a case, time was taken to pronounce the consonants distinctly and separately as in the modern Italian *bel-la*, *quel-la*, &c.

This will illustrate the modern confusion of emphasis with time, and the utter absence of such rules of time or quantity in English as regulated Greek poetry. In the word "imprisonment," for example, the penultimate syllable, although the vowel precedes two consonants very difficult of utterance together, is pronounced short, and the antepenultimate is made equivalent to a long syllable, and is enunciated with the stress or emphasis.

As, however, a real distinction is to be drawn between time or prosodial quantity, and the elevation or depression of the voice; and as it is plain that they are two properties of vocal utterance, perfectly consistent with one another, it is easy to imagine that well-tuned ears, and a delicate vocal organization could produce both effects simultaneously, although it is difficult to realize the nicety and delicacy with which the Greeks, in their pronunciation, paid attention to both rules at one and the same time.

The English mode of pronunciation is remarkably destitute of varied intonation. Our equable mode of talking constitutes one of the difficulties which we experience, more, perhaps, than other nations, of speaking foreign languages like the natives themselves. Whoever hears a modern Greek speak, cannot but be sensible of the remarkable intonation of voice with which he gives reality and expression to every accentual mark, without error, and without difficulty. The tone of utterance falls upon the ear with a peculiarly pleasing and musical cadence. The neglect of that rhythm and quantity which are essential to Greek poetry is indeed offensive to a classical taste; the more so, as in Greek prose and poetry we, being ignorant of the true pronunciation, have nothing else but these to gratify the ear. But the modern Greeks are improving in this respect; it is not now unusual to hear one who has received a liberal education, read the ancient classical authors of his native land in such a manner as to show that he can combine, to a certain extent, the melodious cadence of intonation with the majestic march or lively step of metre and prosody.

As it is clear that all the rhythmical beauty and melodious cadence of verse would be lost if quantity were neglected, so it is equally certain that both in writing and speaking, quantity as well as accent was rigidly regarded. The passage of Aristotle alluded to in the text is a proof of this assertion. In it he states that the foot called the Pæan, which consists of four syllables, one of which is long and the other three short, is peculiarly suitable to the rhythm of prose composition. He adds, that if the first of the four syllables be long, it is suitable to the commencement of a sentence ; if the last, its cadence is fit for the termination. On the other hand, there is abundant evidence that the Athenian ear was acutely sensitive to the accentuation of every syllable. No intonation was too unimportant to escape notice ; it could discover the slightest deviation from the recognized and established rules.

Frequently the accent determined the different senses in which the same word might be used. Οὐκουν, for example, as is well-known, is affirmative or negative, according as it is accentuated on the ultimate or penultimate syllable. And this is the case, not because accentuation, i. e, intonation of voice could destroy the negative force of the οὐ, but because the former accentuation showed that it was to be used interrogatively, the latter indicatively, a difference naturally exhibited by the intonation of the voice, and, therefore, capable of being denoted by accentuation. Hence, therefore, as a negative used interrogatively it became equivalent to an affirmative.

Again, we have another example in the following anecdote, which tradition has handed down to us. When Demosthenes, in his oration on the Crown, exclaimed, "Do you think that Æschines is Alexander's hireling (μισθωτος) or his guest-friend ?" he is said to have pronounced the word as if it had been accentuated μίσθωτός, instead of μισθωτός. One of his auditors, in order to correct his pronunciation, cried out μισθωτός. The orator immediately with great shrewdness and tact took it as an answer to his question, and turning to his adversary, triumphantly exclaimed, "You hear what they say of you." This anecdote shows how important accentuation was, and how sensitive the Attic ear was in judging of the correct and proper use of it.

It is difficult to fix for certain, the period at which the accents which we now have came into use. Their object undoubtedly was, when the Greek language began to decline, and when there was reason to fear that the true pronunciation would be gradually yet rapidly forgotten, to fix and perpetuate, if possible, the beautiful cadences and musical intonations, of which it was capable. Quantity spoke for itself, the rules of prosody could be accurately laid down. Intonation was beyond the reach of such means, it could only be exhibited by the imperfect method of outward symbols.

With this view, it is believed by Voss, that a rude system was invented by Aristophanes, the grammarian, who flourished about B. C. 264, in the reigns of the Ptolemies, IV. and V., but that these accents were not the same which are in use now. The present system of accentuation was not completed and perfected until some time in the tenth century of the Christian era.

INDEX.

for tuition; his orations; their character, 373.

Islands, the Happy, described by Homer; by Hesiod, 123.

Ismenias, one of the founders of Smyrna, 57.

Isocrates, his character of popular demagogue, 361; his compositions; Cicero's opinion of, 366, 372; founder of most flourishing school of rhetoric; his pupils; style, 372; native of Athens; son of Theodorus; first school at Chios; Isæus pupil of; death, 373; not tutor of Demosthenes, 376; Hyperides, pupil of, 381; his contest with Aristotle, 467.

Ithaca, scene of part of Odyssey, 80; how changed in appearance, 112.

Jews, their early historical writings, 319.

Job, his astronomical knowledge compared with that of Homeric age, 111.

Jonson, Ben, his imitation of epigram of Euripides, 256.

Josephus, his statement respecting poems of Homer, 62.

Knight, Paine, revives theory of separators, 60.

Knights of Aristophanes; attack on Cleon; Callistratus afraid to act in; Aristophanes supports principal character; analysis of, 310.

Koppa, the letter, how compounded; how recognizable after disuse, 44.

Lacedæmon, the Hollow, 80.

Lachmann, most sagacious of modern critics; endeavors to disprove unity of Homer's poems; his opinion that the Iliad is made up of eighteen lays, 68.

Lamachus, how represented in Acharnians, 310; in the Clouds, 311.

Language, its connection with literature; two great divisions of; comparison of, with sculpture; the Greek, its origin, harmony, variety, and fitness for poetry, suited to oral transmission, 36; addressed to the ear; its grammar, 37; result of regular plan, 38; how affected by physical character of the country; origin of, 38; facility of composition in, 231; the Pelasgic, its character and affinities, 38; the Latin, resembles Greek in earliest phase, 39; Hellenic, its introduction into Greece, 39; amalgamation with Pelasgic; the German, facility of composition compared with Greek, 231.

Languages, of ancient Europe, the origin of; vocabulary and grammatical structure of; alphabet of, and means of committing them to writing, 35; the classical, varied inflexion of, in sense and sound; philosophic exactness of; Mül-

ler's comparison of, with the modern, 36; their relative adaptation to poetry, 36.

Laws, written in verse; application of word νόμος to, 174; against license of comic poets, 301; limiting ages of public orators, 308.

Lays, Homeric; poems compiled from, 61.

Leake, Col., finds Homer a topographical guide, 292.

Lee-singers, why so called, 297.

Lenæa, Dionysiac festival of, when celebrated, 276; place, why so called, 276.

Lesbian poets, character of their lyrics, 143.

Lesches of Lesbos, cyclic poet, 125.

Letters, transition from Semitic to Greek, 42; the Greek, Donaldson's theory of; difficulties respecting it, 45; at firs sixteen; how long that number used, 45.

Leucadian promontory, the; leap of Sappho from; origin of legend, 156.

Linus, hymns to, their character, 48; when sung, 48; hymn of, sung in Egypt, 49; similar traditions to those of, 49.

Literature, classical, its era, 33; two divisions of Grecian; connection of language with; its character; origin of; vehicles for, amongst ancient Greeks; poetry, earliest species of, 46; none before Homer; of monarchical age; of free institutions, 127; its change from poetry to prose, 172; causes of; how affected by political changes, 173; influence of Chthonian worship upon, 178; offspring of Ionian mind, 180; prose, how wrought out of poetry, 181; philosophy similar in origin to, 193; resemblance of, to national character; different kinds of, 194; national, established in time of Pisistratus, 209; synchronous with appearance of drama, 210; its origin, 215; not Semitic, 216; Greek, truthfulness, essence of, 294; eloquence, characteristic of, 357; classical era of, closes with Aristotle, 501.

Liturgies, the theatrical, 277.

Litotes, grammatical figure; its common use, indicates truthfulness of Greek mind, 295.

Lochus, term applied to chorus by Æschylus, 279.

Logographers, their work, 181; how esteemed; works of, not historical, 181.

Longinus, opinion of unity of Iliad and Odyssey, 59; his opinion of Ion, 265; example for rhythm of Demosthenes, 365; panegyric on Demosthenes, 379; opinion of style of Hyperides, 382.

Love, its character in Homeric age; how

conclusion; conduct after condemnation, 413; we are indebted to the interval for treatise on immortality of soul, embodied in Phædo of Plato; his last words, 413; extolled by Christians as well as heathens; his death; signal for dispersion of his friends; his character as a philosopher, 414; his instructions; how delivered; comparison of his teaching with that of sophists, 415; cause of political coloring of his teaching, 415; his character as contemplated by Plato and Xenophon, 416; true conception of from combination of two views; why he appears to undervalue physical science, 417; difficulties in the way of eliciting Socratic system; use to be made of the writings of Aristotle, 418; exposes immoral tendency of teaching of Sophists; religious character of his philosophy, 419; his doctrines arranged under three heads; his idea of God directed to his relation to man; doctrine of immortality of soul, 420; shown in narrative of Plato; his moral theory correspondent to, 421; idea of object of life; paradox consequent on; refuted by Aristotle; danger of; great schools of Greece; opening from his reformation of philosophy; whom founded by, 421; his occasional coarseness, 435; followed by Plato; importance assigned to ethics and politics, 455.

Solon, laws of, how written, 45; collects poems of Homer, 93; his archonship; his poetry; one of the gnomic poets, 130; poem of Salamis, 131; specimens preserved by Stobæus, 134; one of Seven Sages, 175; an Athenian; related to Pisistratus; his wisdom, how obtained; institutions; poems; philosophical acquirements, 177; celebrated by Cicero for his oratory, 359; Plato descended from, 430; basis of his constitutional timocracy, 492.

Sophists, their professions; contrasted with Socrates, 312; improved prose composition, 358; most celebrated as rhetorical teachers; have left no fragments; obligation of Greek literature to; first directed man to the study of himself; consciousness of identity first taught by, 401; review of circumstances of their times, 401; adopt the false ideas of education prevalent in Athens after Peloponnesian war; education given by them superficial; many of them acquainted with philosophy; examples; generally men of ability; influence of on society, 403; profit, avowed motive for teaching; taught only the wealthier classes; went with tide of popular error, 404; their dialectics, 404; whence

origin of their system; their selfishness, 405; in many respects incompetent; nature of their acquirements; why their works have not been transmitted to posterity, 406; exception; specimen of sophistry of Gorgias; Plato's view of, 406; Socrates, why classed with, 415.

Sophocles, time of his death, 226; belief in necessity for purification, 228; vanquishes Æschylus, 229; attached to cause of freedom, 237; compared with Æschylus; dramatic skill of, 241; his life; son of Sophilus; father's trade; his education; his beauty, 242; contests prize with Æschylus; the Triptolemus; the Antigone, when first exhibited; elected one of ten generals, 242; unfitness for office; forms intimacy with Herodotus; political inconsistency, 243; love of his country; accusation of son; how set aside, 244; chorus of Œdipus Coloneus; quotation from Horace, illustrative of, 244; uncertainty respecting his death; epigram of Simonides; ditto by Simmias; translation of; his plays; perfection of Greek tragic drama; his appellation, the Bee; compared with Æschylus, 246; observation of Aristotle on realization of character in poetry; examples from plays of Sophocles, 246; his morals; essentially ethical; a dramatic reformer; essay on the chorus, 247; number of dramas; dates nuocertain; order of, by Müller, 248; his descriptive accuracy, 293; friendship of Herodotus for; commands expedition to Samos, 328; Herodotus borrows from, 329.

Sparta did not produce one orator, 367; why unable to maintain her ascendency in Greece, 398.

Speusippus, his epigram on Plato, 432; nephew and successor of Plato; his works purchased by Aristotle; succeeded by Xenocrates, 464.

Stage in Greek theatre, 268.

Stars, the, not distinguished from planets in Homeric age; Venus; the constellations; the Milky Way, 111; Sirius; seasons of year marked by; use of, to agriculturist and mariner, 112.

Stasima, all odes, except parode, so called, 279.

Stasinus of Cyprus, cyclic poet, 136.

Stesichorus, contemporary with Sappho; native of Himera; son of Hesiod; legend, how accounted for, 158; originally called Tisias; name, why changed; his use of epode; adapts epic subjects to lyric verse; Quinctilian's opinion of; Müller's, 159; how far correct; bucolic or pastoral poet, 159.

THE END.

CATALOGUE

OF

BLANCHARD & LEA'S PUBLICATIONS.

CAMPBELL'S LORD CHANCELLORS. New Edition—(Now Ready.)

LIVES OF THE LORD CHANCELLORS

AND

KEEPERS OF THE GREAT SEAL OF ENGLAND.

FROM THE EARLIEST TIMES TO THE REIGN OF KING GEORGE IV.

BY LORD CHIEF JUSTICE CAMPBELL, A. M., F. R. S. E.

Second American, from the Third London Edition.

Complete in seven handsome crown 8vo. volumes, extra cloth, or half morocco.

This has been reprinted from the author's most recent edition, and embraces his extensive modifications and additions. It will therefore be found eminently worthy a continuance of the great favor with which it has hitherto been received.

Of the solid merit of the work our judgment may be gathered from what has already been said. We will add, that from its infinite fund of anecdote, and happy variety of style, the book addresses itself with equal claims to the mere general reader, as to the legal or historical inquirer; and while we avoid the stereotyped commonplace of affirming that no library can be complete without it, we feel constrained to afford it a higher tribute by pronouncing it entitled to a distinguished place on the shelves of every scholar who is fortunate enough to possess it.—*Frazer's Magazine.*

A work which will take its place in our libraries as one of the most brilliant and valuable contributions to the literature of the present day.—*Athenæum.*

The brilliant success of this work in England is by no means greater than its merits. It is certainly the most brilliant contribution to English history made within our recollection; it has the charm and freedom of Biography combined with the elaborate and careful comprehensiveness of History.—*N. Y. Tribune.*

BY THE SAME AUTHOR—TO MATCH.

LIVES OF THE

CHIEF JUSTICES OF ENGLAND,

From the Norman Conquest to the Death of Lord Mansfield.

In two very neat vols., crown 8vo., extra cloth, or half morocco.

To match the "Lives of the Chancellors" of the same author.

In this work the author has displayed the same patient investigation of historical facts, depth of research, and quick appreciation of character which have rendered his previous volumes so deservedly popular. Though the "Lives of the Chancellors" embrace a long line of illustrious personages intimately connected with the history of England, they leave something still to be filled up to complete the picture, and it is this that the author has attempted in the present work. The vast amount of curious personal details concerning the eminent men whose biographies it contains, the lively sketches of interesting periods of history, and the graphic and vivid style of the author, render it a work of great attraction for the student of history and the general reader.

Although the period of history embraced by these volumes had been previously traversed by the recent work of the noble and learned author, and a great portion of its most exciting incidents, especially those of a constitutional nature, there narrated, yet in "The Lives of the Chief Justices" there is a fund both of interesting information and valuable matter, which renders the book well worthy of perusal by every one who desires to obtain an acquaintance with the constitutional history of his country, or aspires to the rank of either a statesman or a lawyer. Few lawyers of Lord Campbell's eminence could have produced such a work as he has put forth. None but lawyers of his experience and acquirements could have compiled a work combining the same interest as a narration, to the public generally, with the same amount of practical information for professional aspirants more particularly.—*Britannia.*

1

NIEBUHR'S ANCIENT HISTORY—(A new work, now ready.)

LECTURES ON ANCIENT HISTORY,

FROM THE EARLIEST TIMES TO THE TAKING OF ALEXANDRIA BY OCTAVIANUS,

CONTAINING

The History of the Asiatic Nations, the Egyptians, Greeks, Macedonians, and Carthaginians.

BY B. G. NIEBUHR.

TRANSLATED FROM THE GERMAN EDITION OF DR. MARCUS NIEBUHR,
BY DR. LEONHARD SCHMITZ, F. R S. E.,

With Additions and Corrections from his own MSS. notes.

In three very handsome volumes, crown octavo, extra cloth, containing about fifteen hundred pages.

From the Translator's Preface.

"The Lectures on Ancient History here presented to the English public, embrace the history of the ancient world, with the exception of that of Rome, down to the time when all the other nations and states of classical antiquity were absorbed by the empire of Rome, and when its history became, in point of fact, the history of the world. Hence the present course of Lectures, together with that on the History of Rome, form a complete course, embracing the whole of ancient history. * * * * We here catch a glimpse, as it were, of the working of the great mind of the Historian, which imparts to his narrative a degree of freshness and suggestiveness that richly compensate for a more calm and sober exposition. The extraordinary familiarity of Niebuhr with the literatures of all nations, his profound knowledge of all political and human affairs, derived not only from books, but from practical life, and his brilliant powers of combination, present to us in these Lectures, as in those on Roman history, such an abundance of new ideas, startling conceptions and opinions, as are rarely to be met with in any other work. They are of the highest importance and interest to all who are engaged in the study, not only of antiquity, but of any period in the history of man."

The value of this work as a book of reference is greatly increased by a very extensive Index of about fifty closely printed pages, prepared by John Robson, B. A., and containing nearly ten thousand references; in addition to which each volume has a very complete Table of Contents.

MEMOIRS OF THE LIFE OF WILLIAM WIRT.

BY JOHN P. KENNEDY.

SECOND EDITION, REVISED.

In two handsome 12mo. volumes, with a Portrait and fac-simile of a letter from John Adams. Also,

A HANDSOME LIBRARY EDITION, IN TWO BEAUTIFULLY PRINTED OCTAVO VOLUMES.

In its present neat and convenient form, the work is eminently fitted to assume the position which it merits as a book for every parlor table and for every fireside where there is an appreciation of the kindliness and manliness, the intellect and the affection, the wit and liveliness which rendered William Wirt at once so eminent in the world, so brilliant in society, and so loving and loved in the retirement of his domestic circle. Uniting all these attractions, it cannot fail to find a place in every private and public library, and in all collections of books for the use of schools and colleges; for the young can have before them no brighter example of what can be accomplished by industry and resolution, than the life of William Wirt, as unconsciously related by himself in these volumes.

HISTORY OF THE PROTESTANT REFORMATION IN FRANCE.

BY MRS. MARSH,

Author of "Two Old Men's Tales," "Emilia Wyndham," &c.

In two handsome volumes, royal 12mo., extra cloth.

NEW AND IMPROVED EDITION.
LIVES OF THE QUEENS OF ENGLAND,
FROM THE NORMAN CONQUEST.
WITH ANECDOTES OF THEIR COURTS.

Now first published from Official Records, and other Authentic Documents, Private as well as Public.

NEW EDITION, WITH ADDITIONS AND CORRECTIONS.
BY AGNES STRICKLAND.

In six volumes, crown octavo, extra crimson cloth, or half morocco, printed on fine paper and large type.

Copies of the Duodecimo Edition, in twelve volumes, may still be had.

A valuable contribution to historical knowledge, to young persons especially. It contains a mass of every kind of historical matter of interest, which industry and resource could collect. We have derived much entertainment and instruction from the work.—*Athenæum.*

The execution of this work is equal to the conception. Great pains have been taken to make it both interesting and valuable.—*Literary Gazette*

A charming work—full of interest, at once serious and pleasing.—*Monsieur Guizot.*

THE COURT AND REIGN OF FRANCIS THE FIRST, KING OF FRANCE. By Miss Purdoe, author of "Louis XIV." &c. In two very neat volumes, royal 12mo., extra cloth.

WOMAN IN FRANCE IN THE EIGHTEENTH CENTURY. By Julia Kavanagh, author of "Nathalie," "Madeline," &c. In one very neat volume, royal 12mo.

MEMOIRS OF AN HUNGARIAN LADY. By Theresa Pulszky. With an Historical Introduction, by Count Francis Pulszky. In one vol., royal 12mo., extra cloth.

MIRABEAU; a Life History. In Four Books. In one neat vol., royal 12mo., extra cloth

HISTORY OF TEN YEARS, 1830—1840, OR FRANCE UNDER LOUIS PHILIPPE. By Louis Blanc. In two handsome volumes, crown 8vo., extra cloth.

Perhaps no work ever produced a greater or more permanent effect than this. To its influence, direct and indirect, may in a great measure be attributed the movements which terminated in the Revolution of February, 1848.

HISTORY OF THE FRENCH REVOLUTION OF 1789. By Louis Blanc. In one volume, crown 8vo., extra cloth.

PROFESSOR RANKE'S HISTORICAL WORKS.
HISTORY OF THE POPES, THEIR CHURCH AND STATE, IN THE 16TH AND 17TH CENTURIES. Complete in one large 8vo volume.
HISTORY OF THE TURKISH AND SPANISH EMPIRES, IN THE 16TH CENTURY. AND BEGINNING OF THE 17TH. Complete in one 8vo volume, paper. Price 75 cents.
HISTORY OF THE REFORMATION IN GERMANY. Parts I. II. and III. Price $1.

HISTORY OF THE HUGUENOTS. A new Edition, continued to the Present Time. By W. S. Browning. In one octavo volume, extra cloth.

HISTORY OF THE JESUITS, from the Foundation of their Society to its Suppression by Pope Clement XIV. Their Missions throughout the World; their Educational System and Literature; with their Revival and Present State. By Andrew Steinmetz, author of "The Novitiate," "Jesuit in the Family," &c. In two handsome volumes, crown 8vo., extra cloth.

WRAXALL'S HISTORICAL MEMOIRS OF HIS OWN TIMES. In one octavo volume, extra cloth.
WRAXALL'S POSTHUMOUS MEMOIRS OF HIS OWN TIMES. In one octavo volume, extra cloth.

THE ENCYCLOPÆDIA AMERICANA;

A POPULAR DICTIONARY OF ARTS, SCIENCES, LITERATURE, HIS-
TORY, POLITICS, AND BIOGRAPHY.

In fourteen large octavo volumes of over 600 double-columned pages each.

For sale very low, in various styles of binding.

Some years having elapsed since the original thirteen volumes of the ENCY-
CLOPÆDIA AMERICANA were published, to bring it up to the present day,
with the history of that period, at the request of numerous subscribers, the publishers have issued a

SUPPLEMENTARY VOLUME (THE FOURTEENTH),
BRINGING THE WORK THOROUGHLY UP.

Edited by HENRY VETHAKE, LL. D.

In one large octavo volume, of over 650 double-columned pages, which may be
had separately, to complete sets.

MURRAY'S ENCYCLOPÆDIA OF GEOGRAPHY.

THE ENCYCLOPÆDIA OF GEOGRAPHY, comprising a Complete Description
of the Earth, Physical, Statistical, Civil, and Political; exhibiting its Relation to the Heavenly Bodies, its Physical Structure, The Natural History of
each Country, and the Industry, Commerce, Political Institutions, and Civil
and Social State of all Nations. By HUGH MURRAY, F. R. S. E., &c. Assisted
in Botany, by Professor Hooker—Zoology, &c., by W. W. Swainson—Astronomy, &c., by Professor Wallace—Geology, &c., by Professor Jameson. Revised, with Additions, by THOMAS G. BRADFORD. The whole brought up, by
a Supplement, to 1843. In three large octavo volumes various styles of
binding.

This great work, furnished at a remarkably cheap rate, contains about NINETEEN
HUNDRED LARGE IMPERIAL PAGES, and is illustrated by EIGHTY-TWO SMALL MAPS and a
colored MAP OF THE UNITED STATES, after Tanner's, together with about ELEVAN HUN-
DRED WOOD-CUTS executed in the best style.

PHILOSOPHY IN SPORT MADE SCIENCE IN EARNEST. In one handsome volume, royal 18mo, crimson cloth, with numerous illustrations.

ENDLESS AMUSEMENT. A Collection of Four Hundred Entertaining Ex-
periments. In one handsome volume, royal 18mo., with illustrations, crimson cloth.

MOORE'S MELODIES, SPLENDIDLY ILLUSTRATED.

IRISH MELODIES. By Thomas Moore, Esq. In one magnificent volume,
imperial quarto, with ten large steel plates, by Finden. Handsomely bound in extra
cloth, gilt.

LANGUAGE OF FLOWERS, with illustrative poetry. Eighth edition. In
one beautiful volume, royal 18mo., crimson cloth, gilt, with colored plates.

CAMPBELL'S COMPLETE POETICAL WORKS. Illustrated Edition. One
volume crown 8vo., various bindings.

ROGERS'S POEMS. Illustrated Edition. One volume, royal 8vo., calf gilt.

KEBLE'S CHRISTIAN YEAR. One vol. 18mo., extra cloth.

KEBLE'S CHILD'S CHRISTIAN YEAR. One vol. 18mo., cloth.

POEMS, by Ellis, Currer, and Acton Bell, (Authors of Jane Eyre, &c.) In one
18mo. volume, boards.

POEMS, by Lucretia Davidson. One vol. royal 12mo., paper or extra cloth.

POEMS, by Margaret M. Davidson. One vol. royal 12mo., paper or extra cloth.

SELECTIONS FROM THE WRITINGS OF MRS. DAVIDSON. One vol.
royal 12mo, paper or extra cloth.

LIBRARY OF ILLUSTRATED SCIENTIFIC WORKS.

A series of beautifully printed volumes on various branches of science, by the most eminent men in their respective departments. The whole printed in the handsomest style, and profusely embellished in the most efficient manner.

☞ No expense has been or will be spared to render this series worthy of the support of the scientific public, while at the same time it is one of the handsomest specimens of typographical and artistic execution which have appeared in this country.

DE LA BECHE'S GEOLOGY—(Just Issued.)

THE GEOLOGICAL OBSERVER.

BY SIR HENRY T. DE LA BECHE, C. B., F. R. S.,
Director-General of the Geological Survey of Great Britain, &c.

In one very large and handsome octavo volume.

WITH OVER THREE HUNDRED WOOD-CUTS.

We have here presented to us, by one admirably qualified for the task, the most complete compendium of the science of geology ever produced, in which the different facts which fall under the cognizance of this branch of natural science are arranged under the different causes by which they are produced. From the style in which the subject is treated, the work is calculated not only for the use of the professional geologist, but for that of the uninitiated reader, who will find in it much curious and interesting information on the changes which the surface of our globe has undergone, and the history of the various striking appearances which it presents. Voluminous as the work is, it is not rendered unreadable from its bulk, owing to the judicious subdivision of its contents, and the copious index which is appended.—*John Bull.*

Having had such abundant opportunities, no one could be found so capable of directing the labors of the young geologist, or to aid by his own experience the studies of those who may not have been able to range so extensively over the earth's surface. We strongly recommend Sir Henry De la Beche's book to those who desire to know what has been done, and to learn something of the wide examination which yet lies waiting for the industrious observer.— *The Athenæum.*

KNAPP'S CHEMICAL TECHNOLOGY.

TECHNOLOGY; or, CHEMISTRY APPLIED TO THE ARTS AND TO MANUFACTURES. By Dr. F. KNAPP, Professor at the University of Giessen. Edited, with numerous Notes and Additions, by Dr. EDMUND RONALDS, and Dr. THOMAS RICHARDSON. First American Edition, with Notes and Additions by Prof. WALTER R. JOHNSON. In two handsome octavo volumes, printed and illustrated in the highest style of art, with about 500 wood engravings.

The style of excellence in which the first volume was got up is fully preserved in this. The treatises themselves are admirable, and the editing, both by the English and American editors, judicious; so that the work maintains itself as the best of the series to which it belongs, and worthy the attention of all interested in the arts of which it treats.— *Franklin Institute Journal.*

WEISBACH'S MECHANICS.

PRINCIPLES OF THE MECHANICS OF MACHINERY AND ENGINEERING. By PROFESSOR JULIUS WEISBACH. Translated and Edited by PROF. GORDON, of Glasgow. First American Edition, with Additions by PROF. WALTER R. JOHNSON. In two octavo volumes, beautifully printed, with 900 illustrations on wood.

The most valuable contribution to practical science that has yet appeared in this country.—*Athenæum.*

Unequalled by anything of the kind yet produced in this country—the most standard book on mechanics, machinery, and engineering now extant.— *N. Y. Commercial*

In every way worthy of being recommended to our readers.—*Franklin Institute Journal.*

ILLUSTRATED SCIENTIFIC LIBRARY—(*Continued.*)

CARPENTER'S COMPARATIVE PHYSIOLOGY—(Just Issued.)

PRINCIPLES OF GENERAL AND COMPARATIVE PHYSIOLOGY; intended as an Introduction to the Study of Human Physiology, and as a Guide to the Philosophical Pursuit of Natural History. By WILLIAM B. CARPENTER, M. D., F. R. S., author of "Human Physiology," "Vegetable Physiology," &c. &c. Third improved and enlarged edition. In one very large and handsome octavo volume, with several hundred beautiful illustrations.

MULLER'S PHYSICS.

PRINCIPLES OF PHYSICS AND METEOROLOGY. By PROFESSOR J. MULLER, M. D. Edited, with Additions, by R. EGLESFELD GRIFFITH, M. D. In one large and handsome octavo volume, with 550 wood-cuts and two colored plates.

The style in which the volume is published is in the highest degree creditable to the enterprise of the publishers. It contains nearly four hundred engravings executed in a style of extraordinary elegance. We commend the book to general favor. It is the best of its kind we have ever seen.—*N. Y. Courier and Enquirer.*

MOHR, REDWOOD, AND PROCTER'S PHARMACY.

PRACTICAL PHARMACY: Comprising the Arrangements, Apparatus, and Manipulations of the Pharmaceutical Shop and Laboratory. By FRANCIS MOHR, Ph. D., Assessor Pharmaciæ of the Royal Prussian College of Medicine, Coblentz; and THEOPHILUS REDWOOD, Professor of Pharmacy in the Pharmaceutical Society of Great Britain. Edited, with extensive Additions, by PROF. WILLIAM PROCTER, of the Philadelphia College of Pharmacy. In one handsomely printed octavo volume, of 570 pages, with over 500 engravings on wood.

THE MILLWRIGHT'S GUIDE.

THE MILLWRIGHT'S AND MILLER'S GUIDE By OLIVER EVANS. Eleventh Edition. With Additions and Corrections by the Professor of Mechanics in the Franklin Institute, and a description of an improved Merchant Flour Mill. By C. and O. Evans. In one octavo volume, with numerous engravings.

HUMAN HEALTH; or, the Influence of Atmosphere and Locality, Change of Air and Climate, Seasons, Food, Clothing, Bathing, Mineral Springs, Exercise. Sleep, Corporeal and Mental Pursuits, &c. &c., on Healthy Man. constituting Elements of Hygiene. By Robley Dunglison, M. D. In one octavo volume.

THE ANCIENT WORLD; OR, PICTURESQUE SKETCHES OF CREATION. By D. T. Ansted, author of "Elements of Geology," &c. In one neat volume, royal 12mo , with numerous illustrations.

A NEW THEORY OF LIFE. By S T. Coleridge. Now first published from the original MS. In one small 12mo volume, cloth.

ZOOLOGICAL RECREATIONS. By W. T. Broderip, F. R. S. From the second London edition. One volume, royal 12mo., extra cloth.

AN INTRODUCTION TO ENTOMOLOGY; or, Elements of the Natural History of Insects. By the Rev. Wm. Kirby, and Wm. Spence, F. R S. From the sixth London edition. In one large octavo volume, with plates, plain or colored

THE RACES OF MEN; a Fragment. By John Knox. In one royal 12mo. volume, extra cloth.

AMERICAN ORNITHOLOGY. By Charles Bonaparte, Prince of Canino. In four folio volumes, half bound, with numerous magnificent colored plates.

LECTURES ON THE PHYSICAL PHENOMENA OF LIVING BEINGS. By Carlo Matteucci. Edited by Jonathan Peretra, M. D. In one royal 12mo. volume, extra cloth, with illustrations.

GRAHAM'S CHEMISTRY, NEW EDITION.　Part I.—(Now Ready.)

ELEMENTS OF CHEMISTRY;

INCLUDING THE APPLICATIONS OF THE SCIENCE IN THE ARTS.

BY THOMAS GRAHAM, F. R. S., &c.,

Professor of Chemistry in University College, London, &c.

Second American, from an entirely Revised and greatly Enlarged English Edition.

WITH NUMEROUS WOOD ENGRAVINGS.

EDITED, WITH NOTES, BY ROBERT BRIDGES. M. D.,
Professor of Chemistry in the Philadelphia College of Pharmacy, &c.

To be completed in Two Parts, forming one very large octavo volume.
PART I, now ready, of 430 large pages, with 185 engravings.
PART II, preparing for early publication.

From the Editor's Preface.

The "Elements of Chemistry," of which a second edition is now presented, attained, on its first appearance, an immediate and deserved reputation. The copious selection of facts from all reliable sources, and their judicious arrangement, render it a safe guide for the beginner, while the clear exposition of theorotical points, and frequent references to special treatises, make it a valuable assistant for the more advanced student.

From this high character the present edition will in no way detract. The great changes which the science of Chemistry has undergone during the interval have rendered necessary a complete revision of the work, and this has been most thoroughly accomplished by the author. Many portions will therefore be found essentially altered, thereby increasing greatly the size of the work, while the series of illustrations has been entirely changed in style, and nearly doubled in number.

Under these circumstances but little has been left for the editor. Owing, however, to the appearance of the London edition in parts, some years have elapsed since the first portions were published, and he has therefore found oc casion to introduce the more recent investigations and discoveries in some subjects, as well as to correct such inaccuracies or misprints as had escaped the author's attention, and to make a few additional references.

INTRODUCTION TO PRACTICAL CHEMISTRY, including Analysis. By John F. Bowman, M. D. In one neat royal 12mo. volume, extra cloth, with aumerous illustrations.

DANA ON CORALS.

ZOOPHYTES AND CORALS. By James D. Dana. In one volume imperial quarto, extra cloth, with wood-cuts.

Also. an Atlas to the above, one volume imperial folio, with sixty-one magnificent plates, colored after nature. Bound in half morocco.

These splendid volumes form a portion of the publications of the United States Exploring Expedition. As but very few copies have been prepared for sale, and as these are nearly exhausted, all who are desirous of enriching their libraries with this, the most creditable specimen of American Art and Science as yet issued, will do well to procure copies at once.

THE ETHNOGRAPHY AND PHILOLOGY OF THE UNITED STATES EX-PLORING EXPEDITION. By Horatio Hale. In one large imperial quarto volume, beautifully printed, and strongly bound in extra cloth.

BARON HUMBOLDT'S LAST WORK.

ASPECTS OF NATURE IN DIFFERENT LANDS AND DIFFERENT CLIMATES With Scientific Elucidations. By Alexander Von Humboldt Translated by Mrs. Sabine. Second American edition. In one handsome volume, large royal 12mo., extra cloth.

CHEMISTRY OF THE FOUR SEASONS, SPRING, SUMMER, AUTUMN, AND WINTER By Thomas Griffith. In one handsome volume, royal 12mo, extra cloth, with numerous illustrations.

HANDBOOKS
OF NATURAL PHILOSOPHY AND ASTRONOMY.

BY DIONYSIUS LARDNER, LL. D., ETC.

FIRST COURSE, containing

Mechanics, Hydrostatics, Hydraulics, Pneumatics, Sound, and Optics.

In one large royal 12mo. volume of 750 pages, strongly bound in leather, with over 400 wood-cuts, (Just Issued.)

THE SECOND COURSE, embracing

HEAT, MAGNETISM, ELECTRICITY, AND GALVANISM,

Of about 400 pages, and illustrated with 250 cuts, is just ready.

THE THIRD COURSE, constituting
A COMPLETE TREATISE ON ASTRONOMY

THOROUGHLY ILLUSTRATED, IS IN PREPARATION FOR SPEEDY PUBLICATION.

The intention of the author has been to prepare a work which should embrace the principles of Natural Philosophy, in their latest state of scientific development, divested of the abstruseness which renders them unfitted for the younger student, and at the same time illustrated by numerous practical applications in every branch of art and science. Dr. Lardner's extensive acquirements in all departments of human knowledge, and his well known skill in popularizing his subject, have thus enabled him to present a text-book which, though strictly scientific in its groundwork, is yet easily mastered by the student, while calculated to interest the mind, and awaken the attention by showing the importance of the principles discussed, and the manner in which they may be made subservient to the practical purposes of life. To accomplish this still further, the editor has added to each section a series of examples, to be worked out by the learner; thus impressing upon him the practical importance and variety of the results to be obtained from the general laws of nature. The subject is still further simplified by the very large number of illustrative wood-cuts which are scattered through the volume, making plain to the eye what might not readily be grasped by the unassisted mind. and every care has been taken to render the typographical accuracy of the work what it should be.

Although the first portion only has been issued, and that but for a few months, yet it has already been adopted by many academies and colleges of the highest standing and character. A few of the numerous recommendations with which the work has been favored are subjoined.

From Prof. Millington, Univ. of Mississippi, April 10, 1852.

I am highly pleased with its contents and arrangement. It contains a greater number of every day useful practical facts and examples than I have ever seen noticed in a similar work, and I do not hesitate to say that as a book for teaching I prefer it to any other of the same size and extent that I am acquainted with. During the thirteen years that I was at William and Mary College I had to teach Natural Philosophy, and I should have been very glad to have such a text-book.

From Edmund Smith, Baltimore, May 19, 1852.

I have a class using it, and think it the best book of the kind with which I am acquainted.

From Prof. Cleveland, Philadelphia, October 17, 1851.

I feel prepared to say that it is the fullest and most valuable manual upon the subject that has fallen under my notice, and I intend to make it the text book for the first class in my school.

From S. Schooler, Hanover Academy, Va.,

The "Handbooks" seem to me the best popular treatises on their respective subjects with which I am acquainted. Dr. Lardner certainly popularizes science very well, and a good text-book for schools and colleges was not before in existence.

From Prof. J. S. Henderson, Farmer's College, O., Feb. 16, 1852.

It is an admirable work, and well worthy of public patronage. For clearness and fulness it is unequalled by any that I have seen.

NEW AND IMPROVED EDITION.—(Now Ready)

OUTLINES OF ASTRONOMY.

BY SIR JOHN F. W. HERSCHEL, F. R. S., &c.

A NEW AMERICAN FROM THE FOURTH LONDON EDITION.

In one very neat crown octavo volume, extra cloth, with six plates and numerous wood-cuts.

This edition will be found thoroughly brought up to the present state of astronomical science, with the most recent investigations and discoveries fully discussed and explained.

We now take leave of this remarkable work, which we hold to be, beyond a doubt, the greatest and most remarkable of the works in which the laws of astronomy and the appearance of the heavens are described to those who are not mathematicians nor observers, and recalled to those who are. It is the reward of men who can descend from the advancement of knowledge to care for its diffusion, that their works are essential to all, that they become the manuals of the proficient as well as the text-books of the learner.—*Athenæum.*

There is perhaps no book in the English language on the subject, which, whilst it contains so many of the facts of Astronomy (which it attempts to explain with as little technical language as possible), is so attractive in its style, and so clear and forcible in its illustrations.—*Evangelical Review.*

Probably no book ever written upon any science, embraces within so small a compass an entire epitome of everything known within all its various departments, practical, theoretical, and physical.—*Examiner.*

A TREATISE ON ASTRONOMY.

BY SIR JOHN F. W. HERSCHEL. Edited by S. C. WALKER. In one 12mo. volume, half bound, with plates and wood-cuts.

A TREATISE ON OPTICS.

BY SIR DAVID BREWSTER, LL. D., F. R. S., &c.

A NEW EDITION.

WITH AN APPENDIX, CONTAINING AN ELEMENTARY VIEW OF THE APPLICATION OF ANALYSIS TO REFLECTION AND REFRACTION.

BY A. D. BACHE, Superintendent U. S. Coast Survey, &c.

In one neat duodecimo volume, half bound, with about 200 illustrations.

BOLMAR'S FRENCH SERIES.

New editions of the following works, by A. BOLMAR, forming, in connection with "Bolmar's Levizac," a complete series for the acquisition of the French language:—

A SELECTION OF ONE HUNDRED PERRIN'S FABLES, accompanied by a Key, containing the text, a literal and free translation, arranged in such a manner as to point out the difference between the French and English idiom. &c. In one vol 12mo.

A COLLECTION OF COLLOQUIAL PHRASES, on every topic necessary to maintain conversation. Arranged under different heads, with numerous remarks on the peculiar pronunciation and uses of various words; the whole so disposed as considerably to facilitate the acquisition of a correct pronunciation of the French. In one vol. 18mo

LES AVENTURES DE TELEMAQUE, PAR FENELON, in one vol. 12mo., accompanied by a Key to the first eight books. In one vol. 12mo., containing, like the Fables, the Text, a literal and free translation, intended as a sequel to the Fables. Either volume sold separately.

ALL THE FRENCH VERBS, both regular and irregular, in a small volume.

ELEMENTS OF NATURAL PHILOSOPHY;

BEING

AN EXPERIMENTAL INTRODUCTION TO THE PHYSICAL SCIENCES.

Illustrated with over Three Hundred Wood-cuts.

BY GOLDING BIRD, M.D.,

Assistant Physician to Guy's Hospital.

From the Third London edition. In one neat volume, royal 12mo.

We are astonished to find that there is room in so small a book for even the bare recital of so many subjects. Where everything is treated succinctly, great judgment and much time are needed in making a selection and winnowing the wheat from the chaff Dr. Bird has no need to plead the peculiarity of his position as a shield against criticism, so long as his book continues to be the best epitome in the English language of this wide range of physical subjects.—*North American Review*, April 1, 1851.

From Prof John Johnston, Wesleyan Univ , Middletown, Ct.

For those desiring as extensive a work, I think it decidedly superior to anything of the kind with which I am acquainted.

From Prof. R. O. Currey, East Tennessee University.

I am much gratified in perusing a work which so well, so fully, and so clearly sets forth this branch of the Natural Sciences. For some time I have been desirous of obtaining a substitute for the one now used—one which should embrace the recent discoveries in the sciences, and I can truly say that such a one is afforded in this work of Dr. Bird's.

From Prof. W. F. Hopkins, Masonic University, Tenn.

It is just the sort of book I think needed in most colleges, being far above the rank of a mere popular work, and yet not beyond the comprehension of all but the most accomplished mathematicians.

ELEMENTARY CHEMISTRY;

THEORETICAL AND PRACTICAL.

BY GEORGE FOWNES, Ph.D.,

Chemical Lecturer in the Middlesex Hospital Medical School, &c. &c.

WITH NUMEROUS ILLUSTRATIONS.

Third American, from a late London edition. Edited, with Additions,

BY ROBERT BRIDGES, M.D.,

Professor of General and Pharmaceutical Chemistry in the Philadelphia College of Pharmacy, &c. &c.

In one large royal 12mo. volume, of over five hundred pages, with about 180 wood-cuts, sheep or extra cloth.

The work of Dr. Fownes has long been before the public, and its merits have been fully appreciated as the best text-book on Chemistry now in existence. We do not, of course, place it in a rank superior to the works of Brande, Graham, Turner, Gregory, or Gmelin. but we say that, as a work for students, it is preferable to any of them.—*London Journal of Medicine.*

We know of no treatise so well calculated to aid the student in becoming familiar with the numerous facts in the science on which it treats, or one better calculated as a text-book for those attending Chemical Lectures. * * * * The best text-book on Chemistry that has issued from our press.—*American Med Journal.*

We know of none within the same limits, which has higher claims to our confidence as a college class-book, both for accuracy of detail and scientific arrangement.—*Augusta Med. Journal.*

ELEMENTS OF PHYSICS.

OR, NATURAL PHILOSOPHY, GENERAL AND MEDICAL Written for universal use, in plain, or non-technical language By NEILL ARNOTT, M.D. In one octavo volume, with about two hundred illustrations.

SOMERVILLE'S PHYSICAL GEOGRAPHY.

PHYSICAL GEOGRAPHY.

BY MARY SOMERVILLE.

SECOND AMERICAN FROM THE SECOND AND REVISED LONDON EDITION.

WITH AMERICAN NOTES, GLOSSARY, ETC.

In one neat royal 12mo. volume, extra cloth, of over five hundred and fifty pages.

The great success of this work, and its introduction into many of our higher schools and academies, have induced the publishers to prepare a new and much improved edition. In addition to the corrections and improvements of the author bestowed on the work in its passage through the press a second time in London, notes have been introduced to adapt it more fully to the physical geography of this country; and a comprehensive glossary has been added, rendering the volume more particularly suited to educational purposes. The amount of these additions may be understood from the fact, that not only has the size of the pages been increased, but the volume itself enlarged by over one hundred and fifty pages.

Our praise comes lagging in the rear, and is wellnigh superfluous. But we are anxious to recommend to our youth the enlarged method of studying geography which her present work demonstrates to be as captivating as it is instructive. We hold such presents as Mrs Somerville has bestowed upon the public, to be of incalculable value, disseminating more sound information than all the literary and scientific institutions will accomplish in a whole cycle of their existence.—*Blackwood's Magazine.*

From Thomas Sherwin, High School, Boston.

I hold it in the highest estimation. and am confident that it will prove a very efficient aid in the education of the young, and a source of much interest and instruction to the adult reader.

From Erastus Everett, High School, New Orleans.

I have examined it with a good deal of care, and am glad to find that it supplies an important desideratum. The whole work is a masterpiece. Whether we examine the importance of the subjects treated, or the elegant and attractive style in which they are presented. this work leaves nothing to desire. I have introduced it into my school for the use of an advanced class in geography, and they are greatly interested in it. I have no doubt that it will be used in most of our higher seminaries.

From W. Smyth, Oswego Academy.

So much important, accurate, and general information I have never seen in a volume of its extent. In fine, I believe it to be a work which will soon take a high place in the academies and colleges of America, as well as in the libraries of every individual desirous of accurate information respecting the planet on which we dwell. I have recommended it to those connected with the District School Libraries, for which I consider it exceedingly well adapted.

JOHNSTON'S PHYSICAL ATLAS.

THE PHYSICAL ATLAS

OF NATURAL PHENOMENA.

FOR THE USE OF COLLEGES, ACADEMIES, AND FAMILIES.

BY ALEXANDER KEITH JOHNSTON, F. R. G. S., F. G. S.

In one large volume, imperial quarto, handsomely and strongly bound. With twenty-six plates, engraved and colored in the best style. Together with one hundred and twelve pages of Descriptive Letter-press, and a very copious Index.

A work which should be in every family and every school-room, for consultation and reference. By the ingenious arrangement adopted by the author, it makes clear to the eye every fact and observation relative to the present condition of the earth arranged under the departments of Geology, Hydrography, Meteorology, and Natural History. The letter-press illustrates this with a body of important information, nowhere else to be found condensed into the same space, while a very full Index renders the whole easy of reference.

SCHMITZ AND ZUMPT'S CLASSICAL SERIES.

Under this title BLANCHARD & LEA are publishing a series of Latin School-Books, edited by those distinguished scholars and critics, Leonhard Schmitz and C. G. Zumpt. The object of the series is to present a course of accurate texts, revised in accordance with the latest investigations and MSS., and the most approved principles of modern criticism, as well as the necessary elementary books, arranged on the best system of modern instruction. The former are accompanied with notes and illustrations introduced sparingly, avoiding on the one hand the error of overburdening the work with commentary, and on the other that of leaving the student entirely to his own resources. The main object has been to awaken the scholar's mind to a sense of the beauties and peculiarities of his author, to assist him where assistance is necessary, and to lead him to think and to investigate for himself. For this purpose maps and other engravings are given wherever useful, and each author is accompanied with a biographical and critical sketch. The form in which the volumes are printed is neat and convenient, while it admits of their being sold at prices unprecedentedly low, thus placing them within the reach of many to whom the cost of classical works has hitherto proved a bar to this department of education; while the whole series being arranged on one definite and uniform plan, enables the teacher to carry forward his student from the rudiments of the language without the annoyance and interruption caused by the necessity of using text-books founded on varying and conflicting systems of study.

CLASSICAL TEXTS PUBLISHED IN THIS SERIES.

I. CÆSARIS DE BELLO GALLICO LIBRI IV., 1 vol. royal 18mo., extra cloth, 232 pages, with a Map, price 50 cents.

II. C. C. SALLUSTII CATILINA ET JUGURTHA, 1 vol. royal 18mo., extra cloth, 168 pages, with a Map, price 50 cents.

III. P. OVIDII NASONIS CARMINA SELECTA, 1 vol. royal 18mo., extra cloth, 246 pages, price 60 cents.

IV. P. VIRGILII MARONIS CARMINA, 1 vol. royal 18mo., extra cloth, 438 pages, price 75 cents.

V. Q. HORATII FLACCI CARMINA EXCERPTA, 1 vol. royal 18mo., extra cloth, 312 pages, price 60 cents.

VI. Q. CURTII RUFI DE ALEXANDRI MAGNI QUÆ SUPERSUNT, 1 vol. royal 18mo., extra cloth, 326 pages, with a Map, price 70 cents.

VII. T. LIVII PATAVINI HISTORIARUM LIBRI I., II., XXI., XXII., 1 vol. royal 18mo., ex. cloth, 350 pages, with two colored Maps, price 70 cents.

VIII. M. T. CICERONIS ORATIONES SELECTÆ XII., 1 vol. royal 18mo., extra cloth, 300 pages, price 60 cents.

ELEMENTARY WORKS PUBLISHED IN THIS SERIES.

I.

A SCHOOL DICTIONARY OF THE LATIN LANGUAGE. By DR. J. H. KALTSCHMIDT. In two parts, Latin-English and English-Latin.

Part I., Latin-English, of nearly 500 pages, strongly bound, price 90 cents.

Part II., English-Latin, of about 400 pages, price 75 cents.

Or the whole complete in one very thick royal 18mo. volume, of nearly 900 closely printed double-columned pages, strongly bound in leather, price only $1 25.

II.

GRAMMAR OF THE LATIN LANGUAGE. BY LEONHARD SCHMITZ, Ph. D., F. R. S. E., Rector of the High School, Edinburgh, &c. In one handsome volume, royal 18mo., of 318 pages, neatly half bound, price 60 cents.

SCHMITZ AND ZUMPT'S CLASSICAL SERIES—Continued.

III.

ELEMENTARY GRAMMAR AND EXERCISES. By Dr. Leonhard Schmitz, F. R. S. E., Rector of the High School, Edinburgh, &c. In one handsome royal 18mo. volume of 246 pages, extra cloth, price 50 cents. (Just Issued.)

PREPARING FOR SPEEDY PUBLICATION.

LATIN READING AND EXERCISE BOOK, 1 vol., royal 18mo.
A SCHOOL CLASSICAL DICTIONARY, 1 vol., royal 18mo.
CORNELIUS NEPOS, with Introduction, Notes, &c., 1 vol., royal 18mo.

It will thus be seen that this series is now very nearly complete, embracing eight prominent Latin authors, and requiring but two more elementary works to render it sufficient in itself for a thorough course of study, and these latter are now preparing for early publication. During the successive appearance of the volumes, the plan and execution of the whole have been received with marked approbation, and the fact that it supplies a want not hitherto provided for, is evinced by the adoption of these works in a very large number of the best academies and seminaries throughout the country. From among several hundred testimonials with which they have been favored, and which they are every day receiving, the publishers submit a few of the more recent.

But we cannot forbear commending especially both to instructors and pupils the whole of the series, edited by those accomplished scholars, Drs. Schmitz and Zumpt. Here will be found a set of text-books that combine the excellences so long desired in this class of works. They will not cost the student, by one half at least, that which he must expend for some other editions. And who will not say that this is a consideration worthy of attention? For the cheaper our school-books can be made, the more widely will they be circulated and used. Here you will find, too, no useless display of notes and of learning, but in foot notes on each page you have everything necessary to the understanding of the text. The difficult points are sometimes elucidated, and often is the student referred to the places where he can find light, but not without some effort of his own. We think that the punctuation in these books might be improved; but taken as a whole, they come nearer to the wants of the times than any within our knowledge.—*Southern College Review.*

From W. J. Rolfs, Wrentham, Mass., March 22, 1852.

They seem to me the best and the cheapest school editions of the classics that I have yet seen. The notes are all that a teacher could, and all that a student should desire. On classical history and antiquities I think them p   rich, and the maps add very much to the merit of the books Kaltschmidt's Dictionary I adopted as a matter of course. It is so much superior to all the other school dictionaries that no one who has examined it can hesitate to recommend it.

From Prof. R. N. Newell, Masonic College, Tenn., June 2, 1852.

I can give you no better proof of the value which I set on them than by making use of them in my own classes, and recommending their use in the preparatory department of our institution. I have read them through carefully that I might not speak of them without due examination, and I flatter myself that my opinion is fully borne out by fact, when I pronounce them to be the most useful and the most correct, as well as the cheapest editions of Latin Classics ever introduced in this country. The Latin and English Dictionary contains as much as the student can want in the earlier years of his course; it contains more than I have ever seen compressed into a book of this kind. It ought to be the student's constant companion in his recitations. It has the extraordinary recommendation of being at once portable and comprehensive.

From Prof. D. Duncan, Randolph Macon College, Va., May 25, 1852.

It is unnecessary for me to say anything respecting the text of Schmitz and Zumpt's series. The very names of the editors are a sufficient guarantee of their purity. The beauty of the typography, and the judicious selection of notes will insure their use by every experienced teacher, whilst their cheapness and convenient size will be a sure recommendation to every parent. I think, gentlemen that by the republication of this excellent series you have laid the public under strong obligations to you. We will use them as far as they come into our course, and I will recommend them to our numerous preparatory schools. From the merits above mentioned, they are destined, in my opinion, to supersede most of the editions now in use in our schools.

SCHMITZ AND ZUMPT'S CLASSICAL SERIES—Continued.

From the Rev. L. Van Bokkelen, Principal of St. Timothy's Hall, Md, Feb. 18, 1852.

Since you commenced the series I have invariably adopted the different works in preference to all others, and I now use them all, with the exception of "Q. Curtius."

From W. F. Wyers, New London Academy, Feb. 14, 1852.

I have used no other editions but yours since they made their first appearance, and shall certainly continue to do so.

Among the various editions of the Latin Classics, Schmitz and Zumpt's series, so far as yet published, are at all times preferred, and students are requested to procure no other.—*Announcement of Bethany College, Va.*

Uniform with SCHMITZ AND ZUMPT'S CLASSICAL SERIES.—(Now Ready.)

THE CLASSICAL MANUAL;

AN EPITOME OF ANCIENT GEOGRAPHY, GREEK AND ROMAN MYTHOLOGY, ANTIQUITIES, AND CHRONOLOGY.

CHIEFLY INTENDED FOR THE USE OF SCHOOLS.

BY JAMES S. S. BAIRD, T. C. D.,
Assistant Classical Master, King's School, Gloucester.

In one neat volume, royal 18mo., extra cloth, price Fifty cents.

This little volume has been prepared to meet the recognized want of an Epitome which, within the compass of a single small volume, should contain the information requisite to elucidate the Greek and Roman authors most commonly read in our schools. The aim of the author has been to embody in it such details as are important or necessary for the junior student, in a form and space capable of rendering them easily mastered and retained, and he has consequently not incumbered it with a mass of learning which, though highly valuable to the advanced student, is merely perplexing to the beginner. In the amount of information presented, and the manner in which it is conveyed, as well as its convenient size and exceedingly low price, it is therefore admirably adapted for the younger classes of our numerous classical schools.

From Mr. B. F. Stem, Fredericksburg, Va, July 30, 1852.

The Classical Manual I have perused with delight, and shall at once introduce in my school. It is a book that has long been needed, and I know of none where so much varied matter can be found in so small a space.

From Mr. C. Hammond, Monson, Mass, Aug. 6, 1852.

I shall introduce it into my school at once. It is just what we have needed for a long, long time.

From Prof. Trimble, Kenyon College, O., Aug 30, 1852.

It must recommend itself to the teachers in all the classical institutions within the Union, not only on account of its cheapness, but also for its excellent arrangement; and it will be a *sine qua non* compendious class-book for every student wishing to enter our colleges.

From Mr. J. H. Nourse, Washington, Aug. 17, 1852.

I shall require every classical student to possess a copy of "Baird's Manual."

From Mr. W. W. Clarke, Gouverneur Wes. Sem, N. Y, Aug. 17, 1852.

I admire it very much for the large amount of classical information so concisely and clearly set forth. It is just the thing for students in their early studies, and has long been a desideratum.

From Mr. W. S. Bogart, Tallahassee, Fl., Aug. 7, 1852.

It contains a vast amount of geographical and classical information in a most concise compass, which adapts it equally to the pupil and the advanced student who wishes to review his classical knowledge.

A HISTORY OF GREEK CLASSICAL LITERATURE.

BY THE REV. R. W. BROWNE, M. A.,

Professor of Classical Literature in King's College, London.

In one very neat volume, crown 8vo., extra cloth.

To be shortly followed by a similar volume on Roman Literature.

From Prof. J. A. Spencer, New York, March 10, 1852.

It is an admirable volume, sufficiently full and copious in detail, clear and precise in style, very scholar-like in its execution, genial in its criticism, and altogether displaying a mind well stored with the learning genius, wisdom, and exquisite taste of the ancient Greeks. It is in advance of everything we have, and it may be considered indispensable to the classical scholar and student.

From Prof. N. H. Griffin, Williams College, Mass., March 22, 1852.

A valuable compend, embracing in a small compass matter which the student would have to go over much ground to gather for himself.

From Prof. M. F. Hyde, Burlington College, N. J., Feb. 10, 1852.

This book meets a want that has long been felt of some single work on the subject presenting to the student and general reader, in a popular form, information widely dispersed through a great variety of publications, and nowhere combined into one whole. Mr. Browne's selection of materials is judiciously made, and presented in a perspicuous, elegant, and agreeable manner.

From Prof. Gessner Harrison, University of Va., Feb. 28, 1852.

I am very favorably impressed with the work from what I have seen of it, and hope to find in it an important help for my class of history. Such a work is very much needed.

In this field, following the successful assiduity of others, Mr. Browne enters with the relish of an amateur and the skill of a connoisseur, profiting by the labors of his predecessors, and bringing the tested results into the compass of a most valuable book; one very much to our taste, giving a satisfactory account of the language, the authors, the works which, while Greece herself has passed away, render her name immortal. The history is divided into two periods; the first extends from the infancy of its literature to the time of the Pisistratidæ; the other commences with Simonides, and ends with Aristotle. We commend our author to the favorable regard of professors and teachers.—*Methodist Quarterly Review, South.*

Mr Browne's present publication has great merit. His selection of materials is judiciously adapted to the purpose of conveying within a moderate compass some definite idea of the leading characteristics of the great classical authors and their works. * * * * Mr. Browne has the happy art of conveying information in a most agreeable manner. It is impossible to miss his meaning, or be insensible to the charms of his polished style. Suffice it to say, that he has in a very readable volume, presented much that is useful to the classical reader. Besides biographical information in reference to all the classical Greek authors, he has furnished critical remarks on their intellectual peculiarities, and an analysis of their works when they are of sufficient importance to deserve it.—*London Athenæum.*

This book will be of great value to the student.—*Examiner.*

GEOGRAPHIA CLASSICA:

OR, THE APPLICATION OF ANCIENT GEOGRAPHY TO THE CLASSICS.

By SAMUEL BUTLER, D. D., late Lord Bishop of Litchfield. Revised by his Son. Sixth American, from the last London Edition, with Questions on the Maps, by JOHN PAGET, LL. D. In one neat volume, royal 12mo., half bound.

AN ATLAS OF ANCIENT GEOGRAPHY.

By SAMUEL BUTLER, D D., late Lord Bishop of Litchfield. In one octavo volume, half bound, containing twenty-one quarto colored Maps, and an accentuated Index.

ELEMENTS OF UNIVERSAL HISTORY.

On a new plan; from the Creation of the World to the Congress of Vienna, with a Summary of the Leading Events since that time. By H WHITE. Edited, with a Series of Questions, by JOHN S HART, Principal of the Philadelphia High School In one very large royal 12mo. volume, half bound.

NEW AND IMPROVED EDITION—(Now Ready.)

OUTLINES OF ENGLISH LITERATURE.

BY THOMAS B. SHAW.

Professor of English Literature in the Imperial Alexander Lyceum, St. Petersburg.

SECOND AMERICAN EDITION.

WITH A SKETCH OF AMERICAN LITERATURE.

BY HENRY T. TUCKERMAN,

Author of "Characteristics of Literature," "The Optimist," &c.

In one large and handsome volume, royal 12mo., extra cloth, of about 500 pages.

The object of this work is to present to the student a history of the progress of English Literature. To accomplish this, the author has followed its course from the earliest times to the present age, seizing upon the more prominent "Schools of Writing," tracing their causes and effects, and selecting the more celebrated authors as subjects for brief biographical and critical sketches, analyzing their best works, and thus presenting to the student a definite view of the development of the language and literature, with succinct descriptions of those books and men of which no educated person should be ignorant. He has thus not only supplied the acknowledged want of a manual on this subject, but by the liveliness and power of his style, the thorough knowledge he displays of his topic, and the variety of his subjects, he has succeeded in producing a most agreeable reading-book, which will captivate the mind of the scholar, and relieve the monotony of drier studies.

This work having attracted much attention, and been introduced into a large number of our best academies and colleges, the publishers, in answering the call for a new edition, have endeavored to render it still more appropriate for the student of this country, by adding to it a sketch of American literature. This has been prepared by Mr. Tuckerman, on the plan adopted by Mr. Shaw, and the volume is again presented with full confidence that it will be found of great utility as a text-book, wherever this subject forms part of the educational course; or as an introduction to a systematic plan of reading.

From Prof. R. P. Dunn, Brown University, April 22, 1852.

I had already determined to adopt it as the principal book of reference in my department. This is the first term in which it has been used here; but from the trial which I have now made of it, I have every reason to congratulate myself on my selection of it as a text-book.

From the Rev. W. G. T. Shedd, Professor of English Literature in the University of Vt.

I take great pleasure in saying that it supplies a want that has long existed of a brief history of English literature, written in the right method and spirit, to serve as an introduction to the critical study of it. I shall recommend the book to my classes.

From James Shannon, President of Bacon College, Ky.

I have read about one-half of "Shaw's Outlines," and so far I am more than pleased with the work. I concur with you fully in the opinion that it supplies a want long felt in our higher educational institutes of a critical history of English literature, occupying a reasonable space, and written in a manner to interest and attach the attention of the student. I sincerely desire that it may obtain, as it deserves, an extensive circulation.

HANDBOOK OF MODERN EUROPEAN LITERATURE.

British, Danish, Dutch, French, German, Hungarian, Italian, Polish and Russian, Portuguese, Spanish, and Swedish. With a full Biographical and Chronological Index. By Mrs. FOSTER. In one large royal 12mo. volume, extra cloth. Uniform with "Shaw's Outlines of English Literature."

Lightning Source UK Ltd.
Milton Keynes UK
UKHW020134040219
336575UK00026B/734/P